*Quantitative
Decision-Making
for Business*

Quantitative

Decision-Making

for Business

GILBERT GORDON
ISRAEL PRESSMAN

Department of Statistics
Baruch College, C.U.N.Y.

PRENTICE-HALL, INC., *Englewood Cliffs, N.J. 07632*

Library of Congress Cataloging in Publication Data

Gordon, Gilbert (date)
  Quantitative decision-making for business.

  Bibliography: p.
  Includes index.
  1. Decision-making—Mathematical models.
2. Operations research. 3. Statistical decision.
I. Pressman, Israel (date)   joint author.
II. Title.
HD30.23.G67   658.4'03   77-25381
ISBN 0-13-746701-X

Printed in the United States of America

10 9 8 7 6 5 4 3 2

Prentice-Hall International, Inc., *London*
Prentice-Hall of Australia Pty. Limited, *Sydney*
Prentice-Hall of Canada, Ltd., *Toronto*
Prentice-Hall of India Private Limited, *New Delhi*
Prentice-Hall of Japan, Inc., *Tokyo*
Prentice-Hall of Southeast Asia Pte. Ltd., *Singapore*
Whitehall Books Limited, *Wellington, New Zealand*

To Our Parents

and

To Rachel Leah Pressman

CONTENTS

vii

CHAPTER 15 *Competitive Situations: Game Theory* **516**

PREFACE

This text results from many years of teaching an introductory quantitative methods course at Baruch College, C.U.N.Y. The intention is to provide a clear readable presentation of the essential topics of quantitative decision making. The authors have deliberately developed the basic assumptions within each area before proceeding to the models and applications.

The book is aimed at the student with a low-to-moderate level of mathematical sophistication and stresses comprehension of the techniques and interpretation of the results rather than the underlying theories. For this reason, most concepts are first developed through realistic numerical problems and then followed by more formal material. Many examples are given and all mathematical methods, beyond basic algebra, are discussed as they are used. A knowledge of calculus is not a prerequisite for the use of this book.

Chapters 1–15 contain the topics that are covered by most one-term introductory or survey courses in quantitative decision making—either at the undergraduate or graduate level. However, there is sufficient material in both the text of each chapter and the chapter problems for the book to be used in a two-semester quantitative methods sequence.

A major innovation has been incorporated in this text. For most topics, the book describes the use of the computer in making decisions. Instructors who adopt this text will be able to receive a package of computer programs that cover these topics and a computer guide for using these programs. The intent is to provide the student the opportunity to supplement the lecture and the assigned pencil and paper problems with a set of practical application problems that have a real-life point of view.

In addition to the problems to be solved by using the computer, there are comprehensive sets of problems designed to reinforce the material of each chapter. These problems are in reality an extension of the chapter material and may be thought of (for certain groups of problems) as mini-cases.

Many people deserve our thanks for their contributions to the various stages of this project. A special thanks to our colleagues in the Statistics Department of Baruch College, C.U.N.Y., for their encouragement. Thanks to the following reviewers whose comments and suggestions proved to be invaluable: Professor John J. Bernardo (University of Kentucky); Professor William F. Hamilton (University of Pennsylvania); Professor Mildred G. Massey (California State University); Professor Christopher K. McKenna (The Pennsylvania State University); Professor Eliezer Naddor (The Johns Hopkins University); Professor John J. Neuhauser (Boston College); Professor Richard G. Newman (Indiana University Northwest); Professor Richard Panicucci (Fairleigh Dickinson University); and Professor David Valinsky (Baruch College, C.U.N.Y.).

We would like to express special thanks to the many typists: Ellen Adams, Donna Anderson, Leah Fisher, and especially Michele Millstein for the many typing hours devoted to preparing the various drafts of this book.

Finally, to our families, our deepest thanks for their encouragement, patience, and sacrifice. Their moral support was essential to the completion of this project.

GILBERT R. GORDON
ISRAEL PRESSMAN

CHAPTER ONE

Introduction:
Decisions and Models

OBJECTIVES: The purpose of this chapter is to introduce you to the following concepts which are basic to obtaining a clear understanding of quantitative decision-making.

1. *The framework for decision problems.*
2. *The form of a mathematical model.*
3. *The fundamental techniques of model building.*
4. *Model solution and interpretation.*
5. *The basic elements of sensitivity analysis.*

Complex organizations generate complex decision problems. Today's society is composed of a variety of such organizations—those in business, government, education, and health care, for example. They must frequently make decisions which involve a complex array of factors and which will, in turn, affect many other factors. A common example is a company's decision to introduce a new product, which will be influenced by such considerations as market conditions, labor rates and availability, and investment requirements and availability of funds. The decision will be a multidimensional response, including the production methodology, cost and quality of the product, package design, price, and marketing and advertising strategy. The results of the decision could conceivably affect every phase of the organization. Clearly, this is a complex problem.

As organizations and their decision problems become more complicated and involved, it has become increasingly more difficult for administrators (decision makers) to handle all the factors affecting the decision and to determine the results to be expected from all possible decision alternatives. What is needed is a more scientific method of investigating and analyzing these problems and thus arriving at "better" decisions.

The earliest evidence of interest in this area is the growth of the accounting discipline, which developed systematic procedures for "accounting for" the monetary operations of an organization in order that administrators could develop a clearer picture of this important business behavior. In fact, we can consider accounting statements as a "model" of the organization, a term that will be more fully discussed later in the chapter.

The logical next step after providing information for decisions is to develop decision-making aids which facilitate the investigation of these problems. The birth of this discipline, bearing such names as "quantitative decision making," "operations research," and "management science," occurred during World War II, when the general crisis situation aroused strong interest in methods of making better decisions, both military and economic. The success of the procedures developed during that period encouraged other organizations, particularly businesses and social services, to adopt these approaches to their decision problems. Since that time, the field has grown dramatically and is being applied by a wide variety of organizations to solve a myriad of decision problems.

1.2.1. Introduction. We shall develop a generalized framework for decision problems which will be useful in investigating all types of decision problems. This will facilitate the use of the techniques to be discussed later.

1.2.2. Objective of the Decision. All decision problems must have an objective—or else no problem would exist. One of the most difficult aspects of a problem is usually the choice of the specific objective to be used. For example, in the case of the introduction of a new product, some reasonable objectives might be:

1. Make the greatest profit next year.
2. Make the greatest profit over the next 10 years.
3. Make the greatest return on investment over the next 10 years.
4. Increase the net worth of the company as much as possible at the end of 10 years.
5. Obtain the greatest market share possible with a profit not lower than $10,000 per year.
6. Achieve the highest possible sales given a profit not lower than $10,000 per year.

Naturally, these are only a few of the almost infinite possibilities that could be used. Each different objective will strongly affect the amount of satisfaction to be realized by making a given decision. One decision may yield very satisfactory results when evaluated by one objective and very poor results when evaluated by another. The problem becomes even more complex when some of the factors affecting the decision are variable (i.e., are not known with certainty). For example, for a new product introduction, which includes decisions about price, quality, package, and so on, demand cannot be known with certainty. A forecast could be made, but it would be an estimate at best and thus would be subject to error.

Another aspect which complicates matters is that within an organization there are usually several suborganizations (production, marketing, warehousing, advertising), each with its own objectives, which may be (and usually are) in conflict with other suborganizations' objectives. Salespersons may want to sell any product that any customer will buy, whereas production may wish to manufacture only a few large-volume products. Production may prefer large runs of a single product, which would create large inventories troublesome to the warehousing department. The objective or goal of the decision problem should be one that considers the overall or composite objectives of the total organization.

1.2.3. Decision Activities. The action of making a decision consists of making a choice from among a number of activities, each of which is under the control of the decision maker. These will be referred to as *decision activities* or *controllable activities*. The terms "decision variable" and "controllable variable" will also be used since, when we discuss models, variables (such as x and y) will be used to represent these as-yet-unknown quantities. For example, in the new-product-introduction problem, some possible decision activities might be:

1. The price to be charged.
2. The package design.
3. The marketing–distribution policy to be used (e.g., direct, toward jobbers and wholesalers).
4. The number of machines to purchase for producing the product.
5. The amount of ingredient x as a percentage of the total mix of ingredients (e.g., cashews in a nut mix, gold in jewelry).

In each case the decision maker has the ability to "do" what he decides, and therefore these activities are considered controllable, that is, are subject to the human decision process of choice.

Decision variables, and variables in general, may be divided into two types: discrete and continuous. *Discrete variables* are those that can only take on one of a finite (or discrete) set of possibilities. Each of these possibilities is commonly referred to as a *strategy*.

For example, for the decision activity concerning the package design, we might have several strategies:

STRATEGY 1:   White with large gold letters.

STRATEGY 2:   White with small gold letters.

STRATEGY 3:   White with large black letters.

⋮   ⋮

The decision activity for the number of machines to purchase might be:

STRATEGY 1:   Buy one machine.

STRATEGY 2:   Buy two machines.

STRATEGY 3:   Buy three machines.

⋮   ⋮

Continuous variables, on the other hand, are those for which one of an infinite number of possible values must be chosen. For example, the price to be charged could be $100.00, $120.00, $127.00, $127.50, $127.53, ...

Making a decision, therefore, involves selecting a strategy for each discrete decision variable and selecting a value for each continuous decision variable.

1.2.4. Uncontrollable Activities. Decision problems frequently contain activities that are not under the control of the decision maker. These will be called *uncontrollable activities* or *uncontrollable variables*. For example, in the new-product-introduction problem, the uncontrollable activities might be the raw-material costs, economic conditions in the future, the number of other companies who will also market a similar product, or other factors of this type. These will be determined by "forces" not completely under the control of the decision maker. Uncontrollable variables can also be either discrete (number of other companies marketing a similar product) or continuous (the cost of raw materials).

We shall consider uncontrollable activities of two types:

1. *Known value.* These are usually referred to as the *parameters* of the problem. If we know that our raw-material cost is $0.50 per pound, we may simply use the value 0.50 in considering the problem.
2. *Unknown value.* These values are not known with certainty.

The manner in which a value is selected for an uncontrollable variable with unknown value is an important part of a decision problem. The two extreme cases are called state-of-nature and competitive-strategy types of variables.

State-of-nature variables are those which are determined by a process that does not consider the decision maker at all. For example, the general economic conditions which will exist in the future will not be determined (most likely) by a process that concerns itself with the interests of the decision maker. Rather, there are an almost infinite number of other factors which will determine this outcome. The same is true for a farmer who is deciding which crops to plant. His decision problem may have as an uncontrollable variable, the weather. It is safe to assume that the rainfall during the growing season will be determined by a process (nature) that will "make its decision" without regard to the likes or dislikes of the farmer.

Competitive strategies, on the other hand, exist where an individual's decision will be influenced by a second decision maker, who is in competition with the first decision maker. The competitor's decision will be made so as to improve his own satisfaction, which, owing to the competition, will indirectly act so as to reduce the satisfaction of the first decision maker. The price that is charged by one's competitor for a similar product is an example of a competitive-strategy type of uncontrollable variable.

1.2.5. Partially Controllable Activities. In some cases an activity is neither completely controllable or uncontrollable, and these will be called *partially controllable activities* or *partially controllable variables*. In these cases some of the decision activities of the decision maker affect the outcome of the activity but do not completely determine it. For example, the price to be charged for a new product will affect the demand for the product (not controllable), but many other factors will also affect it. In investigating the decision problem, we cannot neglect either the controllable portion or the uncontrollable portion.

1.2.6. Certainty, Uncertainty, and Risk. When some aspect of a problem is known "for sure," we say that for this aspect of the problem, a situation known as *certainty* exists. For example, if we are considering a number of investment opportunities and can assume that we know (more or less) all the costs and revenues precisely, this would be an example of decision making under certainty, since the decision as to which unique investment opportunity to choose would be evident.

When the outcome of an activity is not known (i.e., is uncontrollable), the situation is very different. The state of *uncertainty* exists when we know nothing about the likelihood (probability distribution) of the possible outcomes for the uncontrollable activity. For example, a farmer who has moved to a new area (where no records are kept) will know nothing about the likelihood of heavy rainfall, moderate rainfall, or light rainfall. This will be a condition of uncertainty.

On the other hand, if the farmer has lived in the same place for many years, he will "know" quite well the likelihood of the various possible levels of rainfall. This assumes that the rainfall next season will be determined by the same process which has determined the rainfall over the past periods of time during which the farmer kept records and developed his "knowledge."

Clearly, this situation, which we are calling *risk*, has much more information for the decision maker and therefore must be handled in a different manner than the uncertainty case.

1.2.7. Constraints. In many cases the decision maker will not be able to pick any values he chooses for his decision variables since not all values will be feasible. For instance, the price he can charge for the new product may be limited by government regulation so as not to exceed $30. In this case one of the *constraints* under which he must make his decision is that the price must be less than or equal to $30. In the case of discrete decision variables, the decision maker simply does not include strategies for consideration which are not feasible. This may be considered as an *implied constraint*.

In other cases, such as with many uncontrollable variables, the constraints may be more complex and require equations to express them. For example, where the decision concerns how much of each of 10 products to produce, a constraint on maximum total production of all 10 products is best expressed by an equation that sums all these variables and specifies that the sum must be less than the given maximum quantity.

1.2.8. Outline of the Decision Process. The decision process may be considered as consisting of the following steps:

1. Define the objective.
2. Determine the controllable activities.
3. Define the uncontrollable activities and determine whether they are state-of-nature or competitive-strategy type.
4. Define the partially controllable variables and their relationships to the controllable variables.
5. Determine the effect of each possible decision (strategy or value for each controllable activity) with respect to the objective—find the best decision.
6. Make a decision, that is, select:
   (a) A strategy for each discrete controllable activity.
   (b) A value for each continuous controllable activity.
7. Observe the results.
8. Repeat the decision process over time.

The process may seem quite simple from the outline given, but in fact it may be extremely complex. Steps 4 and 5 hint at rather complicated procedures involving relationships among many activities (variables) and the objective. In general, without the aid of quantitative techniques, these operations are too difficult to accurately perform, and decision makers have traditionally resorted to rough guesses, estimates, and simplifying assumptions.

It is precisely for these reasons that quantitative methods have been used for making better decisions. In general, the major tool of quantitative decision making is the analytical model, which will be discussed next.

SECTION 1.3. *Models*

1.3.1. What Is a Model? A *model* may be defined as a representation of some process or system that incorporates only those elements of the process or system that affect the objectives of interest. Thus, a model is not a perfect duplicate of the process, but contains sufficient detail so that we can study the model instead of the process itself.

Investigation and analysis of the model is usually more convenient and practical than manipulating the actual process. For instance, architects build scale models of buildings to try to determine their esthetic appeal. In this case the system (building) does not exist and a model is the only means of experimentation. Similarly, naval and aircraft designers build scale models of the boats and airplanes under design and simulate conditions of storms, damage, and so on, to determine their effects. These types of models, called *physical models*, actually resemble in appearance the systems to be investigated. However, these models are not the types used in quantitative decision making.

1.3.2. Analytical Models. An *analytical model* (or *mathematical model*) is one in which numbers and variables represent the elements of the process or system under investigation. It is therefore an abstract model. Every equation that we use is, in fact, itself an analytical model. For example, the equation that gives the future worth of money invested at an interest rate of $i\%$ for n years is

$$(1) \qquad F = P (1 + i)^n$$

where F = money returned to the investor at the end,
         after n years (future worth)
    P = money invested at the beginning (present worth)
    n = number of years
    i = interest rate

This equation is a model of the process of investment and interest paid on an investment. It in no way resembles the process of investing money in a bank, waiting n years, and withdrawing the money. It simply predicts the amount of money that will be available at the end of the n years. One advantage of a mathematical model is that once it is developed it may be used to represent many investment situations (i.e., different beginning investments, numbers of years, and interest rates). All we have to do to model these various processes is to substitute different values for P, n, and i and solve for the value of F.

Consider the difficulty of investigating this investment process without a model, that is, by simply experimenting with the actual system (bank). We would have to make many investments, at different interest rates, and wait different lengths of time to determine the return in each case. Then we would have to try to use these results to predict the return for a different P, n, and i, which would be a difficult, time-consuming process.

In this case using a mathematical model has simplified the investigation considerably and has provided us with a powerful, flexible tool for predicting returns. Another general advantage of model building is that it forces us to investigate the detail structure of the process being studied and thereby to learn a great deal about it. This is not usually the case in physical experimentation, where we simply "use" the actual system. At first glance this second advantage appears insignificant; however, very often, knowledge of the structure is almost as valuable as the analytical results provided by the model. It is usually through greater understanding of our environment—its structures and interactions—that better decisions are made.

1.3.3. Constructing Models of Decision Problems. In constructing models of decision problems we wish to incorporate all factors relevant to the objective and then experiment with the model mathematically (instead of physically) to determine a good decision, or if possible the best (optimal) decision. In general, this will require:

1. Defining variables for
   (a) Decision (controllable) activities.
   (b) Uncontrollable activities.
   (c) The objective, known as the payoff measure or the measure of performance.
2. Developing the relationship among the variables—in particular, how the measure of performance relates to the decision variables.
3. Developing the constraint equations (if any) which assure that only feasible decisions will be considered.

1.3.4. Defining the Variables. The definition of the variables is one of the most important steps in formulating a model, although this is not evident at the outset. It is important to choose variables for the decision activities which will actually give an answer to the problem and at the same time yield an accurate formulation of the model. This will become clearer as the problems of the text are considered.

In general, one variable must be chosen which acts as a measure of how "good" the outcome is with respect to the objective. This variable is usually referred to as the *payoff measure* or *measure of performance*. The formulation of this variable can be as difficult as the formulation of the objective itself, since it must adequately reflect how any outcome will be judged. Whenever possible it should be a variable that takes on numeric values and has the implication that either a high value or a low value is judged "good."

The uncontrollable activities may initially be defined as variables, but some approaches will permit eliminating uncontrollable variables from the final equations. For example, the uncontrollable variable demand, given together with its probability distribution, may be replaced by the average demand that is acceptable, if our objective can be stated as "earning the best *expected* (average) profit."

1.3.5. Expressing the Relationships Among the Variables. The job of developing equations that describe the process under study is most challenging. The function served by these equations is to assure that for given inputs to the process, the outputs (results) of the model will be identical to that of the process. The most important of these equations is the one that relates the payoff measure (objective) to the other variables. This equation is called the *objective function* and is used to evaluate all possible decisions.

1.3.6. Constraints. If all values of the variables are not meaningful, we must include in the problem equations that restrict the variables to taking on only meaningful (feasible) values. These equations will frequently be of the form of inequalities. For example, the selling price to be charged for new products cannot be negative. Thus we do not wish to consider negative values as the selling price. If the variable s is used to represent the selling price, the equation $s \geqslant 0$ (read "s greater than or equal to zero") assures this restriction and should be included as part of the model.

Another example might be an investment decision problem wherein the decision maker could invest different amounts in any or all of three investments (x_1, x_2, x_3) as long as the total investment does not exceed the $10,000 available for investment. The equation $x_1 + x_2 + x_3 \leqslant 10,000$ assures this and should be included in the problem as a constraint. If the decision maker did not wish to consider any decision that would invest less than $1,000 in investment number 1, the appropriate constraint would be $x_1 \geqslant 1,000$.

1.3.7. Sample Decision Problem—Model Construction. Let us consider a problem, to illustrate the concepts we have been discussing. A street peddler buys apples each day and sells them on a street corner. He buys them at 30 cents/pound and can choose a different selling price each day if he so wishes; however, he will keep the same price for the entire day. All unsold apples at the end of the day must be sold for a salvage value of 20 cents/pound, that is, at a loss of 10 cents/pound. The peddler must decide how many pounds of apples to buy each day and what price to charge for them. He obviously wants to earn the highest possible profit each day.

Let us begin by choosing our variables. We choose the variables for the decision activities as follows:

Let $b =$ number of pounds of apples
      the apple peddler will buy each day

    $s =$ selling price per pound

Let us assume that these are continuous variables. If we get an answer $s = 1.5632$, we can charge $1.56 or $1.57/pound without affecting our profit very much.

The uncontrollable variables are as follows:

Let $d =$ demand (in pounds) for apples

    $c =$ cost per pound
       (30 cents for this problem)

    $v =$ salvage value of unsold apples
       (20 cents for this problem)

There is a partially controllable variable, sales, which is affected by the amount purchased and therefore available for sale (b, controllable) and by the demand (d, uncontrollable). Thus, if $x =$ sales (in pounds) of apples, the payoff measure, profit, can be stated as follows:

(2) $P =$ profit (\$) per day

This completes the definition of the variables. The objective function may be formulated as follows:

(3) $$P = \begin{cases} x(s-c) & \text{(if } d \geqslant b) \\ x(s-c)-(b-x)(c-v) & \text{(if } d < b) \end{cases}$$

Stated verbally, if demand (d) is greater than or equal to the quantity purchased (b), sales will equal demand and profit will equal sales (x) times profit per unit, where profit per unit is selling price minus cost ($s-c$). If demand (d) is less than the amount purchased (b), there is a profit of ($s-c$) on the sold units (x) and a loss of ($c-v$) on the unsold units ($b-x$).

Next, let us formulate the relationships among the variables. Notice, that in its present form, the objective function is not a function of the decision variables alone.

First, let us relate sales (x) to demand (d) and quantity bought (b).

(4) $$x = \begin{cases} b & \text{(if } d \geqslant b) \\ d & \text{(if } d < b) \end{cases}$$

If the demand (d) is greater than the quantity bought (b), the peddler "sells out"; that is, $x = b$. Otherwise, sales (x) = demand (d).

What is still needed is a relationship between demand (d) and the controllable variables. No information has as yet been given regarding the relationship between demand (d) and selling price (s). Let us assume that the peddler knows from experience that the relationship between d and s is as shown in Figure 1.3.1, which stated mathematically is

(5) $$d = \frac{20}{s^2} \qquad \text{(for all } s > 0)$$

For example, if selling price (s) = \$2.00/pound, then

$$d = \frac{20}{(s)^2} = \frac{20}{4} = 5 \text{ lb}$$

Let us assume that this is certain; that is, if the peddler charges \$2.00/pound each day, he will sell exactly (or close enough to so that the difference is negligible) 5 lb. This actually removes d from the category of being uncontrollable, for it is, in fact, indirectly completely controllable. This precise relationship between demand and sales is in general unrealistic, but since we are investigating model construction and not marketing

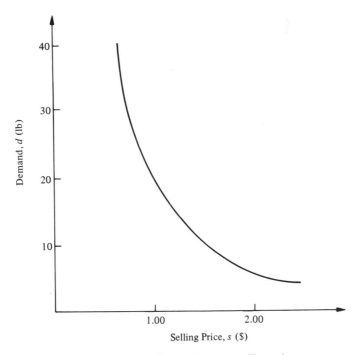

FIGURE 1.3.1. *Demand versus selling price.*

theory, let us not be disturbed by this fact. Also, notice that once the peddler chooses a selling price (s), he knows the demand (d), and will therefore buy (b) exactly a quantity equal to his demand each day (i.e., $b = d = 20/s^2$) so as not to forego a profit on unfilled demand or have a loss on unsold units. Also, since he always buys exactly his demand, $x = b = d = 20/s^2$. We can thus substitute b and s for x and d and derive an objective function consisting only of the decision variables. Finally, since knowing one decision variable (say s) tells us the value of the other ($b = 20/s^2$), we really need only consider one of the two and, after deciding on its value, find the value for the other. Thus, the problem reduces to one having only a single continuous decision variable. Substituting the value of $20/s^2$ for x into the objective function, and considering only the case where $d = b$, we obtain

(6)
$$P = \frac{20}{s^2}(s - c) = \frac{20}{s} - \frac{20c}{s^2}$$
and

(7)
$$b = d = \frac{20}{s^2}$$

For this problem $c = 30$ cents, and therefore equation (6) becomes

(8)
$$P = \frac{20}{s} - \frac{6}{s^2}$$

It should be noted that equation (7) is not an objective function but merely expresses a relationship between one decision variable and the other. Furthermore, the only constraint that need be stated is $s \geqslant 0$; that is, a negative selling price is not to be considered.

We have thus developed a model [equations (7) and (8)] of the decision problem. For any value of selling price (s), the model gives the profit obtained (P) and the quantity to buy (b).

1.3.8. Obtaining Solutions from Models. Obtaining a solution from a model [i.e., finding a decision that gives a good (or even the best) payoff measure value] is highly dependent on the particular model involved. In some cases various mathematical techniques have been developed to find the optimal solution. Examples of such techniques are linear programming (discussed later) and the calculus (which is neither covered nor required for an understanding of the material of this text). Other types of models require experimentation to try and find a good decision. Trial and error can be time-consuming, so numerical procedures for searching out the optimal solution have been developed for certain cases. These have been programmed for computers, which carry out the involved operations in seconds. In general, computers are necessary to carry out the many time-consuming operations of optimization procedures for most real-life problems.

Let us reconsider the apple peddler problem again and discuss how to find a good or optimal decision. We can now state the problem mathematically as:

$$\underset{s}{\text{maximize}} \left\{ P = \frac{20}{s} - \frac{6}{s^2} \right\}$$

(9)
$$\text{s.t.} \quad s \geqslant 0$$

$$b = \frac{20}{s^2}$$

The term "maximize" means find the value of s which yields the highest value for the expression that follows P. The term "s.t." means subject to the constraint equations that follow.

Let us use trial and error to investigate the objective function. Clearly, the more values we try, the better the chance of finding the best one. In general, trial and error does not find the exact optimal solution, but it may find one extremely close to it which is good enough for practical purposes. We shall evaluate the objective function for values of s equal to 0.25, 0.50, 0.75, and so on. The results are shown in Table 1.3.1. From the table it would appear that $s = 75$ cents/pound would be a

TABLE 1.3.1. *Trial and Error Evaluations of
the Profit Objective Function*

s	$20/s$	$6/s^2$	$P = (20/s) - 6/s^2$ ($)
0.25	80.00	96.00	−16.00
0.50	40.00	24.00	16.00
0.75	26.67	10.67	16.00
1.00	20.00	6.00	14.00
1.25	16.00	3.84	12.16
1.50	13.33	2.67	10.66
1.75	11.43	1.96	9.47
2.00	10.00	1.50	8.50

"good" price to charge. The peddler would then buy (b) and sell

$$x = \frac{20}{s^2} = \frac{20}{(0.75)^2} = 35.56$$

pounds of apples each day.

Drawing a graph of the objective function will perhaps indicate more clearly the nature of the optimization. The graph of P versus s is shown in Figure 1.3.2. This curve indicates that there is a value of s which yields a profit greater than $16. This decision is the optimal one, $s*$ (the * indicating the optimal), which yields a higher profit $P*$ than any other.

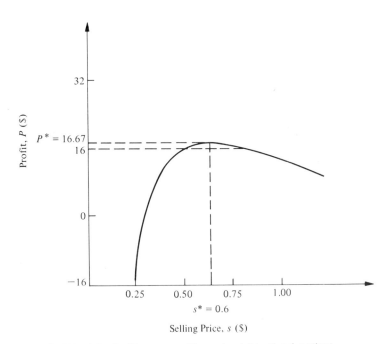

FIGURE 1.3.2. *Profit versus selling price (objective function).*

This value s^* may be found, by use of the calculus,[†] to be

$$s^* = 2c = (0.30) = \$0.60$$

and

$$P^* = \frac{5}{c} = \frac{5}{0.3} = \$16.67.$$

Another way of finding P^* is to substitute $s = 0.60$ into the equation $P = (20/s) - (6/s^2) = 20/0.6 - 6/(0.6)^2 = 16.67$. Thus, the apple peddler should price his apples at 60 cents/pound, he should buy (and consequently sell) $b^* = 20/s^2 = 20/(0.60)^2 = 20/0.36 = 55.56$ lb of apples per day, and earn a daily profit of \$16.67. Notice that this profit is higher than any other found.

One advantage of this analytical model is that if the peddler's cost changes, the new values for s^* and P^* are easily found, since the results $s^* = 2c$, $P^* = 5/c$, and $b = 20/s^2$ apply for all values of c greater than zero. Hence, if the cost changes from day to day, he can compute the optimal selling price and quantity to buy each day. If the cost on one day is $c = 40$ cents/pound, he merely computes $s^* = 2c = 80$ cents/pound, $b = 20/(0.80)^2 = 31.25$, and $P^* = 5/c = \$12.50$. Thus, he buys 31.25 lb, sells them for 80 cents/pound, and earns \$12.50 profit for the day.

1.3.9. Sensitivity Analysis. In many instances it is advantageous to know how the optimal solution changes as the parameters of the problem change. For example, in the apple peddler problem, what is the optimal solution for the purchase price $c = 0.10$, $c = 0.20$, $c = 0.40, \ldots$? This type of study is known as *sensitivity analysis*. It is frequently an important aspect of a decision problem, since it is possible that the cost of the apples has been incorrectly estimated and is, in fact, a value other than the assumed value, $c = 30$ cents/pound. It is also of interest to know the actual profit that will be earned if the optimal solution, assuming $c = 30$ cents/pound, is used despite the fact that c is actually not equal to 30 cents.

Let us perform sensitivity analysis for the apple peddler problem. There are three parameters for this problem:

1. The purchase price c, assumed to be 30 cents.
2. The parameter relating demand to selling price, that is, $d = k/s^2$, where k was assumed to be 20.
3. Salvage value of unsold units (v).

The optimal values, s^*, b^*, and P^*, are derived using the calculus (see Appendix 1) for general values of the two parameters c and k (v had no effect on the optimal, since the quantity purchased equaled the known demand).

$$s^* = 2c \qquad b^* = \frac{k}{4c^2} \qquad P^* = \frac{k}{4c}$$

[†]We repeat that calculus is neither covered nor required for an understanding of this text.

Let us tabulate optimal values of s^*, b^*, P^*, and the actual profit for using the assumed values $c=0.30$, $k=20$, and $v=0.10$ for various values of k, c, and v to determine how sensitive the optimal solution is to the values of these parameters. Let us also tabulate the profit obtained by using $s=0.60$ and $b=55.56$, the assumed optimal values using equation (3). These results are shown in Figure 1.3.3.

For example, assume that the demand constant k changes from $k=20$ to $k=10$. The new optimal values are

$$k=10 \qquad c=0.30 \qquad v=0.20$$

$$s^*=2c=2(0.30)$$

$$=0.60$$

$$b^*=\frac{10}{4c^2}=\frac{10}{4(0.3)^2}=\frac{10}{0.36}$$

$$=27.78 \text{ lb}$$

$$P^*=\frac{k}{4c}=\frac{10}{4(0.30)}=\frac{10}{1.20}$$

$$=8.33$$

What would happen if the apple peddler did not know that his demand had fallen (i.e., $k=10$)? He would still sell at $s=60$ cents and buy $b=55.56$ lb as before. Let us compute the profit he would earn using these "assumed" optimal, but now truly nonoptimal, values. His demand is now

$$d=\frac{k}{s^2}=\frac{10}{(0.60)^2}=27.78 \text{ lb}$$

However, he buys $b=55.56$ lb as before. Thus, from equation (3), since $d<b$,

$$P=d(s-c)-(b-d)(c-v)$$

$$=27.78(0.60-0.30)-(55.56-27.78)(0.30-0.20)$$

$$=8.34-2.78$$

$$=\$5.56$$

He could have earned a profit of $8.33 if he had perfect information about the marketplace. Since his information is not correct, he earns only $5.56. The difference, referred to as *opportunity loss*, is $8.33-\$5.56=\$2.77.

SENSITIVITY ANALYSIS FOR THE APPLE PEDDLER PROBLEM

ASSUMED VALUES					
ASSUMED OPTIMAL	C* =	0.30	K =	20.00	V = 0.20
	S* =	0.60	B* =	55.56	P* = 16.67

CASE	C	S*	K	V	B*	S*	P*	PROFIT FOR ASSUMED OPTIMAL
1	0.15	0.15	10.00	0.10	111.11	0.30	16.67	11.11
2	0.15	0.15	10.00	0.20	111.11	0.30	16.67	13.89
3	0.15	0.15	10.00	0.40	111.11	0.30	16.67	19.44
4	0.15	0.15	20.00	0.10	222.22	0.30	33.33	25.00
5	0.15	0.15	20.00	0.20	222.22	0.30	33.33	25.00
6	0.15	0.15	20.00	0.40	222.22	0.30	33.33	25.00
7	0.15	0.15	40.00	0.10	444.44	0.30	66.67	25.00
8	0.15	0.15	40.00	0.20	444.44	0.30	66.67	25.00
9	0.15	0.15	40.00	0.40	444.44	0.30	66.67	25.00
10	0.30	0.30	10.00	0.10	27.78	0.60	8.33	2.78
11	0.30	0.30	10.00	0.20	27.78	0.60	8.33	5.56
12	0.30	0.30	10.00	0.40	27.78	0.60	8.33	11.11
13	0.30	0.30	20.00	0.10	55.56	0.60	16.67	16.67
14	0.30	0.30	20.00	0.40	55.56	0.60	16.67	16.67
15	0.30	0.30	40.00	0.10	111.11	0.60	33.33	16.67
16	0.30	0.30	40.00	0.20	111.11	0.60	33.33	16.67
17	0.30	0.30	40.00	0.40	111.11	0.60	33.33	16.67
18	0.60	0.60	10.00	0.10	6.94	1.20	4.17	-13.89
19	0.60	0.60	10.00	0.20	6.94	1.20	4.17	-11.11
20	0.60	0.60	10.00	0.40	6.94	1.20	4.17	-5.56
21	0.60	0.60	20.00	0.10	13.89	1.20	8.33	-0.00
22	0.60	0.60	20.00	0.20	13.89	1.20	8.33	-0.00
23	0.60	0.60	20.00	0.40	13.89	1.20	8.33	-0.00
24	0.60	0.60	40.00	0.10	27.78	1.20	16.67	0.00
25	0.60	0.60	40.00	0.20	27.78	1.20	16.67	0.00
26	0.60	0.60	40.00	0.40	27.78	1.20	16.67	0.00

FIGURE 1.3.3. Computer solution to apple peddler problem showing sensitivity analysis.

Notice the wide variation in the optimal profit obtainable (P^*) and the optimal solution (s^*, b^*) as the parameter values, c, k, and v, change. Naturally, since $s^* = 2c$, the variable s^* is completely insensitive to k and v and sensitive only to c. Since $b^* = k/4c^2$, the variable b^* is insensitive to v and is sensitive to k and extremely sensitive to c.

The actual profits for using the assumed optimal decision (i.e., $s^* = 0.60$, $b^* = 55.56$) tend to be drastically lower than for using the true optimal decision, indicating the forgone profits for incorrectly estimating the parameter values of the problem. However, the optimal profit is also insensitive to v, as it does not appear in the total-cost equation.

Since many decision problems use estimated parameter values in the process of model formulation, sensitivity analysis is an important part of decision analysis. An optimal solution that is not overly sensitive to the parameter values of the problem may be considered more reliable than one which is highly sensitive.

**SECTION 1.4. *Scope of Quantitative Decision-Making
in Business***

The simple example presented indicates the power of using models in decision problems. For this reason quantitative techniques are often used whenever the complexity of the problem makes it difficult to find a good decision by general reasoning. If in such situations one can construct an accurate model, then the techniques of quantitative decision-making can be useful.

These techniques have been applied in a wide variety of decision problems in many areas. In some cases practitioners have developed specific techniques for solving classes of problems that have the same model structure. Examples of this are decision theory and linear programming. In other cases specific models have been developed to handle specific problem areas, such as inventory control, queueing, and project scheduling. Both of these types of applications are covered in the text.

Throughout the text examples are shown to indicate the relevant problem areas where these techniques can be used. However, no text in this area could cover all the possible application areas since new ones are being explored every day. It is expected that the examples will not only clarify the material but will actually show how real decision problems are handled using quantitative methods. The examples presented will be elementary compared to complex real-world applications, but they will contain the essential elements of these complex types of decision problems. The diverse selection of problems should give the reader an idea of the possible areas of application and how they can be approached in general.

Frequently, the computations involved in using and solving models for real-world problems are numerous and time-consuming and the prospect of carrying them out by hand makes practical use of the model all but impossible. In these cases, the speed, accuracy, and flexibility of computers makes them a necessary tool for problem solving. In fact, the development of the field of quantitative decision-making is closely interconnected with the development of computers.

Throughout the text sample computer results will be shown to indicate how computers can be used to solve the types of problems being discussed. Since computers are used to such a great extent in the real world, it will be worthwhile to relate the computer solutions to the problems at hand or, if possible, to solve some problems using the computer oneself.

A computer program has been written which performs sensitivity analysis for the apple peddler problem as an example of how computers can be used. The program reads in the assumed parameter values of c, k, and v and solves for the assumed optimal solution s^*, b^*, and P^*. Then the program reads values for c, k, and v and performs sensitivity analysis using the values read. The output is shown as Figure 1.3.3. The program quickly performs the somewhat complex computations of the sensitivity analysis and facilitates using this approach.

PROBLEMS

1.1. For the following situations, describe the controllable variables, state-of-nature variables, competitive-strategy variables, partially controllable variables, the objective, the payoff measure, and any constraints. (*Note:* There may be many possible answers.)

(a) A company considering introducing a new product.
(b) An investor trying to decide how much to invest in stocks, bonds, real estate, bank deposits, and so on.
(c) A company considering the alternatives of building a new plant or expanding existing plants.
(d) A supermarket deciding how many units of each item to buy and how frequently.
(e) A bank deciding how many tellers to hire.
(f) A company considering how much to spend on several types of advertising (e.g., radio, television, newspaper, magazines).

1.2. For each of the situations of Problem 1.1, indicate whether the controllable variables are discrete or continuous and indicate some possible strategies or ranges of values for them.

1.3. For each of the uncontrollable variables of Problem 1.1, indicate whether certainty, uncertainty, or risk is the most appropriate assumption.

1.4. Reconsider the apple peddler problem (Section 1.3.7) but assume that the purchase price of apples is 25 cents per pound, the demand equals $30/s^2$, and the salvage value equals 10 cents/pound. What is the optimal solution and optimal profit?

1.5. (Problem 1.4 continued) Assume that the apple peddler thinks that the demand equals:
(a) $d = 15/s^2$.
(b) $d = 60/s^2$.
What (assumed optimal) decision does he make? How much does he sell and what is his profit for this decision? How much has the improper estimation of demand cost him?

1.6. (Problem 1.4 continued) Perform sensitivity analysis using the computer program for the following values (in cents):

$$c = 15, 25, 35$$
$$k = 15, 30, 60$$
$$v = 5, 10, 15$$

1.7. The Horizon Chemical Company has just received an order for 2,400 grams of a special alloy which must be produced using their special reducer. The reducer may be operated over a wide range of temperatures which affects the hourly yield of the product being produced. Higher temperatures tend to give higher hourly yields, but it costs more to run the reducer at higher temperatures. Another feature of the reducer is that the time duration must be selected in advance. Horizon's Production Department is trying to determine how to set up this production run in the most efficient manner.
(a) State the objective of the decision problem.
(b) Define the controllable variables.
(c) What is the payoff measure?
(d) What other factors exist in addition to the controllable variables?

1.8. (Problem 1.7 continued) Assume the hourly cost ($/hour) equals $0.1x^2 + 1,440$, where x equals temperature in degrees C, and the yield per hour (grams/hour) equals $2x$.
(a) Formulate the objective function for this problem.
(b) If a temperature of $x = 100°C$ is used, how long a production run is required and what is the cost for the run?
(c) Repeat (b) for temperature (x) equal to 50°C and 150°C.

1.9. (Problem 1.7 continued) It can be shown that for Horizon's decision problem if the hourly cost is given as

$$Ax^2 + B$$

and the hourly yield is given as

$$Cx$$

then the optimal operating temperature (x) equals

$$x^* = \sqrt{\frac{B}{A}}$$

(a) Find the optimal temperature, duration, and cost for Horizon's decision problem.

(b) Is the optimal cost lower than all others examined in Problem 1.8?

1.10. (Problems 1.7–1.9 continued) Assume that by mistake the company thinks that the hourly cost equals $0.2x^2 + 1{,}440$. What decision do they make? How much do they lose by not knowing the correct cost equation?

**BOOKS OF
INTEREST**

Ackoff, R. L. and M. W. Sasieni, *Fundamentals of Operations Research.* New York: John Wiley & Sons, Inc., 1968.

Anderson, D. R., D. J. Sweeney, and T. A. Williams, *An Introduction to Management Science: Quantitative Approaches to Decision Making.* St. Paul, Minn.: West Publishing Co., 1976

Churchman, C. West, Russell L. Ackoff, and E. L. Arnoff, *Introduction to Operations Research.* New York: John Wiley & Sons, Inc., 1957.

Eck, R. D., *Operations Research for Business.* Belmont, California: Wadsworth Publishing Co., Inc., 1976.

Hillier, F. S. and Gerald J. Lieberman, *Introduction to Operations Research.* San Francisco: Holden-Day, Inc., 1974.

Levin, Richard I. and Charles A. Kirkpatrick, *Quantitative Approaches to Management* (3rd ed.). New York: McGraw-Hill Book Co., 1975.

Miller, David W. and Martin K. Starr, *Executive Decisions and Operations Research* (2nd ed.). Englewood Cliffs, N.J.: Prentice-Hall, Inc., 1969.

Sasieni, M., A. Yaspan, and L. Friedman, *Operations Research: Methods and Problems.* New York: John Wiley & Sons, Inc., 1959.

Teichrow, D., *An Introduction to Management Science: Deterministic Models.* New York: John Wiley & Sons, Inc., 1964.

Thierauf, Robert J. and R. C. Klekamp, *Decision Making through Operations Research.* New York: John Wiley & Sons, Inc., 1975.

Wagner, H. M., *Principles of Operations Research.* 2nd ed. Englewood Cliffs, N.J.: Prentice-Hall, Inc., 1975.

Derivation of the Optimal Selling Price,
Optimal Purchase Quantity,
and Optimal Profit

If we assume that demand $d = k/s^2$, the profit equation is given by

$$P = \frac{k}{s} - \frac{kc}{s^2}$$

Taking a first derivative of P with respect to s and setting the result equal to zero, we obtain

$$\frac{dP}{ds} = -\frac{k}{s^2} + \frac{2kc}{s^3} = 0$$

For s not equal to zero, we obtain

$$-k = -\frac{2kc}{s}$$

$$s = 2c$$

Taking the second derivative, we obtain

$$\frac{d^2P}{ds^2} = \frac{2k}{s^3} - \frac{6kc}{s^4} = \frac{2ks - 6kc}{s^4} = \frac{2k(s-3c)}{s^4}$$

For $s = 2c$, the second derivative equals

$$-\frac{2kc}{s^4}$$

and so the value $s = 2c$ is a maximum value. Therefore,

$$s^* = 2c$$
$$b^* = \frac{k}{s^2} = \frac{k}{4c^2}$$
$$P^* = \frac{k}{2c} - \frac{kc}{4c^2} = \frac{k}{4c} .$$

CHAPTER 2

Essentials of Probability and Statistics

OBJECTIVES: The purpose of this chapter is to acquaint you with the following concepts which are fundamental to understanding probability and statistics and which form the necessary background for understanding this text.

1. *The basic elements of random processes.*
2. *The fundamentals of probability and computational methods.*
3. *Conditional probabilities and the revision of probabilities.*
4. *The notion of a random variable.*
5. *Discrete and continuous probability distributions.*
6. *Expected value or mean and standard deviation.*
7. *The basic elements of statistics.*

Many decision problems involve elements whose result cannot be predicted with certainty, such as demand for a new product or the cost of a product that has never been produced. Mathematicians have established a set of methods for describing and handling such situations. These methods are generally referred to as *probability* and *statistics*. This chapter presents those essential elements of these topics which form the necessary background for understanding the remainder of the text.

SECTION 2.2. *Random Processes and Events*

We shall consider a *random process* as one which has outcomes that are not predictable with certainty each time the process is conducted. We shall call one observation of the process a *trial*. Examples of random processes are:

1. The demand for a given product during a 1-day period.
2. The per-unit cost of a product that has never been produced.
3. The number of persons arriving to buy tickets to a movie during a 1-hour period.
4. The price of a stock at the end of a day.
5. The number of pounds of iron ore obtained from a mine during a day shift.
6. The survival time (i.e., life) of a light bulb produced by a certain production process.
7. The number of spots showing on a die (singular of dice) that is rolled.
8. The suit and number (face value) of a card drawn randomly from a deck.

All of these examples demonstrate random processes which may give different results each time the process occurs (i.e., each time a new trial is conducted). For example, the demand for a product on Monday will probably be different from the demand on Tuesday. We can thus consider each day to be a separate trial of the random process.

Each of these random processes has certain *events* that can occur as a result of a trial. For example, for the daily demand random process, the events might be:

EVENT 1: Demand $= 0$.

EVENT 2: Demand $= 1$.

EVENT 3: Demand $= 2$.

This is a case of a random process with discrete values, in other words, one that has only a discrete set of possible events. The random process describing the number of pounds of iron ore mined in a day might have as some of its possible events 1,000 lb, 1,000.1 lb, 1,000.11 lb,.... This is an example of a random process with values that are continuous. When a random process is discrete, we can enumerate the events; when it is continuous, however, we can only specify the range of the values that it can assume.

The enumeration of all the possible events that can occur for a trial of a random process is essential to a description of the process. The complete set of all possible events for a random process is called the *event space* or *sample space*.

Figures 2.2.1 and 2.2.2 show the event spaces for the random processes of rolling a die and selecting a card at random from a deck of 52 playing cards. When convenient we may use such symbols as A, B, E_1, and E_2 to denote events.

$$E_1 = 1 \quad \boxed{\cdot} \qquad E_4 = 4 \quad \boxed{\vcenter{\hbox{$\cdot\ \cdot$}}}$$

$$E_2 = 2 \quad \boxed{\cdot\,\cdot} \qquad E_5 = 5 \quad \boxed{\vcenter{\hbox{$\cdot\,\cdot$}}}$$

FIGURE 2.2.1. *Event space for roll of a die.*

$$E_3 = 3 \quad \boxed{\cdot\,\cdot} \qquad E_6 = 6 \quad \boxed{\vcenter{\hbox{$\cdot\,\cdot$}}}$$

	Hearts ♥	Diamonds ♦	Clubs ♣	Spades ♠
Aces:	1H	1D	1C	1S
2's:	2H	2D	2C	2S
3's:	3H	3D	3C	3S
4's:	4H	4D	4C	4S
5's:	5H	5D	5C	5S
6's:	6H	6D	6C	6S
7's:	7H	7D	7C	7S
8's:	8H	8D	8C	8S
9's:	9H	9D	9C	9S
10's:	10H	10D	10C	10S
Jacks:	JH	JD	JC	JS
Queens:	QH	QD	QC	QS
Kings:	KH	KD	KC	KS

FIGURE 2.2.2. *Event space for card drawn at random.*

The events shown in Figures 2.2.1 and 2.2.2 have the following two properties:

1. If any event occurs, no other event of the event space can occur at the same time. We refer to such events as being *mutually exclusive*. For example, a 2 *and* a 3 cannot occur on the roll of a die.
2. No other events other than those enumerated can occur. We refer to a list of such events as being *exhaustive*. Thus, a 7 cannot come up on the roll of a die.

SECTION 2.3. *Elements of Probability*

2.3.1. Introduction. One of the most important characteristics of a random process is the frequency with which each of the possible events occurs, that is, the fraction of time that each event occurs when a trial is conducted.

> *DEFINITION. The probability of an event occurring is the long-run fraction of the time that the event occurs.*

We use the term "long run" since if we conduct only a few trials, the frequency of occurrence may differ from the probability. For example, if the probability that demand = 0 units is $\frac{1}{2}$, we do not expect that for every 2 days we examine, exactly one of the 2 days ($\frac{1}{2}$ of 2) will have zero demand. Yet we would expect that if we examined many, many days, approximately $\frac{1}{2}$ of them would have zero demand. In the long run (i.e., theoretically an infinite number of days) exactly $\frac{1}{2}$ will have zero demand. We shall use the notation

$$P(A) \text{ is the probability that event } A \text{ occurs.}$$

We can also write $P(\text{demand} = 2 \text{ units})$, $P(\text{cost} = \$1.75)$, and so on.

2.3.2. Probability of Mutually Exclusive and Exhaustive Events. Consider the random process defined as the number of spots showing on the face of a die. The mutually exclusive and exhaustive events for this process were shown in Figure 2.2.1.

If the die is fair, then on any trial each event is equally likely to occur. We call these events *equiprobable*. Since there are six equiprobable exhaustive events, each will occur $\frac{1}{6}$ of the time, and therefore the probability of any one event occurring is $\frac{1}{6}$. In general, for a random process with n mutually exclusive, exhaustive, equiprobable events, the probability of any of the events is equal to $1/n$.

Similarly, for the process of selecting a card at random, each event (card) is mutually exclusive, exhaustive, and equiprobable. The probability of selecting any one card on a trial is equal to $\frac{1}{52}$, since there are 52 cards.

Any *impossible event*, such as a 7 coming up on a roll of a fair die, has probability zero, since it can never happen (i.e., the fraction of the time is zero).

2.3.3. Event Sets. Sometimes we are interested in the probability of a number of different events occurring: for example, the probability that the number on the die is even or the card drawn is a spade. These are events composed of a group of the simple mutually exclusive events possible for the process. We call these composite events *event sets*.

The event set "an even number is rolled" is actually a 2 *or* a 4 *or* a 6. We call this "or" relationship the *union* of the events "a 2," "a 4," and "a 6." Similarly, the event set "a spade is drawn" is the union of the 13 mutually exclusive events 1S, 2S,..., 10S, JS, QS, KS.

2.3.4. Addition Rule for Mutually Exclusive Event Sets. There is more than one way to compute probabilities of event sets composed of mutually exclusive, exhaustive, equiprobable events. In the die-rolling example, the event set "even" is really the union of three of the six possible events. The probability is therefore $\frac{3}{6} = \frac{1}{2}$. However, we can also use a general relationship for the union of mutually exclusive events. Denoting the events $A, B, C, \ldots$, we can write

$$P(A \text{ or } B \text{ or } C \text{ or } \ldots) = P(A) + P(B) + P(C) + \cdots$$

Thus

$$P(2 \text{ or } 4 \text{ or } 6) = \frac{1}{6} + \frac{1}{6} + \frac{1}{6} = \frac{3}{6} = \frac{1}{2}$$

This result is known as the Addition Rule for Mutually Exclusive Event Sets. Similarly, for the event set the card drawn at random is a spade, we can compute its probability of $\frac{13}{52}$ or $\frac{1}{4}$ as

$$P(\text{spade}) = P(1S) + P(2S) + \cdots + P(KS)$$

$$= \frac{1}{52} + \frac{1}{52} + \cdots + \frac{1}{52} = \frac{13}{52} = \frac{1}{4}$$

Suppose we are interested in the probability that the face showing on the roll of a die is between 1 and 6 (i.e., 1, 2, 3, 4, 5, or 6). The occurrence of this result is a certainty since it constitutes the entire event space. Its probability can be computed using the Addition Rule.

$$P(\text{between 1 and 6}) = P(1) + P(2) + P(3) + P(4) + P(5) + P(6)$$

$$= \frac{1}{6} + \frac{1}{6} + \frac{1}{6} + \frac{1}{6} + \frac{1}{6} + \frac{1}{6}$$

$$= 1$$

Thus, it can be inferred that the probability of a *certainty event* is 1.

Suppose we are interested in the probability that the face showing is "not a 3," which may be written $P(\bar{3})$. This is clearly $\frac{5}{6}$, the probability of a 1, 2, 4, 5, or 6. It is also equal to $1 - P(3)$ or $1 - \frac{1}{6} = \frac{5}{6}$. In general,

$$P(\bar{A}) = 1 - P(A)$$

2.3.5. Intersection of Event Sets. We may also define event sets whose members are those events which are members of two or more other event sets. For example, consider the probability that a card drawn at random is a "spade" *and* a "picture card (J, Q, K)." Clearly, this is an event set composed of JS, QS, and KS. We may also consider it as those events which belong simultaneously to the following two event sets:

1. The card is a spade.
2. The card is a picture card (J, Q, K).

Event Set 2: Spade;
$$P(A) = \frac{13}{52}$$

	Hearts ♥	Diamonds ♦	Clubs ♣	Spades ♠
Aces:	1H	1D	1C	1S
2's:	2H	2D	2C	2S
3's:	3H	3D	3C	3S
4's:	4H	4D	4C	4S
5's:	5H	5D	5C	5S
6's:	6H	6D	6C	6S
7's	7H	7D	7C	7S
8's:	8H	8D	8C	8S
9's:	9H	9D	9C	9S
10's:	10H	10D	10C	10S
Jacks:	JH	JD	JC	JS
Queens:	QH	QD	QC	QS
Kings:	KH	KD	KC	KS

Event Set 2:
Picture Card;
$P(B) = \frac{12}{52}$

Event Set 3: Intersection
of Spade and Picture Card;
$$P(A \text{ and } B) = \frac{3}{52}$$

FIGURE 2.3.1. *Event set of intersection of two event sets.*

The "and" relationship is called the *intersection* of event sets and is shown diagrammatically in Figure 2.3.1. The probability of this event set is written P(picture card *and* spade) and is called a *joint probability*. The probability can be computed from the fact that this event set is composed of three mutually exclusive equiprobable events (JS, QS, and KS) out of the 52 and therefore has probability $\frac{3}{52}$.

2.3.6. Union of Non-Mutually-Exclusive Events. Let us now consider the probability that the card drawn at random is either a picture card *or* a spade, in other words, the *union* of two non-mutually-exclusive events.

This composite event set is composed of all the spades (13 cards) and all the remaining club, heart, and diamond picture cards (9 cards). Clearly, the probability is equal to $(13+9)/52 = \frac{22}{52}$. Let us develop a probability rule to compute the "or" relationship between non-mutually-exclusive events. Define the following event sets:

A: card is a spade; $P(A) = \frac{13}{52}$

B: card is a picture card; $P(B) = \frac{12}{52}$

If we add the probabilities of the two event sets, yielding

$$P(A) + P(B) = \frac{13}{52} + \frac{12}{52} = \frac{25}{52},$$

we **do not** obtain the correct answer, which is $\frac{22}{52}$. Thus, the addition rule (Section 2.3.4) is valid only if the event sets A and B are mutually exclusive. In our problem there is an overlap in the two event sets. The three spade picture cards are members of both event sets and their contribution to the total probability has been added twice (see Figure 2.3.1) if we simply add $P(A)$ to $P(B)$. We previously discussed that this overlap is the intersection, or $(A$ and $B)$, which has probability $\frac{3}{52}$. We can compute the probability of the card being either a spade *or* a picture card, A or B, by eliminating the overlap as follows:

$$P(A \text{ or } B) = P(A) + P(B) - P(A \text{ and } B)$$
$$= \frac{13}{52} + \frac{12}{52} - \frac{3}{52}$$
$$= \frac{22}{52}$$

Notice that in Figure 2.3.1, there are 22 cards contained within the outer boundaries of the two event sets A and B. This rule may be termed the *General Addition Rule* and will also apply to mutually exclusive event sets since, for them, $P(A$ and $B) = 0$.

2.3.7. Conditional and Marginal Probabilities. Suppose that we remove from the deck all the spades and all the club picture cards, leaving 36 cards. The event space is shown in Figure 2.3.2. If a card is drawn at random, the probability of it being red (R) is different from that of it being black (B). Since there are 26 red cards, $P(R) = \frac{26}{36}$, and since there are 10 black cards, $P(B) = \frac{10}{36}$.

Assume we are told that the card drawn is a 4 but are not told its suit. We would like to determine the probability of the card being red (R) under these new conditions. Clearly, there are two red 4's in the deck (4H and 4D) and one black 4 (4C) (see Figure 2.3.2). The probability of red, given that the card is a 4, is therefore $\frac{2}{3}$. This probability is called a *conditional probability*; that is, it is conditional, on the card being a 4. We write this $P(R|4)$. The probability that the card is black given that it is a

	Hearts ♥	Diamonds ♦	Clubs ♣
Aces:	1H	1D	1C
2's:	2H	2D	2C
3's:	3H	3D	3C
4's:	4H	4D	4C
5's:	5H	5D	5C
6's	6H	6D	6C
7's	7H	7D	7C
8's:	8H	8D	8C
9's:	9H	9D	9C
10's:	10H	10D	10C
Jacks:	JH	JD	
Queens:	QH	QD	
Kings:	KH	KD	

FIGURE 2.3.2. *Event space for card drawn at random from a reduced deck of 36 cards.*

4, $P(B|4) = \frac{1}{3}$. Notice that

$$P(R|4) + P(B|4) = \frac{2}{3} + \frac{1}{3} = 1$$

Hence, given that the card is a 4, it must be either red or black, and these conditional probabilities must therefore add to 1.

Similarly, it can be shown that the probability that the card is a 4 given that it is red, $P(4|R) = \frac{2}{26} = \frac{1}{13}$, since there are 26 red cards, two of which are 4's. This is also a conditional probability and different from $P(R|4)$.

The probabilities $P(R) = \frac{26}{36}$, $P(B) = \frac{10}{36}$, and so on, are called *marginal probabilities* and are not conditional on the value $(1, 2, \ldots)$ of the card. The same is true for probabilities (from the event space in Figure 2.3.2) such as $P(4) = \frac{3}{36}$ or $P(J) = \frac{2}{36}$, which are not conditional on the suit or color of the card. [We have already discussed the concept of the intersection of event sets, such as the probability of a 4 and red card, that is, $P(4 \text{ and } R) = \frac{2}{36}$. These were called *joint probabilities*.]

Thus, if the event space is known, we can compute all the marginal, conditional, and joint probabilities. Sometimes, however, only the joint probabilities are known, and we wish to determine marginal and conditional probabilities. The probability rules for these computations are covered in the next section.

SECTION 2.4. *Probability Rules for Computing Joint, Marginal, and Conditional Probabilities*

Assume that a company has 200 employees and has an index card for each employee. Among other information the card contains information about age and sex. The company is interested in the employee distribution by sex and by whether the employee is under 30, 30 to 50, or over 50.

We define the following event sets for a card selected at random:

A_1: male B_1: under 30 years

A_2: female B_2: 30 to 50 years

                     B_3: over 50 years

The number of employees by category is shown in Figure 2.4.1.

	B_1 Under 30	B_2 30 to 50	B_3 Over 50	
A_1: Male	20	80	0	Total Male: 100
A_2: Female	40	40	20	Total Female: 100
	60 Total under 30	120 Total 30 to 50	20 Total over 50	Total Employees: 200

FIGURE 2.4.1. *Number of employees by age and sex.*

Let us first compute the joint probabilities. Since there are 20 of 200 employees who are male and under 30, the probability that a card selected at random is for a male and under 30 employee is $\frac{20}{200} = 0.1$, which is shown as $P(A_1 \text{ and } B_1)$ in Figure 2.4.2. The other joint probabilities are computed in the same fashion, by dividing the number of specific employees by 200, the total number of employees.

Let us next compute a marginal probability, for example, the probability that the card drawn at random is for a male employee, $P(A_1)$. Of the 200 employees, 100 are male, making the probability

$$P(A_1) = \tfrac{100}{200} = 0.5,$$

which is shown in Figure 2.4.2. Notice that we can also find this and all marginal probabilities directly from the joint probability table by simply adding rows and columns. Summing across the rows, we obtain

$$P_1(A_1) = P(A_1 \text{ and } B_1) + P(A_1 \text{ and } B_2) + P(A_1 \text{ and } B_3)$$
$$= \quad 0.1 \quad + \quad 0.4 \quad + \quad 0$$
$$= 0.5$$

$$P(A_2) = P(A_2 \text{ and } B_1) + P(A_2 \text{ and } B_2) + P(A_2 \text{ and } B_3)$$
$$= \quad 0.2 \quad + \quad 0.2 \quad + \quad 0.1$$
$$= 0.5$$

Thus we may write in general

$$P(A_i) = \sum_j P(A_i \text{ and } B_j) \quad \text{(for any } i)$$

	B_1 Under 30	B_2 30 to 50	B_3 Over 50	
A_1: Male	$P(A_1 \text{ and } B_1)$ $= 0.1$	$P(A_1 \text{ and } B_2)$ $= 0.4$	$P(A_1 \text{ and } B_3)$ $= 0$	$P(A_1) = 0.5$
A_2: Female	$P(A_2 \text{ and } B_1)$ $= 0.2$	$P(A_2 \text{ and } B_2)$ $= 0.2$	$P(A_2 \text{ and } B_3)$ $= 0.1$	$P(A_2) = 0.5$
	$P(B_1) = 0.3$	$P(B_2) = 0.6$	$P(B_3) = 0.1$	

FIGURE 2.4.2. *Joint and marginal probabilities by age and sex.*

Summing down the columns, we obtain

$$P(B_1) = P(A_1 \text{ and } B_1) + P(A_2 \text{ and } B_1)$$

$$= \quad 0.1 \quad + \quad 0.2$$

$$= 0.3$$

$$P(B_2) = P(A_1 \text{ and } B_2) + P(A_2 \text{ and } B_2)$$

$$= \quad 0.4 \quad + \quad 0.2$$

$$= 0.6$$

$$P(B_3) = P(A_1 \text{ and } B_3) + P(A_2 \text{ and } B_3)$$

$$= \quad 0 \quad + \quad 0.1$$

$$= 0.1$$

Hence we may write, in general,

$$P(B_j) = \sum_i P(A_i \text{ and } B_j) \qquad \text{(for any } j\text{)}$$

Let us next compute the conditional probabilities for the two sexes, given the different age categories. Consider the probability of a card drawn at random being for a male employee given that the card is known to be for an employee under 30, or $P(A_1|B_1)$. Since we know that the card is for an employee under 30, it must be one of 60 such cards.

	B_1 Under 30	B_2 30 to 50	B_3 Over 50
A_1: Male	$P(A_1|B_1)$ $= 0.333$	$P(A_1|B_2)$ $= 0.667$	$P(A_1|B_3)$ $= 0$
A_2: Female	$P(A_2|B_1)$ $= 0.667$	$P(A_2|B_2)$ $= 0.353$	$P(A_2|B_3)$ $= 1$
	Sum = 1	Sum = 1	Sum = 1

FIGURE 2.4.3. *Conditional probabilities of sex given age P(A|B).*

Moreover, 20 of these 60 cards are for male employees and therefore

$$P(A_1|B_1) = \tfrac{20}{60} = \tfrac{1}{3} = 0.333.$$

This is shown in Figure 2.4.3. However, we can obtain the same result from the joint probabilities, Figure 2.4.2. If we divide each joint probability by the column marginal probability, we obtain the conditional probabilities conditional on age (B).

$$P(A_1|B_1) = \frac{P(A_1 \text{ and } B_1)}{P(B_1)}$$

$$= \frac{0.1}{0.3}$$

$$= 0.333$$

$$P(A_2|B_1) = \frac{P(A_2 \text{ and } B_1)}{P(B_1)}$$

$$= \frac{0.2}{0.3}$$

$$= 0.667$$

Notice that

$$P(A_1|B_1) + P(A_2|B_1) = 0.333 + 0.667 = 1$$

which is logical, since if the card is for an employee under 30 (B_1), it must be either for a male or a female employee. The probabilities conditioned on a 30- to 50-year-old employee (B_2) are

$$P(A_1|B_2) = \frac{P(A_1 \text{ and } B_2)}{P(B_2)}$$

$$= \frac{0.4}{0.6}$$

$$= 0.667$$

$$P(A_2|B_2) = \frac{P(A_2 \text{ and } B_2)}{P(B_2)}$$

$$= \frac{0.2}{0.6}$$

$$= 0.333$$

with

$$P(A_1|B_2) + P(A_2|B_2) = 0.667 + 0.333 = 1$$

The probabilities conditioned on an over-50-year-old employee (B_3) are

$$P(A_1|B_3) = \frac{P(A_1 \text{ and } B_3)}{P(B_3)}$$

$$= \frac{0}{0.1}$$

$$= 0$$

$$P(A_2|B_3) = \frac{P(A_2 \text{ and } B_3)}{P(B_3)}$$

$$= \frac{0.1}{0.1}$$

$$= 1$$

with

$$P(A_1|B_3) + P(A_2|B_3) = 0 + 1 = 1$$

The general formula for conditional probabilities may be written

$$P(A_i|B_j) = \frac{P(A_i \text{ and } B_j)}{P(B_j)}$$

where

$$\sum_i P(A_i|B_j) = 1 \qquad \text{(for any } j)$$

The conditional probabilities are sometimes written, omitting the i and j subscripts, as follows:

$$P(A|B) = \frac{P(A \text{ and } B)}{P(B)}$$

Notice that the operation of finding $P(A|B)$ is simply dividing each joint probability value, $P(A \text{ and } B)$, by the marginal probability, $P(B)$, which is given at the bottom of each column in Figure 2.4.2.

In a similar fashion, we can compute the conditional probabilities of a card drawn at random being any age group (B) given the sex (A). Consider $P(\text{under } 30|\text{male}) = P(B_1|A_1)$. There are 100 male employees and of these 100 there are 20 who are under 30. Therefore, $P(B_1|A_1) = \frac{20}{100} = 0.2$, which is shown in Figure 2.4.4. An alternative computation for the conditional probability of B_1 given A_1 is

$$P(B_1|A_1) = \frac{P(A_1 \text{ and } B_1)}{P(A_1)}$$

$$= \frac{0.1}{0.5}$$

$$= 0.2$$

	B_1 Under 30	B_2 30 to 50	B_3 Over 50	
A_1: Male	$P(B_1\|A_1)$ $= 0.2$	$P(B_2\|A_1)$ $= 0.8$	$P(B_3\|A_1)$ $= 0$	Sum = 1
A_2: Female	$P(B_1\|A_2)$ $= 0.4$	$P(B_2\|A_2)$ $= 0.4$	$P(B_3\|A_2)$ $= 0.2$	Sum = 1

FIGURE 2.4.4. *Conditional probabilities of age given sex, P(B|A).*

It should be clear that $P(B_1 \text{ and } A_1)$ is the same as $P(A_1 \text{ and } B_1)$. Similarly,

$$P(B_2|A_1) = \frac{P(A_1 \text{ and } B_2)}{P(A_1)}$$

$$= \frac{0.4}{0.5}$$

$$= 0.8$$

$$P(B_3|A_1) = \frac{P(A_1 \text{ and } B_3)}{P(A_1)}$$

$$= \frac{0}{0.5}$$

$$= 0$$

with

$$P(B_1|A_1) + P(B_2|A_1) + P(B_3|A_1) = 0.2 + 0.8 + 0 = 1$$

The probabilities of age (B) conditioned on female (A_2) are

$$P(B_1|A_2) = \frac{P(A_2 \text{ and } B_1)}{P(A_2)}$$

$$= \frac{0.2}{0.5}$$

$$= 0.4$$

$$P(B_2|A_2) = \frac{P(A_2 \text{ and } B_2)}{P(A_2)}$$

$$= \frac{0.2}{0.5}$$

$$= 0.4$$

$$P(B_3|A_2) = \frac{P(A_2 \text{ and } B_3)}{P(A_2)}$$

$$= \frac{0.1}{0.5}$$

$$= 0.2$$

with

$$P(B_1|A_2) + P(B_2|A_2) + P(B_3|A_2) = 0.4 + 0.4 + 0.2 = 1$$

The general formula may be written

$$P(B_j|A_i) = \frac{P(A_i \text{ and } B_j)}{P(A_i)}$$

or

$$P(B|A) = \frac{P(A \text{ and } B)}{P(A)}$$

where

$$\sum_j P(B_j|A_i) = 1 \qquad \text{(for any } i)$$

The operation of finding $P(B|A)$ consists of dividing each joint probability by the marginal probability, $P(A)$, to the right of each row of Figure 2.4.2.

Thus, given the joint probabilities, we can compute both marginal and conditional probabilities for event sets. These techniques are often referred to as *Bayes' Rule*.

SUMMARY OF MARGINAL AND
CONDITIONAL PROBABILITY FORMULA

(1) $$P(A_i) = \sum_j P(A_i \text{ and } B_j) \qquad \text{(for any } i)$$

(2) $$P(B_j) = \sum_i P(A_i \text{ and } B_j) \qquad \text{(for any } j)$$

(3) $$P(A_i|B_j) = \frac{P(A_i \text{ and } B_j)}{P(B_j)}$$

or

$$P(A|B) = \frac{P(A \text{ and } B)}{P(B)}$$

where

$$\sum_i P(A_i|B_j) = 1 \qquad \text{(for any } j)$$

(4) $$P(B_j|A_i) = \frac{P(A_i \text{ and } B_j)}{P(A_i)}$$

or

$$P(B|A) = \frac{P(A \text{ and } B)}{P(A)}$$

where

$$\sum_j P(B_j|A_i) = 1 \qquad \text{(for any } i)$$

A pharmaceutical company is developing a new drug which at present seems to have a 75% chance of being effective against a certain disease. The company is planning to conduct a test to refine their estimate of the likelihood that the drug is effective. The test is only 80% reliable; that is, if the drug is effective, the test will yield a positive result 80% of the time; if the drug is not effective, the test will yield a negative result 80% of the time. The company wants to determine revised estimates of the probabilities that the drug is effective, given that the test result was positive or negative, since the test is expensive and can be performed only once.

Let us use the following notation for the events:

E_1: drug effective

E_2: drug not effective

T_1: positive test result

T_2: negative test result

This notation will be used later (Chapter 4).

The information given in the problem is summarized in Figure 2.5.1, which shows the conditional probabilities of the various test results (T) given the actual drug effectiveness (E), that is, $P(T|E)$ and the marginal probabilities of the actual drug effectiveness, $P(E)$.

	E_1 Drug Effective	E_2 Drug Not Effective
T_1: Test Positive	$P(T_1 \mid E_1)$ $= 0.8$	$P(T_1 \mid E_2)$ $= 0.2$
T_2: Test Negative	$P(T_2 \mid E_1)$ $= 0.2$	$P(T_2 \mid E_2)$ $= 0.8$
	$P(E_1) = 0.75$	$P(E_2) = 0.25$

FIGURE 2.5.1 *Given information for the drug test problem, P(T|E).*

To find $P(E|T)$ we can use equation (2.4.4):[†]

(1)
$$P(E_j|T_i) = \frac{P(T_i \text{ and } E_j)}{P(T_i)}$$

where we have substituted T for A and E for B. However, we are missing the values for $P(T_i \text{ and } E_j)$ and $P(T_i)$. We can use equation (2.4.3) to find the joint probabilities $P(T_i \text{ and } E_j)$:

$$P(T_i|E_j) = \frac{P(T_i \text{ and } E_j)}{P(E_j)}$$

37   [†]Equation (2.4.4) means equation (4) of Section 2.4.

which can be written

(2)
$$P(T_i \text{ and } E_j) = P(T_i|E_j) \cdot P(E_j)$$

This is equivalent to multiplying each $P(T_j|E_i)$ value of Figure 2.5.1 by the marginal probability $P(E_i)$ written at the bottom of each column. This yields the joint probability values, $P(E_i \text{ and } T_j)$, shown in Figure 2.5.2. Summing across the rows we obtain $P(T_i)$, which is equivalent to using equation (2.4.2). We can now apply equation (1) to find $P(E_j|T_i)$. This is equivalent to dividing each $P(T_i \text{ and } E_j)$ value by the marginal probability $P(T_i)$ shown at the right of each row. The results are shown in Figure 2.5.3.

	E_1 Drug Effective	E_2 Drug Not Effective	
T_1: Test Positive	$P(T_1 \text{ and } E_1)$ $= 0.60$	$P(T_1 \text{ and } E_2)$ $= 0.05$	$P(T_1) = 0.65$
T_2: Test Negative	$P(T_2 \text{ and } E_1)$ $= 0.15$	$P(T_2 \text{ and } E_2)$ $= 0.20$	$P(T_2) = 0.35$
	$P(E_1) = 0.75$	$P(E_2) = 0.25$	

FIGURE 2.5.2. *Joint probability table for the drug test problem,* P(T and E).

	E_1 Drug Effective	E_2 Drug Not Effective
T_1: Test Positive	$P(E_1|T_1)$ $= 0.92$	$P(E_2|T_1)$ $= 0.08$
T_2: Test Negative	$P(E_1|T_2)$ $= 0.43$	$P(E_2|T_2)$ $= 0.57$

FIGURE 2.5.3. *Revised probabilities of drug effectiveness for the drug test problem, P(E|T).*

Prior to performing the test the company estimates the probability of the drug being effective, $P(E_1)$, as 0.75. After the test, given a positive outcome, they can estimate the probability of effectiveness $P(E_1|T_1)$ as 0.92; if the test yields a negative outcome, the revised estimate is

$$P(E_1|T_2) = 0.43.$$

Thus, their probabilities of drug effectiveness will have been revised, depending upon the test outcome.

SECTION 2.6. *Independent Events*

2.6.1. Introduction. When considering two events or event sets, sometimes the occurrence of one does not alter the probability of the other occurring. For example, knowing that the card drawn from a full 52-card deck is a jack does not alter the probability that it is a heart, which is still $\frac{1}{4}$. Under such conditions the events or event sets are called *independent*. Mathematically, this is written

(1) $$P(A|B) = P(A)$$

(2) $$P(B|A) = P(B)$$

for two events or event sets A and B; that is, the conditional probabilities equal the unconditional or marginal probabilities.

In the preceding sections we developed the following results for the intersection of event sets:

(3) $$P(A \text{ and } B) = P(A|B) \times P(B) = P(B|A) \times P(A)$$

For independent events, applying equations (1) and (2), we get

(4) $$P(A \text{ and } B) = P(A) \times P(B)$$

Since the event set "jack" is independent of the event set "heart," we can write that the probability that a card drawn at random from a deck of 52 cards is a jack of heart is

$$P(\text{JH}) = P(\text{J and H}) = P(\text{J}) \times P(\text{H})$$
$$= \tfrac{1}{13} \times \tfrac{1}{4} = \tfrac{1}{52}$$

However, if we consider the altered deck of 36 playing cards as shown in Figure 2.3.2, the event sets jack and heart are no longer independent. We have

$$P(\text{J}) = \tfrac{2}{36} = \tfrac{1}{18}$$
$$P(\text{H}) = \tfrac{13}{36}$$
$$P(\text{J}|\text{H}) = \tfrac{1}{13}$$
$$P(\text{H}|\text{J}) = \tfrac{1}{2}$$

and

$$P(\text{J and H}) = P(\text{J}) \times P(\text{H}|\text{J}) = P(\text{H}) \times P(\text{J}|\text{H})$$
$$= \tfrac{1}{18} \times \tfrac{1}{2} = \tfrac{13}{36} \times \tfrac{1}{13}$$
$$= \tfrac{1}{36}$$

2.6.2. Multiple Trials with Independent Events. Let us consider a problem where we toss a fair coin twice and find the probability that the coin shows heads on both tosses.

There are two ways of formulating this problem:

1. One trial consisting of two tosses, or
2. Two trials consisting of one toss each.

The event space for the formulation of the problem as one trial consists of the following four events: HH, HT, TH, and TT. These are four equiprobable, mutually exclusive, and exhaustive events, each having a probability of $\frac{1}{4}$.

Consider now the formulation of the problem as consisting of two trials. The first trial (toss) has the following event space:

A_1: H

A_2: T

and the second trial has the following event space:

B_1: H

B_2: T

The events for each trial are *independent* of the other trial; that is, the outcome of the first toss is unaffected by the outcome of the second toss. In such cases we can use equation (4). Thus, the probability of a head on both tosses is

$$P(A_1 \text{ and } B_1) = P(A_1) \times P(B_1) = \tfrac{1}{2} \times \tfrac{1}{2}$$

$$= \tfrac{1}{4}$$

2.6.3. Multiple Trials with Nonindependent Events. If the events are not independent, we must use equation (3) to compute probabilities:

$$P(A \text{ and } B) = P(A) \times P(B|A)$$

For example, let us compute the probability of randomly drawing 2 jacks from a deck of 52 playing cards without replacing the first card drawn. This can be computed using the following event-set notation:

J_1: jack on first draw

J_2: jack on second draw

$$P(J_1 \text{ and } J_2) = P(J_1) \times P(J_2|J_1)$$

$$= \frac{4}{52} \times \frac{3}{51} = \frac{12}{2,652}$$

$$= \frac{1}{221}$$

2.7.1. Introduction. When the outcomes of a random process are numerical, we can define the outcome results of the process by a variable, called a *random variable*. Thus, we can let

$$X = \text{number of spots showing}$$
$$\text{when a die is rolled}$$

The random variable X has possible outcomes or events 1, 2, 3, 4, 5, and 6, which constitutes the event space. All the properties and relationships developed concerning probabilities of events also hold for outcomes of a random variable. However, since the latter events are numerically valued, they have other useful properties. When we have defined a process by a random variable and have enumerated all the possible outcomes and their probabilities, we call this relationship a *probability distribution*, denoted by $P(X)$. Table 2.7.1 shows the probability distribution for the random variable X, the number of spots showing when a die is rolled. It should be noted that any letter can be used to denote a random variable as long as its interpretation is clearly stated.

TABLE 2.7.1. *Probability Distribution for X,
the Number of Spots Showing
When a Die is Rolled*

X	Probability of X, $P(X)$
1	$\frac{1}{6}$
2	$\frac{1}{6}$
3	$\frac{1}{6}$
4	$\frac{1}{6}$
5	$\frac{1}{6}$
6	$\frac{1}{6}$

2.7.2. Estimating Probability Distributions. Assume that we are interested in estimating the probability distribution for a random variable D, daily demand for a product. To do this we would compile a sample of, say, 200 daily demands and use these data to estimate the probability distribution. The estimation would be made by counting the number of occurrences of each possible outcome for the daily demand (called the *frequency*) and converting these numbers to probabilities. Table 2.7.2 presents a possible result of this estimation procedure. The relative frequency for each outcome is computed as the frequency (i.e., number of days of occurrence) divided by the total number of observations, 200 days. It can be shown that for a random sample, the relative frequency is an unbiased estimator of the probability.

TABLE 2.7.2. *Frequency Function and Estimated Probability*
Distribution for Daily Demand

Daily Demand, D	Frequency (number of days)	Relative = Estimated Frequency Probability	
0	30		0.15
1	60		0.30
2	60		0.30
3	40		0.20
4	8		0.04
5	2		0.01
	200		1.00

2.7.3. Cumulative Probability Distribution. We may sometimes be interested in the likelihood that the outcome of a random variable is not more than some given numerical value. For example, what is the probability that the number of spots showing on a rolled die is not more than 3, that is, shows three or fewer spots? This is known as a *cumulative probability* and is written $C(X)$. The probability distribution $P(X)$ and cumulative probability distribution $C(X)$ for the random variable X are shown in Table 2.7.3. The $C(X)$ is found as follows. The probability of 1 or fewer, $C(1)$, is simply the probability of 1, $P(1) = \frac{1}{6}$, since $0, -1, \ldots$ are impossible and have probability zero. The cumulative probability of 2, $C(2)$ (i.e., the probability of 2 or fewer) is simply the probability of 1 or 2. These are mutually exclusive events and therefore

$$C(2) = P(1 \text{ or } 2) = P(1) + P(2)$$

$$= \frac{1}{6} + \frac{1}{6}$$

$$= \frac{2}{6}$$

TABLE 2.7.3.. *Probability Distribution and*
Cumulative Probability Distribution for
Random Variable X. Number of Spots Showing
When a Die is Rolled

X	Probability, P(X)	Cumulative Probability ($\leqslant X$), C(X)
1	$\frac{1}{6}$	$\frac{1}{6}$
2	$\frac{1}{6}$	$\frac{2}{6} = \frac{1}{3}$
3	$\frac{1}{6}$	$\frac{3}{6} = \frac{1}{2}$
4	$\frac{1}{6}$	$\frac{4}{6} = \frac{2}{3}$
5	$\frac{1}{6}$	$\frac{5}{6}$
6	$\frac{1}{6}$	$\frac{6}{6} = 1$

Another way of finding it is to state that

$$P(2 \text{ or fewer}) = P(1 \text{ or fewer}) + P(2)$$

or

$$C(2) = C(1) + P(2)$$

$$= \tfrac{1}{6} + \tfrac{1}{6}$$

$$= \tfrac{2}{6} \text{ or } \tfrac{1}{3}$$

Similarly,

$$C(3) = C(2) + P(3)$$

$$= \tfrac{2}{6} + \tfrac{1}{6}$$

$$= \tfrac{3}{6} = \tfrac{1}{2}$$

$$C(4) = C(3) + P(4)$$

$$= \tfrac{3}{6} + \tfrac{1}{6}$$

$$= \tfrac{4}{6} = \tfrac{2}{3}$$

$$C(5) = C(4) + P(5)$$

$$= \tfrac{4}{6} + \tfrac{1}{6}$$

$$= \tfrac{5}{6}$$

$$C(6) = C(5) + P(6)$$

$$= \tfrac{5}{6} + \tfrac{1}{6}$$

$$= \tfrac{6}{6} = 1$$

For the daily demand random variable D, we use the relative frequency function, which we call $P(D)$, to find the cumulative relative frequency function, $C(D)$. The cumulative relative frequency function is an unbiased estimator of the cumulative probability distribution, the probability of D or fewer units of demand on a given day. Thus,

$$C(0) = P(0) = 0.15$$
$$C(1) = C(0) + P(1) = 0.15 + 0.30 = 0.45$$
$$C(2) = C(1) + P(2) = 0.45 + 0.30 = 0.75$$
$$C(3) = C(2) + P(3) = 0.75 + 0.20 = 0.95$$
$$C(4) = C(3) + P(4) = 0.95 + 0.04 = 0.99$$
$$C(5) = C(4) + P(5) = 0.99 + 0.01 = 1.00$$

Assume for the moment that we are playing a game where we roll a die and win in dollars an amount equal to the number of spots showing on the die. Let us define a random variable X, the winnings each time the die is rolled. The probability distribution of X is the same as that for the number of spots showing on a rolled die, given in Table 2.7.1. Suppose that we were asked to pay \$3 each time we wished to play this game. We would like to know if this game is profitable in the long run. We recognize that sometimes there will be only one or two spots showing, and therefore for that game we will lose money. However, what is of interest to us is the long run *average* winnings. If they are greater than \$3, it pays to play the game; if they are less than \$3, it does not. The *expected value* or *mean* of a random variable is the long-run average outcome of the random variable and is written $E(X)$ or μ (Greek lower case mu). Let us develop a method for computing the expected value of a discrete random variable such as the winnings in the die game just described. If we played the game many, many times, we would expect approximately $\frac{1}{6}$ of the outcomes to be 1's, $\frac{1}{6}$ to be 2's, $\frac{1}{6}$ to be 3's, and so on. Over a long period of time, our average winnings would be

$$\tfrac{1}{6}(1)+\tfrac{1}{6}(2)+\tfrac{1}{6}(3)+\tfrac{1}{6}(4)+\tfrac{2}{6}(5)+\tfrac{1}{6}(6)=\tfrac{1}{6}+\tfrac{2}{6}+\tfrac{3}{6}+\tfrac{4}{6}+\tfrac{5}{6}+\tfrac{6}{6}$$

$$=\tfrac{21}{6}$$

$$=\$3.50/\text{game}$$

Thus, the game is profitable to us, since the average cost per game is only \$3.

In general, we can write

$$\mu=E(X)=\sum X \cdot P(X)$$

That is, the expected outcome or mean of a random variable is the sum of each outcome times its probability.

Let us apply this rule to find the average daily demand, $E(D)$, for the random-variable data given in Table 2.7.2. We write the expression for the expected value as

$$E(D)=\sum D \cdot P(D)$$

and the computations are shown in Table 2.8.1. We would therefore expect that, if we computed the average demand for many, many days, the average would approach 1.71 units/day.

The expected value or mean is sometimes referred to as a *measure of central tendency* of a random variable, since it defines a unique value about which the outcomes tend to cluster.

44

D (units)	P(D)	D·P(D)
0	0.15	0.00
1	0.30	0.30
2	0.30	0.60
3	0.20	0.60
4	0.04	0.16
5	0.01	0.05
		$E(D) = 1.71$ units

SECTION 2.9. *Standard Deviation—Discrete Random Variable*

The mean or expected value of a probability distribution describes its central tendency. The measure used to describe its variability or spread is the *variance* σ^2 or the *standard deviation* σ, the square root of the variance (Greek lower case sigma). The standard deviation is defined by

$$\sigma = \sqrt{E(X-\mu)^2}$$

the expected value of $(X-\mu)^2$. For discrete random variables, we get

$$\sigma = \sqrt{\Sigma(X-\mu)^2 P(X)}$$

The standard deviation gives a measure of the spread of the distribution, since it reflects deviations from the mean. A simpler form for computing σ for discrete random variables is

$$\sigma = \sqrt{[\Sigma X^2 P(X)] - \mu^2}$$

Consider the two probability distributions presented in Tables 2.9.1 and

TABLE 2.9.1. *Computation of μ and σ for a Probability Distribution with Little Variation*

X	P(X)	X·P(X)	X−μ	(X−μ)²·P(X)	X²·P(X)
19	0.25	4.75	−1	0.25	90.25
20	0.50	10.00	0	0	200.00
21	0.25	5.25	1	0.25	110.25

$$\mu = \Sigma\ X \cdot P(X)$$
$$\mu = \quad 20.00$$

$$\sigma^2 = \Sigma(X-\mu)^2 P(X)$$
$$\sigma^2 = \quad 0.50$$
$$\sigma = \quad 0.707$$

$$\sigma^2 = \Sigma X^2 P(X) - \mu^2$$
$$400.50$$
$$-400.00$$

$$\sigma^2 = \quad 0.50$$
$$\sigma = \quad 0.707$$

2.9.2. The comnputations for the means and the two methods of comput-ing σ are also given. The distributions are similar in that they each have three values, the same set of probabilities, and equal means. However, the distribution of Table 2.9.2 has greater variability, since its values tend to be farther from the mean; that is, 10 and 30 are farther from the mean than 19 and 21. This fact is reflected in its larger variance, σ^2, and standard deviation, σ.

TABLE 2.9.2. *Computation of μ and σ for
a Probability Distribution with Greater Variation*

X	$P(X)$	$X \cdot P(X)$	$X - \mu$	$(X-\mu)^2 \cdot P(X)$	$X^2 \cdot P(X)$
10	0.25	2.50	-10	25.0	25.0
20	0.50	10.00	0	0	200.0
30	0.25	7.50	10	25.0	225.0

$$\mu = \Sigma X \cdot P(X) \qquad \sigma^2 = \Sigma(X-\mu)^2 P(X) \qquad \sigma^2 = \Sigma X^2 P(X) - \mu^2$$

$$\mu = 20.00 \qquad \sigma^2 = 50.00 \qquad 450$$

$$\sigma = 7.07 \qquad -400$$

$$\sigma^2 = 50.00$$

$$\sigma = 7.07$$

SECTION 2.10. *Discrete Probability Distributions*

2.10.1. The Binomial Distribution. Consider a situation or experiment that consists of multiple trials, each of which is independent of the others. For example, we may toss a fair coin 10 times and be interested in determining the probability of exactly 0 heads out of 10 tosses, exactly 1 head out of 10 tosses, and so on. Or we may be interested in determining the probability of zero demand for either 0 days during a 5-day week, for 1 day during a 5-day week, for 2 days during a 5-day week, and so on. The *binomial distribution* can be used to compute these probabilities.

The binomial distribution states that for n independent trials where the probability of some outcome occurring on each trial is p (and $1-p$ of not occurring), the probability of r occurrences out of the n trials is

$$P(r \text{ out of } n) = B(r; n, p) = \frac{n!}{r!(n-r)!} p^r (1-p)^{(n-r)}$$

where $n =$ number of independent trials

$p =$ probability of the outcome of interest
occurring on one trial

$r =$ number of trials out of n
for which the outcome occurs

$a! = a(a-1)(a-2)\cdots 1$

$0! = 1$

Let us find the probability of exactly two out of three rolls of a fair die showing 1's. The event of interest is "toss is a 1." We have

$$n = 3$$
$$p = \tfrac{1}{6}$$
$$r = 2$$

$$P(2 \text{ out of } 3) = B\left(2; 3, \tfrac{1}{6}\right) = \frac{3!}{2!(3-2)!}\left(\frac{1}{6}\right)^2\left(\frac{5}{6}\right)^{3-2}$$

$$= \frac{3!}{(2!)(1!)}\left(\frac{1}{6}\right)^2\left(\frac{5}{6}\right)^1$$

$$= \frac{3\cdot2\cdot1}{(2\cdot1)(1)}\cdot\frac{1}{36}\cdot\frac{5}{6}$$

$$= \frac{6}{2\cdot1}\cdot\frac{1}{36}\cdot\frac{5}{6}$$

$$= \tfrac{5}{72}$$

We can check this result using the probability rules for multiple trials with independent events. We can consider each trial as consisting of two events; a "1" with probability $\tfrac{1}{6}$ and "not a 1" ($\bar{1}$) with probability $\tfrac{5}{6}$. The event sets for the three trials that yield 1's as an outcome in two out of three trial tosses are as follows:

A: $(1 \quad 1 \quad \bar{1})$ probability $= \tfrac{1}{6}\cdot\tfrac{1}{6}\cdot\tfrac{5}{6} = \tfrac{5}{216}$

B: $(1 \quad \bar{1} \quad 1)$ probability $= \tfrac{1}{6}\cdot\tfrac{5}{6}\cdot\tfrac{1}{6} = \tfrac{5}{216}$

C: $(\bar{1} \quad 1 \quad 1)$ probability $= \tfrac{5}{6}\cdot\tfrac{1}{6}\cdot\tfrac{1}{6} = \tfrac{5}{216}$

$$P(2 \text{ out of } 3) = P(A \text{ or } B \text{ or } C)$$

Since A, B, and C are mutually exclusive,

$$P(2 \text{ out of } 3) = P(A) + P(B) + P(C)$$

$$= \tfrac{5}{216} + \tfrac{5}{216} + \tfrac{5}{216}$$

$$= \tfrac{5}{72}$$

It can be shown that for the binomial distribution the following results hold:

mean: $\mu = np$

standard deviation: $\sigma = \sqrt{np(1-p)}$

   Thus, if we wish to determine the mean and standard deviation for the number of 1's out of three tosses of the die, we get

$$\mu = np = 3\left(\tfrac{1}{6}\right)$$

$$= \tfrac{1}{2}$$

$$\sigma = \sqrt{np(1-p)} = \sqrt{3\left(\tfrac{1}{6}\right)\left(\tfrac{5}{6}\right)} = \sqrt{\tfrac{5}{12}}$$

$$= 0.65$$

2.10.2. The Poisson Distribution. Another discrete distribution that is sometimes useful for describing random processes is the *Poisson distribution*. One of its primary uses is to compute the probability for the number of occurrences, X, of a given event during a specific time period. The Poisson distribution is given by[†]

$$P(x) = e^{-a}\frac{a^x}{x!} \qquad (x = 0, 1, 2, \ldots)$$

where $e = 2.7183$. The mean of the distribution is a and the standard deviation can be shown to be $\sqrt{a}$. Thus

$$\mu = a$$

$$\sigma = \sqrt{a}$$

As an example, suppose that cars arrive at a toll booth according to a Poisson distribution at a mean rate of three cars per minute. Let us find the probability of exactly four cars arriving during a 1-minute period.

$$P(4 \text{ arrivals during a 1-minute period}) = \frac{(e^{-3})3^4}{4!}$$

$$= \frac{(0.04978)(81)}{4 \cdot 3 \cdot 2 \cdot 1}$$

$$= 0.168$$

If we consider a 2-minute period, we would expect the mean number of arrivals to be twice as great; that is, $a = 2(3) = 6$ arrivals/2 minutes. This is true for a random process that follows a Poisson distribution. The probability of four cars arriving during a 2-minute period is therefore

$$P(4 \text{ arrivals during a 2-minute period}) = \frac{e^{-6}(6)^4}{4!}$$

$$= \frac{(0.00248)(1,296)}{4 \cdot 3 \cdot 2 \cdot 1}$$

$$= 0.13$$

[†]A table of e to various powers is given in Appendix A.

The interesting property of the Poisson distribution is that it assumes that if the distribution of the number of events occurring during a time period is Poisson, then if we consider a time period of different length, the distribution of number of events is still Poisson, with mean proportional to the length of the time period.

SECTION 2.11. *Continuous Probability Distributions*

2.11.1. Introduction. Up to this point we have examined only random processes with discrete events. There are, however, many random processes with continuous numerically valued events, such as the daily heating-fuel consumption of a home or the weight of ore removed from a mine each day. Such processes may be described by continuous random variables.

In order to compute the likelihood of occurrence of the various outcomes, a *probability density function* (often also called a *probability distribution*) is used instead of a discrete probability distribution. Figure 2.11.1 shows a continuous probability density function for a continuous random variable, X. The function is written simply as $f(X) = \frac{1}{10}$ for X between 1 and 11. In treating continuous random variables, mathematicians have at times chosen to define another variable, for example x, to denote a general value assumed by the random variable and therefore often write the probability density functions as $f(x)$ instead of $f(X)$. However, for simplicity we will not differentiate between the two.

The assumption is that this random variable cannot have outcomes with values lower than 1 or higher than 11; that is, its range is 1 through 11. The constant height of the function is indicative of the fact that all outcomes are equiprobable. This type of probability density function (i.e., a constant value) is called a *uniform distribution*.

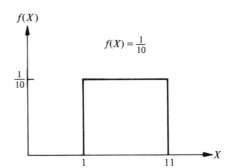

FIGURE 2.11.1. *A continuous probability density function.*

Since X is a continuous random variable, there are an infinite number of values between 1 and 11. The probability of any one value, for instance 2.00000..., is zero since the sum of probabilities for all values between 1 and 11 must add to 1. However, when we ask for the probability that $X = 2$, perhaps we really mean to determine the probability that X is between 1.95 and 2.05; that is, that it falls within a range of values. The way we determine the probability that the random variable falls between any two values, a and b in general, is by finding the area beneath the probability density function between the values a and b. For the function of Figure 2.11.2, this area is given as

$$P(a \leqslant X \leqslant b) = \frac{b-a}{10}$$

For example, the probability that X is between 1 and 2 is

$$P(1 \leqslant X \leqslant 2) = \frac{2-1}{10}$$

$$= \tfrac{1}{10}$$

The probability that X is between 2 and 3 is

$$P(2 \leqslant X \leqslant 3) = \frac{3-2}{10}$$

$$= \tfrac{1}{10}$$

Clearly, the probability that the X falls in any interval that is one unit wide is $\tfrac{1}{10}$. Thus, all equal interval values are equiprobable. For example, the probability that X is between 1.95 and 2.05 is

$$P(1.95 \leqslant X \leqslant 2.05) = \frac{2.05 - 1.95}{10} = \frac{0.1}{10}$$

$$= 0.01$$

as is true for any interval of width 0.1.

The area underneath the entire probability function must always equal 1, since one of the possible values must always occur. In our example X must be a value between 1 and 11:

$$P(1 \leqslant X \leqslant 11) = \frac{11-1}{10} = \frac{10}{10}$$

$$= 1.$$

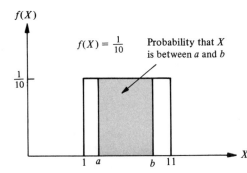

FIGURE 2.11.2. *The probability
that X is between a and b.*

2.11.2. The Cumulative Probability Distribution. We are often interested in finding the probability that the random variable X takes on values less than or equal to a given value x, $P(X \leqslant x)$. These probabilities are found from the *cumulative probability distribution*, which is written $F(x)$. The cumulative probability distribution for our random variable X is shown in Figure 2.11.3. The general method of computing the cumulative function requires the calculus and will not be covered in this text.

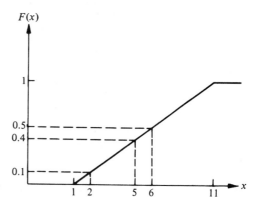

FIGURE 2.11.3. *The cumulative probability distribution $F(x)=P(X \leqslant x)$.*

Note x is a general value of the random variable X

Let us find the probability that $X \leqslant 5$. This is equivalent to the probability that X is between 1 and 5, since values less than 1 are impossible and have zero probability. From the probability density function we find that

$$P(1 \leqslant X \leqslant 5) = \frac{5-1}{10} = 0.4$$

which is precisely the value of the cumulative probability distribution, $F(x)$, for $x=5$ of Figure 2.11.3.

The cumulative probability function can also be used to compute probabilities. For example, assume that we wish to find $P(2 \leqslant X \leqslant 6)$. From the probability density function we compute

$$P(2 \leqslant X \leqslant 6) = \frac{6-2}{10}$$
$$= 0.4$$

It can be shown that

$$P(a \leqslant X \leqslant b) = F(b) - F(a)$$

so that

$$P(2 \leqslant X \leqslant 6) = F(6) - F(2)$$
$$= 0.5 - 0.1$$
$$= 0.4$$

The computation of the expected value or mean and standard deviation of a continuous random variable requires the use of the calculus and will not be covered in this text.

2.11.3. The Standard Normal Distribution. The normal distribution is one of the most important continuous probability distributions (density functions) and is often referred to as the "bell-shaped curve." One such normal distribution, the *standard normal distribution*, has a mean $\mu = 0$ and a standard deviation $\sigma = 1$ and is shown in Figure 2.11.4. The variable Z is usually used to denote the standard normal random variable. As with all probability density functions, the probability of the random variable falling between any two values is given by the area under the function between the two values. For example, it can be shown that $P(0 \leqslant Z \leqslant 1) = 0.3413$, $P(0 \leqslant Z \leqslant 2) = 0.4772$, $P(0 \leqslant Z \leqslant 3) = 0.4987$, and so on. The standard normal distribution is a symmetrical distribution, and therefore $P(0 \leqslant Z \leqslant a) = P(-a \leqslant Z \leqslant 0)$ for any value a. Thus,

$$P(-1 \leqslant Z \leqslant 1) = 0.6826,$$

$$P(-2 \leqslant Z \leqslant 2) = 0.9544,$$

and

$$P(-3 \leqslant Z \leqslant 3) = 0.9974,$$

Since the standard deviation $\sigma = 1$, we can state that 68.3% of the time, the values of the random variable Z will fall between plus or minus $(\pm)1$ standard deviation away from the mean, 95.4% of the time they fall

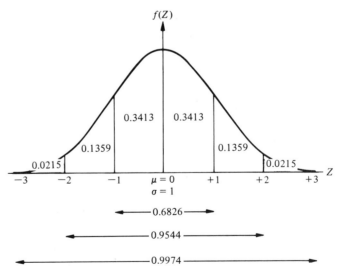

FIGURE 2.11.4. *The standard normal distribution f(Z). ($\mu = 0$ and $\sigma = 1$.)*

between ±2 standard deviations away from the mean, and 99.7% of the time they fall between ±3 standard deviations away from the mean. These statements can be shown to be true for all normally distributed random variables even if $\mu\neq0$ and $\sigma\neq1$.

The actual method of determining probabilities for the random variable Z is to use the *cumulative normal probabilities* table shown as Appendix B. It gives values for $A(z)=P(Z\leqslant z)$ for many values of z, that is, the probability that the random variable Z takes on a value less than or equal to z.[†] This cumulative table is then used to find the probability of a standard normal variable taking on values within any given range.

Let us find the probability that a standard normal random variable Z takes on values between $+1$ and $+2$. This will be equal to

$$P(1\leqslant Z\leqslant2)=P(Z\leqslant2)-P(Z\leqslant1)$$
$$=A(2)-A(1)$$

This is shown diagrammatically in Figure 2.11.5. Using Appendix B we find that $A(2)=0.9772$ and $A(1)=0.8413$, and therefore

$$P(1\leqslant Z\leqslant2)=0.9772-0.8413$$
$$=0.1359$$

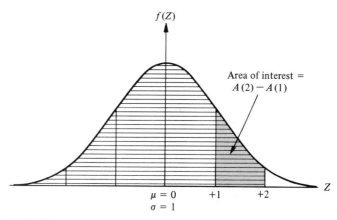

FIGURE 2.11.5. Diagram of finding $P(1\leqslant Z\leqslant2)$ for standard normal distribution.

Since $\sigma=1$ for the standard normal distribution, it can be shown that the probability of any normal random variable (X) falling between 1σ above the mean and 2σ above the mean is 0.1359, or

$$P(\mu+1\sigma\leqslant X\leqslant\mu+2\sigma)=0.1359$$

[†]For the standard normal distribution, $A(Z)$ will be used to denote the cumulative distribution.

2.11.4. The Normal Distribution. In the preceding section we discussed the standard normal distribution, which is the normal distribution with mean $\mu = 0$ and standard deviation $\sigma = 1$. However, most random variables that obey the normal distribution do not have means of $\mu = 0$ and standard deviations of $\sigma = 1$. It will be seen that the cumulative normal probabilities table can still be used to compute probabilities for these normal random variables.

Assume that the daily demand for a product, a random variable X, has mean $\mu = 10$ units and standard deviation $\sigma = 2$. This is often written $N(10, 2)$. Let us find the probability that the demand on a given day is between 12 and 14 units.

In the prior subsection we determined the probability that a standard normal random variable is between $+1$ and $+2$ and, using the cumulative tables, found it to be 0.1359. We further stated that for any normal random variable (X),

$$P(\mu + 1\sigma \leqslant X \leqslant \mu + 2\sigma) = 0.1359$$

since for the standard normal random variable Z, $\mu = 0$ and $\sigma = 1$. For the daily demand random variable with $\mu = 10$ and $\sigma = 2$, the value $X = 12$ is 1σ above the mean. This is calculated as follows: $12 - 10 = 2$ is the distance above the mean. Since $\sigma = 2$, the 2 units above the mean are $\frac{2}{2} = 1\sigma$ above the mean. Similarly, daily demand $X = 14$ units is 2 standard deviations (2σ) above the mean. In general, we may convert any numerical value (X) from a normal distribution to its equivalent standard normal value (Z) by

(1)
$$Z = \frac{x - \mu}{\sigma}$$

Thus

$$P(12 \leqslant X \leqslant 14) = P(1 \leqslant Z \leqslant 2)$$

This is shown diagrammatically in Figure 2.11.6.

Notice that the daily demand distribution is shifted to the right since $\mu = 10$ and is more spread out since $\sigma = 2$. The total area beneath each of the curves must be 1, as is true with all probability density functions.

Thus, to find probabilities involving normal random variables, we simply need to convert our probability question from one involving actual values to one involving the number of standard deviations away from the mean. Let us find the probability that daily demand is between 9 and 13 units, $P(9 \leqslant X \leqslant 13)$. We stated earlier that

$$P(9 \leqslant X \leqslant 13) = F(13) - F(9)$$

We must convert the values 13 and 9, X values, to number of standard deviations away from the mean, Z values. This can be done by using the conversion formula given by equation (1). Thus, the value $X = 9$ is

$$Z = \frac{9 - 10}{2} = -\frac{1}{2}$$

$$= -0.5$$

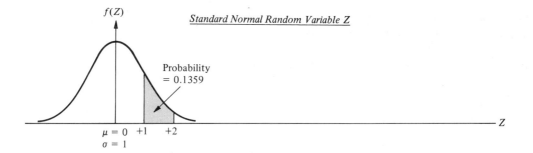

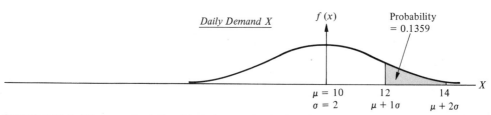

FIGURE 2.11.6. *Diagram of relationship between standard and non-standard normal probabilities. (Z is the standard normal random variable. X is the daily demand, normal, μ = 10, σ = 2.)*

or 0.5 standard deviation below the mean. The value $X = 13$ is

$$Z = \frac{13 - 10}{2} = \frac{3}{2}$$
$$= 1.5$$

or 1.5 standard deviations above the mean. Therefore,

$$P(9 \leqslant X \leqslant 13) = P(-0.5 \leqslant Z \leqslant 1.5)$$
$$= A(1.5) - A(-0.5)$$
$$= 0.9332 - 0.3085$$
$$= 0.6247$$

2.11.5. The Exponential Distribution. One important continuous probability distribution useful in describing many processes is the *exponential distribution*. For example, the duration of telephone calls has been shown to often be exponentially distributed.

The exponential distribution is given by

$$f(T) = be^{-bT} \qquad (\text{for } T \geqslant 0)$$

where $e = 2.7183$. The mean μ or $E(T)$ equals $1/b$. Thus, b defines the mean. The cumulative probability distribution is

$$F(t) = P(T \leqslant t) = 1 - e^{-bt}$$

For example, assume that telephone calls are exponentially distributed with a mean duration of 10 minutes, $\frac{1}{6}$ hour. We shall use hours as a time unit.

The parameter b equals $1/\text{mean}$:

$$b = \frac{1}{\frac{1}{6}} = 6$$

The probability density function is therefore

$$f(T) = 6e^{-6T}$$

The cumulative distribution, $F(t)$, gives the probability that a telephone call takes less than or equal to a general value t hours, or

$$F(t) = 1 - e^{-6t}$$

Thus,

$$P(T \leqslant 0.1 \text{ hour}) = 1 - e^{-6(0.1)} = 0.45$$

$$P(T \leqslant 0.2 \text{ hour}) = 1 - e^{-6(0.2)} = 0.70$$

$$P(T \leqslant 0.3 \text{ hour}) = 1 - e^{-6(0.3)} = 0.83$$

Hence, using the exponential distribution, we would expect 45% of the telephone calls to be finished in less than 6 minutes ($t = 0.1$ hour), 70% in 12 minutes or less ($t = 0.2$ hour), and 83% in 18 minutes or less ($t = 0.3$ hour).

SECTION 2.12. *Sums of Independent Random Variables*

Assume that we are interested in the value of a random variable which is determined as the sum of other independent random variables. For example, weekly demand for a product may be the sum of five independent daily demands, or the length of a certain manufactured product may be the sum of the lengths of several other manufactured parts, each of whose lengths is random and independent. In such cases the mean is the sum of the means and the variance is the sum of the variances or, mathematically stated,

$$\mu_T = \sum_{i=1}^{n} \mu_i$$

$$\sigma_T^2 = \sum_{i=1}^{n} \sigma_i^2$$

where n = number of random variables summed

μ_i = mean of ith random variable

σ_i^2 = variance of ith random variable

μ_T = mean of the resultant random variable

σ_T^2 = variance of the resultant random variable

As an example, consider three parts joined together in a production process to form a final product. The mean and variance of the length of each part is

$$\mu_1 = 10 \quad \sigma_1^2 = 9 \quad \text{or} \quad \sigma_1 = 3$$
$$\mu_2 = 22 \quad \sigma_2^2 = 25 \quad \text{or} \quad \sigma_2 = 5$$
$$\mu_3 = 15 \quad \sigma_3^2 = 16 \quad \text{or} \quad \sigma_3 = 4$$

The mean, variance, and standard deviation of the resultant part is

$$\mu_T = \mu_1 + \mu_2 + \mu_3$$
$$= 10 + 22 + 15$$
$$= 47$$

$$\sigma_T^2 = \sigma_1^2 + \sigma_2^2 + \sigma_3^2$$
$$= 9 + 25 + 16$$
$$= 50$$

$$\sigma_T = \sqrt{\sigma_T^2} = \sqrt{50}$$
$$= 7.1$$

As a second example, assume that daily demand has a mean of 10 units with a standard deviation of 2 units. Weekly demand is the sum of five independent random variables (daily demand) all having the same distribution. The mean weekly demand will be

$$\mu = \mu_1 + \mu_2 + \mu_3 + \mu_4 + \mu_5$$
$$= 10 + 10 + 10 + 10 + 10$$
$$= 5(10)$$
$$= 50 \text{ units}$$

and the variance of weekly demand will be

$$\sigma^2 = \sigma_1^2 + \sigma_2^2 + \sigma_3^2 + \sigma_4^2 + \sigma_5^2$$
$$= 4 + 4 + 4 + 4 + 4$$
$$= 5(4)$$
$$= 20 \text{ units}$$

Therefore, the standard deviation of weekly demand is

$$\sigma = \sqrt{\sigma^2} = \sqrt{20}$$
$$= 4.47 \text{ units}$$

Thus, if the independent random variables being summed have identical distributions, the mean and variance are merely n times the mean and variance of each random variable:

$$\mu_T = n\mu_i$$

$$\sigma_T^2 = n\sigma_i^2$$

and

$$\sigma_T = \sqrt{n}\ \sigma_i$$

One important property of the normal distribution is that if several normally distributed random variables are summed, the resultant variable is also normally distributed. Thus, if in the two examples above the daily demands and part lengths are normally distributed, we have found not only the mean and variance of the resultant variable, but also its probability distribution, which is the normal distribution. For most other probability distributions, however, the resultant random variable will not have the same probability distribution as the individual random variables.

SECTION 2.13. *The Central Limit Theorem*

The *central limit theorem* states that when many independent random variables are summed, no matter what their underlying probability distribution is like, the resultant random variable will approach the normal distribution. The greater the number of random variables summed, the more closely the approximation will hold. In fact, summing relatively few random variables will tend to give a resultant random variable that is extremely close to being normally distributed. For example, summing 12 equiprobable (uniformly distributed) continuous random variables yields a resultant variable that is virtually normally distributed. If the individual random variables have distributions which more closely obey the normal distribution, even fewer than 12 of them summed together will give a resultant variable that is virtually normally distributed.

SECTION 2.14. *Independent Random Samples*

Frequently, in order to make estimates of the mean and variance of the probability distribution of a random variable, independent random samples are taken. For example, to estimate the mean μ and standard deviation σ of daily demand, we may take a randomly selected sample of daily demands from past history. If we denote the n sample values X_1, $X_2, \ldots, X_n$, we can compute two quantities known as the *sample mean* or *average*, $\overline{X}$, and the *sample variance S^2* or *sample standard deviation, S*, which can be shown to be good estimators of the mean μ and variance σ^2

or standard deviation σ of the random variable. These are computed as follows:

$$(1) \qquad \bar{X} = \frac{\sum\limits_{i=1}^{n} X_i}{n}$$

$$(2) \qquad S^2 = \frac{\sum\limits_{i=1}^{n} (x_1 - \bar{X})^2}{n-1}$$

A simpler form for computing S^2 is

$$(3) \qquad S^2 = \frac{\sum\limits_{i=1}^{n} X_i^2 - n\bar{X}^2}{n-1}$$

and

$$S = \sqrt{S^2}$$

Assume that a mining company's daily demands for a metal ore are independent and we have obtained a random sample of 10 daily demands. Let us estimate the mean μ and standard deviation σ of the daily demand. Table 2.14.1 shows the sample values of daily demand in tons

TABLE 2.14.1. *Computation of Sample Average $\bar{X}$
and Sample Standard Deviation S for
a Sample of n = 10 Daily Demands of Metal Ore (in tons)*

Day No. (i)	X_i	$X_i - \bar{X}$	$(X_i - \bar{X})^2$	$(X_i)^2$
1	8.8	−1.43	2.045	77.44
2	11.7	1.47	2.161	136.89
3	10.4	0.17	0.029	108.16
4	6.6	−3.63	13.177	43.56
5	9.6	−0.63	0.397	92.16
6	14.2	3.97	15.761	201.64
7	11.6	1.37	1.877	134.56
8	9.3	−0.93	0.865	86.49
9	9.4	−0.83	0.689	88.36
10	10.7	0.47	0.221	114.49

$$\sum X = 102.3 \qquad \sum(X_i - \bar{X})^2 = 37.222 \qquad \sum X_i^2 = 1{,}083.75$$

$$\bar{X} = \frac{\sum X}{n} \qquad S^2 = \frac{\sum(X_i - \bar{X})^2}{n-1} \qquad S^2 = \frac{\sum X_i^2 - n\bar{X}^2}{n-1}$$

$$= \frac{102.3}{10} \qquad = \frac{37.222}{9} \qquad = \frac{1{,}083.75 - 10(10.23)^2}{9}$$

$$= 10.23 \qquad = 4.136 \qquad = \frac{1{,}083.75 - 1{,}046.529}{9}$$

$$S = \sqrt{S^2} \qquad = \frac{37.221}{9}$$

$$= 2.03 \qquad = 4.136$$

$$S = \sqrt{S^2}$$

$$= 2.03$$

and the computations. Notice that the same result for S^2 and S is obtained whether we use equation (2) or equation (3). The $\overline{X}$ value of 10.23 is an estimate of the true mean daily demand μ. The S value of 2.03 is an estimate of the true standard deviation σ.

SECTION 2.15. *Sampling Distributions*

If we took a second independent random sample of the 10 daily demands, we would not, in general, obtain the same set of sample values, and thus would obtain different values for $\overline{X}$ and S. This will be true for each independent set of 10 daily demands. Therefore, our estimators $\overline{X}$ and S are considered random variables themselves; that is, they are not predictable with certainty *even if we know μ and σ*. It can be shown that the mean of the probability distribution for the random variable $\overline{X}$ is μ:

$$E(\overline{X}) = \mu$$

and the mean of the distribution for the random variable S^2 is σ^2:

$$E(S^2) = \sigma^2$$

For this reason $\overline{X}$ and S^2 are called *unbiased estimators* of the unknown parameters mean μ and variance σ^2.

It is usually also important to know the standard deviation of the distribution of $\overline{X}$, since it measures its variability. This quantity is denoted as $\sigma_{\overline{X}}$ and is often called the *standard error of the mean*. If $\sigma_{\overline{X}}$ is small, we expect $\overline{X}$ to be closer to the true mean than if $\sigma_{\overline{X}}$ is large.

We can show that

$$\sigma_{\overline{X}} = \frac{\sigma}{\sqrt{n}}$$

where n is the sample size. Thus, as we increase the sample size, the standard deviation of the sample average $\sigma_{\overline{X}}$ decreases, and $\overline{X}$ becomes a more precise estimator of the mean. Figure 2.15.1 illustrates this concept.

It was pointed out in the previous section that as the number of summed random variables becomes larger, the distribution of the sum becomes approximately normal. If we examine the expression for $\overline{X}$, $\sum_{i=1}^{n} X_i / n$, we see that it is a sum of random observations of the random variable X divided by a constant, n. The sum, therefore, is approximately normally distributed for large samples from the central limit theorem. Since $\overline{X}$ is simply the sum divided by a constant, it can be shown that $\overline{X}$ is also normally distributed. Thus, we can state that the distribution of $\overline{X}$ is approximately normal with mean μ and standard deviation $\sigma_{\overline{X}} = \sigma/\sqrt{n}$.

If σ is unknown, as is usually the case, we may use S to estimate σ and state that

$$\sigma_{\overline{X}} \approx S_{\overline{X}} = \frac{S}{\sqrt{n}}$$

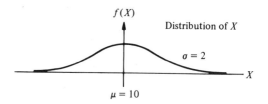

$f(X)$

Distribution of X

$\sigma = 2$

X

$\mu = 10$

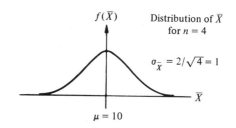

$f(\bar{X})$

Distribution of $\bar{X}$
for $n = 4$

$\sigma_{\bar{X}} = 2/\sqrt{4} = 1$

$\bar{X}$

$\mu = 10$

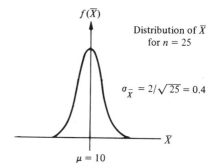

$f(\bar{X})$

Distribution of $\bar{X}$
for $n = 25$

$\sigma_{\bar{X}} = 2/\sqrt{25} = 0.4$

$\bar{X}$

$\mu = 10$

FIGURE 2.15.1. *Relationship between σ and $\sigma_{\bar{x}}$ for $n=4$ and $n=25$ where $\mu=10$ and $\sigma=2$.*

However, in this case the distribution of $\bar{X}$ is no longer normally distributed but follows a distribution, known as the *t distribution*, which looks very much like the normal but changes as n, the number of observations in the sample, changes. However, for n greater than 40, the t distribution is extremely close to the normal distribution. Thus, when $n > 40$ we may as an approximation state that

$\bar{X}$ is approximately normally distributed with mean μ and standard deviation $S_{\bar{x}} = S/\sqrt{n}$.

The standard deviation of S (the sample standard deviation) is far more complicated and will not be covered in this text. However, the variation in S is far less than the variation in $\bar{X}$ and is frequently not even considered; that is, S is used as a point estimate of σ. It is for this reason that the t distribution becomes approximately normal for a sample size of $n > 40$.

In the preceding section we stated that the sample average, $\overline{X}$, is an unbiased estimator of the mean μ but that it has variation as measured by its standard deviation $\sigma_{\overline{x}} = \sigma / \sqrt{n}$. Thus, when we use $\overline{X}$ as an estimate of μ, we do not really believe that $\overline{X}$ does exactly equal μ. In some cases it is preferable to acknowledge this fact by estimating μ as falling within a certain range of values, known as *a confidence interval*, with end points called *confidence limits*. Since $\overline{X}$ is used to estimate these limits and $\overline{X}$ is a random variable, the probability of the interval actually containing μ differs depending on the interval we choose. In general, we choose an interval such that the probability of μ being within it is equal to a prespecified value. One such value usually used is 0.95. Thus, the probability of μ falling outside the confidence limits is 0.05. We call this interval the 95% *confidence limits for μ.*

Let us find the 95% confidence limits for μ if a random sample of 400 items from the population yielded

$$\overline{X} = 200$$
$$S = 40$$

We estimate the distribution of $\overline{X}$ as being approximately normal since $n > 40$ with mean μ unknown and standard deviation approximately equal to $S_{\overline{x}} = S / \sqrt{n} = 40 / \sqrt{400} = 2$. This estimated distribution is shown in Figure 2.16.1. We are looking for the confidence interval, let us call it from a to b, such that

$$P(a \leqslant \mu \leqslant b) = 0.95$$

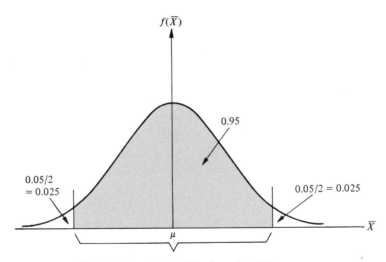

$\overline{X}$ falls in this region for 95% of sample means

FIGURE 2.16.1. *Distribution of $\overline{X}$ for n = 400 and S = 40.*

This is equivalent to stating that

$$P(\mu < a) = 0.025$$

$$P(\mu > b) = 0.025$$

It should be noted that our estimate of *a* and *b* may be very poor—and that the true value of μ *is* greater than *b* or less than *a*. The confidence level would then appear as in Figure 2.16.2. However, the probability of this is only 5%.

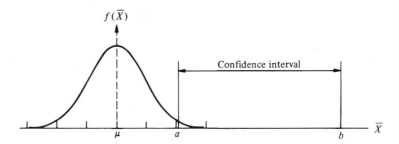

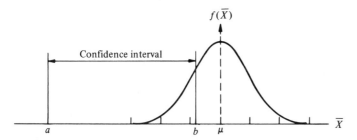

FIGURE 2.16.2. *Possible computed confidence limits for* μ *where* μ *is not within the interval.*

Given our estimate of the distribution of $\overline{X}$ as approximately normal with mean μ and standard deviation $S_{\overline{x}} = S/\sqrt{n} = 2$, we can find a value Z such that the probability that $\overline{X}$ is more than Z standard deviations below the mean μ is 0.025 and the probability that $\overline{X}$ is more than Z standard deviations above the mean μ is also 0.025. Mathematically, we write this as

$$P\left(\overline{X} \leqslant \mu - ZS_{\overline{x}}\right) = 0.025$$

$$P\left(\overline{X} \geqslant \mu + ZS_{\overline{x}}\right) = 0.025$$

The value of Z is found using our cumulative normal probabilities table.

The value Z is the value of the standard normal random variable which has area 0.025 to the right and 0.975 to the left. From Appendix B we find this value to be $Z = 1.96$. Thus, we can write

$$P\left(\overline{X} \leqslant \mu - 1.96 S_{\bar{x}}\right) = 0.025$$

$$P\left(\overline{X} \geqslant \mu + 1.96 S_{\bar{x}}\right) = 0.025$$

Rearranging terms within the parentheses, we obtain

$$P\left(\mu \geqslant \overline{X} + 1.96 S_{\bar{x}}\right) = 0.025$$

$$P\left(\mu \leqslant \overline{X} - 1.96 S_{\bar{x}}\right) = 0.025$$

or

$$P\left(\overline{X} - 1.96 S_{\bar{x}} \leqslant \mu \leqslant \overline{X} + 1.96 S_{\bar{x}}\right) = 0.95$$

Thus,

$$a = \overline{X} - 1.96 S_{\bar{x}}$$

$$b = \overline{X} + 1.96 S_{\bar{x}}$$

For our numerical example we can write the 95% confidence limits for μ as

$$200 - (1.96)(2) \leqslant \mu \leqslant 200 + (1.96)(2)$$

$$196.18 \leqslant \mu \leqslant 203.92$$

If we took a different sample of 400 items, the $\overline{X}$ and S would be different, and so would the a and b. However, we can claim that 95% of the confidence intervals so generated will actually contain the true population mean μ. It should be noted that it is *incorrect* to write the numerical interval in a probability form such as $P(196.18 \leqslant \mu \leqslant 203.92) = 0.95$, since μ *is not a random variable* and has no probability distribution associated with it. Either μ is in the interval or it is not in the interval. The interval $196.18 \leqslant \mu \leqslant 203.92$ is one of the possible 95% confidence intervals that could be constructed.

If we define the *level of confidence* as the probability that the confidence interval contains the mean μ and denote it as $(1 - \alpha)$, we can write

$$P\left(\overline{X} - Z_{\alpha/2} S_{\bar{x}} \leqslant \mu \leqslant \overline{X} + Z_{\alpha/2} S_{\bar{x}}\right) = 1 - \alpha$$

as the general statement of the confidence interval, where $Z_{\alpha/2}$ is defined as the standard normal value, Z, such that the area to the *right* of Z is $\alpha/2$.

The probability that the confidence interval does not contain the mean μ is therefore α, which is sometimes called the *level of significance*.

In this chapter we have provided a review of the basic topics in probability and statistics required for this text. Coverage of these topics is not meant to be comprehensive, but rather to permit readers to become familiar with or to refresh their memories on those topics that are prerequisite for understanding the remaining chapters. Students wishing further coverage are referred to the many excellent texts on probability and statistics given in the Bibliography.

The chapter was divided into three major groupings. In Sections 2.1–2.6 we introduced the basic elements of probability theory, showing how various computations are made. In Sections 2.7–2.12 we presented the concept of a random variable, the definition of a probability distribution, and several important discrete and continuous probability distributions. In Sections 2.13–2.16 several special topics in statistics were discussed.

PROBLEMS

2.1. Define all the possible events for the following random processes:

(a) A 50-page book is opened at random and the page number is observed.

(b) A card is selected at random from a deck containing 10 black cards numbered 1–10 and 5 red cards numbered 1–5.

(c) A chess piece is selected at random from a full set.

(d) The fraction of defective light bulbs in a shipment of 1,000.

(e) The weight of cement in a randomly selected 50-lb bag of cement.

(f) The length of a randomly selected 12-inch ruler.

2.2. (Problem 2.1 continued) Which of the random processes are discrete and which are continuous?

2.3. (Problem 2.1 continued) For those random processes that are discrete, find the probability of each possible event.

2.4. (Problem 2.1b continued) Two cards are drawn at random from the reduced deck in the following way. After the first card is drawn and observed it is replaced, the deck is shuffled, and the second card is drawn. Find the following probabilities:

(a) Both cards are red.

(b) Both cards are even.

(c) A red and a black card are drawn.

(d) The sum of the cards is 6.

(e) Are the first- and second-card results independent? Explain.

2.5. (Problem 2.1b continued) Two cards are drawn from the reduced deck, where the first card drawn is *not* replaced before the second card is drawn. Find the following probabilities:

(a) The second card is red given that the first is red.
(b) The second card is red given that the first is black.
(c) Both cards are red.
(d) Both cards are even.
(e) The second card is black. (The color of the first card is unknown.)
(f) Are the first- and second-card results independent? Explain.

2.6. (Problem 2.1b continued) A single card is drawn at random from the revised deck. Find the probability that the card drawn at random is:

(a) Red
(b) Black
(c) Black and a 2
(d) Red and an 8
(e) Odd
(f) Red and even

(g) Red or a 2
(h) Black or an 8
(i) Red or even
(j) Black or odd
(k) Red given it is an 8
(l) Red given it is an even

2.7. A store has selected records of 800 customers with charge accounts and classified them according to marital status and how soon they pay their bills. The classifications and their frequencies are shown in Figure P2.7.

	Less Than 30 Days	30–60 Days	Over 60 Days	
Married	400	125	75	600
Single	100	75	25	200
	500	200	100	

FIGURE P2.7

(a) For a randomly selected customer:
 (1) Find the joint and marginal probabilities of marital status and payment time.
 (2) Find the following conditional probabilities
  (i) P(marital status | payment time).
  (ii) P(payment time | marital status).
(b) If existing customers are representative of new customers, what is the probability that a new customer:
 (1) Is single and will pay within 30 days?
 (2) Is not married?
 (3) Will pay between 30 and 60 days given that the customer is married?
 (4) Is married given that the customer does not pay between 30 and 60 days?

2.8. An investor currently holds a piece of land on which there may be oil. She is considering arranging for a geological survey, which will indicate whether the land formation is one of three types: I, II, or III. In the past the land classified as a type I formation yielded oil 80% of the time; type II formation, 50% of the time; and type III formation, 10% of the time. For land in this area, 20% of the tests have yielded type I formations, 50% have yielded type II formations, and 30% have yielded type III formations. Find:

(a) The probability of oil.

(b) The probability that given oil is found, the geological survey predicted a (1) type I, (2) type II, or (3) type III formation.

2.9. Given that we have defined the events

A_1: person reads *Time* magazine

A_2: person reads *Newsweek* magazine

B_1: person is a white-collar worker

B_2: person is a blue-collar worker

and that in the population under study the following probabilities hold:

$$P(A_2)=0.7, \qquad P(B_1)=0.4, \qquad P(B_2|A_2)=0.45$$

A person is chosen at random from the population. Find the probability that:

(a) A person reads *Time* and is a blue-collar worker.

(b) A person reads *Newsweek* or is a white-collar worker.

(c) A person reads *Newsweek* given that he is a blue-collar worker.

(d) Determine mathematically whether reading *Newsweek* and being a white-collar worker are independent events.

2.10 Of 250 employees in a company, 130 smoke cigarettes. Of the 150 males working for the company, 85 smoke cigarettes. What is the probability that an employee chosen at random:

(a) Does not smoke cigarettes?

(b) Is female and smokes cigarettes?

(c) Is male or smokes cigarettes?

(d) Let us say that we meet a female employee of the company. What, then, is the probability that she does not smoke cigarettes?

(e) Determine mathematically whether cigarette smoking and sex are independent.

2.11. An order is to be shipped from the East Coast to Denver by way of St. Louis. From past experience it is estimated that the probability that such an order will arrive in St. Louis on time is 0.75, and the probability that it will be late arriving in St. Louis and on time arriving in Denver is 0.10. Suppose an inquiry shows that the order arrived late in St. Louis. What is the probability that it arrived on time in Denver?

2.12. Suppose that a new quick test is available to test a person's cholesterol level. The test is 90% accurate; that is, if a person has a high cholesterol level, there is a 90% chance the test will be positive, while if a person has a low cholesterol level, the test will be negative 90% of the time. It is known that high cholesterol occurs in about 1 of 100 persons.

(a) What is the probability of a test result being positive?
(b) Assume that the test result was positive. What is the probability that the person has high cholesterol?

2.13. A marketing manager is considering the introduction of a new product. He believes that establishing whether the product will be successful depends on the future sales, which will be high (probability = 0.4), medium (probability = 0.5), or low (probability = 0.1). Before introducing the product on a large scale, he market-tests it in a typical urban neighborhood. Past neighborhood market tests have produced the following performance:

Test Neighborhood Demand Reaction	ACTUAL SALES VOLUME		
	High	*Medium*	*Low*
High	0.8	0.3	0.1
Medium	0.2	0.5	0.3
Low	0	0.2	0.6

(a) What is the probability that the test-neighborhood demand will be high? Medium?
(b) Suppose that the test-neighborhood demand for the new product is low; what is the probability that sales will be medium? High?

2.14. Suppose that we do not know whether a die is fair or unfair. If the die is fair, the probability of any of the six numbers is $\frac{1}{6}$; if the die is unfair, the probability of any number showing on the die, X, is given by

$$P(X) = \frac{X}{21}$$

Assume we believe that the probability the die is fair equals 0.90. The die is rolled once and a six appears. What is the probability that the die is fair?

2.15. Five hundred families were surveyed with respect to the number of television sets they owned. The results were as follows:

Number of TV Sets Owned	*Number of Families*
0	75
1	100
2	200
3	60
4	50
5	15

(a) Estimate the probability distribution and cumulative probability distribution of the number of sets owned.
(b) What is the probability that 4 or fewer sets are owned?
(c) What is the probability that a family owns 2–4 sets?
(d) What is the expected number of sets owned?
(e) Find the standard deviation of the number of sets owned.

2.16. Two dice are rolled. Find the probability distribution of the number of spots showing on the dice. Determine the expected number of spots showing on the two dice.

2.17. The following grades were achieved by 40 students taking an exam:

Grade	Frequency
50	2
60	8
70	20
80	3
90	3
100	4

Find:
(a) The probability distribution.
(b) The expected exam grade.
(c) The variance of the exam grade.

2.18. The E. Z. Exam Co. produces sample study exams during the exam season. The exams cost $0.50 to produce and are sold for $1.00 each. All unsold exams are scrapped for $0.25 each. The probabilities of various levels of sales of the E. Z. Exam Co. are as follows:

Sales	Probability
100	0.1
200	0.3
500	0.4
1,000	0.2

(a) Find the expected number of exams that will be sold.
(b) What will be the company's profit if they produce 500 exams and the demand equals the expected number?

2.19. In a marketing experiment, a man is shown a pair of belts, a pair of shirts, and a pair of suits. In each case he is asked to identify the more expensive item of the two. Assume that the person has a probability of 0.8 of identifying the more expensive item correctly.

(a) What is the probability that the person will make correct identifications for all three pairs? For at least one pair?
(b) What is the mean number of correct identifications made? What is the variance?

2.20. The probability of finding at least one typographical error on any page in a book is 0.2. What is the probability that on five pages chosen from the book:

(a) Exactly two pages have typographical errors?

(b) At most four pages have typographical errors?

(c) What is the expected numbers of pages with typographical errors?

2.21. The probability that a patient recovers from delicate open heart surgery is 0.6. Four patients are to have open heart surgery in the next week.

(a) What is the probability that at least two of these patients recover? At most three?

(b) What is the average number of these patients that could be expected to recover from open heart surgery?

2.22. Suppose that customers arrive at a supermarket according to a Poisson distribution. If there are on the average 4 arrivals per minute, find the probability of:

(a) Exactly 2 arrivals in a 1-minute period.

(b) Less than 2 arrivals in a 1-minute period.

(c) More than 1 arrival in a 1-minute period.

2.23. Assume that the probability of any house being destroyed by fire during a given year is 1 in 10,000. Find the probability that of 20,000 houses:

(a) Exactly 1 will be destroyed by fire during a year.

(b) More than 1 will be destroyed by fire during a year.

(Use the binomial to estimate the mean number of fires and use the Poisson distribution as an approximation which is valid if n is large and p is small.)

2.24. A machine-shop lathe is set to produce parts at a length of 100 cm. Because the machinery is old, the actual lengths deviate from 100 cm by small amounts. These deviations are normally distributed with a mean of zero and a standard deviation of 1 cm. Find the probability that for the next part produced, the deviation from 100 cm will be

(a) Between 0 and +0.5 cm

(b) More than +1.5 cm

(c) Less than −0.75 cm

(d) Between −0.5 and +1.25 cm

(e) Between −1.0 and 0.3 cm

(f) More than 1.5 cm or less than −1.0 cm

(g) More than −1.25 cm

2.25. A mail-order crew can fill 1,000 orders in an 8-hour day and will work overtime to fill all orders the day they are received. All orders for the day are received first thing in the morning. If the number of orders received each day is normally distributed with a mean of 750 orders and a standard deviation of 250 orders, then:

(a) What is the probability that overtime work will be required to complete the orders on any given day?

(b) What is the probability according to the normal distribution that the number of orders to be filled in a given day is less than zero? What does this result suggest about the validity of using the normal distribution in this problem?

2.26. In a certain building trade the average wage is $3.60/hour and the standard deviation is 45 cents. If the wages are assumed to follow a normal distribution, what percent of the workers receive wages between

(a) $3.00 and $3.50 per hour?

(b) $2.70 and $3.95 per hour?

(c) Above what wage do 25% of the wages occur?

2.27. The length of time needed to service a car at a gas station is normally distributed with a mean of 15 minutes and a standard deviation of 4 minutes. What is the probability that the time needed to service a car will be:

(a) Between 15 and 20 minutes?

(b) Between 9 and 12 minutes?

(c) Less than 5 minutes?

(d) How long per car will it take to service 95% of the cars?

2.28. Reconsider Problem 2.26. Assume that a sample of 225 workers are taken and the average wage $\overline{X}$ is computed. Find the probability that $\overline{X}$ will be:

(a) Between $3.60 and $3.64.

(b) Above $3.54.

(c) Between $3.55 and $3.58.

2.29. A manufacturer of bulbs tests 144 bulbs to estimate the mean life of the bulbs. From previous studies the standard deviation was determined to be 30 hours and is assumed to be the same on these bulbs.

(a) What is the probability that the sample mean will be within 5 hours of the population mean?

(b) Suppose that the manufacturer tests 400 bulbs. What is the probability that the sample mean will be greater than the population mean by 3 hours?

2.30. (Problem 2.29 continued) Suppose that the estimated mean life turns out to be 160 hours. Determine a 95% confidence interval estimate of the true average life of a bulb:

(a) If the sample size is 144.

(b) If the sample size is 400.

Compare the interval estimates and interpret your results.

2.31. A Florida citrus grower claims that the average weight of his grapefruits is 15 oz. A large distributor samples 100 grapefruits. If the population standard deviation is known to be 3 oz, what is the probability that the sample mean is

(a) Less than 15.5 oz?

(b) Between 14.8 and 15.3 oz?

(c) Below what weight will 99% of the sample means be?

2.32. (Problem 2.31 continued) If the sample of 100 grapefruits yielded an average weight of 16 oz, determine a 98% confidence interval estimate for the true average weight of the Florida grapefruit. If the citrus grower's claim is truly accurate, what can we say about the interval estimate?

2.33. A random sample of 10 Graduate Record Exam scores of students of a large university yielded the following results:

Sample	1	2	3	4	5	6	7	8	9	10
Score	585	517	457	631	551	722	449	473	680	473

(a) Find an estimate for the population mean exam score.

(b) Find an estimate for the population standard deviation of exam scores.

2.34. Eight bags of a commercial fertilizer randomly selected from a large production lot had the following weights:

$$50.7, 49.8, 49.6, 50.3, 50.1, 49.1, 49.9, 51.0 \quad \text{(lb)}$$

(a) Estimate the mean weight of a bag of fertilizer.

(b) Estimate the population standard deviation of fertilizer bag weights.

2.35. A random sample of 100 accounts of a large East Coast utility company indicated that on the average $18.55 was overdue with a standard deviation of $5.28. Construct a 99% confidence interval for the average amount owed on all the company's overdue accounts.

2.36. A very large airline wishes to determine the average weight of passengers suitcases on cross-country trips. A random sample of 81 suitcases are weighed, yielding a mean of 31.5 lb and a standard deviation of 7.2 lb.

(a) Find a 95.44% confidence interval for the population average weight of a suitcase.

(b) How large a sample would the airline have to take so that the 95.44% confidence interval would be from 31 to 32 lb?

2.37. A five-question exam is graded by five instructors. Each instructor compiles the individual exam grade by summing the five numbers provided. In addition, each instructor provides the average and standard deviation for the question graded. The results for the five questions are as follows:

Question	Average	Standard Deviation
1	15.4	2.1
2	12.8	4.6
3	17.3	2.5
4	18.1	1.6
5	16.5	1.9

(a) Find the average grade.
(b) Find the standard deviation.

2.38. A company manufactures four products whose weekly demands (in units) are random with the following means and standard deviations:

Product	Mean	Standard Deviation
1	1,210	25
2	975	16
3	426	11
4	678	19

(a) What is the overall average demand for all company products?
(b) What is the overall standard deviation of the company demand?

BOOKS OF
INTEREST

Burr, Irving W., *Applied Statistical Methods*. New York: Academic Press, Inc., 1974.

Chao, L. L., *Statistics: Methods and Analyses*. New York: McGraw-Hill Book Co., 1969.

Clark, C. T., and L. L. Schkade, *Statistical Methods for Business Decisions*. Cincinnati, Ohio: South-Western Publishing Co., 1969.

Feller, William, *An Introduction to Probability Theory and Its Applications*. vol. I (2nd ed.), 1957; vol. II (3rd ed.), 1968, New York: John Wiley & Sons, Inc.

Freund, J. E. and F. J. Williams, *Elementary Business Statistics—the Modern Approach*. Englewood Cliffs, N.J.: Prentice-Hall, Inc., 1977.

Lapin, L. L., *Statistics for Modern Business Decisions*. New York: Harcourt Brace Jovanovich, 1973.

Parzen, Emmanuel, *Modern Probability Theory and Its Applications*. New York: John Wiley & Sons, Inc., 1960.

CHAPTER THREE

Simple Decision

Problems

OBJECTIVES: The purpose of this chapter is to introduce to you the following concepts essential to the solution of simple decision problems.

1. *The characteristics of the simple decision problem.*
2. *The payoff table.*
3. *The decision criteria under certainty, uncertainty, and risk.*
4. *The expected value in decision problems.*
5. *The concept of opportunity loss.*
6. *The expected value of perfect information.*
7. *Incremental analysis.*
8. *The importance of subjective probabilities.*

In Chapter 1 a generalized framework for solving decision problems was structured. The elements of the decision problem were defined, and the steps in the decision process were outlined. We further classified decision problems with respect to the amount of information known about various aspects of the problem. These classifications were termed certainty, uncertainty, and risk. In this chapter we deal with a decision problem with the following characteristics:

1. The decision maker must make his decision from among a set of defined alternative *actions* or *strategies*. These strategies may be described numerically (order 100 units) or nonnumerically (conduct a market survey).
2. A set of one or more specified *events* exist that are not within the control of the decision maker. As with strategies, events may be described numerically or nonnumerically. Thus, an event may be a demand of 50 units, or it could represent the introduction of a competitive product.
3. For each strategy chosen by the decision maker, a known outcome (payoff) will result that is conditional on which event has occurred. Although outcomes may also be described both numerically and nonnumerically, the usual representation of outcomes is in terms of a conditional payoff, a conditional profit, a conditional cost, or a conditional opportunity-loss value.

This class of problems, which we term *simple decision problems*, will be analyzed for all three classifications: certainty, uncertainty, and risk.

3.2.1. Statement of the Problem. The apple peddler finds that he can only order apples in boxes of 100 lb each and that his storage facilities requirements allow a maximum order of 400 lb. His past experience has taught him that the daily demand ranges from 0 to 400 lb in lots of 100 lb. The peddler has decided to sell the apples at a price of 50 cents/pound. Since the cost per pound is 30 cents, the peddler earns 20 cents for every pound that he sells. For each pound that he does not sell, he loses 10 cents, since all apples not sold each day are bought by a salvage company for 20 cents/pound. The apple peddler's objective is to determine the quantity of apples to buy each day that will maximize his profits.

3.2.2. Payoff Matrix. In order to present the information in a clear and concise manner and to ease the computations necessary to make a decision, an outcome or payoff matrix is developed. The general form of this matrix is shown in Table 3.2.1 and consists of three parts: the strategies, the events, and the conditional payoff values. The strategies consist of M alternative actions for the decision maker; the events consist of N possible outcomes of a random phenomenon outside the control of the decision maker; and the conditional payoff values are numerical values assigned to each strategy i conditional on each event j.

TABLE 3.2.1. *General Form of Payoff Matrix*

Strategies \ *Events*	$E_1 \cdots E_j \cdots E_N$
S_1	
$\vdots$	
S_i	conditional outcome (payoff) values
$\vdots$	
S_M	

For the apple peddler problem there are five strategies from which to choose; buy 0 lb of apples, buy 100, buy 200, buy 300, or buy 400. There are five events that can take place. These are the five possible values of the daily demand for apples, which are 0 lb, 100 lb, 200 lb, 300 lb, or 400 lb. Let us use profit as the payoff measure for this problem. To find the conditional payoff values it is necessary to determine for each strategy–event combination the total revenue and the total cost yielding the conditional profit (CP). Thus, if the decision is the strategy "buy 0 lb," there is $0 revenue independent of the demand, and the CP values for that decision will all be $0. If the decision is "buy 100 lb," then the costs are $100 \times 0.30 = \$30$. The revenues depend on how many he sells at 50 cents/pound and on how many are salvaged at 20 cents/pound. For a demand of 0 lb, all 100 lb are salvaged, producing a revenue of $20. The conditional profit is thus equal to $\$20 - 30 = -\$10$. If the demand is 100 lb (or more), all apples are sold, producing a revenue of $50. The conditional profit is then $\$50 - 30 = \$20$.

If the decision is to "buy 200," we get the following conditional profit values:

buy 200 – demand = 0; conditional profit = $0 + 40 – 60 = –$20
buy 200 – demand = 100; conditional profit = $50 + 20 – 60 = $10
buy 200 – demand = 200 or more; conditional profit = $100 + 0 – 60 = $40

The entire matrix (table) of conditional profit values is presented in Table 3.2.2. The apple peddler can thus see at a glance what the payoff will be if he makes a specific decision and any of the possible events occur. However, which decision to make is a difficult choice. Should he close his business (buy 0) and thus neither earn or lose anything, or should he take some risk of a loss and thereby increase his chance for an overall profit? In the next sections this problem is examined in greater detail, and several decision rules are presented. The notational form of the conditional payoff values that we will use is CP (strategy i|event j); that is, the conditional payoff for selecting strategy i given that event j occurs. Thus,

$$CP(\text{buy } 200\,|\,\text{demand} = 300) = CP(S_3\,|\,E_4) = \$40$$

That is, the conditional profit of choosing strategy S_3: buy 200 lb of apples when the demand that day is 300 lb of apples (E_4) equals $40.

TABLE 3.2.2. *Conditional Profit Payoff Matrix for Apple Peddler Problem (in dollars)*

Events Strategies	E_1: Demand = 0	E_2: Demand = 100	E_3: Demand = 200	E_4: Demand = 300	E_5: Demand = 400
S_1: buy 0	0	0	0	0	0
S_2: buy 100	–10	20	20	20	20
S_3: buy 200	–20	10	40	40	40
S_4: buy 300	–30	0	30	60	60
S_5: buy 400	–40	–10	20	50	80

SECTION 3.3. *Decision under Certainty*

Let us assume that the apple peddler does not have to buy the apples until the end of each day after he has collected all the orders for that day. His agreement with the customers is to deliver the ordered apples after the close of each day's business. Thus, the uncontrollable variable, demand, although still uncontrollable, is no longer unknown, but is known with complete certainty in the same way that he knows the cost per pound of apples. This class of problems is termed *decision under certainty* problems. The method of analysis for these type of problems is as follows:

1. Determine which event takes place.
2. For this event examine the conditional payoff values for all possible strategies. (These numbers will be one·column of the payoff matrix, Table 3.2.2.)
3. The optimal decision is to choose the strategy that yields the best value for the conditional payoff of those examined in step 2. If the payoffs are profits, the best is the maximum value; if the payoffs are costs, the best is the minimum value.

Thus, if the demand during a given day is 0 lb, the conditional payoff values, which in our problem are profit values, are those of the first column of Table 3.2.2, ranging from $-\$40$ to $\$0$. His decision is clearly select S_1: buy 0 with a net profit of $\$0$. If the demand during a day is 100 lb of apples, the conditional payoff values are those of the second column of Table 3.2.2, ranging from $-\$10$ to $\$20$. His decision is thus to select S_2: buy 100 with a net profit of $\$20$.

Hence, the decision maker in this class of problems will always receive the maximum payoff possible. However, most simple decision problems will not be situations with the demand known for certain, but rather they will involve uncertainty or at best risk. Thus, the apple peddler must make his decision before he knows what the day's event will be.

SECTION 3.4. *Decision under Uncertainty*

3.4.1. Introduction. With no knowledge regarding the likelihood (probability) of any of the events occurring, the decision maker must base his decision solely on the actual conditional payoff values, together with his attitude or anticipation toward earning those values. Four decision criteria reflecting different attitudes will be discussed: the pessimistic, the optimistic, the equally likely, and the Savage opportunity-loss decision criteria. These criteria may lead to different decisions for the same problem; thus, it is important that the decision maker select his appropriate criterion at the outset. We shall discuss each of the uncertainty decision criteria with respect to the apple peddler problem.

3.4.2. Pessimistic Decision Criterion. The *pessimistic decision criterion*, or what is sometimes called the *minimax* or *maximin criterion*, assures the decision maker that he will earn no less (or pay no more) than some specified amount. It is a very conservative approach to decision making, in that we anticipate the worst possible outcome (minimum for profit and maximum for cost) for any strategy that we might choose. The optimal strategy chosen is then the best (maximin or minimax) of the anticipated outcomes. The formal procedure for finding the pessimistic decision is as follows:

1. For each possible strategy, identify the worst payoff value. This will be the row minimum for a profit table and the row maximum for a cost table. Record this number in a new column (see Table 3.4.1).
2. Select the strategy with the best anticipated payoff value (maximum for profit and minimum for cost).

This procedure is applied to the apple peddler problem, as shown in Table 3.4.1. For a decision of buy 0, the worst that can occur is $0 profit. If he decides to buy 100 lb, the worst event is a demand of 0 lb, which causes a loss of $10. The row minimum for buy 200 is −$20; for buy 300 it is −$30; and for buy 400 it is −$40. The optimum decision using this criterion is thus strategy S_1, to buy 0 lb, since this guarantees that he will incur no losses. Notice that the pessimistic criterion leads to a "do-nothing" strategy, to avoid the risk of losses.

TABLE 3.4.1. *Apple Peddler Problem with*
Pessimistic Decision Rule (in dollars)

Events / Strategy	E_1: Demand $=0$	E_2: Demand $=100$	E_3: Demand $=200$	E_4: Demand $=300$	E_5: Demand $=400$	Worst Payoff	Optimum
S_1: buy 0	0	0	0	0	0	⃞ 0	Select S_1
S_2: buy 100	−10	20	20	20	20	−10	
S_3: buy 200	−20	10	40	40	40	−20	
S_4: buy 300	−30	0	30	60	60	−30	
S_5: buy 400	−40	−10	20	50	80	−40	

It should be pointed out that this decision rule does not consider the utility values of the various outcomes nor does it allow for the superimposing of the decision maker's subjective feelings about the likelihood of the various events. Rather, this criterion is best suited for those situations where the probabilities are not easily evaluated and the decision maker is very conservative.

3.4.3. Optimistic Decision Criterion. The *optimistic decision criterion*, or what is sometimes called the *maximax* or *minimin criterion*, assures the decision maker that he will not miss the opportunity to achieve the greatest possible payoff or lowest possible cost. However, this decision-making behavior usually involves the risk of a large loss. The approach is optimistic in that we anticipate the best (maximum profit or minimum cost) possible payoff for any strategy we might choose. The optimal strategy is then the best (maximum for a profit table and minimum for a cost table) of the anticipated outcomes. The formal procedure for finding the optimistic decision is as follows:

1. For each possible strategy, identify the best payoff value. Record this number in a new column (see Table 3.4.2).
2. Select the strategy with the best anticipated payoff value. This will be a maximum for a profit table and minimum for a cost table.

This procedure is applied to the apple peddler problem as shown in Table 3.4.2. For a decision of buy 0, the best that can occur is $0 profit. If the peddler decides to buy 100 lb, the best event is a demand of 100 lb or more, which results in a payoff of $20. The row maximum for buy 200 is $40; for buy 300 it is $60; and for buy 400 it is $80. The optimum decision using this criterion is thus strategy S_5, to buy 400 lb, since this guarantees that he will not miss the opportunity to earn the largest payoff. Note, however, that with a decision of buy 400 lb, he takes the risk of a loss of $-$40 or $-$10 if the actual demand is, respectively, 0 or 100 lb.

TABLE 3.4.2. *Apple Peddler Problem with Optimistic Decision Rule (in dollars)*

Events / Strategies	E_1: Demand $=0$	E_2: Demand $=100$	E_3: Demand $=200$	E_4: Demand $=300$	E_5: Demand $=400$	Best Payoff	Optimum
S_1: buy 0	0	0	0	0	0	0	
S_2: buy 100	-10	20	20	20	20	20	
S_3: buy 200	-20	10	40	40	40	40	
S_4: buy 300	-30	0	30	60	60	60	
S_5: buy 400	-40	-10	20	50	80	$\boxed{80}$	Select S_5

3.4.4. Equally Likely Decision Criterion. The *equally likely decison criterion* is based on the *principle of insufficient reason* and is attributed to Laplace. The approach assumes that the decision maker has no knowledge as to which event will occur, and thus he considers the likelihood of the different events occurring as being equal. In effect, the decision maker has assigned the same probability value to each event. This probability is equal to 1/number of events. Hence an average or expected payoff can be computed for each possible strategy and the optimal decision will be the one with the best average payoff value. The formal procedure for finding the equally likely decision is as follows:

1. For each possible strategy, find the average or expected payoff by

adding all the possible payoffs and dividing by the number of possible events. Record this number in a new column (see Table 3.4.3).

2. Select the strategy with the best average payoff value: maximum for profit and minimum for cost.

This procedure is applied to the apple peddler problem as shown in Table 3.4.3. For a decision "buy 0 lb," the average payoff is $0. If the peddler decides to buy 100 lb, the average payoff is

$$\frac{-10+20+20+20+20}{5} = \$14$$

The average payoff for buy 200 is

$$\frac{-20+10+40+40+40}{5} = \$22$$

for buy 300 the average payoff is $24; and for buy 400 the average payoff is $20. The optimum decision using this criterion is thus strategy S_4, buy 300, since this yields the largest average payoff. The equally likely criterion is rarely used since decision makers usually have some subjective feeling about which events are more likely to occur.

TABLE 3.4.3. *Apple Peddler Problem with
Equally Likely Decision Rule (in dollars)*

Strategies \ Events	E_1: Demand = 0	E_2: Demand = 100	E_3: Demand = 200	E_4: Demand = 300	E_5: Demand = 400	Equally Likely Decision: Averages	Optimum
S_1: buy 0	0	0	0	0	0	0	
S_2: buy 100	−10	20	20	20	20	14	
S_3: buy 200	−20	10	40	40	40	22	
S_4: buy 300	−30	0	30	60	60	24	Select S_4
S_5: buy 400	−40	−10	20	50	80	20	

3.4.5. Savage Opportunity-Loss Decision Criterion. The *opportunity-loss decision criterion*, sometimes called the *Savage minimax regret decision criterion*, was proposed by the economist Savage. It assures the decision maker that the opportunities for payoff that he has missed (or lost) because of the random occurrence of a possible unfavorable event will be as small a value as is possible. The approach assumes that for each strategy–event pair, a regret (or opportunity loss) value can be computed equal to the difference between what the payoff could have been (had he chosen the optimal strategy for this event) and what it actually is for the strategy chosen and the event that has occurred. These values are summarized in a conditional opportunity-loss table, with a structure similar to the conditional payoff table, as shown in Table 3.4.4.

TABLE 3.4.4. *Conditional Opportunity-Loss Table*

Strategies \ Events	$E_1 \cdots E_j \cdots E_N$
S_1	
.	
.	conditional
S_i	opportunity
.	loss values
.	
S_M	

The decision process then anticipates the worst (maximum) opportunity loss for each possible strategy and chooses as the optimal strategy the one with the minimum anticipated opportunity loss. The formal procedure for finding the opportunity-loss decision is as follows:

1. From the conditional payoff table, develop the conditional opportunity-loss table as follows:
   (a) For the first possible event, identify the best possible payoff value.
   (b) For each possible strategy, subtract the actual conditional payoff value from this best value. These results are the regret or opportunity loss values for this event.
   (c) Repeat steps (a) and (b) for all possible events.
2. For each possible strategy, identify the worst or maximum regret value. Record this number as a new column.
3. Select the strategy with the smallest (minimum) anticipated opportunity-loss value.

Let us apply this procedure to the apple peddler problem. Consider the occurrence of the event "demand equals 0 lb." The maximum payoff occurs with the decision "buy 0 lb," yielding a payoff of $0. Thus, if the peddler's actual decision is to buy 0, the payoff is maximum and he incurs no regret or lost opportunity. If his decision is to buy 100 lb, he earns a profit of $-$10 and thus his opportunity loss is $10. For a decision of buy 200, the opportunity loss is $20; for buy 300, the opportunity loss is $30; and for buy 400, the opportunity loss is $40. Consider now the occurrence of the event "demand equals 100 lb." The maximum payoff occurs with the decision "buy 100 lb," yielding a profit of $20. Thus, if his actual decision is to buy 100 lb, the payoff is maximum and no regret is incurred. If the decision is to buy 0, his profit is $0 and he has a missed opportunity of $20. For a decision of buy 200, the profit is $10, and therefore the opportunity loss is only $20 $-$ 10 = $10; for buy 300, the opportunity loss is $20 $-$ 0 = $20, and for buy 400, the opportunity loss is $20-(-10)=\$30$. The entire set of conditional opportunity-loss values is summarized in Table 3.4.5. The decision maker now considers his options. If he chooses S_1, the worst opportunity loss that he can incur is \$80. On the other hand, if he chooses S_2, his risk is only a maximum of \$60. He thus records the maximum opportunity loss that he might incur for each possible strategy and selects the strategy with the minimum opportunity-loss risk. These results are shown in Table 3.4.6 and indicate that the opportunity loss decision is S_4: buy 300 lb.

TABLE 3.4.5. *Conditional Opportunity-Loss Table for Apple Peddler Problem (in dollars)*

Events　　　　Strategies	E_1: Demand $=0$	E_2: Demand $=100$	E_3: Demand $=200$	E_4: Demand $=300$	E_5: Demand $=400$
S_1: buy 0	0	20	40	60	80
S_2: buy 100	10	0	20	40	60
S_3: buy 200	20	10	0	20	40
S_4: buy 300	30	20	10	0	20
S_5: buy 400	40	30	20	10	0

TABLE 3.4.6. *Apple Peddler Problem with Opportunity-Loss Decision Rule (in dollars)*

Strategies	Worst Opportunity Loss	Optimum
S_1: buy 0	80	
S_2: buy 100	60	
S_3: buy 200	40	
S_4: buy 300	30	Select S_4
S_5: buy 400	40	

The notational form that we shall use for the conditional opportunity loss is OL(strategy i|event j). Thus, $OL(S_4|E_3)=\$10$.

3.5.1. Introduction. The major underlying assumption of the uncertainty decision criteria discussed in Section 3.4 is that no information is available with regard to the probabilities of the various events. Thus, the decisions are made solely on the basis of the conditional payoff values. Let us suppose that the apple peddler has recorded the actual demands for the last 100 days and formed the following frequency distribution:

Demand (lb)	Frequency of Occurrence (days)
0	10
100	20
200	40
300	20
400	$\dfrac{10}{100}$

From the frequency distribution he can estimate the probability distribution of the demand as

Demand (lb)	0	100	200	300	400
Probability	0.1	0.2	0.4	0.2	0.1

The availability of the probabilities of the various demands reduces the uncertainty in the problem to a level of risk that allows the application of the *Bayes decision rule*. This rule will be applied to the conditional payoff table, yielding the *expected monetary value* (EMV) *rule* and to the conditional opportunity-loss table, yielding the *expected opportunity-loss* (EOL) *rule*.

3.5.2 The Bayes Decision Rule. Suppose that the decision maker decides to choose strategy S_4, buy 300 lb. He will earn $-\$30$ if the demand is 0, which occurs 10% of the time. He will earn $0 if the demand is 100, and this occurs 20% of the time. Similarly, he will earn $30 40% of the time (demand $= 200$), $60 20% of the time (demand $= 300$), and $60 10% of the time (demand $= 400$). This information is summarized in Table 3.5.1.

TABLE 3.5.1. *Payoffs and Probabilities for Strategy S_4 (in dollars)*

	E_1	E_2	E_3	E_4	E_5
Strategy S_4	-30	0	30	60	60
Probability	0.1	0.2	0.4	0.2	0.1

The peddler's expected earnings will be the sum of (payoff $\times$ probability):

$$-\$30(0.10) + 0(0.20) + 30(0.40) + 60(0.20) + 60(0.10) = \$27$$

He will use strategy S_4 if these expected earnings are the best that he can achieve. However, he can determine this fact only if all possible expected earning values are available, one for each strategy. Thus, he will examine each possible strategy to evaluate what its expected payoff will be and choose as the optimal strategy the one with the best expected value. This is the essential concept of the Bayes decision rule. We may apply this approach to either the payoff table or the opportunity-loss table. When applying it to the payoff table we call it the expected monetary value (EMV) decision rule and when applying it to the opportunity-loss table, we call it the expected opportunity-loss (EOL) decision rule. It will be shown later that these two rules are equivalent in that they always select the same strategy as optimal.

The formal procedure for applying the Bayes decision rule is as follows:

1. *EMV*. For each possible strategy, multiply each payoff (CP) value by its probability. The sum of these products is the EMV for that strategy.[†] The strategy with the best EMV (EMV*) is the optimum strategy.
2. *EOL.* For each possible strategy, multiply each opportunity-loss (OL) value by its probability. The sum of these products is the EOL for that strategy.[‡] The strategy with the smallest EOL (EOL*) is the optimum strategy.

These decision rules are applied to the apple peddler problem and the results are shown in Tables 3.5.2 and 3.5.3. For the EMV rule the maximum value for EMV's (EMV*) occurs for strategy 3: buy 200 lb, with an expected value of $28. For the EOL rule the minimum value of the EOL's (EOL*) occurs for strategy 3: buy 200 lb, with an expected regret of $12. In the next section we will show that this result (same optimal strategy using EMV or EOL) is not a mere coincidence but an integral property of the Bayes decision rule structure.

The interpretation of the EMV and EOL results is that of a best "long-run average" value. Thus, if the peddler repeated his decision

---

[†]The EMV for a given strategy i may be written, $EMV(S_i) = \Sigma_j CP(S_i|E_j)P(E_j)$.
[‡]The EOL for a given strategy i may be written, $EOL(S_i) = \Sigma_j OL(S_i|E_j)P(E_j)$.

TABLE 3.5.2. *Computation of EMV for Apple Peddler Problem*

	E_1: Demand $=0$	E_2: Demand $=100$	E_3: Demand $=200$	E_4: Demand $=300$	E_5: Demand $=400$	
			Probabilities			
	0.1	0.2	0.4	0.2	0.1	$EMV = \Sigma\,(\text{payoff} \times \text{probability})$
Strategy 1: payoffs (payoff $\times$ probability)	0 0 +	0 0 +	0 0 +	0 0 +	0 0	$= \$0$
Strategy 2: payoffs (payoff $\times$ probability)	-10 -1 +	20 4 +	20 8 +	20 4 +	20 2	$= 17$
Strategy 3: payoffs (payoff $\times$ probability)	-20 -2 +	10 2 +	40 16 +	40 8 +	40 4	$EMV^* = \boxed{28}$ S_3 is optimum
Strategy 4: payoffs (payoff $\times$ probability)	-30 -3 +	0 0 +	30 12 +	60 12 +	60 6	$= 27$
Strategy 5: payoffs (payoff $\times$ probability)	-40 -4 +	-10 -2 +	20 8 +	50 10 +	80 8	$= 20$

problem many times using strategy S_3, he would earn a profit of $-\$20$ approximately 10% of the time; $10 approximately 20% of the time; and $40 approximately 70% (40% + 20% + 10%) of the time. Over a long period of time the S_3 decision would yield an average profit of about $28 per decision. Similarly, the use of strategy S_3 would lead to an opportunity loss of $0 approximately 40% of the time; $10 approximately 20% of the time; $20 approximately 30% (20% + 10%) of the time; and $40 approximately 10% of the time. Over a long period of time the S_3 decision would yield an average opportunity loss of about $12 per decision.

The expected value (Bayes) decision criterion is one of the most powerful for decision making since it guarantees the best long run payoff. However, even if the decision is one that is to be made only once, there is still strong justification for using expected value. If this criterion is used for all decision problems, then in the long run, the total payoff from all those problems will be optimal.

TABLE 3.5.3. *Computation of EOL for Apple Peddler Problem*

	E_1: Demand $=0$	E_2: Demand $=100$	E_3: Demand $=200$	E_4: Demand $=300$	E_5: Demand $=400$	$EOL=\Sigma$(opportunity loss $\times$ probability)
	Probabilities					
	0.1	0.2	0.4	0.2	0.1	
Strategy 1 opportunity losses (opportunity loss $\times$ probability)	0 0 +	20 4 +	40 16 +	60 12 +	80 8	$=\$40$
Strategy 2 opportunity losses (opportunity loss $\times$ probability)	10 1 +	0 0 +	20 8 +	40 8 +	60 6	$=23$
Strategy 3 opportunity losses (opportunity loss $\times$ probability)	20 2 +	10 2 +	0 0 +	20 4 +	40 4	$EOL^*= \boxed{12}$ S_3 is optimum
Strategy 4 opportunity losses (opportunity loss $\times$ probability)	30 3 +	20 4 +	10 4 +	0 0 +	20 2	$=13$
Strategy 5 opportunity losses (opportunity loss $\times$ probability)	40 4 +	30 6 +	20 8 +	10 2 +	0 0	$=20$

SECTION 3.6. *Value of Perfect Information*

In Section 3.5 we assumed that the apple peddler knew the probability of demand for apples. However, he did not know exactly what the demand would be each day. Let us now assume that the apple peddler can predict each day's demand with certainty. Thus, he will predict those 10% of the days with a 0-lb demand; those 20% of the days with a 100-lb demand; those 40% of the days with a 200-lb demand; those 20% of the days with a 300-lb demand, and those 10% of the days with a 400-lb demand. Hence, for each day he will buy the quantity that will yield the maximum profit. On those days when the demand will be 0 lb he buys 0 lb for a profit of $0. When the demand will be 100 lb he buys exactly 100 lb for a profit of $20. Table 3.6.1 summarizes the apple peddler's strategy and payoff for each possible event and his total expected profit with perfect information, EPPI. Mathematically, we define EPPI as the weighted average of the best payoff possible for each event $CP^*(E_j)$ with the weights equal to probability of each event $P(E_j)$. Thus,

$$(1) \qquad \text{EPPI} = \sum_j P(\text{event } j) \times CP^*(\text{event } j)$$

The value EPPI = $40 represents the average payoff to the apple peddler if, over a long period of time, he always selected the optimal strategy based on perfect information. However, this expectation value must be considered for the decision problem as a prior expectation, that is, before the perfect information is available. Once the information is available, there is no expected payoff; rather, exactly one of five payoffs occurs: $0, 20, 40, 60, or 80.

TABLE 3.6.1. *Computation of Expected Payoff with Perfect Information (EPPI),*
for Apple Peddler Problem

	E_1: Demand = 0	E_2: Demand = 100	E_3: Demand = 200	E_4: Demand = 300	E_5: Demand = 400	
$P(\text{event } j)$	0.1	0.2	0.4	0.2	0.1	
Optimal strategy with perfect information	S_1: buy 0	S_2: buy 100	S_3: buy 200	S_4: buy 300	S_5: buy 400	
Profit with perfect information $CP^*(\text{event } j)$	$0	20	40	60	80	$\text{EPPI} = \sum_j P(E_j) \times CP^*(E_j) = \$40$
$P(E_j)CP^*(E_j)$	$0	4	16	12	8	

It is thus apparent that the apple peddler can increase his optimal expected payoff from EMV* = $28 to EPPI = $40 by having available the necessary perfect information regarding the demand. Clearly, the apple peddler should be willing to pay up to the difference between EPPI and EMV* to obtain this perfect information. We define this number as the *expected value of perfect information*, EVPI. Thus,

$$\text{EVPI} = \text{EPPI} - \text{EMV}^*$$
$$(2) \qquad\qquad = \$40 - 28$$
$$= \$12$$

Another way to look at the value of perfect information is that it reduces the level of the expected opportunity loss. Recall that EOL is in essence the difference between what we earn and what we would like to earn. Thus, if perfect information permits us to earn the maximum, the EOL should become zero, since no opportunities are missed. Consider the relationship between EMV and EOL for the apple peddler problem as shown in Table 3.6.2. If no opportunities were missed, the maximum profit that could be expected is $40. This is precisely EPPI.[†]

TABLE 3.6.2. *Relationship Between EMV and EOL*

Strategies	*Expected Monetary Value, EMV*	*Expected Opportunity Loss, EOL*	*EMV + EOL*
S_1: buy 0	$ 0	$40	$40
S_2: buy 100	17	23	40
S_3: buy 200	28*	12*	40
S_4: buy 300	27	13	40
S_5: buy 400	20	20	40

Hence,

$$EPPI = EMV + EOL$$

(3)
$$= EMV^* + EOL^*$$

Substituting equation (3) into (2), we obtain

$$EVPI = EMV^* + EOL^* - EMV^*$$

$$= EOL^*$$

Thus, the expected value of perfect information is exactly equal to the optimum expected opportunity loss.

[†]Mathematically,

$$EOL(\text{strategy } i) = \sum_j P(\text{event } j) OL(\text{strategy } i | \text{event } j)$$

$$= \sum_j P(\text{event } j)[CP^*(\text{event } j) - CP(\text{strategy } i | \text{event } j)]$$

$$= \sum_j P(\text{event } j) CP^*(\text{event } j) - \sum_j P(\text{event } j) CP(\text{strategy } i | \text{event } j)$$

The first summation is EPPI; the second summation is EMV(strategy i). Thus,

$$EOL(\text{strategy } i) = EPPI - EMV(\text{strategy } i)$$

Knowledge of the EVPI allows the decision maker to evaluate his information-acquiring opportunities in terms of what he can expect to gain from such information. It places an upper bound on what he should spend to obtain information that in practice is rarely perfect.

SECTION 3.7. *Incremental Analysis*

For such problems as the apple peddler problem, which involve analysis of expected values related to an inventory type of strategy, a method known as *incremental* (or *marginal*) *analysis* can be used to find the optimum decision. This approach assumes that the decision process is a series of steps, where at each step a decision is made whether or not to add additional units. The decision is based on whether the additional units produce additional profit. The decision can also be viewed from an opportunity-loss point of view. Units are added as long as the cost of adding the units is less than the cost of not adding them. Let k_u be the unit cost of underordering (i.e., the opportunity cost of a unit demanded but not available). Let P be the probability that the actual demand will be greater than the number of units on hand. Thus, the expected incremental opportunity cost of not buying an additional unit, $\Delta EOL'$, is $k_u P$. The extra unit will not be needed if the actual demand is equal to or less than the units on hand. The probability of this event is $1 - P$. If k_o is the unit cost of overordering (i.e., the opportunity cost of a unit available but not demanded), the expected incremental opportunity cost of buying the extra unit, ΔEOL, is $k_o(1 - P)$. If the cost of not buying, $\Delta EOL'$, is greater than the cost of buying, ΔEOL, the extra unit should be bought. If $\Delta EOL' = \Delta EOL$, the decision maker should be indifferent as to buying or not buying the extra unit. Let P_c be the critical probability which is found when $\Delta EOL' = \Delta EOL$. Thus,

$$k_u \cdot P_c = k_o(1 - P_c)$$

Solving for P_c, we get

$$P_c = \frac{k_o}{k_o + k_u}$$

The decision rule is thus to continue buying additional units as long as $P > P_c$, with the optimum number to buy, d^*, equal to the largest number to buy, d, such that $P > P_c$. If $P = P_c$, we buy d^* or $d^* + 1$.

For the apple peddler problem we define a unit as 100 lb, and therefore k_u equals the lost profit by missing a sale and equals $100(0.20) = \$20$. The term k_o is the cost of buying a unit and not selling it, less the salvage value, and equals $100(0.10) = \$10$. Thus, $P_c = 10/(10 + 20) = 0.333$. The values of P are found from the demand distribution and are given in Table 3.7.1. The probability of selling more than 0 equals the probability that the demand is 100 or 200 or 300 or 400, and equals $0.2+0.4+0.2+0.1=0.9$. Since $P=0.9>P_c=0.333$, order the next unit (i.e., buy 100). The probability of selling more than 100 lb equals $0.4+0.2+0.1=0.7$. Since $P=0.7>P_c=0.333$, order the next unit (i.e., buy 200). The probability of selling more than 200 lb equals $0.2+0.1=0.3$. Since $P=0.3<P_c=0.333$, do not order the next unit, and the optimum strategy is: buy 200.

TABLE 3.7.1. *Demand Distribution and Values of P*

Demand	Probability of Demand	Cumulative Probability of Greater Than Demand, P
0	0.1	0.9
100	0.2	0.7
200	0.4	0.3
300	0.2	0.1
400	0.1	0

SECTION 3.8. *Subjective Probabilities*

As the previous sections have made evident, there is a significant advantage to making decisions when the probabilities of the various events are known. Unfortunately, very often these probabilities are not known but are guessed at by the decision maker. This is true in practice, as is seen by the favoritism that is extended to the likelihood of any single event. If the decision maker can rank all the events in proportion to one event, it is possible by a simple normalizing process to derive a set of subjective probabilities. Once these numbers are known, it is possible to measure the sensitivity of selecting a particular strategy with changes in the probabilities. If variations in the probabilities generate no changes in the optimal decision, he need go no further. If, however, the optimal strategy changes with small changes in probabilities, the estimates used in the decision process must be very carefully chosen.

Suppose that the apple peddler thinks that the event demand $=200$ lb is most likely, assigns it a value 1.0 and makes the following judgments:

a demand of 0 lb is one-fourth as likely   (0.25)

a demand of 100 lb is three-fourths as likely   (0.75)

a demand of 300 lb is half as likely   (0.5)

a demand of 400 lb is half as likely   (0.5)

To find the subjective probabilities we sum the factors or weights and divide the number into each individual factor to estimate the probabilities. Thus, the sum equals $1+0.25+0.75+0.5+0.5=3$ and

$$P(0) \quad = \frac{0.25}{3} = 0.08$$

$$P(100) = \frac{0.75}{3} = 0.25$$

$$P(200) = \frac{1}{3} \quad = 0.33$$

$$P(300) = \frac{0.5}{3} \quad = 0.17$$

$$P(400) = \frac{0.5}{3} \quad = \underline{0.17}$$
$$\phantom{P(400) = \frac{0.5}{3} \quad = } 1.00$$

Using these probabilities to calculate the EMV, we get

$$\text{EMV}(0) \quad = 0$$
$$\text{EMV}(100) = 17.6$$
$$\text{EMV}(200) = 27.7$$
$$\text{EMV}(300) = 27.9$$
$$\text{EMV}(400) = 28.0$$

with the optimum strategy now "buy 400 lb." Hence, the use of subjective probabilities can lead to different decision rules, depending on the individual who is choosing the probabilities.

At first glance, subjective probabilities may not seem very scientific. However, when a decision maker has established in his own mind the relative likelihood of the various events, he uses them in making a decision, with or without a model. Therefore, it is quite logical to quantify these "feelings" and use them in our modeling process.

SECTION 3.9. *Competitive Situations*

In the previous sections we presented decision problems wherein the uncontrollable variables, if unknown, were considered state-of-nature variables: for example, the demand for a product, or the weather conditions—where the decision maker has no control on the unknown elements. However, in many situations there are two decision makers, whose interests are in conflict. A decision considered optimal by one person may affect the choice by his competitor and thereby generate nonoptimal choices by both individuals. These types of problems are solved by techniques of *game theory*. For these problems a payoff table for each competitor must be developed and the special decision rules applied. This material will be treated in Chapter 15.

SECTION 3.10. *Summary*

This chapter has presented an introduction to simple decision problems. The payoff table structure was given and a number of decision rules were explained for the cases of certainty, uncertainty, and risk. In addition, we showed how to find the value of additional information and to analyze when this information should be obtained. Finally, we introduced the method of marginal analysis for solving a class of problems involving risk.

Many decision problems are more complex than have been presented here. Furthermore, the payoff table does not lend itself very readily to solving these problems. In Chapter 4 we shall introduce the decision-tree form, which allows for a more general approach to solving decision problems. We shall also discuss the notion of survey information, which plays an important role in decision theory.

PROBLEMS

3.1. The local bookstore wishes to order copies of the latest national best-seller. Past experience has indicated that the demand for a new book will be 50, 100, 150, or 200 books. The books cost the store $4 and are sold for $6.

(a) Construct the conditional profit payoff table.

(b) Determine the number of books the bookstore should buy, using:
   (1) The pessimistic decision criterion.
   (2) The optimistic decision criterion.
   (3) The equally likely decision criterion.

3.2. (Problem 3.1 continued)

(a) Construct the conditional opportunity-loss table.

(b) Determine the number of books the bookstore should buy, using the Savage regret decision criterion.

3.3. (Problem 3.1 continued) Assume that the bookstore owner has analyzed her previous book sales and has compiled the following data:

Demand for a New Book	Number of Times Demand Occurred
50	10
100	20
150	15
200	5

(a) Find the probability distribution of demand.
(b) Determine the number of books the bookstore should buy, using:
    (1) The EMV criterion.
    (2) The EOL criterion.

3.4. (Problem 3.1 continued) Suppose that the bookstore owner can obtain perfect information about the demand for a new book.
(a) What is the expected profit under perfect information?
(b) What is the expected value of perfect information?

3.5. (Problem 3.1 continued) Solve the local bookstore's problem using incremental analysis and the probabilities of Problem 3.3.

3.6. (Problem 3.1 continued) The bookstore owner, having lost her previous sales data, estimates the probabilities of demand as follows:

> The most likely event is a demand of 100 books,
>
> A demand of 150 books is one-half as likely,
>
> A demand of 50 books is one-fourth as likely,
>
> A demand of 200 books is one-fourth as likely.

(a) Find the probability distribution of demand.
(b) Using the EMV criterion, determine the number of books the bookstore should buy.
(c) What is the EVPI?

3.7. (Problem 3.1 continued) The bookstore owner has learned that she can *sell all* unsold books to a book discount outlet for $1. Resolve Problems 3.1–3.6.

3.8. The Exact Time Watch Company is planning to sell a new low-cost watch through its network of distributors. The price charged to the distributors will be $10. The choice of the watch-movement design will depend only on the overall profit. A windup movement will involve a fixed production setup cost of $100,000 and a variable cost of $5 per unit. An automatic movement will have a somewhat larger fixed cost, $160,000, with a lower per-unit variable cost, $4. A battery-driven movement will have the highest fixed cost, $250,000, with variable costs of $3/unit. The demand for these watches is uncertain, but the company feels that one of the following events will take place:

> E_1: demand = 30,000 units
>
> E_2: demand = 120,000 units
>
> E_3: demand = 200,000 units

(a) Construct the conditional profit payoff table.
(b) Determine the company's optimum decision using the pessimistic decision criterion.

(c) Determine the company's optimum decision using the optimistic decision criterion.

(d) Determine the company's optimum decision using the equally likely decision criterion.

3.9. (Problem 3.8 continued)

(a) Construct the conditional opportunity-loss table.

(b) Determine the company's optimum decision using the Savage regret decision criterion.

3.10. (Problem 3.8 continued) Suppose that the watch manufacturer has determined the probabilities for the three demand events as follows:

Event	P(event)
E_1	0.15
E_2	0.75
E_3	0.10

(a) Determine the company's optimum decision using the EMV criterion.

(b) Determine the company's optimum decision using the EOL criterion.

(c) Suppose that the manufacturer is able to perfectly predict the demand. What is the expected profit under these conditions?

3.11. (Problem 3.8 continued) A market research company offers to provide a model for perfectly predicting the demand for watches. How much should the watch manufacturer be willing to pay the market research company for its model?

3.12. A local farmer must decide on which of three crops to plant: potatoes, tomatoes, or corn. The yield depends on the weather, which may be termed good, variable, or bad. The dollar yields of the three crops under the different weather conditions are summarized in the following payoff table:

Events / Strategies	Weather		
	E_1: Good	E_2: Variable	E_3: Bad
S_1: plant potatoes	$20,000	$15,000	$12,000
S_2: plant tomatoes	30,000	10,000	8,000
S_3: plant corn	25,000	18,000	10,000

(a) Which crop should the farmer plant using the uncertainty decision rules?

(b) Weather records indicate that the probability of good weather is 0.3 and for variable weather is 0.4. Which crop should the farmer plant using the Bayes decision rule?

(c) A weather-predicting service offers to provide a guaranteed weather prediction for a fee of $500. Should the farmer buy the service?

3.13. A company with assets of $100,000 is considering the possibility of moving its plant to one of two locations. The total cost of the move will be $15,000. The company estimates its annual profit for the three locations, present, new location 1, and new location 2, as follows:

PRESENT LOCATION		NEW LOCATION 1		NEW LOCATION 2	
Annual Profit	*Probability*	*Annual Profit*	*Probability*	*Annual Profit*	*Probability*
$5,000	0.2	$ 9,000	0.3	$ 6,000	0.4
6,000	0.5	10,000	0.4	12,000	0.3
8,000	0.3	12,000	0.2	15,000	0.3

(a) Compute the expected dollar values of total assets at the end of 1 year for each strategy.
(b) If the optimum decision is based on the total assets at the end of 4 years, what decision should the company make?
(c) How long is required before the total assets obtained by moving to location 1 are the same as if no move were made?

3.14. A large consulting firm is contemplating selling 10,000 shares of company stock, currently selling at $20 per share, to raise the capital needed for expansion. The company is facing two crucial situations, both of which may influence the future price of the stock:

(1) A Justice Department lawsuit, which could decrease the value of the stock.
(2) A large Defense Department contract, which could increase the value of the stock.

Thus, there are four state-of-nature events:

E_1: contract obtained, no lawsuit—shares rise to $24
E_2: contract obtained, lawsuit occurs—shares rise to $22
E_3: no contract, no lawsuit—shares remain the same
E_4: no contract, lawsuit occurs—shares decrease to $16

We consider three possible strategies:

S_1: sell all the stocks immediately
S_2: sell the stocks only after the two pending actions have occurred
S_3: hedge by selling only 5,000 shares now and the other 5,000 only after the two pending actions have occurred

The objective of the consulting firm is to maximize the proceeds on the sale of the stock.

(a) Construct the conditional profit payoff table.
(b) Determine which strategy the company will use if the choice is based on:
(1) The pessimistic decision criterion.
(2) The optimistic decision criterion.
(3) The equally likely decision criterion.
(4) The Savage regret criterion.

3.15. (Problem 3.14 continued) Suppose it is known that the probability of the consulting company winning the contract is 70% and that the probability of a lawsuit is 60%.

(a) Find the event probability distribution.
(b) What is the optimal strategy based on EMV?
(c) What is the EVPI?

3.16. The Quick Computing Company is planning to introduce a new pocket calculator. Three types of advertising strategy are considered: newspaper ads, radio and television spots, and a mail campaign. The profit for each strategy depends on the company's ability to fill the orders. Three different events will occur. The order will be filled either on time, 1 week late, or 2 weeks late. The conditional payoff table is as follows:

Events Strategies	E_1: On Time	E_2: 1 Week Late	E_3: 2 Weeks Late
S_1: newspaper	$10,000	$20,000	$15,000
S_2: radio and TV	15,000	18,000	20,000
S_3: mail	5,000	15,000	25,000

The company considers the delivery on time as the most likely event, 1-week-late delivery $\frac{2}{3}$ as likely, and 2-week-late delivery $\frac{1}{3}$ as likely.

(a) Estimate the event probability distribution.
(b) What is the optimum strategy using EMV?
(c) The trucking company offers to provide guaranteed delivery dates for an additional fee. Should the company take advantage of this service?

3.17 The Postal Service requires that all parcel post packages mailed on any day be processed the same day. From Postal Service records the following probability distribution of packages mailed was developed:

Number of Packages Mailed	Probability
41–50	0.10
51–60	0.15
61–70	0.30
71–80	0.25
81–90	0.20

A postal clerk processes, on the average, four packages per hour and earns $5 per hour. A 50% premium is paid for overtime. A regular working day is 7 hours and a maximum of 5 hours of overtime per worker per day is allowed.

(a) How many postal clerks should be employed using the EMV criterion?
(b) For the optimum strategy, what is the expected idle-time cost?
(c) For the optimum strategy, what is the expected overtime cost?

3.18. A large printing company wishes to determine how many extra rollers to purchase with its new printing presses. In the event that the machine breaks down and there are no extra rollers, the downtime would cost $20,000. The cost of an additional roller at the time the presses are purchased is $500. Subsequent to this, however, a roller would cost $1,500. The probability distribution of roller failures during the lifetime of the presses is given by the manufacturer as follows:

Number of Failures	Probability
0	0.73
1	0.12
2	0.07
3	0.04
4	0.02
5	0.015
6	0.005

How many rollers should be purchased with the presses in order to minimize total costs?

3.19. A company must decide whether to modernize its plant now in anticipation of higher demands, or to wait until later. The conditional payoff matrix (in $000) is as follows:

Events Strategies	E_1: Demand High	E_2: Demand Medium	E_3: Demand Low
S_1: modernize now	80	60	−15
S_2: modernize later	60	50	10

(a) Find the optimum strategy, using:
   (1) The pessimistic decision criterion.
   (2) The Savage regret decision criterion.
(b) If the probability of demand is 0.2 for high, 0.5 for medium, and 0.3 for low, find the optimum decision using EMV.
(c) What is the value of perfect information?

3.20. A car service company has been cited for its poor-quality tires. To rectify the problem, the company is considering three different tires. The premium tire cost $100 and is guaranteed for 2 years. The first-line tire costs $75 and is guaranteed for 1 year, although the probability of its lasting 1 year is only 0.5. The second-line tire is not guaranteed, costs $50, and lasts 6 months (probability = 0.6), 1 year (probability = 0.3), or 2 years (probability = 0.1). What decision should the company make?

BOOKS OF INTEREST

Brown, R. V., A. S. Kahr, and C. Peterson, *Decision Analysis for the Manager*. New York: Holt, Rinehart and Winston, 1974.

Chernoff, H. and L. E. Moses, *Elementary Decision Theory*. New York: John Wiley & Sons, Inc., 1957.

Hadley, George, *Introduction to Probability and Statistical Decision Theory*. San Francisco: Holden-Day, Inc., 1967.

Jedamus, P. and R. Frame, *Business Decision Theory*. New York: McGraw-Hill Book Co., 1969.

Luce, R. D. and H. Raiffa, *Games and Decisions*. New York: John Wiley & Sons, Inc., 1957.

Morris, W. T., *Management Science: A Bayesian Introduction*. Englewood Cliffs, N.J.: Prentice-Hall, Inc., 1968.

Pratt, J. W., H. Raiffa, and R. Schlaifer, *Introduction to Statistical Decision Theory*. New York: McGraw-Hill Book Co., 1965.

Raiffa, H., *Decision Analysis: Introductory Lectures on Choices Under Uncertainty*. Reading, Mass.: Addison-Wesley, 1968.

Schlaifer, R., *Analysis of Decisions Under Uncertainty*. New York: McGraw-Hill Book Co., 1969.

CHAPTER FOUR

Decision Trees and Survey Information

OBJECTIVES: The purpose of this chapter is to acquaint you with the following concepts regarding decision trees and survey information.

1. *Sequential decision problems.*
2. *The use of decision trees to solve sequential decision problems.*
3. *The backward induction method.*
4. *The effect of survey information.*
5. *The use of revised probabilities in decision problems.*

In Chapter 3 we dealt with decision problems that could be structured in the form of a payoff table. A single decision was required to be made from among a set of alternatives with payoffs conditional on a set of events with unknown likelihoods or at best a known probability distribution. However, many decision problems do not fall into this category. For example, the apple peddler may actually have two separate decisions to make. The first decision is whether to sell his apples uptown or downtown; the second decision is how many apples to buy. Furthermore, if he sells his apples uptown, there may be less likelihood of competition, whereas downtown the competition is much keener, leading to two different probability distributions.

As a second example, the loan officer of a bank, in making a decision about a loan, makes two separate decisions. The first decision is whether to order a special investigation. The second decision is whether to grant the loan.

In both these examples the decision process is referred to as *sequential decision-making* and is usually solved by methods other than the use of a single payoff table. Each complete strategy will require a complex statement as to what action to take at each decision point. For example, a complete strategy for the apple peddler might be: sell downtown and buy 200 lb of apples. A complete strategy for the loan officer might be: order an investigation and if positive, grant the loan; if negative, do not grant the loan. To organize the elements of these complex strategies into a meaningful arrangement, we introduce the concept of a *decision-tree* diagram. The decision tree, with its many branches, allows us to portray every possible action and to display every possible outcome.

The decision-tree diagram will also be useful in a type of decision problem wherein the set of possible events is not the same for each possible strategy or, even if the set of events is the same, their likelihoods are different for each strategy. For example, if the apple peddler has only two strategies—sell uptown or sell downtown—it is possible that uptown three events can occur: demand equals 100, 200, or 300 lb of apples, and downtown five events can occur: demand equals 0, 100, 200, 300, or 400 lb of apples. In addition, even if the demand possibilities are the same in both locations, the probabilities associated with each event may be different. In these cases the decision is easily found using the tree analysis.

101

A third use of decision trees is for those situations wherein the decision maker has the opportunity to experiment or perform a survey before making the decision. For example, you may wish to perform market research before deciding whether to introduce a new product. The rectangular format of the payoff table is quite cumbersome and inconvenient for this type of decision problem, but decision trees handle them easily.

In this chapter we shall present a detailed methodology for solving decision problems that require decision-tree analysis. In addition, we will show how to analyze a decision problem when additional information is available through testing or surveys, and finally we shall analyze the value of obtaining such additional information.

SECTION 4.2. *Decision-Tree Form*

The decision tree is composed of four elements: branches, decision nodes, event nodes, and outcomes (payoffs). A branch is a single strategy or event possibility which connects either two nodes or a node and an outcome. A decision node is a point on the tree represented by a square, □, from which two or more branches emerge. Each branch from a decision node will thus represent a possible single strategy to be taken by the decision maker. An event node is a point on the tree represented by a circle, ○, from which two or more branches emerge. Each of these branches will represent a possible event that might take place. The outcomes are the results (payoffs) of a sequence of strategies and events that form a unique path in the tree from the initial point to the end point. In Figure 4.2.1 a possible decision-tree diagram is presented. The initial node of the tree starts with the first decision, a choice between strategies 1 and 2. Following the choice of a strategy a random event occurs, either event 1 or 2. The decision maker is now at one of the four decision nodes at which a second decision must be made between strategies 3 and 4. Following this decision a second random event occurs, event 3 or 4. Depending on which path has been followed, one of 16 possible payoffs will result. For example, the sequence: strategy 1, event 2, strategy 3, event 4 results in a payoff of CP_6.

The optimal decision for such a decision problem is to choose a set of single strategies that yields the best expected value for the initial node. This solution assumes that the expected value can be determined at each event node and that the decision maker will make a complex decision which depends on the various random events. For example,

FIRST DECISION: STRATEGY 1

1. If event 1 occurs, select STRATEGY 4 as the SECOND DECISION,
2. If event 2 occurs, select STRATEGY 3 as the SECOND DECISION,

with a calculated expected value at the initial node. This expected value

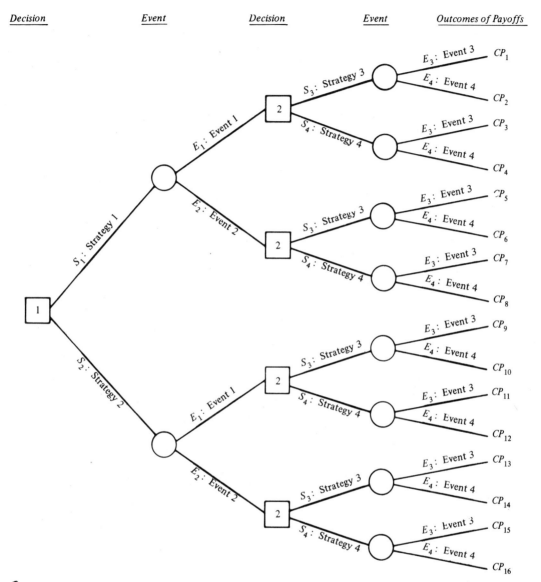

FIGURE 4.2.1. *Decision-tree diagram.*

must be thought of as a long-term average return were the same decision rule to be used many times. The actual outcome of this decision (for this example) will be one of the four payoffs CP_3, CP_4, CP_5, or CP_6.

SECTION 4.3. *Decision-Tree Solution*

In order to show how to solve decision problems using the tree diagram, let us consider several problems. Assume that the apple peddler has a fixed supply of 200 lb of apples daily and must decide whether to sell

103

uptown or downtown. If he sells uptown, there will be no competition, and demand may be 100, 200, or 300 lb of apples. If he sells downtown, there may be competition, in which case the demand for his apples will be only 0, 100, or 200 lb of apples. Figure 4.3.1 presents this problem in decision-tree form.

The first step in solving this problem is to determine the payoffs for each path in the tree. Assume that the payoff measure is the net profit. Since the apples cost 30 cents/pound, the total cost is $200 \times 0.30 = \$60$. Let us assume that the selling price is fixed at 50 cents/pound. Then,

$$CP_1 = 100 \times 0.5 - 60 = -\$10$$

$$CP_2 = 200 \times 0.5 - 60 = \$40$$

The payoff values are shown at the terminal points in Figure 4.3.2. Note that for CP_3 and CP_9, the number sold is only 200 lb, even though the demand was 300 lb.

If no other information is given (likelihoods or probabilities), we must treat this problem as in Section 3.4, using one of the rules for

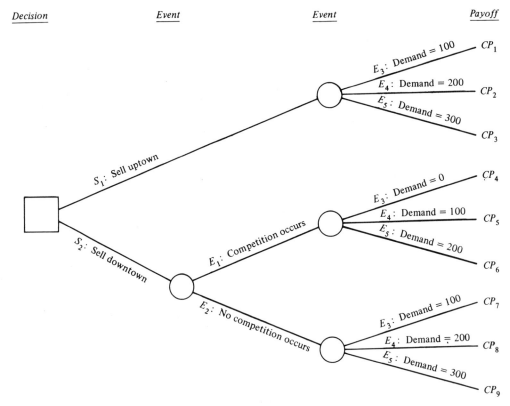

Decision	Event	Event	Payoff

FIGURE 4.3.1. *Tree diagram for apple peddler problem.*

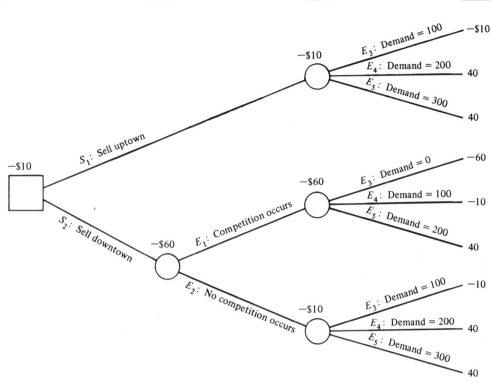

Decision	Event	Event	Payoff

FIGURE 4.3.2. *Tree diagram for apple peddler problem with payoffs and pessimistic decision criterion.*

decisions under uncertainty. If we apply the pessimistic criterion, we would determine the worst outcome at each event node. If the peddler sells uptown, the worst payoff is −$10. If he sells downtown and competition occurs, the minimum payoff is −$60, while if no competition occurs, the minimum payoff is −$10. Hence, the worst payoff for downtown sales is −$60. The peddler will choose to sell uptown, since the payoff −$10 is better than the payoff −$60. In Figure 4.3.2 these numbers are shown above each node. The strategies not chosen are shown with the path broken by two parallel lines.

Assume now that the peddler knows from past experience the probabilities of each possible event. These numbers appear in parentheses along each branch emerging from an event node (Figure 4.3.3). The peddler can now use expected value as his decision criterion, and thus he must determine the expected value of the two possible strategies, sell uptown or sell downtown. For sell uptown we have

$$\text{EMV}(S_1: \text{sell uptown}) = 0.5(-10) + 0.4(40) + 0.1(40) = \$15$$

For sell downtown, we must first calculate the EMV for the two events

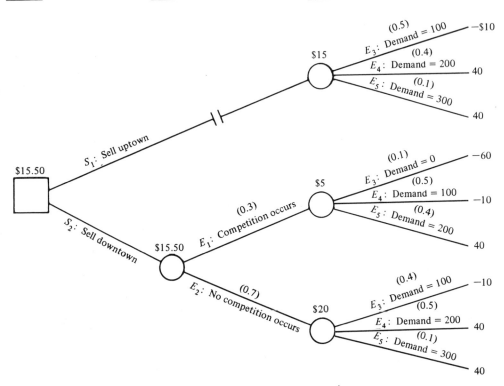

FIGURE 4.3.3. *Tree diagram for apple peddler problem with expected value solution.*

"competition occurs" and "no competition occurs." We get

$$\text{EMV}(E_1\text{: competition occurs})=0.1(-60)+0.5(-10)+0.4(40)$$

$$=\$5$$

$$\text{EMV}(E_2\text{: no competition occurs})=0.4(-10)+0.5(40)+0.1(40)$$

$$=\$20$$

Therefore,

$$\text{EMV}(S_2\text{: sell downtown})=0.3(5)+0.7(20)=\$15.5$$

and the optimal decision is

S_2: *sell downtown, with an expected return of* $15.5.

The method of analysis used in solving the decision-tree problem is called *backward induction.* It assumes that to evaluate an initial strategy, it is necessary to consider all later decisions and events which result from that choice. Thus, the latest possible event and decision nodes are analyzed first, and then the earlier nodes are examined, eventually arriving at the initial node. Using this technique, optimal actions for every eventuality are established throughout the tree diagram, and thus a complete, although complex, decision rule can be stated.

To make this analysis methodology clearer, consider the same problem, where we assume that the apple peddler, on choosing to sell downtown and observing the competition, must decide whether to buy 100 or 200 lb of apples. This problem is represented by the tree diagram of Figure 4.3.4. Notice that the boxed segments of the tree denoted by I and II are in reality simple decision problems that can be solved by the methods of Chapter 3. The payoff table for box I is shown in Table 4.3.1. Similarly, the payoff table for box II is shown in Table 4.3.2. The backward-induction methodology requires that the solution for these two simple decision problems be found first, yielding results CP_{16} and CP_{17}. The decision tree then reduces to that shown in Figure 4.3.5. The solution is found by evaluating the two event nodes and choosing the best value for the optimal solution.

TABLE 4.3.1. *Payoff Table for Box I of Figure 4.3.4*

Events Strategies	E_6: Demand $= 0$	E_7: Demand $= 100$	E_8: Demand $= 200$
S_3: buy 100 lb S_4: buy 200 lb	$CP_4 = -30$ $CP_7 = -60$	$CP_5 = 20$ $CP_8 = -10$	$CP_6 = 20$ $CP_9 = 40$

TABLE 4.3.2. *Payoff Table for Box II of Figure 4.3.4*

Events Strategies	E_9: Demand $= 100$	E_{10}: Demand $= 200$	E_{11}: Demand $= 300$
S_3: buy 100 lb S_4: buy 200 lb	$CP_{10} = 20$ $CP_{13} = -10$	$CP_{11} = 20$ $CP_{14} = 40$	$CP_{12} = 20$ $CP_{15} = 40$

In Figure 4.3.6 we show the payoff values of the terminal branches together with the probabilities of all the event possibilities. Solving the box I decision problem, we get

$$\text{EMV}(S_3: \text{buy } 100) = 0.1(-30) + 0.5(20) + 0.4(20) = \$15$$
$$\text{EMV}(S_4: \text{buy } 200) = 0.1(-60) + 0.5(-10) + 0.4(40) = \$5$$

Therefore, the optimal decision for box I is S_3: buy 100 lb, with an EMV of \$15. Solving the box II decision problem, we get

$$\text{EMV}(S_3: \text{buy } 100) = 0.4(20) + 0.5(20) + 0.1(20) = \$20$$

$$\text{EMV}(S_4: \text{buy } 200) = 0.4(-10) + 0.5(40) + 0.1(40) = \$20$$

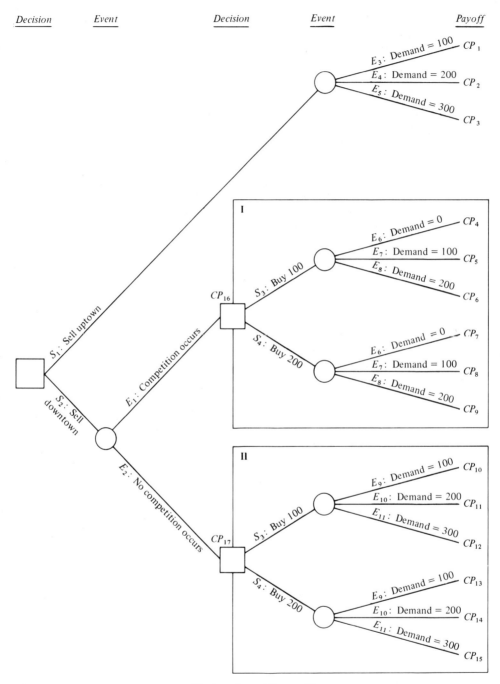

FIGURE 4.3.4. *Tree diagram for modified apple peddler problem.*

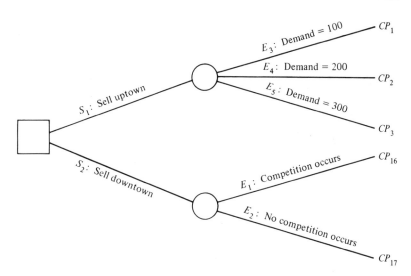

Decision	Event	Payoff

FIGURE 4.3.5. *Reduced tree diagram for modified apple peddler problem.*

Thus, the optimal decision for box II is S_3 or S_4: buy either 100 or 200 lb.

Having solved the two simple decision problems we can now solve the overall decision problem. We get

$$\text{EMV}(S_1: \text{sell uptown}) = 0.5(-10) + 0.4(40) + 0.1(40) = \$15$$

$$\text{EMV}(S_2: \text{sell downtown}) = 0.3(15) + 0.7(20) = \$18.5$$

Hence, the decision is S_2: sell downtown.

The full statement of the decision is as follows:

1. Decision 1: sell downtown.

   If competition occurs, then

2. Decision 2: buy 100 lb of apples.

   If no competition occurs, then

3. Decision 2: buy either 100 or 200 lb of apples.

The expected payoff will be $18.50.

It should be noted that giving a full statement of the decision is just as important as solving the problem and should not be passed over lightly in solving complex decision problems.

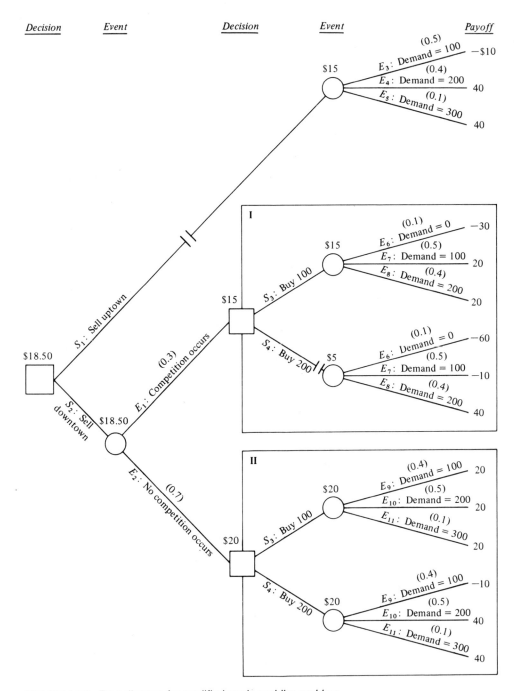

FIGURE 4.3.6. *Tree diagram for modified apple peddler problem.*

4.4.1. Introduction. In Section 4.3 decision trees were used to solve two types of problems. In the first, only one decision was to be made, with event likelihoods represented by different probability distributions. In the second problem, two separate decisions were required at different times. This second class of problems, involving multiple decisions over time, is generally referred to as a *sequential decision problem*. In this section we present a more complicated decision problem, introducing a somewhat more formal solution procedure.

4.4.2. Statement of Problem. The General Products Company (GPC) is planning to introduce a new line of wall paneling in either the economy price range or the deluxe price range. Since a competitive firm exists, the selling price is not chosen until after GPC observes whether the competitive line materializes. If the competitor does introduce its line of paneling, the competing firm chooses its prices after GPC chooses theirs. The economy price line is $5 or $6, and the deluxe price line is $8 or $9. The GPC sales department has analyzed the market and, based on costs and sales figures, have determined the possible annual payoffs as shown in Table 4.4.1. The company must choose which wall-paneling line to introduce and which price to charge.

TABLE 4.4.1. *Payoffs to GPC for Each Possible Strategy Conditional on the Price Choice of the Competitor.*

GPC STRATEGIES	COMPETITOR PRICES (EVENTS)				
	E_1: ECONOMY LINE		E_2: DELUXE LINE		E_3: NO COMPETITION
	E_4: $5 Price	E_5: $6 Price	E_6: $8 Price	E_7: $9 Price	
S_1: economy line					
S_4: $5 price	$CP_1 = \$5,000$	$CP_2 = \$6,000$	$CP_5 = \$5,500$	$CP_6 = \$6,500$	$CP_9 = \$10,000$
S_5: $6 price	$CP_3 = 4,800$	$CP_4 = 5,400$	$CP_7 = 6,000$	$CP_8 = 6,800$	$CP_{10} = 12,000$
S_2: deluxe line					
S_6: $8 price	$CP_{11} = 3,000$	$CP_{12} = 4,000$	$CP_{15} = 7,000$	$CP_{17} = 6,500$	$CP_{19} = 12,000$
S_7: $9 price	$CP_{13} = 2,400$	$CP_{14} = 3,000$	$CP_{16} = 8,000$	$CP_{18} = 7,500$	$CP_{20} = 15,000$

4.4.3. Solution Using Decision Trees. The criterion used by GPC in making its decisions is the EMV rule. The use of this rule assumes that all the probabilities for the various events are known. The detailed decision tree showing all strategies, events, the event probabilities, and the conditional payoff values are shown in Figure 4.4.1. Note that the probability of the competitor's price being $5 is not the same value throughout but depends on GPC's decision.

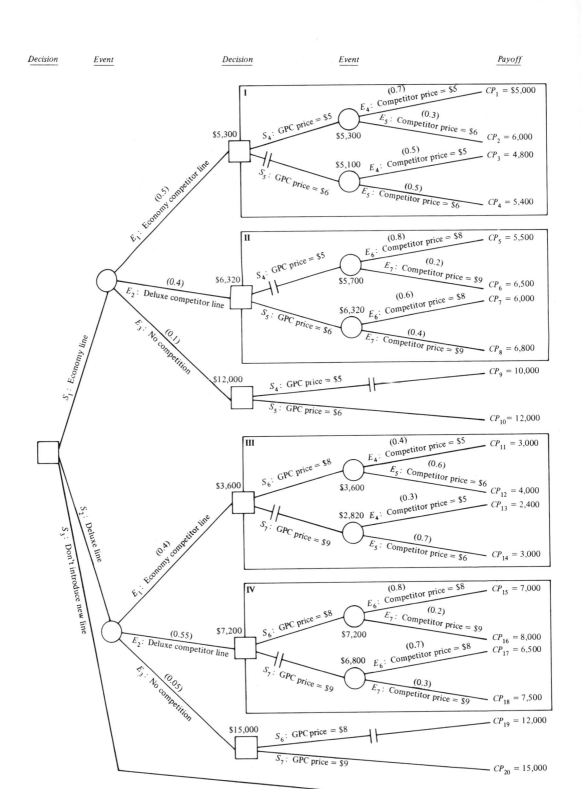

Decision	Event	Decision	Event	Payoff

I

S_4: GPC price = $5 $5,300

(0.7) E_4: Competitor price = $5 CP_1 = $5,000
(0.3) E_5: Competitor price = $6 CP_2 = 6,000

S_5: GPC price = $6 $5,100

(0.5) E_4: Competitor price = $5 CP_3 = 4,800
(0.5) E_5: Competitor price = $6 CP_4 = 5,400

$5,300

(0.5) E_1: Economy competitor line

II

S_4: GPC price = $5 $5,700

(0.8) E_6: Competitor price = $8 CP_5 = 5,500
(0.2) E_7: Competitor price = $9 CP_6 = 6,500

S_5: GPC price = $6 $6,320

(0.6) E_6: Competitor price = $8 CP_7 = 6,000
(0.4) E_7: Competitor price = $9 CP_8 = 6,800

$6,320

(0.4) E_2: Deluxe competitor line

(0.1) E_3: No competition

$12,000 S_4: GPC price = $5 CP_9 = 10,000
S_5: GPC price = $6 CP_{10} = 12,000

S_1: Economy line

III

S_6: GPC price = $8 $3,600

(0.4) E_4: Competitor price = $5 CP_{11} = 3,000
(0.6) E_5: Competitor price = $6 CP_{12} = 4,000

S_7: GPC price = $9 $2,820

(0.3) E_4: Competitor price = $5 CP_{13} = 2,400
(0.7) E_5: Competitor price = $6 CP_{14} = 3,000

$3,600

(0.4) E_1: Economy competitor line

IV

S_6: GPC price = $8 $7,200

(0.8) E_6: Competitor price = $8 CP_{15} = 7,000
(0.2) E_7: Competitor price = $9 CP_{16} = 8,000

S_7: GPC price = $9 $6,800

(0.7) E_6: Competitor price = $8 CP_{17} = 6,500
(0.3) E_7: Competitor price = $9 CP_{18} = 7,500

$7,200

(0.55) E_2: Deluxe competitor line

(0.05) E_3: No competition

$15,000 S_6: GPC price = $8 CP_{19} = 12,000
S_7: GPC price = $9 CP_{20} = 15,000

S_2: Deluxe line

S_3: Don't introduce new line CP_{21} = 0

SECTION 4.4

New-Product Decision Problem

In order to solve complex decision-tree problems, one should always attempt to simplify the tree by identifying the subproblems, which will usually be in the form of simple decision problems. For our example the subproblems are identified by boxes I, II, III, and IV. Solving decision problem I we must decide between S_4 and S_5, using EMV. Thus,

$$\text{EMV}(S_4) = 0.7(5{,}000) + 0.3(6{,}000) = \$5{,}300$$

$$\text{EMV}(S_5) = 0.5(4{,}800) + 0.5(5{,}400) = \$5{,}100$$

Hence, the decision for box I is strategy S_4: GPC price = \$5.

For decision problem II we have the following:

$$\text{EMV}(S_4) = 0.8(5{,}500) + 0.2(6{,}500) = \$5{,}700$$

$$\text{EMV}(S_5) = 0.6(6{,}000) + 0.4(6{,}800) = \$6{,}320$$

Hence, the decision for box II is strategy S_5: GPC price = \$6.

On comparing S_6 and S_7 for subproblem III, we get

$$\text{EMV}(S_6) = 0.4(3{,}000) + 0.6(4{,}000) = \$3{,}600$$

$$\text{EMV}(S_7) = 0.3(2{,}400) + 0.7(3{,}000) = \$2{,}820$$

Thus, the decision for box III is S_6: GPC price = \$8. Finally, solving decision problem IV, we have the following:

$$\text{EMV}(S_6) = 0.8(7{,}000) + 0.2(8{,}000) = \$7{,}200$$

$$\text{EMV}(S_7) = 0.7(6{,}500) + 0.3(7{,}500) = \$6{,}800$$

Hence, the decision for subproblem IV is strategy S_6: GPC price = \$8. The decision problem is now reduced to the simple decision problem presented in Figure 4.4.2.

To solve the reduced decision-tree problem we evaluate strategies S_1, S_2, and S_3. We get

$$\begin{aligned}\text{EMV}(S_1) &= 0.5(5{,}300) + 0.4(6{,}320) + 0.1(12{,}000)\\ &= \$6{,}378\\ \text{EMV}(S_2) &= 0.4(3{,}600) + 0.55(7{,}200) + 0.05(15{,}000)\\ &= \$6{,}150\\ \text{EMV}(S_3) &= 0\end{aligned}$$

Thus, the GPC decision will be S_1: introduce the economy line. The full

← FIGURE 4.4.1. *Decision tree for new product problem.*

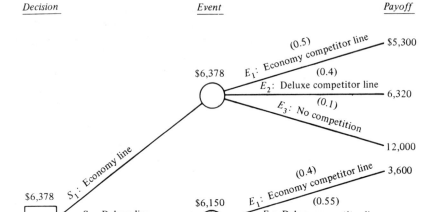

FIGURE 4.4.2. *Reduced decision tree for new product problem.*

decision rule for GPC is as follows:

1. Decision 1; strategy S_1: introduce economy line.

   If competitor introduces an economy line, then

2. Decision 2; strategy S_4: set price at $5.

   If competitor introduces a deluxe line, then

3. Decision 2; strategy S_5: set price at $6.

   If no competition develops, then

4. Decision 2; strategy S_5: set price at $6.

The total expected profit is $6,378.

SECTION 4.5. *Decisions with Survey Information*

In general, a better-informed decision maker should be able to reduce the level of uncertainty in his problem and thereby make a more meaningful decision. To obtain this information, the decision maker can perform a controlled experiment or conduct a survey. The results of the experiment or survey are used to revise his knowledge about the likelihood of the occurrence of the uncertain events. For example, suppose that a bet is to be placed as to the outcome of the toss of a coin, heads or tails. However, you suspect that the coin is not a fair one and you request the opportunity to experiment with the coin. You toss the coin two times and observe the results. If both tosses show heads or both show tails, your suspicion is strengthened and you would bet based on this revised information. If, however, the results were one head and one tail, it is more likely that the coin is truly fair, and your betting would be based on this additional knowledge.

The questions that will be answered in this section are as follows: How does one use the revised information for decision-making? When does it pay to conduct a survey or perform an experiment? In the next section we shall answer the following questions: When is it necessary to revise the initial judgments as a result of survey experimental data? How does one revise probabilities based on a survey?

To assist in developing the methodology, let us examine a simple bank-loan problem. Consider a bank officer faced with the problem of deciding whether or not to grant or deny an application for a 1-year loan. He has two strategies; grant a 1-year $50,000 loan outright ($S_1$) at 12% or deny loan ($S_2$).

If the loan is granted, the bank estimates that the lender will either pay on time, E_1 (probability = 0.96) or default, E_2 (probability = 0.04). If the loan is denied, the money is invested in government bonds at 6%, thus yielding a payoff of $3,000. If the loan is made and repaid, a profit of $6,000 occurs.

The decision tree and payoff table are shown in Figure 4.5.1. The choice between S_1 and S_2 reduces to comparing the EMV of S_1 with the EMV of S_2. Thus,

$$EMV(S_1) = 0.96(6,000) + 0.04(-50,000) = \$3,760$$
$$EMV(S_2) = \$3,000$$

It is clear that without any additional knowledge, the bank is advised to grant the loan and can expect to earn more ($3,760) by following this policy. However, the bank feels that if better information about the lenders were available, the likelihood of a default could be lessened and a reasonable additional profit made when making loans. In order to make their decision, the bank must determine how much additional profit (over the $3,760) they could make if better information were available. To find this, the bank must first reevaluate the probability of a lender either paying on time or defaulting, given that this better information is being used for evaluating loan applications.

Let us assume that to obtain better information the bank engages a special investigation unit at a cost of $500 that will recommend making a loan (T_1) or recommend denying loan (T_2). Furthermore, we assume that the bank is not required to abide by these recommendations but may grant a loan when the recommendation is negative.

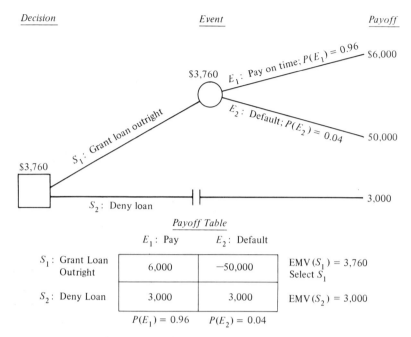

Payoff Table

	E_1: Pay	E_2: Default	
S_1: Grant Loan Outright	6,000	−50,000	EMV $(S_1) = 3,760$ Select S_1
S_2: Deny Loan	3,000	3,000	EMV $(S_2) = 3,000$
	$P(E_1) = 0.96$	$P(E_2) = 0.04$	

FIGURE 4.5.1. *Simplified bank loan problem.*

The decision tree for the problem is shown in Figure 4.5.2. We have introduced a slightly different notation which will be useful for analyzing decision problems that involve a decision on whether to obtain additional information:

A_1, A_2:   strategies regarding the decision to obtain information

T_1, T_2, etc: possible test, experiment, or survey outcomes

This leaves $E_1, E_2, \ldots$, and $S_1, S_2, \ldots$, as having the same meaning as for the decision problem without the decision whether to obtain additional information.

We have also attached a small triangle to the "A_2: order investigation" decision, which represents the cost of the investigation. This quantity, \$500, will not be included in computing the payoffs at the end points of tree and will be incorporated into the analysis only when considering the A_1 versus A_2 decision at the end. Notice that the end of the tree is divided into three sections: I, II, III. These three sections represent almost identical decision problems. The only difference between them is the probabilities of the events E_1: pay and E_2: default.

Section I, where no additional information has been obtained, shows $P(E_1)$ and $P(E_2)$, the bank's initial estimates for payment and default.

116

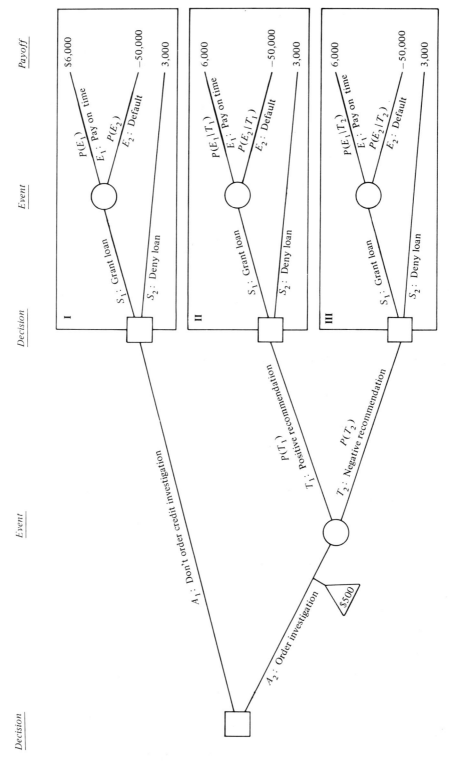

FIGURE 4.5.2. Bank loan problem decision tree.

Section II represents the identical decision being made after receiving a positive recommendation from the investigation, T_1. The probabilities of payment and default are noted as $P(E_1|T_1)$ and $P(E_2|T_1)$.[†] These are conditional probabilities, conditional on receiving a T_1: positive investigation result. We would expect a positive recommendation to indicate a greater likelihood for this individual to pay and should therefore find $P(E_1|T_1) > P(E_1)$. Similarly, for section III, after T_2: negative recommendation, we would expect the probability of paying, $P(E_1|T_2)$, to be lower than without information $P(E_1)$. This *revision of probabilities* is precisely the improved information we receive by taking a test or survey. The original probabilities $P(E)$ are referred to as *prior probabilities* and the probabilities after the survey $P(E|T)$ are called *posterior probabilities*.

Past experience with this investigator yields the data for 200 applicants shown in Table 4.5.1. Out of 156 who received positive recommendations, 154 paid on time and 2 defaulted. From these data it is possible to determine the joint probabilities $P(T$ and $E)$ and the marginal probabilities $P(T)$ and $P(E)$. Dividing all elements of Table 4.5.1 by 200, we get Table 4.5.2. The probabilities of a loan applicant paying his

TABLE 4.5.1. *Results of Past 200 Credit Investigations*

Events Recommendations	E_1: Pay	E_2: Default	Total
T_1: pos. recomm.	154	2	156
T_2: neg. recomm.	38	6	44
Total	192	8	200

TABLE 4.5.2. *Joint Probability Table: P(T and E) with Marginals*

Events Recommendations	E_1: Pay	E_2: Default	$P(T)$
T_1: pos. recomm.	0.77	0.01	0.78
T_2: neg. recomm.	0.19	0.03	0.22
$P(E)$	0.96	0.04	1.00

loan $P(E_1)$ or defaulting on his loan $P(E_2)$ are 0.96 and 0.04, respectively, as given earlier. The probabilities of the credit check yielding a positive recommendation $P(T_1)$ or a negative recommendation $P(T_2)$ are 0.78 and 0.22, respectively. Finally, it is possible to determine the conditional probability of an applicant paying or defaulting on his loan given the recommendation results of the survey. Mathematically, this is represented by $P(E|T)$ and the values are given in Table 4.5.3. They are

[†]A presentation of conditional probabilities is given in Sections 2.3–2.5.

found by using the relationship

$$P(E|T) = \frac{P(T \text{ and } E)}{P(T)}$$

that is, by dividing each value in Table 4.5.2 by $P(T)$, which is shown to the right of each row.

TABLE 4.5.3. *Conditional Probability of Events E
Given Recommendation T: P(E|T)*

Recommendations	Events	E_1: Pay	E_2: Default	Sum
T_1: pos. recomm.		0.987	0.013	1.00
T_2: neg. recomm.		0.865	0.135	1.00

These probability values can now be used to evaluate the strategy of ordering a special investigation A_1 as an alternative to proceeding without the credit check. The analysis of this decision problem and the determination of the value of the added information is aided by the decision tree of Figure 4.5.3. The choice between granting the loan and denying the loan after the special investigation is determined by finding the EMV for S_1 and S_2 in boxes II and III.

For Box II we have

$$\text{EMV}(S_1) = 0.987(6{,}000) + 0.013(-50{,}000)$$
$$= \$5{,}280$$
$$\text{EMV}(S_2) = \$3{,}000$$

Thus, the decision is S_1: grant 1-year loan.

For Box III we have

$$\text{EMV}(S_1) = 0.865(6{,}000) + 0.135(-50{,}000)$$
$$= -\$1{,}567.57$$
$$\text{EMV}(S_2) = \$3{,}000$$

Thus, the decision is S_2: deny loan.

It is now possible to evaluate the alternative actions—A_1: no credit check or A_2: order special investigation, by using EMV. We get

$$\text{EMV}(A_1) = \$3{,}000$$
$$\text{EMV}(A_2) = 0.78(5{,}280) + 0.22(3{,}000) - \text{cost of the investigation}$$
$$= \$4{,}774 - 500$$
$$= \$4{,}274$$

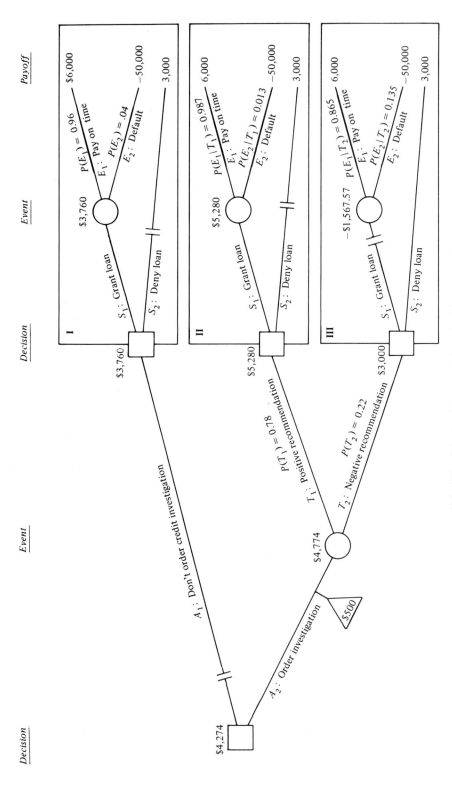

FIGURE 4.5.3. *Bank loan problem decision tree.*

The expected profit assuming that the special investigation has been taken (i.e., neglecting the cost of the special investigation is $4,774, or a $1,014 improvement due to the special investigation). Thus, it pays to make a special investigation since the expected profit will be $514 more than if no credit check is taken. Moreover, as long as the cost of the special investigation is less than $1,014, it is advantageous to the bank to screen out the high-risk applicants by investigating each loan application and thereby earn an expected return of more than $3,760. On the other hand, if the special investigation would cost, say, $2,000, the bank should choose A_1: no credit check. The full general decision rule is as follows:

1. If the cost of the special investigation is $1,014 or more:
   Decision 1 is choose A_1: no credit check.
   Decision 2 is choose S_1: grant loan.
2. If cost of special investigation is less than $1,014:
   Decision 1 is choose A_2: order special investigation.
   Decision 2: if investigation result is a positive recommendation T_1, choose S_1: grant loan; if result is a negative recommendation T_2, then choose S_2: deny loan.

SECTION 4.6. *Computing Revised Probabilities*

Assume now that the bank is opening a new branch in an area where it has no performance record on loan repayments. It estimates the probability of payments for these customers as only $P(E_1)=0.85$ and the probability of default $P(E_2)=0.15$. It expects to use a credit-investigating group whose reliability is already proved. Since the marginal probabilities of paying, $P(E_1)$, and defaulting $P(E_2)$, are different for these new customers, we cannot accept the computations of paying given various investigation outcomes, $P(E|T)$, which were performed using the 200 past histories. This is because those past histories were composed of 96% customers who paid the loan and 4% who did not. However, we may still feel that the investigation is precisely as accurate as before in predicting people's tendency to pay their loans. We refer to this accuracy of prediction as *survey reliability*.

The 200 past histories *can* be used to estimate survey reliability. Looking at Table 4.5.1 we see that of the 192 persons who paid (E_1), 154 received positive recommendations (T_1) and 38 received negative recommendations (T_2). We can estimate $P(T_1|E_1)$ as $\frac{154}{192}=0.80$ and $P(T_2|E_1)$ as $\frac{38}{192}=0.20$. These probabilities of test results given actual loan payment results, $P(T|E)$, are still valid and measure survey reliability. The full set of survey reliability values are given in Table 4.6.1.

Hence, if a loan will eventually default, the probability that the investigative unit will recommend denying the loan is 0.75 (i.e., it is 75% effective). The decision problem of the new bank loan department

TABLE 4.6.1. *Recommendation Reliability Values:*
        P(T|E)

Recommendations	Events	E_1: Pay	E_2: Default
T_1: pos. recomm.		0.80	0.25
T_2: neg. recomm.		0.20	0.75
Sum		1.00	1.00

depends on the type of customers it has. If the new customers would have the same characteristics as the ones in the old branches (i.e., the probability of paying on time was $P(E_1)=0.96$), the decision tree of Figure 4.5.2 would be valid for solving the decision problem of the new bank loan department. However, since the probability of paying on time for the new customer is estimated to be only 0.85, new values for the conditional probabilities must be determined based on the reliability information given in Table 4.6.1.

For example, we must now determine the probability that a loan will default if the recommendation was positive. Symbolically, we must determine $P(E|T)$ if we have information about $P(T|E)$. Using a procedure outlined in Section 2.5, we first calculate $P(T$ and $E)$, that is, the joint probability of each test result and actual event both occurring. This is found from

$$P(T \text{ and } E) = P(E)P(T|E)$$

The $P(E)$ values are called the *prior probabilities* and are the probability values that are estimated when no additional information is available. These values are:

Events	E_1: pay	E_2: default
$P(E)$	0.85	0.15

Thus,

$$P(T_1 \text{ and } E_2) = P(T_1|E_2)P(E_2)$$

$$= 0.25 \times 0.15$$

$$= 0.038$$

That is, we multiply each value in Table 4.6.1 by the appropriate $P(E)$ value. The joint probability table is shown in Table 4.6.2. From the tables the marginal probabilities of E and of T are found by adding the probabilities in a row or a column. Thus, we find that

$$P(T_1)=0.718$$

$$P(T_2)=0.282$$

TABLE 4.6.2. *Joint Probability Table: P(T and E)*

Recommendations / Events	E_1: Pay	E_2: Default	Row Sum $P(T)$
T_1: pos. recomm.	0.680	0.038	0.718
T_2: neg. recomm.	0.170	0.112	0.282
Column sum $P(E)$	0.85	0.15	1.00

This means that based on data already available, the probability that an applicant of the new branch screened by the investigative unit will receive a positive recommendation is 0.718. Note that this is somewhat less than the 0.8 for the old customers. From the values of $P(T$ and $E)$ we can now find $P(E|T)$ using the relationship

$$P(E|T) = \frac{P(T \text{ and } E)}{P(T)}$$

The $P(E|T)$ values are conditional probabilities of the events E given a survey prediction T and we have called them the *posterior probabilities*. The values are presented in Table 4.6.3. For example,

$$P(E_2|T_2) = \frac{P(T_2 \text{ and } E_2)}{P(T_2)}$$

$$= \frac{0.112}{0.282} = 0.398$$

That is, we divide each value in Table 4.6.2 $P(T$ and $E)$ by the appropriate $P(T)$ value. These new revised probability values can now be used to solve the bank-loan decision problem for the new branch. The analysis is aided by the decision tree of Figure 4.6.1, which is exactly the same as Figure 4.5.3 except for the probability values. We first solve the decision problems of boxes I, II, and III. These yield

Box   I—choose S_2: deny loan; EMV = $3,000
Box II—choose S_1: grant loan; EMV = $3,073
Box III—choose S_2: deny loan; EMV = $3,000

We then choose between A_1 and A_2 by finding the EMV values. Thus,

$$EMV(A_1) = \$3,000$$
$$EMV(A_2) = 0.718(3,073) + 0.282(3,000) - 500$$
$$= \$2,552.50$$

Hence the decision is A_1: no credit investigation with an expected payoff of $3,000. Thus, based on the reliability information and our present

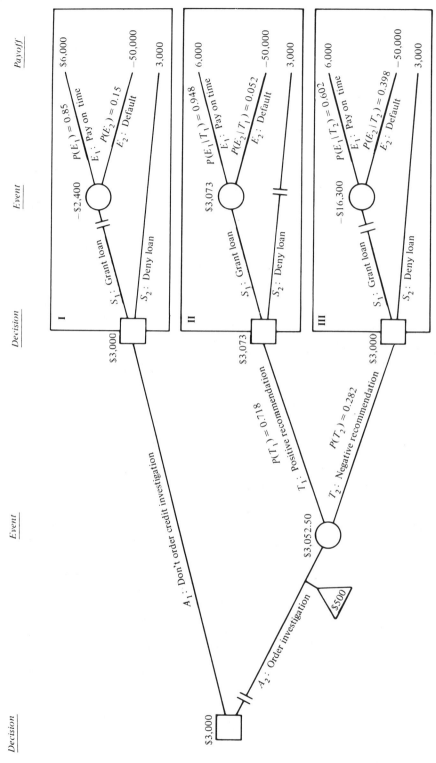

FIGURE 4.6.1. *Bank loan problem decision tree.*

estimates of the probability of a default, there is no advantage at this time to performing credit checks, and all loans should be denied until either better information becomes available or the cost of the investigation is reduced to a value below $52.50.

TABLE 4.6.3. *Conditional Probability of Events E
Given Recommendation T: P(E|T)*

Recommendations	Events	E_1: Pay	E_2: Default
T_1: pos. recomm.		0.948	0.052
T_2: neg. recomm.		0.602	0.398

SECTION 4.7. *Decision Problem with Cost Payoffs*

Let us now consider a second problem to solidify the approach to solving decision problems with test or survey information.

A motel owner has learned that his water supply has gone dry. He is now faced with the options of connecting to city water at a cost of $11,000 or drilling a new well with an expected cost of $10,000 (probability = 0.3), $11,000 (probability = 0.3), or $12,000 (probability = 0.4), depending on the land formation and depth of the waters. A local water survey company offers to perform on-site tests to determine the favorability or unfavorability of a low-cost well. These tests cost $150. The reliability of the company's recommendations based on past experience is given in Table 4.7.1. We have defined the following notation for this problem:

Decision 1 $\begin{cases} A_1 = \text{action 1: do not perform test} \\ A_2 = \text{action 2: order on-site test} \end{cases}$

Decision 2 $\begin{cases} S_1 = \text{strategy 1: drill new well} \\ S_2 = \text{strategy 2: connect to city water} \end{cases}$

$E_1 = $ event 1: cost = $10,000

$E_2 = $ event 2: cost = $11,000

$E_3 = $ event 3: cost = $12,000

$T_1 = $ test result 1: favorable recommendation for low-cost well

$T_2 = $ test result 2: unfavorable recommendation for low-cost well

Recommendations \ Events	E_1: Cost = $10,000	E_2: Cost = $11,000	E_3: Cost = $12,000
T_1: favorable	0.8	0.6	0.2
T_2: unfavorable	0.2	0.4	0.8
	1.0	1.0	1.0

The decision tree for this problem in notational form, including the known data, is presented in Figure 4.7.1. The three subdecision problems in boxes I, II, and III are identical except for the data values. In addition, the events in boxes II and III are conditional on the test results, and thus the $P(E)$ values of box I cannot be used, but new values must be determined. Hence, before proceeding with solving the decision problem, let us determine the various $P(E|T)$ values. As was shown earlier in this chapter, we first determine the joint probability values $P(T \text{ and } E)$ by multiplying the conditional probabilities $P(T|E)$ of Table 4.7.1 by the prior probabilities $P(E)$, shown in Figure 4.7.1. (Box I) The results are tabulated in Table 4.7.2. From the table we find the marginal probabilities by adding the rows and columns. Thus,

$$P(T_1) = 0.5$$
$$P(T_2) = 0.5$$

This means that the probability that the on-site tests will yield a favorable recommendation for a low-cost well is 0.5. It is now possible to compute the posterior probabilities, which are the conditional probabilities of the actual events E given the test predicts a recommendation T. These $P(E|T)$ values are tabulated in Table 4.7.3.

TABLE 4.7.2. *Joint Probability Tables: P(T and E)*

Recommendations \ Events	E_1	E_2	E_3	Row Sum
T_1	0.24	0.18	0.08	0.50
T_2	0.06	0.12	0.32	0.50
Column sum	0.30	0.30	0.40	1.00

TABLE 4.7.3. *Conditional Probability of Events E Given Recommendation T: P(E|T)*

Recommendations \ Events	E_1	E_2	E_3
T_1	0.48	0.36	0.16
T_2	0.12	0.24	0.64

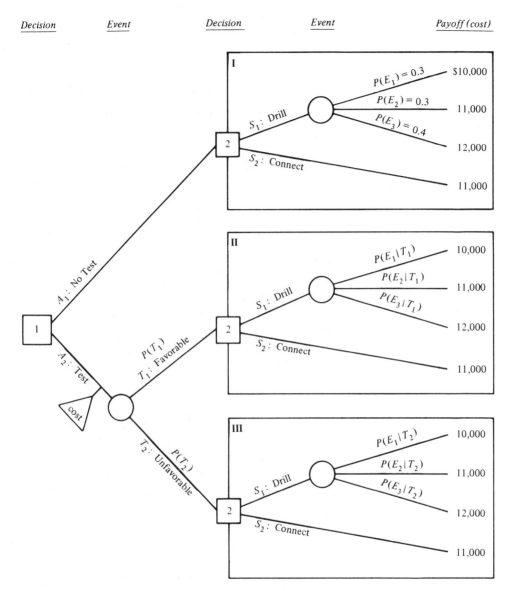

Decision   Event   Decision   Event   Payoff (cost)

FIGURE 4.7.1. *Decision tree for motel water problem.*

The decision tree with the values for the revised probabilities is shown in Figure 4.7.2. To solve this problem we first solve the three subproblems. For subproblem I we have

$$\text{EMV}(S_1) = 0.3(10{,}000) + 0.3(11{,}000) + 0.4(12{,}000)$$

$$= \$11{,}100$$

$$\text{EMV}(S_2) = \$11{,}000$$

Decision   Event   Decision   Event   Payoff (cost)

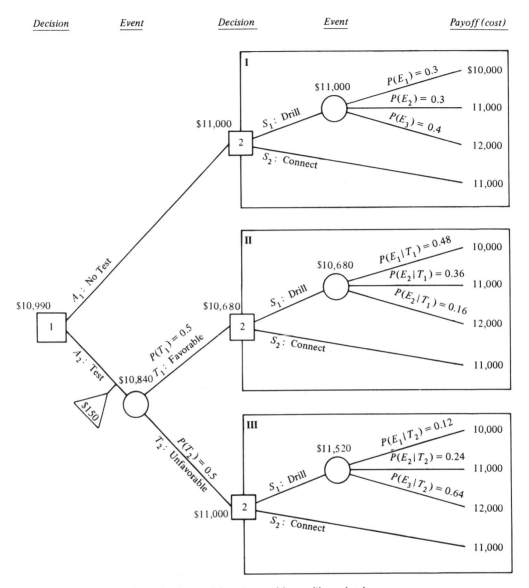

FIGURE 4.7.2. *Decision tree for motel water problem with revised probabilities.*

Thus, the decision is to choose S_2: connect to city water, since that strategy yields the lowest cost. For subproblem II we have

$$\text{EMV}(S_1) = 0.48(10,000) + 0.36(11,000) + 0.16(12,000)$$
$$= \$10,680$$
$$\text{EMV}(S_2) = \$11,000$$

128

Thus, the decision is to choose S_1: drill a new well. For subproblem III
we have

$$EMV(S_1) = 0.12(10,000) + 0.24(11,000) + 0.64(12,000)$$
$$= \$11,520$$
$$EMV(S_2) = \$11,000$$

Thus, the decision is to choose S_2: connect to city water.

Our problem now reduces to the decision problem shown in Figure
4.7.3. Hence, we must evaluate actions A_1 and A_2. We get

$$EMV(A_1) = \$11,000$$
$$EMV(A_2) = 0.5(10,680) + 0.5(11,000) + 150$$
$$= \$10,840 + 150$$
$$= \$10,990$$

Thus, the decision is to choose A_2: order on-site tests. The full decision is

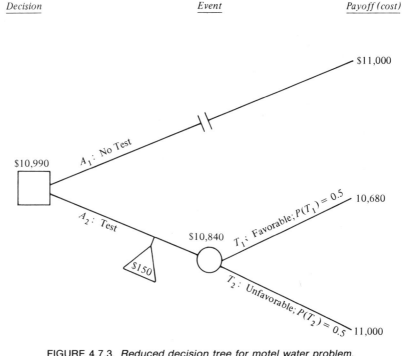

FIGURE 4.7.3. *Reduced decision tree for motel water problem.*

as follows:

1. *Decision 1:* order on-site tests.

   If recommendation is favorable, then

2. *Decision 2:* drill new well.

   If recommendation is unfavorable, then

3. *Decision 2:* connect to city water.

The total expected cost is $10,990.

It should be noted that this decision is valid as long as the cost of the on-site tests is less then $160 (i.e., up to $10 more than the stated $150 price). If, however, the cost of the test goes above $160, the decision will not be to perform an on-site test but to connect to city water, with a total expected cost of $11,000.

SECTION 4.8. *Using the Computer*

A computer program has been prepared which analyzes the standard decision problem with the added option that the decision maker can decide whether he wishes to purchase additional information.

The program requires as input the following information:

1. A code indicating cost or profit payoffs.
2. Number of strategies, events, and test outcomes.
3. The cost of taking the test.
4. The payoff matrix for the decision problem.
5. The marginal probabilities of events, $P(E)$.
6. The conditional probabilities, $P(T|E)$ (i.e., the test reliability).

The output of the program is shown in two parts in Figures 4.8.1 and 4.8.2. Figure 4.8.1 shows as program output the payoff matrix of the simple decision problem and all probabilities, both those that were inputs, $P(E)$ and $P(T|E)$, and those computed, $P(T$ and $E)$, $P(T)$, and $P(E|T)$. Figure 4.8.2 shows the decision-tree analysis, where the program considers each box of the tree separately, the first being box I, A_1: no test. For each strategy, the expected value is computed and the best strategy is indicated. Thus, under alternative A_1 we choose S_2, with EMV = $3,000.

The same analysis is performed for the other boxes of the tree: II and III, which refer to test outcome T_1 and T_2 for action A_2: take test alternative. For T_1 we choose S_1 with EMV = $3,073.17 and for T_2 we choose S_2 with EMV = $3,000. The program also prints the expected value assuming that the test is taken, $3,052.50, and finally the optimal

DECISION TREE ANALYSIS

A1 - NO TEST

STRATEGY	EXPECTED VALUE
S1	-2400.00
S2	3000.00
SELECT S2	EXPECTED VALUE = 3000.00

A2 - TAKE TEST

TEST OUTCOME T1   PROBABILITY = 0.717

STRATEGY	EXPECTED VALUE
S1	3073.17
S2	3000.00
SELECT S1	EXPECTED VALUE = 3073.17

TEST OUTCOME T2   PROBABILITY = 0.282

STRATEGY	EXPECTED VALUE
S1	-16300.88
S2	3000.00
SELECT S2	EXPECTED VALUE = 3000.00

EXPECTED VALUE ASSUMING TEST TAKEN = 3052.50
COST OF TEST = 500.00
EXPECTED VALUE OF A2 - TEST = 2552.50

OPTIMAL DECISION IS A1 - NO TEST   EXPECTED VALUE = 3000.00
SELECT S2

FIGURE 4.8.2. Computer output for bank loan problem. Decision-tree analysis.

DECISION PROBLEM WITH TEST INFORMATION

PROFIT PAYOFF MATRIX

STRATEGY	EVENTS E1	E2
S1	6000.00	-5000.00
S2	3000.00	3000.00
PROBABILITY	0.850	0.150

TEST INFORMATION
COST= 500.00

PROBABILITY OF T GIVEN E

TEST OUTCOME	E1	E2
T1	0.800	0.250
T2	0.200	0.750

PROBABILITY OF T AND E

	E1	E2	P(T)
T1	0.680	0.037	0.717
T2	0.170	0.112	0.282

PROBABILITY OF E GIVEN T

	E1	E2
T1	0.948	0.052
T2	0.602	0.398

FIGURE 4.8.1. Computer output for bank loan problem. Payoff table and probabilities

alternative, A_1: test or A_2: no test is given. This final optimal decision takes into account the cost of the test. For our problem the optimal decision is A_1: no test, with EMV = $3,000, and S_2: no loan, since the cost of the test reduces the EMV to below $3,000.

SECTION 4.9. *Summary*

In this chapter we have presented a method for solving decision problems that are not of the "simple" type. To handle the many variations that might take place we introduced the decision-tree form and showed how, using backward induction, a complex decision could be made.

One class of complex decision problems covered was the sequential decision problem, wherein one of the decisions is whether to perform a test or survey. If the test is performed, other decisions are based on its results. If the conditional probabilities of the various events are known, the EMV solution is easily found. If these probabilities are not known, it is necessary to compute revised probabilities, called posterior probabilities, given the prior probabilities, by using the survey reliability information. This information is usually more readily available to the decision maker. A detailed computation procedure was presented for calculating the posterior probabilities from the survey reliability information.

A computer program was developed that performs the necessary computations for the decision-tree analysis. These computations include the probability computations as well as the expected value computations for each branch of the decision tree.

We note once again that for any decision problem the full decision must be given. This means that all possible outcomes that might be considered must be stated as part of the decision rule.

PROBLEMS

4.1. A toy manufacturer must decide on which of two new games to manufacture, A or B. If he chooses to make game B, there is a 60% chance that a competitive game will appear on the market. Sales for the company are classified as high (100,000 units), medium (50,000 units), or low (10,000 units). Marketing has determined that for game A the probability of high sales is 0.3 and for medium sales is 0.6. If game B is marketed, the probability of high sales is 0.5 if no competition develops and 0.2 if the competitive game appears. The probability of low sales is 0.2 whether or not competition occurs. Game A cost $2 to produce and will be sold for $4. Game B cost $3 to produce and will be sold for $6 if no competition occurs and $5 if competition occurs.

(a) Draw the detailed decision-tree diagram for this problem.
(b) Determine the optimum decision for the toy manufacturer if he wishes to maximize his total profit.
(c) What should be his decision if he is interested only in maximizing the number of units he sells?

4.2. (Problem 4.1 continued) A toy consultant is engaged to analyze the chance of a competitive game to game *B* appearing on the market. In the past this consultant has been accurate 75% of the time; that is, 75% of the time he predicted competition when competition actually occurred, and 75% of the time he predicted no competition when competition actually did not occur. The consultant reports to the manufacturer that competition will not occur.

(a) What is the probability of competition occurring?

(b) What should the manufacturer decide if maximum profit is his objective?

4.3. A knitting company operates many knitting machines with a useful life of 10 years. These machines cost $1,000, with a yearly maintenance cost of $150. A manufacturer offers the company a new improved model which costs $2,000, with maintenance costs that vary from machine to machine. The probability distribution of maintenance costs for this new model is as follows:

Maintenance Cost/Year ($)	0	100	200
Probability	0.4	0.4	0.2

The manufacturer offers to permit the knitting company to test *each* machine before deciding whether to accept or reject it. Since the delivery time for the new machines is 1 month, a decision to reject a new machine will force the company to purchase one of the older-model machines, which are available on instant notice. The manufacturer provides the results of tests and yearly costs on 500 of its new models, as shown in Figure P4.3.

		Yearly Cost			
		$0	$100	$200	Total
Test Result	Satisfactory	150	100	0	250
	Unsatisfactory	50	100	100	250
	Total	200	200	100	500

FIGURE P4.3

(a) What is the probability that the test result will be satisfactory?

(b) What is the probability that the yearly cost will be $100 if the test result proved satisfactory?

(c) Construct the decision tree for this problem.

(d) What should the knitting company do, assuming that the test is free?

(e) What is the most the company should be willing to pay for the test?

4.4. (Problem 4.3 continued) Assume that the manufacturer has revised his new model and claims that the probabilities for the various maintenance costs are as follows:

Maintenance Cost/Year ($)	0	100	200
Probability	0.4	0.5	0.1

Since the model has just come out, he has no test results to offer. However, he claims that the test reliability of his testing process is the same as it was for the unrevised new model.

(a) Determine the conditional probabilities of the yearly costs, given the various test results.

(b) Find the knitting company's optimal decision, assuming that the test is free.

4.5. An oil driller owns oil rights on a piece of property that he can drill for oil or sell now for $10,000. The costs of drilling are $20,000. If oil is found, he can sell the rights for $100,000. He has the option of having a geological survey performed, which will classify his land as good, fair, or poor. The survey costs $500. The test results for 200 wells in the area of his proposed well are shown in Figure P4.5. By law the survey is done in strictest confidence and therefore does not affect the selling price of the rights. What should the oil driller do?

	Land Contains	
	Oil	No Oil
Test Result Good	50	10
Test Result Fair	20	30
Test Result Poor	10	·80

FIGURE P4.5

4.6. (Problem 4.5 continued) Assume that the land is located in a different area than the ones for which the tests were taken. In this area the probability that oil will be found is 0.2. What should the oil driller do?

4.7. The Household Products Company is considering the development and introduction of a new kitchen slicer. If the sales of this product prove successful (probability $= 0.4$), the company will earn $100,000. If the sales are poor (probability $= 0.6$), the company will lose $50,000. To assist in the planning process the company is considering hiring a market survey company to predict what the sales will be. The results of the survey predictions and actual sales for 50 other products tested are as shown in Figure P4.7.

(a) Draw the decision tree for this problem.

(b) What is the full decision of the Household Products Company?

Actual Sales

Survey Prediction of Sales		Successful	Poor
	Successful	32	4
	Poor	8	6

FIGURE P4.7

4.8. A "Think Tank" consulting firm must decide on which of two government proposals they should respond to, the Job Corps analysis or the Employment Service study. If they bid on the Job Corps analysis, they have a 40% chance of winning the contract. If they bid on the Employment Service study, the chance of winning the contract is 60%. The government indicates that the amount of the award will be cost plus either 8% or 9%, with probabilities 0.7 and 0.3, respectively. The consulting firm estimates the cost for the Job Corps analysis as $200,000 and for the Employment Service study as $300,000. The cost to prepare the Job Corps proposal is $4,000, and the Employment Service proposal, $8,000.

(a) Draw the decision-tree diagram for this problem.

(b) Use backward induction to determine which proposal the consulting firm should bid on.

4.9. (Problem 4.8 continued) The Think Tank hires a proposal consultant to analyze the company's chances of winning the contracts. The consultant's record shows that she predicts correctly 80% of the time.

(a) On which proposal should the company bid if the consultant predicts that they will win both contracts?

(b) On which proposal should the company bid if the consultant predicts that they will lose both contracts?

4.10. An investor is considering two possible investments for a 1-year period, at the end of which the investments will be sold. The investments are (1) a bank savings certificate which pays 6% interest, or (2) a stock whose selling price and dividend at the end of the year are dependent on the state of the industry, as follows:

State of Industry	Probability	Stock Price at End of 1 Year	Dividend (%)
Good	0.1	Up 20%	20%
Fair	0.5	Same	10%
Bad	0.4	Down 20%	0

Since the investor is going to invest only $1,000 he decides to purchase an economic outlook recommendation from a major investment firm for $10. The report published by the Accurate Investment Firm shows the results of their prediction for 1,000 customers as shown in Figure P4.10.

Actual State of the Industry

		Good	Fair	Bad	Total
Accurate Investment Firm Prediction	Good	80	100	20	200
	Fair	15	350	135	500
	Bad	5	50	245	300
	Total	100	500	400	1000

FIGURE P4.10

(a) Draw the decision tree for this problem.
(b) Use backward induction to determine which investment the investor should make if he wishes to maximize his cash on hand at the end of the year.

4.11. (Problem 4.10 continued) A friend of the investor from a foreign country would like to make a similar investment in her country. However, she feels that in her country, the probability that the economy will be good is only 0.05, while the probability that the economy will be fair is 0.7. Since no investment prediction service is available in her country, she intends to use the prediction reliability data of the Accurate Investment Firm, which she obtains at no cost. Which investment should the investor's friend make?

4.12. A manufacturer must buy rolls of material for next year's spring season. He can sign a contract now at the rate of $1.20 per yard *or* wait and pay the existing price during the fall when he takes delivery. His demand for the material and the existing price will depend on whether the fall weather will be cold (C), seasonal (S), or warm (W), as follows:

Weather	C	S	W
Price/Yard ($)	0.75	1.00	1.60
Demand (yards)	1,000	2,000	4,000
Probability	0.3	0.4	0.3

The manufacturer can buy a weather forecast for $25, which will predict good or bad fall weather. He estimates the probabilities of the forecast as shown in Figure P4.12.

(a) Draw the decision tree for the problem.
(b) Find the revised probabilities of weather given the forecast outcomes.
(c) What is the manufacturer's optimal decision if he wishes to minimize his material cost?

Actual Weather

		C	S	W
Forecast	Good	0.1	0.5	0.9
	Bad	0.9	0.5	0.1

FIGURE P4.12

4.13. The Normal Oil Company is considering bidding for an offshore oil drilling contract to be awarded by the government. Company management have determined the bid price to be $300 million, with a 60% chance of winning. If they win the contract, they must decide whether to set up a new drilling operation or to move an existing operation, which had been proved successful, to the new site. With either operation the probability of success and the financial return is as follows:

	NEW DRILLING OPERATION		OLD OPERATION MOVED	
Outcome	Probability	Revenue (millions of $)	Probability	Revenue (millions of $)
Success	0.7	400	0.8	350
Failure	0.3	100	0.2	175

If they do not bid, or they lose the contract, the company will use the $300 million to modernize its operations, with the increased profit to the company being either 5% or 6%, with respective probabilities 0.4 and 0.6.

(a) Draw the decision tree for this problem.
(b) Should the Normal Oil Company bid for the contract?
(c) An oil surveyor offers to predict success or failure of a new drilling project for a fee of $10,000. The past performance of the oil surveyor is a prediction reliability of 90%. Draw the decision tree and determine the optimal decision of the Normal Oil Company.

4.14. You are trying to decide about choosing among three business opportunities: *A*, *B*, or *C*. If you choose *A*, there is a 50–50 chance of going broke or earning $50,000. If you choose opportunity *B*, there is an 80% chance of earning $25,000. If business *B* fails, you still have the option of either settling for $500 or taking a stock option in a company that will be worth $50,000 (probability=0.1) or zero (probability=0.9). If business *A* fails, you have three choices: accept a debt of $2,000, embezzle $35,000 of company money and leave the country, or file for personal bankruptcy and place yourself in the hands of a court-appointed trustee. If you leave the country, there is a 95% chance of being extradited and fined $10,000. If you file for personal bankruptcy, there is a 95% chance that your debts will be wiped out and a 60% chance you will have to pay back $4,000. Finally, if you choose opportunity *C*, you will earn $10,000 (probability=0.6) or be in debt for $1,000 (probability= 0.4). Draw the decision tree for this problem and determine the optimal decision that you should make.

4.15. A civil service worker is trying to decide whether she should take an exam for a higher position. If she passes the exam, her lifetime earnings will increase by $5,000, whereas if she fails the exam, her work will suffer and her lifetime earnings will be $1,000 lower than if she had not taken the exam. After studying for the exam she feels that she has a 60% chance of passing the test. A local training school offers to provide an intensive brush-up test on the exam material for a fee of $100. The results of the school test performance in relation to actual civil service test performance for 500 persons is shown in Figure P4.15.

(a) Draw the decision tree for this problem.

(b) Determine what decision the civil service worker should make.

		Actual Result in Civil Service Test		
		Pass	Fail	Total
Training School Test Exam	Pass	100	50	150
	Fail	200	150	350
	Total	300	200	500

FIGURE P4.15

4.16. Reconsider Problems 3.8–3.10. The marketing department of the Exact Time Watch Company informs the management that it can conduct a survey to estimate the demands for the new watches. To support their claim they provide a table of the results of past survey predictions in probabilities (see Figure P4.16).

(a) Compute the revised probabilities of demand given the survey predictions.

(b) Determine whether the company should conduct the survey. Write the complete decision rule.

		Actual Demand		
		E_1	E_2	E_3
Survey Prediction of Demand	T_1	0.8	0.2	0.1
	T_2	0.15	0.7	0.3
	T_3	0.05	0.1	0.6
		1.0	1.0	1.0

FIGURE P4.16

4.17. Reconsider Problem 3.20. The manufacturer of the tires offers the car service company the opportunity to run a test on the second line tires. In the past such tests have been performed on 400 second line tires, with the results shown in Figure P4.17. If the test cost $10, should the car service perform the test?

	Actual Time Tire Lasted			
	6 Months	1 Year	2 Years	Total
Test Prediction — Short life	180	60	0	240
Test Prediction — Long life	20	60	80	160
Total	200	120	80	400

FIGURE P4.17

4.18. The Social Security Administration intends to build a new computer facility at either site A or site B. A blue ribbon commission will recommend one of the two sites within 1 year. Thereafter, the S.S. Administration will make a final choice of the site; however, it need not be the commission-recommended one.

Land adjacent to the two sites is selling rapidly and Model Homes, Inc., would like to build homes near the new computer facility. Present and estimated future value of developable land are as given below:

Site	Present Value ($)	Future Value if Computer Built at Location ($)	Future Value if Computer Not Built at Location ($)
A	600,000	800,000	400,000
B	1,000,000	1,200,000	700,000

Model Homes has two alternatives. It can purchase land now or it can take a 1-year option on both locations for $100,000. If it purchases land now, it can purchase either at A only, B only, or at both. If land is purchased and the computer facility is not built in that location, the land is resold at a loss. The options will allow Model Homes to purchase the land at current prices. If the land is not purchased now or the options picked up, the land will not be available to Model Homes.

Model Homes hires a real estate consultant to assist in the decision. The consultant establishes that site A will eventually be chosen with a probability 0.6. In addition, the probability of the commission recommending a site given that the S. S. Administration will choose that site is given in Figure P4.18. What should the consultant recommend to Model Homes?

		Given that the S.S. Administration Chooses Site	
		A	B
Probability of Commission Recommending Site	A	0.8	0.1
Probability of Commission Recommending Site	B	0.2	0.9

FIGURE P4.18

4.19. The City Fire Commissioner is considering converting the city's call boxes to a new telephone-operated type. He feels that the overall economic effects of the new call boxes will save the city $600,000 (probability = 0.7), have no effect at all (probability = 0.2), or cost the city $400,000 (probability = 0.1). The call-box manufacturer provides the results of a pilot study on predicted overall savings as compared to actual savings as shown in Figure P4.19. Draw the decision tree and determine the Commissioner's optimum decision.

		\$600,000	\$0	−\$400,000
Pilot Test Will Predict	Savings	0.7	0.1	0.1
	No Change	0.2	0.6	0.2
	Loss	0.1	0.3	0.7

Given Actual Savings Will Be

FIGURE P4.19

BOOKS OF INTEREST

Bross, I. D. J., *Design for Decision*. New York: Macmillan Co., 1953.

Dyckman, T. R., Smidt, S., and McAdams, A. K., *Managerial Decision Making under Uncertainty*. New York: Macmillan Co., 1969.

IEEE Transactions on Systems Science and Cybernetics (Special Issue on Decision Analysis), Vol. SSC-4, No. 3 (September 1968).

Lapin, L. L., *Quantitative Methods for Decision Making*. New York: Harcourt Brace Jovanovich, 1976.

Magee, J. F., "Decision Trees for Decision-Making," *Harvard Business Review*, July-August, 1964; and "How to Use Decision Trees in Capital Investment," *Harvard Business Review*, September-October, 1964.

Spurr, W. A. and Bonini, C. P., *Statistical Analysis for Business Decisions*. Rev. ed. Homewood, Ill.: Richard D. Irwin, Inc., 1973.

Thrall, R. M., Coombs, C. H., and Davis, R. L. (eds.), *Decision Processes*. New York: John Wiley & Sons, Inc., 1954.

Weiss, L., *Statistical Decision Theory*. New York: McGraw-Hill Book Co., 1961.

Winkler, R. L., *Introduction to Bayesian Inference and Decision*. New York: Holt, Rinehart and Winston, Inc., 1972.

CHAPTER FIVE

Utility Measures
in Decision-Making

OBJECTIVES: The purpose of this chapter is to present
to you the following basic concepts of
utility theory, useful in decision-making.

1. *Shortcomings of the expected monetary
   value criterion in some decision
   problems.*
2. *The concept of a utility measure.*
3. *Computation of utility measures for
   a decision maker.*
4. *Use of utility measures.*

In the preceding chapters the use of expected value or the Bayes decision criterion has been shown to be very useful for purposes of decision-making. However, there are situations where decision makers knowingly act contrary to this criterion. For example, most people buy insurance on valuable objects such as houses, automobiles, jewelry, and so on. They essentially understand that their expected value from such a purchase (as an investment) is negative; that is, there will be a long-run expected cost in buying insurance. It is precisely this expected cost that assures insurance companies a profit in the long run.

Similarly, many individuals choose to gamble, such as playing state lotteries, knowing that their long-run expected value of such an investment is negative (i.e., a loss). If it were not for this expected loss, the state would derive no income from lotteries.

What is it about these situations that make them attractive to some (but not all individuals)? In both cases there is the prospect of large "one-time" gains or losses versus relatively small payments with certainty. Many individuals are willing to pay relatively small amounts in order to have the opportunity to either win relatively large gains or to forego relatively large losses, even though these events have a low probability of occurring and the investment (payment) has an expected cost associated with it.

Clearly, the actual monetary (dollar) values do not completely express the desirability or undesirability of the various incomes and costs to all individuals in the same way. In fact, most individuals differ in their attractiveness for different amounts of money and their willingness to accept risk in order to gain these monies or to forego their payment. Utility theory is an attempt to devise means of measuring the true attractiveness (utility) of various monetary incomes or losses to different individuals and their willingness to accept risk.

This chapter presents the basic concepts of utility theory and its usefulness in decision-making.

SECTION 5.2. *Decision Problems with Monetary Payoffs*

5.2.1. Introduction. As previously mentioned, two examples where expected value leads to decisions that some decision makers would consider irrational are insurance and lotteries. Two common decision problems will be given to illustrate this basic concept. A third example will also be given, to demonstrate decision makers' differing attitudes toward various monetary gains and their willingness to accept risk. These examples will be reconsidered later in the chapter after the concepts of utility have been developed.

5.2.2. Example 1: Insurance.

A company is shipping a package containing an item whose value is $5,000. They can buy insurance for $10 which will pay for replacing the item if it is lost in shipment. The probability of the item being lost is 0.001.

There are two strategies:

S_1: don't buy insurance
S_2: buy insurance

and two events:

E_1: shipment not lost
E_2: shipment lost

Let us form the payoff table for this problem. We will consider losses as negative income, as this will be more convenient later in the chapter. If the company buys insurance, their cost will be $10, whether or not the shipment is lost, since insurance will pay for replacement if it is lost. The payoff matrix is shown in Figure 5.2.1 along with the expected monetary value (EMV) computations. Using the EMV criterion we would select S_1: don't buy insurance. Yet most of us would buy insurance, indicating that our aversion to a loss of $5,000 is greater than the value of 5,000 would indicate.

However, what if the shipper was a very large company that made many of these shipments all the time? It would be better not to insure each package and lose one in every 1,000 shipments rather than pay the $10 insurance premium each time. Expected value generally holds for decisions that are repeated many times. However, where the decision is

	E_1 Shipment not Lost	E_2 Shipment Lost	*Expected Values*
S_1: Don't Buy Insurance	$0	−$5,000	$\text{EMV}^*(S_1) = -\$5$; Select S_1
S_2: Buy Insurance	−$10	−$10	$\text{EMV}(S_2) = -\$10$
Probabilities	$P(E_1) = 0.999$	$P(E_2) = 0.001$	

FIGURE 5.2.1. *Payoff table for insurance problem using monetary value.*

made only once and there are payoffs of large losses or gains, it may not be rational to simply use expected value.

5.2.3. Example 2: A Lottery. A lottery is being conducted where 1,000 tickets are being sold for $10 each. The winner will be drawn at random and receive a $5,000 prize and the return of the $10 purchase price (or a $5,010 prize).

The two strategies are:

S_1: buy a ticket

S_2: don't buy a ticket

and the two events are

E_1: your ticket not drawn

E_2: your ticket drawn

The payoff matrix is shown in Figure 5.2.2 along with the expected-value computations. Using the EMV criterion, we would not buy the ticket. Yet in practice many individuals would and actually do purchase lottery tickets. The prospect of a $5,000 win somehow outweighs the $10 loss and the low probability of winning.

	E_1 Don't Win	E_2 Win	*Expected Values*
S_1: Don't Buy Ticket	0	0	EMV*(S_1) = $0; Select S_1
S_2: Buy Ticket	−$10	$5,000	EMV(S_2) = −$4.99
Probabilities	$P(E_1) = 0.999$	$P(E_2) = 0.001$	

FIGURE 5.2.2. *Payoff table for lottery using monetary values.*

5.2.4. Example 3: An Investment Problem. An investor has $10,000 to invest for 1 year and is considering two strategies:

S_1: invest in a very safe loan paying 20% per year

S_2: invest in a speculative stock that will either remain at the same price or go up by 50% at the end of the year

The problem will be considered with two different sets of probabilities of stock prices. The events are:

E_1: stock price remains the same

E_2: stock price goes up by 50%

We consider the following two sets of probabilities:

1. $P(E_1)=0.5, P(E_2)=0.5$
2. $P(E_1)=0.7, P(E_2)=0.3$

The two payoff tables and expected-value calculations are shown in Figure 5.2.3.

	E_1 Stock Price Same	E_2 Stock Price up 50%
S_1: Loan	$2,000	$2,000
S_2: Stock	$0	$5,000
Probabilities	(a) $P(E_1) = 0.5$ (b) $P(E_1) = 0.7$	$P(E_2) = 0.5$ $P(E_2) = 0.3$

Expected Values

(a) $P(E_1) = 0.5$ $P(E_2) = 0.5$	(b) $P(E_1) = 0.7$ $P(E_2) = 0.3$
EMV(S_1) = $2,000	EMV(S_1) = $2,000; Select S_1
EMV(S_2) = $2,500 Select S_2	EMV(S_2) = $1,500

FIGURE 5.2.3. *Payoff tables for investment problem using two alternative sets of probabilities.*

For the case where $P(E_1)=0.5$, the expected monetary value of strategy S_2: buy stock is the higher one, so the EMV criterion would select it as optimal. Yet there are many individuals who would be conservative and make the loan rather than risk earning zero. We call these individuals *risk-averters*.

For the case where $P(E_1)=0.7$, the expected monetary value of S_1 is the higher one. Yet many individuals would prefer S_2 so as to be able to have a chance of earning the $5,000. We call these individuals *risk-seekers*. What influences their decisions is the relative attractiveness or utility to them of $0, $2,000, and $5,000. It is precisely these tendencies that utility theory attempts to measure and include in the decision model.

SECTION 5.3. *Utility Measures*

In order to more adequately measure the desirability or undesirability (utility) of various gains or losses to a decision maker, we define a new measure called *utility*. This measure is represented by a numerical value associated with each monetary gain and loss in order to indicate the utility of these monetary values to the decision maker. We can also assign these utility measures to outcomes that have no monetary value, but for the moment let us restrict ourselves to monetary payoff situations which are conceptually more straightforward.

We therefore assign numbers to payoffs (which may be dollar gains or losses) so as to reflect their relative utility to the decision maker. In order for our utility measures to be consistent, they must obey the following rules:

1. The more desirable an outcome, the higher its utility measure will be. For example, winning $100 will have a higher utility measure than winning $50.
2. If a decision maker prefers outcome 1 to outcome 2, and he prefers outcome 2 to outcome 3, he prefers outcome 1 to outcome 3.
3. If a decision maker is indifferent between two outcomes, they have equal utility.
4. In a situation involving risk, the expected utility of the decision equals the true utility of the decision. Thus, we can use the Bayes decision rules with utility as we did with monetary values. For example, assume that a particular strategy has outcome O_1 with probability P_1 and outcome O_2 with probability $P_2 = 1 - P_1$. If we define the utility of O_1 as $U(O_1)$ and the utility of O_2 as $U(O_2)$, the expected utility of the strategy, which we define as EU(strategy), is

$$\text{EU(strategy)} = P_1 \cdot U(O_1) + (1 - P_1) \cdot U(O_2)$$

In a sense, selecting utility values for a decision maker is similar to developing a measure for temperature. If we are told that the temperature is 30° in the room, we must also know whether that figure is given in terms of Fahrenheit or Centigrade. Both of these temperature scales were developed by defining two points, such as the boiling and freezing points of water and making all other measurements relative to those points. The utility values will be chosen in the same way as in the case with temperature and will depend mainly on which scale we set up.

Let us examine what might be utility measures for three different decision makers, A, B, and C. The graph of utility versus monetary value for each individual is shown in Figure 5.3.1. Notice that all three curves intersect at two points: the utility of $0 is 0 and the utility of $10,000 is 100. We have arbitrarily selected these two points as reference points. All other values are referenced to these. Earnings are indicated as a positive $(+)$ value and losses as a negative $(-)$ value. Thus, using zero as a reference point, all losses will have negative utility values. The utility values of 0 and 100 are truly arbitrary. We could have used, for example, 1,000 and 2,000, but zero for $0 and 100 for the highest gain ($10,000 in our case) seems convenient.

Notice the different pattern of the curves for the three decision makers, A, B, and C. These differences are related to the different

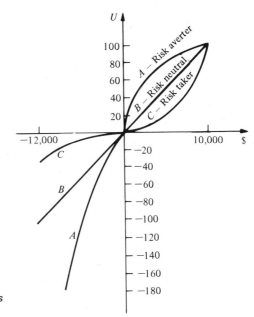

FIGURE 5.3.1. *Utility functions for three decision makers.*

attitudes toward earnings up to $10,000. It will be shown that *A* can be called a risk-averter, *B* can be called a risk-neutral, and *C* can be called a risk-taker. The slope of the utility curve will indicate which tendency an individual has.

Consider decision maker *B*. Each additional $1,000 of income increases his utility by an equal amount. For example, earning $1,000 yields a utility of 10. Earning an additional $1,000 (i.e., going from $1,000 to $2,000) also yields an additional 10 units of utility (i.e., the utility goes from 10 to 20). The same is true for increases up to $10,000. This type of individual will be termed *risk-neutral*.

A different attitude occurs for decision maker *A*. Small incomes have high utility, but *additional* incomes always bring *smaller increases* in utility. The first $1,000 income has utility of approximately 44. The utility of a $2,000 income is 60. The additional $1,000 of income has increased this utility by only $60 - 44 = 16$ units. This is smaller than the 44-unit increase for the initial $1,000 income. Decision maker *A* is called a risk-averter, since larger amounts yield for him smaller gains in utility and he will not be anxious to take the risk to get these larger amounts.

The reverse is true for decision maker *C*. Each *additional* dollar of income always increases his utility by larger and larger amounts. He will thus take more risk to gain these larger values and is called a risk-seeker.

In general, the greater the increase in utility that is achieved through an outcome, the greater is the willingness to take risk to achieve it. This will be more clearly seen when we consider the procedures for computing utility functions for decision makers.

147

The procedures for determining utility values rely on the rule that the expected utility of a risky investment equals the utility of the investment. We begin by picking any two monetary values and assigning utility values to them. We shall assign a utility value of 0 to a $0 gain and a utility value of 100 to a $10,000 gain. We can choose any values for utility as long as the higher income receives a higher utility value. We shall use the following notation. The utility of any dollar value is written $U(\$)$. Thus,

$$U(\$0) = 0$$

$$U(\$10,000) = 100$$

Let us next concern ourselves with finding the utility value for an income between $0 and $10,000, say $4,000, for decision maker A. In order to determine $U(\$4,000)$ we offer him a choice between accepting one of two alternatives:

ALTERNATIVE 1: $4,000 income (for certain)

ALTERNATIVE 2:   one chance to play a game. A coin will be flipped. If it comes up heads, he wins $10,000; if it comes up tails, he wins nothing ($0). The probability of the coin coming up heads is as-yet unspecified and will be called p.

Notice that the lottery contains outcomes ($0 and $10,000) with known utility, and the certainty amount ($4,000) is in between the other two values.

Clearly, any decision maker's preference between the two alternatives will depend upon the probability, p, of the coin coming up heads. If p is very low, a decision maker will choose alternative 1 and receive $4,000 for certain. If p is very high (i.e., extremely close to 1), a decision maker will choose alternative 2, a chance to play the game once. At some value of p between 0 and 1 a decision maker will be indifferent between the two alternatives (i.e., they will have equal utility for him). This will determine his utility for a $4,000 gain. We, therefore, adjust the value of p until the decision maker is indifferent between the two alternatives. Then, by definition,

$$U(\$4,000) = EU(\text{alternative } 2) = p \cdot U(\$10,000) + (1-p) \cdot U(\$0)$$

Since there are three decision makers, A, B, and C, we use a subscript with the symbol p to indicate which decision maker is being referenced. Let us assume that decision maker A is indifferent between alternatives 1 and 2 when $p_A = 0.8$. This means that if p is greater than 0.8, he will choose alternative 2: the game, and when p is less than 0.8, he will choose alternative 1: $4,000 for certain. With $p=0.8$, the expected value of the game is

$$E(\text{game}) = 0.8(\$10,000) + 0.2(\$0) = \$8,000$$

The $4,000 for certain has such a relatively high utility for him that not until the game has an expected value of greater than $8,000 does the choice of alternative 2: the game, become preferable. It is for this reason that we call decision maker A a risk-averter. Since he is indifferent with $p_A = 0.8$, let us compute the utility of a $4,000 gain as being the expected utility of the game. Thus,

$$U(\$4,000) = 0.8\,U(\$10,000) + (1 - 0.8)U(\$0)$$
$$= 0.8(100) + 0.2(0)$$
$$= 80$$

It can be seen that this agrees with the curve for decision maker A of Figure 5.3.1.

Let us see how decision maker B views the two alternatives. We called him risk-neutral, which means that the dollar values truly express utility for him. He will take alternative 2: the game, only when its expected value is higher than $4,000. With $p_B = 0.4$, the game has expected value of $4,000,

$$E(\text{game}) = 0.4(\$10,000) + 0.6(\$0) = \$4,000$$

Therefore, he will be indifferent between the two alternatives when $p_B = 0.4$. For him,

$$U(\$4,000) = 0.4\,U(\$10,000) + (1 - 0.4)U(\$0)$$
$$= 0.4(100) + 0.6(0)$$
$$= 40$$

Decision maker C, on the other hand, was called a risk-seeker. We stated that larger incomes always brought increasingly greater increases in utility. This means that for him, the prospect of a $10,000 win is so attractive that he will often choose alternative 2: the game, even though the expected value is somewhat below $4,000. For example, a person of his type will choose the game even with $p = 0.2$. The expected value of the game with $p = 0.2$ is

$$E(\text{game with } p = 0.2) = 0.2(\$10,000) + 0.8(\$0) = \$2,000$$

It is this tendency that makes him a risk-seeker. Let us state that he will be indifferent between the two alternatives when $p_C = 0.08$. That is, if p is greater than 0.08, he chooses the game; if it is less than 0.08, he chooses the $4,000. His utility for $4,000 is therefore

$$U(\$4,000) = 0.08\, U(\$10,000) + (1 - 0.08)U(\$0)$$
$$= 0.08(100) + 0.92(0)$$
$$= 8$$

This value agrees with the curve of Figure 5.3.1.

We now have utility values for three monetary values

Monetary Value ($)	0	4,000	10,000
Utility for *A*	0	80	100
Utility for *B*	0	40	100
Utility for *C*	0	8	100

Consider now finding utility values for a $2,000 gain. The general approach is to offer the decision maker a choice between two alternatives. The first is an amount with certainty, and the second is a game with two outcomes and a given probability of one of the outcomes (the probability of the second outcome is always 1 minus the probability of the first). As long as the utility of two of the dollar outcomes are known, the third may be found. We have found three utility values and can use three different alternatives to find the utility of $2,000. Table 5.4.1 presents these possibilities and the equations that are used to find the utility of a $2,000 gain for each alternative. In each case the utility values for two of the monetary amounts are known, and if the decision maker specifies the probability for which he is indifferent (p) we can find the utility of a $2,000 gain. Whichever of the methods is used, we should always arrive at the same utility value for a $2,000 gain, or else there is an inconsistency. Table 5.4.2 shows the value of p_A and the computation of $U(\$2,000)$ for each of the three methods for decision maker A. If decision maker A is consistent in his responses, he would have to give as his indifference probabilities (p_A) exactly the values shown for each of the three methods.

TABLE 5.4.1. *Various Methods for Finding the Utility of $2,000 Gain*

Method	Alternative 1: Certain Amount	Alternative 2: Game	Equation
1	$2,000	$10,000 with probability p, $0 with probability $(1-p)$	$U(\$2,000) = p \cdot U(\$10,000) + (1-p) \cdot U(\$0)$
2	$2,000	$4,000 with probability p, $0 with probability $(1-p)$	$U(\$2,000) = p \cdot U(\$4,000) + (1-p) \cdot U(\$0)$
3	$4,000	$10,000 with probability p, $2,000 with probability $(1-p)$	$U(\$4,000) = p \cdot U(\$10,000) + (1-p) \cdot U(\$2,000)$

TABLE 5.4.2. *Computation of Utility of $2,000 for Decision Maker A Using Three Methods*

Method	p_A	Computation of U ($2,000)
1	0.6	$U(\$2,000) = p_A \cdot U(\$10,000) + (1 - p_A) \cdot U(\$0)$ $= 0.6(100) + 0.4(0)$ $= 60$
2	0.75	$U(\$2,000) = p_A \cdot U(\$4,000) + (1 - p_A) \cdot U(\$0)$ $= 0.75(80) + 0.25(0)$ $= 60$
3	0.5	$U(\$4,000) = p_A \cdot U(\$10,000) + (1 - p_A) \cdot U(\$2,000)$ $80 = 0.5(100) + 0.5\,U(\$2,000)$ $30 = 0.5\,U(\$2,000)$ $U(\$2,000) = 60$

As a next step, consider finding utility values for losses, in particular, the utility of a loss of, say, $5,000, that is, $U(-\$5,000)$. There are many possible methods for finding it, as with the previous example. Consider the following:

ALTERNATIVE 1: $0 for certain (don't play)

ALTERNATIVE 2:   A game:
Win $10,000 with probability p
Lose $5,000 with probability $(1-p)$

Since the utility of $0 and $10,000 are known, we can use the equation

$$U(\$0) = p \cdot U(\$10,000) + (1-p) \cdot U(-\$5,000)$$

to solve for $U(-\$5,000)$ if the indifference probability p is known. Assume that decision maker A is indifferent between the two alternatives for $p_A = 0.6$. This means that if p is less than 0.6, he will not play the game (i.e., accept $0), whereas if p is greater than 0.6, he will play the game. Thus,

$$U(\$0) = 0.6\,U(\$10,000) + (1 - 0.6)\,U(-\$5,000)$$

$$0 = 0.6(100) + 0.4\,U(-\$5,000)$$

$$-60 = 0.4\,U(-\$5,000)$$

$$U(-\$5,000) = -150$$

Using this procedure we can develop a utility function for a decision maker by finding utility values for many monetary values and plotting a curve such as in Figure 5.3.1. These utility values can then be used in place of monetary values when analyzing decision problems.

Let us reconsider the decision problems of Section 5.2 using the utility values of Figure 5.3.1 for each decision maker.

Monetary Value

		E_1 Shipment not Lost	E_2 Shipment Lost	*Expected Monetary Value*
S_1:	Don't Buy Insurance	$0	−$5,000	EMV*(S_1) = −$5; Select S_1
S_2:	Buy Insurance	−$10	−$10	EMV(S_2) = −$10
Probabilities:		$P(E_1) = 0.999$	$P(E_2) = 0.001$	

Utility–Decision Maker A

		E_1 Shipment not Lost	E_2 Shipment Lost	*Expected Utility*
S_1:	Don't Buy Insurance	0	−150	EU(S_1) = −0.150
S_2:	Buy Insurance	−0.11	−0.11	EU*(S_2) = −0.11; Select S_2
Probabilities:		$P(E_1) = 0.999$	$P(E_2) = 0.001$	

Utility–Decision Maker B

		E_1 Shipment not Lost	E_2 Shipment Lost	*Expected Utility*
S_1:	Don't Buy Insurance	0	−50	EU*(S_1) = −0.05; Select S_1
S_2:	Buy Insurance	−0.1	−0.1	EU(S_2) = −0.1
Probabilities:		$P(E_1) = 0.999$	$P(E_2) = 0.001$	

Utility–Decision Maker C

		E_1 Shipment not lost	E_2 Shipment Lost	*Expected Utility*
S_1:	Don't Buy Insurance	0	−6	EU*(S_1) = −0.006; Select S_1
S_2:	Buy Insurance	−0.01	−0.01	EU(S_2) = −0.010
Probabilities:		$P(E_1) = 0.999$	$P(E_2) = 0.001$	

FIGURE 5.5.1. *Insurance problem using monetary value and utility values for decision makers A, B, and C.*

EXAMPLE 1. Insurance Problem. The payoff table and expected-value calculations using monetary values and utility values for decision makers A, B, and C are shown in Figure 5.5.1. The utility of a $10 loss to decision maker C is actually extremely close to zero, but is shown as -0.01. The loss of $10 to decision maker A is close to that of decision maker B and is shown

Monetary Value	E_1 Don't Win	E_2 Win	Expected Monetary Value
S_1: Don't Buy Ticket	0	0	$EMV^*(S_1) = 0$; Select S_1
S_2: Buy Ticket	$-\$10$	$-\$5,000$	$EMV(S_2) = -4.99$
Probabilities	$P(E_1) = 0.999$	$P(E_2) = 0.001$	

Utility–Decision Maker A

	E_1 Don't Win	E_2 Win	Expected Utility
S_1: Don't Buy Ticket	0	0	$EU^*(S_1) = 0$; Select S_1
S_2: Buy Ticket	-0.11	87	$EU(S_2) = -0.109$
Probabilities	$P(E_1) = 0.999$	$P(E_2) = 0.001$	

Utility–Decision Maker B

	E_1 Don't Win	E_2 Win	Expected Utility
S_1: Don't Buy Ticket	0	0	$EU^*(S_1) = 0$; Select S_1
S_2: Buy Ticket	-0.1	50	$EU(S_2) = -0.0499$
Probabilities	$P(E_1) = 0.999$	$P(E_2) = 0.001$	

Utility–Decision Maker C

	E_1 Don't Win	E_2 Win	Expected Utility
S_1: Don't Buy Ticket	0	0	$EU(S_1) = 0$
S_2: Buy Ticket	-0.01	13	$EU^*(S_2) = 0.003$; Select S_2
Probabilities	$P(E_1) = 0.999$	$P(E_2) = 0.001$	

FIGURE 5.5.2. *Lottery problem using monetary value and utility values for decision makers A, B, and C. See Example 2 on p. 155.*

Monetary Value	E_1 Stock Price Same	E_2 Stock Price up 50%	Expected Monetary Value	Expected Monetary Value
S_1: Loan	$2,000	$2,000	$EMV(S_1) = 2,000$	$EMV^*(S_1) = 2,000$; Select S_1
S_2: Stock	$0	$5,000	$EMV^*(S_2) = 2,500$; Select S_2	$EMV(S_2) = 1,500$
Probabilities	(a) $P(E_1) = 0.5$ (b) $P(E_1) = 0.7$	$P(E_2) = 0.5$ $P(E_2) = 0.3$		

Utility–Decision Maker A

	E_1 Stock Price Same	E_2 Stock Price up 50%	Expected Utility	Expected Utility
S_2: Loan	60	60	$EU^*(S_1) = 60$; Select S_1	$EU^*(S_1) = 60$; Select S_1
S_2: Stock	0	87	$EU(S_2) = 43.5$	$EU(S_2) = 26.1$
Probabilities	(a) $P(E_1) = 0.5$ (b) $P(E_1) = 0.7$	$P(E_2) = 0.5$ $P(E_2) - 0.3$		

Utility–Decision Maker B

	E_1 Stock Price Same	E_2 Stock Price up 50%	Expected Utility	Expected Utility
S_1: Loan	20	20	$EU(S_1) = 20$	$EU^*(S_1) = 60$; Select S_1
S_2: Stock	0	50	$EU^*(S_2) = 25$; Select S_2	$EU(S_2) = 15$
Probabilities	(a) $P(E_1) = 0.5$ (b) $P(E_1) = 0.7$	$P(E_2) = 0.5$ $P(E_2) = 0.3$		

Utility–Decision Maker C

	E_1 Stock Price Same	E_2 Stock Price up 50%	Expected Utility	Expected Utility
S_2: Loan	2	2	$EU(S_1) = 2$	$EU(S_1) = 2$
S_2: Stock	0	13	$EU^*(S_2) = 6.5$; Select S_2	$EU^*(S_2) = 3.9$; Select S_2
Probabilities	(a) $P(E_1) = 0.5$ (b) $P(E_1) = 0.7$	$P(E_2) = 0.5$ $P(E_2) = 0.3$		

FIGURE 5.5.3. *Investment problem using monetary value and utility for decision makers A, B, and C. Two sets of probabilities used.* *(a) $P(E_1) = 0.5$; $P(E_2) = 0.5$. (b) $P(E_1) = 0.7$; $P(E_2) = 0.3$.*

as −0.11. Using EMV the decision maker should accept the risk of losing the parcel, which is the actual choice made by decision makers *B* and *C*, the risk-neutral and risk-taker. However, decision maker *A*, the risk-averter, will buy insurance. Utility theory has thus included the individual attitudes toward different gains and losses and the individual risk preferences into the model.

EXAMPLE 2. A Lottery. The payoff table and expected-value calculations are shown in Figure 5.5.2. Decision maker *C* ignores the EMV result and chooses to take the risk in order to have a chance of winning the $5,000.

EXAMPLE 3. The Investment Problem with Two Alternative Sets of Probabilities. The payoff table and expected-value calculations are shown in Figure 5.5.3. Notice that decision maker *A* averts the risky investment in favor of a certain $5,000 income even when the expected value is higher than the certain $2,000. Decision maker *C*, on the other hand, takes the risky investment even when the expected value is lower than the certain $2,000.

Thus, once we have established utility measures for a decision maker, we can use these values as payoffs in any decision problem. Utility values become important when the decision maker's attitude toward the monetary payoffs is different from that of decision maker *B*, the risk-neutral decision maker. It is worthwhile to mention again that where decisions are made over and over again, the expected value criterion guarantees the best long-run average payoffs. But where decisions are made once, and there are large losses or gains involved, utility measures become important.

SECTION 5.6. *Typical Utility Function*

Most individuals tend to follow a general pattern of utility relationships or functions with respect to losses or gains. A representative pattern is shown in Figure 5.6.1. No numerical values are shown since they would differ according to the individual selected.

Initially, small gains hold small appeal, but as the amount increases, they have increasingly greater attractiveness for the individual. In this situation (region I of Figure 5.6.1) the individual will take risks to gain larger amounts. At a certain point the amount gained guarantees a standard of living (or a goal) which is relatively acceptable, and additional amounts bring relatively smaller utility (region II). In this region the individual will not take risks to get these incomes.

At some point, however, the gains guarantee even a higher standard of living (or goal) and again become increasingly more desirable. In this region (III), the individual again becomes a risk-seeker. This continues until a certain standard of living is achieved and again the individual is relatively satisfied. Further gains hold less utility for him and he becomes

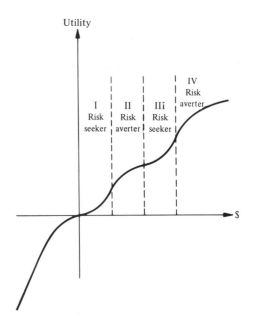

FIGURE 5.6.1. *Representative utility function for an individual.*

a risk-averter (region IV). The pattern of risk-seeking and risk-averting may be repeated again several times, depending on the individual.

Concerning losses, most individuals exhibit a pattern similar to that of Figure 5.6.1. Larger losses always being larger reductions in utility, although small losses still have very small negative utility.

In general, individuals have varying attitudes and are at some times risk-seekers and at other times risk-averters, depending on the quantities of money involved.

SECTION 5.7. *Outcomes Without Monetary Value*

The concept of utility becomes even more important when we concern ourselves with decision problems where the outcomes (payoffs) do not have monetary values and there is an element of risk. Without a numerically valued payoff we cannot compute expected values—which we have seen to be very useful for decision-making purposes. Let us consider such a decision problem and see how utility measures can be used to solve it.

A director of a remedial reading program must decide which of two possible texts to purchase for use in the program. The effectiveness of the texts depends upon the attitude of the students toward the program. From past classes he estimates that 30% of the time the classes are interested, 50% of the time they are indifferent, and 20% of the time they are disinterested. The overall per cent improvement in reading scores for each text (strategy) is shown in Figure 5.7.1.

156

	E_1	E_2	E_3
	Interested	Indifferent	Disinterested
S_1: Use Text 1	100%	30%	0%
S_2: Use Text 2	30%	60%	30%
Probabilities	0.3	0.5	0.2

FIGURE 5.7.1. *Payoff table for remedial reading problem, showing percent improvement in reading scores*

Since the payoffs are not monetary values, we cannot compute expected values. (It is improper to compute expected values of percentages.) Let us find the utility of each of the results (payoffs) to the director. We first rank the alternatives:

Ranked Outcomes
100% increase
60% increase
30% increase
0% increase

We next assign utility values to the best and worst alternatives. Let us assign a utility value of zero to a 0% increase and a value of 10 to a 100% increase (10 is chosen so as to be different from the value of 100 used in the preceding sections). Let us next find the utility of an increase of 60%. We offer the director the following choice:

ALTERNATIVE 1:   Increase of 60% with certainty

ALTERNATIVE 2:   A game with two outcomes:
A: 100% increase with probability p
B: 0% increase with probability $(1-p)$

The director must choose one or the other and his choice will be affected by the value of p. Assume that when p is 0.9, he is indifferent between the two alternatives. Then

$$U(60\% \text{ increase}) = p \cdot U(100\% \text{ increase}) + (1-p) \cdot U(0\% \text{ increase})$$

$$= 0.9(10) + 0.1(0)$$

$$= 9$$

We have thus determined the utility to the director of an increase of 60%. Let us next find the utility of a 30% increase. We offer him a choice

157

of one of the following two alternatives:

ALTERNATIVE 1: Increase of 30% with certainty

ALTERNATIVE 2: A game with two outcomes:
A: 60% increase with probability p
B: 0% increase with probability $(1-p)$

Assume that the director is indifferent between the two alternatives when $p = \frac{2}{3}$. Then

$$U(30\% \text{ increase}) = p \cdot U(60\% \text{ increase}) + (1-p) \cdot U(0\% \text{ increase})$$

$$= \frac{2}{3}(9) + \frac{0.1}{3}(0)$$

$$= 6$$

The utility function for the director is shown in Figure 5.7.2. The payoff table using utilities and the expected utility computations are shown in Figure 5.7.3. On this basis he would select text 2.

	E_1 Interested	E_2 Indifferent	E_3 Disinterested	*Expected Utility*
S_1: Use Text 1	10	6	0	6
S_2: Use Text 2	6	9	6	7.5; Select S_2
Probabilities	$P(E_1) = 0.3$	$P(E_2) = 0.5$	$P(E_3) = 0.2$	

FIGURE 5.7.2. *Utility function for the director of the remedial reading program.*

FIGURE 5.7.3. *Payoff table using utility values. Remedial reading problem.*

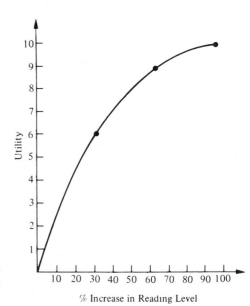

Utility

% Increase in Reading Level

Thus, although no specific monetary payoff values were available, the director could make an intelligent choice by using utility theory.

SECTION 5.8. *Summary*

The importance of utility measures in both decision problems with monetary and nonmonetary payoffs has been demonstrated. The procedure for computing utility measures for decision makers has been presented, together with their use in solving decision problems. A general discussion of the attitudinal behavior of individuals with respect to risk was given. The relationship among risk, utility, and probability was shown for the basic utility model.

PROBLEMS

5.1. Mr. A assigns a utility value of 1 to a loss of $500 and a value of 10 to a gain of $1,000. He claims that he is indifferent between $5 for certain and the following lottery: a $500 loss with probability 0.3 and a $1,000 gain with probability 0.7. What is his utility value for $5?

5.2. Mr. B assigns a utility value of 0.1 to $-$10 and his value for $200 is 0.5. He claims that he is indifferent between $200 for certain and the following lottery: a 0.7 chance at $-$10 and a 0.3 chance at $20,000. What is his utility value for $20,000?

5.3. Mr. C assigns a utility value of 0 to $1,000 and -150 to $500. He maintains that he is indifferent between a certainty of $500 and the following lottery: a 0.8 chance at a gain of $1,000 and a 0.2 chance of a loss of $1,000. What is his utility value for a loss of $1,000?

5.4. Mr. D assigns the following utility values: 10 for $2,000, 6 for $500, and 0 for $-$100. Find the probability p such that he will be indifferent between $500 for certain and the following lottery: a gain of $2,000 with probability p and a loss of $100 $(-$100) with probability $1-p$.

5.5. Mr. A has a utility index of 50 for a loss of $1,000 and 120 for a profit of $3,000. He says he is indifferent between $10 for certain and the following lottery: a 0.4 chance at a $1,000 loss and a 0.6 chance at a $3,000 profit. Mr. T has the same utility indices as Mr. A at $-$1,000 and $10, but he is indifferent between $10 for certain and the following lottery: a 0.8 chance at a $1,000 loss and a 0.2 chance at a $3,000 profit.

(a) What is Mr. A's utility index for $10?
(b) What is Mr. T's utility index for $3,000?
(c) Sketch a rough graph of the utility curves for Mr. A and Mr. T. Describe their risk-taking personalities.

5.6. The Fresh Milk Dairy is considering enlarging their plant now or waiting until next year. The payoff for each strategy, in thousands of dollars, depends on the demand for their product which may be high, moderate, or low. The profit in thousands of dollars and the demand probabilities are as follows:

Events \ Strategies	E_1: High Demand $P(E_1)=0.2$	E_2: Moderate Demand $P(E_2)=0.5$	E_3: Low Demand $P(E_3)=0.3$
S_1: enlarge now	100	80	-10
S_2: enlarge next year	80	60	10

The company has decided that a $10,000 loss will be a utility of zero and a $100,000 profit has a utility of 100. Furthermore, they are indifferent among:

(1) $80,000 for certain and a lottery
$$\begin{cases} \$100,000 \text{ profit;} \\ \text{probability} = 0.9. \\ \$10,000 \text{ loss;} \\ \text{probability} = 0.1. \end{cases}$$

(2) $60,000 for certain and a lottery
$$\begin{cases} \$100,000 \text{ profit;} \\ \text{probability} = 0.80. \\ \$10,000 \text{ loss;} \\ \text{probability} = 0.20. \end{cases}$$

(3) $10,000 for certain and a lottery
$$\begin{cases} \$100,000 \text{ profit;} \\ \text{probability} = 0.25. \\ \$10,000 \text{ loss;} \\ \text{probability} = 0.75. \end{cases}$$

(a) Find the best decision using the EMV decision rule.
(b) Construct the utility matrix.
(c) What strategy should the dairy adopt using the expected utility decision rule?

5.7. A car manufacturer is considering a change in design of two of its models, regular and premium. The company can decide to change the designs of both, only one, or neither of the two models. The profits that the manufacturer expects to earn are as follows, in millions of dollars:

Events \ Strategies	E_1: Redesign of Regular Model Successful	E_2: Redesign of Premium Model Successful	E_3: Both Redesigns Successful	E_4: Neither Redesign Successful
S_1: redesign regular	20	-20	20	-20
S_2: redesign premium	-10	20	20	-20
S_3: redesign both	-6	-10	30	-50
S_4: redesign neither	5	5	5	5

The management of the company feels that a redesign of the regular model has a 60% chance of being successful and that the redesign of the premium model has a 50% chance of success. Furthermore, the success or failure of one car redesign will have no effect on the success or failure of the other.

Assume that the following utilities have been assigned: -10 to a loss of $50 million; 0 to a loss of $10 million; and 50 to a profit of $20 million. In addition, the company is indifferent between the following situations:

For Certain	Lottery
(1) $3 million profit	70% chance of $20 million profit 30% chance of $10 million loss
(2) $10 million loss	20% chance of $50 million loss 80% chance of $6 million loss
(3) $6 million loss	96% chance of $10 million loss 4% chance of $30 million profit
(4) $3 million profit	40% chance of $20 million loss 60% chance of $30 million profit

(a) Construct the utility matrix.
(b) Determine the optimum strategy using expected utility.
(c) Compare the result in part (b) with the optimum strategy using EMV.

5.8. Suppose that you have a total capital of $20,000. You have the opportunity to make an investment of $10,000 which will be either entirely lost or worth $40,000 in 2 years.

(a) Using expected values, what is the maximum probability of a total loss that would make this investment profitable?
(b) Assume that your utility function is of the form

$$U(M) = \sqrt{M + 30,000}$$

where M (monetary value) $\geqslant -30,000$. What is the maximum probability of a total loss that would make this investment profitable?

5.9. Suppose that the General Products Company of Section 4.4 has a utility function for money (M) of the form

$$U(M) = \frac{M + 5,000}{100}$$

(a) Redraw Figure 4.4.1 and calculate the utility for each payoff value.
(b) What is the optimal decision based on these new utility values?

5.10. Assume that the local bookstore of Problem 3.1 has the following utility function for money (M):

$$U(M) = \sqrt{\frac{M + 1{,}000}{1{,}000}}$$

(a) Construct the utility table.
(b) Using the probability distribution of demand from Problem 3.3, determine the optimal number of books the bookstore should buy.

5.11. A student is confronted with the problem of deciding which of two courses to take. If she takes the statistics course, she estimates her probable grades as 20% chance for an A, 40% chance for a B, and 40% chance for a C. If she takes the management course, the estimates are

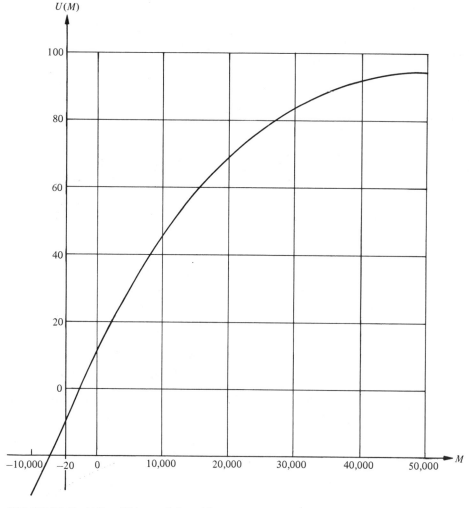

FIGURE P5.12. *Utility, U(M), vs. dollars, M.*

50% chance for a B, 40% chance for a C, and 10% chance for a D. She has assigned a utility of -10 to the C grade and a utility of 30 to an A grade. In addition, she states that she is indifferent between

(1) a C for certain and a lottery $\begin{cases} \text{A with probability 0.20} \\ \text{D with probability 0.80} \end{cases}$

(2) a B for certain and a lottery $\begin{cases} \text{A with probability 0.60} \\ \text{C with probability 0.40} \end{cases}$

Which course should she take?

5.12. Reconsider Problem 4.14. Assume your utility for money $U(M)$ is as given in Figure P5.12. Estimate your utility value for the various payoffs and determine your optimum decision based on the expected utility criterion.

**ARTICLES
AND BOOKS**

Aitchison, J., *Choice Against Chance*. Reading, Mass.: Addison-Wesley, 1970.

Edwards, W. and Tversky, A. (eds.). *Decision Making*. Baltimore: Penguin Books, Inc., 1967.

Fishburn, P. C., *Utility Theory for Decision Making*. New York: John Wiley & Sons, Inc., 1970.

Friedman, M. and Savage, L. J., "The Utility Analysis of Choices Involving Risk," *Journal of Political Economy*, August 1948.

Hammond, J. S., "Better Decisions with Preference Theory," *Harvard Business Review*, November–December 1967.

Savage, L. J., *The Foundations of Statistics*. New York: John Wiley & Sons, Inc., 1954.

CHAPTER SIX

Introduction to

Linear Programming

OBJECTIVES: The purpose of this chapter is to acquaint you with the following introductory concepts of linear programming.

1. *The characteristics of a linear programming problem.*
2. *The graphic solution of linear programming problems.*
3. *The interpretation of slack and surplus variables.*
4. *The shadow price and its relationship to resources.*
5. *Sensitivity analysis.*
6. *The form and meaning of a basic solution.*

In many business settings a manager finds himself in a position of trying to meet specified goals, but being restricted by the limitation of available resources. For example, a firm manufactures two different products with different per-unit profits. The number of units of each product that can be produced is limited by the availability of raw materials, manufacturing time, and labor. The firm would like to produce a quantity of each product such that the total profit is as large as possible and in such a manner that none of the limitations are exceeded.

This type of situation is an example of a class of problems known as *allocation problems*, which are solvable, under certain conditions, by the techniques of linear programming (LP). More formally, we shall define a *linear programming problem* as an allocation problem wherein the values of a set of continuous controllable variables must be determined to meet a prescribed objective or goal, but which are subject to a set of limitations based on available resources, capabilities, or activities. Let us consider a specific problem to illustrate these concepts.

SECTION 6.2. *Linear Programming Production Problem*

6.2.1. Problem Description. The owner of a small appliance manufacturing company that specializes in clocks must decide what types and quantities of output to manufacture for each day's sale. Let us assume that he manufactures only two kinds of clocks—regular clocks and alarm clocks—from which he may select his product mix. We also assume that tomorrow's product mix can only be produced with the labor, facilities, and parts currently on hand. These supplies are as follows:

number of labor hours	1,600
number of processing hours	1,800
number of alarm assemblies	350

The resources are related to the two alternative manufactured outputs, regular clocks and alarm clocks, in the following way: Each unit of regular clocks produced requires 2 hours of labor and 6 hours of processing, while each unit of alarm clocks produced requires 4 hours of labor and 2 hours of processing. Finally, the profit per unit of regular clocks manufactured is $3.00, while the profit per unit of alarm clocks manufactured is $8.00. How many of each type of clock should the owner manufacture to maximize his profit?

6.2.2. The Variables and Objective Function. Let

x_1 = number of regular clocks manufactured
x_2 = number of alarm clocks manufactured
Z = profit per day for total production of regular and
  alarm clocks (i.e., the measure of performance variable)

Then $3x_1$ is the total profit from manufacturing x_1 units of regular clocks and $8x_2$ is the total profit from manufacturing x_2 units of alarm clocks. Thus, the total profit from this production process is

$$Z = 3x_1 + 8x_2 \quad \text{dollars}$$

and the owner's objective is to find values of x_1 and x_2 so as to make Z as large as possible. Written mathematically, we have for the objective function

(1) $$\max Z = 3x_1 + 8x_2$$

Thus, if $x_1 = 5$ clocks and $x_2 = 7$ alarm clocks, the profit is $Z = 5(3) + 8(7) = \$71$. From equation (1), however, one cannot determine the best values for x_1 and x_2, since the more that is produced, the greater the profit will be. It should be noted, in addition, that $x_1 = 0$ and $x_2 = 0$ are possible (*feasible*) values that yield zero profit. However, assigning negative values to x_1 and x_2 makes no sense whatsoever.

6.2.3. The Constraints. From the stated problem it is clear that there are three restrictions to the production process; (1) the number of labor hours available—1,600 hours, (2) the number of processing hours available—1,800 hours, and (3) the number of alarm assemblies available—350 assemblies. Let us consider each restriction in turn.

LABOR CONSTRAINT. The number of labor hours required to produce 1 unit of regular clock is 2 hours. Thus, to produce x_1 clocks will require $2x_1$ hours. Similarly, the number of labor hours for producing one alarm clock is 4 hours and for x_2 alarm clocks it is $4x_2$ hours. Hence, the total labor hours required to produce x_1 and x_2 clocks is $2x_1 + 4x_2$ hours. Since only 1,600 labor hours are available, only as many clocks in total can be manufactured such that the total labor hours used in production does not exceed the hours available. Mathematically, this is written

166 (2) $$2x_1 + 4x_2 \leqslant 1,600$$

This *inequation* should be read: "$2x_1$ plus $4x_2$ must be less than or equal to 1,600." This means that $x_1 = 100$ regular clocks and $x_2 = 250$ alarm clocks is a possible answer since $2(100) + 4(250) = 1,200$, which is less than 1,600. In addition, $x_1 = 200$ clocks and $x_2 = 300$ alarm clocks is a possible answer, since it uses exactly 1,600 labor hours. In the former case 400 labor hours are unused, but in the latter case no labor hours remain idle. Unused resources should not be viewed as unusual, but rather may be necessary in order to obtain the maximum profit.

PROCESSING CONSTRAINT.   The number of processing hours required to produce 1 unit of regular clocks is 6 hours. Thus, to produce x_1 clocks will require $6x_1$ processing hours. Similarly, the number of processing hours for producing one alarm clock is 2 hours and for x_2 alarm clocks it is $2x_2$ hours. Hence, the total processing hours required to produce x_1 and x_2 clocks is $6x_1 + 2x_2$ hours. Since only 1,800 processing hours are available, we require that the total processing hours used in production do not exceed the hours available. Mathematically, this is written

$$(3) \qquad\qquad 6x_1 + 2x_2 \leqslant 1,800$$

As in the case of the labor constraint, it is possible to define values for x_1 and x_2 such that not all the processing time will be utilized.

ALARM ASSEMBLIES CONSTRAINT.   The problem states that only a supply of 350 alarm assemblies are available. Thus, the number of alarm clocks that can be produced is limited to a maximum of 350. Note, however, that this restriction will not affect the number of regular clocks that can be produced. Mathematically, this constraint is written

$$(4) \qquad\qquad x_2 \leqslant 350$$

Once again we point out that it may be to the manufacturer's advantage not to use all the available alarm assemblies in this production situation and to produce less than 350 alarm clocks.

CONSTRAINTS EXCLUDING NEGATIVE PRODUCTION.   Since negative production (i.e., x_1 or x_2 assuming negative values) is meaningless, let us add the following two constraints:

$$(5) \qquad\qquad x_1 \geqslant 0$$

$$(6) \qquad\qquad x_2 \geqslant 0$$

This is interpreted as follows: The variables x_1 and x_2 can assume any value zero or greater. In fact, for all LP problems, all variables may not assume negative values.

6.2.4. The Model. We can now summarize the manufacturer's production problem as follows: produce x_1 units of regular clocks and x_2 units of alarm clocks such that the profit

(1) $$Z = 3x_1 + 8x_2 \text{ is a maximum}$$

and subject to the constraints

(2) $\qquad 2x_1 + 4x_2 \leqslant 1{,}600 \qquad$ (labor hours)

(3) $\qquad 6x_1 + 2x_2 \leqslant 1{,}800 \qquad$ (processing hours)

(4) $\qquad x_2 \leqslant 350 \qquad$ (alarm assemblies)

(5) $\qquad x_1 \qquad \geqslant \quad 0 \qquad$ (nonnegativity)

(6) $\qquad x_2 \geqslant \quad 0 \qquad$ (nonnegativity)

The manufacturer must now determine the values of x_1 and x_2.

SECTION 6.3. *Characteristics of the Linear Programming Problem*

We have already formulated one linear programming problem and have therefore seen something of the basic structure of these problems. Let us, however, consider in more detail linear programming's general characteristics.

The linear programming problem can be characterized by its three components—the variables, the objective, and the constraints. The *variables* are continuous, controllable, and nonnegative (may not take on negative values). Using the notation x_1 to represent the first variable, x_2 to represent the second variable, and so on, the continuity and nonnegativity aspect of the problem will be represented by

(1)
$$
\begin{aligned}
x_1 &\geqslant 0 \\
x_2 &\geqslant 0 \\
&\;\vdots \\
x_n &\geqslant 0
\end{aligned}
$$

This is interpreted as follows. If there are n different variables to be considered, each one's value must be greater than or equal to zero. These constraints are so common that they are defined as being part of the linear programming problem and need not necessarily be stated each time.

An example of a possible solution to an LP problem with three variables ($n = 3$) that is concerned with the purchase of three raw materials might be $x_1 = 2$ lb, $x_2 = 3.17$ lb, $x_3 = 0$ lb. On the other hand, the solution $x_1 = 5$ lb, $x_2 = -2.5$ lb, $x_3 = 0$ lb is not acceptable.

The *objective* of the linear programming problem is a mathematical representation of the goal in terms of a measurable objective such as profit, cost, revenue, or distance. It must be a linear function[†] and is represented in one of two forms:

$$\text{maximize } Z = c_1 x_1 + c_2 x_2 + \cdots + c_n x_n$$

or

(2)
$$\text{minimize } Z = c_1 x_1 + c_2 x_2 + \cdots + c_n x_n$$

where Z is the measure-of-performance variable, which is a function of $x_1, \ldots, x_n$, the controllable variables; $c_1, c_2, \ldots, c_n$ are parameters or uncontrollable variables that give the contribution of a unit of the respective variable $x_1, \ldots, x_n$ to the measure of performance, Z.

Maximizing or minimizing depends on the objective chosen. Thus, a profit or revenue objective will be maximized and a cost or distance objective will be minimized. If, for example, there are two controllable variables x_1 and x_2 representing the number of units of regular clocks and alarm clocks, respectively, to be produced and the profit per unit is $c_1 = \$3$ for clocks and $c_2 = \$8$ for alarm clocks, the objective function will be

(3)
$$\text{maximize } Z = 3x_1 + 8x_2$$

That is, produce a quantity of regular clocks and alarm clocks such that the total profit from the production is as large as possible. On the other hand, x_1 and x_2 might represent the number of board-feet of pine and walnut, respectively, to purchase to meet some objective like building a piece of furniture, with $c_1 = \$0.50/$board-foot for pine and $c_2 = \$3.00/$board-foot for walnut. The objective function then will be

(4)
$$\text{minimize } Z = 0.5x_1 + 3x_2$$

That is, purchase a quantity of board-feet of pine and walnut such that the total cost of purchasing the raw materials is as small as possible.

The constraints are the set of expressions representing the restrictions imposed on the controllable variables and thereby limiting the

---

[†]A linear function is one that is of the form given by equation (2):

$$Z = c_1 x_1 + c_2 x_2 + \cdots + c_n x_n$$

Examples of nonlinear functions are

$$Z = c_1 x_1 x_2$$

$$Z = c_1 x_1^2 + c_2 x_2$$

$$Z = \frac{c_1 x_1}{x_2} \quad \text{etc.}$$

If either the objective function or any of the constraints are nonlinear, the problem is a nonlinear programming problem, which also falls under the general category of mathematical programming.

possible values of those variables. The expressions can be given either as linear equations or as linear inequations. An example of a linear equation is

(5) $$x_1 + x_2 = 10$$

Thus, if x_1 is the number of color-television sets to be purchased and x_2 is the number of black-and-white sets to be purchased, equation (5) states that exactly 10 units total are to be purchased. Furthermore, the number of color sets and the number of black-and-white sets purchased will be restricted to a range of 0 to 10 if equation (1) is imposed (i.e., $x_1 \geqslant 0, x_2 \geqslant 0$).

A *linear inequation* is an expression where the equal sign ($=$) is replaced by one of the following four symbols: $<$, $>$, $\leqslant$, or $\geqslant$. Equation (5) written as an inequation would appear possibly as one of the following:

(6a) $x_1 + x_2 < 10$ (i.e., $x_1 + x_2$ must be less than 10)

(6b) $x_1 + x_2 > 10$ (i.e., $x_1 + x_2$ must be greater than 10)

(6c) $x_1 + x_2 \leqslant 10$ (i.e., $x_1 + x_2$ must be less than or equal to 10)

(6d) $x_1 + x_2 \geqslant 10$ (i.e., $x_1 + x_2$ must be greater than or equal to 10)

Equation (6a) states the restriction that total television units purchased must be less than 10. Equation (6b) states the restriction that total units purchased must be greater than 10. Equation (6c) states the restriction that total units purchased must be at most 10. Finally, equation (6d) states the restriction that total units purchased must be at least 10.

The number of constraints written for any particular linear programming problem is a function of the number of different restrictions stated. Thus, if two raw materials are used in producing a product and each is available only in limited quantities, there will be a constraint for each raw material. If, in addition, total labor available is restricted, a labor constraint will be written.

An example of a resource constraint is as follows: Each regular clock produced requires 2 hours of labor, and each alarm clock produced requires 4 hours of labor. The available supply of labor is 1,600 hours. The constraint would read

(7) $$2x_1 + 4x_2 \leqslant 1,600$$

That is, the amount of labor to produce the regular clocks ($2x_1$) plus the amount of labor to produce the alarm clocks ($4x_2$) must not exceed 1,600 hours. However, it may be less than 1,600 hours, in which case some labor hours will be left over.

In summary, a linear programming model will be structured so as to find values of controllable variables that maximize or minimize a defined linear objective function subject to a set of defined linear constraints and subject to the nonnegativity restrictions.

There is a mathematical technique which is used to solve linear programming problems, known as the simplex method, which is discussed in Chapter 8. However, when there are only two variables, a graphical approach can be used. Since the graphical approach also reveals much about the structure of LP problems, let us examine this approach in some detail.

SECTION 6.4. *Graphical Solution Technique*

It might seem possible to find the solution to an LP problem by total enumeration. That is, pick pairs of values for x_1 and x_2, respectively, that satisfy equations (6.2.2)–(6.2.6), substitute these values into the objective function (6.2.1), and record the corresponding value of Z. When all the Z values are recorded, the solution will be the x_1 and x_2 pair that yields the largest value of Z. Brief reflection on this procedure will prove the impossibility of this technique. It is thus necessary to limit the number of possible answers and to choose a best solution from among this much smaller set of candidate solutions. For those problems that have only two variables, it is possible to visually display the entire set of possible solutions, to reduce this set to a finite number of candidate solutions, and then to determine a best solution. The technique that does this is called the *graphical solution technique for LP problems with two variables*. The procedure is divided into four steps; (1) graph the constraints, (2) determine the feasible solution region, (3) graph the objective function, and (4) determine the "optimum" or best solution.

GRAPHING THE CONSTRAINTS. The first step is to set up a graph that will act as a map of all feasible solutions (i.e., the values of x_1, x_2 which satisfy all the constraints). We begin with a map that expresses only the nonnegativity constraints, which is shown in Figure 6.4.1. Since equations (6.2.5) and (6.2.6) require that x_1 and x_2 be greater than or equal to zero, the axes themselves are the lines necessary to display these two constraints. The x_1 axis is the equation of the line $x_2 = 0$. Point A, $x_1 = 300, x_2 = 0$, point B, $x_1 = 0, x_2 = 350$, and point C, $x_1 = 100, x_2 = 100$ are all points that satisfy the nonnegativity constraints. Hence, the nonnegativity constraints restrict the values of x_1 and x_2 to only those points on or above the x_1 axis and on or to the right of the x_2 axis. Thus, any values of x_1 and x_2 that are nonnegative are *candidate solutions*. The next step is to graph the remaining constraints. Since these constraints are linear inequations, the graphing procedure is as follows. Find the points (x_1, x_2) that

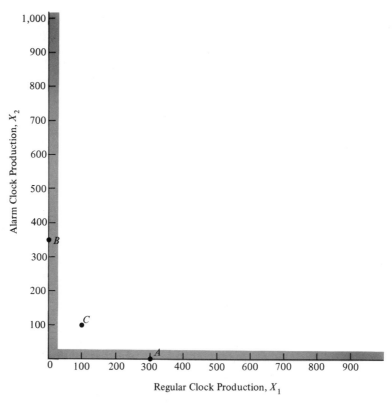

FIGURE 6.4.1. *Coordinate system and scale.*

make the equations just hold as an equality. These act as a boundary of the region of points which obey the constraint as an inequality. The labor constraint thus becomes

(1) $$2x_1 + 4x_2 = 1,600$$

This is the equation of a straight line which can easily be drawn if two points on the line are known. These two points are found by first letting $x_1 = 0$ and solving for x_2 or

$$2(0) + 4x_2 = 1,600$$
$$x_2 = 400$$

Thus, the first point $(x_1, x_2) = (0, 400) = D$. We then let $x_2 = 0$ and solve for x_1. Hence,

$$2x_1 + 4(0) = 1,600$$
$$x_1 = 800$$

Thus, the second point $(x_1, x_2) = (800, 0) = E$. These two points, D and E, are then connected by a straight line as in Figure 6.4.2. This straight line

172

has the effect of dividing the set of possible solution points found from Figure 6.4.1 into two groups; (1) those points that satisfy the labor constraint [equation (6.2.2)] and (2) those points that violate that constraint. It is clear that points on the line fall into the former group, since the constraint reads "less than or equal to." Consider point C. Substituting the values of $(x_1, x_2) = (100, 100)$ into equation (6.2.2), we get

$$2(100) + 4(100) = 600 < 1,600$$

Thus, point C satisfies the constraint. On the other hand, substituting point $F = (x_1, x_2) = (0, 900)$ into equation (6.2.2) gives

$$2(0) + 4(900) = 3,600 > 1,600$$

Thus, point F violates the constraint. On continuing this process, one would conclude that all points on the same side of the labor line as point C satisfy the constraint and all points on the same side of the line as point F will violate the constraint. Thus, the nonnegativity and labor constraints yield a *feasible region* of solution possibilities, as shown by the darkened region in Figure 6.4.2.

A simple method for determining which side of a line graphed from an inequation constraint is in the feasible region is to examine whether

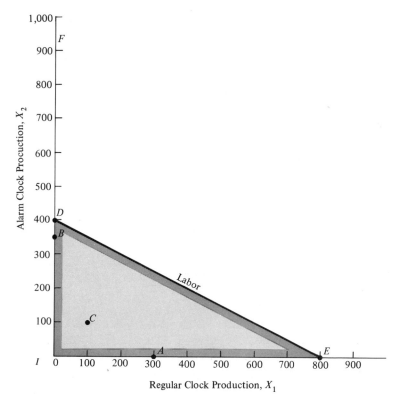

FIGURE 6.4.2. *Labor constraint.*

the origin $(0,0)$ satisfies the constraint. If it does, all points on the same side of the line as the origin are feasible points. If the origin violates the constraints, all points on the same side of the line as the origin are infeasible. For example, substituting $(x_1, x_2) = (0,0)$ into equation (6.2.2), we get

$$2(0) + 4(0) = 0 < 1,600$$

Thus, the origin satisfies the constraint, as do all points *below* the line. Points A, B, C, D, and E are all called *feasible solution point*.

Continuing with the processing and alarm assembly constraints we have the two equality equations

(2) $6x_1 + 2x_2 = 1,800$

and

(3) $x_2 = 350$

Following the graphing procedure just outlined gives the processing line shown in Figure 6.4.3, with a reduced feasible region (shown darkened), and the alarm assembly line shown in Figure 6.4.4, with a further reduced feasible solution region (shown darkened).

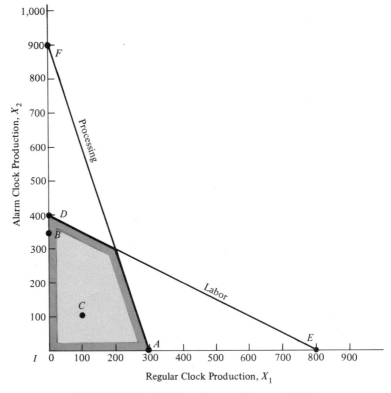

FIGURE 6.4.3. *Addition of processing constraint.*

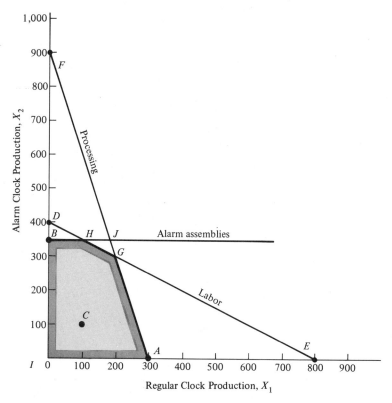

FIGURE 6.4.4. *Feasible solution region as defined by all the constraints.*

THE FEASIBLE REGION. Since all constraints have been examined and graphed, we define the feasible solution region for our production problem as the darkened region of Figure 6.4.4. Thus, points A, B, and C are still feasible points, whereas points D, E, and F are now infeasible.

GRAPHING THE OBJECTIVE FUNCTION. The next step in the graphical procedure is to graph the objective function equation, which is for our problem

$$(4) \qquad Z = 3x_1 + 8x_2$$

Solving for x_2 in terms of x_1 and Z, we get

$$(5) \qquad x_2 = -\frac{3}{8}x_1 + \frac{Z}{8}$$

Equation (5) is the equation of a line with a slope of $-\frac{3}{8}$, an x_2-axis intercept of $Z/8$, and the line is uniquely defined for each value of Z. Since two lines are parallel if their slopes are equal, equation (5) will generate a set of parallel lines which differ only by the value of the

175

intercept $Z/8$. For example,

(6) $$x_2 = -\frac{3}{8}x_1 + \frac{1,200}{8}$$ (earn \$1,200 profit)

and

(7) $$x_2 = -\frac{3}{8}x_1 + \frac{2,400}{8}$$ (earn \$2,400 profit)

are the parallel lines $Z=1,200$ and $Z=2,400$ shown in Figure 6.4.5. Equation (6) may be interpreted as the set of points (x_1, x_2) that yield as a solution to the production problem, $Z=\$1,200$ profit, while equation (7) is the set of points (x_1, x_2) with a solution, $Z=\$2,400$ profit.

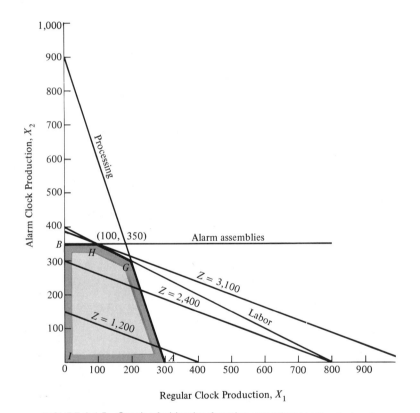

FIGURE 6.4.5. *Graph of objective function superimposed onto feasible region.*

FINDING THE OPTIMUM SOLUTION.   Since we desire Z to be a maximum, the solutions as shown by equation (7) are superior to those of equation (6). This process can be continued and a parallel line drawn with an increased value of Z as long as the set of points (x_1, x_2) that satisfy this line contains at least one point that is feasible. Thus, Z can be increased until the parallel line

176

(8) $$x_2 = -\frac{3}{8}x_1 + \frac{3,100}{8}$$ (earn \$3,100 profit)

This line has only one point $(x_1, x_2) = (100, 350)$ that is feasible. Since every other feasible point yields a value of Z less than 3,100 and values of Z greater than 3,100 yield parallel lines with no feasible points, we conclude that the point $(x_1, x_2) = (100, 350)$ is the optimum or best point and the optimum Z will be \$3,100. In terms of our original production problem we thus have the following solution or decision strategy for the manufacturing plant owner:

$$\text{Produce:} \quad x_1^* = 100 \qquad \text{(regular clocks)}$$

$$x_2^* = 350 \qquad \text{(alarm clocks)}$$

$$\text{Yield:} \quad Z^* = \$3,100 \qquad \text{(profit)}$$

where the superscript * is used to indicate the optimal value.

To show how a different point might have been the optimal one, let us consider what happens if the objective function equation (6.2.1) is replaced by a different objective function, say,

$$(9) \qquad \text{maximize } Z = 3x_1 + 2x_2$$

Then the set of parallel lines to be drawn would be

$$(10) \qquad x_2 = -\frac{3}{2}x_1 + \frac{Z}{2}$$

Figure 6.4.6 shows parallel lines for $Z = 600$, $Z = 1,000$, and $Z = 1,200$. Following the analysis presented earlier, it is evident that the optimum point is at $(x_1^*, x_2^*) = (200, 300)$ with the optimum $Z^* = 1,200$. In terms of the original problem, this would be interpreted as the following decision strategy for the owner:

$$\text{Produce:} \quad x_1^* = 200 \qquad \text{(regular clocks)}$$

$$x_2^* = 300 \qquad \text{(alarm clocks)}$$

$$\text{Yield:} \quad Z^* = \$1,200 \qquad \text{(profit)}$$

It is worthwhile to note at this point that the two solutions we have examined have both occurred at corner points or extreme points of the feasible region. Linear programming theory proves that for any linear programming problem, the solution must occur at one of the extreme points of the feasible region. Thus, for our two-variable problem, the graphical solution method can be simplified as follows: Evaluate the objective function at each extreme point of the feasible region. The optimum solution occurs at the extreme point that yields the best value for the objective function. Since reading the values from a graph is usually not precise, let us solve algebraically for the x_1, x_2 values for each

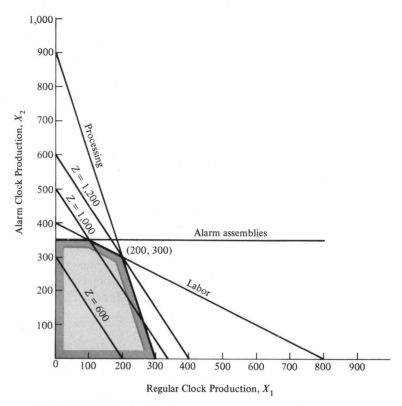

FIGURE 6.4.6. *Graph of feasible region with objective function given by equation (9).*

point. Points I, A, and B were found precisely during our graphical procedure and the results are given in Table 6.4.1.

TABLE 6.4.1. *Evaluation of Objective Function for All Extreme Points*

Point	Coordinates (x_1, x_2)	$Z = Profit = 3x_1 + 8x_2$
I	0, 0	$3(0) + 8(0) = 0$
A	300, 0	$3(300) + 8(0) = 900$
B	0, 350	$3(0) + 8(350) = 2,800$
G	200, 300	$3(200) + 8(300) = 3,000$
H	100, 350	$3(100) + 8(350) = 3,100$

POINT G. From the graph of Figure 6.4.5 it can be seen that point G is defined as the point of intersection of the labor hour and processing hour constraints, where each holds as an equality. Thus

(1) $\qquad 2x_1 + 4x_2 = 1,600 \qquad$ (labor hours)

178 (2) $\qquad 6x_1 + 2x_2 = 1,800 \qquad$ (processing hours)

Multiplying equation (1) by -3, we obtain

(11) $$-6x_1 - 12x_2 = -4,800$$

Adding equation (11) to equation (2), we obtain

$$0x_1 - 10x_2 = -3,000$$

Thus,

(12) $$x_2 = 300$$

Substituting $x_2 = 300$ into equation (1), we obtain

$$2x_1 + 4(300) = 1,600$$

$$2x_1 \qquad = 400$$

(13) $$x_1 = 200$$

Thus point G has x_1, x_2 values of $(200, 300)$.

POINT H. In a similar fashion, point H is the intersection of the labor hour and alarm assemblies constraints:

(1) $\qquad 2x_1 + 4x_2 = 1,600 \qquad$ (labor hours)

(3) $\qquad \qquad x_2 = 350 \qquad$ (alarm assemblies)

Substituting $x_2 = 350$ into equation (1), we obtain

$$2x_1 + 4(350) = 1,600$$

$$2x_1 \qquad = 200$$

(14) $$x_1 = 100$$

Thus, point H has x_1, x_2 values of $(100, 350)$.

Let us now evaluate the objective function for each extreme point. We return to our original problem, where

(4) $$Z = 3x_1 + 8x_2$$

Clearly, the optimum point is $(x_1^*, x_2^*) = (100, 350)$, with the maximum value of Z^* equal to \$3,100 profit.

Later we shall define these points as *basic feasible solution points* and will show that the analytic techniques for solving linear programming problems examine these points only, and choose the optimum solution from among this finite set of feasible solutions.

Let us return to the clock and alarm clock production problem. We now know that the optimal production mix is to produce 100 regular clocks and 350 alarm clocks. Let us discuss how this production mix has utilized the resources of labor hours, processing hours, and alarm assemblies.

We can see from the graph of Figure 6.4.5 that the solution, point H, lies on the labor-hours constraint line. Recall that this constraint line was drawn assuming that the constraint held as an equality (i.e., all labor hours are used up). Thus, the solution, to produce 100 regular clocks and 350 alarm clocks, should use up all the labor hours. Let us verify this by substituting $x_1 = 100$ and $x_2 = 350$ into the labor-hours constraint. We get

$$2(100) + 4(350) = 1,600$$

The left-hand side represents the actual utilization of labor hours, which in this case is equal to the available labor hours, the right-hand side. There are no slack (i.e., unused) labor hours. The same is true for alarm assemblies.

Let us check the utilization of processing hours:

$$6(100) + 2(350) = 1,300 < 1,800$$

Hence, there are $1,800 - 1,300 = 500$ slack processing hours. This is economically important information since these slack processing hours can be used to produce another product or perhaps can be sold to another company. Thus, it is useful to obtain both the optimal variable values and the utilization of resources from an LP resource-allocation problem solution. It is therefore convenient to modify the LP problem in such a way that the new problem is equivalent to the original one, but yields information about resource utilization more directly.

Consider the conversion of the labor constraint

$$(1) \qquad\qquad 2x_1 + 4x_2 \leqslant 1,600$$

into its equality form given by

$$(2) \qquad\qquad 2x_1 + 4x_2 = 1,600$$

We state that this conversion is not an equivalent conversion since the set of values (x_1, x_2) that satisfy equation (1) are not the same as those which satisfy equation (2). This can easily be seen, since all the values that satisfy equation (2) will also satisfy equation (1). However, there are many values of (x_1, x_2) that satisfy equation (1), for example $(x_1, x_2) = (100, 100)$ or $(0, 350)$, but they do not satisfy equation (2).

It is possible, however, to convert equation (1) into an *equivalent linear equality equation* in such a way that the feasible values for equation

(1) are preserved in the equivalent equation. This is possible by adding another variable, known as a *slack variable*, whose value will be the difference between the resources actually used and those available. Consider the following equality equation:

(3) $$2x_1 + 4x_2 + x_3 = 1,600$$

For every set of points (x_1, x_2) that satisfies equation (1), equation (3) will be satisfied with an appropriate value for x_3. For example, if $(x_1, x_2) = (100, 100)$, then $2(100) + 4(100) + x_3 = 1,600$ and $x_3 = 1,000$. If $(x_1, x_2) = (0, 350)$, then $x_3 = 200$. Since x_1 and x_2 are nonnegative variables, the smallest value of x_1 and x_2 is zero. Thus, the largest value for x_3 is 1,600. Furthermore, every set of values (x_1, x_2) chosen must satisfy equation (1). Therefore, the smallest value of x_3 is zero. Hence, x_3 is a nonnegative variable with a defined range, 0 to 1,600. Variables such as x_3 that convert linear inequations such as equation (1) (i.e., with a less-than-or-equal-to symbol) into equivalent linear equations will be called *slack variables*.

In addition to the usefulness of slack variables in the analytical solution of linear programming (see Chapter 8), slack variables have a special economic interpretation. Consider the labor constraint of equation (1). If $x_1 = 100$ regular clocks and $x_2 = 350$ alarm clocks, the total labor hours used for the production equals 1,600 hours, the exact total amount of available resource. Hence, from equation (3), $x_3 = 0$, or the amount of unused labor hours is zero. On the other hand, if $x_1 = 0$ regular clocks and $x_2 = 350$ alarm clocks, the total labor hours used for the production equals 1,400 hours and $x_3 = 200$ labor hours that are unused and still available.

If $x_3 = 0$, we will say that the labor constraint is a *binding constraint*; and if $x_3 > 0$, the constraint will be *nonbinding*. A study of several example points shows that a constraint is binding if the point (x_1, x_2) is exactly on the constraint line [for example, $(x_1, x_2) = (100, 350)$ satisfies $2x_1 + 4x_2 = 1,600$]. The constraint is not binding if the point (x_1, x_2) is inside the feasible region but is not on the constraint line.

Similar analyses of the processing and alarm assemblies constraints yields the following equivalent equations:

(4) $\qquad 6x_1 + 2x_2 + x_4 = 1,800 \qquad$ (processing constraint)

(5) $\qquad\qquad x_2 + x_5 = 350 \qquad$ (alarm assembly constraint)

The slack variables x_4 and x_5 are interpreted, respectively, as the amount of unused processing hours and the number of alarm clocks that could have been produced but were not produced. The variable x_5 could also be interpreted as the number of unused alarm assemblies.

A reexamination of the five extreme points in Figure 6.4.4 in terms of the slack variables reveals the following results.

1. For point I, $x_1 = x_2 = 0$, and therefore all constraints are not binding. Thus, $x_3 = 1,600$ unused labor hours, $x_4 = 1,800$ unused processing hours, and $x_5 = 350$ unused alarm assemblies.
2. For point A, $x_1 = 300$ and $x_2 = 0$. Thus, the processing constraint is binding, but the labor and alarm assemblies constraints are not binding. Hence, $x_3 = 1,600 - 2(300) = 1,000$ unused labor hours, $x_4 = 0$ unused processing hours, and $x_5 = 350$ unused alarm assemblies.
3. For point B, $x_1 = 0$ and $x_2 = 350$. Thus, only the alarm assemblies constraint is binding. Hence, $x_3 = 200$ unused labor hours, $x_4 = 1,100$ unused processing hours, and $x_5 = 0$ unused alarm assemblies.
4. For point G, $x_1 = 200$ and $x_2 = 300$. Thus, both the labor and processing constraints are binding, while the alarm assemblies constraint is not binding. Hence, $x_3 = 0$ unused labor hours, $x_4 = 0$ unused processing hours, and $x_5 = 50$ unused alarm assemblies.
5. For point H, $x_1 = 100$ and $x_2 = 350$. Thus, both the labor and alarm assemblies constraints are binding, while the processing constraint is not binding. Hence, $x_3 = 0$ unused labor hours, $x_4 = 500$ unused processing hours, and $x_5 = 0$ unused alarm assemblies.

The optimal solution of the production problem therefore yields the following decision policy for the owner:

Produce: $x_1^* = 100$ (regular clocks)

$x_2^* = 350$ (alarm clocks)

Resources unused: $x_3^* = 0$ (labor hours)

$x_4^* = 500$ (processing hours)

$x_5^* = 0$ (alarm assemblies)

Yield: $Z^* = \$3,100$ (profit)

On closer examination of these five results, one noteworthy characteristic emerges. For each of the five points examined, five variables were defined, of which exactly two yielded values of zero and exactly three yielded values that were positive. This concept will be discussed and developed further in Section 6.7, where we discuss *basic solutions*.

In general, not all constraints are like equation (1) (i.e., with $\leqslant$ symbology). Very often a constraint will be of the $\geqslant$ type, such as

182   (6) $x_1 \geqslant 50$

If this were a constraint in our production problem, it would be interpreted as meaning that at least 50 regular clocks must be produced. Converting equation (6) to its equivalent equality equation yields

(7)
$$x_1 - x_6 = 50$$

The variable x_6 is called a *surplus variable* and is interpreted as the excess resource used or the excess product produced over and above the minimum required by the problem. If, for example, $x_1^* = 100$, then $x_6^* = 50$ clocks produced over the minimum. A negative sign is used in front of a surplus variable in order that they be defined as continuous nonnegative variables, as are the slack variables and the original problem variables. Mathematically, the slack and surplus variables will be treated in an identical fashion, with no special distinctions between them.

SECTION 6.6. *Sensitivity Analysis*

6.6.1. Introduction. As discussed in Chapter 1, sensitivity analysis is concerned with the question of how the solution changes if we change the parameters of the problem (e.g., the objective function coefficients, the right-hand sides of the constraints, etc.). The simplex method for solving linear programming problems yields valuable information regarding sensitivity analysis. Two of the most important pieces of information are values called *shadow prices* and the *parameter ranges* both for the objective function coefficients and the right-hand sides of the constraints. In this section we shall discuss the meaning and economic interpretation of these quantities. In Chapter 8 the analytical methods for computing them are presented.

6.6.2. Incremental Value of Resources—Shadow Prices. Returning once again to the clock manufacturer problem, we have determined that for our optimal solution ($x_1 = 100, x_2 = 350$) all labor hours are used up ($x_3 = 0$), there are 500 unused processing hours ($x_4 = 500$), and all alarm assemblies are used up ($x_5 = 0$). Suppose that the manufacturer is considering making more resources available, thereby producing more clocks and making higher profits. To expand resources would require, for example, using overtime hours or obtaining more alarm assemblies. Since this requires expenditure of funds, an important question is how much additional profit can be achieved if additional resources are available. This additional profit is usually referred to as the *incremental value*, the *marginal profit*, or the *shadow price of resources*. To be specific, if 1 more labor hour is available (i.e., 1,601 labor hours instead of 1,600 labor hours) how much higher than our old optimal profit of $3,100 would the new optimal profit be? If the optimal profit with 1,601 labor hours is

$3,101.50, the incremental value of the additional labor hours is $1.50. The simplex method for solving LP problems, covered in Chapter 8, yields these values as part of the solution and calls them *dual-variable values*. There is one dual variable for each constraint, and its value is the incremental value or shadow price.

In general, we have the following definition:

> *DEFINITION. The dual variable or shadow price is defined as the change in the optimal value of the objective function per unit increase in the right-hand side of the constraint.*

For resource constraints, the shadow price has the economic interpretation of an incremental value of an additional unit of resource. This is due to the fact that for a resource constraint, an increase in the right-hand side of 1 is interpreted as an additional unit of resource available. The new optimal objective function value will indicate the increased profit due to this additional unit available.

Consider the following two possibilities:

1. An additional 100 hours of labor are available.
2. An additional 120 hours of processing are available.

The question is then whether the optimum solution has changed with the change in resources and if so what is the new optimal policy? A second question that might be asked is whether the owner should purchase additional resources and if so, how much should he pay for them? In order to answer these questions we shall consider each of these changes separately.

If an additional 100 hours of labor are available, constraint (6.2.2) becomes

$$(1) \qquad 2x_1 + 4x_2 \leqslant 1,700$$

The revised feasible region together with the objective function lines are shown in Figure 6.6.1. The optimum solution occurs at the intersection of the labor and alarm assemblies constraints and is equal to the following decision policy:

$$
\begin{aligned}
\text{Produce:} \quad & x_1^* = 150 && \text{(regular clocks)} \\
& x_2^* = 350 && \text{(alarm clocks)} \\
\text{Yield:} \quad & z^* = 3,250 && \text{(dollars profit)}
\end{aligned}
$$

The number of alarm clocks produced has not changed, and all the additional labor hours were used to produce an additional 50 regular clocks, with an increase in profit of $150. Thus the increase in profit for each additional hour of labor available, called the *incremental value*, is $\frac{150}{100} = $1.50/$labor hour. An examination of the solution point indicates

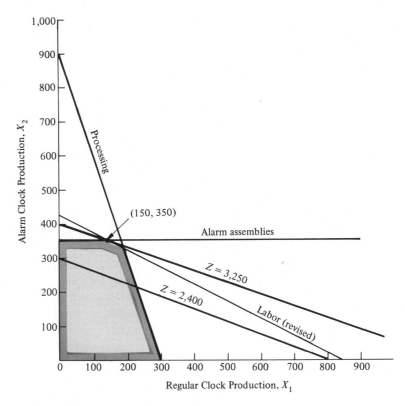

FIGURE 6.6.1. *Optimal solution to production problem with revised labor constraint (6.6.1).*

that the labor and alarm assemblies constraints are still binding and the processing constraint is still not binding. Thus, the unused resources, which are given by the slack variables, are

$$x_3 = 0 \qquad \text{(unused labor hours)}$$

$$x_4 = 200 \qquad \text{(unused processing hours)}$$

$$x_5 = 0 \qquad \text{(unused alarm assemblies)}$$

The marginal profit of labor, \$1.50/labor hour, is the *shadow price* or incremental value of 1 hour of labor. The owner would be willing to pay any amount up to \$1.50 for obtaining 1 additional hour of labor, since his profit increases by \$1.50 for each hour of labor. Although it might appear that the owner would buy as many additional labor hours as possible, closer examination shows that buying more than 166.67 additional hours of labor would not be wise. The reasoning for this is as follows. Since he is already producing as many alarm clocks as is possible, all additional labor will go toward regular clock production. Moreover, each regular clock requires 2 hours of labor and 6 hours of processing. Only 500 hours of processing are still available ($x_4 = 500$), and therefore only $\frac{500}{6} = 83.33$ additional clocks could physically be produced. These clocks would require the 166.67 additional labor hours. Any further purchase of labor hours will yield no further profit, since no additional clocks or alarm clocks could be produced.

Consider now the second option, 120 additional hours of processing. Constraint (6.2.3) becomes

(2) $$6x_1 + 2x_2 \leqslant 1,920$$

The revised feasible region together with the objective function lines are shown in Figure 6.6.2. The optimum point is exactly the same as the solution given in Section 6.4, that is, $(x_1, x_2) = (100, 350)$, and $Z = \$3,100$ profit. Thus, the increase in profit by adding 120 processing hours is zero. Hence, the shadow price or incremental value of processing hours is zero. This means that the owner would be willing to pay zero dollars to buy additional hours of processing. This conclusion can be further understood by noting that from the original problem unused processing hours (x_4)

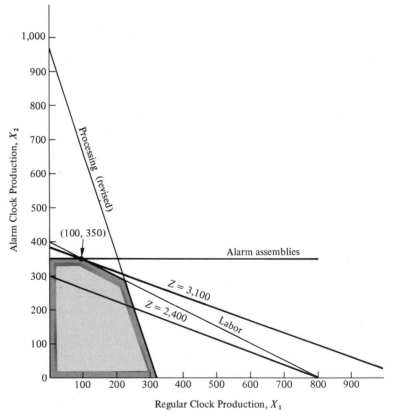

FIGURE 6.6.2. *Optimal solution to production problem with revised processing constraint (6.6.2).*

equals 500 hours, and since the owner already has extra hours that could be used, he would never rationally buy more hours. It can be shown by similar analysis that the shadow price for alarm assemblies is $2.00. That is, the owner should be willing to pay any amount less than $2.00 for additional alarm assemblies.

Let us consider a nonresource constraint and interpret the shadow price. Let us assume that at least 50 regular clocks must be produced. This would add a fourth constraint to our problem,

$$x_1 \geqslant 50$$

which, when the surplus variable is added, becomes

$$x_1 - x_6 = 50$$

For the optimal solution, $x_1^* = 100$, $x_2^* = 350$, x_1 is already greater than 50. Thus, the solution is still feasible and therefore still optimal. The surplus variable x_6 will equal 50, indicating that we have chosen to produce an additional 50 alarm clocks over the minimum required. If our minimum production requirement were 51 instead of 50 (an increase in the right-hand side of 1 unit), no change would occur to the solution or optimal profit since $x_1^* = 100$. The only change would be $x_6 = 49$ instead of 50. Since the change in the optimal objective function for this unit increase in the right-hand side is zero, the dual variable or shadow price for this constraint is zero.

If the minimum production quantity were 150 units, the constraint would be

$$x_1 - x_6 = 150$$

and the old optimal solution is no longer feasible. The new optimal solution can be shown to be (see Figure 6.6.3)

$$x_1^* = 150$$
$$x_2^* = 325$$
$$Z^* = \$3,050$$

Notice that adding this constraint has reduced our profit ($Z^* = \$3,050$ instead of $3,100$), since our old optimal solution is no longer feasible. Also, we will produce only the minimum required ($x_1 = 150$) and no more. We would actually like to produce fewer units ($x_1 = 100$), but we are not permitted to because of the constraint. In this case, increasing the right-hand side by 1 unit (i.e., requiring a minimum of 151 units of product 1) will cause a further decrease of the optimal value of the objective function. Thus, the dual variable or shadow price for the row will be negative. It can be shown that each additional unit of required regular clock production will cause a decrease in the optimal value of the objective function of $1, and therefore the dual variable or shadow price for the constraint is -1. Conversely, *decreasing* the minimum required production to 149 will cause an *increase* in the optimal value of the objective function of $1.

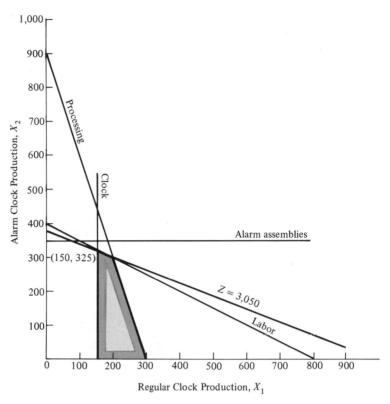

FIGURE 6.6.3. *Optimal solution to production problem with additional clock constraint.*

From these two examples it is possible to derive the following rules:

1. If a constraint is binding in the optimum solution (i.e., slack or surplus variable = 0), the shadow price of that constraint will be nonzero. If it is a resource constraint, it pays for the owner to purchase additional units of that resource at any price less than the shadow price.
2. If a constraint is not binding in the optimum solution (i.e., slack or surplus variable greater than zero), the shadow price of that constraint is zero. If it is a resource constraint, no additional units of that resource should be purchased at any price.

6.6.3. Right-Hand-Side Ranges. In Section 6.6.2 we saw that it is often advantageous to increase or decrease the right-hand sides of various constraints, that is, "relax" the constraint somewhat. The dual-variable or shadow price indicated the per-unit improvement obtained. For example, it was shown that for each additional labor hour, an additional $1.50 in profit could be gained; and conversely, each 1-hour reduction in available labor hours causes a $1.50 reduction in profit. One might ask: Over what range of available labor hours (right-hand sides) does the $1.50

shadow price remain valid? For example, we would suspect that adding an additional 100,000 labor hours would not yield $1.50 \times 100{,}000 = \$150{,}000$ in profit. We suspect that the production required to utilize the 100,000 additional labor hours would require using more than the available units of the other resources. This is the case. We can obtain relatively easily, using the results of the simplex method, the range of right-hand-side values for each constraint within which the shadow price applies (see Chapter 8 for the analytical techniques). These are known as *right-hand-side ranges*. They are an extremely valuable aspect of sensitivity analysis.

For example, it can be shown that the right-hand-side range for the labor-hours constraint is 1,400 to 1,766.67. Thus, if we are considering increasing labor hours by 100 hours (from 1,600 to 1,700), our new optimal profit will be $1.50 \times 100 = \$150$ higher, or $3,250. However, an increase of 200 hours, to 1,800 hours, would *not* yield an additional profit of $1.50 \times 200 = \$300$, since 1,800 is outside the right-hand-side range for this constraint.

6.6.4. Objective-Function-Coefficient Ranges. Similar to the defining of right-hand-side ranges, we can define a range of values for the objective function coefficients. The interpretation, however, is somewhat different than for right-hand-side ranges. For example, as we change the profit per unit for regular or alarm clocks, the shadow prices for all resources change, since the resources now are used to produce products with different profits. Therefore, the objective function ranges will not relate to constant shadow-price values. However, as we change the objective function coefficients (let us assume they are per-unit profits), it may no longer be optimal to produce the same number of units of each product as before; that is, the optimal solution may shift to a new corner point of the feasible region. The objective-function-coefficient ranges tell us for which range of values the solution (excluding the optimal value of the objective function and the dual variables) remains the same. For example, it can be shown (the analytical methods are given in Chapter 8) that as long as the per-unit profit for alarm clocks is at least $6, the optimal solution is still $x_1 = 100$, $x_2 = 350$. Thus, if we increase the per-unit profit for alarm clocks by $1, the optimal solution is still $x_1 = 100$, $x_2 = 350$, but our new optimal-objective-function value is increased by $350, since 350 alarm clocks are produced. However, for regular clocks, the per-unit profit must be between $0 and $4 for our optimal solution to remain the same.

6.6.5. Parametric Linear Programming. The logical extension to the sensitivity analysis we have just discussed is to vary either right-hand sides or objective function coefficients outside their ranges or to vary more than one element at a time (e.g., to increase both labor hours and production hours simultaneously). This is known as *parametric linear programming*. This approach affords greater flexibility in sensitivity analysis. Owning to its complexity, it will not be covered here, but many of the commercially available computer programs for solving linear programming include this feature.

SECTION 6.7. *Basic Solutions*

In Section 6.4 we found that solutions to the production problem would be found only at the extreme points or corner points of the feasible region. In Section 6.5 we found that the set of inequality constraints could be written in an equivalent equality format, introducing new variables called slack or surplus variables. Furthermore, we observed that the solutions corresponding to the extreme points all have the same underlying structure: Two variables have value zero and three variables have positive values. Let us examine this property of the linear programming problem in greater detail.

The production problem in the equality equivalent format is

$$(1) \qquad \text{maximize } Z = 3x_1 + 8x_2 + 0x_3 + 0x_4 + 0x_5$$
$$\text{s.t.}$$
$$(2) \qquad 2x_1 + 4x_2 + x_3 \qquad\qquad = 1{,}600$$
$$(3) \qquad 6x_1 + 2x_2 \qquad + x_4 \qquad = 1{,}800$$
$$(4) \qquad\qquad x_2 \qquad\qquad + x_5 = 350$$

and the nonnegativity requirements

$$x_1, x_2, x_3, x_4, x_5 \geqslant 0$$

The slack variables x_3, x_4, and x_5 have been introduced into the objective function. Their contribution to profit is zero, however; thus the original objective is not altered. The problem is then to find a set of variables $(x_1, x_2, x_3, x_4, x_5)$ that satisfy equations (2), (3), and (4) and for which profit is a maximum. Equations (2), (3), and (4) are a set of three equations with five unknowns, and it is a well-known fact that there are an infinite number of solutions to this equation set. The reader can easily verify this fact by choosing arbitrary values for x_1 and x_2 and solving for x_3, x_4, and x_5. For example, $x_1 = 100$, $x_2 = 200$ gives $x_3 = 600$, $x_4 = 800$, and $x_5 = 150$.

Among this infinite set of solutions are a group of solutions that have a unique property; that is, for each solution, three of the variables are greater than zero and two of the variables are exactly equal to zero. For our production problem there will be exactly 10 of these type of solutions, since there are exactly 10 different ways in which three variables that are permitted to take on values greater than zero can be chosen from among five variables. These are listed in Table 6.7.1. These 10 solutions are called the *basic solutions* of the problem, and in general every linear programming problem will have a set of basic solutions. Later in this section a general methodology for finding basic solutions will be outlined.

TABLE 6.7.1. *Variables for the Basic Solutions for Clock Production Problem*

Solution No.	Variables Permitted to Take on Values Other Than Zero	Variables Set Equal to Zero
1	x_3, x_4, x_5	x_1, x_2
2	x_2, x_4, x_5	x_1, x_3
3	x_2, x_3, x_5	x_1, x_4
4	x_2, x_3, x_4	x_1, x_5
5	x_1, x_4, x_5	x_2, x_3
6	x_1, x_3, x_5	x_2, x_4
7	x_1, x_3, x_4	x_2, x_5
8	x_1, x_2, x_5	x_3, x_4
9	x_1, x_2, x_4	x_3, x_5
10	x_1, x_2, x_3	x_4, x_5

Let us now examine the 10 basic solutions.

SOLUTION 1

$$x_3, x_4, x_5 \neq 0; \quad x_1, x_2 = 0$$

From equations (2)–(4), we find that

$$x_3 = 1,600$$
$$x_4 = 1,800$$
$$x_5 = 350$$

Thus solution 1, $(x_1, x_2, x_3, x_4, x_5) = (0, 0, 1600, 1800, 350)$, corresponds to point I on Figure 6.4.4 and is a feasible solution point. We will call such points *basic feasible solutions*.

SOLUTION 2

$$x_2, x_4, x_5 \neq 0; \quad x_1, x_3 = 0$$

From equation (2) we have

$$2(0) + 4x_2 + 0 = 1,600$$

or

$$x_2 = 400$$

Therefore, from equations (3) and (4), we get

$$6(0) + 2(400) + x_4 \quad = 1,800$$

$$400 + x_5 = 350$$

or

$$x_4 \quad = 1,000$$

$$x_5 = -50$$

This solution, $(x_1, x_2, x_3, x_4, x_5) = (0, 400, 0, 1,000, -50)$, corresponds to point D on Figure 6.4.4; however, it is not a feasible solution point. We thus conclude that not all basic solutions are feasible solutions.

SOLUTION 3

$$x_2, x_3, x_5 \neq 0; \quad x_1, x_4 = 0$$

From equation (3) we have

$$6(0) + 2x_2 + 0 = 1,800$$

or

$$x_2 \quad = 900$$

Therefore, from equations (2) and (4), we get

$$2(0) + 4(900) + x_3 \quad = 1,600$$

$$900 + x_5 = 350$$

or

$$x_3 \quad = -2,000$$

$$x_5 = -550$$

This solution, $(x_1, x_2, x_3, x_4, x_5) = (0, 900, -2,000, 0, -550)$, corresponds to point F on Figure 6.4.4 and is also a nonfeasible solution point.

SOLUTION 4

$$x_2, x_3, x_4 \neq 0; \quad x_1, x_5 = 0$$

From equation (4) we have

$$x_2 + 0 = 350$$

or

$$x_2 = 350$$

Therefore, from equations (2) and (3), we get

$$2(0) + 4(350) + x_3 = 1,600$$

$$6(0) + 2(350) + x_4 = 1,800$$

$$x_3 = 200$$

$$x_4 = 1,100$$

This solution, $(x_1, x_2, x_3, x_4, x_5) = (0, 350, 200, 1,100, 0)$, corresponds to point B on Figure 6.4.4 and is a basic feasible solution point.

Continuing in this fashion, we obtain Table 6.7.2. The reader should verify solutions 5–10. We find that of the 10 basic solutions, only five will be feasible, and these correspond exactly to the extreme points of the feasible region.

From this discussion, a nongraphic solution to a linear programming problem emerges.

Step 1. Convert all inequation constraints to equivalent equality constraints.

Step 2. Determine all basic solutions.

TABLE 6.7.2. *Basic Solutions for the Clock Production Problem*

Solution No.	x_1	x_2	x_3	x_4	x_5	Comment
1	0	0	1,600	1,800	350	Feasible— point I
2	0	400	0	1,000	−50	Not feasible— point D
3	0	900	−2,000	0	−550	Not feasible— point F
4	0	350	200	1,100	0	Feasible— point B
5	800	0	0	−3,000	350	Not feasible— point E
6	300	0	1,000	0	350	Feasible— point A
7	[a]	0	[a]	[a]	0	Impossible[a]
8	200	300	0	0	50	Feasible— point G
9	100	350	0	500	0	Feasible— point H
10	183.3	350	−166.7	0	0	Not feasible— point J

[a]We might conceive of this basic solution as the intersection of the alarm assemblies constraint with the x_1 axis, two parallel lines that intersect in theory at infinity.

Step 3. Determine all basic feasible solutions. These are found by examining all basic solutions and discarding as infeasible those solutions that contain a negative value for one of the variables.

Step 4. Evaluate the objective function for each of the basic feasible solutions.

Step 5. Determine the optimum solution as the one that maximizes (minimizes) the objective function.

Let us consider now a somewhat general procedure for finding the basic solutions. First convert all inequations to equivalent linear equations by introducing slack or surplus variables. We now have a linear system of M equations[†] containing a total of $(N+M)$ variables, N original and M slack or surplus. For example, our production problem contains three equations and five variables $(3+2)$. Each basic solution will be made up of no more than M variables with value greater than zero and the remainder of the variables with zero value. Next, choose a subset of M variables which may take on values other than zero and set the remainder equal to zero. For example, $x_3, x_4, x_5 \neq 0$; $x_1, x_2 = 0$. The resulting system of equations will be M equations with M unknowns, which can be solved algebraically. Continue choosing different subsets of M variables and solving each different resulting system of M equations until no more subsets of M variables can be chosen. All basic solutions will then have been determined. The number of basic solutions must be finite, since there are a finite number of ways that M variables can be chosen from a set of $(N+M)$ variables. This concept in probability theory is called *combinations* and is given by the formula $(N+M)!/M!(N)!$ with $N! = N(N-1)(N-2)\cdots(2)(1)$ and $0! = 1$. Thus, if $N=2$ and $M=3$, the number of basic solutions will be

$$\frac{5!}{3!2!} = \frac{(5)(4)(3)(2)(1)}{(3)(2)(1)(2)(1)} = \frac{120}{12} = 10$$

The actual computation of the basic solutions will be similar to the procedure followed earlier in the section for our production problem.

SECTION 6.8. *Linear Programming Minimization Problems*

Let us consider an allocation problem wherein it is desirable to meet a specific objective at the lowest possible cost. This will result in a *minimization objective function.*

Assume that the clock manufacturer has the same resources available (1,600 labor hours, 1,800 processing hours, 350 alarm assemblies) and needs to produce at least 50 regular clocks, at least 100 alarm clocks, and

---

[†]We assume here that all equations are "different" in the sense that one equation cannot be derived from the others and that the equations are not parallel.

that the total production must be at least 300 clocks (either type). Assume that he wishes to do so in the least expensive way. The cost to produce a regular clock is $2, and the cost to produce an alarm clock is $6. We may formulate the problem as follows:

(1)   minimize $Z = 2x_1 + 6x_2$
        s.t.

(2) $2x_1 + 4x_2 \leqslant 1{,}600$ (labor hours)

(3) $6x_1 + 2x_2 \leqslant 1{,}800$ (processing hours)

(4) $x_2 \leqslant 350$ (alarm assemblies)

(5) $x_1 \quad\quad \geqslant 50$ (required regular clock production)

(6) $x_2 \geqslant 100$ (required alarm clock production)

(7) $x_1 + \ x_2 \geqslant 300$ (required total production)

(8) $x_1, \ x_2 \geqslant 0$ (nonnegativity)

In this case our measure-of-performance variable Z represents total cost and we wish to find values of x_1 and x_2 that yield the lowest possible value for total cost, Z, and still satisfy all the constraints. Notice that the last three constraints are "greater-than-or-equal-to" constraints.

Proceeding as before, and graphing the constraints and the objective function for varying values of Z, we obtain Figure 6.8.1. Since our objective is to achieve the lowest possible value of Z, the minimum occurs at point (200, 100), where $Z = \$1{,}000$ cost.

No additional procedures are necessary for minimization problems, since every minimization problem can be converted to an equivalent maximization problem for which procedures have been developed. This conversion is quite simple and is obtained by multiplying the minimization objective function by -1 and then maximizing the result. Clearly, minimizing Z is the same as maximizing $-Z$, since the higher Z gets, the lower $-Z$ gets. Thus, our minimization LP problem can be stated as

(1)   maximize $Z = -2x_1 - 6x_2$
                    s.t.

(2) $2x_1 + 4x_2 \leqslant 1{,}600$

(3) $6x_1 + 2x_2 \leqslant 1{,}800$

(4) $x_2 \leqslant 350$

(5) $x_1 \quad\quad \geqslant 50$

(6) $x_2 \geqslant 100$

(7) $x_1 + \ x_2 \geqslant 300$

(8) $x_1, \ x_2 \geqslant 0$

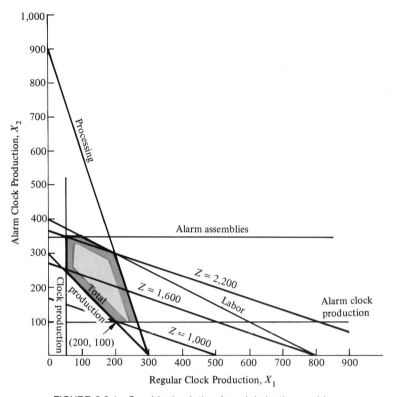

FIGURE 6.8.1. *Graphical solution for minimization problem.*

The constraints have remained the same; the objective function is now the negative of what it was before. Solving this problem, we would obtain

$$x_1^* = 200 \quad \text{(regular clocks)}$$

$$x_2^* = 100 \quad \text{(alarm clocks)}$$

$$Z^* = -\$1,000$$

The optimal values for the controllable variables, x_1 and x_2, are the same. All we need to realize is that our optimal total cost is, in fact, $+\$1,000$ instead of $-\$1,000$. This technique will prove helpful if, for instance, we have at our disposal a computer program that solves only the LP maximization problem and we wish to solve a minimization problem.

SECTION 6.9. *Using the Computer*

There are available many computer programs for solving linear programming problems. A sample output for one of them is shown in Figure 6.9.1 using the production problem of this chapter.

```
                    LINEAR  PROGRAMMING

MAXIMIZE Z =                    3.000        8.000

SUBJECT TO THE FOLLOWING CONSTRAINTS

NO.  TYPE        RHS            CONSTRAINT COEFFICIENTS

 1    LE      1600.000        2.000        4.000

 2    LE      1800.000        6.000        2.000

 3    LE       350.000        0.0          1.000


VARIABLES
    ORIGINAL VARIABLES 1 THROUGH  2
    SLACK VARIABLES  3 THROUGH  5 ADDED TO CONSTRAINTS 1 THROUGH  3



                    OPTIMAL SOLUTION


OBJECTIVE FUNCTION      3100.000

BASIS VARIABLES    1    4    2

                 SOLUTION        OBJECTIVE FUNCTION RANGES
VARIABLE          VALUE       LOWER       GIVEN        UPPER
   1            100.000        0.0        3.000        4.000
   2            350.000        6.000      8.000   999999.000
   3              0.0     -999999.000     0.0          1.500
   4            500.000       -0.200      0.0          0.500
   5              0.0     -999999.000     0.0          2.000



                 SHADOW        RIGHT HAND SIDE RANGES
CONSTRAINT        PRICE       LOWER       GIVEN        UPPER
   1              1.500      1400.000    1600.000     1766.667
   2              0.0        1300.000    1800.000   999999.000
   3              2.000       300.000     350.000      400.000
```

FIGURE 6.9.1. *Computer solution to production problem.*

The program requires as input four elements:

1. The number of variables (not including slack and surplus) and the number of $\leqslant$, $\geqslant$, and = constraints. We have read in 2, 3, 0, and 0.
2. The objective function entries. We have read in 3. and 8.
3. The coefficients of the constraint equations, not including the right-hand sides. The constraints must be in the order of $\leqslant$ constraints first, $\geqslant$ constraints second, and = constraints last. We have read in 2. and 4.; 6. and 2. and 0. and 1.
4. The right-hand sides of the constraints. We have read in 1,600.; 1,800., and 350.

Note that this program assumes a maximization objective. The program output is as follows:

1. The statement of the problem as read in.
2. The variable names used. Variables 1 and 2 are used to represent x_1 and x_2, and variables 3, 4, and 5 are used to represent the slack variables x_3, x_4, and x_5.
3. The optimum (i.e., highest value) of the objective function (Z^*). The value for our problem is 3,100.
4. The basis variables (i.e., those permitted to take on values greater than zero).
5. The answers (i.e., the optimum values for all the variables).
6. The dual-variable or shadow-price values for each constraint (row). The shadow price for the first row (labor hours) is 1.5, for the second row (process hours) it is 0, and for the third row (alarm assemblies) it is 2. The program also prints the range of right-hand-side values for which the basis remains the same.

This particular program also allows for sensitivity analysis (i.e., changing the right-hand sides, objective function, or any of the constraints, and rerunning to find the new solution). We have rerun the problem increasing the right-hand side of the labor-hour constraint (number 1) from 1,600 to 1,700 hours, an increase of 100 hours. According to our dual variable for the labor-hour constraint, the objective function should go up by 1.5 for each additional labor hour available, or a net increase of 150 for 100 additional labor hours. The output for this run is presented in Figure 6.9.2 and shows the revised results. All labor hours, including the additional 100, have been fully utilized, as evidenced by noting that the slack variable for the labor-hours row, x_3, has value zero, and in addition the dual variable is still 1.500. The new optimum-objective-function value is 3,250, 150 higher than before.

A third run (see Figure 6.9.3) was performed, increasing the number of labor hours from 1,700 to 1,800 to show that we cannot achieve this 1.5-per-unit increase forever. The value 1,800 is greater than the right-hand-side upper limit for the labor-hours constraint of 1,766.667. The results show that the slack variable for the labor-hours row, x_3, has a value of 33.333, indicating that 33.33 labor hours were unused (i.e., the usage was $1,800 - 33.333 = 1,766.667$). Naturally, the dual variable for this constraint is now zero. Notice also that slack variable x_4 is now zero, meaning that all process hours are fully utilized; that is, the process constraint is binding and the associated dual-variable value is 0.5. Finally, note that the dual variable for the alarm assemblies is 7, quite a high value, indicating that additional alarm assemblies would contribute $7 each toward the profit.

We can conclude that if the manufacturer wishes to increase profits by adding resources, he can do so by adding 166.67 labor hours. After

NEW RIGHT HAND SIDES
    1700.000   1800.000   350.000

                    OPTIMAL SOLUTION

OBJECTIVE FUNCTION   3250.000

BASIS VARIABLES   1   4   2

| | SOLUTION | OBJECTIVE FUNCTION RANGES | | |
VARIABLE	VALUE	LOWER	GIVEN	UPPER
1	150.000	0.0	3.000	4.000
2	350.000	6.000	8.000	999999.000
3	0.0	-999999.000	0.0	1.500
4	200.000	-0.200	0.0	0.500
5	0.0	-999999.000	0.0	2.000

| | SHADOW | RIGHT HAND SIDE RANGES | | |
CONSTRAINT	PRICE	LOWER	GIVEN	UPPER
1	1.500	1400.000	1700.000	1766.667
2	0.0	1600.000	1800.000	999999.000
3	2.000	330.000	350.000	425.000

FIGURE 6.9.2. *Computer solution with increased labor hour resource.*

NEW RIGHT HAND SIDES
    1800.000   1800.000   350.000

                    OPTIMAL SOLUTION

OBJECTIVE FUNCTION   3350.000

BASIS VARIABLES   3   1   2

| | SOLUTION | OBJECTIVE FUNCTION RANGES | | |
VARIABLE	VALUE	LOWER	GIVEN	UPPER
1	183.333	0.0	3.000	24.000
2	350.000	1.000	8.000	999999.000
3	33.333	-999999.000	0.0	1.500
4	0.0	-999999.000	0.0	0.500
5	0.0	-999999.000	0.0	7.000

| | SHADOW | RIGHT HAND SIDE RANGES | | |
CONSTRAINT	PRICE	LOWER	GIVEN	UPPER
1	0.0	1766.667	1800.000	999999.000
2	0.500	700.000	1800.000	1900.000
3	7.000	0.0	350.000	360.000

FIGURE 6.9.3. *Optimum solution for production problem with 1800 labor hours available.*

that, greater profits can be achieved by adding either process hours or alarm assemblies. However, the costs of the additional resources are not shown, and these would enter into the decision process. Only if additional labor hours cost less than $1.50 should they be added.

By performing sensitivity analysis in this fashion, the decision maker can explore various scales of operation and determine which is most profitable. Many computer programs perform this type of sensitivity analysis more efficiently by using a technique known as parametric linear programming. The availability of computers to carry out these computations allows a decision maker to investigate many possibilities that would not be possible otherwise.

SECTION 6.10. *Summary*

In this chapter we have attempted to give the reader an understanding of the general nature of linear programming problems. Beginning with a definition and the general structure of the LP problem, we formulated a typical problem. The problem was solved by the graphical approach, which served as the springboard for many additional concepts. The existence of slack and surplus variables and their interpretations were given; the notion of a shadow price was introduced and its explanation given in economic terms. A nongraphic approach was established through the concept of a basic solution. Finally, procedures for using the computer for linear programming problems were stated and explained.

PROBLEMS

6.1. Graph each of the following sets of inequations, identifying the feasible region and recording the extreme points:

(a) $\quad 5X_1 + 10X_2 \leqslant 50$

$\quad\quad 6X_1 + 2X_2 \leqslant 30$

$\quad\quad X_1 \quad\quad\quad \leqslant 3$

(b) $\quad 3X_1 + 2X_2 \leqslant 30$

$\quad\quad 4X_1 + 5X_2 \leqslant 60$

$\quad\quad\quad\quad X_2 \leqslant 10$

(c) $\quad 2X_1 - 4X_2 \leqslant 0$

$\quad\quad X_1 + X_2 \leqslant 50$

$\quad\quad X_1 \quad\quad\quad \geqslant 10$

$\quad\quad\quad\quad X_2 \geqslant 15$

6.2. (Problem 6.1 continued) For each of the sets of inequations, graph the following lines, indicating their maximum and minimum values:

(a) $Z = X_1 + X_2$
(b) $Z = 3X_1 + 4X_2$
(c) $Z = 2X_1 - X_2$

6.3. (Problem 6.1 continued) Convert each of the sets of inequations to the equality equivalent form and find all basic solutions. Indicate which of the solutions are feasible.

6.4. A television manufacturer must decide how many black-and-white and how many color sets he should produce for each day's sale so as to maximize his daily profit. Each day he has available the following supplies:

TV chassis	24
production hours	160
color tubes	10

Each black-and-white set requires 5 production hours and yields a profit of $6. Each color set requires 10 production hours and yields a profit of $15.

(a) Formulate the manufacturer's problem as a linear program.
(b) Solve the problem graphically.

6.5. (Problem 6.4 continued) Write the constraint set in equality equivalent form and find all the basic solutions. Associate each basic solution with a point on your graph.

6.6. (Problem 6.4 continued) Find the slack-variable values for the optimal solution and discuss their economic interpretation.

6.7. (Problem 6.4 continued) Suppose that the profit for each color set is only $12. How many of each type of set should he manufacture?

6.8. (Problem 6.4 continued) Suppose that the profit for black-and-white sets increases to $8 per unit. What should be his optimal daily product mix?

6.9. (Problem 6.4 continued) Give an economic interpretation for each shadow price or dual variable and indicate whether its value is $+$, $-$, or 0 for the optimal solution.

6.10. (Problem 6.4 continued) Solve the television manufacturer's problem using the computer and interpret the output. Resolve the problem using the computer for available production hours of 165 and 200. Compare and interpret your results.

6.11. (Problem 6.4 continued) A competitive firm goes bankrupt and offers to sell the television manufacturer some of his stock. Consider the following offers and determine if the manufacturer should accept the offer:

(a) 5 TV chassis at $2.00 each.
(b) 10 TV chassis at $0.20 each.
(c) 4 color-set tubes at $4.00 each.
(d) 6 color-set tubes at $2.50 each.
(e) 15 color-set tubes at $1.00 each.

6.12. (Problem 6.4 continued) A job shop offers our television manufacturer production time at $1.00/hour for 5 hours, $0.75/hour for 15 hours, or $2.00/hour for 3 hours. Should the manufacturer accept any of these offers?

6.13. (Problem 6.4 continued) Assume that the minimum number of television sets produced must be 23 units.

(a) Write the new constraint and add it to the LP problem.
(b) Find the optimal solution to this revised LP problem.
(c) Give an economic interpretation of the dual variable for this new constraint.

6.14. (Problem 6.4 continued) The sales manager requires that the number of color sets manufactured be at least twice that of the number of black-and-white sets.

(a) Write this new constraint and add it to the LP problem.
(b) Find the optimal solution to this revised LP problem.

6.15. (Problem 6.14 continued) Solve this revised problem using the computer and interpret your results.

6.16. A printing company is considering the purchase of two different types of presses, *A* and *B*. Type *A* occupies 40 square feet of floor space, cost $2,000, and requires three full-time operators. Type *B* occupies 60 square feet of floor space, cost $6,000, and requires three full-time operators. The company has available 720 square feet of usable floor space and $60,000 cash. The union requires that work be provided for at least 48 operators at all times. Type *A* can print at a rate of 100 sheets/minute, while type *B* can print at a rate of 300 sheets/minute. The company will purchase a mix of presses *A* and *B* that maximize its production output.

(a) Formulate this problem as a linear program.
(b) Solve the problem graphically.

6.17. (Problem 6.16 continued) Write the constraint set in equality equivalent form and find all the basic solutions. Indicate which basic solutions are feasible.

6.18. (Problem 6.16 continued) Find the slack-variable values for the optimum solution and discuss their economic interpretation.

6.19. (Problem 6.16 continued) Give an economic interpretation for each shadow price or dual variable and indicate whether its value is $+$, $-$, or 0 for the optimal solution.

6.20. (Problem 6.16 continued) Solve the printing company's problem using the computer and interpret the output.

6.21. (Problem 6.16 continued) Suppose that the type A press is improved and now has a production rate of 250 sheets/minute. How many of each type of machine should the company purchase?

6.22. (Problem 6.16 continued) The printing company's landlord offers to rent the company additional space on a different floor. How much space should they rent, and what is the value to the company in renting this space?

6.23. (Problem 6.16 continued) The union offers to renegotiate its contract with the printing company to require only 42 operators. Should the company accept the union's offer?

6.24. (Problem 6.16 continued) A bank offers to lend the company $6,000 with a daily charge of $1.00. Assume an 8-hour day and that the printing company earns $0.01 for each 100 sheets it prints. Should the company make this loan? Assume no restriction on number of operators.

6.25. (Problem 6.16 continued) Suppose that the supplier informs the printing company that it will only supply orders of 17 or more presses (either type).
(a) Write this new constraint.
(b) Find the new optimal basic feasible solution.
(c) Give an economic interpretation for the dual of this new constraint.

6.26. A hand-drill manufacturer that produces two models, regular and portable, must assemble at least 100 drills for each day's delivery. The regular drill requires 2 hours of preparation and costs $10 and the portable requires 5 hours of preparation and costs $15. The dealer's objective is to minimize his total cost of preparation given that he has 400 preparation hours available each day and at least 40 portables must be assembled each day.
(a) Formulate this problem as a linear program.
(b) Solve the problem graphically.

6.27. (Problem 6.26 continued) Find the slack-variable values and give their economic interpretation.

6.28. (Problem 6.26 continued) Interpret the dual variables and indicate whether their values are $+$, $-$, or 0 for the optimal solution.

6.29. (Problem 6.26 continued) Solve the hand-drill manufacturer's problem using the computer and interpret the output.

6.30. (Problem 6.26 continued) Suppose that the manufacturer can produce no more than 50 regular drills each day. What should be his product mix?

6.31. The Wood Products Company produces two major products, desks and cabinets. The profit margin is $5 per desk and $6 per cabinet. All products must go through three processes—cutting, assembling, and finishing—which have an upper capacity of 48, 40, and 50 hours per week. The two products require the following process time, in hours:

Process	Desks	Cabinets	Weekly Capacity
Cutting	2	4	50
Assembling	5	2	40
Finishing	4	4	52

(a) Formulate this problem as a linear program.
(b) Solve the problem graphically.
(c) Find the slack-variable values and give their economic interpretation.
(d) Interpret the dual variables and indicate whether their values are +, −, or 0 for the optimal solution.

**BOOKS OF
INTEREST**

Charnes, Abraham and W. W. Cooper, *Management Models and Industrial Applications of Linear Programming*. New York: John Wiley & Sons, Inc., 1961.

Dantzig, G. B., *Linear Programming and Extensions*. Princeton, N.J.: Princeton University Press, 1963.

Driebeek, Norman J., *Applied Linear Programming*. Reading, Mass.: Addison-Wesley Publishing Co., Inc., 1969.

Garvin, W. W., *Introduction to Linear Programming*. New York: McGraw-Hill Book Co., 1960.

Gass, S. I., *Linear Programming: Methods and Applications*, 2nd ed. New York: McGraw-Hill Book Co., 1964.

Hadley, G. *Linear Programming*. Reading, Mass.: Addison-Wesley Publishing Co., Inc., 1962.

Kim, C., *Introduction to Linear Programming*. New York: Holt, Rinehart and Winston, Inc., 1971.

Kwak, N. K., *Mathematical Programming with Business Applications*. New York: McGraw-Hill Book Co., 1973.

Naylor, T. H., E. T. Byrne, and J. M. Vernon. *Introduction to Linear Programming: Methods and Cases*. Belmont, Ca.: Wadsworth Publishing Co., 1971.

CHAPTER SEVEN

Linear Programming Applications

OBJECTIVES: The purpose of this chapter is to present to you the following basics in applying linear programming techniques.

1. *The relevance of linear programming to business problems.*
2. *The formulation of linear programming models of decision problems.*
3. *The use of the computer to solve linear programming problems.*
4. *The interpretation of computer solutions.*
5. *Sensitivity analysis and its economic implications.*

In Chapter 6 we presented the general structure of the linear programming problem and its solution characteristics. In practice, using linear programming consists of the following steps:

1. Defining the problem.
2. Formulating the linear programming model mathematically.
3. Running the problem on the computer.
4. Interpreting the solution.
5. Performing sensitivity analysis and additional computer runs to investigate changes in the problem, such as additional resources available. (These analyses constitute *postoptimality analysis.*)

This chapter will present a wide variety of decision problems, each of which can be represented as a linear programming model. The LP models will be formulated so as to present the techniques of formulation as applied to realistic decision problems. A computer solution for each problem will be presented and interpreted so as to indicate the practical application of many of the concepts discussed in Chapter 6. In each case additional runs will be presented where some constraint has been altered to investigate its effect on the solution. The additional runs will be those which are suggested by examining the initial solution itself, as is done in actual practice.

As mentioned previously, linear programming does not necessarily yield integer-valued answers to a decision problem. In many situations this does not pose a problem, since the solution values are large, and rounding causes negligible inaccuracies. However, we shall not be concerned in this chapter with noninteger results and will assume that the integer answer, when necessary, is easily obtainable.

Finally, the problems presented, although designed to illustrate both the techniques of model formulation and the application of linear programming to real-world types of decision problems, are generally smaller than those handled in practice so as not to be overly complex. In real-world decision problems there might be hundreds or even thousands of variables or constraints. However, the procedure for solving these problems is similar to the methodology presented in this chapter.

Formulating a linear programming model for a problem can sometimes prove more difficult than it might at first appear. The most important feature of a proper formulation is that, when solved, it provides the correct answer to the decision problem. This may sound obvious, but it is an important guiding principle.

In general, we may divide formulation into the following steps:

1. Define the objective. This must include precisely what decisions must be made and with what objective in mind. For example, for the clock-production problem of Chapter 6, we can state the objective as: "Determine how many regular clocks and alarm clocks to produce so as to maximize profit." A properly stated objective will make the remaining steps of formulation more straightforward.

2. Define the variables, including their dimensions. For example, "Let x_1 = number of regular clocks to produce." We could also have formulated the production in dimensions of dozens, thousands, dollars worth, or (for some decision problems) tons, gallons, and so on. It is important to define each variable clearly, including its dimensions, so that when the solution is obtained, for example, $x_1 = 50$, we know precisely what it means.

3. Formulate the constraints. The inequality or equality equations which prevent the variables of the problem from taking on infeasible values must be developed. It is important that these equations also define the range of values which the variables can actually assume. The constraints must be in an acceptable linear inequality format, e.g.,

$$a_1 x_1 + a_2 x_2 + a_3 x_3 + \cdots \leqslant b$$

where $a_1, a_2, a_3, \ldots$ are constants
$\quad b$ is a nonnegative constant $\quad$ (zero or positive)

The relation may be $\leqslant$, $\geqslant$, or $=$. In general, an inequality constraint is preferable to an equality constraint, since an equality constraint gives no indication, for purposes of sensitivity analysis, whether increasing or decreasing the right-hand side improves the objective function. Incorrect constraint formulation can lead to solutions which are not feasible or to excluding solutions from consideration which are really feasible (and possibly optimal). It may be necessary or convenient when formulating the constraints to define additional variables which were not foreseen in advance. This is perfectly permissible as long as they are carefully defined as described in step 2.

4. Formulate the objective function. The objective function should yield the payoff measure value for all possible feasible solution values.

7.3.1. Statement of the Problem. A company has $180,000 available for purchase of machines to produce a new product. The manufacturer of the machines offers three models: the regular model, costing $3,000; the deluxe model, costing $5,000, and the super model, costing $10,000. The regular model occupies 15 square feet of floor space, requires one operator to run, and can produce 4 units of product per hour. The deluxe model occupies 20 square feet of floor space, requires two operators to run, and can produce 5 units of product per hour. The super model occupies 30 square feet of floor space, requires five operators to run, and can produce 20 units of product per hour. The company insists that at least half of the machines purchased be the deluxe model. A unit of product is expected to have a gross profit of $10, excluding the labor cost of the operators. It is felt that all product that can be produced can be sold at the $10-per-unit profit figure. The company has available 500 square feet of floor space for the machines and 100 operators to run the machines. Operators are paid $4 per hour.

7.3.2. Statement of the Objective. The manufacturer needs to determine the number of each type of machine to purchase. Since a per-unit profit for final product is given, our objective can be to maximize profit. The statement of the objective is therefore:

Determine the number of regular, deluxe, and super machines to purchase so as to maximize profit.

7.3.3. Definition of the Variables. Given the objective, let:

x_1 = number of regular machines to purchase

x_2 = number of deluxe machines to purchase

x_3 = number of super machines to purchase

We would have used other variable names instead of x_1, x_2, x_3 (e.g., R, D, S, or x_R, x_D, x_S). However, since the computer program references the variables simply as number $1, 2, 3$, and so on, the names we have chosen will be easiest to use.

7.3.4. The Constraints and the Objective Function. In general, constraints need to be formulated one at a time, and we shall consider each restriction in sequence.

208

AVAILABLE FUNDS. We need to write an inequation which states that the sum of the cash spent on each type of machine must be less than or equal to the $180,000 available. For example, the cash spent on regular machines is equal to

$$\left(\begin{array}{c}\text{number of regular}\\\text{machines purchased}\end{array}\right) \times \left(\begin{array}{c}\text{cost per}\\\text{regular machine}\end{array}\right)$$

Thus, the constraint will read

$$\left(\frac{\$3,000}{\text{machine}}\right)(x_1 \text{ machines}) + \left(\frac{\$5,000}{\text{machine}}\right)(x_2 \text{ machines})$$

$$+ \left(\frac{\$10,000}{\text{machine}}\right)(x_3 \text{ machines}) \leqslant \$180,000$$

or

$$3,000x_1 + 5,000x_2 + 10,000x_3 \leqslant 180,000$$

Notice that the dimension of each term of the constraint is $; that is,

$$\$ + \$ + \$ \leqslant \$$$

It is critical when formulating constraints that the dimensions be consistent.

It is also possible to divide both sides of the constraint by a positive number so as to reduce the size of the numbers. For example, we can divide both sides by 1,000, giving

$$3x_1 + 5x_2 + 10x_3 \leqslant 180$$

which is an exact equivalent constraint. We need only keep in mind that the dimension of the constraint is thousands of dollars ($000). This will be important when interpretating the solution received from the computer. This approach of "scaling" constraints is helpful, owing to the rounding error involved in numerical computations.

FLOOR SPACE. The floor space required by the machines purchased must be less than or equal to the available floor space of 500 square feet. Thus,

$$15x_1 + 20x_2 + 30x_3 \leqslant 500$$

The dimensions of the constraint are square feet.

OPERATORS. The number of operators required to run the machines may not exceed the number of available operators. Thus,

$$1x_1 + 2x_2 + 5x_3 \leqslant 100$$

MINIMUM NUMBER OF DELUXE MACHINES. The requirement is that at least $\frac{1}{2}$ of the total number of machines purchased be deluxe models. Let us write an expression in terms of the variables $x_1, x_2,$ and x_3, which indicates the fraction of the total number of machines purchased which are deluxe machines:

$$\left(\begin{array}{c}\text{fraction}\\\text{deluxe}\end{array}\right) = \frac{\text{number of deluxe machines}}{\text{total number of machines}}$$

$$= \frac{x_2}{x_1 + x_2 + x_3}$$

Since this fraction must be no less than 0.5,

$$\frac{x_2}{x_1 + x_2 + x_3} \geqslant 0.5$$

In its present form this constraint is not acceptable since we must have a constraint in a linear form with all variables on the left-hand side. Multiplying both sides by $x_1 + x_2 + x_3$ (which is nonnegative), we obtain

$$x_2 \geqslant 0.5(x_1 + x_2 + x_3)$$

Subtracting the right-hand side from both sides, we obtain

$$-0.5x_1 + 0.5x_2 - 0.5x_3 \geqslant 0$$

which is an acceptable linear inequality constraint.

THE OBJECTIVE FUNCTION.   Our objective is to maximize profit, and we must therefore develop a profit measure associated with the purchase of a machine. The profit is related to output rate, gross profit per unit of product, number of operators required, and the operator's salary. Since we are given the output rate and operator's salary rate in per-hour figures, let us use as a profit measure the dimension \$/hour. The hourly profit associated with the purchase of a machine is

$$\left(\begin{array}{c}\text{output}\\\text{rate}\end{array}\right) \times \left(\begin{array}{c}\text{gross profit}\\\text{per unit}\end{array}\right) - \left(\begin{array}{c}\text{number of}\\\text{operators}\end{array}\right) \times \left(\begin{array}{c}\text{operator's}\\\text{salary}\end{array}\right)$$

For each regular machine the hourly profit is

$$\left(\frac{4 \text{ units}}{\text{hour}}\right) \times \left(\frac{\$10}{\text{unit}}\right) - (1 \text{ operator}) \times \left(\frac{\$4}{\text{operator hour}}\right) = 40 - 4 = \frac{\$36}{\text{hour}}$$

For each deluxe machine the hourly profit is

$$\left(\frac{5 \text{ units}}{\text{hour}}\right) \times \left(\frac{\$10}{\text{unit}}\right) - (2 \text{ operators}) \times \left(\frac{\$4}{\text{operator hour}}\right) = 50 - 8 = \frac{\$42}{\text{hour}}$$

For each super machine the hourly profit is

$$\left(\frac{20 \text{ units}}{\text{hour}}\right) \times \left(\frac{\$10}{\text{unit}}\right) - (5 \text{ operators}) \times \left(\frac{\$4}{\text{operator hour}}\right) = 200 - 20$$

$$= \frac{\$180}{\text{hour}}$$

These are hourly profits per machine purchased. If we multiply each by the number of machines of each type purchased (x_1, x_2, x_3) and add these expressions, we obtain the total hourly profit for all machines purchased. Our objective function is, therefore,

$$Z = 36x_1 + 42x_2 + 180x_3$$

The complete linear programming model is shown in Figure 7.3.1.

x_1 = Number of regular machines to purchase
x_2 = Number of deluxe machines to purchase
x_3 = Number of super machines to purchase

maximize $\{Z = 36x_1 + 42x_2 + 180x_3\}$ Hourly profit
s.t.

No.	Subject	Constraints
1	Cash ($000)	$3x_1 + 5x_2 + 10x_3 \leqslant 180$
2	Floor Space (ft^2)	$15x_1 + 20x_2 + 30x_3 \leqslant 500$
3	Operators	$1x_1 + 2x_2 + 5x_3 \leqslant 100$
4	Min Deluxe	$-0.5x_1 + 0.5x_2 - 0.5x_3 \geqslant 0$
		$x_1, x_2, x_3 \geqslant 0$

FIGURE 7.3.1. *Linear programming model of the equipment purchase problem.*

7.3.5. The Computer Solution. The model as we have developed it is in a proper form for submission to our computer program; that is, we wish to maximize and the constraints are in the order "less than or equal to," "greater than or equal to," "equal to." (See Section 6.9.)

The solution obtained from the computer is shown in Figure 7.3.2.[†] Notice that the program has added slack variables 4, 5, and 6 to the cash, floor space, and operators constraints (numbers 1, 2, and 3), and a surplus variable, 7, to the minimum deluxe constraint (number 4). The optimal decision is to buy zero regular machines (x_1), 10 deluxe machines (x_2), and 10 super machines (x_3). The profit obtained will be $2,220/hour, as shown by the objective function.

7.3.6. Sensitivity and Postoptimality Analysis. The binding constraints are floor space (number 2) and the minimum deluxe constraint (number 4), as shown by the nonzero shadow price and also by the fact that the slack or surplus variables on these constraints (numbers 5 and 7) are zero. The slack variables for the other two constraints indicate the unused resources of cash and operators. The slack variable (number 4) for the cash constraint (number 1) has value 30, indicating that $30,000 of the $180,000 available will not be spent. Recall that the dimension of the

[†]The term *artificial variables* that is shown in the figure is discussed in Section 8.8. However, this material is not necessary for understanding this chapter.

LINEAR PROGRAMMING

MAXIMIZE Z =   36.000   42.000   180.000

SUBJECT TO THE FOLLOWING CONSTRAINTS

NO.   TYPE   RHS   CONSTRAINT COEFFICIENTS

 1   LE   180.000   3.000   5.000   10.000

 2   LE   500.000   15.000   20.000   30.000

 3   LE   100.000   1.000   2.000   5.000

 4   GE   0.0   -0.500   0.500   -0.500

VARIABLES
    ORIGINAL VARIABLES 1 THROUGH   3
    SLACK VARIABLES   4 THROUGH   6 ADDED TO CONSTRAINTS 1 THROUGH   3
    SURPLUS VARIABLES   7 THROUGH   7 ADDED TO CONSTRAINTS   4 THROUGH   4
    ARTIFICIAL VARIABLES   8 THROUGH   8 ADDED TO CONSTRAINTS   4 THROUGH   4

                OPTIMAL SOLUTION

OBJECTIVE FUNCTION   2220.000

BASIS VARIABLES   4   3   6   2

              SOLUTION   OBJECTIVE FUNCTION RANGES
VARIABLE   VALUE   LOWER   GIVEN   UPPER
    1   0.0   -999999.000   36.000   113.400
    2   10.000   -180.000   42.000   120.000
    3   10.000   69.429   180.000   999999.000
    4   30.000   -999999.000   0.0   14.800
    5   0.0   -999999.000   0.0   4.440
    6   30.000   -999999.000   0.0   31.714
    7   0.0   -999999.000   0.0   93.600

              SHADOW   RIGHT HAND SIDE RANGES
CONSTRAINT   PRICE   LOWER   GIVEN   UPPER
    1   0.0   150.000   180.000   999999.000
    2   4.440   0.0   500.000   600.000
    3   0.0   70.000   100.000   999999.000
    4   -93.600   -8.333   0.0   12.500

FIGURE 7.3.2. *Equipment purchase problem. Computer solution.*

cash constraint is thousands of dollars ($000). The slack variable (number 6) on the operators constraint (number 3) has value 30, indicating that 30 of the 100 operators will not be needed.

The shadow price on the floor-space constraint (number 2) of 4.440 is to be interpreted such that each additional square foot of floor space provided (an increase in the right-hand side of 1 unit) would yield an additional $4.44 in hourly profit (change in the objective function). This incremental profit value of $4.44 per additional square foot will apply for up to 600 square feet of floor space, the right-hand-side-range upper limit for constraint 2. Thus, if we performed a run with 600 square feet of floor space, an increase of 100 square feet from our original run, our new optimal profit would be increased by (100 square feet)×($4.44/square foot)=$444. To see the effect of going beyond this limit, let us increase the floor-space availability to 700 square feet and rerun the model. This may be done, using our computer program, by simply changing only the right-hand sides and rerunning. The output of this change is shown in Figure 7.3.3.

```
NEW RIGHT HAND SIDES
       180.000      700.000       100.000         0.0



              OPTIMAL SOLUTION


OBJECTIVE FUNCTION      2664.000

BASIS VARIABLES   3   5   6   2
```

	SOLUTION	OBJECTIVE FUNCTION RANGES		
VARIABLE	VALUE	LOWER	GIVEN	UPPER
1	0.0	-999999.000	36.000	76.400
2	12.000	-180.000	42.000	90.000
3	12.000	104.250	180.000	999999.000
4	0.0	-999999.000	0.0	14.800
5	100.000	-4.848	0.0	4.440
6	16.000	-999999.000	0.0	31.714
7	0.0	-999999.000	0.0	64.000

	SHADOW	RIGHT HAND SIDE RANGES		
CONSTRAINT	PRICE	LOWER	GIVEN	UPPER
1	14.800	0.0	180.000	210.000
2	0.0	600.000	700.000	999999.000
3	0.0	84.000	100.000	999999.000
4	-64.000	-9.000	0.0	15.000

FIGURE 7.3.3. *Equipment purchase problem with 700 square feet of floor space. Computer solution.*

The new solution is to buy zero regular machines (x_1), 12 deluxe machines (x_2), and 12 super machines (x_3). The optimal profit is $2,664/hour. The floor-space constraint (number 2) is no longer binding (zero shadow price). The slack variable on this constraint (number 5) has value 100, indicating that there are 100 square feet of unused floor space, that is, only $700-100=600$ would be used. This is precisely the upper limit for the right-hand side of the floor-space constraint from our first run. Going beyond this upper limit of 600 square feet makes the constraint no longer binding. Notice that our optimal profit is $444 higher than before, since we have in effect added only 100 square feet of floor space to be used. Clearly, some other constraint must now be binding. It is the cash constraint (number 1) with a shadow price of 14.800 and a slack variable (number 4) value of zero. The shadow price of 14.8 is interpreted such that an additional $1,000 available for purchase of machines (increase in right-hand side) will yield $14.80/hour in hourly profit. Recall that the dimension of this constraint is thousands of dollars.

Let us return to our original run shown in Figure 7.3.2. In addition to the floor-space constraint being binding, the minimum deluxe constraint (number 4) is binding, as shown by the nonzero shadow price and the zero surplus variable (number 7). The shadow price of -93.6 has no direct economic interpretation, because changing the right-hand side of the constraint changes the structure of the original constraint. However, we can conclude that forcing half of the machines purchased to be deluxe models restricts our ability to earn profit. Let us relax this constraint somewhat by requiring only that at least 4 deluxe machines be purchased,

$$x_2 \geqslant 4$$

This run may be performed simply by changing constraint 4 and the right-hand sides. The computer output is shown in Figure 7.3.4.

Our new solution is to purchase zero regular machines (x_1), 4 deluxe machines (x_2), and 14 super machines (x_3). The optimal profit is now $2,688/hour, which is higher than before. Notice that the optimal solution again purchases only the minimum required number of deluxe machines. This constraint (number 4) is binding, as indicated by a

```
NEW CONSTRAINT   4
         0.0              1.000           0.0


NEW RIGHT HAND SIDES
      180.000       500.000      100.000        4.000


                     OPTIMAL SOLUTION


OBJECTIVE FUNCTION       2688.000

BASIS VARIABLES    4   3   6   2
```

VARIABLE	SOLUTION VALUE	OBJECTIVE FUNCTION RANGES		
		LOWER	GIVEN	UPPER
1	0.0	−999999.000	36.000	90.000
2	4.000	−999999.000	42.000	120.000
3	14.000	72.000	180.000	999999.000
4	20.000	−999999.000	0.0	18.000
5	0.0	−999999.000	0.0	6.000
6	22.000	−999999.000	0.0	36.000
7	0.0	−999999.000	0.0	78.000

CONSTRAINT	SHADOW PRICE	RIGHT HAND SIDE RANGES		
		LOWER	GIVEN	UPPER
1	0.0	160.000	180.000	999999.000
2	6.000	80.000	500.000	560.000
3	0.0	78.000	100.000	999999.000
4	−78.000	0.0	4.000	25.000

FIGURE 7.3.4. *Equipment purchase problem. Four deluxe machines required. Computer solution.*

nonzero shadow price and a zero surplus variable (x_7). The shadow price of -78 means that if we require the purchase of an *additional* deluxe machine ($x_2 \geqslant 5$) we will *reduce* profit by \$78/hour. It may also be interpreted such that a *reduction* of 1 required deluxe machine ($x_2 \geqslant 3$) will *increase* profit by \$78/hour. This shadow price will apply as long as constraint 4 is anywhere between $x_2 \geqslant 0$ and $x_2 \geqslant 25$, the lower and upper right-hand-side ranges for the constraint.

SECTION 7.4. *Equipment-Purchase Problem Reconsidered*

7.4.1. Statement of the Problem. Let us reconsider the equipment purchase problem of Section 7.3 with a different objective. Instead of a maximizing profit objective, let us assume that the company desires to purchase sufficient equipment so as to be able to produce 200 units of product per hour for the least cash expenditure possible.

7.4.2. Statement of Objective. The objective for the revised problem is therefore:

Determine the number of regular, deluxe, and super machines to purchase so as to be able to produce at least 200 units per hour at minimum purchase cost.

7.4.3. Definition of the Variables. The variables (x_1, x_2, x_3) are the same as in Section 7.3, that is, the quantity of each type of machine to purchase.

7.4.4. The Constraints and the Objective Function

ORIGINAL CONSTRAINTS. Only a few modifications to the formulation of Section 7.3 are necessary. The constraint on available funds is no longer necessary. Either we can meet the objective within the \$180,000 available or not. If we can, the constraint will have no effect. If not, it will cause an infeasible solution. However, it will be better to obtain a solution with a purchase cost in excess of \$180,000 than to be unable to obtain a solution. The other constraints presented are still valid and require no changes.

MINIMUM HOURLY PRODUCTION. We must add a constraint stating that minimum hourly production must be at least 200 units, that is,

$$4x_1 + 5x_2 + 20x_3 \geqslant 200$$

It is logical to assume that the optimal solution will require purchasing machines so as to produce *exactly* 200 units per hour, since additional

215

production over 200 units/hour would require additional machines. However, it is always better to formulate an inequality constraint when possible. It may not always be obvious whether the greater or the equal case is the better.

THE OBJECTIVE FUNCTION. The objective function must reflect the purchase cost of the machines:

$$Z = 3{,}000x_1 + 5{,}000x_2 + 10{,}000x_3$$

This expression measures the purchase cost in dollars. We can also measure it in thousands of dollars ($000),

$$Z = 3x_1 + 5x_2 + 10x_3$$

Since this expression has values more in line with the other constraints, let us use it. We need only recall that all objective function values are in thousands of dollars ($000).

The complete linear programming model is shown in Figure 7.4.1.

x_1 = Number of regular machines to purchase
x_2 = Number of deluxe machines to purchase
x_3 = Number of super machines to purchase

minimize $\{Z = 3x_1 + 5x_2 + 10x_3\}$ Purchase cost ($000)
    s.t.

No.	Subject	Constraints
1	Floor space (sq ft)	$15x_1 + 20x_2 + 30x_3 \leqslant 500$
2	Operators	$1x_1 + 2x_2 + 5x_3 \leqslant 100$
3	Min deluxe	$-0.5x_1 + 0.5x_2 - 0.5x_3 \geqslant 0$
4	Min production (units)	$4x_1 + 5x_2 + 20x_3 \geqslant 200$
		$x_1, x_2, x_3 \geqslant 0$

FIGURE 7.4.1. *Linear programming model of the revised equipment purchase problem.*

7.4.5. The Computer Solution. The change that must be made to the model as given in Figure 7.4.1 is necessary because of the fact that the computer program we are using maximizes instead of minimizes. This requires, however, only a change in the objective function, as was discussed in Section 6.6. Instead of

$$\text{minimize}\{Z = 3x_1 + 5x_2 + 10x_3\}$$

we substitute

$$\text{maximize}\{Z = -3x_1 - 5x_2 - 10x_3\}$$

The solutions to these two problems are exactly equivalent except that whenever the objective is discussed, we must remember that the computer-developed optimal solution is the negative of the true cost. The same is true for the shadow prices, which use objective function values.

LINEAR PROGRAMMING

MAXIMIZE Z =   -3.000   -5.000   -10.000

SUBJECT TO THE FOLLOWING CONSTRAINTS

NO.	TYPE	RHS	CONSTRAINT COEFFICIENTS		
1	LE	500.000	15.000	20.000	30.000
2	LE	100.000	1.000	2.000	5.000
3	GE	0.0	-0.500	0.500	-0.500
4	GE	200.000	4.000	5.000	20.000

VARIABLES
    ORIGINAL VARIABLES 1 THROUGH 3
    .SLACK VARIABLES 4 THROUGH 5 ADDED TO CONSTRAINTS 1 THROUGH 2
    SURPLUS VARIABLES 6 THROUGH 7 ADDED TO CONSTRAINTS 3 THROUGH 4
    ARTIFICIAL VARIABLES 8 THROUGH 9 ADDED TO CONSTRAINTS 3 THROUGH 4

OPTIMAL SOLUTION

OBJECTIVE FUNCTION   -120.000

BASIS VARIABLES   4   5   2   3

VARIABLE	SOLUTION VALUE	OBJECTIVE FUNCTION RANGES LOWER	GIVEN	UPPER
1	0.0	-999999.000	-3.000	-0.400
2	8.000	-999999.000	-5.000	-2.500
3	8.000	-17.222	-10.000	5.000
4	100.000	-0.153	0.0	999999.000
5	44.000	-2.143	0.0	999999.000
6	0.0	-999999.000	0.0	4.000
7	0.0	-999999.000	0.0	0.600

CONSTRAINT	SHADOW PRICE	RIGHT HAND SIDE RANGES LOWER	GIVEN	UPPER
1	0.0	400.000	500.000	999999.000
2	0.0	56.000	100.000	999999.000
3	-4.000	-5.000	0.0	5.000
4	-0.600	0.0	200.000	250.000

FIGURE 7.4.2. *Revised equipment purchase problem. Computer solution.*

The computer solution to the problem is shown in Figure 7.4.2. The program has added slack variables 4 and 5 to the square feet and operators constraints (number 1 and 2) and surplus variables 6 and 7 to the min deluxe and min production constraint (numbers 3 and 4).

The optimal solution is to purchase zero regular machines (x_1), 8 deluxe machines (x_2), and 8 super machines (x_3). The optimal objective function value is -120. This is to be interpreted as a minimum purchase cost of $120,000.

7.4.6. Sensitivity and Postoptimality Analysis. The minimum deluxe constraint (number 3) is binding, as evidenced by a nonzero shadow price and its surplus variable (number 6) having value 0. The minimum hourly production constraint (number 4) is also binding as shown by a nonzero shadow price and its surplus variable (number 7) having value 0. The other two constraints are not binding (zero shadow prices and nonzero slack variables). The slack variable (number 4) on the floor-space constraint (number 1) has value 100, indicating 100 unused square feet of floor space. The slack variable (number 5) on the operators constraint (number 2) having value 44 indicates 44 unused operators.

As discussed in Section 7.3.6, the shadow price of the minimum deluxe constraint (number 3) does not have a direct economic interpretation. It merely indicates an improvement for relaxing the constraint (i.e., requiring fewer deluxe machines).

The shadow price of -0.6 for the minimum production constraint requires careful interpretation. It states that increasing the right-hand side by 1 unit (i.e., requiring an additional unit of production) *decreases* the objective function by 0.60 thousand dollars (since the dimension of the objective function is $000), or $600. However, the objective function is the negative of purchase cost ($000). Thus, the shadow price is to be interpreted such that each additional unit of hourly production required will *increase* purchase cost by $600.

```
NEW RIGHT HAND SIDES
    500.000      100.000        0.0         225.000
```

```
                    OPTIMAL SOLUTION


OBJECTIVE FUNCTION      -135.000

BASIS VARIABLES    4    5    2    3
```

	SOLUTION	OBJECTIVE FUNCTION RANGES		
VARIABLE	VALUE	LOWER	GIVEN	UPPER
1	0.0	-999999.000	-3.000	-0.400
2	9.000	-999999.000	-5.000	-2.500
3	9.000	-17.222	-10.000	5.000
4	50.000	-0.153	0.0	999999.000
5	37.000	-2.143	0.0	999999.000
6	0.0	-999999.000	0.0	4.000
7	0.0	-999999.000	0.0	0.600

	SHADOW	RIGHT HAND SIDE RANGES		
CONSTRAINT	PRICE	LOWER	GIVEN	UPPER
1	0.0	450.000	500.000	999999.000
2	0.0	63.000	100.000	999999.000
3	-4.000	-5.625	0.0	2.500
4	-0.600	0.0	225.000	250.000

FIGURE 7.4.3. *Revised equipment purchase problem. Required 225 units of production. Computer solution.*

Let us investigate the effect of increasing the required production. The shadow price applies up to a required production level of 250 units. Let us illustrate the meaning of the shadow price by increasing the required production to a value within this range, say 225 units. The output for this run is shown in Figure 7.4.3. We would purchase 9 deluxe and 9 super machines. Our optimal cost is now $135,000 (objective function -135). The objective function has gone down by 15, $-135-(-120) = -15$. This equals the change in the right-hand side ($+25$) times the shadow price (-0.6).

Notice that the same constraints are binding; that is, the minimum deluxe and minimum production constraints and the basis are the same (variables 2, 3, 4, and 5). Therefore, the same shadow prices still apply.

SECTION 7.5. *Portfolio Selection Problem*

7.5.1. Statement of the Problem. An investor has $100,000 which he wishes to invest in income-producing securities and government bonds so as to maximize his annual return. He has selected five possible investments, all of which he considers to have reasonably high yields and stability:

1. Oil company *A* stock, paying 11% annual dividend.
2. Oil company *B* stock, paying 7.5% annual dividend.
3. Electric utility *A* stock, paying 8% annual dividend.
4. Electric utility *B* stock, paying 6% annual dividend.
5. Government bonds, paying 5% annual interest.

Since he has no plans to sell the stocks in the future, he is not concerned with their selling price. Based on the various risk levels involved, he has made the following decisions:

1. The total investment in oil stocks may not exceed $30,000.
2. The total investment in electric utilities may not exceed $50,000.
3. The investment in oil company *A* may not exceed $20,000.
4. The investment in electric utility *A* may not exceed $30,000.
5. The total investment in oil stocks may not exceed the total investment in electric utilities.
6. The investment in oil company *A* and electric utility *A* combined may not exceed the investment in government bonds.

7.5.2. Statement of the Objective. The objective of the decision maker is:

Determine how much money to invest in each investment so as to maximize annual return.

7.5.3. Definition of the Variables. The variables must specify the amount of money invested in each alternative. Since these will be large values, let us define their dimensions as thousands of dollars ($000). Thus, let

$$x_1 = \text{investment in oil company } A \ (\$000)$$

$$x_2 = \text{investment in oil company } B \ (\$000)$$

$$x_3 = \text{investment in electric utility } A \ (\$000)$$

$$x_4 = \text{investment in electric utility } B \ (\$000)$$

$$x_5 = \text{investment in government bonds } (\$000)$$

7.5.4. The Constraints and the Objective Function

AVAILABLE FUNDS. Since the investor has only $100,000 to invest,

$$x_1 + x_2 + x_3 + x_4 + x_5 \leqslant 100$$

The right-hand side is 100, since the variables are defined in terms of thousands of dollars.

MAXIMUM OIL STOCK INVESTMENT. The investment in oil stocks may not exceed $30,000.

$$x_1 + x_2 \leqslant 30$$

The right-hand side is 30 instead of 30,000, since the variables have been defined in terms of thousands of dollars.

MAXIMUM ELECTRIC UTILITY INVESTMENT. The investment in electric utility stocks may not exceed $50,000.

$$x_3 + x_4 \leqslant 50$$

MAXIMUM OIL COMPANY A. The investment in oil company A may not exceed $20,000,

$$x_1 \leqslant 20$$

MAXIMUM ELECTRIC UTILITY A. The investment in electric utility A may not exceed $30,000,

$$x_3 \leqslant 30$$

OIL–UTILITY RELATIONSHIP. The total investment in oil stocks may not exceed the total investment in electric utilities. Thus,

$$x_1 + x_2 \leqslant x_3 + x_4$$

220   Since this constraint is not in proper form, let us subtract the right-hand side from both sides, giving

$$x_1 + x_2 - x_3 - x_4 \leqslant 0$$

which is an acceptable linear inequality constraint.

GOVERNMENT BONDS VERSUS OIL COMPANY *A* AND ELECTRIC UTILITY *A*.
The investments in oil company *A* and electric utility *A* combined may
not exceed the investment in government bonds,

$$x_1 + x_3 \leqslant x_5$$

Since this is not an acceptable form, subtract x_5 from both sides, giving

$$x_1 + x_3 - x_5 \leqslant 0$$

THE OBJECTIVE FUNCTION.   The objective function must express the annual return to the investor:

$$Z = 0.11x_1 + 0.075x_2 + 0.08x_3 + 0.06x_4 + 0.05x_5$$

Since the variables x_1 through x_5 have dimensions of thousands of
dollars, the objective function value will also be in thousands of dollars
($000).

The complete linear programming model is shown in Figure 7.5.1.

x_1 = Investment in oil co. *A* ($000)
x_2 = Investment in oil co. *B* ($000)
x_3 = Investment in electric utility *A* ($000)
x_4 = Investment in electric utility *B* ($000)
x_5 = Investment in government bonds ($000)

Maximize $\{z = 0.11x_1 + 0.075x_2 + 0.08x_3 + 0.06x_4 + 0.05x_5\}$ Return ($000)
s.t.

No.	Subject	Constraints	
1	Cash	$x_1 + x_2 + x_3 + x_4 + x_5$	$\leqslant 100$
2	Max oil	$x_1 + x_2$	$\leqslant 30$
3	Max electric	$x_3 + x_4$	$\leqslant 50$
4	Max oil co. *A*	x_1	$\leqslant 20$
5	Max electric *A*	x_3	$\leqslant 30$
6	Oil – utility	$x_1 + x_2 - x_3 - x_4$	$\leqslant 0$
7	Bonds	$x_1 + x_3 - x_5$	$\leqslant 0$

FIGURE 7.5.1. *Linear programming model of the portfolio selection
problem.*

7.5.5. The Computer Solution. The linear programming model is in an
acceptable form for submission to the computer program. The solution is
shown in Figure 7.5.2. The program has added slack variables 6–12 to the
constraints.

LINEAR PROGRAMMING

| MAXIMIZE Z = | | 0.110 | 0.075 | 0.080 | 0.060 | 0.050 |

SUBJECT TO THE FOLLOWING CONSTRAINTS

NO.	TYPE	RHS	CONSTRAINT COEFFICIENTS				
1	LE	100.000	1.000	1.000	1.000	1.000	1.000
2	LE	30.000	1.000	1.000	0.0	0.0	0.0
3	LE	50.000	0.0	0.0	1.000	1.000	0.0
4	LE	20.000	1.000	0.0	0.0	0.0	0.0
5	LE	30.000	0.0	0.0	1.000	0.0	0.0
6	LE	0.0	1.000	1.000	−1.000	−1.000	0.0
7	LE	0.0	1.000	0.0	1.000	0.0	−1.000

VARIABLES
   ORIGINAL VARIABLES 1 THROUGH 5
   SLACK VARIABLES 6 THROUGH 12 ADDED TO CONSTRAINTS 1 THROUGH 7

OPTIMAL SOLUTION

OBJECTIVE FUNCTION   7.167

BASIS VARIABLES 2 7 8 3 10 5 1

VARIABLE	SOLUTION VALUE	OBJECTIVE FUNCTION RANGES		
		LOWER	GIVEN	UPPER
1	20.000	0.093	0.110	999999.000
2	6.667	0.065	0.075	0.080
3	26.667	0.077	0.080	0.100
4	0.0	−999999.000	0.060	0.062
5	46.667	0.047	0.050	0.070
6	0.0	−999999.000	0.0	0.068
7	3.333	−0.005	0.0	0.010
8	23.333	−0.005	0.0	0.055
9	0.0	−999999.000	0.0	0.017
10	3.333	−0.020	0.0	0.003
11	0.0	−999999.000	0.0	0.007
12	0.0	−999999.000	0.0	0.018

CONSTRAINT	SHADOW PRICE	RIGHT HAND SIDE RANGES		
		LOWER	GIVEN	UPPER
1	0.068	80.000	100.000	110.000
2	0.0	26.667	30.000	999999.000
3	0.0	26.667	50.000	999999.000
4	0.017	10.000	20.000	25.000
5	0.0	26.667	30.000	999999.000
6	0.007	−10.000	0.0	5.000
7	0.018	−20.000	0.0	10.000

FIGURE 7.5.2. *Portfolio selection problem. Computer solution.*

The solution calls for the following investments:

Variable	Investment	Amount
1	Oil company A	$20,000
2	Oil company B	$6,667
3	Electric utility A	$26,667
4	Electric utility B	0
5	Government bonds	$46,667
		$100,001

with an annual return of $7,167, or 7.167%.[†] Suppose that the investor were required to invest in $1,000 units; that is, he could invest $6,000 or $7,000 but not $6,667. He might be tempted to round each answer to the nearest thousand and invest $20,000, $7,000, $27,000, and $47,000. These investments would add to $101,000 and would not technically be feasible. The exact solution would require a technique known as *integer programming*. The investor in this case would probably adjust the $47,000 investment in government bonds to $46,000, with little change to the objective function (annual return) of $7,167.

7.5.6. Sensitivity and Postoptimality Analysis. The binding constraints are those with zero slack-variable values and nonzero shadow prices, and are the cash (number 1), the maximum oil company A (number 4), the oil–utility (number 6), and bonds (number 7) constraints. All of the available $100,000 has been spent, as expected.

The shadow price for the cash constraint of 0.068 indicates that each additional $1,000 of cash available (constraint 1 has dimensions of $000) will yield an additional 0.068 thousand dollars ($68, or 6.8%) in annual return, which is lower than the 7.167% overall return. This 6.80% figure applies to cash investments up to a level of $110,000 in cash available, since the right-hand-side upper limit for the cash constraint (number 1) is 110. If more than $110,000 is available, the basis will change. Let us demonstrate this by performing another run with $120,000 available. We simply change the right-hand side of the cash constraint (number 1) to 120 and rerun. The computer solution is shown in Figure 7.5.3.

The new solution is to invest $20,000, $10,000, $30,000, $10,000, and $50,000, respectively, in each investment, with an annual return of $8,450 on the $120,000 investment, or 7.04%. The basis of the solution has changed. For example, the solution now calls for investing in electric utility $B(x_4)$, which it did not require before. The shadow price on the cash constraint (number 1) is 0.06, and it applies up to a level of $130,000

[†]The total of $100,001, instead of $100,000, is due to rounding.

NEW RIGHT HAND SIDES

| 120.000 | 30.000 | 50.000 | 20.000 | 30.000 | 0.0 | 0.0 |

OPTIMAL SOLUTION

OBJECTIVE FUNCTION   8.450

BASIS VARIABLES   4   2   8   3   11   5   1

VARIABLE	SOLUTION VALUE	OBJECTIVE FUNCTION RANGES		
		LOWER	GIVEN	UPPER
1	20.000	0.085	0.110	999999.000
2	10.000	0.060	0.075	0.100
3	30.000	0.070	0.080	999999.000
4	10.000	0.050	0.060	0.065
5	50.000	0.040	0.050	0.060
6	0.0	−999999.000	0.0	0.060
7	0.0	−999999.000	0.0	0.015
8	10.000	−0.010	0.0	0.010
9	0.0	−999999.000	0.0	0.025
10	0.0	−999999.000	0.0	0.010
11	10.000	−0.010	0.0	0.008
12	0.0	−999999.000	0.0	0.010

CONSTRAINT	SHADOW PRICE	RIGHT HAND SIDE RANGES		
		LOWER	GIVEN	UPPER
1	0.060	110.000	120.000	130.000
2	0.015	20.000	30.000	35.000
3	0.0	40.000	50.000	999999.000
4	0.025	10.000	20.000	30.000
5	0.010	20.000	30.000	35.000
6	0.0	−10.000	0.0	999999.000
7	0.010	−10.000	0.0	10.000

FIGURE 7.5.3. *Portfolio selection problem with $120,000 available cash. Computer solution.*

cash available. Note that the shadow price tells the investor the return he can expect on *additional* (incremental) investments.

Let us return to our original problem (shown in Figure 7.5.2) and examine the objective function ranges. Notice, for example, that if the return from electric utility $B(x_4)$ were 0.062 or higher, instead of 0.06, the solution would change. Most likely, it would then be worthwhile to invest in electric utility B. Let us examine the effect if the return from electric utility B is 0.065 instead of 0.06. The computer solution for this case is shown in Figure 7.5.4. The solution calls for investments of $20,000, $10,000, $20,000, $10,000, and $40,000, respectively, in oil companies A and B, electric utilities A and B, and government bonds. Notice that there is an investment in electric utility B of $10,000, which was not the case when the return was only 6%. The overall return is now $7,200, or 7.2%.

CPTIMAL SOLUTION

OBJECTIVE FUNCTION   7.200

BASIS VARIABLES   2   4   8   3   10   5   1

VARIABLE	SOLUTION VALUE	OBJECTIVE FUNCTION RANGES		
		LOWER	GIVEN	UPPER
1	20.000	0.090	0.110	999999.000
2	10.000	0.065	0.075	0.095
3	20.000	0.065	0.080	0.085
4	10.000	0.062	0.065	0.080
5	40.000	-0.015	0.050	0.055
6	0.0	-999999.000	0.0	0.065
7	0.0	-999999.000	0.0	0.010
8	20.000	-999999.000	0.0	0.010
9	0.0	-999999.000	0.0	0.020
10	10.000	-0.005	0.0	0.015
11	0.0	-999999.000	0.0	0.0
12	0.0	-999999.000	0.0	0.015

CONSTRAINT	SHADOW PRICE	RIGHT HAND SIDE RANGES		
		LOWER	GIVEN	UPPER
1	0.065	80.000	100.000	110.000
2	0.010	26.667	30.000	40.000
3	0.0	30.000	50.000	999999.000
4	0.020	10.000	20.000	30.000
5	0.0	20.000	30.000	999999.000
6	0.0	-20.000	0.0	5.000
7	0.015	-20.000	0.0	10.000

FIGURE 7.5.4. *Portfolio selection problem. Return from electric utility B equals 6.5%. Computer solution.*

SECTION 7.6. *Advertising Selection Problem*

7.6.1. Statement of the Problem. A new restaurant is opening and the owners have budgeted $50,000 for advertising in the coming month. They are considering four types of advertising:

1. 30-second television commercials.
2. 30-second radio commercials.
3. Full-page advertisement in a local newspaper.
4. Full-page advertisements in a local magazine which is published weekly and will appear four times during the coming month.

The restaurant owners wish to reach families with incomes both over and under $20,000. The number of exposures to families of each type and the cost for each of the media is shown in Table 7.6.1.

225

TABLE 7.6.1. *Exposures and Cost for Media*

Media	Cost of Advertisement ($)	Number of Exposures to Families with Annual Income over $20,000	Number of Exposures to Families with Annual Income under $20,000
Television	2,500	2,000	5,000
Radio	1,000	300	2,000
Newspaper	400	500	100
Magazine	750	1,000	1,000

To have a balanced campaign, the owners have determined the following restrictions:

1. No more than eight television advertisements.
2. No more than 60% of the total advertisements may be newspaper and magazine advertisements.
3. There must be at least 30,000 exposures to families with incomes over $20,000.
4. There must be at least 80,000 exposures to families with incomes under $20,000.

7.6.2. Statement of the Objective. The owners wish to reach (expose) as many families as possible, so we shall state the objective as follows:

Determine the number of each type of advertisement to purchase so as to maximize the total number of exposures.

7.6.3. Definition of the Variables. The variables should describe the number of advertisements of each type to purchase. We can define them in terms of number of advertisements or in terms of how much to spend in dollars for each type. Since most of the information of the problem is given per advertisement, it will be simpler to use number of advertisements. Therefore, let

x_1 = number of television advertisements to purchase

x_2 = number of radio advertisements to purchase

x_3 = number of newspaper advertisements to purchase

x_4 = number of magazine advertisements to purchase

7.6.4. The Constraints and the Objective Function

AVAILABLE CASH.   The total cost may not exceed $50,000. Therefore,

$$2,500x_1 + 1,000x_2 + 400x_3 + 750x_4 \leqslant 50,000$$

226

MAXIMUM TELEVISION ADVERTISEMENTS. The number of television advertisements may not exceed 8; therefore,

$$x_1 \leqslant 8$$

MAXIMUM NEWSPAPER AND MAGAZINE ADVERTISEMENTS. The number of newspaper and magazine advertisements may not exceed 60% of the total. The fraction of the total which are newspaper and magazine advertisements is

$$\frac{x_3 + x_4}{x_1 + x_2 + x_3 + x_4}$$

Thus,

$$\frac{x_3 + x_4}{x_1 + x_2 + x_3 + x_4} \leqslant 0.6$$

Rearranging to form an acceptable linear inequality constraint, we get

$$x_3 + x_4 \leqslant 0.6(x_1 + x_2 + x_3 + x_4)$$

or

$$-0.6x_1 - 0.6x_2 + 0.4x_2 + 0.4x_3 \leqslant 0$$

MAXIMUM MAGAZINE ADVERTISEMENTS. Since the magazine only comes out four times in the next month,

$$x_4 \leqslant 4$$

MINIMUM EXPOSURES TO FAMILIES WITH INCOMES OVER $20,000. This constraint must express the total number of exposures to families with incomes over $20,000. Thus,

$$2,000x_1 + 300x_2 + 500x_3 + 1,000x_4 \geqslant 30,000$$

MINIMUM EXPOSURES TO FAMILIES WITH INCOMES UNDER $20,000. In a similar fashion to the preceding constraint, we have

$$5,000x_1 + 2,000x_2 + 100x_3 + 1,000x_4 \geqslant 80,000$$

THE OBJECTIVE FUNCTION. The objective function must express the total number of exposures, which includes all families (over $20,000 plus under $20,000). Therefore,

$$Z = 7,000x_1 + 2,300x_2 + 600x_3 + 2,000x_4$$

227   The complete linear programming model is shown in Figure 7.6.1.

x_1 = Number of TV advertisements to purchase

x_2 = Number of radio advertisements to purchase

x_3 = Number of newspaper advertisements to purchase

x_4 = Number of magazine advertisements to purchase

$$\text{maximize} \quad \{Z = 7000x_1 + 2300x_2 + 600x_3 + 2000x_4\}$$
$$\text{s.t.}$$

No.	Subject	Constraints
1	Available funds	$2{,}500x_1 + 1{,}000x_2 + 400x_3 + 750x_4 \leqslant 50{,}000$
2	Max TV	$x_1 \leqslant 8$
3	Max newspaper & magazine	$-0.6x_1 - 0.6x_2 + 0.4x_3 + 0.4x_4 \leqslant 0$
4	Max magazine	$x_4 \leqslant 4$
5	Min over \$20,000	$2{,}000x_1 + 300x_2 + 500x_3 + 1{,}000x_4 \geqslant 30{,}000$
6	Min under \$20,000	$5{,}000x_1 + 2{,}000x_2 + 100x_3 + 1{,}000x_4 \geqslant 80{,}000$

$$x_1, x_2, x_3, x_4 \geqslant 0$$

FIGURE 7.6.1. *Linear programming model of media selection problem.*

7.6.5. The Computer Solution.

The model as shown is in an acceptable form for input to the computer program. The solution is shown in Figure 7.6.2. The program has added slack variables 5, 6, 7, and 8 to the first four constraints and surplus variables 9 and 10 to the last two constraints.

The solution calls for 8 television ads (x_1), 25 radio ads (x_2), 5 newspaper ads (x_3), and 4 magazine ads (x_4). The total number of exposures will be approximately 124,500 (the objective function).

7.6.6. Sensitivity and Postoptimality Analysis.

The binding constraints are cash (number 1), maximum television ads (number 2), maximum magazine ads (number 4), and minimum exposures to families with incomes over \$20,000 (number 5). These are indicated by having zero slack or surplus variables and nonzero shadow prices.

Let us study the shadow prices to determine what is most binding in the problem. The shadow price for the maximum television ads constraint (number 2) of 2,302.630 indicates that for each additional television ad we permit (increase of right-hand side by 1), the total number of exposures (objective function) will increase by approximately 2,303 exposures. This certainly deserves consideration. The upper limit on television ads for which this shadow price value is valid is 9.52 television ads. This does not mean that if we allow more than 9.52 ads, they will not be used. It only indicates that the shadow price will not apply past that point.

A similar analysis holds for the maximum magazine ads constraint (number 4). However, the magazine comes out only four times next

LINEAR PROGRAMMING

| MAXIMIZE Z = | | 7000.000 | 2300.000 | 600.000 | 2000.000 |

SUBJECT TO THE FOLLOWING CONSTRAINTS

NO.	TYPE	RHS	CONSTRAINT COEFFICIENTS			
1	LE	50000.000	2500.000	1000.000	400.000	750.000
2	LE	8.000	1.000	0.0	0.0	0.0
3	LE	0.0	−0.600	−0.600	0.400	0.400
4	LE	4.000	0.0	0.0	0.0	1.000
5	GE	30000.000	2000.000	300.000	500.000	1000.000
6	GE	80000.000	5000.000	2000.000	100.000	1000.000

VARIABLES
    ORIGINAL VARIABLES 1 THROUGH 4
    SLACK VARIABLES 5 THROUGH 8 ADDED TO CONSTRAINTS 1 THROUGH 4
    SURPLUS VARIABLES 9 THROUGH 10 ADDED TO CONSTRAINTS 5 THROUGH 6
    ARTIFICIAL VARIABLES 11 THROUGH 12 ADDED TO CONSTRAINTS 5 THROUGH 6

OPTIMAL SOLUTION

OBJECTIVE FUNCTION   124499.875

BASIS VARIABLES   10   1   7   4   3   2

VARIABLE	SOLUTION VALUE	OBJECTIVE FUNCTION RANGES LOWER	GIVEN	UPPER
1	8.000	4697.367	7000.000	999999.000
2	25.000	1500.000	2300.000	4244.441
3	5.000	−999999.000	600.000	920.000
4	4.000	1072.369	2000.000	999999.000
5	0.0	−999999.000	0.0	2.553
6	0.0	−999999.000	0.0	2302.630
7	16.200	−500.000	0.0	999999.000
8	0.0	−999999.000	0.0	927.631
9	0.0	−999999.000	0.0	0.842
10	14500.000	−0.457	0.0	999999.000

CONSTRAINT	SHADOW PRICE	RIGHT HAND SIDE RANGES LOWER	GIVEN	UPPER
1	2.553	44319.586	50000.000	56333.359
2	2302.630	1.703	8.000	9.520
3	0.0	−16.200	0.0	999999.000
4	927.631	0.0	4.000	6.452
5	−0.842	28099.992	30000.000	37871.430
6	0.0	−999999.000	80000.000	94500.000

FIGURE 7.6.2. *Media selection problem. Computer solution.*

month, and we cannot relax this constraint. The shadow price for the cash constraint (number 1) of 2.553 indicates that each additional dollar spent will yield an additional 2.553 exposures up to an expenditure of $56,333.

The shadow price of -0.842 for the minimum exposures to families with incomes over $20,000 (constraint number 5) should be carefully interpreted. If we require one *additional* exposure of this type (right-hand side 30,001 instead of 30,000), our total number of exposures (objective function) will *decrease* by 0.842 exposure. This may at first seem contradictory. However, requiring more exposures to families with incomes over $20,000 will cause a shift of money to ads with relatively larger exposures to the high-income families but relatively lower total exposures.

Let us investigate allowing more television ads, a constraint that has a very high shadow price associated with it. The upper limit for the resource given the current shadow price value is 9.52 ads. Consider the case of allowing 12 ads. The computer output with the new right-hand side of 12 for the maximum television ad constraint (number 2) is shown in Figure 7.6.3.

NEW RIGHT HAND SIDES

50000.000	12.000	0.0	4.000	30000.000	80000.000

OPTIMAL SOLUTION

OBJECTIVE FUNCTION   131099.813

BASIS VARIABLES   9   1   4   10   7   2

	SOLUTION	OBJECTIVE FUNCTION RANGES		
VARIABLE	VALUE	LOWER	GIVEN	UPPER
1	12.000	5749.996	7000.000	999999.000
2	17.000	1500.000	2300.000	2666.667
3	0.0	-999999.000	600.000	920.000
4	4.000	1725.000	2000.000	999999.000
5	0.0	-999999.000	0.0	2.300
6	0. '	-999999.000	0.0	1250.000
7	15.800	-500.000	0.0	323.529
8	0.0	-999999.000	0.0	275.000
9	3100.004	-0.355	0.0	0.842
10	17999.977	-0.457	0.0	0.550

	SHADOW	RIGHT HAND SIDE RANGES		
CONSTRAINT	PRICE	LOWER	GIVEN	UPPER
1	2.300	41000.008	50000.000	999999.000
2	1250.000	9.520	12.000	18.800
3	0.0	-15.800	0.0	999999.000
4	275.000	-0.000	4.000	22.588
5	0.0	-999999.000	30000.000	33100.004
6	0.0	-999999.000	80000.000	97999.938

FIGURE 7.6.3. *Media selection problem. Maximum television ads increased to 12. Computer solution.*

The new solution calls for 12 television ads, 17 radio ads, 0 newspaper ads, and 4 magazine ads. The total number of exposures is now 131,100 (this is slightly different than the objective function, owing to rounding errors). There are excess exposures to families in both income categories (i.e., neither constraint 5 or 6 is binding). The maximum television ad constraint (number 2) is still binding, and the shadow price of 1,250 is valid for up to 18 ads (the right-hand-side upper limit). Thus each additional television ad above 12 we allow will increase the total number of exposures by 1,250.

SECTION 7.7. *Transportation Problem*

7.7.1. Statement of the Problem. A company has three factories, at which it produces its product. It distributes the product through four warehouses, which are located at distances from the factories. Each month the warehouses supply the central office with their demands for the product and management must determine from which factories to supply each warehouse. Warehouses may be supplied from more than one factory. The factories have the following availability (or capacity) each month:

Factory	A	B	C	Total
Available Units Each Month	50	55	70	175

For the coming month, the warehouses have the following demand:

Warehouse	1	2	3	4	Total
Demand	30	60	20	40	150

The per-unit cost of shipping a unit from each factory to each warehouse is shown in Figure 7.7.1.

	To Warehouse			
	1	2	3	4
From Factory A	15	18	19	13
From Factory B	21	14	15	17
From Factory C	25	12	17	22

FIGURE 7.7.1. *Per-unit shipping costs.*

The company wishes to find the best way to supply each warehouse's demand without exceeding the availability of product at each factory. This problem, known as the *transportation problem*, has a special methodology for its solution, which will be presented in Chapter 9. However, we shall treat it here as a linear programming problem.

7.7.2. Statement of the Objective. The objective of the decision maker is to determine how to supply each warehouse's demand. It is tempting to define the objective in terms of how much to take from each factory and how much to supply each warehouse. However, this suggests an improper formulation which does not truly answer the problem of how much to ship from each factory to each warehouse. We will state the objective as:

> Determine how much to ship from *each* factory to *each* warehouse so as to minimize cost.

7.7.3. Definition of the Variables. It is necessary to define a variable expressing the number of units shipped from each factory to each warehouse. Since there are three factories and four warehouses, there will be a total of $3 \times 4 = 12$ variables. The simplest way of naming the variables is to use two subscripts; one indicating the source (factory) and another indicating the destination (warehouse). Thus, we have:

	NUMBER OF UNITS SHIPPED	
Variable	*From Factory*	*To Warehouse*
x_{A1}	A	1
x_{A2}	A	2
x_{A3}	A	3
x_{A4}	A	4
x_{B1}	B	1
x_{B2}	B	2
x_{B3}	B	3
x_{B4}	B	4
x_{C1}	C	1
x_{C2}	C	2
x_{C3}	C	3
x_{C4}	C	4

7.7.4. The Constraints and the Objective Function. We will have two types of constraints. The first type will state that, for each factory, the sum of the shipments from that factory to all warehouses may not exceed the available units. The second type will state that, for each warehouse, the sum of shipments to that warehouse must be at least equal to its demand.

FACTORY CONSTRAINTS

$$\text{Factory } A: \quad x_{A1} + x_{A2} + x_{A3} + x_{A4} \leqslant 50$$

$$\text{Factory } B: \quad x_{B1} + x_{B2} + x_{B3} + x_{B4} \leqslant 55$$

$$\text{Factory } C: \quad x_{C1} + x_{C2} + x_{C3} + x_{C4} \leqslant 70$$

WAREHOUSE CONSTRAINTS

$$\text{Warehouse 1:} \quad x_{A1} + x_{B1} + x_{C1} \geqslant 30$$

$$\text{Warehouse 2:} \quad x_{A2} + x_{B2} + x_{C2} \geqslant 60$$

$$\text{Warehouse 3:} \quad x_{A3} + x_{B3} + x_{C3} \geqslant 20$$

$$\text{Warehouse 4:} \quad x_{A4} + x_{B4} + x_{C4} \geqslant 40$$

THE OBJECTIVE FUNCTION. The objective function must state the total cost of the shipments. Thus,

$$Z = 15x_{A1} + 18x_{A2} + 19x_{A3} + 13x_{A4}$$
$$+ 21x_{B1} + 14x_{B2} + 15x_{B3} + 17x_{B4}$$
$$+ 25x_{C1} + 12x_{C2} + 17x_{C3} + 22x_{C4}$$

The complete linear programming model is shown in Figure 7.7.2.

x_{A1} = Number of units shipped from factory A to warehouse 1

.
.
.

x_{C4} = Number of units shipped from factory C to warehouse 4

minimize $\left\{ Z = 15x_{A1} + 18x_{A2} + 19x_{A3} + 13x_{A4} + 21x_{B1} + 14x_{B2} + 15x_{B3} + 17x_{B4} \right.$
s.t. $\left. + 25x_{C1} + 12x_{C2} + 17x_{C3} + 22x_{C4} \right\}$

No.	Subject	Constraints			
1	Factory A	$x_{A1} + x_{A2} + x_{A3} + x_{A4}$			$\leqslant 50$
2	Factory B	$x_{B1} + x_{B2} + x_{B3} + x_{B4}$			$\leqslant 55$
3	Factory C	$x_{C1} + x_{C2} + x_{C3} + x_{C4}$			$\leqslant 70$
4	Warehouse 1	x_{A1}	$+ x_{B1}$	$+ x_{C1}$	$\geqslant 30$
5	Warehouse 2	x_{A2}	x_{B2}	$+ x_{C2}$	$\geqslant 60$
6	Warehouse 3	x_{A3}	x_{B3}	x_{C3}	$\geqslant 20$
7	Warehouse 4	x_{A4}	x_{B4}	x_{C4}	$\geqslant 40$

$$x_{A1}, x_{A2}, x_{A3}, x_{A4}, x_{B1}, x_{B2}, x_{B3}, x_{B4}, x_{C1}, x_{C2}, x_{C3}, x_{C4} \geqslant 0$$

FIGURE 7.7.2. *Linear programming model of the transportation problem.*

7.7.5. The Computer Solution. The model shown in Figure 7.7.2 is not in quite an acceptable form for submission to the computer program for solution. We have found it convenient to use variable names such as x_{A1}, x_{B1}, and so on. We shall have to convert them to simple variable numbers:

Variable Name	Variable Number	Variable Name	Variable Number
x_{A1}	1	x_{B3}	7
x_{A2}	2	x_{B4}	8
x_{A3}	3	x_{C1}	9
x_{A4}	4	x_{C2}	10
x_{B1}	5	x_{C3}	11
x_{B2}	6	x_{C4}	12

Second, our computer program maximizes and we wish to minimize. As previously discussed, all we need do is multiply the objective function by -1 and maximize. Thus we shall state the objective as

$$\text{maximize}\{ Z = -15x_1 - 18x_2 - 19x_3 - 13x_4 - 21x_5 - \cdots \}$$

The model is now in a proper form for submission to the computer program. The solution obtained from the program is shown in Figure 7.7.3.

Notice that the program has added slack variables 13–15 to the factory constraints and surplus variables 16–19 to the Warehouse constraints.

The solution is tabulated in Figure 7.7.4. The total cost is $2,070, the negative of our objective function. Notice further that not all the capacity of factories B and C will be used.

7.7.6. Sensitivity and Postoptimality Analysis. The only binding factory constraint is factory A (number 1), whereas all the warehouse constraints (numbers 4–7) are binding.

The shadow-price value of 4 for the factory A constraint (number 1) is interpreted as follows. If an additional unit of product is available from factory A (increase in right-hand side of 1 unit), the objective function will increase by 4. Since the objective function is the negative of cost, this means a decrease in cost of $4. This value applies for factory A capacity (right-hand side) up to a level of 70 units.

The shadow price of -19 for the warehouse 1 constraint (number 4) is interpreted as follows. If an increase in the required supply to warehouse 1 of 1 unit (increase in right-hand side) is made, the objective function will *decrease* by 19, that is, the cost will increase by $19. A similar analysis holds for the other warehouse constraints.

LINEAR PROGRAMMING

MAXIMIZE Z =

-15.000	-18.000	-19.000	-13.000	-21.000	-14.000	-15.000
-17.000	-25.000	-12.000	-17.000	-22.000		

SUBJECT TO THE FOLLOWING CONSTRAINTS

CONSTRAINT COEFFICIENTS

NO.	TYPE	RHS							
1	LE	50.000	1.000	1.000	0.0	0.0	0.0	0.0	0.0
			0.0	0.0	0.0	0.0	0.0		
2	LE	55.000	0.0	0.0	1.000	1.000	0.0	0.0	0.0
			1.000	1.000	0.0	0.0	0.0		
3	LE	70.000	0.0	0.0	0.0	0.0	1.000	1.000	1.000
			0.0	0.0	1.000	1.000	0.0		
4	GE	30.000	1.000	0.0	1.000	0.0	1.000	0.0	0.0
			0.0	0.0	0.0	0.0	0.0		
5	GE	60.000	0.0	0.0	0.0	0.0	0.0	0.0	0.0
			1.000	0.0	1.000	0.0	1.000		
6	GE	20.000	0.0	1.000	0.0	1.000	0.0	1.000	0.0
			0.0	0.0	0.0	0.0	0.0		
7	GE	40.000	0.0	0.0	0.0	0.0	0.0	0.0	1.000
			0.0	1.000	0.0	1.000	0.0		

VARIABLES
ORIGINAL VARIABLES 1 THROUGH 12
SLACK VARIABLES 13 THROUGH 15 ADDED TO CONSTRAINTS 1 THROUGH 3
SURPLUS VARIABLES 16 THROUGH 19 ADDED TO CONSTRAINTS 4 THROUGH 7
ARTIFICIAL VARIABLES 20 THROUGH 23 ADDED TO CONSTRAINTS 4 THROUGH 7

FIGURE 7.7.3. Transportation problem. Computer solution.

OBJECTIVE FUNCTION   -2070.000

BASIS VARIABLES   14   7   15   1   10   4   8

VARIABLE	SOLUTION VALUE	OBJECTIVE FUNCTION RANGES LOWER	GIVEN	UPPER
1	30.000	-17.000	-15.000	4.000
2	0.0	-999999.000	-18.000	-8.000
3	0.0	-999999.000	-19.000	-11.000
4	20.000	-17.000	-13.000	-11.000
5	0.0	-999999.000	-21.000	-19.000
6	0.0	-999999.000	-14.000	-12.000
7	20.000	-17.000	-15.000	0.0
8	20.000	-19.000	-17.000	-13.000
9	0.0	-999999.000	-25.000	-19.000
10	60.000	-14.000	-12.000	0.0
11	0.0	-999999.000	-17.000	-15.000
12	0.0	-999999.000	-22.000	-17.000
13	0.0	-999999.000	0.0	4.000
14	15.000	-2.000	0.0	2.000
15	10.000	-2.000	0.0	2.000
16	0.0	-999999.000	0.0	19.000
17	0.0	-999999.000	0.0	12.000
18	0.0	-999999.000	0.0	15.000
19	0.0	-999999.000	0.0	17.000

CONSTRAINT	SHADOW PRICE	RIGHT HAND SIDE RANGES LOWER	GIVEN	UPPER
1	4.000	35.000	50.000	70.000
2	0.0	40.000	55.000	999999.000
3	0.0	60.000	70.000	999999.000
4	-19.000	10.000	30.000	45.000
5	-12.000	0.0	60.000	70.000
6	-15.000	0.0	20.000	35.000
7	-17.000	20.000	40.000	55.000

FIGURE 7.7.3. *Continued.*

TO

		1	2	3	4	Slack	Total
F	A	$x_1 = 30$			$x_4 = 20$		50
R O	B			$x_7 = 20$	$x_8 = 20$	$x_{14} = 15$	55
M	C		$x_{10} = 60$			$x_{15} = 10$	70
Total:		30	60	20	40	25	

FIGURE 7.7.4. *Tabulation of solution for the transportation problem.*

Consider the effect of increasing the factory A Capacity above the limit of 70 units to 80 units. The solution is shown in Figure 7.7.5. The tabulation of the solution is shown in Figure 7.7.6. The cost is now $1,990, which is lower than previously. This is explained by the fact that

236

NEW RIGHT HAND SIDES
    80.000   55.000   70.000   30.000   60.000   20.000   40.000

OPTIMAL SOLUTION

OBJECTIVE FUNCTION   -1990.000

BASIS VARIABLES   13   7   15   1   10   4   14

VARIABLE	SOLUTION VALUE	OBJECTIVE FUNCTION RANGES		
		LOWER	GIVEN	UPPER
1	30.000	-21.000	-15.000	0.0
2	0.0	-999999.000	-18.000	-12.000
3	0.0	-999999.000	-19.000	-15.000
4	40.000	-17.000	-13.000	0.0
5	0.0	-999999.000	-21.000	-15.000
6	0.0	-999999.000	-14.000	-12.000
7	20.000	-17.000	-15.000	0.0
8	0.0	-999999.000	-17.000	-13.000
9	0.0	-999999.000	-25.000	-15.000
10	60.000	-14.000	-12.000	0.0
11	0.0	-999999.000	-17.000	-15.000
12	0.0	-999999.000	-22.000	-13.000
13	10.000	-4.000	0.0	4.000
14	35.000	-2.000	0.0	2.000
15	10.000	-2.000	0.0	2.000
16	0.0	-999999.000	0.0	15.000
17	0.0	-999999.000	0.0	12.000
18	0.0	-999999.000	0.0	15.000
19	0.0	-999999.000	0.0	13.000

CONSTRAINT	SHADOW PRICE	RIGHT HAND SIDE RANGES		
		LOWER	GIVEN	UPPER
1	0.0	70.000	80.000	999999.000
2	0.0	20.000	55.000	999999.000
3	0.0	60.000	70.000	999999.000
4	-15.000	0.0	30.000	40.000
5	-12.000	0.0	60.000	70.000
6	-15.000	0.0	20.000	55.000
7	-13.000	0.0	40.000	50.000

FIGURE 7.7.5. Transportation problem. Factory A availability increased to 80 units. Computer solution.

TO

		1	2	3	4	Slack	Total
F R O M	A	$x_1 = 30$			$x_4 = 40$	$x_{13} = 10$	80
	B			$x_7 = 20$		$x_{14} = 35$	55
	C		$x_{10} = 60$			$x_{15} = 10$	70
	Total:	30	60	20	40	55	

FIGURE 7.7.6. Tabulation of solution for the transportation problem. Factory A availability expanded to 80 units.

having extra capacity allows more freedom in the choice of less expensive routes. Notice, in addition, that none of the factory constraints (numbers 1, 2, and 3) are binding; each has excess capacity.

SECTION 7.8. *Blending Problem*

7.8.1. Statement of the Problem. A heating-oil distributor blends two grades of heating oil (regular and nontoxic) from three products (called distillates 1, 2, and 3) produced in the crude-oil refining process. The distillates are purchased from a local refinery. The heating oils are simply blends of the three distillates, but must conform to certain specifications particularly with regard to their sulfur content and vapor pressure. The data concerning the heating oils are shown in Table 7.8.1 and the data for the distillates is shown in Table 7.8.2. We assume that a blend of distillates has specifications (sulfur content, vapor pressure) equal to the weighted average of the components. This assumption is not in general true, for example, with octane rating.

TABLE 7.8.1. *Heating-Oil Data*

	Maximum Sulfur Content (grams / barrel)	Minimum Vapor Pressure	Maximum Distillate 3 Content (%)	Selling Price ($/barrel)	Maximum Monthly Sales (barrels)
Regular	14	6	80	12.00	10,000
Nontoxic	8	12	30	16.00	4,000

TABLE 7.8.2. *Distillate Data*

	Sulfur Content (grams / barrel)	Vapor Pressure	Cost ($/barrel)	Maximum Available (barrels / month)
Distillate 1	6	16	10.00	3,000
Distillate 2	10	8	14.00	2,000
Distillate 3	18	4	6.00	10,000

7.8.2. Statement of Objective. The heating-oil distributor wishes to know how to blend his heating oils each month so as to maximize profit. Let us be more specific in our statement of objective so as to better formulate the problem. Blending heating oil means combining certain quantities of distillates together. It is these quantities which truly specify the blend. Let us therefore state the objective as:

Determine how much of each distillate to combine (blend) in each heating oil so as to maximize profit.

7.8.3. Definition of the Variables. The variables must reflect the quantities of each distillate and its use, that is, for the regular or nontoxic heating-oil blend. Figure 7.8.1 portrays the blending operation and a logical way to define the decision variables. For example, let

$$x_{1R} = \text{number of barrels of distillate 1 used}$$
$$\text{to blend regular heating oil, etc.}$$

Thus, the variables of our problem are

$$x_{1R}, x_{2R}, x_{3R}, x_{1N}, x_{2N}, x_{3N}$$

and all have dimensions of number of barrels. This formulation of the decision variables leads to the simplest possible formulation of the constraints and objective function.

We could also define additional variables to represent the quantity of each distillate used and the quantity of each heating oil blended. For example, we could define x_1 as the quantity of distillate 1 used. We would then need a constraint which stated $x_1 = x_{1R} + x_{1N}$. This would only add variables and constraints to the problem. It will be much simpler to add together the values of x_{1R} and x_{1N} to find the quantity of distillate 1 used after a solution is obtained. The same is true for the quantities of the heating oils blended. For example, we would define x_R as the quantity of regular heating oil blended and have a constraint stating $x_R = x_{1R} + x_{2R} + x_{3R}$. Thus, we shall use only the variables shown in Figure 7.8.1.

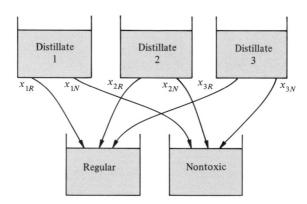

FIGURE 7.8.1. *Diagram of the blending operation.*

7.8.4. The Constraints and the Objective Function. We must formulate constraints which prevent the heating oils from being blended in a fashion that violates the specifications. As previously mentioned, we assume that when distillates are blended, the mixture has a specification (sulfur content or vapor pressure) which is the weighted average of the combined distillates. For example, if we mixed 1 barrel of distillate 1 (sulfur content 6) with 2 barrels of distillate 2 (sulfur content 10) with 3 barrels of distillate 3 (sulfur content 18), the resulting blend would have a sulfur content equal to

$$\frac{(6)(1)+(10)(2)+(18)(3)}{1+2+3} = \frac{6+20+54}{6} = \frac{80}{6} = 13.3$$

MAXIMUM SULFUR CONTENT

Regular heating oil—sulfur content may not exceed 14 grams/barrel

$$\frac{6x_{1R}+10x_{2R}+18x_{3R}}{x_{1R}+x_{2R}+x_{3R}} \leqslant 14$$

$$6x_{1R}+10x_{2R}+18x_{3R} \leqslant 14(x_{1R}+x_{2R}+x_{3R})$$

$$-8x_{1R}-4x_{2R}+4x_{3R} \leqslant 0$$

which is an acceptable linear inequality constraint.

Nontoxic heating oil—sulfur content may not exceed 8 grams/barrel:

$$\frac{6x_{1N}+10x_{2N}+18x_{3N}}{x_{1N}+x_{2N}+x_{3N}} \leqslant 8$$

$$6x_{1N}+10x_{2N}+18x_{3N} \leqslant 8(x_{1N}+x_{2N}+x_{3N})$$

$$-2x_{1N}+2x_{2N}+10x_{3N} \leqslant 0$$

MINIMUM VAPOR PRESSURE

Regular heating oil—minimum vapor pressure is 6.

$$\frac{16x_{1R}+8x_{2R}+4x_{3R}}{x_{1R}+x_{2R}+x_{3R}} \geqslant 6$$

$$16x_{1R}+8x_{2R}+4x_{3R} \geqslant 6(x_{1R}+x_{2R}+x_{3R})$$

$$10x_{1R}+2x_{2R}-2x_{3R} \geqslant 0$$

Nontoxic heating oil—minimum vapor pressure is 12.

$$\frac{16x_{1N}+8x_{2N}+4x_{3N}}{x_{1N}+x_{2N}+x_{3N}} \geqslant 12$$

$$16x_{1N}+8x_{2N}+4x_{3N} \geqslant 12(x_{1N}+x_{2N}+x_{3N})$$

$$4x_{1N}-4x_{2N}-8x_{3N} \geqslant 0$$

MAXIMUM DISTILLATE 3 CONTENT

Regular heating oil—80%.

$$\frac{x_{3R}}{x_{1R}+x_{2R}+x_{3R}} \leqslant 0.8$$

$$x_{3R} \leqslant 0.8(x_{1R}+x_{2R}+x_{3R})$$

$$-0.8x_{1R}-0.8x_{2R}+0.2x_{3R} \leqslant 0$$

Nontoxic heating oil—30%.

$$\frac{x_{3N}}{x_{1N}+x_{2N}+x_{3N}} \leqslant 0.3$$

$$x_{3N} \leqslant 0.3(x_{1N}+x_{2N}+x_{3N})$$

$$-0.3x_{1N}-0.3x_{2N}+0.7x_{3N} \leqslant 0$$

MAXIMUM HEATING-OIL SALES. Recall that each barrel of distillate mixed into a heating oil becomes a barrel of heating oil (see Figure 7.8.1). The total amount of heating oil blended is thus the sum of the amounts of distillate blended.

Regular heating oil—maximum sales 10,000.

$$x_{1R}+x_{2R}+x_{3R} \leqslant 10,000$$

Nontoxic heating oil—maximum sales 4,000.

$$x_{1N}+x_{2N}+x_{3N} \leqslant 4,000$$

MAXIMUM DISTILLATE AVAILABILITY. In a similar fashion, the total amount of each distillate used is the sum of the amount used to blend regular and nontoxic heating oils.

Distillate 1—maximum availability 3,000 barrels.

$$x_{1R}+x_{1N} \leqslant 3,000$$

Distillate 2—maximum availability 2,000 barrels.

$$x_{2R}+x_{2N} \leqslant 2,000$$

Distillate 3—maximum availability 10,000 barrels.

$$x_{3R}+x_{3N} \leqslant 10,000$$

OBJECTIVE FUNCTION. To find the objective function we must find the profit associated with each activity (variable). For example, what profit is obtained by taking 1 barrel of distillate 1 and adding it to the regular blend? This additional barrel of distillate 1 costs the company $10. It increases the volume of regular heating oil by 1 barrel, which is sold for $12. The net profit equals $12 - 10 = \$2/\text{barrel}$. Thus, for each variable the objective function coefficient (profit) is revenue minus cost.

$$Z = (12-10)x_{1R} + (12-14)x_{2R} + (12-6)x_{3R} + (16-10)x_{1N}$$

$$+ (16-14)x_{2N} + (16-6)x_{3N}$$

$$= 2x_{1R} - 2x_{2R} + 6x_{3R} + 6x_{1N} + 2x_{2N} + 10x_{3N}$$

The complete formulation is shown in Figure 7.8.2. We have placed the minimum vapor-pressure constraints, which are "greater-thans," last, as required by the computer program.

x_{1R} = No. of barrels of distillate 1 to be blended into regular heating oil

$\vdots$

x_{3N} = No. of barrels of distillate 2 to be blended into non-toxic heating oil

maximize $\{Z = 2x_{1R} - 2x_{2R} + 6x_{3R} + 6x_{1N} + 2x_{2N} + 10x_{3N}\}$
s.t.

No.	Subject	Constraints	
	Max Sulphur Content		
1	Regular	$-8x_{1R} - 4x_{2R} + 4x_{3R}$	$\leqslant 0$
2	Nontoxic	$-2x_{1N} + 2x_{2N} + 10x_{3N}$	$\leqslant 0$
	Max Distillate 3 Content		
3	Regular	$-0.8x_{1R} - 0.8x_{2R} + 0.2x_{3R}$	$\leqslant 0$
4	Nontoxic	$-0.3x_{3N} - 0.3x_{2N} + 0.7x_{3N}$	$\leqslant 0$
	Max Sales		
5	Regular	$x_{1R} + x_{2R} + x_{3R}$	$\leqslant 10,000$
6	Nontoxic	$+ x_{1N} + x_{2N} + x_{3N}$	$\leqslant 4,000$
	Max Availability		
7	Distillate 1	$x_{1R} + x_{1N}$	$\leqslant 3,000$
8	Distillate 2	$x_{2R} + x_{2N}$	$\leqslant 2,000$
9	Distillate 3	$x_{3R} + x_{3N}$	$\leqslant 10,000$
	Min Vapor Pressure		$\geqslant 0$
10	Regular	$10x_{1R} + 2x_{2R} - 2x_{3R}$	
11	Nontoxic	$4x_{1N} - 4x_{2N} - 8x_{3N}$	$\geqslant 0$

$$x_{1R} \cdot x_{2R} \cdot x_{3R} \cdot x_{1N} \cdot x_{2N} \cdot x_{3N} \geqslant 0$$

FIGURE 7.8.2. *Linear programming formulation of the blending problem.*

7.8.5. The Computer Solution. The model as shown in Figure 7.8.2 is in an acceptable form for submission to our computer program except for the names of the variables. Therefore, we make the following equivalences:

Variable Number	Variable Name
1	x_{1R}
2.	x_{2R}
3	x_{3R}
4	x_{1N}
5	x_{2N}
6	x_{3N}

The computer solution is shown in Figure 7.8.3. Notice that the program has added slack variables 7–15 to the first 9 constraints and surplus variables 16 and 17 to constraints 10 and 11. A tabulation of the solution is shown in Figure 7.8.4.

Notice that 3,800 barrels of distillate 3 are unused and will not be purchased. Also, 2,800 barrels of demand for nontoxic fuel will be unfilled. Clearly, there is no way to use the excess 3,800 barrels of distillate 3 in a profitable manner and still meet the specifications.

7.8.6. Sensitivity and Postoptimality Analysis. The binding constraints are: regular sulfur content (number 1), nontoxic sulfur content (number 2), regular maximum sales (number 5), distillate 1 availability (number 7), and distillate 2 availability (number 8). The shadow price for distillate 1 availability (constraint 7) of $8 is quite high. This indicates that each additional barrel of distillate 1 (purchased at $10 per barrel) would increase profit by $8, and this would apply up to a level of 5,333 barrels of distillate 1 available, the right-hand-side upper limit. This means that a premium of up to $8 should be paid for extra distillate 1, that is, up to $10 + 8 = \$18$ per barrel. Let us perform a computer run assuming an additional 1,000 barrels of distillate 1 are available (i.e., 4,000 barrels is available). The computer solution is shown in Figure 7.8.5. Notice that the new optimal profit is $52,000, which is $8,000 higher than previously. The increase is, in fact, equal to the 1,000 additional barrels times the shadow price of $8.00.

LINEAR PROGRAMMING

MAXIMIZE Z =

SUBJECT TO THE FOLLOWING CONSTRAINTS

CONSTRAINT COEFFICIENTS

NO.	TYPE	RHS	2.000	-2.000	6.000	6.000	2.000	10.000
1	LE	0.0	-8.000	-4.000	4.000	0.0	0.0	0.0
2	LE	0.0	0.0	0.0	0.0	-2.000	2.000	10.000
3	LE	0.0	-0.800	-0.800	0.200	0.0	0.0	0.0
4	LE	0.0	0.0	0.0	0.0	-0.300	-0.300	0.700
5	LE	10000.000	1.000	1.000	1.000	0.0	0.0	0.0
6	LE	4000.000	0.0	0.0	0.0	1.000	1.000	1.000
7	LE	3000.000	1.000	0.0	0.0	1.000	0.0	0.0
8	LE	2000.000	0.0	1.000	0.0	0.0	1.000	0.0
9	LE	10000.000	0.0	0.0	1.000	0.0	0.0	1.000
10	GE	0.0	10.000	2.000	-2.000	0.0	0.0	0.0
11	GE	0.0	0.0	0.0	0.0	4.000	-4.000	-8.000

VARIABLES
ORIGINAL VARIABLES 1 THROUGH 6
SLACK VARIABLES 7 THROUGH 15 ADDED TO CONSTRAINTS 1 THROUGH 9
SURPLUS VARIABLES 16 THROUGH 17 ADDED TO CONSTRAINTS 10 THROUGH 11
ARTIFICIAL VARIABLES 18 THROUGH 19 ADDED TO CONSTRAINTS 10 THROUGH 11

FIGURE 7.8.3. Blending problem. Computer solution.

OBJECTIVE FUNCTION   43999.977

BASIS VARIABLES   3   6   9   10   16   12   17   2   15   1   4

VARIABLE	SOLUTION VALUE	OBJECTIVE FUNCTION RANGES		
		LOWER	GIVEN	UPPER
1	2000.001	−4.000	2.000	14.000
2	2000.000	−999999.000	−2.000	999999.000
3	6000.000	3.000	6.000	999999.000
4	999.999	−2.000	6.000	12.000
5	0.0	−999999.000	2.000	2.000
6	200.000	−0.000	10.000	40.000
7	0.0	−999999.000	0.0	1.000
8	0.0	−999999.000	0.0	1.000
9	1999.999	−15.000	0.0	12.000
10	160.000	−50.000	0.0	14.286
11	0.0	−999999.000	0.0	2.000
12	2800.004	−5.000	0.0	6.667
13	0.0	−999999.000	0.0	8.000
14	0.0	−999999.000	0.0	0.0
15	3799.996	−999999.000	0.0	3.333
16	12000.016	−1.000	0.0	1.000
17	2400.000	−3.333	0.0	1.250

CONSTRAINT	SHADOW PRICE	RIGHT HAND SIDE RANGES		
		LOWER	GIVEN	UPPER
1	1.000	−11999.941	0.0	12000.004
2	1.000	−1999.999	0.0	2285.713
3	0.0	−1999.999	0.0	999999.000
4	0.0	−160.000	0.0	999999.000
5	2.000	4000.004	10000.000	12999.988
6	0.0	1199.996	4000.000	999999.000
7	8.000	2000.002	3000.000	5333.336
8	0.0	500.004	2000.000	5000.000
9	0.0	6200.004	10000.000	999999.000
10	0.0	−999999.000	0.0	12000.016
11	0.0	−999999.000	0.0	2400.000

FIGURE 7.8.3. *continued.*

DISTILLATE		TO		Slack (unused distillate)	*Total Distillate*
		Regular	Nontoxic		
	1	$x_1 = 2,000$	$x_4 = 1,000$	$x_{13} = 0$	3,000
	2	$x_2 = 2,000$	$x_5 = 0$	$x_{14} = 0$	2,000
	3	$x_3 = 6,000$	$x_6 = 200$	$x_{15} = 3,800$	10,000
Slack (unfilled demand)		$x_{11} = 0$	$x_{12} = 2,800$		
	Total Product	10,000	4,000		

FIGURE 7.8.4. *Tabulation of solution for the blending problem.*

NEW RIGHT HAND SIDES
0.0   0.0   0.0   0.0   10000.000   4000.000   4000.000   2000.000   10000.000   0.0   0.0

OPTIMAL SOLUTION

OBJECTIVE FUNCTION   51999.980

BASIS VARIABLES   3   6   9   10   12   17   16   2   15   1   4

VARIABLE	SOLUTION VALUE	OBJECTIVE FUNCTION RANGES		
		LOWER	GIVEN	UPPER
1	2000.000	-4.000	2.000	14.000
2	2000.000	-999999.000	-2.000	999999.000
3	5999.996	3.000	6.000	999999.000
4	2000.000	-2.000	6.000	12.000
5	0.0	-999999.000	2.000	2.000
6	400.000	0.000	10.000	40.000
7	0.0	-999999.000	0.0	1.000
8	0.0	-999999.000	0.0	1.000
9	1999.998	-15.000	0.0	12.000
10	320.000	-50.000	0.0	14.286
11	0.0	-999999.000	0.0	2.000
12	1600.000	-5.000	0.0	6.667
13	0.0	-999999.000	0.0	8.000
14	0.0	-999999.000	0.0	0.0
15	3599.997	-999999.000	0.0	3.333
16	12000.004	-1.000	0.0	1.000
17	4799.996	-3.333	0.0	1.250

CONSTRAINT	SHADOW PRICE	RIGHT HAND SIDE RANGES		
		LOWER	GIVEN	UPPER
1	1.000	-23999.973	0.0	12000.004
2	1.000	-4000.001	0.0	4571.430
3	0.0	-1999.998	0.0	999999.000
4	0.0	-320.000	0.0	999999.000
5	2.000	5999.996	10000.000	15999.992
6	0.0	2400.000	4000.000	999999.000
7	8.000	2000.001	4000.000	5333.332
8	0.0	0.000	2000.000	4000.001
9	0.0	6400.000	10000.000	999999.000
10	0.0	-999999.000	0.0	12000.004
11	0.0	-999999.000	0.0	4799.996

FIGURE 7.8.5. Blending problem. Distillate 1 availability increased to 4000 barrels. Computer solution.

7.9.1. Statement of the Problem. An investor is considering several investments which extend over the next 5 years, at which time he will need all his capital. The investments are all to be made only on the first day of each year. The investments are:

1. Investment A, which is available on the first of each year and yields a 15% return at the end of 2 years.
2. Investment B, which is available only 2 years from now (the beginning of the third year) and yields a 25% return at the end of 3 years. The maximum the investor will consider is $40,000.
3. Investment C, which is available only 1 year from now (the beginning of the second year) and yields a 40% return at the end of 4 years. The maximum investment, however, is $30,000.
4. One-year government bonds, paying 6%/year.

The investor currently has $100,000 to invest.

7.9.2. Statement of Objective. This problem is considered dynamic; that is, we are concerned with the performance of the investment over time. For example, we must decide on how much to invest in government bonds at the beginning of each year. The objective is therefore:

Determine how much to invest in each investment at each point in time so as to maximize his cash in hand at the end of the 5-year period.

7.9.3. Definition of the Variables. We need variables which indicate the amount of money invested in each investment (A, B, C, or government bonds) at each point in time. Let us use a time scale calling the beginning of the first year (now) point-in-time 1, the beginning of the second year point-in-time 2, and so on. The end of the planning horizon is the end of year 5 or the beginning of year 6.

Our decision variables will have to indicate both time $(1, 2, \ldots, 6)$ and investment (A, B, C, and G for government bonds). One convenient method is to use variables with two subscripts: the first indicating which point-in-time and the second indicating which investment. For example, x_{1A} is the amount of money invested in investment A at the beginning of the first year. We also need a variable to express the return to the investor at the end of the fifth year. Let us call this x_{6R}. Table 7.9.1 illustrates the possible investments and their points in time. We assume that all money returned during the 5-year period is immediately reinvested so as to increase his return at the end. Notice that variable x_{5B} is not allowed, since it would return the funds 1 year after the end.

Since the investments will tend to be large numbers, let us define them in terms of thousands of dollars ($000). Thus,

$$x_{1A} = \text{investment in } A \text{ at time period 1 (\$000)}$$

$$\vdots \qquad\qquad \vdots$$

$$x_{6R} = \text{return to the investor at the end of}$$
$$\text{the fifth year (\$000)}$$

TABLE 7.9.1. *Investment and Variables Dynamic Investment Problem*

Point in Time	1	2	3	4	5	6
Investments	x_{1A}	x_{2A}	x_{3A}	x_{4A}	x_{5G}	Return x_{6R}
	x_{1G}	x_{2C}	x_{3B}	x_{4G}		
		x_{2G}	x_{3G}			

7.9.4. The Constraints and the Objective Function. We shall need a constraint for each point in time to balance the flow of cash, to be certain that investments are less than or equal to cash available. Although he will always invest all available cash (i.e., we could use an equality constraint), no harm is done by using a less-than constraint. At the beginning of the first year the cash available is simply the investor's $100,000. After that, the cash available is the sum of returns of all investments which end at that point in time. All investments that end at the end of the fifth year will constitute the investor's total cash in hand (x_{6R}), since all intermediate returns are reinvested.

YEAR 1

Σ investments $\leqslant$ available cash

$$x_{1A} + x_{1G} \leqslant 100$$

Note that the right-hand side is 100 (not 100,000) since the variables are defined in terms of thousands of dollars.

YEAR 2

Σ investments $\leqslant$ available cash

In this case the available cash is only the money that is returned to the investor from his investment in government bonds in year 1 (x_{1G}). Since government bonds pay 6% interest, the amount he receives after 1 year is 1.06 times the amount invested (i.e., $1.06x_{1G}$). Therefore,

$$x_{2A} + x_{2C} + x_{2G} \leqslant 1.06x_{1G}$$

Subtracting the right-hand side from both sides gives

$$-1.06x_{1G} + x_{2A} + x_{2C} + x_{2G} \leqslant 0$$

which is an acceptable linear inequality constraint.

YEAR 3

Σ investments $\leqslant$ available cash

In this case the available cash is from two sources, x_{2G} and x_{1A}, since investment A has a 2-year life. Thus,

$$x_{3A} + x_{3B} + x_{3G} \leqslant 1.15x_{1A} + 1.06x_{2G}$$

$$-1.15x_{1A} - 1.06x_{2G} + x_{3A} + x_{3B} + x_{3G} \leqslant 0$$

YEAR 4

Σ investments $\leqslant$ available cash

$$x_{4A} + x_{4G} \leqslant 1.15x_{2A} + 1.06x_{3G}$$

$$-1.15x_{2A} - 1.06x_{3G} + x_{4A} + x_{4G} \leqslant 0$$

YEAR 5

Σ investments $\leqslant$ available cash

$$x_{5G} \leqslant 1.15x_{3A} + 1.06x_{4G}$$

$$-1.15x_{3A} - 1.06x_{4G} + x_{5G} \leqslant 0$$

END OF YEAR 5.   We must set our return variable (x_{6R}) equal to the cash available.

$$1.15x_{4A} + 1.40x_{2C} + 1.25x_{3B} + 1.06x_{5G} = x_{6R}$$

$$1.15x_{4A} + 1.40x_{2C} + 1.25x_{3B} + 1.06x_{5G} - x_{6R} = 0$$

MAXIMUM B INVESTMENT.   The maximum investment in B is \$40,000; therefore,

$$x_{3B} \leqslant 40$$

since the variables are defined in terms of thousands of dollars.

MAXIMUM C INVESTMENT

$$x_{2C} \leqslant 30$$

THE OBJECTIVE FUNCTION.   The investor wishes to maximize his cash in hand at the end of the 5 years. We have already defined a variable expressing this quantity (x_{6R}); therefore,

$$Z = x_{6R}$$

The complete linear programming formulation is shown in Figure 7.9.1. Notice that we have placed all less-than constraints first, which is a requirement of the computer program we are using.

x_{1A} = Investment in A at the beginning of year 1, etc.

.
.
.

x_{6R} = Return to the investor at the end of year 5 (beginning of year 6)

maximize $\{Z = \qquad\qquad\qquad\qquad\qquad\qquad x_{6R}\}$
s.t.

No.	Subject	Constraints	
1	Year 1	$x_{1A} + x_{1G}$	$\leqslant 100$
2	Year 2	$-2.06x_{1G} + x_{2A} + x_{2C} + x_{2G}$	$\leqslant 0$
3	Year 3	$-1.15x_{1A} \qquad\qquad -1.06x_{2G} + x_{3A} + x_{3B} + x_{3G}$	$\leqslant 0$
4	Year 4	$-1.15x_{2A} \qquad\qquad -1.06x_{3G} + x_{4A} + x_{4G}$	$\leqslant 0$
5	Year 5	$-1.15x_{3A} \qquad\qquad -1.06x_{4G} + x_{5G}$	$\leqslant 0$
6	Max B	x_{3B}	$\leqslant 40$
7	Max C	x_{2C}	$\leqslant 30$
8	Return	$1.4x_{2C} \qquad +1.25x_{3B} \qquad\qquad +1.06x_{5G} - x_{6R}$	$= 0$

$x_{1A}, x_{1G}, x_{2A}, x_{2C}, x_{2G}, x_{3A}, x_{3B}, x_{3G}, x_{4A}, x_{4G}, x_{5G}, x_{6R} \geqslant 0$

FIGURE 7.9.1. *Linear programming model of the dynamic investment problem.*

7.9.5. The Computer Solution.
The model as shown is in an acceptable form for submission to our computer program, except that the variable names are inconsistent with those used by the program which uses only variable numbers. Let us make the following equivalences:

Variable Names	Variable Number	Variable Names	Variable Number
x_{1A}	1	x_{3B}	7
x_{1G}	2	x_{3G}	8
x_{2A}	3	x_{4A}	9
x_{2C}	4	x_{4G}	10
x_{2G}	5	x_{5G}	11
x_{3A}	6	x_{6R}	12

The solution is shown in Figure 7.9.2. Notice that the program has added slack variables 13–19 to the less-than constraints. A tabulation of the solution is shown in Table 7.9.2. The net return to the investor at the end of the fifth year is $143,750, or 43.75% over 5 years.

LINEAR PROGRAMMING

MAXIMIZE Z =

0.0 / 0.0	0.0 / 0.0	0.0 / 0.0	0.0 / 0.0	0.0 / 1.000	0.0	0.0

SUBJECT TO THE FOLLOWING CONSTRAINTS

CONSTRAINT COEFFICIENTS

NO.	TYPE	RHS							
1	LE	100.000	1.000 / 0.0	1.000 / 0.0	0.0 / 0.0	0.0 / 0.0	0.0 / 0.0	0.0	0.0
2	LE	0.0	0.0 / 0.0	-1.060 / 0.0	1.000 / 0.0	1.000 / 0.0	1.000 / 0.0	0.0	0.0
3	LE	0.0	-1.150 / 1.000	0.0 / 0.0	0.0 / 0.0	0.0 / 0.0	-1.060 / 0.0	1.000	1.000
4	LE	0.0	0.0 / -1.060	0.0 / 1.000	-1.150 / 1.000	0.0 / 0.0	0.0 / 0.0	0.0	0.0
5	LE	0.0	0.0 / 0.0	0.0 / 0.0	0.0 / -1.060	0.0 / 1.000	0.0 / 0.0	-1.150	0.0
6	LE	40.000	0.0 / 0.0	0.0 / 0.0	0.0 / 0.0	0.0 / 0.0	0.0 / 0.0	0.0	1.000
7	LE	30.000	0.0 / 0.0	0.0 / 0.0	0.0 / 0.0	1.000 / 0.0	0.0 / 0.0	0.0	0.0
8	EQ	0.0	0.0 / 0.0	0.0 / 1.150	0.0 / 0.0	1.400 / 1.060	0.0 / -1.000	0.0	1.250

VARIABLES
ORIGINAL VARIABLES 1 THROUGH 12
SLACK VARIABLES 13 THROUGH 19 ADDED TO CONSTRAINTS 1 THROUGH 7
ARTIFICIAL VARIABLES 20 THROUGH 20 ADDED TO CONSTRAINTS 8 THROUGH 8

FIGURE 7.9.2. Dynamic investment problem. Computer solution.

OPTIMAL SOLUTION

OBJECTIVE FUNCTION   143.750

BASIS VARIABLES   3   12   7   9   11   1   2   4

| VARIABLE | SOLUTION VALUE | OBJECTIVE FUNCTION RANGES | | |
		LOWER	GIVEN	UPPER
1	34.783	-0.033	0.0	1.402
2	65.217	-1.402	0.0	0.033
3	39.130	-1.322	0.0	0.034
4	30.000	-0.078	0.0	999999.000
5	0.0	-999999.000	0.0	0.030
6	0.0	-999999.000	0.0	0.0
7	40.000	-0.031	0.0	999999.000
8	0.0	-999999.000	0.0	0.0
9	45.000	-0.026	0.0	0.029
10	0.0	-999999.000	0.0	0.026
11	0.0	-1.060	0.0	0.025
12	143.750	0.0	1.000	999999.000
13	0.0	-999999.000	0.0	1.402
14	0.0	-999999.000	0.0	1.322
15	0.0	-999999.000	0.0	1.219
16	0.0	-999999.000	0.0	1.150
17	0.0	-999999.000	0.0	1.060
18	0.0	-999999.000	0.0	0.031
19	0.0	-999999.000	0.0	0.078

| CONSTRAINT | SHADOW PRICE | RIGHT HAND SIDE RANGES | | |
		LOWER	GIVEN	UPPER
1	1.402	63.085	100.000	999999.000
2	1.322	-39.130	0.0	999999.000
3	1.219	-42.453	0.0	40.000
4	1.150	-45.000	0.0	999999.000
5	1.060	0.0	0.0	999999.000
6	0.031	0.000	40.000	82.453
7	0.078	0.000	30.000	69.130
8	-1.000	-999999.000	0.0	143.750

FIGURE 7.9.2. Continued.

TABLE 7.9.2. Tabulation of Solution to Dynamic Investment Problem

Variable	Variable Number	Amount Invested($)
1	x_{1A}	34,783
2	x_{1G}	65,217
3	x_{2A}	39,130
4	x_{2C}	30,000
5	x_{2G}	0
6	x_{3A}	0
7	x_{3B}	40,000
8	x_{3G}	0
9	x_{4A}	45,000
10	x_{4G}	0
11	x_{5G}	0

7.9.6. Sensitivity and Postoptimality Analysis. All constraints are binding, as indicated by their nonzero shadow prices. Of primary interest are the cash constraint (number 1), the maximum B constraint (number 6), and the maximum C constraint (number 7). The shadow price of 1.402 for the cash constraint (number 1) indicates that each additional $1,000 available for investment will return $1,402 at the end of 5 years. This value is valid for any additional amount of cash, as indicated by the right-hand-side upper limit being 999,999. The shadow price for the maximum B constraint (number 6) of 0.031 indicates that for each *additional* $1,000 of investment in B above $30,000 that we allow, the return (objective function) will go up by (0.031)(1,000), or $31. This increment is valid for B investments up to $82,453. A similar analysis applies for the maximum C constraint (number 7).

Let us verify the shadow-price value for the cash constraint by increasing the available cash from $100,000 to $110,000 (i.e., increase the

NEW RIGHT HAND SIDES

110.000	0.0	0.0	0.0	0.0	40.000	30.000	0.0

OPTIMAL SOLUTION

OBJECTIVE FUNCTION   157.768

BASIS VARIABLES   3 12   7   9 11   1   2   4

VARIABLE	SOLUTION VALUE	OBJECTIVE FUNCTION RANGES LOWER	GIVEN	UPPER
1	34.783	−0.033	0.0	1.402
2	75.217	−1.402	0.0	0.033
3	49.730	−1.322	0.0	0.034
4	30.000	−0.078	0.0	999999.000
5	0.0	−999999.000	0.0	0.030
6	0.0	−999999.000	0.0	0.0
7	40.000	−0.031	0.0	999999.000
8	0.0	−999999.000	0.0	0.0
9	57.190	−0.026	0.0	0.029
10	0.0	−999999.000	0.0	0.026
11	0.0	−1.060	0.0	0.025
12	157.768	0.0	1.000	999999.000
13	0.0	−999999.000	0.0	1.402
14	0.0	−999999.000	0.0	1.322
15	0.0	−999999.000	0.0	1.219
16	0.0	−999999.000	0.0	1.150
17	0.0	−999999.000	0.0	1.060
18	0.0	−999999.000	0.0	0.031
19	0.0	−999999.000	0.0	0.078

CONSTRAINT	SHADOW PRICE	RIGHT HAND SIDE RANGES LOWER	GIVEN	UPPER
1	1.402	63.085	110.000	999999.000
2	1.322	−49.730	0.0	999999.000
3	1.219	−53.953	0.0	40.000
4	1.150	−57.190	0.0	999999.000
5	1.060	0.0	0.0	999999.000
6	0.031	0.000	40.000	93.953
7	0.078	0.000	30.000	79.730
8	−1.000	−999999.000	0.0	157.768

FIGURE 7.9.3. *Dynamic investment problem. Cash available increased to $110,000. Computer solution.*

right-hand side of constraint 1 from 100 to 110). The computer solution is shown in Figure 7.9.3. The new objective function value is $14,020 higher than previously (neglecting rounding errors) as could be predicted by using the shadow price [i.e., $(1.402)(10) = 14.02$ thousands of dollars]. The additional money has gone into government bonds in year 1 (x_{1G} or variable 1) and A investments in years 2 and 4 (variables x_{2A} and x_{4A} or numbers 3 and 9).

SECTION 7.10. *Summary*

This chapter has presented a wide variety of decision problems which were formulated as linear programming problems and solved using the computer. This procedure is similar to the manner in which such decision problems are usually treated in practice. These problems have demonstrated both the relevance of linear programming to decision making and the techniques of formulation.

Each solution has been analyzed to reveal its basic structure. Sensitivity analysis was discussed to reveal its importance in the decision-making process. Additional runs (postoptimality analysis) were performed to indicate the types of further investigations that would be performed by the practitioner in a realistic case study. It is only through exercises such as these that one can come to understand linear programming and its importance.

PROBLEMS

For the following problems:

(1) Formulate the linear programming model of the problem.
(2) Solve the problem using the computer.
(3) State the solution.
(4) Determine which constraints (resources, restrictions, etc.) are binding and discuss the economic implication of all slack and surplus variables.
(5) Perform sensitivity analysis; that is, discuss the economic implication of all shadow prices, right-hand-side ranges, and objective function ranges.
(6) Perform postoptimality analysis; that is, perform additional runs, changing various restrictions and per-unit cost or profit values to determine the effect of such changes.

7.1. XYZ Automobile Engine Block Company makes three sizes of engine blocks—compact, standard, and luxury—which are sold to the auto industry. The blocks are made by casting steel and then milling and polishing. The per-unit utilization of steel and the casting, milling, and polishing shop time per unit are shown in Figure P7.1. Next month there

	Compact	Standard	Luxury
Steel (lb)	300	400	1,000
Casting Hours	3	5	9
Milling Hours	4	5	7
Polishing Hours	4	7	8

FIGURE P7.1

are 56,000 lb of steel, 620 casting hours, 600 milling hours, and 670 polishing hours available. The company has existing contracts with one automaker to deliver 20 compact blocks and 30 standard blocks per month. Per-unit profits are $20 for compact, $50 for standard, and $80 for luxury blocks.

7.2. (Problem 7.1 continued). Assume that the company operates two separate plants, which both produce the identical engine blocks and require the same resources per block produced. The second plant has 6000 lb of steel, 900 casting hours, 850 milling hours, and 400 polishing hours available next month.

7.3. The Midland Airfreight Company plans to sell its old propeller freight airplanes and invest in new jets. Three types are being considered: large, medium, and small. The company has $120 million available for purchase of the airplanes. The large jets cost $8 million each, the medium cost $5 million each, and the small $2 million each. The company has sufficient pilots to operate 30 airplanes of any type. If only small planes were purchased, the company could maintain 60 planes. However, medium planes require 50% more maintenance than small planes, and the larger ones require $2\frac{1}{2}$ times as much maintenance as the small. Freight shipments are measured in ton-miles. The large planes can transport 450,000 ton-miles/month, the medium planes can transport 200,000 ton-miles/month, and the small ones can transport 80,000 ton-miles/month. Freight rates are 20 cents/ton-mile. The company anticipates a demand of 7 million ton-miles/month. Large planes cost $70,000 per month to operate, medium planes cost $30,000 per month to operate, and small planes cost $10,000 per month to operate.

7.4. (Problem 7.3 continued) Assume that the company has fixed contracts to ship the 7 million ton-miles/month. If they cannot ship all the demand themselves, they must meet the contract by shipping the excess with a competitor at a net loss of 20 cents/ton-mile.

7.5. A chemical company manufactures a product (X) which can be made by processing any (or all) of three raw-material ores. Each pound of ore 1 yields 0.7 lb of X, ore 2 yields 0.4 lb of X, and ore 3 yields 0.6 lb of X. Processing a pound of ore 1 requires 3 hours of distillation; ore 2 requires 2 hours of distillation; ore 3 requires 4 hours of distillation. Each

255

pound of X produced requires 2 hours of cleaning of processed raw materials (1, 2, or 3). There are 4,000 hours available on the distillation unit next month and 2,000 hours available on the cleaning unit next month. Available for purchase next month are 500 lb of ore 1, 1,000 lb of ore 2, and 800 lb of ore 3. Ore 1 costs $4 per pound, ore 2 costs $2 per pound, ore 3 costs $5 per pound. A pound of product X sells for $10. At least 600 lb of X must be produced, but all that is produced can be sold.

7.6. (Problem 7.5 continued) Assume that a by-product of the distillation process which was previously discarded can now be sold for $20 per pound. Each pound of this new product (Y) requires 1 hour of cleaning. When ore 1 is processed, 2% of the yield is product Y; when ore 2 is processed, 40% of the yield is product Y, when ore 3 is processed, 10% of the yield is product Y.

7.7. The Consolidated Grain Company owns two farms, one in Iowa and one in Indiana. The Iowa farm is 300 acres, has available water of 250,000 gallons per season, and costs $100 per planted acre per season to operate. The Indiana farm is 240 acres, has available water of 400,000 gallons per season, and costs $200 per planted acre to operate. Consolidated plants three crops on these farms: wheat, corn, and barley. They estimate that wheat will sell for $25/bushel, requires 1,000 gallons of water per acre, and yields 20 bushels/acre. Corn will sell for $20/bushel, requires 1,500 gallons of water per acre, and yields 15 bushels/acre. Barley will sell for $15/bushel, requires 1,800 gallons of water per acre, and yields 40 bushels/acre. The company forecasts a maximum demand for wheat of 5,000 bushels; for corn, 6,000 bushels; and for barley, 4,000 bushels. However, at least 2,000 bushels of wheat is necessary.

7.8. Acme Dairies is planning its feed mix for their dairy cows. The cows are fed a mixture of hay, mixed grains, and vitamin supplements. Nutritional needs for vitamins A, B_1, and D, and protein, must be met. Figure P7.8 shows the cost and nutritional contents of each feed and the nutritional requirements of each cow.

Feed	Vitamin A	Vitamin B_1	Vitamin D	Protein	Cost
Hay	2 mg/lb	8 mg/lb	3 mg/lb	50 gm/lb	$0.50/lb
Mixed Grains	6 mg/lb	2 mg/lb	5 mg/lb	80 gm/lb	$1.00/lb
Vitamin Supplement	8 mg/oz	4 mg/oz	20 mg/oz	—	$2.00/oz
Min. Required Per Day	20 mg	30 mg	40 mg	200	
Max. Allowed Per Day	50 mg	—	120		

Nutrient

FIGURE P7.8

7.9. The Ajax Answering Service answers telephones for customers. They have found that their load remains the same from day to day but differs during the day.

The number of operators required during the day is as follows:

Time	Number of Operators Required
Midnight–4 A. M.	6
4–8 A. M.	4
8 A. M.–noon	20
Noon–4 P. M.	30
4–8 P. M.	15
8–12 P. M.	8

Operators work an 8-hour continuous shift, but begin work at midnight, 4 A. M., 8 A. M., and so on. Ajax would like to schedule its workshifts so as to minimize the number of operators on the payroll. Neglect holidays, sick days, and so on.

7.10. The Supreme Cabinet Company has just received a large rush order for two styles of kitchen cabinets. The order is for 500 model *A* and 300 model *B* cabinets. The cabinets are made of wood, and since they are to be painted, it does not matter which wood is used. However, because of the different technology involved, the cost to produce each cabinet from the different types of wood varies as shown in Figure P7.10. To produce a unit of each cabinet requires one standard sheet of any of the three woods. Birch sheets cost $4 each, pine sheets cost $3 each, and spruce sheets cost $5 each. Supreme's lumber supplier has 200 birch sheets, 400 pine sheets, and 250 spruce sheets available for immediate delivery.

	Birch	Pine	Spruce
Cabinet A	$12	$16	$8
Cabinet B	$7	$5	$10

FIGURE P7.10

7.11. Eternity Perfumes makes a fragrance called Hidden Treasure in both perfume and toilet water. Both are blends of essence *A*, essence *B*, and a base stock consisting of water, alcohol, coloring, and other ingredients. The requirements for each product are as follows:

Perfume	*Toilet Water*
At least 20% *A*	At least 10% of *A*
At least 40% *A* and *B* combined	No more than 80% base stock

Acidity is measured by a quantity called pH. The pH of both the perfume and toilet water must be between 6.8 and 7.2. The pH values of essence *A*, essence *B*, and the base stock are 7.4, 7.1, and 6.6, respectively.

Assume that the pH value of the mixture is the weighted average of the pH of the blended materials.

Essence *A* cost $6/ounce, essence *B* costs $3/ounce, and the base stock costs $0.50/ounce. The perfume sells for $8/ounce, and the toilet water sells for $5/ounce. Next month's anticipated demand is 400 oz for the perfume and 600 oz for the toilet water. There will be 100 oz of essence *A* and 300 oz of essence *B* available next month.

7.12. The Williams Toy Company is trying to plan its cash needs for the holiday season. The cash income and expenditures for the period October through January are as follows:

	Oct.	*Nov.*	*Dec.*	*Jan.*	*Total*
Cash income ($000)	50	150	600	300	1,100
Cash outflow ($000)	200	600	100	50	950
Net	− 150	− 450	500	250	150

At the end of the period all excess cash will be paid out as taxes and dividends. The company must maintain a minimum balance in its checking account which it will have at the beginning of October. The company can obtain a 4-month loan of up to $400,000 on October 1 at an interest rate of 1%/month paid monthly. They may also borrow on a short-term basis from month to month up to a limit of $300,000. The money will be transfered to or from the company's account on the first of each month so that the loan amount will be whatever the company desires for the month up to the $300,000 limit. This loan will cost 1.2%/month, payable monthly based on the loan balance that exists during the month. Any excess cash may be invested in 1-month government bonds at a rate of 0.7%/month but must be invested on the first of the month.

7.13. The Worldwide Manufacturing Company is floating a stock issue that will yield $12 million dollars for investment within the company. There are five possible projects under consideration.

Purchasing	*Rate of Return (%)*	*Maximum Investment (millions of $)*
1. Improved materials-handling equipment	15	3
2. Automating packaging operations	10	5
3. Purchase raw materials in anticipation of price increase	18	6
4. Paying up outstanding notes	8	4
5. Additional promotion for a new product line	20	1

There is no minimum investment required for any project. Projects 1 and 2 are classified as capital expenditure projects, projects 3 and 5 are speculative investment projects, and project 4 is a financial project. Worldwide insists on the following:

(1) Investment in capital expenditure projects must be at least 40% of the total.

(2) The investment in speculative projects must be no more than 50% of the amount used to pay notes.

7.14. The Ready Mixed Cement Company offers three ready mixed packaged products—mortar, industrial concrete, and residential concrete, which it sells by the pound for $.06, $.065, and $.072, respectively. Each pound of mortar is composed of 10% sand, 80% cement, and 10% gravel. Each pound of industrial concrete is composed of 10% sand, 30% cement, and 60% gravel. The residential concrete is composed of 20% sand, 30% cement, and 50% gravel. The company is running a special promotion and has advance orders for the next month for 2000 pounds of mortar, 1000 pounds of industrial concrete, and 3000 pounds of residential concrete. For next month's sales, they can purchase 2000 pounds of sand at $.06 per pound, 5000 pounds of cement at $.05 per pound, and 4000 pounds of gravel at $.04 per pound. They insist on filling all advance orders, and any extra production can also be sold.

7.15. The General Tape and Twine Company sells its 3-ply reinforced gum tape, which comes in 1000 foot rolls, in four different widths: 1 inch, 2 inches, 3 inches, and 4 inches. All the various widths must be produced by appropriately cutting the base stock which comes only in a 4-inch width. The cutting machine is designed such that it can cut the base stock into a maximum of three strips. The cutting alternatives are as follows:

Cutting Alternative	Type of Rolls Produced
1	2 in., 2 in.
2	1 in., 3 in.
3	1 in., 1 in., 2 in.

The selling price per roll of each type of tape is as follows:

Tape size	1 in.	2 in.	3 in.	4 in.
Selling price per 1000 feet	$5.00	$6.00	$8.00	$10.00

The firm has available an inventory of 50 million feet of the base stock, for which it has paid $4.00 per 1000 feet. It requires a minimum production of 15,000 one-inch rolls, 10,000 two-inch rolls, 5000 three-inch rolls, and 8000 four-inch rolls.

CHAPTER EIGHT

Linear Programming Computational Methods

OBJECTIVES: The purpose of this chapter is to present to you the following computational methods and concepts used in solving linear programming problems.

1. *The simplex method.*
2. *Multiple solutions.*
3. *Problems with no finite solution.*
4. *The need for artificial variables in special cases.*
5. *The dual linear program.*
6. *Economic interpretation of the dual.*
7. *Use of the simplex table for sensitivity analysis.*

In Chapter 6 we found that several methods are available for solving linear programming problems. These procedures, however, are generally impractical or inefficient. The graphical technique is practical only for two-variable, or possibly three-variable, problems. Finding all the basic feasible solutions can be a long and tedious task. For example, a problem with four variables and six constraint equations will have 210 basic solutions to determine and evaluate. Thus, it is clear that an efficient computational procedure is required to solve the general class of linear programming problems. The simplex method meets this computational objective. It is efficient in its computational procedure and it yields the optimal solution in a finite number of steps. It also has the added benefit of giving the shadow-price values when the optimal solution has been found.

In this chapter a detailed description of the simplex method will be presented. This will then be followed by the simplex algorithm and several special computational rules. The chapter will conclude with a discussion of the dual problem and sensitivity analysis.

SECTION 8.2. *Basic Feasible Solutions and*
the Concept of a Basis

In Section 6.7 a procedure was outlined for finding all the basic feasible solutions of an LP problem. In brief, the procedure was as follows. Assuming that there are N variables and M inequality constraints,

1. Write all constraints in equality-equivalent form, adding slack or surplus variables where necessary. There will now be $N + M$ variables.
2. Choose a set of N variables and set their values equal to zero. The remaining M equations with M unknowns are then solved to yield a *basic solution*.
3. Step 2 is repeated until all possible sets of N variables have been chosen and all basic solutions have been found.
4. Those basic solutions with no negative values are termed *basic feasible solutions*.

A basic feasible solution, therefore, has the following characteristic: N variables are zero and M variables are nonzero. This set of M nonzero variables will be called the *basis* of the solution. It tells us which of the $M + N$ variables constitute the present solution. The variables that make up the basis will be called *basic variables*. Thus, every basic feasible solution to an LP problem will be defined by a basis composed of M basic variables.

For example, consider the following set of inequality constraints to a linear programming problem:

$$(1) \qquad\qquad 2x_1 + 4x_2 \leqslant 1{,}600$$

$$(2) \qquad\qquad 6x_1 + 2x_2 \leqslant 1{,}800$$

$$(3) \qquad\qquad x_2 \leqslant 350$$

The equality-equivalent form is

$$(4) \qquad\qquad 2x_1 + 4x_2 + x_3 \qquad\qquad = 1{,}600$$

$$(5) \qquad\qquad 6x_1 + 2x_2 \qquad + x_4 \qquad = 1{,}800$$

$$(6) \qquad\qquad x_2 \qquad\quad + x_5 = 350$$

Here $N = 2$ and $M = 3$; thus a basis will consist of three variables. Since we wish to choose only three out of the five, there are 10 different ways that we can make this choice. Although we cannot write down all 10 basic solutions just by inspection of equations (4)–(6), one basic solution can easily be found by this technique. If we set $x_1 = x_2 = 0$, a solution automatically emerges:

$$(7) \qquad\qquad x_3 = 1{,}600; \qquad x_4 = 1{,}800; \qquad x_5 = 350$$

This solution is both basic and feasible and the basis may be written (x_3, x_4, x_5). The reason this solution is obvious is because each of the basic variables appears only once in all the equations and its coefficient, when it does appear, is exactly 1. Thus, if the equations could be arranged such that the basic variables are isolated, the basic solution would be easily determined by inspection. This rearrangement of the equations can be performed if we apply two basic algebra rules:

1. One equation added to a second equation yields a valid equation.
2. Equations multiplied by a constant are still valid equations.

We will refer to the application of these rules in rearranging our equations as *row operations*. Thus, we can multiply equation (5) by $\frac{1}{6}$ yielding

$$(5a) \qquad\qquad x_1 + \tfrac{1}{3}x_2 \qquad + \tfrac{1}{6}x_4 \qquad = 300$$

Multiplying equation (5a) by -2 gives

(5b) $$-2x_1 - \tfrac{2}{3}x_2 \qquad -\tfrac{1}{3}x_4 \quad = -600$$

Adding equation (5b) to equation (4) gives

(4a) $$\tfrac{10}{3}x_2 + x_3 - \tfrac{1}{3}x_4 \quad = 1{,}000$$

Equations (4), (5), and (6) can now be written as follows:

(4a) $$\tfrac{10}{3}x_2 + x_3 - \tfrac{1}{3}x_4 \quad = 1{,}000$$

(5a) $$x_1 + \tfrac{1}{3}x_2 \qquad + \tfrac{1}{6}x_4 \quad = 300$$

(6) $$x_2 \qquad + x_5 = 350$$

The easily observed basis for these equations is (x_3, x_1, x_5), with x_1 having replaced x_4 from the previously identified basis. The basic solution is then

$$x_1 = 300; \qquad x_3 = 1{,}000; \qquad x_5 = 350$$

with $x_2 = x_4 = 0$. Since none of the values are negative, this solution is a basic feasible solution. Notice that when we identify a basis we do not list them in the numerical order of their subscripts. Rather, they are listed in equation-order format, that is, the variable that is isolated in the first equation, x_3, the isolated variable in the second equation, x_1, and the isolated variable for the third equation, x_5. This arrangement is presented to ease the understanding of the procedures used in the simplex method.

If we refer back to Figure 6.4.4, we note that the basis (x_3, x_4, x_5) corresponds to the point I while the basis (x_3, x_1, x_5) corresponds to point A. These two points are adjacent extreme points. It can be shown in general that if only one basic variable of the basis is changed, the new basis extreme point will always be adjacent to the old basis extreme point. It is thus possible to systematically examine all the extreme points of the feasible region by changing the basis one basic variable at a time. If, in addition to changing the basis, we consider the effect of that new basic solution on the value of the objective function, we can determine the optimal solution in a most efficient way. This entire procedure is called the simplex method and is described in detail in the next section.

SECTION 8.3. *Simplex Method*

The *simplex method* for solving LP problems is based on the following:

1. It is possible to write the original problem in a form that yields a first feasible solution. (We are now assuming only $\leqslant$ constraints.)

2. It is possible to determine if the solution given can be improved or not.
3. If the solution cannot be improved, it will be termed the optimal solution.
4. If the solution can be improved, it is possible to determine exactly which variable should join the basis and which variable should be removed from the basis in order to find the improved solution.
5. The optimal solution must be reached (if it exists) in a finite number of steps since there are a finite number of extreme points.

Let us reconsider the LP production problem of Chapter 6. The mathematical statement of the problem is

(1) $$\text{maximize } Z = 3x_1 + 8x_2$$
$$\text{s.t.}$$

(2) $$2x_1 + 4x_2 \leqslant 1,600$$

(3) $$6x_1 + 2x_2 \leqslant 1,800$$

(4) $$x_2 \leqslant 350$$

(5) $$x_1, x_2 \geqslant 0$$

Equation (1) may be rewritten in the following constraint-like form:

(6) $$Z - 3x_1 - 8x_2 = 0$$

Hence, if we add slack variables to equations (2), (3), and (4), giving equality equivalent equations, and only allow nonnegative values of x_1 and x_2, the problem can be restated as follows. Find the set of nonnegative variables $(x_1, x_2, x_3, x_4, x_5)$ that satisfy

(7) $$2x_1 + 4x_2 + x_3 \qquad = 1,600$$

(8) $$6x_1 + 2x_2 \qquad + x_4 \qquad = 1,800$$

(9) $$x_2 \qquad + x_5 = 350$$

(10) $$Z - 3x_1 - 8x_2 \qquad = 0$$

and for which Z is as large as possible.

From Section 8.2 it is clear that we can write a first feasible solution to the problem by inspection. The basis is (x_3, x_4, x_5), and the solution is

(11) $$x_1 = x_2 = 0; \qquad x_3 = 1,600; \qquad x_4 = 1,800; \qquad x_5 = 350$$
and

(12) $$Z = 0$$

To simplify the presentation of the computations and results of the various basic feasible solutions used to find the optimum solution to our problem, let us present equations (7)–(10) as shown in Table 8.3.1. The equation row numbers are indicated for ease in identification. The basis column will list the basic variables of the current solution. The last

TABLE 8.3.1. *First Solution*

Equation Row Number	Basis	x_1	x_2	x_3	x_4	x_5	Solution
				VARIABLES			
1	x_3	2	4	1	0	0	1,600
2	x_4	6	2	0	1	0	1,800
3	x_5	0	1	0	0	1	350
4	Z	-3	-8	0	0	0	0

element in that column will always be Z. The variables' columns are the coefficients of the variables as given in the equality equivalent equations, (7)–(10), or their revision. The solution column is the right-hand side of equations (7)–(10), or their revision. The solution is read from the table by equating the variables of the basis column with the corresponding values of the solution column. Thus, we have the solution given by equations (11) and (12).

Let us now examine whether this solution can be improved. Since equation (10) actually states that

$$(10) \qquad\qquad Z = 0 + 3x_1 + 8x_2$$

it can be seen that if x_1 is increased by 1 unit, Z will be increased by 3 units, while if x_2 is increased by 1 unit, Z will be increased by 8 units. Hence, there is a definite advantage to including x_2 in the basis. However, since this basis can only contain three variables, if x_2 is included one of the three variables (x_3, x_4, x_5) must be removed (i.e., set equal to zero). To determine which variable to remove, rewrite equations (7)–(9), with $x_1 = 0$, as follows:

$$(13) \qquad\qquad x_3 = 1,600 - 4x_2$$

$$(14) \qquad\qquad x_4 = 1,800 - 2x_2$$

$$(15) \qquad\qquad x_5 = 350 - x_2$$

Since we wish to make x_2 as large as possible, thereby increasing Z by 8 per unit of x_2, let us see how big we can make x_2 before one of the basic variables (x_3, x_4, x_5) becomes zero while the others remain positive and feasible.

If $x_3 = 0$, then from equation (13) we obtain

$$x_2 = \frac{1,600}{4} = 400$$

Thus, when x_2 gets as high as 400, x_3 equals zero and leaves the basis.

If $x_4 = 0$, then from equation (14) we obtain

$$x_2 = \frac{1,800}{2} = 900$$

If $x_5 = 0$, then from equation (15) we obtain

$$x_2 = \frac{350}{1} = 350$$

Thus, the highest we can increase x_2 and have one basis variable become zero while the others remain positive is

$$x_2 = \text{minimum } \{400, 900, 350\} = 350$$

If we make $x_2 = 351$, then from equation (15)

$$x_5 = 350 - 351 = -1$$

which is no longer a feasible solution.

Our new basic feasible solution is, therefore,

$$x_2 = 350$$

$$x_3 = 1,600 - 4(350) = 200$$

$$x_4 = 1,800 - 2(350) = 1,100$$

The second solution can be presented in tabular form by transforming the equations of Table 8.3.1 by the row operations of Section 8.2. Since x_2 is replacing x_5 for the third row, we desire that the x_2 column values contain all zeros except in the third row, where it must be a 1; and the third and fourth columns, for x_3 and x_4, remain unchanged since x_3 and x_4 remain in the basis. Thus, we wish the form of the equations to be

$$?x_1 + 0x_2 + 1x_3 + 0x_4 + ?x_5 = ?$$

$$?x_1 + 0x_2 + 0x_3 + 1x_4 + ?x_5 = ?$$

$$?x_1 + 1x_2 + 0x_3 + 0x_4 + ?x_5 = ?$$

$$Z + ?x_1 + 0x_2 + 0x_3 + 0x_4 + ?x_5 = ?$$

The ? indicates a value that is not yet specified.

Let us consider what rearrangements have to be made to each row so as to have it correspond to this form. We begin with the row corresponding to the variable leaving the basis (x_5) (i.e., row 3). Comparing row 3 [equation (9)] as shown in Table 8.3.1, we see that row 3 already corresponds to the correct form for the new solution. This will not always be the case. In general, a value other than 1 will appear in the column of the entering variable (x_2). In such cases the entire equation (row) should be divided by whatever value appears there, so that the new row will have a 1 in the proper position.

Next consider row 1. Row 1 of Table 8.3.1 differs from the required form for our new solution in that it requires a 0 in the x_1 column (coefficient of x_1 in the equation). A simple way to transform row 1 is suggested by the fact that row 3 contains a 1 in the x_2 position. If we compute [row 1]–4[row3], the resulting equation will have the necessary form. The reason the number 4 is used is because the current value of the row 1/column x_2 value is -4. Therefore,

$$\begin{array}{rl}
\text{[row 1]} & 2x_1 + 4x_2 + 1x_3 + 0x_4 + 0x_5 = 1{,}600 \\
+ & \\
(-4)\text{[row 3]} & \underline{0x_1 - 4x_2 + 0x_3 + 0x_4 - 4x_5 = -1{,}400} \\
=\text{[new row 1]} & 2x_1 + 0x_2 + 1x_3 + 0x_4 - 4x_5 = 200
\end{array}$$

The new row 1 in our second solution table is, therefore:

Equation Row Number	Basis	VARIABLES					Solution
		x_1	x_2	x_3	x_4	x_5	
1	x_3	2	0	1	0	-4	200

Thus, transforming the rows (other than the row corresponding to the variable leaving the basis) can be accomplished by the following rule:

$$\text{new row} = [\text{old row}] + \left[\left(\begin{array}{c} -\text{value of old row element} \\ \text{in "entering variable" column} \end{array} \right) \left(\begin{array}{c} \text{new "leaving} \\ \text{variable" row} \end{array} \right) \right]$$

Multiplying row 3 by -2 and adding to row 2 yields the new row 2:

Equation Row Number	Basis	VARIABLES					Solution
		x_1	x_2	x_3	x_4	x_5	
2	x_4	6	0	0	1	-2	1,100

Multiplying row 3 by 8 and adding to row 4 yields

Equation Row Number	Basis	VARIABLES					Solution
		x_1	x_2	x_3	x_4	x_5	
4	Z	-3	0	0	0	8	2,800

Combining these results, we get Table 8.3.2. The equations corresponding to Table 8.3.2 are

$$\begin{array}{rl}
(16) & 2x_1 + x_3 - x_5 = 200 \\
(17) & 6x_1 + x_4 - 2x_5 = 1{,}100 \\
(18) & x_2 + x_5 = 350 \\
(19) & Z - 3x_1 + 8x_5 = 2{,}800
\end{array}$$

with the solution by inspection given as

$$x_1 = x_5 = 0; \qquad x_2 = 350; \qquad x_3 = 200; \qquad x_4 = 1,100$$

and

$$Z = 2,800$$

TABLE 8.3.2. *Second Solution*

Equation Row Number	Basis	VARIABLES					Solution
		x_1	x_2	x_3	x_4	x_5	
1	x_3	2	0	1	0	−4	200
2	x_4	6	0	0	1	−2	1,100
3	x_2	0	1	0	0	1	350
4	Z	−3	0	0	0	8	2,800

From equation (19) we observe that Z can be further improved by 3 units for each unit of x_1 added to the solution. To determine how much x_1 to add and which variable to remove, we rewrite (16), (17), and (18) as (where $x_5 = 0$)

(20) $$x_3 = 200 - 2x_1$$

(21) $$x_4 = 1,100 - 6x_1$$

(22) $$x_2 = 350$$

Following the rule of maintaining feasibility, as stated earlier, we determine from minimum $(200/2, 1,100/6) = 100$ that x_3 is set equal to zero with $x_1 = 100$, $x_4 = 1,100 - 6(100) = 500$, and $x_2 = 350$. Note that x_2 cannot become zero, since it is unaffected by x_1.

The equation form of the third solution will be

$$1x_1 + 0x_2 + ?x_3 + 0x_4 + ?x_5 = ?$$
$$0x_1 + 0x_2 + ?x_3 + 1x_4 + ?x_5 = ?$$
$$0x_1 + 1x_2 + ?x_3 + 0x_4 + ?x_5 = ?$$
$$Z + 0x_1 + 0x_2 + ?x_3 + 0x_4 + ?x_5 = ?$$

The third solution, Table 8.3.3, is then found as follows. Divide row 1 by row 2, yielding:

Equation Row Number	Basis	VARIABLES					Solution
		x_1	x_2	x_3	x_4	x_5	
1	x_1	1	0	$\frac{1}{2}$	0	−2	100

Multiply the new row 1 by -6 and then by 3, yielding rows 1a and 1b.

Equation Row Number	Basis	VARIABLES					Solution
		x_1	x_2	x_3	x_4	x_5	
1	x_1	1	0	$\frac{1}{2}$	0	-2	100
1a		-6	0	-3	0	12	-600
1b		3	0	$\frac{3}{2}$	0	-6	300

Add row 1a to row 2 of Table 8.3.2, yielding:

Equation Row Number	Basis	VARIABLES					Solution
		x_1	x_2	x_3	x_4	x_5	
2	x_4	0	0	-3	1	10	500

Add row 1b to row 4 of Table 8.3.2, yielding:

Equation Row Number	Basis	VARIABLES					Solution
		x_1	x_2	x_3	x_4	x_5	
4	Z	0	0	$\frac{3}{2}$	0	2	3,100

Row 3 remains unchanged.

The equations corresponding to Table 8.3.3 are

$$(23) \qquad x_1 + \tfrac{1}{2}x_3 \quad - 2x_5 = 100$$

$$(24) \qquad - 3x_3 + x_4 + 10x_5 = 500$$

$$(25) \qquad x_2 \qquad + x_5 = 350$$

$$(26) \qquad Z + \tfrac{3}{2}x_3 \quad + 2x_5 = 3,100$$

with the solution by inspection given as

$$(27) \qquad x_3 = x_5 = 0; \quad x_1 = 100; \quad x_2 = 350; \quad x_4 = 500$$

and

$$(28) \qquad Z = 3,100$$

From equation (26) it is clear that no positive values of x_3 or x_5 could improve the value of Z. Hence, equations (27) and (28) yield the optimum solution to our problem. Although there are 10 possible basic solutions, the simplex method chose to examine only three of them and, in a systematic computational procedure, find the optimum solution.

TABLE 8.3.3. *Third Solution*

Equation Row Number	Basis	VARIABLES					Solution
		x_1	x_2	x_3	x_4	x_5	
1	x_1	1	0	$\frac{1}{2}$	0	-2	100
2	x_4	0	0	-3	1	10	500
3	x_2	0	1	0	0	1	350
4	Z	0	0	$\frac{3}{2}$	0	2	3,100

On referring once again to Figure 6.4.4, we note that the three solutions presented correspond to points I, B, and H, respectively, which are all adjacent points. Point I, the origin, is the first solution. Points A and B are then examined to evaluate the per-unit increase in the objective function Z. Since B shows a greater per-unit improvement, the next solution point is B. The method then evaluates the adjacent points of B (i.e., I and H). Since H shows a greater per-unit improvement, the next solution point is H. On evaluating the adjacent points of H, no improvement can be made in Z; therefore, H is the optimum point. This last fact must be true if both the constraints and the objective function are linear (i.e., straight lines).

It should be apparent that the simplex method follows an orderly and systematic procedure that might be described by a set of computational rules. This set of rules, called an *algorithm*, is described in the next section.

SECTION 8.4. *Simplex Algorithm*

Let us review the basic steps of the simplex method.

1. Find a first feasible solution.
2. Determine which variable, if any, should join the basis to improve the objective function Z.
3. Determine which variable should leave the basis.
4. Transform the set of equations into a format such that the solution is determinable by inspection.
5. Repeat steps 2, 3, and 4 until no further improvement in Z is possible.

We shall now define a set of rules, called the *simplex algorithm*, that accomplishes the five steps listed without the necessity of writing any equations other than the original equality equivalent set.

RULE 1. First Feasible Solution

- Write the inequality constraints in equality equivalent form by adding slack variables. (See Table 8.4.1.)
- Write the objective function in a constraint-like form. (See Table 8.4.1.)

270

TABLE 8.4.1. *Equations for First Feasible Solution*

Original Problem	Equality-Equivalent Equations
Maximize $Z = 3x_1 + 8x_2$ s.t.	
$2x_1 + 4x_2 \leqslant 1{,}600$	$2x_1 + 4x_2 + x_3 \qquad = 1{,}600$
$6x_1 + 2x_2 \leqslant 1{,}800$	$6x_1 + 2x_2 \qquad + x_4 \qquad = 1{,}800$
$x_2 \leqslant 350$	$x_2 \qquad + x_5 = 350$
$x_1, \quad x_2 \geqslant 0$	$Z - 3x_1 - 8x_2 \qquad = 0$

- Prepare the first table as shown in Table 8.4.2.
- The solution is read by equating the basis and solution columns row by row:

$$x_3 = 1{,}600; \qquad x_4 = 1{,}800; \qquad x_5 = 350; \qquad Z = 0$$

TABLE 8.4.2. *First Solution*

Equation Row Number	Basis	VARIABLES					Solution	Ratio
		x_1	x_2	x_3	x_4	x_5		
1	x_3	2	4	1	0	0	1,600	$1{,}600/4 = 400$
2	x_4	6	2	0	1	0	1,800	$1{,}800/2 = 900$
3	x_5	0	1	0	0	1	350	$350/1 = 350$
4	Z	-3	-8	0	0	0	0	

RULE 2. Variable to Enter the Basis

- Examine the values of the last row of the current solution (in the variables columns only). These numbers, if negative, indicate that an improvement in Z is possible. If positive, no improvement is possible.
- Choose as the entering variable the variable whose last-row value is most negative. (Thus, in Table 8.4.2 we choose the column with a -8 in the last row.)
- Box this column.

RULE 3. Variable to Leave the Basis

- Form the ratio of corresponding elements from the solution column to the entering variable column. (In our problem, x_2.) List these ratios only if positive.
- Choose, as the variable to leave the basis, the row with the smallest positive ratio. (In our problem, this is row 3. Therefore, x_5 is removed and replaced by x_2.)
- Box this row.

Notice that one element of the table appears both in the boxed row and boxed column. We call this element the *key element* or the *pivot element*.

RULE 4. *Finding the New Solution*

- If the key element is 1, the boxed row remains the same in the new table.
- If the key element is other than 1, divide all elements in the boxed row by the key element to find the new values for that row.
- To find the values of the remaining rows of the new table, row operations, as in Section 8.2, are performed on all rows so that all elements except the key element in the boxed column are zero.

Thus, we get Table 8.4.3, from which the solution can easily be read:

$$x_3 = 200; \qquad x_4 = 1,100; \qquad x_2 = 350; \qquad Z = 2,800$$

TABLE 8.4.3. *Second Solution*

Equation Row Number	Basis	VARIABLES					Solution	Ratio
		x_1	x_2	x_3	x_4	x_5		
1	x_3	2	0	1	0	-4	200	$200/2 = 100$
2	x_4	6	0	0	1	-2	1,100	$1,100/6 = 183.3$
3	x_2	0	1	0	0	1	350	—
4	Z	-3	0	0	0	8	2,800	

RULE 5. *Finding the Optimum Solution*

- Repeat rules 2, 3, and 4 until one of the two following results occur.
- All elements of the last row are $\geqslant 0$; thus, an optimum solution has been found.
- At least one element of the last row is negative, indicating that improvement is possible but all ratios are nonpositive. We term this solution an *unbounded* solution. (See Section 8.6.)

Applying Rule 5 to Table 8.4.3 we find that x_1 is the new entering variable, x_3 is the variable that leaves the basis, and the key element is 2. We then generate Table 8.4.4 with the solution

$$x_1 = 100; \qquad x_4 = 500; \qquad x_2 = 350; \qquad Z = 3,100$$

TABLE 8.4.4. *Third Solution*

Equation Row Number	Basis	VARIABLES					Solution
		x_1	x_2	x_3	x_4	x_5	
1	x_1	1	0	$\frac{1}{2}$	0	-2	100
2	x_4	0	0	-3	1	10	500
3	x_2	0	1	0	0	1	350
4	Z	0	0	$\frac{3}{2}$	0	2	3,100

Applying rule 5 to Table 8.4.4 shows that this solution is optimum, since all elements of the last row are ≥ 0.

An alternative method exists for finding the table values when going from one solution table to the next. This procedure yields one value at a time, and although it is equivalent to the row operations of Section 8.2, it is more routine and therefore less subject to error.

The first row entered into the new table is, as in rule 4, the boxed row of the old table divided by the key element. The revised procedure is used to find all the other values of the table. Let us consider revising the second solution table and obtaining the third solution. We first find row 1, by dividing the old row 1 (boxed row) by the key element, 2:

$$\text{New row 1:} \quad \tfrac{2}{2} \quad \tfrac{0}{2} \quad \tfrac{1}{2} \quad \tfrac{0}{4} \quad -\tfrac{4}{2} \quad \tfrac{200}{2}$$

To find the new row 2, we perform the row operation

$$\text{new row 2} = \text{old row 2} + (-6)(\text{new row 1})$$

$$= \text{old row 2} - \frac{(6)(\text{old row 1})}{2}$$

We have written the new row 1 as the old row 1 divided by 2, and the value 6 used is the value of the row 2 element in the boxed column. Let us consider what operations are performed on the value in the x_5 column of row 2 by these row operations:

$$\text{old row 2 value} - \frac{(6)(\text{old row 1 value})}{2} = (-2) - \frac{(6)(-4)}{2}$$

$$= (-2) + 12$$

$$= 10$$

The new value in row 2 in the x_5 column is therefore 10. Table 8.4.5 shows these values circled and arrows indicating the flow of the operations. We can first divide 6 by 2, then multiply by -4 and subtract this quantity from -2. All other elements of the table (excluding row 1, the old boxed row) can be found in the same manner. Notice that since the

TABLE 8.4.5. *Second Solution.*
Finding New Row 2–x_5 Column Value

Equation Row Number	Basis	VARIABLES					Solution	Ratio
		x_1	x_2	x_3	x_4	x_5		
1	x_3	2	0	1	0	-4	200	$200/2 = 100$
2	x_4	6	0	0	1	-2	1,100	$1{,}100/6 = 183.3$
3	x_2	0	1	0	0	1	350	—
4	Z	-3	0	0	0	8	2,800	

value in the boxed column of row 3 is zero, all new row 3 values are equal to the old ones. The procedure also works for all values in row 4. Table 8.4.6 illustrates the procedure for finding the new x_3 column–row 4 value, which is as follows:

$$\text{old row 4 value} - \frac{(-3)\,(\text{old row 1 value})}{(2)} = (0) - \frac{(-3)(1)}{2}$$

$$= 0 + \frac{3}{2}$$

$$= \frac{3}{2}$$

Following the flow shown in Table 8.4.6, we first compute $-\frac{3}{2}$, multiply by 1, $= -\frac{3}{2}$, and subtract from 0, $= +\frac{3}{2}$.

TABLE 8.4.6. *Second Solution.
Finding New Row 4–x_3 Column Value*

Equation Row Number	Basis	VARIABLES					Solution	Ratio
		x_1	x_2	x_3	x_4	x_5		
1	x_3	②	0	①	0	−4	200	$\frac{200}{2} = 100$
2	$x_4 \div$	6	0	0	1	−2	1,100	$\frac{1,100}{6} = 183.3$
3	x_2	0	1	0	0	1	350	—
4	Z	−3	0	⓪	0	8	2,800	

SECTION 8.5. *Alternate Optima*

It may occasionally occur that more than one basic feasible solution yields the same optimum value for the objective function Z. We refer to these solutions as *alternate optima*. Consider our production problem with a different objective function as follows:

$$\text{maximize } Z = 3x_1 + 6x_2$$

s.t.

$$2x_1 + 4x_2 \leqslant 1,600$$

$$6x_1 + 2x_2 \leqslant 1,800$$

$$x_2 \leqslant 350$$

$$x_1, x_2 \geqslant 0$$

The equality-equivalent form for the problem is

$$2x_1 + 4x_2 + x_3 \qquad\qquad = 1{,}600$$

$$6x_1 + 2x_2 \qquad + x_4 \qquad = 1{,}800$$

$$x_2 \qquad\qquad + x_5 = 350$$

$$Z - 3x_1 - 6x_2 \qquad\qquad\qquad = 0$$

Applying the rules of the simplex algorithm, we get the first three solutions of Table 8.5.1. Since none of the entries in the fourth (Z) row are negative, the solution is optimal. Of the two variables not in the basis, x_3 and x_5, x_3 could not be considered to enter the basis, since its entrance will result in a reduction of the value of Z. However, x_5 has a zero entry in row 4, indicating a zero improvement in Z for each unit of x_5 that enters the basis. Thus, Z will remain the same whether we introduce x_5 or

TABLE 8.5.1. *Solution Tables. Showing Alternate Optima*

Equation Row Number	Basis	VARIABLES					Solution	Ratio
		x_1	x_2	x_3	x_4	x_5		
		Solution 1						
1	x_3	2	4	1	0	0	1,600	400
2	x_4	6	2	0	1	0	1,800	900
3	x_5	0	1	0	0	1	350	350
4	Z	-3	-6	0	0	0	0	
		Solution 2						
1	x_3	2	0	1	0	-4	200	100
2	x_4	6	0	0	1	-2	1,100	183.3
3	x_2	0	1	0	0	1	350	—
4	Z	-3	0	0	0	6	2,100	
		Solution 3						
1	x_1	1	0	$\frac{1}{2}$	0	-2	100	—
2	x_4	0	0	-3	1	10	500	50
3	x_2	0	1	0	0	1	350	350
4	Z	0	0	$\frac{3}{2}$	0	0	2,400	
		Solution 4						
1	x_1	1	0	$-\frac{1}{10}$	$\frac{2}{10}$	0	200	
2	x_5	0	0	$-\frac{3}{10}$	$\frac{1}{10}$	1	50	
3	x_2	0	1	$\frac{3}{10}$	$-\frac{1}{10}$	0	300	
4	Z	0	0	$\frac{3}{2}$	0	0	2,400	

not. Let us, however, attempt to enter variable x_5. x_4 is removed and the fourth solution is

$$x_1 = 200; \qquad x_5 = 50; \qquad x_2 = 300; \qquad Z = 2{,}400$$

This solution is a different basic feasible solution than the third solution, but the value of Z has remained the same; thus we have an alternate optimum. Note that now x_4 has a zero in the fourth row. Rule 5 can thus be modified to include the following:

> If at least one of the elements in the last row, corresponding to a variable not in the basis, is exactly zero, then alternate optima exist.

It should be noted that, in general, alternate optima will be adjacent extreme points of the feasible region. In our example the alternate optima are points G and H of Figure 6.4.4. Furthermore, alternate optima occur only when the objective function equation is parallel to one of the constraints.

SECTION 8.6. *Unbounded Solutions*

In Section 8.4, rule 5, we noted the possibility of an unbounded solution to a linear programming problem. Let us consider a problem that yields such a solution.

$$\text{maximize } Z = x_1 + x_2$$
$$\text{s.t.}$$
$$-2x_1 + x_2 \leqslant 100$$
$$x_1 - x_2 \leqslant 50$$
$$x_1, \ x_2 \geqslant 0$$

The equality-equivalent equations are

$$-2x_1 + x_2 + x_3 \qquad = 100$$
$$x_1 - x_2 \qquad + x_4 = 50$$
$$Z - \ x_1 - x_2 \qquad = 0$$

Applying the simplex algorithm, we get Table 8.6.1. In the last row of solution 1 there are two negative values which are equal. We arbitrarily chose x_1 to enter but could just as well have chosen x_2 to enter. In general, as long as the last row value corresponding to a variable is negative, that variable is a valid candidate for entering the basis and will always yield an improved solution.

The last row of solution 2 has one negative value, and thus an improvement is indicated. However, no positive ratio can be formed,

TABLE 8.6.1. *Example Showing Unbounded Solution*

Equation Row Number	Basis	VARIABLES x_1	x_2	x_3	x_4	Solution	Ratio
		Solution 1					
1	x_3	-2	1	1	0	100	—
2	x_4	1	-1	0	1	50	50
3	Z	-1	-1	0	0	0	
		Solution 2					
1	x_3	0	-1	1	2	200	
2	x_1	1	-1	0	1	50	
3	Z	0	-2	0	1	50	

since all elements in the boxed column are negative. Thus,

$$x_3 = 200 + x_2$$
$$x_1 = 50 + x_2$$

and x_2 can be made as large as possible. This condition is an indication of an unbounded solution. It means that we can increase the value of the objective function by as much as we wish and the constraints will always be satisfied.

Although an unbounded solution can occur in theory, in practical real-world problems it is a very unlikely occurrence and usually indicates an error in formulation of the linear programming problem.

SECTION 8.7. *Degenerate Solutions*

A solution to a linear programming problem may occur where the values of the basic variables are not all positive (i.e., one or more of the basic variable values is exactly zero). A solution of this type will be called a *degenerate* solution.

Consider the following example, which will show how to handle problems that give rise to degeneracy:

$$\text{maximize } Z = 3x_1 + 8x_2$$

s.t.

(1) $$2x_1 + 4x_2 \leqslant 1,600$$
(2) $$6x_1 + 2x_2 \leqslant 1,800$$
(3) $$x_2 \leqslant 350$$
(4) $$x_1 \leqslant 100$$
(5) $$-x_1 + 3x_2 \leqslant 1,050$$
$$x_1, \ x_2 \geqslant 0$$

Converting this problem to the equality equivalent form, we get the following set of equations representing our problem:

$$2x_1 + 4x_2 + x_3 \qquad\qquad\qquad = 1{,}600$$

$$6x_1 + 2x_2 \qquad + x_4 \qquad\qquad = 1{,}800$$

$$x_2 \qquad\qquad + x_5 \qquad = 350$$

$$x_1 \qquad\qquad\qquad + x_6 \qquad = 100$$

$$-x_1 + 3x_2 \qquad\qquad\qquad + x_7 = 1{,}050$$

$$Z - 3x_1 - 8x_2 \qquad\qquad\qquad = 0$$

The solution to this problem using the simplex algorithm is given in Table 8.7.1. In the first solution the variable to enter the basis is x_2. However, on computing the ratios to determine which variable leaves the basis a tie occurs between variables x_5 and x_7. It is this condition that indicates that a degeneracy will occur. The rule that we will use when a

TABLE 8.7.1. *Solution Tables Showing Degeneracy*

Equation Row Number	Basis	VARIABLES							Solution	Ratio
		x_1	x_2	x_3	x_4	x_5	x_6	x_7		
				Solution 1						
1	x_3	2	4	1	0	0	0	0	1,600	400
2	x_4	6	2	0	1	0	0	0	1,800	900
3	x_5	0	1	0	0	1	0	0	350	350
4	x_6	1	0	0	0	0	1	0	100	— \ tie
5	x_7	−1	3	0	0	0	0	1	1,050	350 /
6	Z	−3	−8	0	0	0	0	0	0	
				Solution 2						
1	x_3	2	0	1	0	−4	0	0	200	100 \
2	x_4	6	0	0	1	−2	0	0	1,100	183.3 tie
3	x_2	0	1	0	0	1	0	0	350	—
4	x_6	1	0	0	0	0	1	0	100	100 /
5	x_7	−1	0	0	0	−3	0	1	0	—
6	Z	−3	0	0	0	8	0	0	2,800	
				Solution 3						
1	x_1	1	0	$\frac{1}{2}$	0	−2	0	0	100	
2	x_4	0	0	−3	1	10	0	0	500	
3	x_2	0	1	0	0	1	0	0	350	
4	x_6	0	0	$-\frac{1}{2}$	0	2	1	0	0	
5	x_7	0	0	$\frac{1}{2}$	0	−5	0	1	100	
6	Z	0	0	$\frac{3}{2}$	0	2	0	0	3,100	

tie occurs for the smallest positive ratio is the following:

Arbitrarily choose a variable to leave the basis from among those variables with equal smallest positive ratios.

If the variable chosen does not lead to a solution, return to the solution where the tie occurred and choose a different variable to leave the basis.

We thus choose x_5 to leave the basis and develop solution 2. The degeneracy now surfaces, in that the value of one of the basic variables, x_7, is equal to zero. On continuing the simplex algorithm, we once again note a tie in the ratio column. We choose x_3 to leave the basis and develop solution 3. The degeneracy is still present, in that basic variable $x_6 = 0$. However, x_7 does not necessarily have to remain at a zero level and is now equal to 100. On examining the last row of solution 3, the indications are that this solution is optimal. We term this solution an *optimal degenerate solution*.

In Figure 8.7.1. we have graphed the five constraints of our problem. Solution 1 is represented by point A. Solution 2 is represented by point B. This point is the intersection of constraints (3) and (5). Further inspection

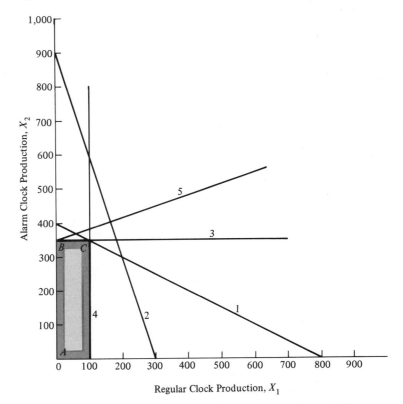

FIGURE 8.7.1. *Feasible region for degenerate solution example.*

shows that in reality constraint (5) is redundant, in that it imposes no additional restrictions to the feasible region than does constraint (3). Thus, one characteristic of degeneracy is redundant constraints. Note, however, that *not* all redundant constraints lead to degeneracy. Solution (3) is represented by point C. This point is the intersection of three constraints: (1), (3), and (4). Thus, the slack variables for these constraints x_3, x_5, and x_6 must equal zero. Hence, a condition of degeneracy occurs. If the solution were nondegenerate, at least one of these three slack variables would be positive.

SECTION 8.8. *Artificial Variables*

Consider the following addition to the production problem of Section 6.2:

At least 300 clocks in total (regular plus alarm) must be produced.

This constraint would be represented by

$$x_1 + x_2 \geqslant 300$$

The production problem is thus:

$$\text{maximize } Z = 3x_1 + 8x_2$$
$$\text{s.t.}$$
$$2x_1 + 4x_2 \leqslant 1,600$$
$$6x_1 + 2x_2 \leqslant 1,800$$
$$x_2 \leqslant 350$$
$$x_1 + x_2 \geqslant 300$$
$$x_1, \ x_2 \geqslant 0$$

The equality-equivalent form of the problem is

$$2x_1 + 4x_2 + x_3 \qquad\qquad = 1,600$$
$$6x_1 + 2x_2 \qquad + x_4 \qquad\qquad = 1,800$$
$$x_2 \qquad + x_5 \quad = 350$$
$$x_1 + x_2 \qquad\qquad - x_6 = 300$$
$$Z - 3x_1 - 8x_2 \qquad\qquad\qquad = 0$$

However, since a basic feasible solution cannot be determined by inspection, no initiation of the simplex algorithm can take place. The usual procedure for obtaining a first solution would yield $x_6 = -300$, which is not feasible. To overcome this difficulty, we make the following modifications.

For each row that does not yield an isolated variable (i.e., a $+1$ in the row and 0's in all other rows as in the fourth row), introduce an artificial variable (for our example, $+x_7$).

Assign a very large negative profit per unit $(-M)$ in the objective function to correspond to this artificial variable, so that it will be highly undesirable to give this variable a positive value.

Hence, the objective function will read

$$\text{maximize } 3x_1 + 8x_2 - Mx_7$$

while the fourth equality-equivalent constraint will read

$$x_1 + x_2 - x_6 + x_7 = 300$$

These artificial variables are not defined in terms of the original problem and are used only as an aid in initiating the simplex algorithm. The $-M$ introduced in the objective function is intended to discourage the solution procedure either from maintaining the artificial variable as one of the basic variables or from choosing the artificial as a candidate entering variable. We thus get as the set of equality-equivalent equations,

$$
\begin{aligned}
2x_1 + 4x_2 + x_3 \quad &\quad = 1{,}600 \\
6x_1 + 2x_2 \quad + x_4 \quad &\quad = 1{,}800 \\
x_2 \quad + x_5 \quad &\quad = 350 \\
x_1 + x_2 \quad - x_6 + \quad x_7 &= 300 \\
Z - 3x_1 - 8x_2 \quad + Mx_7 &= 0
\end{aligned}
$$

Hence, the initial basis is (x_3, x_4, x_5, x_7) and the first solution can be written as in Table 8.8.1. It should be noted that as long as an artificial variable is one of the basic variables of a solution and has a positive value, the solution is nonfeasible for the original problem. Thus, the intent of this procedure, called *the big M method*, is to remove the artificial variable from the basic solution and to keep it from returning. If it turns out that the optimal solution to the modified problem contains an artificial variable at a positive level as one of the basic variables, this means that the original problem has no solution.

Continuing the simplex algorithm through solutions 2, 3, and 4 we arrive at an optimum solution with x_7 not in the basis. This must be the optimal solution to the original problem.

TABLE 8.8.1. *Solution Tables for Artificial-Variables Example*

Equation Row Number	Basis	VARIABLES							Solution	Ratio
		x_1	x_2	x_3	x_4	x_5	x_6	x_7		
					Solution 1					
1	x_3	2	4	1	0	0	0	0	1,600	400
2	x_4	6	2	0	1	0	0	0	1,800	900
3	x_5	0	1	0	0	1	0	0	350	350
4	x_7	1	1	0	0	0	-1	1	300	300
5	Z	-3	-8	0	0	0	0	M	0	
					Solution 2					
1	x_3	-2	0	1	0	0	4	-4	400	100
2	x_4	4	0	0	1	0	2	-2	1,200	600
3	x_5	-1	0	0	0	1	1	-1	50	50
4	x_2	1	1	0	0	0	-1	1	300	—
5	Z	5	0	0	0	0	-8	$M+8$	2,400	
					Solution 3					
1	x_3	2	0	1	0	-4	0	0	200	100
2	x_4	6	0	0	1	-2	0	0	1,100	183.3
3	x_6	-1	0	0	0	1	1	-1	50	—
4	x_2	0	1	0	0	1	0	0	350	—
5	Z	-3	0	0	0	8	0	M	2,800	
					Solution 4					
1	x_1	1	0	$\frac{1}{2}$	0	-2	0	0	100	
2	x_4	0	0	-3	1	10	0	0	500	
3	x_6	0	0	$\frac{1}{2}$	0	-1	1	-1	150	
4	x_2	0	1	0	0	1	0	0	350	
5	Z	0	0	$\frac{3}{2}$	0	2	0	M	3,100	

SECTION 8.9. *Duality*

8.9.1. Primal–Dual Formulation. In Section 6.6 we introduced the concept of a shadow price, which we called the dual variable. We explained that there is one dual variable for each constraint, and that it represents the incremental value of an additional unit of the respective resource. We showed that the dual variable would be positive if the constraint was binding, but would equal zero if the constraint was not binding. These results, however, should be considered as part of a more general problem structure, which we shall refer to as the *dual problem*.

Linear programming theory states that each problem that we formulate is in reality two problems, which we shall call the primal problem and the dual problem. Thus, although we may formulate a specific linear

programming problem and solve it, there exists another linear programming problem, which uses the same data but is called the dual problem.

In general, it makes no difference which of the two problems is
called the primal and which is called the dual. An LP theorem states that
the dual of the dual is the primal. Thus, by applying the rules of duality
to solve one problem, we obtain the solution to the other problem.
However, in order to standardize and simplify the duality procedure we
will establish some definitions and rules. We define the primal problem as
an LP maximization problem with $\leqslant$ constraints and nonnegative variables. Thus, the production problem we have been using as an example
throughout this chapter will represent the typical primal problem.

PRIMAL PROBLEM

$$\text{maximize } Z = 3x_1 + 8x_2$$
$$\text{s.t.}$$
$$2x_1 + 4x_2 \leqslant 1{,}600$$
$$6x_1 + 2x_2 \leqslant 1{,}800$$
$$x_2 \leqslant 350$$
$$x_1, x_2 \geqslant 0$$

Let us use the letter w for the dual variables with one dual variable
for each constraint. Thus, for our problem we have three dual variables:
w_1, w_2, and w_3. The dual problem is a linear programming minimization
problem with $\geqslant$ constraints and nonnegative variables.

DUAL PROBLEM

$$\text{minimize } G = 1{,}600w_1 + 1{,}800w_2 + 350w_3$$
$$\text{s.t.}$$
$$2w_1 + \quad 6w_2 \qquad \geqslant 3$$
$$4w_1 + \quad 2w_2 + \quad w_3 \geqslant 8$$
$$w_1, w_2, w_3 \geqslant 0$$

On examining the primal and dual problems, the following relationships emerge:

The minimization objective function of the dual problem uses the
resources (right-hand side) of the primal problem as the coefficients
of the dual variables.

The right-hand side of the dual constraints are the per-unit profit
coefficients of the primal problem.

283

The coefficients of the constraint equations remain the same *except* that they are transposed. Thus, if the primal coefficients are represented by an array of numbers

$$A = \begin{bmatrix} 2 & 4 \\ 6 & 2 \\ 0 & 1 \end{bmatrix}$$

then the transpose of A, A^T, is given by a new array of numbers,

$$A^T = \begin{pmatrix} 2 & 6 & 0 \\ 4 & 2 & 1 \end{pmatrix}$$

The number of dual variables is equal to the number of primal constraint equations.

The number of dual constraint equations is equal to the number of primal variables.

Thus, given a maximization linear programming problem with N variables and M constraints, which we call the primal problem, there exists a minimization linear programming problem with M variables and N constraints, which we call the dual problem.

It should be noted that not all problems will appear exactly in the primal problem format. For example, consider the following problem:

$$\text{minimize } Z = x_1 + 2x_2$$
$$\text{s.t.}$$
$$2x_1 + 4x_2 \leqslant 1{,}600$$
$$x_1 - x_2 = 300$$
$$x_1 \geqslant 100$$
$$x_1, \ x_2 \geqslant 0$$

From the previous discussion it is not obvious what the dual of this problem is, since the problem differs from the general primal problem format. To find the dual of this problem we must use the following rules:

Transform all minimization linear programming problems to maximization problems, by changing the signs of the coefficients. (See Section 6.8.)

Transform all $\geqslant$ constraints (except the nonnegativity constraints) to $\leqslant$ constraints by multiplying the constraint by -1.

Thus our primal problem becomes

$$\text{maximize } Z = -x_1 - 2x_2$$
$$\text{s.t.}$$
$$2x_1 + 4x_2 \leqslant 1{,}600$$
$$x_1 - x_2 = 300$$
$$-x_1 \leqslant -100$$
$$x_1, \ x_2 \geqslant 0$$

The dual problem is, then:

$$\text{minimize } G = 1{,}600w_1 + 300w_2 - 100w_3$$
$$\text{s.t.}$$
$$2w_1 + w_2 - w_3 \geqslant -1$$
$$4w_1 - 2w_2 \geqslant -2$$

Since all the constraints in the primal problem are $\leqslant$ except the second constraint, all the dual variables except the second will be nonnegative:

$$w_1, w_3 \geqslant 0$$

The dual variable w_2 is unrestricted in sign (positive or negative) because the second primal constraint is an equality constraint.

Thus, a major concern in writing the dual is to determine the range of values for the dual variables. A summary of the general primal–dual relationships is presented in Table 8.9.1.

TABLE 8.9.1. *Primal–Dual Relationships*

If:	*Primal*	*Then*:	*Dual*
1. Objective is to maximize		1. Objective is to minimize	
2. Variables are $\geqslant 0$		2. Corresponding constraints are $\geqslant$ inequalities	
3. Variables are unrestricted		3. Corresponding constraints are $=$ (equalities)	
4. Constraints are $\leqslant$ inequalities		4. Corresponding variables are $\geqslant 0$	
5. Constraints are $=$ (equalities)		5. Corresponding variables are unrestricted	

One final point should be noted in constructing the dual problem. It is possible that some of the primal variables are nonpositive, say $x_1 \leqslant 0$. This is easily handled by introducing a new variable $x_1' = -x_1$; thus, $x_1' \geqslant 0$. We then replace every x_1 in the primal problem with a $-x_1'$ and then apply the general primal–dual relationships.

8.9.2. Solution of Dual Problem. The dual problem can be solved by the simplex method in exactly the same way as the primal problem. Let us rewrite dual problem (D) as a maximization problem. We get:

$$\text{maximize } G = -1,600w_1 - 1,800w_2 - 350w_3$$

s.t.

$$2w_1 + 6w_2 \geqslant 3$$

$$4w_1 + 2w_2 + w_3 \geqslant 8$$

$$w_1, w_2, \quad w_3 \geqslant 0$$

The equality-equivalent equations for this problem are

$$2w_1 + 6w_2 \qquad - w_4 \qquad = 3$$

$$4w_1 + 2w_2 + w_3 \qquad - w_5 = 8$$

$$G + 1,600w_1 + 1,800w_2 + 350w_3 \qquad = 0$$

Applying the big M method of Section 8.8, we obtain the optimum solution:

$$w_1^* = \tfrac{3}{2} \qquad w_2^* = 0 \qquad w_3^* = 2$$

$$w_4^* = 0 \qquad w_5^* = 0 \qquad G^* = -3,100$$

This means that the optimum solution to the minimization problem is $+3,100$, the same optimum solution found for the primal problem. [See equation (8.3.28).] This result is actually a theorem in LP theory which states that:

If either the primal or dual problems has a finite optimal solution, the other problem has a finite optimal solution and that max Z = min G. If either problem has an unbounded optimal solution, the other problem has no feasible solutions.

Thus, solving the primal problem gives the optimum G for the dual problem.

The optimum values of the dual variables can also be found from solving the primal problem. In Table 8.9.2 we have given the final table of the primal problem (Table 8.4.2).

It can be shown from linear programming theory that the values in the last row of the primal optimum solution table are the optimum solution values of the dual problem. Since x_3 is the slack variable of the first constraint, it corresponds to the first dual variable w_1. Therefore, $w_1 = \tfrac{3}{2}$. Likewise, x_4 and x_5 correspond to the dual variables w_2 and w_3, respectively. Hence, $w_2 = 0$ and $w_3 = 2$. Moreover, w_4 and w_5 are surplus variables of the dual problem and they correspond to x_1 and x_2, respectively, of the primal problem. Thus, $w_4 = 0$ and $w_5 = 0$. The correspondence between primal and dual variables is summarized in Table 8.9.3. It

TABLE 8.9.2. *Final Table of Primal Problem*

Equation Row Number	Basis	VARIABLES					Solution
		x_1	x_2	x_3	x_4	x_5	
1	x_1	1	0	$\frac{1}{2}$	0	-2	100
2	x_4	0	0	-3	1	10	500
3	x_2	0	1	0	0	1	350
4	Z	0	0	$\frac{3}{2}$	0	2	3,100

TABLE 8.9.3. *Correspondence Between Primal and Dual Variables*

	Primal	Dual	
Main variables	$\begin{cases} x_1 \\ x_2 \end{cases}$	$\left. \begin{matrix} w_1 \\ w_5 \end{matrix} \right\}$	Surplus variables
Slack variables	$\begin{cases} x_3 \\ x_4 \\ x_5 \end{cases}$	$\left. \begin{matrix} w_1 \\ w_2 \\ w_3 \end{matrix} \right\}$	Main variables

can be seen that it is never necessary to solve both problems independently. Only one of the two need be solved, with the solution to the other problem available by inspection.

8.9.3. Economic Interpretation of Dual. As we discussed in Section 6.6, the optimum dual-variable values are called shadow prices and represent the amount of change in the objective function for a unit increase in the respective right-hand side. Thus, $w_1 = \frac{3}{2}$ means that for each unit of labor added, the profit increases by $1.50. For each unit of processing added, the profit remains the same; thus, $w_2 = 0$. Finally, $w_3 = 2$ means that for each additional alarm assembly added, the profit increases by $2.00. These values for the shadow prices remain stable as long as the current optimal basis of the primal problem remains feasible. If the resources are changed in sufficient quantity, the current solution to the primal problem would no longer be optimal and a new primal basis would be determined. There would then evolve a new set of shadow prices. This was shown in Section 6.9, where the labor resource was increased to 1,800 hours. The new primal basis was $(x_1, x_2, x_3) = (183.33, 350, 33.33)$, with $Z^* = \$3,350$. The shadow prices were computed to be $w_1 = 0$, $w_2 = 0.5$, and $w_3 = 7$.

The shadow prices are also interpreted as the maximum amount of money the manager or decision maker would be willing to pay to buy additional units of an exhausted or scarce resource. Thus, $w_1 = \frac{3}{2}$ means that the manager would be willing to pay $1.50 per additional labor hour, $w_2 = 0$ means that he would be unwilling to buy any additional processing hours, and $w_3 = 2$ means that he would be willing to pay $2.00 per alarm assembly unit. Hence, the shadow prices are, in effect, implied per-unit costs of the resources.

With this interpretation of the dual variables, we can give the following interpretation of the dual problem. Recall that the primal problem is to maximize the profit of a production process subject to restrictions on the input resources. Suppose a second manufacturer believes that he has a more efficient way of using the available resources to produce the output and wants to buy out the first manufacturer. He therefore offers the first manufacturer a payment of w_1 for each unit of labor, w_2 for each unit of processing, and w_3 for each alarm assembly. Thus, the total payment to the first manufacturer (and total cost to the second manufacturer) is

$$G = 1,600w_1 + 1,800w_2 + 350w_3$$

The w values for the payment offer are chosen such that

$$2w_1 + 6w_2 \geqslant 3$$
$$4w_1 + 2w_2 + w_3 \geqslant 8$$

That is, the payment offer for the resources guarantee at least an equivalent value of $3.00 per regular clock and $8.00 per alarm clock. The second manufacturer convinces the first that this payment offer is at least as much as he could obtain from any production decision, since it can be shown that

$$1,600w_1 + 1,800w_2 + 350w_3 \geqslant 3x_1 + 8x_2$$

That is, the dual objective function is always greater than or equal to the primal objective function, and $G = Z$ only at the optimum solution. Thus, the first manufacturer accepts the offer and the competition buys him out at the minimum cost.

8.9.4. Complementary Slackness. From our analysis of the primal–dual problem we can make the following observations. If the dual variable is positive (w_1 and w_3), the corresponding primal constraint is binding and the respective slack variables (x_3 and x_5) are zero. If the primal constraints are strict inequalities (second constraint) and thus the respective slack variable is positive, the corresponding dual variable is zero (w_2). These concepts are referred to as *complementary slackness* and can be represented in the following set of equations using Table 8.9.3:

$$\begin{cases} x_1 w_4 = 0 \\ x_2 w_5 = 0 \end{cases} \qquad \begin{cases} x_3 w_1 = 0 \\ x_4 w_2 = 0 \\ x_5 w_3 = 0 \end{cases}$$

The first two equations state that if the primal main variables are positive, the dual surplus variables must be zero. That would imply that the dual constraints are satisfied as equalities. If, however, a dual constraint is not binding, the primal main variable is zero. The last three equations are interpreted similarly. If the dual variables are positive, the primal constraints are binding and the slack variables are zero. If, however, the primal constraints are satisfied as inequalities, the dual variables are zero.

The concepts of complementary slackness can be used to find the solution of the dual problem if the primal optimal solution is known. Thus, given the solution to the primal problem

$$x_1^* = 100, \quad x_2^* = 350, \quad x_3^* = 0, \quad x_4^* = 500, \quad x_5^* = 0$$

and

$$Z^* = 3,100$$

we conclude the following:

From $x_1 w_4 = 0$ and $x_2 w_5 = 0$, $w_4^* = 0$ and $w_5^* = 0$.
From $x_4 w_2 = 0$, $w_2^* = 0$.

Thus, the dual constraints must be satisfied at the optimum by

$$2w_1 \qquad = 3$$
$$4w_1 + w_3 = 8$$

Therefore, $w_1^* = \frac{3}{2}$ and $w_3^* = 2$. Substituting the optimum values of w into the dual objective function, we get

$$G^* = 1,600\left(\tfrac{3}{2}\right) + 1,800(0) + 350(2)$$
$$= 3,100$$

SECTION 8.10. *Sensitivity Analysis*

8.10.1. Introduction. Quite often a manager is interested in knowing the effect on the optimal solution to the LP problem when the profit per unit of output changes (say, for regular clocks from $3.00/unit to $4.00/unit) or if the amount of resources available changes (say, from 1.600 labor hours to 1,700 labor hours). Moreover, he would like to know the effect of a new product introduction (radio alarm clocks) or a new constraint (total clocks must be at least 300 units) or a change in the coefficients of the constraint equations that measure the usage of resource input per unit of output (say from 2 labor hours per regular clock to 3 labor hours per regular clock). By examining the final optimal table of the primal problem it is possible to answer many of the manager's questions without the necessity of solving the whole problem once again from the beginning. We present in Table 8.10.1 the final table of the primal problem and will now

TABLE 8.10.1. *Final Table of Primal Problem*

Equation Row Number	Basis	x_1	x_2	x_3	x_4	x_5	Solution
				VARIABLES			
1	x_1	1	0	$\frac{1}{2}$	0	-2	100
2	x_4	0	0	-3	1	10	500
3	x_2	0	1	0	0	1	350
4	Z	0	0	$\frac{3}{2}$	0	2	3,100

show how this information can be used to answer the manager's questions.

8.10.2. Changes in Resources. Suppose that after an optimal solution was found, it was learned that more (or less) labor was, in reality, available. If this change in resource is such that the present optimal solution is still feasible, the new optimal value for the profit can be found by multiplying the shadow price of labor, $1.50, by the change in labor resource, $+100$ hours (or -100 hours), yielding an increase of $150.00 profit (or a decrease of $150.00 profit). Thus, what we wish to determine is the range of possible values for the resources such that the current value of the resources' shadow prices are constants. Two cases must be considered: first, the case where there is excess resource at present, and second, the case where all the available resource is being used.

CASE 1. Excess Resource Exists. If the resource is not fully utilized, the corresponding slack variable will be in the basis of the optimal solution. Thus, if not all the processing time is used, x_4 is positive in the optimal basis and increasing the amount of processing time will increase x_4 but will not change the shadow price, which remains at zero. On the other hand, if the processing time is decreased, x_4 will decrease until it reaches zero, at which point the basis changes, x_4 is no longer in the optimal basis, and the shadow price changes. The LP problem would then have to be resolved with the new resource value. Thus, for our problem, the range of values for the change in x_4 is

$$-500 \leqslant \text{change in } x_4 \leqslant \infty$$

and

$$-500 \leqslant \text{change in processing resource} \leqslant \infty$$

and therefore the range of values for the processing resource is

$$1,800 - 500 \leqslant \text{processing time} \leqslant 1,800 + \infty$$

or

$$1,300 \leqslant \text{processing time} \leqslant \infty$$

CASE 2. Resource is Fully Utilized. If the resource is fully utilized, the constraints are binding and the corresponding slack variables are zero in the optimal solution. Thus, for our problem $x_3 = x_5 = 0$, both not in the optimal basis. From Table 8.10.1 ($x_5 = 0$),

$$x_1 + \tfrac{1}{2}x_3 = 100$$

$$-3x_3 + x_4 = 500$$

Solving for x_3, we get

$$x_3 = 200 - 2x_1$$

or

$$x_3 = -166.67 + \frac{x_4}{3}$$

Thus, x_3 can increase until 200, at which time $x_1 = 0$ and a basis change occurs, or x_3 can decrease until -166.67, at which time $x_4 = 0$ and a basis change occurs. Hence,

$$-166.67 \leqslant \text{change in } x_3 \leqslant 200$$

However, an increase in x_3 is to be interpreted as an increase in the number of slack or unused labor hours. This must correspond to an overall decrease in the actual labor hours used for production. Therefore,

$$-200 \leqslant \text{change in usable labor resource} \leqslant 166.67$$

and

$$1,600 - 200 \leqslant \text{available labor hours} \leqslant 1,600 + 166.67$$

or

$$1,400 \leqslant \text{available labor hours} \leqslant 1,766.67$$

Furthermore, from Table 8.10.1 ($x_3 = 0$),

$$x_1 \quad - 2x_5 = 100$$

$$x_4 + 10x_5 = 500$$

$$x_2 + x_5 = 350$$

Solving for x_5, we get

$$x_5 = -50 + \frac{x_1}{2}$$

or

$$x_5 = 50 - \frac{x_4}{10}$$

or

$$x_5 = 350 - x_2$$

Thus, x_5 can increase only until 50, at which time $x_4 = 0$ and a basis change occurs or x_5 can decrease until -50, at which time $x_1 = 0$ and a basis change occurs. Hence,

$$-50 \leqslant \text{change in } x_5 \leqslant 50$$

and

$$-50 \leqslant \text{change in usable alarm assemblies resource} \leqslant 50$$

Therefore,

$$350 - 50 \leqslant \text{available alarm assemblies} \leqslant 350 + 50$$

or

$$300 \leqslant \text{available alarm assemblies} \leqslant 400$$

Table 8.10.2 summarizes the sensitivity analysis for the available resources for which the present basis remains optimal.

TABLE 8.10.2. *Sensitivity Analysis of Resource Values*

		CONSTRAINTS	
	Labor Time	*Processing Time*	*Alarm Assemblies*
Slack variables	x_3	x_4	x_5
Original resource availability	1,600 hr	1,800 hr	350 alarm assemblies
Resource change decrease	−200	−500	50
Lower limit of resource	1,400	1,300	300
Resource change increase	166.67	No limit	50
Upper limit of resource	1,766.67	∞	400
Range	1,400–1,766.67	1,300–∞	300–400
Shadow price	$1.50	0	$2.00

8.10.3. Change in Profit Values. Suppose that after the optimal solution to the LP problem has been determined, the manager realizes that the profit per regular clock is only $2.00. He wishes to know if the present optimal basis is still optimal, if he must resolve the whole problem, or if by some modifications a new optimal solution can be determined. Two cases, in general, must be examined. The first considers the case if the variable associated with the profit change is in the optimal basis, and the second considers the case where the variable associated with the profit change is not in the optimal basis.

CASE 1. *Variable Associated with Profit Change is Not in Final Basis.* In the final table to the production problem, x_3 and x_5 are not in the final basis. Since x_3 and x_5 did not appear in the original objective function, they might be thought of as having a profit per unit of zero. Assume that the profit per unit for x_3 increases by Δc_3. It can be shown that in Table 8.10.1, the last row element corresponding to x_3 would now be $\frac{3}{2} - \Delta c_3$. For the solution to be optimal, $\frac{3}{2} - \Delta c_3 \geqslant 0$ or $\Delta c_3 \leqslant \frac{3}{2}$, with Δc_3 having no lower bound. Thus, c_3 ranges from $-\infty$ to $\frac{3}{2}$. For x_5, we would find in a similar way that $\Delta c_5 \leqslant 2$ and Δc_5 has no lower bound. Thus, c_5 ranges from $-\infty$ to 2.

CASE 2. *Variable Associated with Profit Change is in Final Basis.* Assume that the profit per unit of regular clocks, c_1, is increased to $c_1 + \Delta c_1$. Then, in the last row of the final table, $c_1 + \Delta c_1$ must become zero for the x_1 column. This is accomplished by multiplying the elements in the x_1 row by Δc_1 and adding to every corresponding element in the last row. These new last elements must all remain positive for the solution to still be optimal. Thus, for a change in c_1, we have

$$-2\Delta c_1 + 2 \geqslant 0$$

$$\Delta c_1 \quad \leqslant \frac{-2}{-2} = 1$$

and

$$\tfrac{1}{2}\Delta c_1 + \tfrac{3}{2} \geqslant 0$$

$$\Delta c_1 \geqslant \frac{-\tfrac{3}{2}}{\tfrac{1}{2}} = -3$$

Thus,

$$-3 \leqslant \Delta c_1 \leqslant 1$$

and

$$0 \leqslant c_1 \leqslant 4$$

Thus, if in reality the profit for regular clocks were only $2.00 per unit, the optimal basis would still be optimal.

A similar analysis can be performed for c_2; if the new profit per unit of alarm clocks is $c_2 + \Delta c_2$, then

$$\Delta c_2 + 2 \geqslant 0$$

$$\Delta c_2 \geqslant \frac{-2}{1} = -2$$

and

$$\Delta c_2 \geqslant 0$$

$$\Delta c_2 \leqslant \infty$$

Thus,

$$-2 \leqslant \Delta c_2 \leqslant \infty$$

and

$$6 \leqslant c_2 \leqslant \infty$$

Table 8.10.3 summarizes the sensitivity analysis for the profits per unit for which the present basis remains optimal.

TABLE 8.10.3. *Sensitivity Analysis of Profit-per-Unit Coefficients*

	OUTPUT VARIABLES	
	Regular Clocks	*Alarm Clocks*
Variable name	x_1	x_2
Original objective function coefficient	$3.00	$8.00
Profit change decrease	−3.00	−2.00
Lower limit	0	6.00
Profit change increase	1	No limit
Upper limit	4.00	∞
Range	0–4	6–∞
Effect of unit change on profit	100	350

8.10.4. New Products. Suppose that the manager is considering introducing a new product, alarm clock–radios. He would like to know if this product should be manufactured internally or possibly produced on the outside. If produced internally, it would require the expenditure of available resources; that is, each alarm clock radio requires 3 labor hours, 2 processing hours, and 1 alarm assembly. The variable savings from manufacturing the new product internally are $6.00/unit. The solution to the manager's problem will be as follows:

> If the current optimal basic solution is still optimal after a new product has been considered, the new product should not be manufactured internally.
>
> If the current optimal solution changes, the new product should be considered for internal production.

In general, the current optimal basic solution remains optimal as long as the dual solution is also optimal. Hence, if we examine the dual constraint associated with the new product, it will be obvious what the manager's decision should be. Thus, if the dual constraint is satisfied using the present solution values, the new product should not be produced internally. If the dual constraint is violated with the current optimal values, the new product should be produced internally. For our example the dual constraint that corresponds to the new product is

$$3w_1 + 2w_2 + w_3 \geqslant 6$$

In order to determine if the constraint is satisfied, we substitute the values for the shadow prices, $w_1 = \frac{3}{2}$, $w_2 = 0$, and $w_3 = 2$, yielding

$$3\left(\tfrac{3}{2}\right) + 2(0) + 1(2) = 6.5 > 6$$

Thus, the constraint is satisfied, the present solution is still optimal, and the new product should not be produced internally (i.e., the costs of producing the product internally are greater than the savings).

As a final comment on sensitivity analysis, the following points are noted. It might occur that after an optimal solution to an LP problem has been found, a new constraint is discovered. Two possibilities take place.

> The new constraint is satisfied with the current solution. Thus, the current solution remains optimal.
>
> The new constraint is violated with the current solution. Thus, the problem must be resolved.

It also might occur that the values for the resource usage per unit of output are incorrect and must be changed. The analysis of this sensitivity problem is beyond the scope of this text.

Using computers to solve linear programming problems was discussed in Section 6.9. There are many available computer programs for linear programming. One of the most popular is a program developed by IBM known as MPS (Mathematical Programming System). Most of the large-scale linear programming computer programs allow for as many as thousands of constraints and variables and do far more than simply obtain the optimal solution. In addition, all of the sensitivity analyses described in this chapter (and much more) can be easily performed. These types of analyses are generally known as postoptimality analysis.

The computer program described in Section 6.9 yields more than just the optimal solution. By changing one input parameter, the program prints the initial tableau and the tableau after each iteration. A portion of this extended output is shown in Figure 8.11.1. The final tableau is

SIMPLEX TABLEAU AFTER ITERATION 0

ROW	BASIS VAR	SOLUTION	TABLEAU VALUES				
1	3	1600.000	2.000	4.000	1.000	0.0	0.0
2	4	1800.000	6.000	2.000	0.0	1.000	0.0
3	5	350.000	0.0	1.000	0.0	0.0	1.000
4	Z	0.0	-3.000	-8.000	0.0	0.0	0.0

SIMPLEX TABLEAU AFTER ITERATION 1

ROW	BASIS VAR	SOLUTION	TABLEAU VALUES				
1	3	200.000	2.000	0.0	1.000	0.0	-4.000
2	4	1100.000	6.000	0.0	0.0	1.000	-2.000
3	2	350.000	0.0	1.000	0.0	0.0	1.000
4	Z	2800.000	-3.000	0.0	0.0	0.0	8.000

SIMPLEX TABLEAU AFTER ITERATION 2

ROW	BASIS VAR	SOLUTION	TABLEAU VALUES				
1	1	100.000	1.000	0.0	0.500	0.0	-2.000
2	4	500.000	0.0	0.0	-3.000	1.000	10.000
3	2	350.000	0.0	1.000	0.0	0.0	1.000
4	Z	3100.000	0.0	0.0	1.500	0.0	2.000

FIGURE 8.11.1. *Sample computer output.*

identical to that developed in this chapter and can be used for further sensitivity analysis.

Since real-world linear programming problems tend to be large, without computers it would be impossible to obtain a practical solution. Therefore, the computer is an essential tool of linear programming studies.

SECTION 8.12. *Summary*

This chapter has dealt with the general technique for solving a linear programming problem. The simplex method was developed and a simplex algorithm presented. In theory, a linear programming problem of any size can be solved. Since the simplex computational procedures give rise to several special cases, each of these was discussed separately. These included alternate optima, unbounded solutions, degeneracy, and artificial variables.

The concept of duality and its relationship to the original primal problem was examined fully. The interpretation of the dual variables and the dual problem and complementary slackness concept were presented, as were solution procedures for the dual problem.

An introductory discussion of linear programming sensitivity analysis was presented. Three major areas were examined: the change in available resources, the change in profit per unit, and the introduction of new products.

For further study of the theory and applications of linear programming, the student is referred to the many good books on linear programming listed in the Bibliography.

PROBLEMS

8.1. Reconsider the television manufacturer problem, Problem 6.4. Solve it again, using the simplex algorithm.

8.2. (Problem 8.1 continued) Perform the sensitivity analysis for this problem and determine the range of values for the right-hand-side values such that the shadow prices remain constant.

8.3. (Problem 8.1 continued) Perform the sensitivity analysis for this problem and determine the range of values for the unit profits such that the current optimal basis remains optimal.

8.4. (Problem 8.1 continued)

(a) Write the dual of this problem.
(b) Give an economic interpretation of the dual problem.
(c) Solve the dual problem using the method of Section 8.8.

8.5. (Problem 8.1 continued) Suppose that the profit per unit for each type of television set is the same and equals $8. Solve this revised problem using the simplex algorithm. Interpret your answer.

8.6. (Problem 8.1 continued) Suppose that the manufacturer has only eight color tubes available. Solve this revised problem using the simplex algorithm. Interpret your answer.

8.7. (Problem 8.1 continued) The manufacturer is considering the manufacture of a black-and-white portable line of sets that can use the same chassis. Each of these sets requires 6 production hours and will yield a profit of $8. Should the manufacturer change his output mix to include this new line?

8.8. Consider the following LP problem:

$$\text{maximize } Z = 3X_1 + 4X_2$$
$$\text{s.t.}$$
$$2X_1 - 4X_2 \leqslant 0$$
$$X_1 + X_2 \leqslant 50$$
$$X_1 \qquad \geqslant 10$$
$$X_2 \geqslant 15$$
$$X_1, \quad X_2 \geqslant 0$$

8.9. (Problem 8.8 continued) Write the dual of this problem and find the dual solution using complementary slackness.

8.10. (Problem 8.8 continued) Solve this problem using the computer and give the sensitivity analysis results for the objective function coefficients and the right-hand sides.

8.11. Consider the following linear programming problem:

$$\text{maximize } Z = 4X_1 + 6X_2 + 8X_3$$
$$\text{s.t.}$$
$$-4X_1 + 2X_2 + 2X_3 \leqslant 20$$
$$3X_2 + 6X_3 \geqslant 45$$
$$X_1, \quad X_2 \qquad \geqslant 0$$

Solve this problem using the simplex algorithm.

8.12. (Problem 8.11 continued) Write the dual of this problem and solve using the simplex algorithm.

8.13. Formulate a two-variable problem by which you can show graphically that the simplex algorithm is not the most efficient solution technique (i.e., the minimum number of tableaus needed to reach the optimum solution).

8.14. Reconsider the printing company problem, Problem 6.16. Solve this problem using the simplex algorithm.

8.15. (Problem 8.14 continued) Perform the sensitivity analysis for this problem and determine the range of values for the right-hand-side values such that the shadow prices remain constant.

8.16. Consider the following linear programming problem:

$$\text{maximize } Z = 8X_1 + 3X_2$$
$$\text{s.t.}$$
$$3X_1 + 4X_2 \leqslant 330$$
$$6X_1 + 2X_2 \leqslant 300$$
$$2X_1 \qquad \leqslant 80$$
$$X_1, \quad X_2 \geqslant 0$$

Solve this problem using the simplex algorithm.

8.17. (Problem 8.16 continued) Write the dual of this problem and solve using complementary slackness.

8.18. Consider the following linear programming problem:

$$\text{maximize } Z = 3X_1 + 5X_2 + 4X_3$$
$$\text{s.t.}$$
$$2X_1 + 4X_2 + 2X_3 \leqslant 24$$
$$2X_1 + X_2 + 4X_3 \leqslant 12$$
$$X_1, \quad X_2, \quad X_3 \geqslant 0$$

Solve this problem using the simplex algorithm.

8.19. (Problem 8.18 continued) Write the dual of this problem and solve it graphically.

8.20. (Problem 8.18 continued) Solve the dual problem using the method of Section 8.8.

8.21. The Grape Wine Company produces three types of wine—Sangria, Sherry, and Concord Grape, which it sells by the case for $15, $20, and $25, respectively. Each case of Sangria costs $10 to produce and requires 1 hour to process and 3 hours in the bottling department. Each case of Sherry costs $12 to produce, requires 2 hours to process, and spends 4 hours in bottling. The Concord Grape costs $21 per case to produce, uses 3 hours of processing and 4 hours in bottling. A total of 220 hours of processing time and 240 hours of bottling time are available each week.

The cases of wine are stored in a warehouse with a capacity of 3000 cubic feet and are shipped out in their entirety at the end of each week. The Sherry and Sangria occupy 1.5 cubic feet/case, but the Concord Grape, because of the shape of the bottle, requires 2 cubic feet/case. The company has a contract with a local wine shop to deliver at least 60 cases of Sangria each week.

(a) Formulate the linear programming problem that will determine the optimum number of cases of each wine to produce each week.

(b) Solve the problem using the simplex method.

(c) Write the dual problem, find the dual solution, and interpret the results.

8.22. (Problem 8.21 continued) The company is considering introducing a new Light Tokay wine which will sell for $22/case. This wine cost $18 per case to produce, requires 2 hours of processing, 3 hours of bottling, and occupies 1.4 cubic feet of space. Should any Light Tokay be produced?

8.23. The Holland Bulb Nursery has been operating at a net loss since its formation 5 years ago. Management, in order to promote business, decides it will give away to each customer a bag of their special plant food called "Great Grow." Each bag is a mixture of bone meal, processed vegetable matter, and special vitamins and must contain at least 11 ounces of nitrogen and 6 ounces of phosphorous. Each pound of bone meal contains 2 ounces of phosphorous and 1 ounce of nitrogen, each pound of processed vegetable matter contains 1 ounce of phosphorous and 2 ounces of nitrogen, while each ounce of special vitamins contains 10 percent nitrogen and 8 percent phosphorous. Bone meal costs $1.04 a pound, processed vegetable matter costs $0.76 per pound, and the special vitamins cost $6.40 per pound. The management wishes to produce the bags of Great Grow at a minimum cost.

(a) Formulate the linear programming problem to determine the amount of ingredients to be used in each bag.

(b) Solve the problem using the simplex method.

(c) Write the dual problem and interpret the dual solution.

8.24. The R&L Sportswear Company manufactures skirts and dresses for junior wear. The skirts and dresses are produced of a special blend of polyester, cotton, and rayon. The amount of cones of thread needed for each skirt and dress and the per unit profit are given in the table below:

	UNIT REQUIREMENT (CONES)	
Resource	*Skirt*	*Dress*
Polyester	3	4
Cotton	6	3
Rayon	4	8
Unit profit	$4	5

The B&I Manufacturing Company, a competitor of R&L, receives an emergency order for the same type of dresses and skirts from its best customer. Not having enough resource stock available, B&I offers to buy R&L's stock of 1600 cones of polyester, 2000 cones of cotton, and 2400 cones of rayon at prices that will guarantee that R&L's overall profit will be at least equivalent to $4 per skirt and $5 per dress.

(a) Formulate the linear programming problem that determines what price B&I should pay R&L for the resources.
(b) Solve the problem using the simplex method.
(c) Write the dual problem and interpret the solution.

8.25. The Painting Supplies Manufacturing Company manufactures a paint sprayer which is assembled from three major components: container, handle and spray nozzle. Because of committments to other products the company is unsure whether they will be able to manufacture sufficient quantities of each of the components to meet next year's forecasted demand of 1000 paint sprayers. Since the company policy is to "always meet the demand," the firm considers contracting with a local manufacturer to produce some of the components. Analysis of their production process in terms of production time requirements and manufacturing cost yields the following data:

	COMPONENT			
Process	*Container* (*min*)	*Handle* (*min*)	*Spray Nozzle* (*min*)	*Total Process Time Available* (*min*)
Stamping	2	1.5	3	5,000
Milling	2.5	2	2.5	6,000
Polishing	1.5	2	1	400

Component	*Manufacturing Cost* ($)	*Purchase Cost* ($)
Container	0.60	0.80
Handle	0.30	0.40
Spray Nozzle	1.25	1.50

Formulate this problem as a linear program and solve using the computer.

CHAPTER NINE

Transportation and Assignment Problems

OBJECTIVES: The purpose of this chapter is to acquaint you with the following special linear programming problems.

1. *The basic structure of the transportation problem.*
2. *Solution procedures for the transportation problem.*
3. *The basic structure of the assignment problem.*
4. *Solution procedures for the assignment problem.*

As is evident by the discussions in Chapters 6, 7, and 8, a very broad class of problems can be formulated and solved using the linear programming framework. However, in many of these problem classes, the simplex method, although powerful enough to solve all these problems, is not the most efficient solution technique. One such special type of problem is known as the *transportation problem*. The special procedure for solving this class of problems is applicable to many situations that have the special transportation-type structure in their formulation. A second special type of problem is the *assignment problem*, which is in reality a special case of the transportation problem but with a more refined structure. In this chapter these two problems and their special solution procedures will be described.

SECTION 9.2. *Transportation Problem*

9.2.1. Statement of the Problem. In Chapter 7 we described the transportation problem as follows: a manufacturer produces a single product at M factories (source). These goods must then be shipped to N storage facilities (destination). Each source has a known available supply, and each destination has a known required demand. If the cost of shipping a single unit of the product from each source to each destination is known, our objective is to determine a shipping schedule (or allocation program) from sources to destinations so that the total shipping cost is as small as possible.

Let us reconsider the following transportation problem, which we formulated as a linear programming problem in Chapter 7. A manufac-

TABLE 9.2.1. *Factory Supplies*

Factory	Supply of Clocks
A	50
B	30
C	70
	150

TABLE 9.2.2. *Storage Facility Demands*

Storage Facility	Demand for Clocks
1	30
2	60
3	20
4	40
	150

TABLE 9.2.3. *Unit Shipping Costs (in dollars)*

From \ To	1	2	3	4
A	15	18	19	13
B	20	14	15	17
C	25	12	17	22

turer produces clocks at three factories and ships them to four storage facilities. The supplies, demands, and unit shipping costs are given in Tables 9.2.1, 9.2.2, and 9.2.3.

The manufacturer desires a shipping schedule such that his overall transportation costs will be minimized. Although we can solve this problem using the simplex method, it can be shown that the special structure of this problem lends itself to a simplified special version of the simplex algorithm which we call the *transportation algorithm*. However, before we describe the solution procedures we will present the special tabular structure used in the transportation algorithm.

9.2.2. Transportation Tableau. In order to present the data in a clear and compact manner and to simplify the calculations needed to determine an optimum solution, a transportation tableau is developed. This tableau may be thought of as consisting of six parts; the sources, the destinations, the supplies, the demands, the unit shipping costs, and the shipping allocations. This general structure is presented in Figure 9.2.1. Note in the figure that each source–destination cell is divided into two parts. In the upper part of the cell we will record the unit shipping cost; in the lower part we will record the value of the source-to-destination shipping allocation, if this value is positive. Thus, since many allocations will be zero, many of these spaces will be left blank. However, these

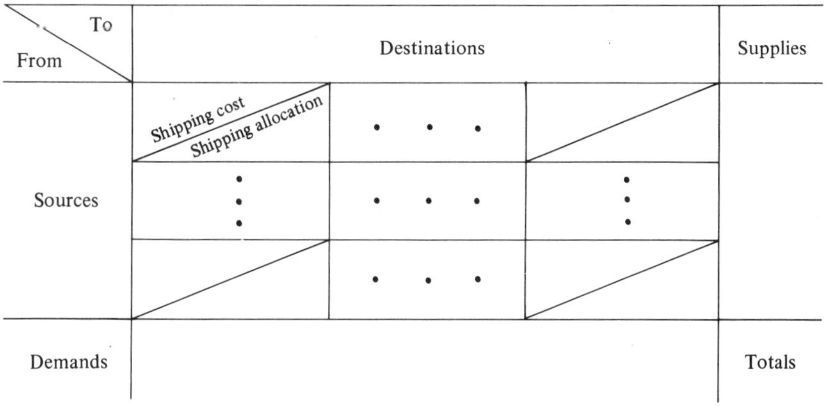

FIGURE 9.2.1. *General structure of transportation tableau.*

blank spaces will not be unused. The transportation procedure will utilize these blank spaces for recording the results of evaluating alternative total shipping allocations to determine if a less costly overall shipping schedule can be found. These evaluation numbers, once derived, will be used in the same way that the last row is used in the simplex algorithm (i.e., to determine if a change in the basis is required). The transportation tableau for our manufacturer problem is given (Figure 9.2.2.). It should be noted that for our problem, total supply is equal to total demand. In Section 9.3 we shall discuss the case of supply not equal to demand.

From \ To	1	2	3	4	Supplies
A	15	18	19	13	50
B	20	14	15	17	30
C	25	12	17	22	70
Demands	30	60	20	40	150 / 150

FIGURE 9.2.2. *Transportation tableau for manufacturer's problem.*

9.2.3. Finding a First Solution. In developing a linear programming formulation of the transportation problem we showed (see Chapter 7) that the number of allowable allocations (i.e., the number of cells in the tableau that can have positive allocations and which we refer to as *basic variables*) for each solution (called a *basic solution*) equals the number of sources plus the number of destinations minus 1 (i.e., $M + N - 1$). This means that only $M + N - 1$ of the possible $M \cdot N$ shipping allocations can be positive, and all the others must be zero. Thus, for our problem, there are $(3)(4) = 12$ possible shipping allocations that could be made, but only $3 + 4 - 1 = 6$ allocations form a basic solution. If a solution consists of more than $M + N - 1$, say 7, allocations, the solution is not basic. If a solution consists of less than $M + N - 1$, say 5, allocations, the solution is *degenerate*. The solution procedure we shall describe will not allow nonbasic solutions. The degeneracy case will be discussed in Section 9.4.

The transportation problem, as we have defined it, always has a first feasible solution and a finite optimum solution. If we start with the transportation tableau in the form of Figure 9.2.2, we define two procedures for establishing this first feasible solution: the northwest-corner technique and the minimum-cost technique.

1. *The northwest-corner technique:*

304
(a) Begin at cell in upper left-hand (northwest) corner of tableau.

(b) Compare available supply and demand for this cell. Allocate the smaller of the two values to this cell. Circle this allocation. Reduce the available supply and demand by this value. (For our problem cell *A*1 has a supply of 50 and a demand of 30. Thus, we allocate 30 units to cell *A*1. (See Figure 9.2.3.)

(c) If the cell just allocated is the southeast corner cell, stop; a first solution has been found. If it is not, go to step (d).

(d) Move to the next cell according to the following rules:

(1) If supply exceeds demand, the next cell is the adjacent cell in the column.

(2) If demand exceeds supply, the next cell is the adjacent cell in the row.

(3) If demand equals supply, the next cell is the adjacent cell diagonally.

(e) Go to step (b).

For our problem (see Figure 9.2.3) we move from cell *A*1 to cell *A*2 since demand (50) is greater than supply (30). We then compare a supply of 20 with a demand of 60. Thus, we allocate 20 to cell *A*2. We then move to cell *B*2, which is allocated 30 units since supply (30) is less than demand (40). In the same manner we move to cell *C*2, with an allocation of 10, and then to cells *C*3 and *C*4 with allocations of 20 and 40, respectively. Thus, we have made six allocations, which is the required number for a basic solution. The first feasible solution and the cost of this first solution are given in Table 9.2.4.

TABLE 9.2.4. *First Feasible Solution and Its Total Cost
Using the Northwest-Corner Technique*

	CELL NAME						
	*A*1	*A*2	*B*2	*C*2	*C*3	*D*3	*Total*
Shipping allocation	30	20	30	10	20	40	150
Unit shipping cost ($)	15	18	14	12	17	22	
Total cost ($)	450	360	420	120	340	880	2,570

2. *The minimum-cost technique:*

(a) Begin at the cell with the lowest transportation cost. If a tie exists, choose this cell arbitrarily.

(b) Compare available supply and demand for this cell. Allocate the smaller of the two values to this cell. Circle this allocation. Reduce the available supply and demand by this value. If either the supply or the demand remaining equals zero, no allocation can be made; go to step (c). [For our problem cell *C*2 has the minimum transportation cost (12), with a supply of 70 and a demand of 60. Thus, we allocate to cell *C*2 60 units. See Figure 9.2.4.]

Stage 1

From \ To	1	2	3	4	Supplies	Supply vs. Demand
A	15 (30)	18	19	13	~~50~~ 20	~~50~~ (30)
B	20	14	15	17	30	
C	25	12	17	22	70	
Demands	~~30~~ 0	60	20	40	150 / 150	

Stage 2

From \ To	1	2	3	4	Supplies	
A	15 (30)	18 (20)	19	13	~~50~~ ~~20~~ 0	(20) 60
B	20	14	15	17	30	
C	25	12	17	22	70	
Demands	~~30~~ 0	~~60~~ 40	20	40	150 / 150	

Stage 3

From \ To	1	2	3	4	Supplies	
A	15 (30)	18 (20)	19	13	~~50~~ ~~20~~ 0	
B	20	14 (30)	15	17	~~30~~ 0	(30) 40
C	25	12	17	22	70	
Demands	~~30~~ 0	~~60~~ ~~40~~ 10	20	40	150 / 150	

Stage 4

From \ To	1	2	3	4	Supplies	
A	15 (30)	18 (20)	19	13	~~50~~ ~~20~~ 0	
B	20	14 (30)	15	17	~~30~~ 0	
C	25	12 (10)	17	22	~~70~~ 60	70 (10)
Demands	~~30~~ 0	~~60~~ ~~40~~ ~~10~~ 0	20	40	150 / 150	

Stage 5

From \ To	1	2	3	4	Supplies	
A	15 (30)	18 (20)	19	13	~~50~~ ~~20~~ 0	
B	20	14 (30)	15	17	~~30~~ 0	
C	25	12 (10)	17 (20)	22 (40)	~~70~~ ~~60~~ ~~40~~ 0	60 (20)
						(40) (40)
Demands	~~30~~ 0	~~60~~ ~~40~~ ~~10~~ 0	~~20~~ 0	~~40~~ 0	150 / 150	

FIGURE 9.2.3. *First solution using northwest-corner technique.*

To / From	1	2	3	4	Supplies	*Supply vs. Demand*
A	15	18	19	13	50	
B	20	14	15	17	30	
C	25	12 (60)	17	22	7̶0̶ 10	70 (60)
Demands	30	6̶0̶ 0	20	40	150 / 150	

To / From	1	2	3	4	Supplies	
A	15	18	19	13 (40)	5̶0̶ 10	50 (40)
B	20	14	15	17	30	
C	25	12 (60)	17	22	7̶0̶ 10	
Demands	30	6̶0̶ 0	20	4̶0̶ 0	150 / 150	

To / From	1	2	3	4	Supplies		
A	15 (10)	18	19	13 (40)	5̶0̶ 1̶0̶ 0	(10)	30
B	20	14	15 (20)	17	3̶0̶ 10	30	(20)
C	25	12 (60)	17	22	7̶0̶ 10		
Demands	3̶0̶ 20	6̶0̶ 0	2̶0̶ 0	4̶0̶ 0	150 / 150		

To / From	1	2	3	4	Supplies		
A	15 (10)	18	19	13 (40)	5̶0̶ 1̶0̶ 0		
B	20 (10)	14	15 (20)	17	3̶0̶ 1̶0̶ 0	(10)	20
C	25	12 (60)	17	22	7̶0̶ 10		
Demands	3̶0̶ 2̶0̶ 10	6̶0̶ 0	2̶0̶ 0	4̶0̶ 0	150 / 150		

To / From	1	2	3	4	Supplies		
A	15 (10)	18	19	13 (40)	5̶0̶ 1̶0̶ 0		
B	20 (10)	14	15 (20)	17	3̶0̶ 1̶0̶ 0		
C	25 (10)	12 (60)	17	22	7̶0̶ 1̶0̶ 0	(10)	(10)
Demands	3̶0̶ 2̶0̶ 1̶0̶ 0	6̶0̶ 0	2̶0̶ 0	4̶0̶ 0	150 / 150		

307   FIGURE 9.2.4. *First solution using minimum-cost technique.*

(c) If no more allocations can be made, stop, a first solution has been found. If more allocations can be made, go to step (d).
(d) Move to the next cell with the lowest transportation cost. If a tie exists, choose the next cell arbitrarily between the tied cells.
(e) Go to step (b).

For our problem (see Figure 9.2.4) we move from cell $C2$ to cell $A4$. We then compare a supply of 50 with a demand of 40. Thus, we allocate 40 to cell $A4$. We then move to cell $B2$, but no allocation can be made here, since all demands have been met for destination 2. We then move to cells $A1$ and $B3$, which we allocate 10 and 20 units, respectively. Continuing the process we find we cannot allocate to cells $B4$, $C3$, or $A2$ and thus move to cell $B1$, with an allocation of 10, and finally to $C1$, with an allocation of 10. The number of allocations equals six, which is the required number for a basic solution. The first feasible solution and the cost of this first solution are given in Table 9.2.5.

TABLE 9.2.5. *First Feasible Solution and Its Total Cost
Using The Minimum-Cost Technique*

	CELL NAME						
	A1	*B1*	*C1*	*C2*	*B3*	*A4*	*Total*
Shipping allocation	10	10	10	60	20	40	150
Unit shipping cost	15	20	25	12	15	13	
Total cost ($)	150	200	250	720	300	520	2,140

Note that the minimum-cost technique yields a lower cost than the northwest-corner technique; however, this is not always the case. It is possible that the northwest-corner technique will yield the smaller cost for a given set of data. In general, however, the northwest-corner technique is usually simpler to find, while the minimum-cost technique will usually yield a smaller first-solution total cost.

9.2.4. Finding an Improved Solution. Assume the first feasible solution as shown in Figure 9.2.5. In order to determine if an improved solution (i.e., lower total cost) can be found, it is necessary to evaluate each unallocated cell to test whether that cell should be included in the overall allocation. The evaluation involves calculating the net change in cost if the unallocated cell is included in the solution. If the overall cost decreases, the indication will be that this cell is to be included in the solution. This procedure is equivalent to the simplex algorithm procedure (see Section 8.4) of finding the variable to enter the solution and become part of the new basis, the variable to be removed from the present solution, and then finding the new solution. Consider cell $A2$. Let us allocate 1 unit to this cell. The cost of this allocation is $+\$18$. However,

To From	1	2	3	4	Supplies
A	15 (10)	18 / 16	19 / 9	13 (40)	50
B	20 (10)	14 / 7	17 (20)	17 / −1	30
C	25 (10)	12 (60)	17 / −3	22 / −1	70
Demands	30	60	20	40	150 / 150

FIGURE 9.2.5. *First feasible solution.*

we now have allocated $10+1+40=51$ units of supply and $1+60=61$ units of demand, an infeasible allocation. Hence, to maintain the feasibility (in supply and demand) the following changes in allocated cells must be made:

	ALLOCATION CHANGE			COST CHANGE	
Cell	From	To		Increases	Decreases
$A1(-1)$	10	9			−$15
$C1(+1)$	10	11		+$25	
$C2(-1)$	60	59			− 12
				+$25	−$27

Thus, the net increase in cost is $\$(18+25)-27=\$16$ for a 1-unit allocation to $A2$. Clearly, we would not make this allocation, since it would lead to an undesirable solution. We record this value, 16, in the lower right-hand portion of cell $A2$ of Figure 9.2.5.

We can view this reallocation as presented in Figure 9.2.6. Cell $A2$ is designated a plus $(+)$ cell. Thus, there is a cost increase of $18 for 1 unit of allocation added to cell $A2$. To compensate for this addition, we

To From	1	2	3	4	Supplies
A	15 − (10)	18 +	19	13 (40)	50
B	20 (10)	14	15 (20)	17	30
C	25 + (10)	12 − (60)	17	22	70
Demands	30	60	20	40	150 / 150

FIGURE 9.2.6. *Evaluation of cell A2 showing reallocation path.*

subtract 1 unit from cell $A1$, designated a minus $(-)$ cell, and save $15. To compensate for this reduction from 10 to 9 units, we add a unit to cell $C1$, designated a plus $(+)$ cell, and change its value from 10 to 11. We thereby incur an added cost of $25. The path is complete (and therefore the allocation is feasible) with the subtracting of 1 unit from cell $C2$, designated a minus $(-)$ cell, and changing its value from 60 to 59, with a saving of $12. The evaluation value is computed by following the path arrows of Figure 9.2.6 and adding or subtracting cost in accordance with the cell designations. Thus, the evaluation of cell $A2$ is

$$+18 - 15 + 25 - 12 = +16$$

Now consider cell $A3$. If we allocate 1 unit to this cell, the additional cost of the allocation is $+19$. However, the feasibility requirements of the problem require the following changes in allocated cells:

	ALLOCATION CHANGE		COST CHANGE	
Cell	*From*	*To*	*Increases*	*Decreases*
$A1(-1)$	10	9		$-\$15$
$B1(+1)$	10	11	$+\$20$	
$B3(-1)$	20	19		-15
			$+\$20$	$-\$30$

Thus, the net increase in cost is $\$(19 + 20) - 30 = \$9$ per unit allocation to $A2$. This value is recorded in the lower right-hand portion of cell $A3$. The evaluation of cells $B2$, $B4$, $C3$, and $C4$ is given in Table 9.2.6, and the values are entered in Figure 9.2.5. We note that three cells, $C3$, $B4$, and $C4$, yield a negative evaluation value. This means that an improvement (i.e., reduction in overall allocation cost) in the solution is possible by reallocating the supplies such that one of these three cells is included in the solution. Since $C3$ gives the largest per unit improvement in the cost, we choose $C3$ as the entering cell. The amount of cost improvement will be $3 for each unit allocated to cell $C3$. This procedure is equivalent to examining the last row in a linear programming simplex table for negative values to determine whether an improved solution can be found and choosing the variable with the largest negative value as the entering variable. Since $C3$ is to enter the solution (basis), one of the cells already in the solution (basis) must be removed in order that the number of allocated cells remains at six and our solution is a basic feasible solution.

To determine the cell that leaves the basis, let us note the following:

We desire to make the allocation to cell $C3$ as large as possible, since that will reduce our cost by the greatest amount.

Feasibility in supply and demand must always be maintained.

The allocation to any cell cannot be negative.

For each unit allocated to cell $C3$, two cells, $C1$ and $B3$, will have their allocations reduced by 1 unit.

TABLE 9.2.6. *Evaluation of Cells B2, B4, C3, and C4*

Evaluated Cell	Cell	From	To	Increases	Decreases
		ALLOCATION CHANGE		COST CHANGE	
$B2$	$B2(+1)$	0	1	+$14	
	$B1(-1)$	10	9		−$20
	$C1(+1)$	10	11	+ 25	
	$C2(-1)$	60	59		− 12
				Total +$39	−$32
				Net +$7	
$B4$	$B4(+1)$	0	1	+$17	
	$A4(-1)$	40	39		−$13
	$A1(+1)$	10	11	+ 15	
	$B1(-1)$	10	9		− 20
				Total +$32	−$33
				Net	−$1
$C3$	$C3(+1)$	0	1	+$17	
	$B3(-1)$	20	19		−$15
	$B1(+1)$	10	11	+ 20	
	$C1(-1)$	10	9		− 25
				Total +$37	−$40
				Net	−$3
$C4$	$C4(+1)$	0	1	+$22	
	$A4(-1)$	40	39		−$13
	$A1(+1)$	10	11	+ 15	
	$C1(-1)$	10	9		− 25
				Total +$37	−$38
				Net	−$1

Thus, we can allocate units to cell $C3$ until the allocation of one of the cells in the basis becomes zero and is removed from the basis. The two cells that are candidates to leave the basis are $C1$ and $B3$ (note the minus sign indicated for these cells), since their allocations are reduced by 1 unit with the addition of 1 unit to $C3$. However, since the current allocation of cell $C1$ is less than that of cell $B3$, the reducing process will cause cell $C1$ to reach zero before cell $B3$ reaches zero. Hence, we allocate 10 units to cell $C3$, the cell entering the basis, and make the following tableau adjustments:

Cell	From	To	Increases	Decreases
	ALLOCATION CHANGE		COST CHANGE	
$C3$	0	10	10×$17=$170	
$B3$	20	10		−10×$15=−$150
$B1$	10	20	10×$20=$200	
$C1$	10	0		−10×$25=−$250
			Total $370	−$400
			Net	−$30

Cell $B3$ is reduced by 10 units, saving \$150; cell $B1$ is increased by 10 units, costing an additional \$200; and cell $C1$ is reduced by 10 units to a level of zero and is thus removed from the basis. The saving here is \$250. Thus, the net saving for the reallocation is $10 \times \$3 = \$30$. The revised allocation is shown in Figure 9.2.7.

To From	1	2	3	4	Supplies
A	15 ⑩	18 13	19 9	13 ㊵	50
B	20 ⑳	14 4	15 ⑩	17 −1	30
C	25 3	12 ㊿	17 ⑩	22 2	70
Demands	30	60	20	40	150 150

FIGURE 9.2.7. *Second solution.*

The second solution and the cost of this solution are given in Table 9.2.7. Note that the total cost has been reduced from \$2,140 to \$2,110, a saving of \$30.

TABLE 9.2.7. *Second Solution and Its Total Cost*

	CELL NAME						
	$A1$	$B1$	$C2$	$B3$	$C3$	$A4$	*Total*
Shipping allocation	10	20	60	10	10	40	150
Unit shipping cost (\$)	15	20	12	15	17	13	
Total cost (\$)	150	400	720	150	170	520	2,110

9.2.5. Finding the Optimum Solution. To determine if this allocation is optimum, we must once again evaluate all the unallocated cells as to whether their inclusion in the basis will further improve the solution. These evaluations are shown in Table 9.2.8 and are entered in the lower right-hand portion of the unallocated cells of Figure 9.2.7. Since cell $B4$ shows a value of -1, we can improve our solution by replacing one of the basis cells with cell $B1$. From Table 9.2.8 we note that for each unit allocated to cell $B4$, the allocations to cells $A4$ and $B1$ must be each reduced by 1 unit to maintain feasibility. Thus, these two cells are candidates to leave the basis. However, the current allocation of cell $B1$ (20) is less than that for cell $A4$ (40). Thus, cell $B1$ will be the first to reach zero on applying the reduction process, and will thus be the cell to leave the basis. Hence, we allocate 20 units to cell $B4$, the cell entering

TABLE 9.2.8. *Evaluation of Unallocated Cells of Second Solution*

| | | ALLOCATION CHANGE | | COST CHANGE | |
Evaluated Cell	Cell	From	To	Increases	Decreases
A2	A2(+1)	0	1	+$18	
	C2(−1)	60	59		−$12
	C3(+1)	10	11	+ 17	
	B3(−1)	10	9		− 15
	B1(+1)	20	21	+ 20	
	A1(−1)	10	9		− 15
			Total	+$55	−$42
			Net	+$13	
A3	A3(+1)	0	1	+$19	
	B3(−1)	10	9		−$15
	B1(+1)	20	21	+ 20	
	A1(−1)	10	9		− 15
			Total	+$39	−$30
			Net	+$9	
B2	B2(+1)	0	1	+$14	
	B3(−1)	10	9		−$15
	C3(+1)	10	11	+ 17	
	C2(−1)	60	59		− 12
			Total	+$31	−$27
			Net	+$4	
B4	B4(+1)	0	1	+$17	
	A4(−1)	40	39		−$13
	A1(+1)	10	11	+ 15	
	B1(−1)	20	19		− 20
			Total	+$32	−$33
			Net	+	−$1
C1	C1(+1)	0	1	+$25	
	C3(−1)	10	9		−$17
	B3(+1)	10	11	+ 15	
	B1(−1)	20	19		− 20
			Total	+$40	−$37
			Net	+$3	
C4	C4(+1)	0	1	+$22	
	A4(−1)	40	39		−$13
	A1(+1)	10	11	+ 15	
	B1(−1)	20	19		− 20
	B3(+1)	10	11	+ 15	
	C3(−1)	10	9		− 17
			Total	+$52	−$50
			Net	+$2	

the basis, and make the following tableau adjustments:

	ALLOCATION CHANGE			COST CHANGE	
Cell	*From*	*To*		*Increases*	*Decreases*
*B*4	0	20		20×$17=$340	
*A*4	40	20			−20×$13=−$260
*A*1	10	30		20×$15=$300	
*B*1	20	0			−20×$20=−$400
				Total $640	−$660
				Net	−$20

The net savings is $20×1=$20. The revised allocation is shown in Figure 9.2.8.

From \ To	1	2	3	4	Supplies
A	15 / (30)	18 / 12	19 / 8	13 / (20)	50
B	20 / 1	14 / 6	15 / (10)	17 / (20)	30
C	25 / 4	12 / (60)	17 / (10)	22 / 3	70
Demands	30	60	20	40	150 / 150

FIGURE 9.2.8. *Third solution.*

The third solution and the cost of the solution are given in Table 9.2.9. The total cost has been reduced from $2,110 to $2,090, a saving of $20.

TABLE 9.2.9. *Third Solution and Its Total Cost*

	CELL NAME						
	*A*1	*C*2	*B*3	*C*3	*A*4	*B*4	*Total*
Shipping allocation	30	60	10	10	20	20	150
Unit shipping cost ($)	15	12	15	17	13	17	
Total cost ($)	450	720	150	170	260	340	2,090

We once again evaluate all the unallocated cells of Figure 9.2.8, and these results are given in Table 9.2.10 and recorded in Figure 9.2.8. Since all the evaluated cell values are nonnegative, we have an indication of optimality (i.e., no further improvement in the allocation can be made).

TABLE 9.2.10. *Evaluation of Unallocated Cells of Third Solution*

Evaluated Cell	ALLOCATION CHANGE			COST CHANGE	
	Cell	From	To	Increases	Decreases
A2	A2(+1)	0	1	+$18	
	A4(−1)	20	19		−$13
	B4(+1)	20	21	+ 17	
	B3(−1)	10	9		− 15
	C3(+1)	10	11	+ 17	
	C2(−1)	60	59		− 12
				Total +$52	−$40
				Net +$12	
A3	A3(+1)	0	1	+$19	
	A4(−1)	20	19		−$13
	B4(+1)	20	21	+ 17	
	B3(−1)	10	9		− 15
				Total +$36	−$28
				Net +$8	
B1	B1(+1)	0	1	+$20	
	A1(−1)	30	29		−$15
	A4(+1)	20	21	+ 13	
	B4(−1)	20	19		− 17
				Total +$33	−$32
				Net +$1	
B2	B2(+1)	0	1	+$14	
	B3(−1)	10	9		−$15
	C3(+1)	10	11	+ 17	
	C2(−1)	60	59		− 12
				Total +$33	−$27
				Net +$6	
C1	C1(+1)	0	1	+$25	
	A1(−1)	30	29		−$15
	A4(+1)	20	21	+ 13	
	B4(−1)	20	19		
	B3(+1)	10	11	+ 15	
	C3(−1)	10	9		− 17
				Total +$53	−$49
				Net +$4	
C4	C4(+1)	0	1	+$22	
	B4(−1)	20	19		−$17
	B3(+1)	10	11	+ 15	
	C3(−1)	10	9		− 17
				Total +$37	−$34
				Net +$3	

Thus, Table 9.2.9 shows the optimal allocation schedule at a minimum cost of $2,090.

9.2.6. Alternate Optimal Solutions. It may occur that one or more of the evaluation values of the unallocated cells of the optimal solution yield a value of zero. This means that that cell could enter the basis, replace one of the existing basis cells, and yield no improvement in the objective function. We shall refer to this situation as the existence of an *alternate optimal solution.* As an example, assume that the optimal allocation to a transportation problem is as given in Figure 9.2.9. The evaluation value for cell $C2$ is zero, meaning that if $C2$ were allocated, no change in the solution would occur. To determine this alternate solution, we follow the procedure discussed in Section 9.2.4. Thus, the two candidate cells for replacement are $B2$ and $C3$. However, since the allocation of $B2$ (15) is less than that of $C3$ (16), we allocate 15 units to $C2$ and make the following adjustments:

	ALLOCATION CHANGE		COST CHANGE	
Cell	From	To	*Increases*	*Decreases*
$C2$	0	15	$+\$11\times 15=\$165$	
$C3$	20	5		$-\$14\times 15=-\$210$
$B3$	5	20	$+\$16\times 15=\$240$	
$B2$	15	0		$-\$13\times 15=-\$195$
			Total $+\$405$	$-\$405$
			Net $\$0$	

The net change in cost is zero, although a different allocation has been found. This solution is shown in Figure 9.2.10.

Since all evaluation values are nonnegative, this solution is optimal, with a minimum cost of $779, no change from the previous solution.

From \ To	1	2	3	Supply
A	10 ⑩	14 5	17 5	10
B	17	13 ⑮	16 ⑤	20
C	12 ⑮	11 0	14 ⑳	35
Demands	25	15	25	65 / 65

FIGURE 9.2.9. *Optimal solution showing existence of alternate optimal solution.*

From \ To	1	2	3	Supply
A	10 ⑩	14 ⟋ 5	17 ⟋ 5	10
B	17 ⟋ 3	13 ⟋ 0	16 ⑳	20
C	12 ⑮	11 ⑮	14 ⑤	35
Demands	25	15	25	65 / 65

Total cost = $779

FIGURE 9.2.10. *Alternate optimal solution.*

SECTION 9.3 *Supply Not Equal to Demand*

In Section 9.2 we discussed a transportation problem where supply equals demand. In most real-world situations, however, this condition is not realized, and either supply exceeds demand or demand exceeds supply. Since our transportation method requires that supply equal demand, we must make some adjustments to the solution procedure to allow for the unequal case.

9.3.1. Supply Exceeds Demand. Let us suppose that in our original problem, Section 9.2.1, the supply exceeds the demand. Thus, the demand is assumed to be 150 clocks, but the supply is now given by Table 9.3.1. Hence, the supply exceeds the demand by 25 units. In order to set up our transportation tableau, we create a dummy storage facility (destination), 5, that will ficticiously receive this excess supply. To facilitate the computation, we assign a unit transportation cost of zero to units shipped from each supply point to this dummy destination. The first solution using the northwest-corner technique is shown in Figure 9.3.1. From this first solution, we can now apply the procedures of Sections 9.2.4 and 9.2.5 to find the optimal solution. In the optimal solution, destination 5 will be allocated 25 units from one or more of the origins. This will be interpreted as one or more factories shipping less than their shipping capacity. For example, in Figure 9.3.1, factory *C* actually ships 45 units and remains with 25 units unshipped.

TABLE 9.3.1. *Factory Supplies*

Factory	Supply of Clocks
A	50
B	55
C	70
	175

From \ To	1	2	3	4	Dummy 5	Supplies
A	15 (30)	18 (20)	19	13	0	50
B	20	14 (40)	15 (15)	17	0	55
C	25	12	17 (5)	22 (40)	0 (25)	70
Demands	30	60	20	40	25	175 / 175

FIGURE 9.3.1. *First solution for assumption that supply exceeds demand.*

9.3.2. Demand Exceeds Supply. Consider now the case where the demand of the original problem of Section 9.2.1 exceeds the supply (i.e., supply equals 150 clocks), but demand is as is given in Table 9.3.2. Thus, demand exceeds supply by 25 units. To set up the transportation tableau, we create a ficticious or dummy supply point, D, to supply the excess demand. We assign a unit transportation cost of zero for shipments from

TABLE 9.3.2. *Storage Facility Demands*

Storage Facility	Demands of Clocks
1	30
2	60
3	45
4	40
	175

From \ To	1	2	3	4	Supplies
A	15 (30)	18 (20)	19	13	50
B	20	14 (30)	15	17	30
C	25	12 (10)	17 (45)	22 (15)	70
Dummy D	0	0	0	0 (25)	25
Demands	30	60	45	40	175 / 175

FIGURE 9.3.2. *First solution for assumption that demand exceeds supply.*

this factory or source to all destinations. The first solution using the northwest-corner technique is given in Figure 9.3.2. We now proceed to solve the problem as was discussed in Sections 9.2.4 and 9.2.5. In the optimal solution a shipping allocation is made from factory D to one or more storage facilities. This is interpreted as one or more storage facilities (destination) not being shipped their required demands. For example, in Figure 9.3.2, facility 4 requires 40 units, of which 15 are actually supplied from factory C and 25 units of demand go unfilled.

SECTION 9.4 *Degeneracy*

In Section 9.2.3 we noted that the transportation method requires making $M + N - 1$ allocations. It sometimes occurs, however, either at the initial solution or during subsequent solutions, that the number of allocations is less than $M + N - 1$. For example, the transportation tableau of Figure 9.4.1 yields only four allocations. Although this solution is feasible, it presents us with a problem of how to evaluate the unallocated cells. For example, if we allocate 1 unit to cell $A3$, increasing the cost by $+\$19$, the allocation of cell $C3$ must be reduced by 1 unit to 9, at a saving of $-\$14$; however, the supply requirement of origin C, 10 units, is violated. An allocation with less than $M + N - 1$ cells with positive allocations is called a *degenerate solution*. Since the transportation procedure works only if $M + N - 1$ defined cells are in the basis, it is necessary to modify our tableau whenever a degeneracy occurs, by introducing unallocated cells into the basis and considering them as if they were allocated.

From \ To	1	2	3	Supplies
A	15 ㉚	20 ⑳	19	50
B	13	21 ㊵	18	40
C	22	16	14 ⑩	10
Demands	30	60	10	100 / 100

FIGURE 9.4.1. *Tableau showing degeneracy.*

Let d equal an infinitesimally small allocation to an unallocated cell such that the cell can be considered in the basis, but not as affecting the total supply and demand balance or the total cost. Thus, if an unallocated cell is given an allocation d, it becomes part of the basis without changing the existing solution. The problem is then to choose which cell(s) should be given this d allocation. Consider Figure 9.4.1. Two types of unallocated cells can be defined. The first type is called an *evaluatable cell*, that is, a cell that can be evaluated as per Section 9.2.4. Cell $B1$ meets this criterion. Adding 1 unit to $B1$ yields the following cost changes:

$$B1: +\$13; \quad B2: -\$21; \quad A2: +\$20; \quad A1: -\$15$$
$$\text{Net change: } -\$3$$

The second type of cell is the unevaluatable cell, such as $A3$, $B2$, $C1$, and $C2$. We can now state a rule for handling the degenerate solution:

If a transportation tableau solution is degenerate, allocate a quantity d to any unevaluatable cell. Repeat this process as many times as is necessary to attain $M + N - 1$ allocations.

Applying this rule to Figure 9.4.1 yields a nondegenerate solution as in Figure 9.4.2. We have allocated d to cell $C2$ and thus all the unallocated cells can be evaluated as is shown in the figure. The solution procedure is then continued as discussed in Sections 9.2.4 and 9.2.5. If in the optimal solution one of the cells has an allocation d, it means that no actual shipment from that origin to the indicated destination actually takes place.

From \ To	1	2	3	Supplies
A	15　(30)	20　(20)	19　1	50
B	13　−3	21　(40)	18　−1	40
C	22　11	16　(d)	14　(10)	10
Demands	30	60	10	100 / 100

FIGURE 9.4.2. *Tableau showing use of d to resolve degeneracy.*

SECTION 9.5 *MODI Method for Evaluating Unallocated Cells*

An alternative method is available for evaluating the unallocated cells of any transportation tableau. This method, called the MODI (modified distribution) *method*, is based on the duality properties of our linear programming formulation of the transportation problem. It can be shown that there exists a set of U_i's for the supplies (one for each supply row i) and a set of V_j's for the demands (one for each demand column j) such that for every allocated cell

$$U_i + V_j = C_{ij}$$

Furthermore, for the unallocated cells, the evaluation value can be found from

$$d_{ij} = C_{ij} - U_i - V_j$$

In practice, the computations are carried out as follows:

Choose a value arbitrarily for any of the U_i's or V_j's, say $U_1 = 0$. Compute the remaining U_i's and V_j's from $U_i + V_j = C_{ij}$.

Thus,

$$V_1 = C_{11} - U_1 = 15 - 0 = 15$$
$$V_4 = C_{14} - U_1 = 13 - 0 = 13$$
$$U_2 = C_{12} - V_1 = 20 - 15 = 5$$
$$U_3 = C_{13} - V_1 = 25 - 15 = 10$$
$$V_2 = C_{32} - U_3 = 12 - 10 = 2$$
$$V_3 = C_{33} - U_2 = 15 - 5 = 10$$

Hence,

$$U_1 = 0, \qquad U_2 = 5, \qquad U_3 = 10$$
$$V_1 = 15, \qquad V_2 = 2, \qquad V_3 = 10, \qquad V_4 = 13$$

Compute the cell evaluation d from

$$d_{ij} = C_{ij} - U_i - V_j$$

The unallocated cells of Figure 9.2.4 can be evaluated as follows:

$$d_{12} = C_{12} - U_1 - V_2 = 18 - 0 - 2 = 16$$
$$d_{13} = C_{13} - U_1 - V_3 = 19 - 0 - 10 = 9$$
$$d_{22} = C_{22} - U_2 - V_2 = 14 - 5 - 2 = 7$$
$$d_{24} = C_{24} - U_2 - V_4 = 17 - 5 - 13 = -1$$
$$d_{33} = C_{33} - U_3 - V_3 = 17 - 10 - 10 = -3$$
$$d_{34} = C_{34} - U_3 - V_4 = 22 - 10 - 13 = -1$$

These results are presented in Figure 9.5.1 and are identical with the evaluations presented in Figure 9.2.5. Once the unallocated cells are evaluated, the procedure for choosing an entering and leaving cell and for determining the optimal solution is exactly the same as presented in Sections 9.2.4 and 9.2.5.

U_i	V_j From \ To	15 **1**	2 **2**	10 **3**	13 **4**	Supplies
0	A	15 (10)	18 16	19 9	13 (40)	50
5	B	20 (10)	14 7	15 (20)	17 −1	30
10	C	25 (10)	12 (60)	17 −3	22 −1	70
	Demands	30	60	20	40	150 / 150

FIGURE 9.5.1. *Evaluation of unallocated cells using MODI method.*

SECTION 9.6. *Transportation Algorithm*

Let us summarize the various solution steps of the transportation problem in the form of a *transportation algorithm*.

Step 1. Construct the transportation tableau showing sources, destinations, supplies, demands, and unit transportation costs.

Step 2. If supply is unequal to demand, add the appropriate dummy origin or destination. Set the unit transportation costs for the dummy equal to zero.

Step 3. Find a first feasible solution using either the northwest-corner technique or the minimum-cost technique.

Step 4. If a degeneracy occurs, allocate an amount d to an un-evaluatable cell.

Step 5. Evaluate all the unallocated cells using either the standard method (Section 9.2.4) or the MODI method (Section 9.5).

Step 6. If all evaluations are nonnegative, an optimal solution has been found. If at least one evaluation is negative, the solution can be improved by changing the allocation.

Step 7. The *entering cell* is the cell with the most negative evaluation.

Step 8. Allocate to the entering cell as many units as is possible (i.e., until the value of one of the existing allocated cells is reduced to zero). This cell is the *exiting cell*.

Step 9. Adjust the allocations so that the supply and demand requirements are satisfied.

322   *Step 10.* Go to step 4.

9.7.1. Statement of the Problem. Consider a transportation problem wherein the number of factories (sources) equals the number of storage facilities (destinations) and where the supply and demand values are exactly 1 unit. Thus, it is possible to supply exactly one unit to only one of the destinations from each source, and each destination receives exactly 1 unit from only one source. Although this problem could be solved using the transportation algorithm of Section 9.6, a more efficient procedure, called the *assignment algorithm*, is available.

In order to develop the assignment-algorithm procedure, consider the following two problems:

1. A supplier has four nuclear reactors stored in four separate warehouses. These reactors must be delivered to four electric company sites. The cost of shipping a reactor from each warehouse to each site is shown in Figure 9.7.1. This tableau arrangement is the general assignment problem format. The objective is to find an assignment of reactors to electric company sites such that the total shipping cost is as small as possible.
2. A job shop has four men available for work on four separate jobs. Only one man can work on any one job. The cost of assigning each man to each job is given in Figure 9.7.1. The objective is to assign men to jobs such that the total cost of the assignment is a minimum.

Electric Company Sites or Jobs

From \ To	1	2	3	4
A	$20	25	22	28
B	15	18	23	17
C	19	17	21	24
D	25	23	24	24

Warehouses or Men

FIGURE 9.7.1. *Unit shipping costs from warehouses to electric company sites (or unit cost of assigning men to jobs).*

These two problems are solved with the identical procedure, and thus only the first problem will be dealt with. A possible assignment might be: $A1$, $B2$, $C3$, $D4$. The total shipping cost for this assignment is

$$\$20 + 18 + 21 + 24 = \$83.$$

The assignment is shown in Figure 9.7.2.

This assignment may not, however, be the optimal one. The solution procedure that we will develop in the next section to find the optimal

323

FIGURE 9.7.2. *Possible solution to assignment problem.*

assignment is based on the following principles:

> The cost tableau can be converted into an equivalent cost tableau for which the optimal assignment solution will be obvious.
>
> A constant may be added or subtracted from any row or column of the cost tableau without changing the optimal assignment.

9.7.2. Assignment-Problem Solution Procedure. Consider the reactor located at warehouse A. It must be shipped to one of the four sites at a cost of at least $20. There is no way this shipment could be made for less cost. Thus, the actual cost might be $20+0=20$ (site 1), $20+5=25$ (site 2), $20+2=22$ (site 3), or $20+8=28$ (site 4). Let us, therefore, subtract 20 from each cell in the first row of Figure 9.7.1 so that the first row of our cost tableau reads as in Figure 9.7.3 and, in addition, let us record the $20 as a fixed irreducible cost which is independent of the assignment made.

In a similar manner, the shipping cost from warehouse B to any site will cost at least $15. Thus, the second row of Figure 9.7.1 can be converted by subtracting $15 from each cell and recording the $15 as a fixed cost. We thus obtain the results shown in Figure 9.7.4. From warehouses C and D the minimum shipping costs to any site will be $17 and $23, respectively. Therefore, if we subtract 17 and 23 from rows 3 and 4 of Figure 9.7.1, we get Figure 9.7.5, which shows a fixed cost of $75 independent of the assignment made. On examining Figure 9.7.5, we note that two assignments could easily be made without any additional cost: for example, cells $A1$ and $C2$, or $B1$ and $C2$. However, to make the

From\To	1	2	3	4	Fixed Cost
A	0	5	2	8	$20

FIGURE 9.7.3

From\To	1	2	3	4	Fixed Cost
A	0	5	2	8	$20
B	0	3	8	2	$15

FIGURE 9.7.4

Electric Company Sites

To / From	1	2	3	4	Fixed Cost
A	0	5	2	8	$20
B	0	3	8	2	15
C	2	0	4	7	17
D	2	0	1	1	23
					Total $75

(Warehouses)

FIGURE 9.7.5. *Cost tableau after subtracting row minimum from each row.*

required four assignments will necessitate additional cost over and above the $75 already fixed. Our objective is, therefore, to add as small an amount of additional fixed cost such that the required number of assignments (in our case, 4) can be made by inspection.

Consider the electric company sites. Each site must receive one reactor from only one warehouse. The *minimum* additional fixed cost to ship a reactor to site 1 is $0 (from A or B) to site 2 is $0 (from C or D) to site 3 is $1 (from D) and to site 4 is $1 (from D). Thus, if we subtract these minimum values from the respective columns of the cost tableau of Figure 9.7.5, we get Figure 9.7.6, which shows a total fixed cost of $77. On inspecting Figure 9.7.6, we find that three assignments can be made with no additional costs: for example, cells A1, C2, D3 or B1, C2, D4. (Notice that we do not assign cell D2, since that would preclude assigning cell D3 or D4, which are desirable assignment cells since they incur zero additional cost.) However, to make a fourth assignment, an additional fixed cost must be added to our total of $77. To determine this *minimum* fixed cost to be added, we proceed as follows. Draw the minimum set of horizontal and vertical lines to cover all *zeros* of the cost

Electric Company Sites

To / From	1	2	3	4	Fixed Cost
A	0	5	1	7	$20
B	0	3	7	1	15
C	2	0	3	6	17
D	2	0	0	0	23
Fixed Cost – $ 0	0	1	1		Total, row $75

(Warehouses)

Total, column 2

Grand total $77

FIGURE 9.7.6. *Cost tableau after subtracting column minimums from each column.*

tableau. This minimum set of lines will exactly equal the number of assignments that could be made without additional fixed cost. For our problem the number of lines equals 3 and is shown in Figure 9.7.7. In the next section a procedure for finding these lines will be given. We then choose the smallest cell value, h, from among the cells that are not covered by a line. The *minimum fixed cost to add* is given by

$$\begin{bmatrix} \text{minimum} \\ \text{fixed cost} \\ \text{to add} \end{bmatrix} = h \left[\begin{pmatrix} \text{number of} \\ \text{horizontal} \\ \text{lines} \end{pmatrix} - \begin{pmatrix} \text{number of} \\ \text{vertical} \\ \text{lines} \end{pmatrix} \right]$$

For our problem $h = 1$ and the minimum fixed cost to add is $1(2-1) = \$1$, bringing the total cost to \$78. To find the new cost tableau, we apply the following revision rules to the lined cost tableau:

1. Subtract h from every uncovered cell.
2. Add h to every cell that is covered by two lines (i.e., the intersection of two lines).
3. Cells that are covered by one line are not changed.

Electric Company Sites

Warehouses

From \ To	1	2	3	4
A	0̸	5	1	7
B	0̸	3	7	1
C	~~2~~	~~0~~	~~3~~	~~6~~
D	~~2~~	~~0~~	~~0~~	~~0~~

FIGURE 9.7.7. *Cost tableau with
3 lines covering zeros.*

Applying these rules to Figure 9.7.7, we obtain the cost tableau of Figure 9.7.8. On examining this table we observe two possible optimal assignments (alternate optima). These solutions are optimal because the number of assignments to be made equals the number of assignments that are required. This cost tableau is thus the equivalent tableau to Figure 9.7.1. The two solutions are: solution 1: cells $A1$, $B4$, $C2$, $D3$, and solution 2:

Electric Company Sites

Warehouses

From \ To	1	2	3	4
A	0	4	0	6
B	0	2	6	0
C	4	0	3	6
D	4	0	0	0

FIGURE 9.7.8. *Revised cost
tableau.*

Cost – Grand total = \$78

cells $A3$, $B1$, $C2$, $D4$. The costs of these solutions can be checked by determining the shipping costs of the solution cells from Figure 9.7.1.

Thus, for solution 1,

$$\text{total cost} = \$20 + 17 + 17 + 24 = \$78$$

and for solution 2,

$$\text{total cost} = \$22 + 15 + 17 + 24 = \$78$$

A pictoral representation of solution 1 is shown in Figure 9.7.9.

Electric Company Sites

From \ To	1	2	3	4
A	20 X			
B				17 X
C		17 X		
D			24 X	

Warehouses

FIGURE 9.7.9. *Optimal assignment.*

SECTION 9.8. *Assignment Algorithm*

The goal of the assignment solution procedure is to find an equivalent cost tableau with a sufficient number of zero cost cells such that the optimal assignment plan can be determined by inspection. The minimum cost is then the fixed cost which was determined to be unavoidable independent of the decision. Let us set up a series of computational steps for solving the assignment problem which we call the *assignment algorithm*:

Step 1. Determine the cost table from the given problem. If the number of origins does not equal the number of destinations, a dummy origin or dummy destination must be added. (See Section 9.3.) The shipping costs for the dummy cells are always zero.

Step 2. Develop the first revised cost tableau by subtracting the minimum cost value of each row from every cell in that row. Repeat for the minimum cost value in each column. Each row and column now has at least one zero value. Sum all the minimum cost values (columns and rows). This is the current value of the minimum fixed cost.

Step 3. Determine an assignment that requires no cost over and above the minimum fixed cost as follows:

• For each row or column with a single zero value cell that has not been assigned or eliminated, box that zero value as an assigned cell.

- For every zero value that becomes assigned, eliminate all other zeros in the same row and/or column.
- If a row and/or column has two or more zeros and one cannot be chosen by inspection, choose the assigned zero cell arbitrarily.
- Continue this process until every zero cell is either boxed (i.e., assigned) or eliminated.

Step 4. If the number of assigned cells equals the number of rows (and columns), an optimal assignment has been found with a cost equal to the minimum fixed cost. If a zero cell was chosen arbitrarily in step 3, there may be an alternate optimum. If no optimum is found, go to step 5.

Step 5. Draw a set of lines, equal to the number of assignments made in step 3, that cover all the zeros of the revised cost tableau using the following procedure:

- For each row that no assignment was made, make a check next to that row.
- Examine the checked rows. If any zero cells occur in those rows, check the respective columns that contain those zeros.
- Examine the checked columns. If any assigned zeros occur in those columns, check the respective rows that contain those assigned zeros.
- Repeat this process until no more rows or columns can be checked.
- Draw a line through each *checked column* and each *unchecked row*.

Step 6. Develop the new revised cost tableau as follows:

- From among the cells not covered by any line, choose the smallest element. Call this value *h*.
- Subtract *h* from every cell not covered by a line.
- Add *h* to every cell covered by two lines (i.e., the intersection of two lines).
- Cells covered by one line remain unchanged.

Step 7. Determine the new value of the minimum fixed cost from the formula

$$\begin{bmatrix} \text{new value} \\ \text{of minimum} \\ \text{fixed cost} \end{bmatrix} = \begin{bmatrix} \text{old value} \\ \text{of minimum} \\ \text{fixed cost} \end{bmatrix} + h \left[\begin{bmatrix} \text{number of} \\ \text{horizontal} \\ \text{lines} \end{bmatrix} - \begin{bmatrix} \text{number of} \\ \text{vertical} \\ \text{lines} \end{bmatrix} \right]$$

Step 8. Go to step 3.

Let us now resolve the problem presented in Section 9.7 using the assignment algorithm.

Step 1. The cost tableau (Figure 9.8.1).

Step 2. The first revised cost tableau (Figure 9.8.2).

Step 3. Determine an assignment.

From \ To	1	2	3	4
A	$20	25	22	28
B	15	18	23	17
C	19	17	21	24
D	25	23	24	24

FIGURE 9.8.1

From \ To	1	2	3	4	
A	0	5	1	7	20
B	0	3	7	1	15
C	2	0	3	6	17
D	2	0	0	0	23
	0	0	1	1	

Minimum fixed cost = $77

FIGURE 9.8.2

We examine row A and note that it has only one zero ($A1$). We box this zero. All zeros in the boxed column are eliminated. Thus, cell $B1$ is eliminated. Row C has one zero ($C2$) and it gets boxed. Thus, cell $D2$ is eliminated. There is one zero in column 3 ($D3$) which gets boxed, and cell $D4$ is eliminated. Thus, all zeros are either boxed (assigned) or eliminated. (See Figure 9.8.3.)

From \ To	1	2	3	4
A	[0]	5	1	7
B	⊠	3	7	1
C	2	[0]	3	6
D	2	⊠	[0]	⊠

FIGURE 9.8.3

Step 4. The solution is not optimal, since only three assignments were made and four are required.

Step 5. Cover the zeros with three lines, since three assignments were made. We check row B, since it has no assignment. We then check column 1, since row B has a zero in column 1. We then check row A, since column 1 has an assigned zero in row A. No other rows or columns can be checked. We then draw our three lines through rows C and D, the unchecked rows, and column 1, the checked column. (See Figure 9.8.4.)

Step 6. Develop the new revised cost tableau.

From \ To	1	2	3	4	
A	[0]	5	1	7	✓
B	0	3	7	1	✓
C	2	[0]	3	6	
D	2	8	[0]	8	

FIGURE 9.8.4

The smallest uncovered element is 1. Therefore, $h=1$. Subtracting h from the uncovered cells and adding h to cells C1 and D1, we get the new revised cost tableau (Figure 9.8.5). The new minimum cost is given by

$$\begin{bmatrix} \text{new value} \\ \text{of minimum} \\ \text{fixed cost} \end{bmatrix} = \$77 + 1(2-1) = \$78$$

From \ To	1	2	3	4
A	0	4	0	6
B	0	2	6	0
C	4	0	3	6
D	4	0	0	0

FIGURE 9.8.5

Step 8. We now go to step 3 to try to find a new and possibly optimal assignment.

Step 3. Determine an assignment.

Only row C has a single zero. We box cell C2 and eliminate D2. All remaining rows and columns have two zeros. Choose a zero arbitrarily, say $B4$, and box this cell. Thus, cells $B1$ and $D4$ are eliminated. Hence, column 1 now has one zero ($A1$), and row D has one zero ($D3$). These are both boxed and cell $A3$ is eliminated. Thus, all zeros are either boxed or eliminated, as shown in Figure 9.8.6.

To From	1	2	3	4
A	[0]	4	✗	6
B	✗	2	6	[0]
C	4	[0]	3	6
D	4	✗	[0]	✗

FIGURE 9.8.6

Step 4. Since the number of assignments (4) equals the number of rows (4), the solution is optimal with a cost of $78, the minimum fixed cost. We note that an optimal solution exists and is determined if cell $B1$ is assigned instead of cell $B4$. This yields the step 3 tableau, shown in Figure 9.8.7. This solution is termed an *alternate optimal solution.*

To From	1	2	3	4
A	✗	4	0	6
B	0	2	6	✗
C	4	0	3	6
D	4	✗	✗	0

FIGURE 9.8.7

SECTION 9.9. *Using the Computer*

Computer programs are available for solving both the transportation and the assignment problems. For the transportation problem the user must read in the following data:

1. The number of rows and columns.
2. The unit shipping costs.
3. The supplies at each source.
4. The demands at each destination.

COSTS

TO

FROM	SUPPLIES	1	2	3	4
A	50.00	15.00	18.00	19.00	13.00
B	30.00	20.00	14.00	15.00	17.00
C	70.00	25.00	12.00	17.00	22.00
	DEMANDS	30.00	60.00	20.00	40.00

OPTIMAL SOLUTION

FROM	TO	AMOUNT	UNIT COST	COST
A	1	30.00	15.00	450.00
A	4	20.00	13.00	260.00
B	3	10.00	15.00	150.00
B	4	20.00	17.00	340.00
C	2	60.00	12.00	720.00
C	3	10.00	17.00	170.00
			TOTAL	2090.00

FIGURE 9.9.1. *Sample output for transportation problem.*

The program prints the optimal shipping allocations and the minimum total cost. A sample output is shown in Figure 9.9.1.

For the assignment problem the user reads in the following data:

1. The number of rows (and columns).
2. The unit assignment costs.

The program prints the optimal assignment and the minimum total cost. A sample output is shown in Figure 9.9.2.

SECTION 9.10. *Summary*

In this chapter we have presented algorithms for solving two special linear programming problems. Although these problems could be solved using the simplex algorithm, the special structure of these problems allows for a more efficient solution technique.

For the transportation problem, the tableau structure is described and two methods are given to find the first feasible solution. Two procedures are presented for evaluating unallocated cells to determine whether an improved solution is attainable. The special cases of supply not equal to demand and degeneracy are also discussed.

For the assignment problem, a procedure is developed such that the solution is optimal whenever a feasible assignment is found (i.e., assignment equals number of rows/columns). This procedure is based on

COSTS

FROM	TO 1	2	3	4
A	20	25	22	28
B	15	18	23	17
C	19	17	21	24
D	25	23	24	24

OPTIMAL SOLUTION

FROM	TO	COST
B	1	15
C	2	17
A	3	22
D	4	24
TOTAL		78

FIGURE 9.9.2. *Sample output for assignment problem.*

maintaining the cost level at the minimum possible value, adding cost only when no other alternative exists.

Computer programs to solve these problems were developed and sample outputs are given.

PROBLEMS

9.1. The EZC Window Company manufactures awning windows in three factories and ships them to four distribution points. The per-window shipping costs are as follows:

From \ *To*	DISTRIBUTION POINT 1	2	3	4	*Capacity (units)*
Factory 1	10	8	12	14	300
Factory 2	6	7	10	11	150
Factory 3	4	9	7	5	250
Demand (units)	350	125	100	125	

(a) Find a first feasible shipping allocation using the northwest-corner technique.
(b) Find a first feasible shipping allocation using the minimum-cost technique.
(c) Starting from the first feasible solution [either (a) or (b)], find the optimum shipping allocation using the transportation algorithm.

9.2. (Problem 9.1 continued) Suppose that the capacity of factory 2 is increased to 200 units. Find the optimum minimum-cost shipping allocation.

9.3. (Problem 9.1 continued) Suppose that the demand at distribution point 3 is increased to 150 units. Find the optimum minimum-cost shipping allocation using the MODI method.

9.4. (Problem 9.1 continued) Suppose that the capacities of factories 1 and 3 are increased to 350 units each. Suppose further that a distribution point 5 is opened with a demand of 150 units and costing $8 for each unit shipped into it regardless of source. Use the transportation algorithm to determine the optimum shipping allocation.

9.5. (Problem 9.1 continued) Formulate this transportation problem as a linear programming problem and solve using the computer. Give an interpretation for the dual variables.

9.6. A truck rental company is concerned about the optimal distribution of its empty trucks. Suppose that the surplus trucks are available at locations 1, 2, 3, and 4, while additional trucks are needed at locations 5, 6, and 7, as follows:

	LOCATION						
	1	2	3	4	5	6	7
Surplus trucks	11	13	17	12			
Required trucks					17	25	11

The per-unit cost of moving a truck is as follows:

From \ To	5	6	7
1	$10	12	14
2	17	12	10
3	14	9	8
4	15	14	9

Determine how the surplus trucks should be distributed so as to minimize the total shipping costs.

9.7. Consider the transportation problem shown in tableau form in Figure P9.7. Solve this problem using the computer.

9.8. Three jobs are to be assigned to three men. The assignment costs in dollars are given in Figure P9.8. Find the optimal minimum cost assignment.

Destination

From \ To	1	2	3	4	5	6	7	Supplies
A	7	6	5	8	8	10	2	300
B	15	21	24	7	14	11	9	200
C	9	9	10	14	8	10	8	400
D	10	16	14	11	11	9	10	200
E	7	8	9	8	12	11	9	300
Demands	200	300	100	200	100	200	300	1400 / 1400

Source (row label), FIGURE P9.7

Men

From \ To	1	2	3
A	15	14	13
B	15	14	11
C	14	14	12

Jobs (row label)

FIGURE P9.8

9.9. The government solicits five companies to bid on five different proposals with the intent of giving one job to each of the companies. The bid amounts in thousands of dollars are given in Figure P9.9 with an $\times$ denoting no bid submitted. Find the optimal assignment of contracts to companies such that the total government cost is a minimum.

Proposal

Company	1	2	3	4	5
1	90	85	100	75	80
2	80	85	95	X	90
3	70	80	85	75	80
4	X	90	95	70	85
5	85	80	90	80	90

FIGURE P9.9

9.10. Given the cost data in Figure P9.10 for an assignment problem, find the optimal assignment using the computer.

	1	2	3	4	5	6	7
A	45	32	70	51	37	62	54
B	56	44	47	38	70	52	63
C	32	39	60	48	57	43	50
D	33	29	41	47	35	56	50
E	46	39	48	66	60	52	45
F	26	17	30	45	34	41	33
G	45	47	69	56	40	61	55

FIGURE P9.10

9.11. Fashion Sportswear Enterprises sells women's knitted sportswear. The company owns knitting machines which produce the sportswear in a semifinished state—i.e., only front and back pieces are made by the company machines. The company solicits local housewives to seam the pieces, sew on buttons, and embroider four sportswear patterns on the semifinished goods. The four patterns are equally difficult to make, but the material costs vary somewhat for the different patterns. The housewives supply all the necessary materials—such as buttons and thread—to be applied to the semifinished goods. Four housewives have submitted their bids per pattern as shown in Figure P9.11.

		Housewife			
		1	2	3	4
	A	$ 7.50	7.80	7.10	7.30
	B	10.20	10.00	10.80	10.50
Pattern	C	5.40	5.20	5.60	5.00
	D	7.00	7.30	7.20	7.40

FIGURE P9.11

The company wants 20 garments with pattern A, 25 with pattern B, 30 with pattern C, and 20 with pattern D, within one month of placing the orders. The housewives estimate that they will have time to make, respectively, 18, 22, 31, and 24 garments each in the one-month period. How should the company place its orders?

9.12. A small computer consulting firm is faced with the problem of its source and application of funds. The funds are available from the following:

(a) $30,000 from bonds at 4% per year.
(b) $120,000 from common stock at 9% per year.
(c) $300,000 from preferred stock at 7% per year.
(d) $200,000 from a bank loan at 8% per year.
(e) $180,000 from a private mortgage at 10% per year.

The money can be invested in one or more of the following projects:

(a) Modernization of operations at a gross profit of 10% up to $29,000.

(b) Research & development at a gross profit of 15% up to $100,000.

(c) Purchase new patent rights at a gross profit of 13% up to $90,000.

(d) Purchase another company at a gross profit of 12% up to $110,000.

(e) Retrain employees at a gross profit of 11% up to $200,000.

How should the company maximize its return on its investment?

BOOKS OF INTEREST

Daellenbach, Hans G. and Earl J. Bell, *User's Guide to Linear Programming*. Englewood Cliffs, N.J.: Prentice-Hall, Inc., 1970.

Dano, Sven, *Linear Programming in Industry: Theory and Applications*, 2nd ed. Vienna: Springer-Verlag, OHG, 1965.

Gupta, Skiv K. and John M. Cozzolino, *Fundamentals of Operations Research for Management*. San Francisco, Calif.: Holden-Day, Inc., 1975.

Hu, T. C., *Integer Programming and Network Flows*. Reading, Mass.: Addison-Wesley Publishing Co., Inc., 1969.

Kwak, N. K., *Mathematical Programming with Business Applications*. New York: McGraw-Hill Book Co., 1973.

Loomba, N. P. and E. Turban, *Applied Programming for Management*. New York: Holt, Rinehart and Winston, 1974.

Di Roccaferrera, Giuseppe M., *Introduction to Linear Programming Processes*. Cincinnati, Ohio: South-Western Publishing Co., 1967.

CHAPTER TEN

Inventory Control

OBJECTIVES: The purpose of this chapter is to acquaint you with the following elements essential to solving inventory problems.

1. *The characteristics of inventory problems.*
2. *Inventory decision rules.*
3. *The basic economic order quantity model.*
4. *Allowing for quantity discounts.*
5. *The make-versus-buy decision, incorporating inventory costs.*
6. *Allowance for backordering.*
7. *Incorporating variability of demand.*
8. *Sensitivity analysis.*
9. *Inventory problems with multiple items.*

Almost all organizations find it necessary to maintain inventories of goods which are either consumed within the organization (office supplies, raw materials) or are supplied to users outside the organization. These inventories are costly to maintain since they represent a dollar investment for goods (inventories) which are essentially just sitting on the shelf. If these dollars were not invested in inventory, they could be used profitably elsewhere. For example, excess cash could be used to purchase interest-bearing notes and thereby earn income. Or the funds could be used to purchase additional equipment, which will yield increased profits. In addition, there are other costs for carrying inventory (storage, insurance, etc.), which will be discussed in detail later. It appears, therefore, that there is an advantage to reducing the level of inventories.

There are, however, advantages afforded by higher inventories. The primary advantage is a reduced likelihood of being out of stock (a *stockout*), which almost always carries with it a penalty of some kind. The penalty for stockouts may be due to customer dissatisfaction or lost sales, or in the case of materials and supplies, a penalty due to delaying the necessary operations of the organization until the goods arrive. Another, less obvious benefit of higher inventory levels, is that they generally mean fewer, but larger, replenishments (i.e., reorders and receipt of goods). If the organization produces the goods itself, there are usually substantial savings when the production runs are large and therefore less frequent. Moreover, even if the goods are purchased from a supplier, each additional order will have an additional cost associated with it, such as the costs of maintaining a larger purchasing department, processing the order, mailing it, handling the goods when they arrive, and so on. Thus, there are tradeoffs between ordering larger quantities, thereby maintaining larger inventories, and ordering smaller quantities and thereby reducing the inventories. Inventory control attempts to determine policies that balance these opposing strategies.

There are two basic types of inventory problems: static and dynamic. *Static problems* are those in which the decision maker has only one opportunity to buy an item and sell it. An example would be the sale of calendars, where orders are placed in advance of the new year and leftovers must be sold at a loss. These types of problems can usually be handled adequately by decision theory models, which were described in

Chapter 3. *Dynamic problems* involve those cases in which there is an on-going need for the item, and ordering must therefore take place periodically. These latter types of problems are much more common in the real world and are the subject matter discussed in this chapter. An inventory control policy generally concerns itself with the answers to the following two questions:

1. How much should be ordered?
2. When should an order be placed?

There are various ways to specify these policy decisions, some of which will be discussed in the next sections. However, the actual inventory decisions (i.e., the actual amount to order and the actual time to order) must be based on the actual costs involved.

SECTION 10.2. *Structure of an Inventory System*

In general, all inventory systems have similar structures and may be described by certain basic elements. Before discussing these elements in detail, picture the following possible view of a dynamic inventory system. Consider a tank of liquid with the liquid representing the inventory (see Figure 10.2.1). Demand for the liquid is represented by a drain on the tank which lowers the level of inventory. In our tank of liquid representation, demand occurs continuously. Replenishment of inventory (liquid) occurs periodically by turning on the faucet, causing the inventory level to rise. This process is then repeated over and over again and can thus be classified as a dynamic inventory problem. Consider now one of the simplest forms of stating an inventory policy (how much, when).

Order Q units when inventory falls to a level of R units.

The quantity ordered (how much) is referred to as the *order quantity* or *lot size* and is denoted by the variable Q. The point in time when an order is

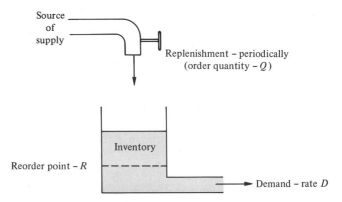

FIGURE 10.2.1. *A view of a dynamic inventory system.*

to be placed (when) is determined by the inventory level itself. Thus, an order is placed (for Q units) when the inventory falls to a specified level, known as the *reorder point*, which is denoted by the variable R. There are other ways of specifying the "how much and when" of an inventory control policy, but this approach, being the simplest and most common, will be the one primarily discussed throughout the chapter. Hence, finding a solution to an inventory decision problem with an order quantity–reorder point inventory policy will involve finding optimum values for the two controllable variables Q and R.

Let us now discuss in some detail the basic elements of inventory systems.

10.2.1. Demand. We shall view the demand as being a rate denoted as D units per time. For example, the demand rate for some product may be $D = 3,600$ units/year. In this case we have selected a time period of 1 year. We could also have selected 1 month ($\frac{1}{12}$ year) as a time period and state that the demand rate is $D = 300$ units/month. This figure is found by dividing 3,600 units/year by 12 months/year and obtaining 300 units/month. We could also convert the demand to a daily rate (assuming 30 days/month) by either of two methods:

1. Divide $D = 3,600$ units/year by 360 days/year, giving $D = 10$ units/ day.
2. Divide $D = 300$ units/month by 30 days/month, giving $D = 10$ units/ day.

In any case, no matter which time period we use to measure the demand, the actual rate must be the same, just as 60 miles/hour is exactly the same as 1 mile/minute.

In some inventory situations demand may fluctuate from day to day. However, although the demand rate varies, the average demand rate may still be constant, and therefore the concept of an average demand rate D will still be meaningful and useful for decision-making purposes.

10.2.2. Cost of the Goods. We shall assume that the goods are either purchased from a supplier or manufactured by the organization itself at a cost of $U\$/unit. Thus, for a given item with a unit cost $U = \$10/$unit (read "10 dollars per unit") we assume that an order of 20 units will cost (20 units) $\times$ ($\$10/$unit) $= \$200$ (over and above any of the fixed costs of placing the order). The importance of this assumption is that over a long period of time, let us say 1 year, the cost of the goods will equal the demand during the year times the cost per unit independent of how much we order each time. For example, if we sell (or use) $D = 3,600$ units/year costing $\$10/$unit, the cost for a 1-year period would be (3,600 units/year)

$\times(\$10/\text{unit}) = \$36,000/\text{year}$. The cost of the goods ($36,000/year) will be the same whether we order 3,600 units once per year, 1,800 units twice per year, or 300 units 12 times per year (once per month), since we have a fixed unit cost. We will consider one inventory model where this assumption is somewhat relaxed, the "price break" or "quantity discount" case, but in general we shall assume that fixed unit costs are the case. Let us next consider some of the costs, which vary depending upon how much and how frequently we order.

10.2.3. Cost of Placing Orders or Setting up for a Production Run.
Each time an order is placed for goods, there is a fixed cost independent of the size of the order itself. It is necessary to have a purchasing department which places orders and handles the invoices, payments, and so on. If a greater number of orders are placed, a larger and more costly department will be required. Each order requires preparing forms, recording the information, mailing the order, receiving the goods, making the payment, and so on, activities that have a definite cost. For example, if we determine that the direct ordering costs associated with placing 1,000 orders/year are $20,000 and the costs for placing 2,000 orders/per year are $30,000, then the additional 1,000 orders/year have cost an additional $10,000, or each additional order has cost the company

$$\frac{\$30,000 - \$20,000}{1,000 \text{ orders}} = \$10/\text{order}.$$

This amount would be considered a direct, incremental ordering cost.

If the product is produced within the company, then each time we require a production run of the item, the production process must stop producing some other product and be set up to produce this item. This will involve a period of time during which no production occurs, thereby incurring a loss of revenues. Moreover, many other costs might be incurred, such as new tools and dyes, wasted product while the process is being tested and adjusted to produce properly, and so on. In this case the cost of placing an order for goods is generally referred to as a *set up cost* and has the same meaning as the order cost, which was defined for the case where the goods are purchased from a supplier.

We shall denote the order cost by the variable K. For example, if $K = \$10/\text{order}$, then placing 12 orders/year (once per month) will cost $12 \times 10 = \$120/\text{year}$.

10.2.4. Carrying Cost.
As was mentioned earlier, there is a cost associated with holding (carrying) inventory. This cost is usually due to many factors, a few of which we shall discuss. The primary factor may be termed the *cost-of-capital* factor. Dollars invested in inventory often must be borrowed; thus, there is an interest cost. However, if the money is on

hand, then by investing in inventory it is unavailable for income-earning investments elsewhere. This is a concept often overlooked by managers in making inventory decisions. Some of the other factors that determine carrying cost are:

1. Storage cost—providing warehouse space to store the goods.
2. Handling costs—salaries, equipment, and so on, to handle the inventory.
3. Insurance—more valuable goods require higher insurance coverages.
4. Taxes—some localities place taxes on inventory.
5. Obsolescence—larger inventories lead to larger losses if the product becomes obsolete (i.e., newer products being introduced).

There are two ways of specifying the carrying cost, which will be shown to be essentially the same.

1. k_c—The cost of carrying 1 unit in inventory for a given length of time. We incur greater costs for carrying more units and/or for carrying them for longer periods of time. For example, if k_c equals 10 dollars per unit per year, then the cost to carry 5 units for 2 years is equal to $[\$10/(\text{unit}\cdot\text{year})]\times(5\text{ units})\times(2\text{ years})=\$100$. To carry 10 units for 2 years would cost \$200, as would the cost to carry 5 units for 4 years. Thus, carrying cost per year $= k_c \times$ (number of units carried in inventory).
2. k_i—The cost to carry 1 dollar's worth of inventory per time. This cost is just like the interest rate charged by banks for lending money and is thus usually expressed as an interest rate. For example, if we borrow \$100 from a bank at an interest rate of 5% (0.05) per year, the interest we would have to pay the bank (neglecting compounding) is (0.05 per year)$\times(\$100)=\$5/\text{year}$. The interest on borrowing \$200 for 1 year would be \$10, as would be the interest for borrowing the \$100 for 2 years. The same concept applies to investing dollars in inventory. If $k_i=5\%/\text{year}$, then carrying \$100 worth of goods in inventory for 1 year would also cost $(0.05)(\$100)=\$5$. Carrying it for 2 years would cost \$10, and carrying \$200 worth of inventory for 1 year would also cost \$10. Thus, carrying cost per year $= k_i \times$ (dollar value of units carried).

If we know the carrying cost per dollar's worth of inventory (k_i), it is a simple matter to find the carrying cost per unit of inventory (k_c) provided we know the cost of a unit (U). Each unit in inventory is effectively $\$U$ worth of inventory and $k_c = Uk_i$. For example, if the unit cost is $U=\$10/\text{unit}$ and the dollar carrying cost is 5%/year, then carrying \$10 worth of goods in inventory for 1 year costs $(\$10)(0.05)=\$0.50$. Carrying 1 unit in inventory is equivalent to carrying \$10 in inventory, since the unit cost $U=\$10/\text{unit}$ and the carrying costs are the same. This is seen by computing $k_c = U \cdot k_i = (10)(0.05) = \$0.50$ per unit per year, and the computed costs are the same.

10.2.5. Stockout Cost. It is certainly an undesirable event to be out of stock when units are demanded, and therefore we will associate a cost with a stockout. These stockouts affect the buyer in two possible ways. Either it causes the buyer to have to wait until the goods arrive in stock (the goods are *backordered*), or the customer must go buy the goods somewhere else (*lost sale*). We shall assume the backordering case throughout this chapter since it is simpler to analyze. Moreover, stockouts of supplies or raw materials may cause production delays, may lead to lost sales, and may even lead to dire consequences. For example, stockouts of anesthetics at a hospital or jet fuel at an airport would probably have serious consequences. Thus, we see that in some cases stockouts are serious and have an associated high cost, while in others they are not so serious and will be assigned a low cost.

Two basic formulations of stockout costs are generally used in inventory modeling.

1. k_s—Stockout cost determined on the basis of how many units and for how long. If $k_s = \$5$ per unit per day and we are out of stock (backordered) for 10 units for 30 days, we would compute the cost of this shortage as $[\$5/(\text{unit} \cdot \text{day})] \times (10 \text{ units}) \times (30 \text{ days}) = \$1,500$. We could have stated this stockout cost on a per-year basis, $k_s = (\$5$ per unit per day$) \times (360 \text{ days per year}) = \$1,800$ per unit per year, and it would have the same meaning. To show this we note that a stockout of 30 days is equivalent to a stockout of $\frac{1}{12}$ year. Therefore, the cost of a 10-unit stockout for 30 days is equal to $[\$1,800/(\text{unit} \cdot \text{year})] \times (10 \text{ units}) \times (\frac{1}{12} \text{ year}) = \$1,500$, the same as before.
2. k_u—Stockout cost per unit independent of how long the stockout exists. Thus, if $k_u = \$25$ per unit and we stocked-out on 10 units, the cost would be $(\$25/\text{unit}) \times (10 \text{ units}) = \$250$, whether the stockout was for 1 day or for 30 days. This formulation is more useful in the lost-sales situation, where it can represent lost profit on the sale; however, it can also be used in the backorder situation as long as it accurately represents the penalty suffered.

10.2.6. Lead Time. There is generally a delay between the time an order is placed and the receipt of the goods. This length of time is known as *lead time* and will be denoted by the variable L. Thus, if the lead time L is 10 days and we wish to receive the goods on March 25, we must place the order on March 15. As the example indicates, lead time causes the placing of orders in advance of the time at which they are to arrive. If both the demand rate and the lead time period are known, the demand during the lead time is known with certainty, and the decision rules can be found with no difficulty whatsoever. If however, either, or both, is variable, the inventory model is quite complex. One case of this latter type of problem will be treated in this chapter.

10.2.7. Production Rate. If the goods are ordered from a supplier, generally they arrive all at once by truck, train, mail, and so on. However, if they are produced by the company, it may be the case that the goods come off the production line "serially" (i.e., one at a time) and are absorbed into inventory uniformly during the course of the production run. The rate at which goods flow into inventory is an important factor in inventory modeling and will be denoted as P units per time. For instance, when the factory is operating, it may turn out 50 units per day, which is equivalent to (50 units/day)×(30 days/months)=1,500 units/month or (1,500)(12)=18,000 units/year. Thus, P is a rate, like the demand rate D. It may be viewed as the inflow rate of liquid in the tank of Figure 10.2.1 when the faucet is turned on.

10.2.8. Quantity Discounts. It is often the case that when goods are ordered from a supplier in large-enough quantities, the unit costs is reduced and is lower than the standard unit cost ($\$U$/unit). For instance, a supplier may state that there will be a 5% discount on the usual $10/unit price on orders of $5,000 or more, giving a new unit cost $U_d=\$9.50$/unit. This quantity discount may make the prospect of ordering in larger quantities more attractive than otherwise. An example of this type of problem will be treated in this chapter.

10.2.9. Other Controllable Variables

1. The number of orders per time. Although the inventory policy has been stated in terms of the order quantity and the reorder point (Q,R), it is still useful to know how many orders per year are to be placed, and this quantity is denoted as n. For example, if demand $D=3,600$ units/year and we order 100 units each time, then the number of orders per year is (3,600 units/year)/(100 units)=36 orders/year, or 3 orders/month or 1 order/(10 days), assuming 360 days/year for simplicity.
2. The time between orders, t, tells how frequently orders are placed, as does the variable n. In fact, t is very closely related to n. If we place 36 orders per year (1 per 10 days), we will place an order every $\frac{1}{36}$ year, which is the same as every 10 days.

10.2.10. *Summary*. The elements of the inventory system which have been defined are shown below. The brackets [ ] indicate the dimensions (unit of measurement) of each. The time period may be a day, week, month, year, or whatever.

Q [units]	order quantity; the number of units to order each time.
R [units]	reorder point; the level of inventory at which time an order is placed.
D [units/time]	demand rate, units per time.
U [$/unit]	cost of a unit, dollars per unit.
K [$/order]	order cost; the fixed cost of placing an order independent of the size of the order, dollars per order.
k_c [$/(unit·time)]	per-unit carrying cost; cost of carrying 1 unit in inventory per time.
k_i [%/time]	per-dollar carrying cost; cost of carrying 1 dollar's worth of inventory per time, usually expressed as a percent of the dollar value of inventory.
k_s [$/(unit·time)]	the per-unit per-time stockout cost; a charge for being out of stock for each unit per time.
k_u [$/unit]	per-unit stockout cost; cost of being out of stock for 1 unit independent of how long the stockout occurs.
L [time]	lead time; time between placing an order and receiving the goods.
P [units/time]	production rate; rate of flow of goods into inventory when production occurs.
n [orders/time]	number of orders per time.
t [time]	time between orders.

SECTION 10.3. *General Methodology of Inventory Modeling*

The aim in building an inventory model is to determine values for the decision variables (how much, when) which are optimal (i.e., yield the lowest cost). Therefore, an objective function must be formulated which relates the measure of performance of the inventory control policy to the decision variables. The measure of performance to be used will be total cost per time, and if we use a time period of 1 year, the measure will be total cost per year. Optimization will then require finding the values of the decision variables which minimize the total cost per year. The total cost used as a measure of performance will actually be a total variable cost figure; that is, only those costs which vary with respect to the decision variables (how much, when) will be included.

Several inventory models will be considered in this chapter, each of which is rather simple compared to real-life inventory problems, but which reveal the important concepts of inventory control.

SECTION 10.4. *Basic EOQ Model*

10.4.1. Definition. The basic economic order quantity (EOQ) model or lot-size model may be defined by the following simple inventory characteristics:

1. One product with a constant demand rate, known with certainty.
2. Goods arrive in lots (i.e., all together) when an order is received.
3. Zero lead time (i.e., instantaneous receipt of goods).
4. No stockouts permitted—this can easily be achieved since lead time is zero, and more goods can be obtained instantaneously whenever desired.

Note, however, that even if lead time were a positive value, zero stockouts can be achieved. This is true because the demand rate is known and constant, and therefore it is known how long any existing inventory will last. Hence, a new supply of goods can always be received before the old supply runs out. Let us consider a specific problem. Assume the following data:

1. Demand rate $D = 3,600$ units/year.
2. Order cost $K = \$10$/order.
3. Unit cost $U = \$4$/unit.
4. Per-dollar carrying cost $k_i = 20\%$/year; thus, the per-unit carrying cost equals $k_c = Uk_i = 4(0.2) = \$0.80$/unit·year.
5. 360 days/year (12 months, 30 days/month) for simplicity.

Assume that we arbitrarily decide to order $Q = 100$ units each time we order. This means that we will order $n = 3,600/100 = 36$ times per year, since over a 1-year period we sell 3,600 units and must order 3,600 units. Thus, in general, $n = D/Q$. Furthermore, if we order 36 times per year, the time between orders is $t = \frac{1}{36}$ year, or 10 days. Hence, in general, $t = 1/n = Q/D$. Notice that by selecting Q, we immediately determine the values of n and t. Since each additional unit carried in inventory over and above the necessary level will cost more as a result of the carrying cost, all orders will be placed so that the goods will arrive just when the inventory level equals zero (i.e., the reorder point, $R = 0$). Ordering goods sooner would cause additional units to be held in inventory, thereby increasing the carrying cost but achieving no other benefits. Since we arbitrarily chose $Q = 100$ units, our inventory policy would be:

Order 100 units when inventory equals 0 units.

A graph of the resulting inventory pattern due to this control policy is shown in Figure 10.4.1. Notice that every 10 days, when inventory $= 0$, an order is placed, goods are received immediately ($L = 0$), and inventory jumps from 0 to $Q = 100$ units.

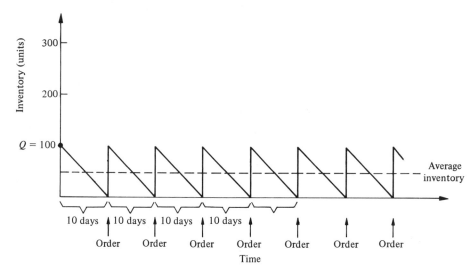

FIGURE 10.4.1. *Graph of inventory over time for Q = 100. Basic* EOQ *model.*

Let us now compute the cost of this inventory policy. We shall adopt as a measure of performance the cost over a reasonably long period of time, 1 year, since our demand rate and carrying costs are stated in terms of time periods of 1 year. We shall then compute the *total cost per year* (TC), which is affected by our choice of a value for the decision variable, the order quantity Q. This cost can also be called a total variable cost since only those costs which are affected by a choice of Q will be included. For example, as previously mentioned, the cost of the goods themselves [i.e., $(3,600 \text{ units/year}) \times (\$4/\text{unit}) = \$14,400/\text{year}$] will not change as we change Q. Therefore, they will not be included in our total cost computation. The two components of total variable cost (TC) are:

1. *Order cost per year* (TOC).
2. *Carrying cost per year* (TCC).

Their relationship can be expressed as

$$(1) \qquad TC = TOC + TCC$$

Let us now consider each of these costs individually.

10.4.2 Order Cost per Year. The order cost per year may be computed by multiplying the number of orders per year by the cost for each order. For our problem the cost per order, K, is \$10, if $Q = 100$, the number of orders per year $n = D/Q = 3,600/100 = 36$. Thus, the order cost per year equals $10 \times 36 = \$360/$year. In general, we may write that the order cost per time equals

$$(2) \qquad TOC = Kn = \frac{KD}{Q}$$

10.4.3. Carrying Cost per Year. The carrying cost per year may be found by multiplying the number of units carried by the per-unit carrying cost (k_c). However, as is seen from Figure 10.4.1, the inventory is always changing. The procedure we shall use is to compute the costs based on the average inventory carried. We could find this value by recording the inventory level at the end of each day for a long time and then average the numbers. It should be clear from Figure 10.4.1 that the average inventory computed over 10 days will be the same as the average inventory computed for 20, 30, or 360 days, since the basic pattern repeats itself over and over. This method is not necessary, however, since there are mathematical techniques which can compute the average value of a curve over time. For the inventory curve of Figure 10.4.1 it can be shown that the average inventory is $\frac{1}{2}$ the maximum value of 100, or 50 units, which is as expected. In general, for the inventory model we are discussing, the average inventory will be $\frac{1}{2}$ the maximum value, or, since the maximum value is equal to Q, the average inventory is $Q/2$. Thus, the carrying cost per year is (\$0.80/unit/year) $\times$ (50 units) $= \$40/$year. In general, the carrying cost per year is given by

$$(3) \qquad TCC = \frac{k_c Q}{2}$$

Thus, for $Q = 100$ the total variable cost per year (TC) equals \$360/year plus \$40/year, which equals \$400/year. Thus, from equations (1), (2), and (3) we get the general relationship

$$(4) \qquad TC = \frac{KD}{Q} + \frac{k_c Q}{2}$$

10.4.4. *Changing the Order Quantity.* Let us now evaluate the cost for a different value of our decision variable (i.e., $q = 200$). As before, we can determine that $n = D/Q = 3,600/200 = 18$ orders/year, half the number of orders per year when $Q = 100$. This result may be clearly seen from Figure 10.4.2, which shows the inventory pattern for both $Q = 100$ and $Q = 200$. The ordering cost per year equals $KD/Q = (10) \times (3,600)/200 = \$180$/year, half of the value for $Q = 100$. The average inventory will be $Q/2 = 100$ units, twice the value for $Q = 100$, and the carrying cost per year will be $k_c Q/2 = (0.8) \times (200)/2 = \$80$/year, also twice the value for $Q = 100$. We could have obtained the same result by simply substituting $Q = 200$ into the total-cost equation (4), which is valid for any value of Q. Thus,

$$TC = \frac{KD}{Q} + \frac{k_c Q}{2}$$

$$= \frac{(10)(3,600)}{200} + \frac{(0.8)(200)}{2}$$

$$= 180 + 80 = \$260/\text{year}$$

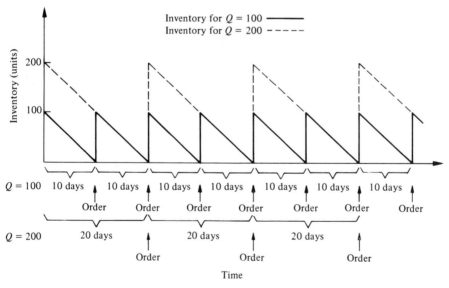

FIGURE 10.4.2. *Graph of inventory over time for Q=100 and Q= 200. Basic* EOQ *model.*

Notice that by going from $Q = 100$ to $Q = 200$, the order cost per year has been cut in half (half as many orders), but the carrying cost has doubled (more units in inventory on the average). Thus, by ordering more each time, thereby reducing the frequency of ordering, the order cost per year goes down, but the carrying cost goes up (i.e., there is a tradeoff between the two costs). Overall, however, the total cost per year has gone down, and therefore ordering $Q = 200$ units each time is better than ordering $Q = 100$ units each time.

Figure 10.4.3 shows the effect of changing Q on the order cost, carrying cost, and total cost. As can be seen, there is a point where the total cost is lowest (i.e., the optimal value of Q, which is denoted as Q^*). Also, this value of Q^* achieves the lowest possible total cost, and this value is denoted TC*. Our aim is to find Q^* and TC*.

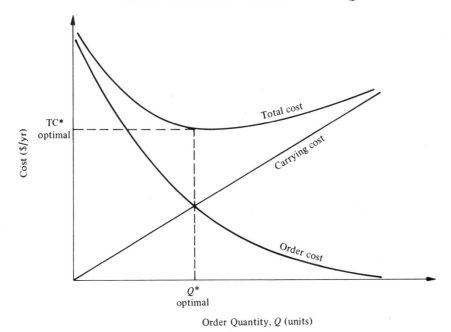

FIGURE 10.4.3. *Effect of order quantity Q on cost.*

10.4.5. *Trial-and-Error Method for Finding the Optimal Order Quantity.*

We can search for the *optimal order quantity* Q^* (sometimes referred to as the *economic order quantity*, EOQ) by evaluating the total cost (TC) for various values of q and selecting the lowest. Trial-and-error methods are generally not used, since they are time consuming and do not guarantee finding the optimal. However, they do illustrate the problem at hand, and we shall use the method here before discussing the analytical results. (See Table 10.4.1.)

It would appear from Table 10.4.1 that ordering $Q = 300$ units each time yields the lowest total cost of \$240/year. However, we cannot be sure that $Q = 280$ or $Q = 320$ is not even lower. Let us consider the analytical results that find the exact optimal order quantity.

$$D = 3{,}600;\ K = 10;\ k_c = 0.8$$

Order Quantity, Q (units)	TOC: Order Costs per Year $= KD/Q$ ($/year)	TCC: Carrying Cost per Year $= k_c Q/2$ ($/year)	TC: Total Cost per Year $= TOC + TCC$ ($/year)
100	360.00	40.00	400.00
200	180.00	80.00	260.00
300	120.00	120.00	240.00
400	90.00	160.00	250.00
500	72.00	200.00	272.00
600	60.00	240.00	300.00
700	51.43	280.00	331.43
800	45.00	320.00	365.00
900	40.00	360.00	400.00
1,000	36.00	400.00	436.00

10.4.6. Optimal Solution to the Basic EOQ Model. The optimal value of
Q may be derived using the calculus, and the method is shown in
Appendix 10-1 for the reader who has had some training in the calculus.
The results will simply be stated here.

The total variable-cost equation is

(4)
$$TC = \frac{KD}{Q} + \frac{k_c Q}{2}$$

The optimal values are

(5)
$$Q^* = \sqrt{\frac{2KD}{k_c}}$$

(6)
$$TC^* = \sqrt{2KDk_c}$$

Let us use these results for our problem where $D = 3{,}600$, $K = 10$, and
$k_c = 0.8$. We get

$$Q^* = \sqrt{\frac{2(10)(3600)}{0.8}}$$

$$= 300 \text{ units}$$

If we order 300 units each time, we shall place

$$n^* = \frac{D}{Q^*} = \frac{3{,}600}{300}$$

352

$$= 12 \text{ orders/year}$$

and

$$t^* = \frac{1}{n^*} = \frac{Q^*}{D} = \frac{1}{12} \text{ year between orders}$$

$$= (\tfrac{1}{12} \text{ year})(360 \text{ days/year})$$

$$= 30 \text{ days or 1 month}$$

The total cost can be found in either of two ways:

1. Substitute Q^* into the equation for total cost, which is valid for any value of Q:

$$TC = \frac{KD}{Q} + \frac{k_c Q}{2}$$

$$= \frac{10(3,600)}{300} + \frac{(0.8)(300)}{2}$$

$$= 120 + 120$$

$$= \$240/\text{year}$$

2. Use the expression for TC^*:

$$TC^* = \sqrt{2KDk_c}$$

$$= \sqrt{2(10)(3,600)(0.8)}$$

$$= \$240/\text{year}$$

Notice that the expression for TC^* enables us to find the optimal total cost without solving for the optimal order quantity.

Thus our optimal inventory policy may be stated as:

Order 300 units when inventory equals 0.

One very interesting fact is indicated by the solution for the optimal order quantity Q^*. It is a function of the square root of the demand rate D. Thus, if demand doubles, the optimal inventory level is not double what it was previously. The new optimal order quantity, and average inventory, is only the $\sqrt{2} = 1.414$ times the old value. For example, if $D = 7,200$ units/year, $Q^* = 424$ units instead of 300 units. The average inventory will then be 212 units instead of 150 units. The fact that inventories should not double if demand doubles is in itself a very important guiding principle and is not obvious at first glance.

10.4.7. Allowing for Lead Time. Let us modify the assumptions of the basic EOQ model just slightly and assume that the lead-time period (L) is not zero. For example, if $L = 10$ days, we must order our goods 10 days before the goods are supposed to arrive. However, let us state our policy the same way (i.e., *order Q units when inventory equals R units*). Figure 10.4.4 represents this variation of the EOQ model. Notice that the graph of inventory is identical to that for zero lead time, except that the orders are placed $L = 10$ days earlier than the point at which inventory hits zero. The optimal order quantity (Q^*) will not change from the basic EOQ model with $L = 0$. This can also be seen from the fact that the total cost equation (TC $= KD/Q + k_cQ/2$), from which Q^* was obtained, did not contain the variable L. Thus, all our results obtained for the basic EOQ model with $L = 0$ are still valid except for the reorder point (R). We need to raise the reorder point so that it "triggers" the order L days early. Solving the lead-time case by adjusting the reorder point is valid for any model as long as both the demand rate (D) and the lead-time period (L) are known and constant. The only additional computation that is necessary is to determine the reorder point that will provide exactly enough inventory to last through the lead-time period of L days.

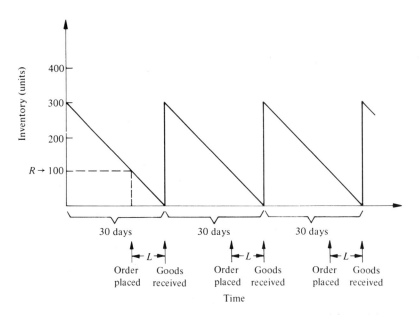

FIGURE 10.4.4. *Graph of inventory versus time. Basic* EOQ *model with lead time L = 10 days.*

Let us consider our prior example. The demand rate $D = 3,600$ units/year which is equivalent to (3,600 units/year)/(360 days/year) = 10 units/day. Assume that the lead-time period $L = 10$ days. During a 10-day period the demand that will occur (which will be denoted as D_L) = (10 units/day) × (10 days) = 100 units. Therefore, 100 units will just be sufficient to last through the lead-time period of 10 days. If we place an order when inventory equals 100 units, then 10 days later, when inventory equals zero, our order will arrive, which is just what is required.

Thus, our reorder point is 100 units. Our new inventory decision rule is then

Order 300 units when inventory equals 100 units

since the old optimal order quantity, $Q=300$ units, is still valid.

SECTION 10.5. *Quantity Discounts*

In the prior example we determined an optimal order quantity ($Q=300$ units), which, since the unit cost $U=\$4/$unit, means that we order $4\times300=\$1,200$ worth of goods from our supplier each time. This is perhaps a fairly small order from our supplier's point of view. Most vendors would prefer larger orders and encourage customers to order larger quantities by offering discounts for larger orders (i.e., *quantity discounts* or *price breaks*). Suppose, for example, that the supplier will give a discount of 2% on orders of $7,200 or more. If we order $7,200 worth of goods, which equals $\$7,200/\$4/$unit)$=1,800$ units each time, we will pay 2% less than $7,200, or $7,056. In effect, our unit cost will have been reduced by 2%. Denoting the discount unit cost by U_d, our unit cost will only be $U_d=\$3.92/$unit if we order $Q_d=1,800$ units each time. We are denoting the quantity we must order to obtain the discount as Q_d. Ordering 1,800 units each time means that we will order $N=D/Q_d=3,600/1,800=2$ orders/year. At first glance this seems very inviting because our cost of goods will go down. However, we previously determined that our variable inventory costs (ordering plus carrying) are lowest when we order $Q^*=300$ units and are equal to $240/year. If we order $Q_d=1,800$ units each time, our inventory costs will be higher. Thus, we need to compare the two situations on the basis of the sum of the variable inventory costs (TC) plus the cost of the goods themselves. Since TC was measured in terms of dollars per year, let us measure all our costs on a per-year basis.

STRATEGY 1: Don't take the discount,
order $Q=300$ units each time.

From our prior calculations we have determined that for $Q=300$, our total variable cost is

$$TC=\$240/\text{year}$$

Let us add to this the cost of the goods for a 1-year period, using the undiscounted unit cost $U=\$4/$unit.

$$\text{cost of goods}=U\times D=(3,600\text{ units/year})\times(\$4/\text{unit})$$
$$=\$14,400/\text{year}$$

355

Our total cost (including goods) is therefore

Total variable cost (TC)	$ 240.00/year
Cost of goods	$14,400.00/year
Total	$14,640.00/year

STRATEGY 2:   Take the discount,
 order $Q_d = 1,800$ units each time.

Our first step is to evaluate the total variable cost for ordering $Q_d = 1,800$ units each time. The total variable cost equation still holds (i.e., TC = $KD/Q + k_c Q/2$). However, the per-unit carrying cost (k_c) was derived from the per-dollar carrying cost (k_i) and the unit cost (U) (i.e., $k_c = k_i U$). We now have a new unit cost (U_d) and must recompute k_c.

$$k_c = (\$3.92/\text{unit})\,(20\%/\text{year}) = \$0.784/(\text{unit}\cdot\text{year})$$

Let us now evaluate TC for $Q = 1,800$ units:

$$TC = \frac{10(3,600)}{1,800} + \frac{(0.784)(1,800)}{2}$$
$$= 20 + 705.60 = \$725.60/\text{year}$$

To this we must add the cost of the goods:

$$\text{cost of goods} = U_d \times D = (\$3.92/\text{unit}) \times (3,600 \text{ units/year})$$
$$= \$14,112/\text{year}$$

Total variable costs	$ 725.60/year
Cost of goods	$14,112.00/year
Total	$14,837.60/year

Thus, the total costs for ordering in sufficient quantities to obtain the discount are higher than maintaining the optimal decision ($Q = 300$) and not taking the discount. The optimal policy is therefore, as before,

Order 300 units, when inventory = 100 units,

if $L = 10$ days.

This would not always be the case. If the discount were 5% instead of 2%, the cost of goods would be $3.80 \times 3,600$ or $13,680/year, which would make the total cost lower than the $14,640/year for strategy 1, and it would then pay to order $Q_d = 1,800$ units each time. In that case (5% discount) our inventory policy decision rule would be (assuming $L = 10$):

Order 1,800 units when inventory equals 100 units

since demand during lead time D_L has not changed.

STRATEGY 3: Take the discount,
order Q_d more than 1,800 units each time.

It may be advantageous to order more than 1,800 each time independent of whether strategy 1 is better than strategy 2 or vice versa. However, this can occur only if the optimum value for the discounted order quantity Q_d^* is greater than the price-break point (for our example, 1,800 units). Thus, it is always necessary to calculate Q_d^* from

$$Q_d^* = \sqrt{\frac{2KD}{k_i U_d}}$$

For our quantity discount problem,

$$Q_d^* = \sqrt{\frac{(2)(10)(3,600)}{(0.20)(3.80)}} = 307.8$$

Therefore, Q_d^* is less than the price-break point (1,800) and strategy 2 is better than strategy 3. It should be pointed out, however, that for any specific problem it is possible that strategy 1 has a lower cost than strategy 2, while strategy 3 has a lower cost than strategy 1. Thus, it is always necessary to compute all three strategies for each price break or quantity discount value.

We have considered only a single price break when $7,200 is ordered. There might be additional price breaks, such as a 4% discount if $15,000 worth of goods is ordered, a 6% discount if $25,000 worth of goods is ordered, and so on. Each of these price breaks (and respective order quantities) would then be considered precisely as the $7,200 price break, to find which yields the lowest total cost, including the cost of the goods.

The quantity discount or price break situation shows how including inventory costs, which in this case are the carrying and ordering costs, can affect a decision. Were it not for inventory costs, ordering in larger quantities to obtain a discount would always be advantageous, an assumption made by many managers.

SECTION 10.6. *Serial-Production Rate Case*

10.6.1. Introduction. Let us consider the case where the organization produces the goods itself instead of ordering them from a supplier. There are two possible descriptions for the manner in which the goods are produced. The first is that all the units of the lot are ready at the same time whenever a "lot" of goods is produced. In this case all the units produced go into inventory at the same time and inventory rises abruptly by Q units. In such cases the results developed for the basic EOQ model still apply. An example of such a production process might be the ceramics industry, where the final step in the production process is baking the units, all together, in an oven for a few days. Clearly, in this case all the units would be ready at the same time.

The second possibility is that the units are produced and are ready "one at a time." This is known as *serial* production at a finite (not infinite) rate and will be considered in some detail in this section. In this case inventory rises gradually during the production instead of abruptly at the end. On referring back to Figure 10.2.1, we can consider inventory replenished through production as if the faucet is turned on and the flow rate into the vat (production rate P) is greater than the flow out (demand rate D) so that the inventory level rises. After Q units have flown into the vat, the faucet is turned off until the next replenishment is scheduled. Figure 10.6.1 shows a graph of inventory versus time for the finite production case.

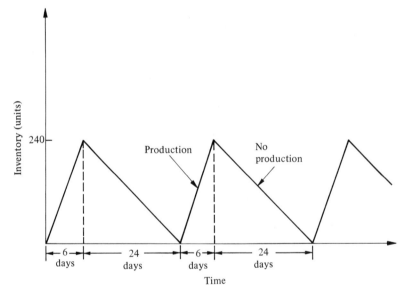

FIGURE 10.6.1. *Inventory versus time for the finite production rate case. D = 10 units/day; P = 50 units/day; Q = 300 units.*

Let us assume that all the essential characteristics stated for the basic EOQ model still apply with the exception that instead of receiving the goods in lots, the organization produces the goods itself at a production rate P units per time. The production rate (P) is assumed to be greater than the demand rate (D); otherwise, inventory would remain constant or decrease. During the period of time when production occurs, at rate P, demand is still depleting inventory at a rate D units per time. Thus, the net rate of increase in inventory during production is $P - D$ units per time. For example, if the demand rate is 3,600 units/year, equivalent to 10 units/day, and the production rate is 50 units/day, during production, the net rate of increase in inventory is $50 - 10 = 40$ units/day. If the order quantity, usually called the "lot size" in the production case, equals 300 units, it will take $\frac{300}{50} = 6$ days to produce. Thus, the maximum inventory level will be $6 \times 40 = 240$ units instead of $Q = 300$ units, which was found when we assumed replenishment in lots. Moreover, if we produce 300 units each time, we will still produce $D/Q = 3,600/300 = 12$ times/year, as before, or $t = 30$ days between orders (production runs). As with the basic EOQ model, the best strategy is to schedule the units to start arriving when the inventory level just hits zero so as not to have any excess inventory.

One slight change from the basic EOQ model occurs with respect to the order cost K. In the serial-production case, each time production occurs there is both a fixed and a variable cost. The variable cost, also denoted by $\$U$/unit, remains the same, no matter how much is produced. However, the fixed cost of production, such as setting up the production process to produce this product, replacing what it was producing before, must be included in the order cost (K). Since setup costs for production tend to be higher than ordering cost from a supplier, the term "setup cost" is usually used instead. However, the variable K has the same meaning as before [i.e., the fixed cost each time an order (to the factory) is placed].

The solution methodology, as before, is to formulate a total-variable-cost-per-year objective function and to find the optimal value for the decision variable. It will be seen that there is only one decision variable, Q, the lot size or order quantity. The objective function will once again be the sum of the ordering and the carrying costs per time.

10.6.2. Ordering Cost. If we produce Q units each time, we will produce $n = D/Q$ times per year, and the time between production runs will be $t = 1/n = Q/D$. For example, if $D = 3,600$ units/year and we produce $Q = 300$ units each time, we will produce $n = 3,600/300 = 12$ times/year, and the time between production runs will be $t = \frac{1}{12}$ year = 30 days.

The setup cost (ordering cost) per time equals (number of production runs per time) $\times$ (setup cost per run). Thus, if we produce $n = 12$ times/ year and the fixed cost of a production run (setup cost) equals $10, the setup cost per time equals $(10)(12) = \$120$/year, or, in general,

(1) $$\text{ordering (setup) cost/time} = \frac{KD}{Q}$$

10.6.3. Carrying Cost. As in the basic EOQ model, it is necessary to find the average inventory carried and hence incur a cost of k_c dollars per unit per year for each unit carried. In order to compute the average inventory, we must first find the "peak" or maximum value of inventory. It has already been pointed out that inventory will increase during the period of time when production occurs at a rate which is the difference between the production and demand rates (i.e., $P - D$). Using the values of $D = 3,600$ units/year $= 10$ units/day, $P = 50$ units/day, $Q = 300$ units, and $t = 30$ days, we concluded that producing $Q = 300$ units would take $Q/P = \frac{300}{50} =$ 6 days. We also saw that during the production period of 6 days, inventory rose by $P - D = 50 - 10 = 40$ units/day. It is important to use the same time unit (days) when using P and D in an equation so that the result makes sense. Otherwise, we are effectively "mixing apples and oranges." Thus, if the production period lasts $Q/P = 6$ days and inventory rises at a rate of $P - D = 40$ units/day, the "peak" inventory value is equal to $(Q/P)[P - D] = Q(1 - D/P) = 240$ units. It can be shown that the average inventory is $\frac{1}{2}$ the peak value, or $Q/2(1 - D/P) = 120$ units.

Therefore, in general,

(2)
$$\text{carrying cost/year} = k_c \left(\frac{Q}{2} \right)\left(1 - \frac{D}{P} \right)$$

10.6.4. Optimal Solution to the Serial-Production Model. Our total variable-cost objective function, in terms of dollars per year, is given by

(3)
$$TC = \frac{KD}{Q} + k_c \left(\frac{Q}{2} \right)\left(1 - \frac{D}{P} \right)$$

It can be shown using the calculus that the optimal values are

(4)
$$Q^* = \sqrt{\frac{2KD}{k_c} \frac{P}{P - D}}$$

(5)
$$TC^* = \sqrt{2KDk_c \left(1 - \frac{D}{P} \right)}$$

Using the values previously given [i.e., $D = 3,600$ units/year $= 10$ units/day, $K = \$10/\text{order}$, $k_c = \$0.80/(\text{unit} \cdot \text{year})$, $P = 50$ units/day] and substituting these values into equation (4) for the optimal value of Q, we obtain

$$Q^* = \sqrt{\frac{2(10)(3,600)}{0.80} \frac{50}{50 - 10}} = 300 \sqrt{\frac{5}{4}}$$

$$= 335 \text{ units}$$

TC^* may be found by either substituting Q^* into equation (3),

$$TC^* = \frac{10(3,600)}{335} + \frac{1}{2}(335)(.8)\frac{50}{50 - 10}$$

$$= 107.33 + 107.33$$

$$= \$214.66/\text{year}$$

or, by substituting into equation (5),

$$TC^* = \sqrt{2(10)(3,600)(0.80)\left(1 - \tfrac{10}{50}\right)}$$

$$= \$214.66/\text{year}$$

Notice that we have used $D = 3,600$ units/year in the expression KD/Q, since the total cost equation is in terms of dollars per year, while we have used $D = 10$ units/day when forming the ratio of D and P (measured in units/day) in order to be consistent.

Let us compare the results for the serial-production case with those of the basic EOQ model. Notice that for the serial-production case the optimal order quantity Q^* is higher and that the total cost per year is lower. This is due to the fact that since inventory rises gradually, instead of abruptly, average inventories, and therefore costs, are lower.

With lead time $L = 0$, our optimal decision rule is

Order 335 units when inventory equals 0 units.

If lead time is positive, the order must be placed earlier as was the case with the basic EOQ model. Thus, if lead time $L = 10$ days, the demand during lead time $D_L = (10 \text{ days}) \times (10 \text{ units/day}) = 100$ units. Our optimal decision rule is then

Order 335 units when inventory equals 100 units.

10.6.5. Incorporating Inventory Costs into the Make-Versus-Buy Decision Problem. Assume that we are confronted with the following decision problem. A certain item that is used in the company can be made (produced) internally or be bought from the outside. Which alternative should be chosen? In general, making the part internally means a lower per-unit cost (U). However, it also generally means a setup cost (K) greater than what the ordering cost would be if the item were purchased from a supplier. Frequently, such decisions are made without considering the difference in inventory costs between the two strategies. Let us solve a simple make-versus-buy decision problem incorporating inventory costs to show their effect on the solution.

Assume that our first strategy is to buy the items from a supplier and that no stockouts are permitted, as described in Section 10.4, the basic EOQ model. We found there that the optimal policy was to order $Q^* = 300$ units each time we order with a total variable cost $TC^* = \$240/\text{year}$. The cost of the goods themselves [i.e., $U \times D = 4(3,600) = \$14,400/\text{year}$] was not included in our total-cost equation. Since the unit cost is different for the second strategy, we must compare the two strategies on the basis of the sum of total variable cost plus cost of

goods.

STRATEGY 1: Buy from the supplier at $U = \$4/$unit,
ordering cost $= \$10/$order:

$$\text{cost} = \$240/\text{year} + \$14{,}400/\text{year} = \$14{,}640/\text{year}$$

STRATEGY 2: Produce the units internally
with a unit cost $U = \$3.75/$unit,
setup cost $K = \$500$,
and production rate $P = 50$ units/day.

Since the unit cost has changed, we must first find the new carrying cost per unit (k_c).

$$k_c = k_i U = (0.20)(3.75) = \$0.75/(\text{unit} \cdot \text{year})$$

The optimal total cost is

$$\text{TC}^* = \sqrt{2KDk_c\left(1 - \frac{D}{P}\right)}$$

$$= \sqrt{2(500)(3{,}600)(0.75)\left(1 - \tfrac{10}{50}\right)}$$

$$= \$1{,}470/\text{year}$$

The cost of goods per year is equal to

$$U \times D = (3.75)(3{,}600) = \$13{,}500/\text{year}$$

Therefore, the total cost is

$$\text{cost} = 1{,}470 + 13{,}500 = \$14{,}970/\text{year}$$

Hence, even though the cost of the goods is lower when we produce them ourselves instead of buying them from a supplier, the total cost for the produce strategy is higher and strategy 1, buy, is optimal. The increase in inventory costs more than offset the reduction in the cost of the goods. Thus, it is clear that inventory costs should always be included in make-versus-buy decisions.

An example of when strategy 2 is preferable is if the unit cost for producing internally is lower (e.g., $3/unit). In that case the savings in costs of the goods is sufficient to make strategy 2 the preferable one. The reader should verify this conclusion mathematically.

In general, the make-versus-buy problem is a very complicated one. For example, producing another product may require large investments in equipment, space, new staff training, and so on, and these additional factors should be included in evaluating the economics of the two alternatives. However, we have oversimplified the problem just to illustrate the possible impact of inventory costs on decision problems.

10.7.1. Introduction. In many cases users who demand the product when none is available (stocked out) will simply wait until it is available to receive it. This condition is known as *backordering*. As soon as an order arrives, the backorders are filled, and the remaining units go into inventory to fill future demand. However, because the customers wait does not mean that there is no cost associated with stocking out. There may be additional handling and shipping costs to fill the backorder. Furthermore, most managers agree that stocking out is an undesirable event, and therefore a penalty is suffered when it does occur, due to loss of goodwill, and so on. Let us model this penalty by a cost. The formulation of stockout cost we shall use penalizes us in two ways. First, we are penalized more the greater the number of units stocked-out, *and* second, the penalty is larger the longer the duration of the stockout. For example, if the cost of stocking out is $k_s = \$1.25$ per unit per year, written $\$1.25/(\text{unit} \cdot \text{year})$, if we are stocked-out on 2 units for 3 years the cost would be

$$\left[\$1.25/(\text{unit} \cdot \text{year})\right] \times (2 \text{ units}) \times (3 \text{ years}) = \$7.50$$

Let us now consider the basic EOQ model with the following modification:

Stockouts are permitted, all units are back-ordered (no lost sales) at a cost of k_s dollars per unit per year.

For this case we have the option of ordering later than the moment when inventory hits zero (i.e., wait until a certain number of backorders exists before placing an order). Let us define the level of backorders that exists when an order arrives as S. Figure 10.7.1 shows the graph of inventory versus time where backordering is permitted and $Q = 300$, $S = 100$. For convenience, backorders are shown as negative inventory; that is, an inventory on the graph of -100 units actually means zero inventory with 100 backorders existing. Notice that when goods arrive, there are 100 backorders existing. The first 100 units of the 300 received fill the backorders and bring the inventory to 0; the remaining units go into inventory and bring inventory to a level of 200 units.

Let us consider the effect of allowing stockouts as compared to the no-stockout case. With no stockouts, the height of the inventory curve was Q instead of $Q - S$ as shown for the stockout case. Furthermore, the average inventory will be lower for the backorder case. It will be even lower than $(Q - S)/2$, since the inventory is actually zero during the portion of the time when backorders exist. Thus, the total carrying costs are reduced. However, there will be a stockout cost which will increase the total cost. This cost increases as more backorders are permitted for longer intervals of time. Thus, our objective will be to select values for the two decision variables, Q and S, such that the total cost is minimized.

363

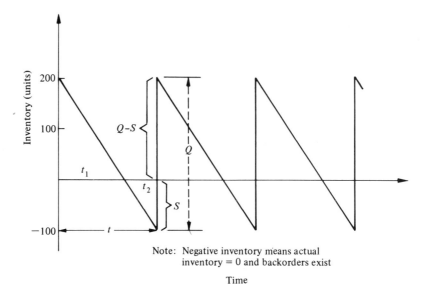

Note: Negative inventory means actual
inventory = 0 and backorders exist

Time

FIGURE 10.7.1. *Graph of inventory versus time, backordering per-*
mitted. Q=300; S=100.

We shall formulate a total variable-cost equation which has three components:

1. Ordering cost per time (TOC).
2. Carrying cost per time (TCC).
3. Stockout cost per time (TSC).

We will once again exclude the cost of the goods, since that cost does not vary as we change the values of our decision variables Q and S. The total cost will be given by

(1) $$TC = TOC + TCC + TSC$$

10.7.2. Ordering Cost. Similar to the basic EOQ model, the ordering cost per year will be given by the cost per order times the number of orders per year, or

(2) $$TOC = Kn = \frac{KD}{Q}$$

This equation is still valid since the number of orders per year has not changed. This can be seen by observing that no matter what number of backorders we permit, if the demand (D) is 3,600 units/year and we order $Q = 300$ units each time, we will always order $D/Q = 12$ orders/year.

10.7.3. *Carrying Cost.* In order to determine the carrying cost, it is necessary to find the average inventory. In this model, however, we need consider only the physical inventory, since backorders existing (shown on the graph as negative inventory) do not affect our inventory carrying costs. Figure 10.7.2 shows the graph of physical inventory over time. It can be shown mathematically that the average of this curve over time is equal to $(Q-S)^2/2Q$. Appendix 10-2 shows the development of the total-cost equation. For the curve shown, $Q=300$ and $S=100$, and the average inventory would equal

$$\frac{(300-100)^2}{2(300)} = \frac{40{,}000}{600} = 66.7 \text{ units}$$

The carrying cost per year is equal to the per-unit carrying cost times the average inventory or

(3)
$$\text{TCC} = \frac{k_c(Q-S)^2}{2Q}$$

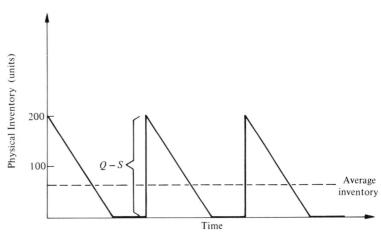

FIGURE 10.7.2. *Graph of physical inventory versus time, backordering permitted. Q=300; S=100.*

10.7.4. *Stockout Cost.* To compute the stockout cost per year we must find the average backorder quantity and multiply by the stockout cost, since, like inventory, backorder levels are changing all the time. Recall that the negative inventory values on the graph of Figure 10.7.1 actually mean a positive level of backorders and positive inventory means zero backorders. Figure 10.7.3 shows a graph of backorders over time. The average can be shown mathematically to be $S^2/2Q$. The stockout cost per year is equal to the stockout cost per unit per year times average stockout, or

(4)
$$\text{TSC} = \frac{k_s S^2}{2Q}$$

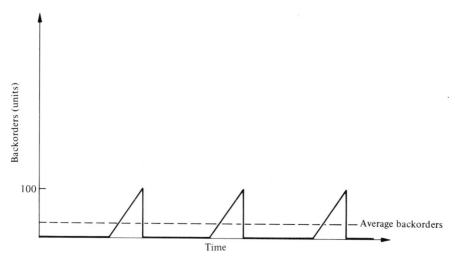

FIGURE 10.7.3. *Graph of backorders versus time, backorders permitted. Q=300; S=100.*

For the case where $Q=300$, $S=100$, and a stockout cost $k_s = \$1.20/(\text{unit}\cdot\text{year})$, the average stockout cost per year is equal to

$$\frac{(1.20)\times(100)^2}{2(300)} = \frac{12,000}{600} = \$20/\text{year}$$

10.7.5. Optimal Solution to the Backorder Model. The total-cost equation is the sum of the three costs, order cost per year, carrying cost per year, and stockout cost per year. Thus, from equations (1)–(4) we get

$$(5) \qquad \text{TC} = \frac{KD}{Q} + \frac{k_c(Q-S)^2}{2Q} + \frac{k_sS^2}{2Q}$$

It can be shown mathematically, using the calculus, that the optimal solution to the backorder model is

$$(6) \qquad Q^* = \sqrt{\frac{2KD}{k_c}\frac{k_c+k_s}{k_s}}$$

$$(7) \qquad S^* = Q^*\frac{k_c}{k_c+k_s}$$

$$(8) \qquad \text{TC}^* = \sqrt{2KDk_c\frac{k_s}{k_c+k_s}}$$

For the example we have been considering, $D=3{,}600$ units/year, $K = \$10/\text{order}$, $k_c = \$0.80/(\text{unit}\cdot\text{year})$ and $k_s = \$3.20/(\text{unit}\cdot\text{year})$. The opti-

366

mal values are

$$Q^* = \sqrt{\frac{2(10)(3,600)}{0.80} \frac{(0.8+3.2)}{3.2}} = 300\sqrt{1.25}$$

$$= 335 \text{ units}$$

$$S^* = 335\frac{0.80}{0.80+3.2} = 335(0.2)$$

$$= 67 \text{ units}$$

TC* may be once again found in either of two ways.

1. Substitute Q^* and S^* into the total-cost equation:

$$\text{TC} = \frac{KD}{Q} + \frac{k_c(Q-S)^2}{2Q} + \frac{k_s S^2}{2Q}$$

$$= \frac{10(3,600)}{335} + \frac{(0.8)(335-67)^2}{2(335)} + \frac{(3.2)(67)^2}{2(335)}$$

$$= 107.46 + 85.76 + 21.44$$

$$= \$214.66/\text{year}$$

2. Use the expression for TC*:

$$\text{TC}^* = \sqrt{2KDk_c\frac{k_s}{k_c+k_s}}$$

$$= \sqrt{2(10)(3,600)(0.8)\frac{3.2}{0.8+3.2}}$$

$$= 240\sqrt{0.8}$$

$$= \$214.66/\text{year}$$

Notice that this total cost is lower than the \$240/year TC computed for the basic EOQ model for which no stockouts were permitted (i.e., S was set equal to zero). The important conclusion is that the inventory control policy that prevents stockouts completely is generally not a least-cost policy. The inventories carried generally do not justify the savings that would occur by having extremely few or no stockouts. Only in situations where stockouts are disasterous ($k_s = \infty$) should a no-stockout policy be considered as optimal.

With leadtime $L=0$ our optimal decision rule is

Order 335 units when the level of backorders equals 67 units.

If leadtime is positive, the order must be placed earlier, as was the case with the basic EOQ model. Thus, if leadtime is $L=5$ days, the demand during leadtime $D_L = (5 \text{ days}) \times (10 \text{ units/day}) = 50$ units. Our optimal decision rule will call for ordering at an inventory level 50-units-of-demand before the level of backorders equals 67, or when the level of backorders $= 67 - 50 = 17$ units. Thus the optimal ordering rule is

Order 335 units when the level of backorders equals 17 units.

If $L=10$ days (i.e., $D_L = 100$ units), there will be an inventory level of 33 units 10 days before the level of backorders equals 67 $(67 - 100 = -33$ units of backorder or 33 units of inventory). Our optimal policy is then

Order 335 units when inventory equals 33 units.

SECTION 10.8. *Variable Demand with Backordering*

In most inventory situations, particularly where items are sold to the public, the demand for an item does not remain constant day after day. Even in cases where the average demand has remained constant at, let us say, 3,600 units/year over many years, each day's demand is not necessarily exactly 10 units. For some days it may be less than 10; for others it may be more than 10; however, over a long period of time, the average demand is 10 units/day or 3,600 units/year. When there is variability in the actual demand, or for that matter when the lead-time period is variable, stockouts are generally tolerated, since usually they cannot be completely prevented without incurring a very high cost. This situation, which now includes conditions of risk, requires us to include the use of expected values in our decision-making process.

Theoretically, to obtain the exact optimal order quantity (Q) and reorder point (R), we would formulate a model for the objective function (TC). This equation would be defined as the *expected cost per year* and would be a function of the two decision variables Q and R. Then, we would find the optimal values, Q^* and R^*, which minimize this function. However, this tends to be a somewhat complicated process, and it would do little to reveal the concepts involved with variable-demand problems.

Let us consider a simple problem and a method for finding a "good" set of values for Q and R (i.e., an approximate optimal solution which tends to be close to the exact one). Assume an inventory problem with the same characteristics as the basic EOQ model with the additional requirement that demand is variable with a known probability distribution (risk), and stockout costs are defined slightly differently. Moreover, all stocked-out units are backordered. Let us also use the same numerical values as before: *average* demand rate $D = 3,600$ units/year; order cost $K = \$10$/order; unit cost $U = \$4$/unit; per-dollar carrying cost $k_i = 20\%$/year, giving a per-unit carrying cost of $\$0.80$/(unit year); and lead time $L = 10$ days. When considering the backorders, we shall use a stockout cost which charges us only for how many units are backordered but not for how long they are backordered as was the case with k_s. We shall denote this stockout cost as k_u and its dimensions are dollars per unit. Assume that $k_u = \$1$/unit. Each unit backordered costs us $\$1$ each time a backorder occurs.

Our inventory policy will once again state:

Order Q units when inventory equals R units.

Thus, we order a fixed quantity, Q units, each time. Since demand is variable, it will take a different amount of time to use up the Q units that have been received at each replenishment. Thus, the number of orders per year and the time between orders will also vary. Therefore, the variables n and t must be used to denote *average* number of orders per year and *average* time between orders, respectively. For example, if we order $Q = 300$ units each time, and the *average* demand during a 30-day period is (10 units/day)×(30 days) = 300 units, then, on the average, the time between orders will be 30 days. Sometimes it will be more, sometimes it will be less. Thus, the type of policy we are considering can be called a fixed order quantity–variable period policy. There are also variable quantity–fixed period policies, which are similar in structure, but we shall not consider them here.

The method for finding a good approximate solution to our variable-demand problem with a Q, R policy is to first "make believe" that demand is constant, that no stockouts are permitted, and solve this assumed problem for the optimal order quantity Q^*. This value will be used as the fixed order quantity of our variable-demand problem. Thus, we essentially apply the basic EOQ model results using the average demand rate as D. The numerical values we are considering here are identical to those considered in Section 10.4 on the basic EOQ model. The results obtained there were:

$$Q^* = 300 \text{ units}$$
$$TC^* = 120 + 120 = \$240/\text{year}$$

The total cost per year is shown broken down into its two components of ordering cost per year and carrying cost per year. Thus, as long as we order 300 units each time, our average number of orders per year will still equal $n = D/Q = 3,600/300 = 12$, and our average ordering cost per year will still equal $Kn = 10(12) = \$120$/year. These will remain the same no matter what reorder point R we select.

When demand was constant we set our reorder point equal to the demand during lead time $L = 10$ days, which was equal to (10 days)×(10 units/day) = 100 units. Our policy was then:

Order 300 units when inventory equals 100 units.

Let us consider what the average total cost per year of this policy would be for the variable-demand case. The total cost figure of $240/year includes in it the two components of ordering cost and carrying cost per year. The average ordering cost, as already discussed, will remain the same. The average carrying costs will be somewhat the same, since the average inventory will be to a reasonable approximation $Q/2$. What has not been included is the stockout cost, which must now be considered. Figure 10.8.1 shows a graph of inventory versus time for the variable-demand problem. The first cycle shows the average demand rate equal to 10 units/day, and the inventory equals zero when the order arrives. This is the exact equivalent of the constant demand rate, basic EOQ model. For the second cycle the demand rate is less than 10 units/day, and a positive inventory exists when the order arrives. The third cycle shows the demand rate greater than 10 units/day, and a backorder condition exists when the order arrives. Actually, the inventory curves would not be straight lines since during each hour of the day demand is different, but

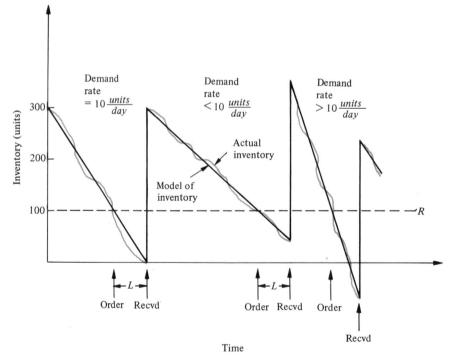

FIGURE 10.8.1. *Inventory versus time for the variable-demand case.*
D=3600 units/year; L=10 days; Q=300 units; R=100 units.

let us approximate them by straight lines. Thus, a stockout, and hence an associated stockout cost, occurs when demand during lead time is greater than the reorder point.

To compute the probability of a stockout each time an order is placed, we must know the probability distribution of demand during lead time. For the purpose of illustrating the concept, let us assume demand during lead time D_L is distributed according to the normal distribution. The two curves of Figure 10.8.2 illustrate the probability of a stockout occurring for two possible reorder-point values: (1) the reorder point R equals the average demand during lead time $= \overline{D}_L = 100$ units; and for (2) $R > \overline{D}_L$. Notice that when the reorder point R is set equal to the mean demand during lead time $\overline{D}_L$, the probability of stockout equals 0.5. Raising R reduces the probability of stockout, and consequently reduces the expected number of units backordered each time an order is placed. However, raising the reorder point (i.e., ordering sooner) increases the number of units carried in inventory. For example, if we reorder when inventory $= 110$ units instead of 100 units, the entire graph of Figure 10.8.1 is raised by 10 units, and consequently our average inventory is 10 units higher. Therefore, increasing the reorder point R reduces the stockout cost but increases the carrying costs.

The number of units by which we raise the reorder point above the average demand during lead time, $\overline{D}_L$, is known as the *buffer stock* or *safety stock* and will be denoted as B. It is approximately this many

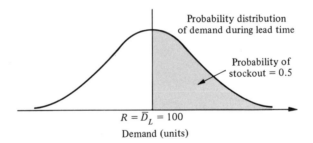

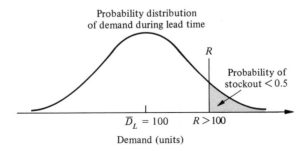

FIGURE 10.8.2. *Probability distribution of demand during lead time, assuming normal distribution probability of stockout shown for $R = \overline{D}_L$ AND $R > \overline{D}_L$.*

additional units that will be carried, on the average, over and above the inventory carried when $R = \overline{D}_L$. The objective is to find the value of R that minimizes the sum of the average (or expected) stockout costs and the carrying cost for the buffer stock.

Let us find the expected stockout cost for the case when $R = \overline{D}_L = 100$ units, which we will call strategy 1. To do this we must know the probability distribution of demand during lead time. We have previously assumed that this distribution is the normal distribution, however, only for the purpose of illustration. The computations, assuming that the normal distribution applies, are rather complex and will not be considered here. We therefore assume that the probability distribution of demand during lead time is as given by the discrete distribution of Table 10.8.1. This assumption is somewhat of an oversimplification, since it does not allow (as an example) for a demand of $91, 92, \ldots, 99$ units, only 90 and 100. However, we could have generated the distribution for all integer values, which would be more accurate but requires more computations. The same technique would apply, however, for any distribution given.

TABLE 10.8.1. *Discrete Probability Distribution of Demand During Lead Time D_L*

Demand (units)	Probability
70	0.01
80	0.04
90	0.20
100	0.50
110	0.20
120	0.04
130	0.01

Let us now evaluate strategy 1, $R = \overline{D}_L = 100$ units, which means that the buffer stock $B = 0$.

STRATEGY 1: $B = 0$,
that is, $R = \overline{D}_L = 100$ units
Expected stockout cost per year:

This will equal the expected number of units backordered each time an order is placed, multiplied by the cost per unit backordered, k_u, multiplied by the average number of times per year orders are placed, n. We must multiply by n in order to make the total cost a per-year figure instead of per order. Thus,

(1) $\left(\begin{array}{c}\text{expected stockout}\\\text{cost per year}\end{array}\right) = \left(\begin{array}{c}\text{expected number}\\\text{of units backordered}\end{array}\right) \cdot (k_u) \cdot (n)$

To find the expected number of units backordered we must find the possible values of backorders, the probability of each, multiply, and form the sum. This computation is shown in Table 10.8.2. Notice that only when demand is greater than R does a stockout occur and the number of units backordered equals demand minus R. All occurrences of demand less than or equal to R contribute zero to the computation. Thus, the expected stockout cost per year is

$$(3.1 \text{ units/order}) \cdot (\$1/\text{unit}) \cdot (12 \text{ orders/year}) = \$37.20/\text{year}$$

The carrying cost for the buffer stock is zero since the buffer stock $B = 0$. Therefore,

$$\begin{bmatrix} \text{Total expected} \\ \text{cost per year---} \\ \text{strategy 1} \end{bmatrix} = \text{stockout cost} + \text{carrying cost}$$

$$= 37.20 + 0 = \$37.20/\text{year}$$

TABLE 10.8.2. *Computation of Expected Number
of Units Backordered*

1. $R = 100$

Demand (units)	Number of Units Backordered	Probability	Backorders × Probability
70	0	0.01	0
80	0	0.04	0
90	0	0.20	0
100	0	0.50	0
110	10	0.20	2.0
120	20	0.04	0.8
130	30	0.01	0.3

Expected number of units backordered = 3.1
$R = 100$

2. $R = 110$

Demand (units)	Number of Units Backordered	Probability	Backorders × Probability
70	0	0.01	0
80	0	0.04	0
90	0	0.20	0
100	0	0.50	0
110	0	0.20	0
120	10	0.04	0.4
130	20	0.01	0.2

Expected number of units backordered = 0.6
$R = 110$

STRATEGY 2: $B = 10$,
that is, $R = \bar{D}_L + B = 100 + 10 = 110$ units
Expected stockout cost per year:

From equation (1) and Table 10.8.2, we find this cost to be

$$= \left[(10)(0.04) + (20)(0.01) \right] \text{ units/order} \times (\$1/\text{unit}) \times (12 \text{ orders/year})$$
$$= (0.6) \times (1) \times (12)$$
$$= \$7.20/\text{year}$$

Carrying cost for buffer stock:

$$= B \times k_c$$
$$= (10 \text{ units}) \left[\$0.8/(\text{unit} \cdot \text{year}) \right]$$
$$= \$8/\text{year}$$

Total expected cost per year—strategy 2:
$$= 7.20 + 8 = \$15.20/\text{year}$$

Since this is lower than the cost for strategy 1, $R = 110$ is better than $R = 100$. On an incremental basis, raising the reorder point by 10 units reduced expected stockout cost by \$30/year (i.e., $37.20 - 7.20$) and only increased carrying cost by \$8/year.

STRATEGY 3: $B = 20$,
that is, $R = 100 + 20 = 120$ units
Expected stockout cost per year:

$$= \left[(10)(0.01) \right] \times (1) \times (12)$$
$$= \$1.20/\text{year}$$

Carrying cost for buffer stock:

$$= (20)(0.8)$$
$$= \$16.00/\text{year}$$

Total expected cost per year—strategy 3:

$$= 1.20 + 16.00$$
$$= \$17.20/\text{year}$$

This is higher than that for $R = 110$ units and therefore less desirable. Adding the 10 additional units of buffer stock reduced stockout cost by \$6/year but added \$8/year to carrying costs. Clearly, adding another 10 units to the reorder point will be even worse, but let us evaluate this strategy anyway, since it represents the "no-stockout" solution.

STRATEGY 4: $B = 30$,

that is, $R = 100 + 30 = 130$ units

Expected stockout cost per year:

$$= (0) \times 1 \times 12$$

$$= \$1/\text{year}$$

Carrying cost for buffer stock:

$$= (30)(0.8)$$

$$= \$24.00/\text{year}$$

Total expected cost per year—strategy 4:

$$= 0 + 24.00$$

$$= \$24.00/\text{year}$$

As expected, it is higher than for strategy 3. The additional 10 units saved only $1.20 stockout costs and added $8 per year in carrying costs. This is a key point. Frequently the no-stockout, or extremely low stockout solution is the one preferred on intuitive grounds. Our analysis shows how protecting against the very rare stockout case is usually economically unjustified. Strategy 4 protects against a stockout occurring for the rare event of demand during lead time = 130 units, an event that occurs only 1 in 100 times.

Of the strategies considered, strategy 2 is best, and using it, our optimum inventory decision rule can be stated as follows:

Order 300 units when inventory equals 110 units.

We have only considered strategies equal to the various demand possibilities (i.e., 100, 110, 120, and 130 units). Perhaps $R = 105$ or $R = 115$ units is still better than $R = 110$ units. In fact, this is not the case. It can be shown that the optimal reorder point will always be equal to one of the actual demands that can occur (i.e., that shifting it from 110 units is not economically justified).

SECTION 10.9. *Variable Demand and Unknown Stockout Cost*

There are practical approaches to determining inventory rules when the stockout cost, which is usually a highly subjective value, is unknown. In such cases the policy may be selected such that the probability of a stockout each time an order is placed is at or below a specified level.

Although this approach does not yield an "optimal" solution, it is a rational approach to the problem and is a relatively straightforward procedure.

Consider the problem of Section 10.8, variable demand with back-ordering, but now assume that the stockout cost is unknown. Since the order cost K is known ($10/order) and the carrying cost k_c is known ($0.80/unit·year) we can still solve for the optimal order quantity, assuming a constant demand rate. This was found equal to $Q^* = 300$ units, and we shall use this value as the order quantity of our inventory decision rule. When the stockout cost was known, we solved for the reorder point, which minimized the sum of expected stockout cost plus carrying cost for the buffer stock. Since it is now assumed to be unknown, we shall have to choose our reorder point based on a different criterion. Let us adopt the following criterion: select a reorder point such that a stockout occurs on the average no more than 5% of the time after an order is placed.

Let us again consider the probability distribution of demand during lead time as shown in Table 10.8.1. Assume for the moment that the reorder point $R = 100$ units. Let us find the probability of a stockout each time an order is placed. A stockout will occur if the demand during lead time exceeds the reorder point value (i.e., demand equals 110 or 120 units). This probability equals $0.20 + 0.04 + 0.01 = 0.25$. Since this probability is greater than 0.05, $R = 100$ units does not meet the criterion as stated.

If we select $R = 110$ units, the probability of a stockout is the probability of demand being 120 or 130 units and is equal to $0.04 + 0.01 = 0.05$. Therefore, the reorder point $R = 110$ units meets the stated criterion and is selected. Our inventory policy therefore states:

Order 300 units when inventory equals 110 units.

If the criterion required a probability of a stockout of no more than 0.04, 0.03, or 0.02, we would then select $R = 120$ as the reorder point.

This approach to determining the reorder point is simple enough that it can be applied when demand follows the normal distribution, a far more reasonable assumption. Assume that *daily demand* is normally distributed with a mean of 10 units and a standard deviation of 3 units. The demand during lead time D_L is just the sum of 10 independent day's demands. For such situations the distribution of the sum is normal, the mean of the sum equals the sum of the means, and the variance of the sum equals the sum of the variances. Thus, the mean demand during lead time equals $10 \times 10 = 100$ units. The variance of daily demand equals $3^2 = 9$ units, and the variance of demand during lead time equals $10 \times 9 = 90$ units. Therefore, the standard deviation of demand during lead time equals $\sqrt{90} = 9.49$ units. This is precisely the same mean and standard deviation of the discrete distribution of demand used in Section 10.8 as shown in Table 10.8.1.

We need to find the reorder point which yields a 0.05 probability that demand during lead time will exceed this value. This situation is depicted by Figure 10.8.2. We shall use the Cumulative Normal Probabilities Table (shown as Appendix B). The standard normal distribution has mean $\mu = 0$ and standard deviation $\sigma = 1$, and the table lists the probability of the random variable being less than or equal to any value (called z). We wish a value z such that the probability of a random variable being less than or equal to z is 0.95 (i.e., 0.05 probability of being greater). From the table it can be seen that the value of z which has approximately a 0.95 probability is $z = 1.65$. We may interpret this as 1.65 standard deviations above the mean. The demand during lead-time distribution we are considering has a mean equal to 100 units and a standard deviation of 9.49 units. The value that is equal to 1.65 standard deviations above the mean for this distribution is

$$\mu + 1.65\sigma = 100 + (1.65)(9.49) = 115.66 \text{ units}$$

Our inventory policy is therefore:

Order 300 units when inventory equals 116 units.

SECTION 10.10 *Sensitivity Analysis—Basic EOQ Model*

In general, many of the cost parameters in an inventory problem are estimated and therefore, sensitivity analysis becomes an important part of an inventory problem. If the actual cost values are different from their assumed values, the true optimal solution is different from that computed using the assumed values. It is thus important to know what effects these differences have on the true optimal solution and what cost per year the assumed optimal solution actually yields. Let us perform sensitivity analysis for the problem considered in Section 10.4, the basic EOQ model.

Our assumed values were $D = 3,600$ units/year, $K = \$10/\text{order}$, and $k_i = 20\%$ per year, and the derived (assumed) optimal solution was $Q^* = 300$ units, $TC^* = \$240/\text{year}$.

Let us examine the effect on the optimal order quantity Q^* of varying the demand rate D, the ordering cost K, and the per dollar carrying cost k_i, and determine the actual cost per year if the assumed optimal value of Q is used. These computations are shown in Table 10.10.1. The values selected for all parameters are $\frac{1}{10}$, $\frac{1}{2}$, 2 times, and 10 times the assumed value. Notice that the optimal solution and even the profit for using the assumed optimal solution of $Q = 300$ is relatively

TABLE 10.10.1. *Sensitivity Analysis for the Basic EOQ Model*

Assumed Parameter Values $D=3{,}600$ $K=10$ $k_i=0.20$

Assumed Optimal $Q^*=300$ $TC^*=240$

Parameter Value	Q^*	TC^*	Total Actual Cost for $Q=300$
$D=$ 300	94.8	75.89	132.00
$D=$ 1,800	212.1	169.68	180.00
$D=$ 7,200	424.2	339.36	360.00
$D=30{,}000$	948.6	758.88	1,320.00
$K=$ 1	94.8	75.89	132.00
$K=$ 5	212.1	169.68	180.00
$K=$ 20	424.2	339.36	360.00
$K=100$	948.6	758.88	1,320.00
$k_i=0.02$	948.6	75.89	132.00
$k_i=0.10$	424.2	169.68	180.00
$k_i=0.40$	212.1	339.36	360.00
$k_i=2.00$	94.8	758.88	1,320.00

insensitive to the values of D, K, and k_i. Even if our estimate of, for example, the carrying cost K is off by 50% our "optimal" policy still yields a "reasonable" total cost.

SECTION 10.11. *Multiple Items with Unknown Costs and Constraints*

When there are multiple items, as is usually the case, the situation is more complex than when a single item's inventory level needs to be controlled. The question of whether to order all items at the same time (same n for all items), or to order each item separately is important. If certain items are all ordered from the same supplier, there may be distinct advantages, such as quantity discounts, lower freight costs, and reduced ordering costs, to ordering all at the same time. If items are ordered from different suppliers, or produced internally, it may be reasonable to consider each separately and to order each at a different time.

Another complexity that frequently arises is that there may be constraints on quantities, such as the total average inventory, the total warehouse space, or the total number of orders per year for all products. There is a calculus technique known as Lagrange multipliers which can be used to solve such problems (where we assume constant demand and lead time), but it is beyond the scope of this book. The general approach is to first neglect the constraint and determine the optimal policy for each item independently. Then the optimal policies are checked to see if the constraint is violated. For example, a constraint of total average inventory investment requires that the sum of average inventory investment ($UQ/2$ for the basic EOQ case) for each item be less than or equal to a given value. If the individual optimal policies yield a sum of average inventory investment which is less than the given value, these policies may be considered feasible and implemented. If the total average inventory is larger than the given value, the policies must be adjusted so as to obey the constraint (i.e., Q must be reduced for each time). The technique of Lagrange multipliers indicates how to do this in an optimal fashion (i.e., so as to minimize the sum of the total costs over all items).

There is, however, a general approach which is not optimal but "reasonable" and may even be used where the order cost K and the per dollar carrying cost k_i are not known. The required assumptions are that k_i and K are the same for all items, orders are received in lots, demand is constant, and no stockouts are permitted (basic EOQ case). The approach is applicable for the following two types of constraints:

1. The sum of average dollar investment in inventory $(U \cdot Q/2)$ over all items must be less than or equal to a value A.
2. The sum of orders per year $(n = D/Q)$ over all items must be less than or equal to a value B.

Assume for the moment that we have three products, all ordered from different suppliers, and that the demand rate for the first product is $D_1 = 3,600$ and the unit cost is $U_1 = 4$; for the second product $D_2 = 400$ and $U_2 = 16$; for the third product $D_3 = 2,000$ and $U_3 = 20$.

If there is a constraint on either total average dollar investment in inventory $(\leqslant A)$ or on total number of orders per year $(\leqslant B)$, it can be shown that a "reasonable" approach is to allocate either the average inventory investment or the number of orders per year to each product so that its fraction of the total is equal to the ratio of the square root of demand in dollars (demand times unit cost) for the product divided by the sum of the square roots of demand in dollars for all products. The square root stems from the square root in the expression for Q^*.

Assume that the total average investment in inventory is limited to $A = \$5,000$. Let us use this approach to distribute the $\$5,000$ investment to each product in a reasonable manner. The computations are shown in Table 10.11.1. The derived order quantities of 750 units, 125 units, and

TABLE 10.11.1. *Allocation of $5,000 Total Average Inventory Investment to Three Products*

Product	D	U	$\sqrt{DU}$	$\sqrt{DU}/\Sigma\sqrt{DU}$	Average Investment, I	$Q = 2I/U$	Number of Orders/Year, $n = D/Q$
1	3,600	4	120	0.3	0.3(5,000) = $1,500	750	4.80
2	400	16	80	0.2	0.2(5,000) = $1,000	125	3.20
3	2,000	20	200	0.5	0.5(5,000) = $2,500	250	8.00
			400		$5,000		16.00

250 units will yield a total average investment in inventory of $5,000, as required, and will cause 16 orders/year to be placed.

What if, on the other hand, the company wished to restrict the total number of orders per year to $B = 10$? Let us allocate these 10 orders/year to the three products. The computations are shown in Table 10.11.2. The derived order quantities of 1200, 200, and 400 yield exactly 10 orders/year and a total average inventory investment of $8,000.

TABLE 10.11.2. *Allocation of 10 Total Orders per Year to Three Products*

Product	D	U	$\sqrt{DU}$	$\sqrt{DU}/\Sigma\sqrt{DU}$	Number of Orders / Year n	$Q = D/n$	Average Investment $I = UQ/2$
1	3,600	4	120	0.3	0.3(10)=3	1,200	$2,400
2	400	16	80	0.2	0.2(10)=2	200	1,600
3	2,000	20	200	0.5	0.5(10)=5	400	4,000
			400		10		$8,000

Notice that that the company cannot achieve both constraints: total number of orders no more than 10 *and* total average investment no more than $5,000. Their preference for one policy over the other indicates something about the relationship of K and k_i even though the costs are not known. Assume that they prefer keeping the total number of orders per year to 10. This means that, to them, reducing the total investment in inventory from $8,000 to $5,000 (a reduction of $3,000) is not worth increasing the number of orders per year from 10 to 16 (an increase of 6). The reduction in carrying cost per year would be $3,000k_i$ and the increased order cost per year would be $6K$. Therefore,

$$3,000k_i < 6K$$

or

$$k_i < 0.002K$$

If they prefer the policy that yields $5,000 total average inventory, then

$$k_i > 0.002K$$

Suppose that the company is indifferent between the two policies and would like to find one that has more total orders per year than 10 and a lower total average inventory investment less than $8,000. Suppose that they decide to allow 13 orders/year. The derived policy is shown in Table 10.11.3. This policy yields 13 total orders/year and a total average investment in inventory of $6,158. If this inventory investment is still not satisfactory, additional policies may be investigated by specifying a total

TABLE 10.11.3. *Allocation of 13 Total Orders per Year to Three Products*

Product	D	U	$\sqrt{DU}$	$\sqrt{DU}/\Sigma\sqrt{DU}$	Number of Orders/Year n	$Q = D/n$	Average Investment $I = UQ/2$
1	3,600	4	120	0.3	0.3(13) = 3.9	923	$1,846
2	400	16	80	0.2	0.2(13) = 2.6	154	1,232
3	2,000	20	200	0.5	0.5(13) = 6.5	308	3,080
			400		13.0		$6,158

number of orders greater than 13 or a total average inventory investment of less than $6,158.

SECTION 10.12. *Using the Computer*

A computer program has been written which performs all the computations for the single-product models treated in this chapter. The program first solves the basic EOQ model given as input the values of:

1. Ordering cost K in terms of $/order.
2. Demand rate D in terms of units/year.
3. Per-dollar carrying cost k_i in terms of %/year.
4. Unit cost U in terms of $/unit.
5. Lead time L in terms of days.
6. Number of days per year to be used.

A series of codes are also read in indicating which additional models are to be solved. The codes are: 1, quantity discounts; 2, serial production, with make versus buy; 3, stockouts permitted; 4, variable demand.

For each additional case to be treated the additional information necessary must be read in:

Quantity discount case. The discount, in per cent, and the quantity that must be ordered, in dollars
Serial production. The setup cost, in terms of $/order; the unit cost, in terms of $/unit; and the production rate, in terms of units/day.
Stockouts permitted. The backorder cost k_s in terms of $/(unit·year).
Variable demand case. The backorder cost k_u in terms of $/unit and the probability distribution of demand during lead time.

Figures 10.12.1–10.12.5 show the output for all the models. The values used as input are those used throughout the chapter. The availability of such a computer program allows a decision maker to quickly determine the optimal policies for a wide variety of inventory situations.

BASIC EOQ MODEL

K =   10.00 $/ORDER   D =   3600.00 UNITS/YEAR
KI =   20.00% U =   4.00 $/UNIT KC =   0.80 $/(UNIT*YEAR)
L =   10.00 DAYS   NO. OF DAYS/YEAR =   360

OPTIMAL VALUES
Q* =   300.00 UNITS   N*=   12.00 ORDERS/YEAR   T* =   30.00 DAYS
TOTAL COST TC* =   240.00 $/YEAR
OPTIMAL POLICY---ORDER   300.00 UNITS WHEN INVENTORY EQUALS   100.00 UNITS

FIGURE 10.12.1

QUANTITY DISCOUNTS

DISCOUNT OF   2.0% ON ORDERS OF   7200.00 $ OR MORE

STRATEGY 1---ORDER   300.00 UNITS EACH TIME   TOTAL COST =   240.00 +   14400.00 =   14640.00 $/YEAR
STRATEGY 2---ORDER   1800.00 UNITS EACH TIME   TOTAL COST =   725.60 +   14112.00 =   14837.60 $/YEAR

OPTIMAL STRATEGY IS STRATEGY 1

FIGURE 10.12.2

PRODUCTION RATE CASE - MAKE VERSUS BUY

P =   50.00 UNITS/DAY   SETUP COST =   500.00 $/ORDER   U =   3.75 $/UNIT

OPTIMAL VALUES
Q* =   2449.49 UNITS   N*=   1.47 ORDERS/YEAR   T* =   244.95 DAYS
TOTAL COST TC* =   1469.69 $/YEAR
OPTIMAL POLICY---PRODUCE 2449.49 UNITS WHEN INVENTORY EQUALS   100.00 UNITS

STRATEGY 1---ORDER   300.00 UNITS EACH TIME   TOTAL COST =   240.00 +   14400.00 =   14640.00 $/YEAR
STRATEGY 2---PRODUCE   2449.49 UNITS EACH TIME   TOTAL COST =   1469.69 +   13500.00 =   14969.69 $/YEAR

OPTIMAL STRATEGY IS STRATEGY 1

FIGURE 10.12.3

STOCKOUTS PERMITTED—BACKORDERS ASSUMED

STOCKOUT COST = 3.20 $/(UNIT*YEAR)

OPTIMAL VALUES

Q* = 335.41 UNITS   N* = 10.73 ORDERS/YEAR   T* = 33.54 DAYS   S* = 67.08 UNITS
        TOTAL COST TC* = 214.66 $/YEAR
        OPTIMAL POLICY—ORDER 335.41 UNITS WHEN INVENTORY EQUALS 32.92 UNITS

FIGURE 10.12.4

VARIABLE DEMAND CASE

STOCKOUT COST = 1.00 $/UNIT

DEMAND	70.00	80.00	90.00	100.00	110.00	120.00	130.00
PROB	0.01	0.04	0.20	0.50	0.20	0.04	0.01

STRATEGY 1   B = 0.00 UNITS   R = 100.00 UNITS   COST = 37.20 + 0.00 = 37.20 $/YEAR
STRATEGY 2   B = 10.00 UNITS   R = 110.00 UNITS   COST = 7.20 + 8.00 = 15.20 $/YEAR
STRATEGY 3   B = 20.00 UNITS   R = 120.00 UNITS   COST = 1.20 + 16.00 = 17.20 $/YEAR
STRATEGY 4   B = 30.00 UNITS   R = 130.00 UNITS   COST = 0.00 + 24.00 = 24.00 $/YEAR

OPTIMAL STRATEGY IS STRATEGY 2 ORDER 300.00 UNITS WHEN INVENTORY = 110.00 UNITS

FIGURE 10.12.5

We have examined the basic structure of inventory-control decision problems and indicated that the form of the decision rule is to find optimum values for how much to order and when to order. The basic costs considered were ordering or setup cost, carrying cost, stockout cost, and cost of goods. The general methodology used is to develop an objective function in terms of the controllable variables and find optimal values. The measure of performance used is total variable cost per time and the types of policies considered were fixed-order-quantity policies.

Five cases were treated in the chapter, each differing slightly with regard to demand, cost of the goods, replenishment structure (i.e., in lots or gradually), and stockouts. Each case is representative of the types of situations encountered in real-world problems. The balance between ordering or setup costs, carrying costs, and stockout costs (where applicable) is illustrated in all cases. The quantity-discount case and the make-versus-buy problem reveal the need to incorporate inventory costs into problems, where they are frequently ignored. The models that permit stockouts reveal the economic advantage of allowing stockouts versus the no-stockout policy.

Although we have considered only a few basic inventory situations, they have illustrated the types of considerations and procedures that are necessary in treating the more complex, real-world inventory problems. The use of computers has been demonstrated through a computer program which performs all the computations necessary in obtaining solutions to many of the cases that have been covered.

PROBLEMS

Problems 10.1–10.11 focus on the following situation with varying assumptions.

BASIC DATA. A company uses a certain product in its production process at a rate of 1,800 units/year. The units are purchased in lots from a supplier at a fixed cost of $2/unit with 5 days required between the time an order is placed and receipt of the goods. The fixed cost of placing an order is $18 and the cost of carrying inventory is 25% of the cost of inventory per year. Assume 360 days/year and no backordering permitted.

10.1. Find the variable inventory costs (ordering plus carrying) for the following decision rules.

(a) Order 100 units each time.

(b) Order twice per year.

(c) Order every 30 days.

10.2. Find the optimal ordering rule and the total variable cost for this rule.

10.3. Sensitivity analysis: repeat Problem 10.2 for the following changes to the problem.

(a) The order cost is $4.50.
(b) The order cost is $72.00.
(c) The demand rate is 16,200 units/year.
(d) The demand rate is 200 units/year.
(e) The unit cost is $50.00.
(f) The unit cost is $0.08.
(g) The carrying cost is 100%/year.
(h) The carrying cost is 6.25%/year.

10.4. Repeat Problem 10.2 assuming that the following restrictions apply.

(a) Average investment in inventory must be no more than $200.
(b) Average investment in inventory must be no more than $500.
(c) The maximum number of orders per year is 20.
(d) The maximum number of orders per year is 2.

10.5. Repeat Problem 10.2 assuming that the following price breaks apply.

(a) 5% discount on orders of $3,600 or more.
(b) 10% discount on orders of $3,600 or more.
(c) 50% discount on orders of $1,000 or more.

10.6. Repeat Problems 10.1–10.3 assuming that instead of purchasing the product, the company manufactures it itself serially, at a rate of 15 units/day. All other costs are the same as the basic data.

10.7. Assume as an alternative to purchasing the product that the company is considering manufacturing it serially at a rate of 15 units/day with the costs as given below. In each case determine whether it is more economical to continue purchasing the product or to manufacture it.

(a) Unit cost $1.80, setup cost $400.
(b) Unit cost $1.50, setup cost $400.
(c) Unit cost $1.80, setup cost $100.

10.8. Repeat Problem 10.2 assuming that the company will allow backorders at a cost of

(a) $2.00/unit·year.
(b) $0.50/unit·year.

Also, indicate the savings achieved versus the "no-stockout" rule.

10.9. Repeat Problem 10.2 assuming that backordering is permitted and demand is variable. The probability distribution of demand during a 5-day period is:

Demand	10	15	20	25	30	35	40
Probability	0.02	0.13	0.20	0.30	0.20	0.13	0.02

The following situations are to be considered:

(a) Backorder cost is $1.50/unit.
(b) Backorder cost is $0.50/unit.
(c) The unit cost is $8/unit and the backorder cost is $5/unit.
(d) The desired probability of a stockout each time an order is placed is 0.15. Find the ordering rule.

10.10. Assume that demand during a 5-day period is normally distributed with mean 25 units and standard deviation 5 units. Find the approximately optimal ordering rule that provides:

(a) A stockout $\frac{1}{4}$ of the time an order is placed.
(b) A stockout $\frac{1}{20}$ of the time an order is placed.
(c) A stockout $\frac{1}{100}$ of the time an order is placed.

10.11. Assume that, in addition to the product already described, the company purchases two other products. The second product has a demand rate of 4,900 units/year and a unit cost of $9; the third product has a demand rate of 300 units/year and a unit cost of $3. Assume that all other basic data also apply to these products, and that each is ordered from a different supplier.

Find the "rational" inventory rule, assuming that:

(a) Total average investment in inventory may not exceed $2,000.
(b) Total average investment in inventory may not exceed $1,500.
(c) Total number of orders may not exceed 30 per year.
(d) Total number of orders may not exceed 20 per year.

10.12. Demand for a product averages 2,400 lb/year. The annual carrying cost is $5/pound and the cost of placing an order is $22. Lead time is 10 days; assume 240 days/year. Find the optimal order rule and the minimum cost for it.

10.13. Consider a lot-size system in which no inventory is carried. Let k_s be the shortage cost of a unit per unit time. Let the other parameters of the system be D and K, as in the basic EOQ model. Write an equation for the total cost of the system and determine the optimum lot size.

10.14. (Problem 10.13 continued) Assume that the yearly demand in a large health salon for sun lamps is 520 units. No inventory is carried; however, the reorder cost is $18 and the shortage cost is $0.10/unit/week. (Assume 52 weeks/year.)

(a) Find the optimum lot size and the minimum cost.
(b) The decision maker is unaware of the true parameter values and assumes that $k_s = \$0.05/$unit/week and $K = \$25/$order. He therefore uses an incorrect value for Q. What is the total cost of the system in this case?

10.15. Usage of a high-speed drill bit in a factory is at the rate of 300 bits each 3 months. The cost of carrying it in inventory is 10%/month. The order cost is $100 and the cost of a bit is $5. Lead time is 3 days. At present the lot size used is 100 bits/order. What would be the potential yearly savings if an optimal lot size were used? What is the optimal policy?

10.16. The production department of a toaster manufacturer must supply annually 3,000 switches. It can produce this part at a rate of 1,000 parts/month. The setup of a production run costs $144 and the part costs $10. The carrying cost is 20%/year.

(a) Determine the optimum number of parts per production run, the corresponding total cost, and how long a production run takes to produce.
(b) The company considers purchasing the parts from an electrical supplier since the order cost will only be $25. However, the unit cost of each part will increase by 20%. Should the company buy the parts or produce them internally?

10.17. An auto-parts supplier stocks batteries according to the EOQ model. The demand for batteries is 6,000 per year, with the reorder cost equal to $100 and the unit cost of a battery $30. The carrying cost is 15%/year. The order department manager when computing the optimal lot size assumes the parameters are: demand, 4,800 units; unit cost, $20, and reorder cost, $120.

(a) What lot size does he order? What does he think the minimum cost of the system is?
(b) What is the true cost of the rule selected by the manager? What is the minimum cost of the system?

10.18. A refinery uses 2,400 parts of a certain item during the year. The part is heavily used and deteriorates often. If a replacement part is not available, damages occur amounting to $9/month for each part not available. Each month 200 parts are purchased at a cost of $80/part. The inventory carrying cost is 15%/year. What should be the level of inventory at the beginning of each month after all backorders have been filled?

10.19. (Problem 10.18 continued). Find the optimal number of parts to order each month if the order cost is $50. How many backorders should accumulate before an order is placed?

10.20. For a new car dealer the demand for automobiles is 25 per month. The carrying cost is $100/car/month. Backorders are allowed at a cost of $20/car/month and the cost to place an order is $48. Find the average inventory, the average shortage, and the time between orders for the optimal solution.

10.21. A plumbing supply company fills orders for faucet units at the rate of 120 per year. The reorder cost is $20 and the annual inventory carrying cost is 25%. The faucet unit cost is $30 each.

(a) Find the optimum EOQ value.

(b) Assume that the manufacturer offers the plumbing supplier the following discount: from 50 to 99 units, a 5% discount; over 99 units, a 10% discount. What order quantity should be purchased?

10.22. Assume the following discount schedule for a product:

Order Size	Discount (%)
0–999	0
1,000–2,499	3
2,500 and over	5

The relevant data for this system are $D = 5,000$ units/year, $k_i = 20\%$/year, $U = \$10$/unit, and $K = \$49$/order. What order quantity should be selected?

10.23. A company expects to use 1,200 cases of small motors during the next 12 months. The cost of each case is $50 and the fixed cost of placing an order is $12. The carrying cost per case per year is $5.

(a) What is the optimum lot size?

(b) The company has the capability of producing the motors internally. With a setup cost of $200 per production run, the assembly line can produce these motors at a rate of 300 cases/month at a savings of 25%/unit. What is the optimum number of cases to produce for each production run?

(c) Determine whether the company should produce the motors internally or buy them from the outside.

10.24. The Hi-Fi Phonograph Company sells 100,000 phonograph records each year. The company analysts have determined that the minimum total cost is achieved when 20 orders are made per year. The cost associated with each EOQ order is $150 and the cost per record is equal to $2.

(a) What is the dollar value of the average inventory carried?

(b) Assume that the demand increases to 150,000 records annually and the order cost decreases to $120/order. How will this affect the optimum order quantity?

10.25. A computer programmer whose salary is $20,000/year has the following salary payment schedule. As long as the employer holds the money, he pays the programmer interest at an annual rate of 6% interest. Each time the programmer requests a salary check there is a charge of $10. If the programmer runs out of money, he has the option of borrowing from a finance company at an annual rate of 8%.

(a) How large should his check be? (Neglect deductions.)

(b) How much should he borrow from the finance company?

(c) How often should the programmer get paid?

BOOKS OF
INTEREST

Arrow, K. J., S. Karlin, and H. Scarf, *Studies in the Mathematical Theory of Inventory and Production*. Stanford, Ca.: Stanford University Press, 1958.

Buffa, Elwood S., *Operations Management: The Management of Productive Systems*. New York: Wiley Hamilton, 1976.

——, *Production-Inventory Systems: Planning and Control*. Homewood, Ill.: Richard D. Irwin, Inc., 1968.

—— and W. Taubert, *Production-Inventory Systems: Planning and Control*. Rev. ed. Homewood, Ill.: Richard D. Irwin, Inc., 1972.

Chase, Richard B. and Nicholas J. Aquilano, *Production and Operations Management: A Life Cycle Approach*. Homewood, Ill.: Richard D. Irwin, Inc., 1973.

Greene, J. H., *Production and Inventory Control Handbook*. New York: McGraw-Hill Book Co., 1970.

Hadley, G. and T. M. Whitin, *Analysis of Inventory Systems*. Englewood Cliffs, N.J.: Prentice-Hall, Inc., 1963.

Holt, C. C., F. Modigliani, J. F. Muth, and H. A. Simon, *Planning Production, Inventories, and Work Force*. Englewood Cliffs, N.J.: Prentice-Hall, Inc., 1960.

Magee, J. R. and D. M. Boodman, *Production Planning and Inventory Control*. 2nd ed. New York: McGraw-Hill Book Co., 1967.

Naddor, Eliezer, *Inventory Systems*. New York: John Wiley & Sons, Inc., 1966.

Shore, Barry, *Operations Management*. New York: McGraw-Hill Book Co., 1973.

Starr, M. K. and D. W. Miller, *Inventory Control: Theory and Practice*. Englewood Cliffs, N.J.: Prentice-Hall, Inc., 1962.

Wagner, H. M., *Statistical Management of Inventory Systems*. New York: John Wiley & Sons, Inc., 1962.

APPENDIX 10-1

***Derivation of
the Optimal Order Quantity Q*
for the Basic EOQ Model***

Our objective is to minimize the total-cost equation with respect to Q, that is,

$$\text{minimize TC} = \frac{KD}{Q} + \frac{k_c Q}{2}$$

Taking a first derivative and setting it equal to zero, we obtain

$$\frac{d(TC)}{dQ} = \frac{-KD}{Q^2} + \frac{k_c}{2} = 0$$

$$Q^2 = \frac{2KD}{k_c}$$

$$Q = \sqrt{\frac{2KD}{k_c}}$$

For a minimum value, the second derivative must be positive:

$$\frac{d^2(TC)}{dQ^2} = \frac{2KD}{Q^3} > 0 \qquad \left(\text{for } Q = \sqrt{\frac{2KD}{k_c}} \right)$$

since K, D, and Q are positive. Therefore, the solution $Q = \sqrt{2KD/k_c}$ is a minimum point on the total-cost equation and

$$Q^* = \sqrt{\frac{2KD}{k_c}}$$

Substituting the optimal value Q^* into the total-cost equation, we obtain

$$TC^* = \frac{K \cdot D}{\sqrt{2KD/k_c}} + \frac{k_c}{2}\sqrt{\frac{2KD}{k_c}}$$

$$TC^* = \frac{\sqrt{KDk_c}}{\sqrt{2}} + \frac{\sqrt{2}}{2}\sqrt{KDk_c}$$

$$= \sqrt{2KDk_c}$$

APPENDIX 10-2

**Derivation of the Average Inventory
and Average Backorder Level
for the Stockouts-Permitted Model**

Referring to Figures 10.7.1–10.7.3, graphs that pertain to this case, let us make the following definitions:

t = time between orders

t_1 = time during which inventory is positive

t_2 = time during which backorders exist
(inventory is zero, shown as negative on Figure 10.7.1)

Therefore,

$$t_1 = (Q - S)/D, \text{ since } Q - S \text{ units are used up}$$
at rate D during time t_1

$$t_2 = S/D, \text{ since the level of backorders accumulated}$$
during time t_2 at rate D is S

$$t = t_1 + t_2 = Q/D, \text{ already known}$$

AVERAGE INVENTORY

During t_1 the average inventory $= \dfrac{Q - S}{2}$

During t_2 the average inventory $= 0$

During t the average inventory

$$= \frac{t_1(Q - S)/2 + t_2 \cdot 0}{t}$$

$$= \frac{[(Q - S)/D](Q - S)/2}{Q/D}$$

$$= \frac{(Q - S)^2}{2Q}$$

AVERAGE BACKORDER LEVEL

In a similar fashion, average backorder level during t

$$= \frac{t_1 \cdot 0 + t_2 S/2}{t}$$

$$= \frac{(S/D) \cdot (S/2)}{Q/D}$$

$$= \frac{S^2}{2Q}$$

CHAPTER ELEVEN

Queueing Problems–
Structure and Relevance
for Business

OBJECTIVES: The purpose of this chapter is to introduce to you the following concepts which are essential to the study of queueing models.

1. *Essential elements of a queueing system.*
2. *The arrival and service processes.*
3. *Measures of system performance.*
4. *Decision making in queueing systems.*
5. *The relevance of analytical solutions.*
6. *The role of simulation.*

In many organizations the need often arises to provide certain services to a special class of customers or users of the service. These users generally arrive in a random fashion, wait for the service in a queue or waiting line if the service providers are busy, receive the service, and then leave. These types of environments will be referred to as *queueing systems*. Examples of such situations include the telephone switchboard in an office, checkout counters in supermarkets, toll booths on a highway, bank tellers in a bank, and doctors in the emergency room of a hospital.

In these types of service environments the major objective of the decision maker is to provide the service in the best and most efficient manner, thereby generating less congestion and waiting and faster processing of the users. On the other hand, to improve the quality of service usually requires the utilization of increased resources and results in a greater cost for providing the service. This class of decision problems (queueing) generally concerns itself with balancing the benefits of improved service with the increased cost of providing the service. In some cases the quality of the service can be related directly to a dollar benefit, whereas in other cases it cannot. For example, what dollar value can we place on the reduction in waiting time at a hospital emergency room or at the checkout counters in a supermarket? Yet the decisions regarding the resources to expend in providing improved service should be made primarily on the basis of some measure of performance. Before discussing the measures of performance of a queueing system, it is necessary to specify a detailed description of the characteristics of the service environment under investigation. This will be referred to as the *system structure*. We shall refer to the part of the service environment that provides the service as the *service system*. The service system is then part of an overall environment concerned with waiting lines or queues. This total environment will be called the *queueing system*.

SECTION 11.2. *Characteristics of Queueing Systems*

A simple queueing system can be represented diagrammatically as in Figure 11.2.1. This figure shows that users or customers arrive from outside the queueing system. If the service system (doctors, ticket sellers,

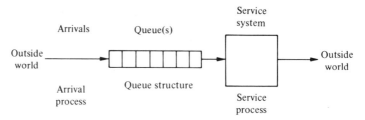

FIGURE 11.2.1. *Simple queueing system structure.*

bank tellers, etc.) is busy, the users must wait in one or more queues until they can be served. When it is their turn to be served and someone is free to serve them, they "enter service" (i.e., are served by one of the service providers). After receiving service, they leave the queueing system.

More complicated queueing-system structures could have many sets of servers, where all (or a portion) of the users go first to one server and then to others, with queues at each server. This chapter will discuss only simple queueing systems.

The manner in which users arrive to receive the service is called the *arrival process*. Service may be provided in many different ways (number of servers, rates of service) and this is called the *service process*. The manner in which users wait (queue) for service can also differ widely, and this is called the *queue discipline*. Specifying these three characteristics of a simple queueing system describes the system in detail. Each of these three characteristics will be discussed in detail in the following sections.

SECTION 11.3. *Arrival Process*

The arrival processes of most queueing systems are random; that is, the users do not arrive in a perfectly orderly manner. Thus, to describe the occurrence of an arrival, it is necessary to define a probability distribution of arrivals. There are two ways of defining the arrival process, which are more or less equivalent.

1. A probability distribution is used to define the *arrival rate*, that is, the number of arrivals per unit time. For example, there may be 100 arrivals the first hour, 140 arrivals the second hour, and so on. The mean arrival rate might be 120 arrivals/hour, which is equivalent to 60 per half-hour or 2 per minute.
2. A probability distribution is used to define the *interarrival time*, that is, the time between arrivals. For example, the time between the first and the second user's arrivals might be 45 seconds, while between the second and the third user's arrivals it might be only 15 seconds. The mean interarrival time would then be 30 seconds.

The equivalency between the arrival-rate approach and the inter-arrival-time approach is fairly straightforward. If, on the average, there are 2 arrivals/minute, we would expect that on the average there is $\frac{1}{2}$ minute between each arrival. This relationship always holds true:

$$\text{mean interarrival time} = \frac{1}{\text{mean arrival rate}}$$

In some cases the arrival-rate approach will be more convenient; in others, the interarrival time approach will be preferred. However, many different arrival processes could have the same means and yet differ greatly in the way people arrive. For instance, one process could have more variability than another (i.e., a larger standard deviation). Therefore, the mean arrival rate and the mean interarrival time values are not fully sufficient to describe the arrival process. To specify the arrival process more completely, the entire probability distribution of the arrival process must be used.

DESCRIBING THE ARRIVAL PROCESS BY A PROBABILITY DISTRIBUTION. Suppose that we were interested in describing the arrival process (both the arrival rate and interarrival time) by using a probability distribution. The first step would be to observe exactly how the system is being used. To do this we would stand by the entrance to the system (door of the bank, entrance to the emergency room of the hospital) and note the time that the users arrived. Let us assume that we collected the data shown in Table 11.3.1.

Notice that we have divided the samples into time periods of exactly 1 minute. We could easily have divided them into 5-minute, 10-minute, half-hour, or 1-hour intervals and then have computed a mean arrival rate for the particular period being used. Naturally, the mean arrival rate

TABLE 11.3.1. *Samples of Arrivals*

Time Period	Time of Arrival for Each Arrival (hr:min:sec)	Number of Arrivals During Period	Interarrival Time for Each Arrival (sec)[a]
9:00–9:01	9:00:28, 9:00:39	2	36, 11
9:01–9:02	9:01:02, 9:01:48, 9:01:54	3	23, 46, 6
9:02–9:03	9:02:48	1	54
9:03–9:04	9:03:15, 9:03:57	2	27, 42
9:04–9:05	—	0	—
9:05–9:06	9:05:02, 9:05:04, 9:05:42, 9:05:56	4	65, 38, 14
.	.	.	.
.	.	.	.
.	.	.	.
1:59–2:00	1:59:02, 1:59:27, 1:59:38	2	8, 25, 11
There are 300 one-minute periods	Sum of observations (Σx): Mean ($\Sigma x / n$):	600 arrivals 2.00 arrivals/minute	18,000 seconds 30.00 seconds/arrival

[a]Assume that the arrival just prior to 9:00 o'clock occurred at 8:59:52. Thus, the first interarrival time number is 36 seconds.

for a 5-minute interval of time would be 5 times the mean for a 1-minute interval. Furthermore, note that the interarrival time for the first arrival after 9:00 o'clock uses the time of arrival of the user just prior to 9:00 o'clock, which is given in the table footnote.

The samples of the number of arrivals during a 1-minute interval can only be integer values (i.e., 0 arrivals, 1 arrival, 2 arrivals, etc.). This is an example of discrete data. The interarrival times, on the other hand, are in reality continuous, although we have recorded them to the nearest second. For example, the interarrival time could be 20 seconds, 20.4 seconds, 20.43 seconds, 20.432 seconds, and so on. It all depends on how precisely we choose to measure the time.

The next step is to obtain the total number of arrivals and the total interarrival time. We then compute the mean arrival rate and mean interarrival time, which are, respectively, $600/300 = 2.00$ arrivals per minute (or 120 arrivals per hour), and $18,000/600 = 30.00$ seconds ($\frac{1}{2}$ minute) between arrivals.

We next consider estimating the probability distributions of the arrival rate and interarrival time. To do this we construct frequency distributions of the number of arrivals per minute and of interarrival times. Since interarrival times are continuous, we choose intervals of 30-second width (i.e., 0.00–29.99 seconds, 30.00–59.99 seconds, etc.). The frequency distributions are shown in Table 11.3.2. The frequency distribution is an estimate of the probability distribution we are seeking and describes the arrival process quite completely. The importance of the probability distribution in describing the arrival process may be seen by considering another arrival process, which also has a mean arrival rate of

TABLE 11.3.2. *Frequency Distributions for Arrival Data of Table 11.3.1*

	ARRIVAL RATE (ARRIVALS/MINUTE)			INTERARRIVAL TIME (TIME BETWEEN ARRIVALS)	
Arrivals / Minute	*Number of Observations*	*Fraction of Observations (Probability)*	*Seconds*	*Number of Observations*	*Fraction of Observations (Probability)*
0	40	0.133	0–29.99	379	0.632
1	81	0.270	30–59.99	140	0.233
2	81	0.270	60–89.99	51	0.085
3	54	0.180	90–119.99	19	0.032
4	27	0.090	120–149.99	7	0.012
5	11	0.037	150–179.99	3	0.005
6	4	0.013	180–209.99	1	0.002
7	2	0.007			

Number of observations = 300 at 1-minute intervals Number of observations = 600 arrivals
Mean = 2.00 arrivals/minute Mean = 30.00 seconds
Standard deviation = 1.41 arrivals/minute Standard deviation = 30.00 seconds

2.00 arrivals/minute:

Arrivals per Minute	Probability	
1	0.05	Mean = 2.00
2	0.90	Standard devi-
3	0.05	ation = 0.10

Although the means for the two processes are the same, the second one has considerably less variation in the number of arrivals per unit time. This reduced variability is of course indicated by a smaller standard deviation.

SECTION 11.4. *The Queue Structure*

There are many ways that users of a system will wait for service. We shall list some of the questions that can be asked concerning the queue structure, which will give us an indication of some of those ways.

1. Do all users wait in a single queue or are there many (multiple) queues?
2. If there are multiple queues, how do users choose a queue (at random, shortest one, etc.)? Do they remain in the same queues or do they switch from queue to queue? If they switch, what is the switching rule (i.e., after how long, to which other queue, etc.)?
3. Is service on a *first-in, first-out* (FIFO) basis, or are there *priority* users who are served first? An example of a priority queue structure is the police department, where calls for police assistance in an emergency are given priority over nonemergency calls.
4. Do all users who arrive when service is busy join the queue or do some leave immediately (*balk*)? If there is balking, how does it occur? For example, arrivals may leave immediately when there are at least five users waiting.
5. Do all users wait for service once they join the queue, or do some leave after waiting some amount of time (*reneging*)? If there is reneging, how does it occur, for example, after waiting 10 minutes?
6. Is there a limit to the size of the queue, so that when it is full (i.e., has reached the specified limit) all arrivals are turned away? A limited queue may occur where there is limited space, as in a waiting room or where there are limited facilities, or on a telephone switchboard, where callers receive a busy signal when all the automatic answering machines are busy.

These considerations should give some indication of the various possibilities that a queue structure can have. In many situations the behavior of the users is not known with certainty and must be described by a probability distribution. For example, if there is reneging, some users will wait 5 minutes before reneging, some 6 minutes, 7, 8, and so on. A probability distribution can be used to describe the likelihood of reneging occuring at different time values.

Clearly, there are many possibilities for queue structures and it is important to study carefully the structure of the system under investigation. An apparently small change in queue behavior can sometimes change the system performance drastically. For example, some banks with multiple tellers have instituted procedures whereby customers wait in a single queue and go the the first available teller instead of at separate queues at each teller's window. It can be shown that the mean waiting time for customers is reduced with a single queue and therefore yields a better level of service.

SECTION 11.5. *The Service System*

In many respects the methods of specifying how servers provide service is similar to the arrival process and queue structure. As with the queue structure, certain questions must be asked about the service system structure in order that it be fully specified. These questions are:

1. Is there one server or multiple servers?
2. If multiple servers;
   (a) Do they all serve all customers, or are some specialized (e.g., savings and checking tellers in a bank)?
   (b) Do they all work at the same speed, or are some faster and some slower?
3. Do some users go first to one server and then to another (e.g., receptionist and then specialized servers) or does one server handle the total service of the user? In general, we must examine these aspects of the service system in great detail. For instance, the division of bank tellers into checking, savings, express deposit only, check cashing only, and so on, is a change in the service system structure which has proved useful. The same is true of exact-change toll booths on highways, bridges, and tunnels.

A second important consideration in specifying the service system is determining how long it takes a server to provide service to a user. However, this will usually vary from user to user and is therefore best described by a probability distribution. A method virtually identical to that used for specifying the arrival process can be used here. We specify the speed of the server by either of two descriptions:

1. *Service rate.* The number of services per unit time, assuming that the server is kept busy during the entire time period. For example, a typist

who on the average types 10 letters per hour when busy is faster than one who can only type 5 per hour on the average. The service rate (services per time) is analogous to the arrival rate (arrivals per time). It is also a rate (i.e., 180 services/hour, or 3 services/minute).

2. *Service time.* The time required to perform a service. For example, a typist who, on the average, can type 10 letters per hour (service rate) takes an average of $\frac{1}{10}$ hour or 6 minutes per letter (service time). This is analogous to the interarrival time (time between arrivals), since, if the server is always kept busy, the service time is the same as the time between completing one service and completing the next.

In order to estimate the probability distributions of these two measures of service speed we observe a server in operation and collect sample data just as we did with the arrival process. It is, however, necessary to be certain that the server is always busy (never idle) during the period of observation. This may require observing the system during an unusually heavy period or artificially creating an all-busy situation. Assume this is the case, the server is observed for 3 hours, and we obtain the data shown in Table 11.5.1. For each user served, we record the time the service was completed and count the number of services during each 1-minute period. The service times are derived as the time between service completions. As shown, the mean service rate is $540/180 = 3.00$ services/minute (180 services/hour) and the average service time is $10,800/540 = 20.00$ seconds ($\frac{1}{3}$ minute).

As with the arrival process, the probability distributions of service rate and service time can be determined and are shown in Table 11.5.2. These tables show clearly that there exists an analogy between the service rate and the arrival rate and between the service time and the interarrival time.

TABLE 11.5.1. *Samples of Services for One Server During an "Always Busy" Period*

Time Period	Time of Service Completion for Each User (hr: min: sec)	Number of Completions During Period	Service Time for Each User (sec)[a]
2:00–2:01	2:00:22, 2:00:37	2	27, 15
2:01–2:02	2:01:07, 2:01:22, 2:01:44, 2:01:57	4	30, 15, 22, 13
2:02–2:03	2:02:47	1	50
2:03–2:04	2:03:03, 2:03:37, 2:03:56	3	16, 34, 19
2:04–2:05	—	0	—
2:05–2:06	2:05:21, 2:05:44	2	85, 23
.	.	.	.
.	.	.	.
.	.	.	.
4:59–5:00	5:59:15, 4:59:34, 4:59:42	3	24, 19, 8
There are 180 one-minute periods	Sum of observations (Σx) Mean ($\Sigma x/n$)	540 services 3.00 services/minute	10,800 seconds 20.00 seconds/service

[a]Assume that the service completion just prior to 2:00 o'clock occurred at 1:59:55.

TABLE 11.5.2. *Frequency Distribution for Service Data of Table 11.5.1*

	SERVICE RATE (*Services / Minute*)			SERVICE TIME (*Time to Complete a Service*)	
Services / Minute	*Number of Observations*	*Fraction of Observations (Probability)*	*Seconds*	*Number of Observations*	*Fraction of Observations*
0	9	0.050	0–29.99	420	0.777
1	27	0.150	30–59.99	94	0.174
2	40	0.222	60–89.99	21	0.039
3	40	0.222	90–119.99	5	0.009
4	31	0.173	120–149.99	1	0.002
5	18	0.100			
6	9	0.050			
7	4	0.022			
8	2	0.011			
	180	1.000			

Number of observations = 180 at 1-minute intervals
Mean = 3.00 services/minute
Standard deviation = 1.73 services/minute

Number of observations = 540 services
Mean = 20.00 seconds/service
Standard deviation = 20.00 seconds/service

SECTION 11.6. *Measures of Performance of a Queueing System*

In order to measure the performance (level of service) of a queueing system, various statistics can be used. The statistics generally fall into two categories: user-oriented and system-oriented statistics.

A *user-oriented statistic* measures performance related to "what the user experiences." Each user of the system will, for instance, experience a certain amount of waiting time in the queue. Each user's waiting time will most likely be different, owing to the randomness of the process. A probability distribution (and its mean and standard deviation) can be used to describe the variation in user waiting times. An example of a waiting-time probability distribution might be as in Table 11.6.1. Notice that the waiting time is a continuous variable.

The major types of user-oriented statistics are:

1. *Waiting times.* Time spent waiting in the queue for service.
2. *Time spent in the system.* Time between arrival and leaving after completing service (or leaving before receiving service). It includes the time spent waiting in the queue plus the service time.
3. If there is balking, reneging, or a limited queue, the likelihood (probability) of a user leaving without being served.

Clearly, a system that provides, on the average, smaller waiting time, less time spent in the system, or a smaller probability of leaving without being served is providing better service, at least from the user's point of

TABLE 11.6.1. *Probability Distribution*
for Waiting Times

Waiting Time (minutes)	Probability
0–0.499	0.393
0.5–0.999	0.239
1.0–1.499	0.145
1.5–1.999	0.088
2.0–2.499	0.053
2.5–2.999	0.032
3.0–3.499	0.020
3.5–3.999	0.012
4.0–4.499	0.007
4.5–4.999	0.005
5.0–5.499	0.002
⋮	⋮
Mean = 1.00	

view. The general means of providing better service is to have more and/or faster servers. Speeding up the service time usually requires additional technology (computers in banks, faster machines on an assembly line), more highly skilled employees (higher wage rates or additional training, procedures, etc.) or simply more servers (hiring more people or adding another exact-change toll booth). In general, this service improvement will cost more money. Therefore, the economics of queueing decision problems will focus on the balancing of the improvement in service with the cost to provide the better service.

System-oriented statistics attempts to describe characteristics of the system as a whole, for instance, the number of users in the queue. These types of statistics have the characteristic that they have unique values at each point in time, and these values change with changes in time. They differ from user-oriented statistics, wherein each user provides data for only one discrete sample point. For example, for the user-oriented-statistic waiting time, each user experiences a given waiting time. If we were to observe 50 users using the system, we would obtain 50 discrete observations of waiting time. On the other hand, if a graph of the number of users in the queue versus time were drawn as in Figure 11.6.1, this system-oriented statistic (variable) has a value at each time point and it changes over time as shown by the graph. This type of variable, which changes over time in a random fashion, is known as a *stochastic variable*. We can still describe it by a probability distribution; however, it must be interpreted slightly differently than the probability distribution for a variable with discrete samples, such as waiting time. A probability distribution for number of users in the queue appears as shown in Table 11.6.2. In this case the probability of there being two users in the queue must be interpreted as the fraction of time that there are two users in the

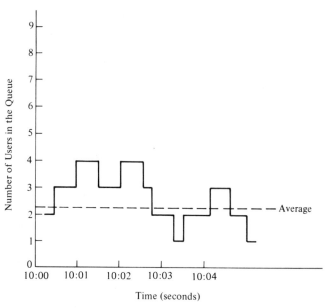

FIGURE 11.6.1. *Graph of number of users in the queue versus time.*

TABLE 11.6.2. *Probability Distribution of Number of Users in the Queue*

Number in Queue	Probability (Fraction of the Time)
0	0.555
1	0.148
2	0.099
3	0.066
4	0.044
5	0.029
6	0.020
7	0.013
8	0.009
9	0.007
10	0.005
Mean = 1.33	

queue. We can calculate a mean and standard deviation as with any distribution, and they have the usual meanings. The mean number of users in the queue is the long-run average number in the queue, the average being shown on Figure 11.6.1.

The main system-oriented statistics used to measure the performance of a queueing system are:

1. The *number of users in the queue* (probability distribution, mean, standard deviation).

2. The *number of users in the system*, which includes those in the queue plus those receiving service (probability distribution, mean, standard deviation).

3. *Server usage*. This is a variable that has only two values (busy or idle). The probability of the server being busy (fraction of the time busy or average utilization) is usually used.

4. Probability that a user has to wait before being served (i.e., the probability that the server, or all servers, are busy).

These measures give a general description of the system. A system with more users waiting in a queue is quite different from one with a shorter queue. A system with a higher server-idle time means an opportunity for servers to take on added responsibilities (clerical, etc.), while one with little server-idle time does not.

It is appropriate to note that the means (or averages) of either user- or system-oriented variables are the measures of performance of the system used most often, since they do reveal the overall or long-run status of the system.

SECTION 11.7. *Economic Example*

To get a better understanding of how to deal with decision problems concerning queueing systems, let us consider a simple problem. A large automobile repair company maintains a parts supply room to supply all the mechanics with the necessary parts to fix the automobiles on which they are working. The mechanics must leave the cars on which they are working and go to the parts supply room, where they are served by attendants who give them the parts they need, fill out the required forms, and so on. If no attendant is free, the mechanics wait (in a queue) until an attendant is free to serve them. They wait in a single queue and are served on a first-come, first-served basis. The mean arrival rate at the supply room is two mechanics per minute, and an attendant can serve an average of three mechanics per minute (i.e., an average service time of 20 seconds). The mechanics are paid $9/hour and the attendants are paid $3/hour.

While the mechanics are at the supply room, either waiting or being served, they are not fixing cars, yet since they are paid on an hourly basis, they are still being paid for that time. Reducing the time they spend at the supply room saves the company money. Let us assume that the only way this can be done is by hiring more attendants, which will also cost more money. The decision problem in this case centers on how many attendants to hire so as to minimize the total cost of mechanics' lost time plus attendants' salary. Another way of viewing the problem is that each additional attendant we hire reduces the mechanics' lost-time cost but increases the personnel cost. It pays to add attendants as long as the savings in mechanics' lost-time cost is greater than the additional attendants' salaries. It was given that each additional attendant costs $3 per hour. To find the mechanics' lost-time cost per hour, we multiply the number of mechanics per hour who arrive to be served by the average time they spend at the supply room and by the mechanics' salary per hour:

$$\begin{pmatrix} \text{mechanics'} \\ \text{lost-time cost} \end{pmatrix} = \begin{pmatrix} \text{arrival} \\ \text{rate} \end{pmatrix} \times \begin{pmatrix} \text{mean time spent} \\ \text{in the system} \end{pmatrix} \times \begin{pmatrix} \text{mechanics'} \\ \text{pay rate} \end{pmatrix}$$

Thus, to evaluate the mechanics' lost-time cost we need to know the mean time mechanics will spend in the system for different numbers of attendants (servers). As previously mentioned, this is one of the major user-oriented statistics which measures the performance of the system. Let us not concern ourselves with how these statistics could be obtained, but assume that the company asked its quantitative methods department to study the problem. The following results were developed:

Number of Attendants	1	2	3	4
Mean Time Spent in the System	1.00	0.37	0.34	0.33

Notice that the mean time spent in the system approaches (can be no lower than) the mean service time, since even if there is no waiting, all mechanics must spend the time required to be served, which is on the average 0.33 minute. Let us now evaluate the total cost to the company for different numbers of attendants. The cost is composed of attendants' salaries per hour and mechanics' lost-time costs per hour. We must convert all per-minute figures to per-hour figures, or vice versa, to be consistent.

STRATEGY 1:   Hire one attendant:

$$\begin{pmatrix} \text{total cost} \\ \text{per hour} \end{pmatrix} = \begin{bmatrix} \text{attendants'} \\ \text{salary} \\ \text{per hour} \end{bmatrix} + \begin{bmatrix} \text{mechanics'} \\ \text{lost-time cost} \\ \text{per hour} \end{bmatrix}$$

$$= \begin{pmatrix} \text{number of} \\ \text{attendants} \end{pmatrix} \begin{pmatrix} \text{attendants'} \\ \text{salary} \end{pmatrix} + \begin{pmatrix} \text{arrival} \\ \text{rate} \end{pmatrix}$$

$$\times \begin{pmatrix} \text{mean time spent} \\ \text{in the system} \end{pmatrix} \begin{pmatrix} \text{mechanics'} \\ \text{salary} \end{pmatrix}$$

$$= (1)(\$3/\text{hour}) + (120/\text{hour})(1.00 \text{ min})$$

$$\times \left(\frac{1}{60} \frac{\text{hr}}{\text{min}} \right)(\$9/\text{hour})$$

$$= \$3.00/\text{hour} + \$18.00/\text{hour}$$

$$= \$21.00/\text{hour}$$

Notice that we must convert mean time in the system measured in minutes to an hourly figure by dividing by 60 minutes/hour to be consistent.

STRATEGY 2: Hire two attendants:

$$\left(\begin{array}{c}\text{total cost}\\\text{per hour}\end{array}\right) = (2)(\$3/\text{hour}) + (120/\text{hour})$$

$$\times (0.37 \text{ min})\left(\frac{1}{60} \frac{\text{hr}}{\text{min}}\right)(\$9/\text{hour})$$

$$= \$6/\text{hour} + \$6.66/\text{hour}$$

$$= \$12.66/\text{hour}$$

Since the cost for two attendants is less than that for one attendant, it is better to hire two attendants than one. From an incremental point of view, adding the second attendant added \$3/hour in salary cost but saved \$11.34/hour (\$18.00 minus \$6.66) in mechanics' lost-time cost.

STRATEGY 3: Hire three attendants:

$$\left(\begin{array}{c}\text{total cost}\\\text{per hour}\end{array}\right) = (3)(\$3/\text{hour}) + (120/\text{hour})$$

$$\times (0.34 \text{ min})\left(\frac{1}{60} \frac{\text{hr}}{\text{min}}\right)(\$9/\text{hour})$$

$$= \$9/\text{hour} + \$6.12/\text{hour}$$

$$= \$15.12/\text{hour}$$

Adding the third attendant is not justified, since the total cost per hour for three attendants is higher than for two attendants. The additional attendant costs \$3/hour more but only saves \$0.54/hour in lost-time cost. Additional attendants will be even less profitable.

Thus, the optimal strategy is to hire two attendants.

SECTION 11.8. *Applications of Queueing Models*

There have been a wide variety of applications of queueing models where decisions must be made regarding queueing systems. As already mentioned, the general objective is to evaluate the measures of performance of various queueing-system structures and establish a balance between the costs and the benefits of improved service.

One of the earliest applications of queueing models was performed at Bell Laboratories in trying to develop procedures for determining how many telephone lines were required between telephone company offices. The telephones represented multiple servers in the service system. Users were people calling between the two offices (calls). The calls arrived randomly to the telephone offices and the length of times of the phone calls (service times) were random. There was no queueing (queue limited to zero), since all callers who found the lines busy received a busy signal and hung up. Their studies showed that both the arrival and service distributions tended to follow a given probability distribution known as the Poisson probability distribution. The major difference between the studies was a different arrival rate. They were able to develop and to solve an analytical model of this general queueing system and to use it throughout the Bell System to determine how many lines are needed, for a given arrival rate, to achieve a desired service level. One criterion of performance was that callers should not find all lines busy more than a stated fraction of the time [i.e., the probability of all servers' (lines) busy less than a stated value].

The banks have used queueing theory to determine the number of tellers necessary during given periods of demand (arrivals) and to compare single versus multiple queues. Computer systems have been modeled as queueing systems. The various portions of the computer are the servers (core storage, tape drives, etc.) and jobs to be run are the users. This has helped determine how big and fast a computer is required for a given load of processing.

Traffic studies have modeled cars on a roadway and toll booths as queueing systems. The sections of roadway or the toll booths are the servers, and cars are the users. The types of decisions considered are how many lanes (multiple servers) to build, how many toll booths are required, and how to set the timing of lights at an intersection. Much of traffic systems theory is connected with queueing theory.

Queueing models have been used to help in designing such hospital facilities as emergency, operating, or maternity rooms. The patients are the users and the facilities are servers. Queueing models can help predict waiting times or the probability that the facilities are all in use. (Women ready to give birth cannot wait until the maternity room is free and will give birth either in the waiting room or in a regular operating room.)

The police emergency response system has been modeled as a queueing system. The servers are telephone operators who answer calls and dispatch patrol cars to aid the caller. The object is to determine the waiting times (response time) for police assistance for various demand levels, number of operators, and police cars on patrol.

These are but a few of the many possible situations that are essentially queueing-type systems, for which queueing models can be used to help in the design process.

An analytical solution to a queueing system simply means that algebraic expressions or formulas are derived for the measures of performance of the system (mean, standard deviation, probability distribution), by mathematical or quantitative methods. These methods usually require complex mathematical models of the system and arithmetic manipulations of these models to solve for the desired quantities. For example, for one very specific queueing system[†] it can be shown that the analytic solution for the mean number of users in the system is given by

$$(1) \quad \left(\begin{array}{c} \text{mean number of} \\ \text{users in system} \end{array} \right) = \frac{\text{mean arrival rate}}{(\text{mean service rate}) - (\text{mean arrival rate})}$$

If it is possible to derive an analytical solution to a queueing problem, it is certainly a distinct advantage. For instance, the expression for the mean number of users in the system, equation (1), is extremely useful, since it applies to a great variety of queueing systems, all of which have the same structure but different mean arrival and service rates. To solve for the mean number of users in the system for any system whose structure is identical with that of the one for which equation (1) was derived, we substitute the particular mean arrival and service rates into equation (1) and evaluate it.

In practice, however, general analytical solutions are difficult to obtain and have been developed for only a very limited class of queueing systems. A brief description of analytical solutions to a simple queueing system is presented in the next section. More detailed treatment of general analytic methods is presented in Chapter 12.

Since most real-life queueing systems are far too complex to be analyzed analytically, an alternative method must be utilized to derive measures of performance of a queueing system. This other technique, known as *simulation*, has been developed and is extremely useful in deriving the desired measures of performance for queueing systems as well as in assisting to solve other probability and stochastic problems. Although simulation will be covered in greater detail in Chapter 13, it is worthwhile to discuss it briefly here. A simulation model "imitates" the system it represents, and results are found by a procedure known as "running" the model rather than by solving the model. Since the number of computations in a simulation are usually very large, the model is usually run on a computer. As part of the simulation process, it generates samples of arrival times, wait times, service times, number of users in the system, and so on, in exactly the way that the actual system would generate them. If the simulation model is properly constructed, the

407   [†]This case is discussed in detail in the next section.

samples generated are representative (i.e., are exactly like the observations we would make if we conducted a study of the actual queueing system). The computer simulation model also collects statistics, as we would do, and these data are used to estimate the measures of performance of the system. If the model is run to simulate longer periods of time, more simulated samples are generated, and our estimates are more precise (lower standard deviation). Changes to the system, such as adding additional servers or a second queue, are made by making slight changes in the simulation model and running it again on the computer. Thus, the researcher uses a computer simulation model to "experiment" with different system structures in the same way that the actual system would be investigated as to the effects of different structures.

Although simulation requires the expenditure of considerable computer time (which, of course, involves considerable cost), since simulation models are generally easier to construct than analytical models and yield solutions when an analytical solution is just not possible, it is usually worth the effort to model a system using simulation. It should be kept in mind, however, that simulation models are far less general than analytical models. This is because each change to the system requires a corresponding change in the model (usually just a slight one) and rerunning the whole model on the computer.

SECTION 11.10. *Using Analytical Results—The Basic Models*

To illustrate the use of analytical results to find measures of performance for a queueing system, let us consider the following problem. A police department is building a new precinct house and plans to install one phone and an automatic answering–holding device at the telephone company for callers who call when the line is busy. People will phone this number to report crimes, ask questions, and the like. The police department estimates that during most of the day they will receive an average of 120 calls/hour and that the operator can handle 180 calls/hour, on the average, if he is always busy. (Notice that these conform to the mean arrival and service values given in earlier sections.) Calls are handled on a first-come, first-served basis due to the automatic call answering–holding machine, which can accommodate "more than enough" callers and answers the calls in sequence. The police department assumes that all persons who find the line busy when they call will wait until their call is answered. The telephone company assures them (having performed many studies of such situations) that the arrival rates and service rates are distributed according to the Poisson probability distribution,[†] and the police department can use the telephone company results for their new system.

[†]We shall not be concerned here with what the Poisson probability distribution is.

The police department is interested in knowing if one telephone is sufficient and would like to see some measures of performance of the system with one telephone prior to actually building the precinct house (more telephones mean more employees, desk space, etc.)

This problem can be represented by a queueing system with calls or callers being the users, a telephone (and operator) being the server, and the automatic answering–holding machine acting as the (assumed unlimited) queue. The queueing system structure may be described technically as follows:

1. Poisson probability distribution for arrival rate.
2. Single queue, FIFO, no balking or reneging.
3. Single server, Poisson probability distribution for service rate.

Analytical solutions have been derived for this particular system and we shall simply present them and use the results for our problem. A detailed discussion of how these results are obtained will be presented in Chapter 12. These results have been derived for general arrival rate λ (Greek lowercase lambda) and service rate μ (Greek lowercase mu). For our particular problem $\lambda = 120$ arrivals/hour $= 2$ arrivals/minute and $\mu = 180$ services/hour $= 3$ services/minute. We shall use these values and solve for the measures of performance of this system.

USER-ORIENTED STATISTICS

1. The mean time spent in the system (T_s), that is, the average time spent by a caller for both waiting and being answered, is given by

$$(1) \qquad T_s = \frac{1}{\mu - \lambda}$$

Using $\lambda = 120$ arrivals/hour and $\mu = 180$ services/hour,

$$T_s = \frac{1}{180 - 120} = \frac{1}{60} \text{ hour}$$
$$= 1 \text{ minute}$$

Notice that the result we obtain is in terms of hours, since both λ and μ are measured in terms of hours. We can then convert to minutes if we wish. We can derive the same result by using $\lambda = 2$ arrivals/minute and $\mu = 3$ services/minute. Thus,

$$T_s = \frac{1}{3 - 2} = 1 \text{ minute}$$

Since this appears to be easier, let us use $\lambda = 2$ and $\mu = 3$ from here

on.

2. The mean time spent in the queue (T_q), that is, the time a caller spent waiting to be answered, is given by

$$T_q = \frac{\lambda}{\mu(\mu - \lambda)} = \frac{2}{3(3-2)} = \frac{2}{3} \text{ minute}$$

(2)

$$= 40 \text{ seconds}$$

SYSTEM-ORIENTED STATISTICS

1. The mean number of users (calls) in the system (L_s), that is, the total number of callers in the queue plus in service, is given by

(3)
$$L_s = \frac{\lambda}{\mu - \lambda} = \frac{2}{3-2} = 2 \text{ users}$$

2. The mean number of users in the queue who are waiting for service (L_q) is given by

(4)
$$L_q = \frac{\lambda^2}{\mu(\mu - \lambda)} = \frac{(2)^2}{3(3-2)} = \frac{4}{3} = 1.33 \text{ users}$$

3. The probability (fraction of the time) that the server (operator) is busy (P_b) is given by

(5)
$$P_b = \frac{\lambda}{\mu} = \frac{2}{3} = 0.67$$

Note that P_b is also the probability that a caller must wait before being answered, since a caller waits only when the operator is busy.

From these results an administrator obtains a fairly clear picture of how the system will perform. He can then utilize this information to assist in deciding whether or not an additional telephone is necessary. For example, one design criterion might be that no more than 1 out of 10 (0.10) callers must wait before being answered, and that the average waiting time must be less than 10 seconds ($\frac{1}{6}$ minute). To achieve this, additional phones and operators must be added. This can be seen from the fact that the design requires $P_b = 0.10$, whereas the system calculates it as $P_b = 0.67$. Furthermore, the design requires $T_q = 10$ seconds, but the system yields the larger value, $T_q = 40$ seconds. Thus, the design criteria are not being met by a single telephone. The addition of servers, however, changes the service system structure from single to multiple servers, but fortunately analytical solutions are also available for the multiple-server case. To reanalyze our telephone needs, we use two values from that solution: (1) the probability that all servers are busy (P_b), which will equal the fraction of customers who must wait before being answered; and (2) the mean waiting time T_q. However, the analytical solutions themselves are quite complicated, and there is no point in our presenting them here. Since there is a computer program available which evaluates most of the major performance statistics of the multiple-server system, this program was run for the data of the telephone problem. The results are tabulated in Table 11.10.1.

TABLE 11.10.1. *Measures of Performance for Various Numbers of Operators*

Number of Operators	*Mean Waiting Time*	*Probability that All Servers Are Busy*
1	0.67 min = 40 sec	0.67
2	0.04 min = 2 sec	0.17
3	Approximately 0	0.03
4	Approximately 0	0.01

From this table we observe that the lowest number of servers which achieves *both* design criteria is 3. Therefore, the police department should install three telephones.

SECTION 11.11. *Using the Computer*

As an example of the types of computer applications possible for queueing models, a computer program has been developed for queueing systems with the following characteristics: (1) Poisson arrival and service process, (2) single-queue FIFO, and (3) no balking or reneging. This is precisely the system considered in the prior section. The functions performed by this program are as follows:

1. Developing the probability distributions (if desired) of arrival rate, interarrival time, service rate, and service time.
2. Computing various measures of performance of the queueing system for up to 10 servers.
3. Performing the economic evaluations (if desired) as described in Section 11.7.

The required input to the program is:

1. Mean arrival rate.
2. Mean service rate.
3. Options (i.e., whether the probability distributions and/or the economic evaluations are desired).
4. Cost per server and lost-time cost if economic evaluations are desired.

A sample output for the problem considered throughout this chapter with arrival rate equal to 2 arrivals/minute, service rate equal to 3 services/minute, cost per server equal to $3/hour, and lost-time cost equal to $9/hour is shown in Figures 11.11.1–11.11.3. These are the same results that were used throughout this chapter.

The program identifies no specific time units of its own, and the user must express all input values in terms of a uniform time unit, such as hours, tenths of hours, minutes, seconds. The program was run using a time unit of 1 minute, and arrival and service rates are stated as 2 and 3, respectively. The costs must also be expressed on a per-minute basis, and therefore $3/hour is $0.05/minute and $9/hour is $0.15/minute.

The first part of the output, Figure 11.11.1, is the probability distributions of arrival rate, interarrival time, service rate, and service time. Notice that these distributions are almost exactly equal to the distributions derived from the sample data and shown in Sections 11.3 and 11.5. In fact, these sample data were designed to fit a Poisson probability distribution. The probability of the number of arrivals and services per time are shown for 0 up to 10. It is advisable, when the distributions are of interest, to choose a time unit such that the mean rate is less than 5, so that the probability of more than 10 arrivals or services is low. For example, for our problem the mean arrival rate is 120 arrivals/hour, which is equivalent to 2 arrivals/minute. We have used a time unit of 1 minute so that the mean arrival rate is a value lower than 5.

The second portion of the output, Figure 11.11.2, contains various measures of performance of the system for different numbers of servers up to 10. These data were used in Section 11.10, which considered the use of analytical results.

The third portion of the output, Figure 11.11.3, is the economic evaluations considered in Section 11.7. Notice that the results are in terms of dollars per minute instead of dollars per hour used in the text.

```
BASIC QUEUEING MODELS WITH ECONOMIC ANALYSIS,
    POISSON ARRIVALS AND SERVICE, FIFO QUEUE UNLIMITED


MEAN ARRIVAL RATE=        2.00 ARRIVALS/TIME
MEAN SERVICE RATE=        3.00 SERVICES/TIME


                    PROBABILITY DISTRIBUTIONS
```

ARRIVAL RATE		INTER ARRIVAL TIME		SERVICE RATE		SERVICE TIME	
NO. OF ARR/TIME	PROB	TIME BET ARRIVALS	PROB	NO. OF SVC/TIME	PROB	TIME BET SERVICES	PROB
0	0.1353	0.0– 0.5	0.6321	0	0.0498	0.0– 0.5	0.7769
1	0.2707	0.5– 1.0	0.2325	1	0.1494	0.5– 1.0	0.1733
2	0.2707	1.0– 1.5	0.0855	2	0.2240	1.0– 1.5	0.0387
3	0.1804	1.5– 2.0	0.0315	3	0.2240	1.5– 2.0	0.0086
4	0.0902	2.0– 2.5	0.0116	4	0.1680	2.0– 2.5	0.0019
5	0.0361	2.5– 3.0	0.0043	5	0.1008	2.5– 3.0	0.0004
6	0.0120	3.0– 3.5	0.0016	6	0.0504	3.0– 3.5	0.0001
7	0.0034	3.5– 4.0	0.0006	7	0.0216	3.5– 4.0	0.0000
8	0.0009	4.0– 4.5	0.0002	8	0.0081	4.0– 4.5	0.0000
9	0.0002	4.5– 5.0	0.0001	9	0.0027	4.5– 5.0	0.0000

FIGURE 11.11.1. *Computer output for probability distributions.*

NO. OF SERVERS	MEAN NO. IN SYSTEM	MEAN NO. IN QUEUE	PROB ALL SERV BUSY	MEAN WAIT TIME	MEAN TIME IN SYSTEM
1	2.00	1.33	0.66667	0.67	1.00
2	0.75	0.08	0.16667	0.04	0.37
3	0.68	0.01	0.03252	0.00	0.34
4	0.67	0.00	0.00507	0.00	0.33
5	0.67	0.00	0.00065	0.00	0.33
6	0.67	0.00	0.00007	0.00	0.33
7	0.67	0.00	0.00001	0.00	0.33
8	0.67	0.00	0.00000	0.00	0.33
9	0.67	0.00	0.00000	0.00	0.33
10	0.67	0.00	0.00000	0.00	0.33

FIGURE 11.11.2. *Computer output for measures of performance.*

ECONOMIC EVALUATION

COST PER SERVER =   0.05 $/TIME
COST OF LOST TIME =   0.15 $/TIME

NO. OF SERVERS	SERVICE COST	LOST TIME COST	TOTAL COST
1	0.0500	0.3000	0.3500
2	0.1000	0.1125	0.2125
3	0.1500	0.1014	0.2514
4	0.2000	0.1002	0.3002
5	0.2500	0.1000	0.3500
6	0.3000	0.1000	0.4000
7	0.3500	0.1000	0.4500
8	0.4000	0.1000	0.5000
9	0.4500	0.1000	0.5500
10	0.5000	0.1000	0.6000

FIGURE 11.11.3. *Computer output for economic evaluation.*

Multiplying them by 60 minutes/hour will yield identical numerical results.

This program illustrates how results that would otherwise take hours to obtain with a calculator are obtained in a very short time. A decision maker concerned with a queueing decision problem would find the analytical results that are programmed on a computer an invaluable aid. Although simulation has been just briefly mentioned, the importance of computers when using simulation is even more critical. It would be almost impossible without the aid of a computer to construct a simulation model that yielded useful results.

SECTION 11.12. *Summary*

Queueing systems are to be found as part of many organizations, and decision problems arise with respect to their performance. The tradeoffs in the decision problem apply to the cost of providing service and the performance of the system. Models have been developed to evaluate the measures of performance of queueing systems and are used as part of the decision-making process.

413

Constructing a model entails describing the components of the system in detail (i.e., arrival process, queue structure, and service process) and solving for the measures of performance. The two general approaches to obtaining these results are analytical methods and simulation.

The decision criterion can be based upon these measures of performance so that the resulting system meets certain stated levels of service. In addition, if certain measures of performance can be related to dollar costs or income, an objective function can be developed and an optimal solution obtained.

The chapter has presented the basic techniques for describing the system, measuring the performance of the system, using analytical results to design a system to meet stated performance criteria, and finding an economically optimum system. It has also presented a brief discussion of applications of queueing models which relates the techniques discussed to real-world problems. The use of the computer has been demonstrated through a computer program that evaluates analytical results to obtain measures of performance of a simple type of queueing system.

PROBLEMS

11.1. Find examples of queueing systems and describe generally their structure, arrival process, queue discipline, and service process.

11.2. Given the following 10 times of arrival to a queueing system, estimate the mean arrival rate and mean interarrival time. The arrival times are given to the nearest minute: 9:01, 9:27, 9:58, 10:12, 10:48, 11:34, 12:04, 12:16, 12:35, 12:59.

11.3. A taxicab company runs its own repair and maintenance facility. Taxicabs arrive at an average of 3 per hour and require, on the average, 15 minutes for maintenance. Taxicabs yield $10/hour profit when operating. The company currently has only one mechanic performing maintenance and is considering hiring additional ones. Mechanics are paid $5/hour. The mean time spent by a taxicab at the facility (waiting and maintenance) for different numbers of mechanics available is:

Number of Mechanics	1	2	3	4
Mean Time Spent (min)	45	20	16	15

11.4. (Problem 11.3 continued) Assume that the arrival rate and service rate are Poisson-distributed and there is only one mechanic. Find:

(a) The mean time spent in the queue (mean wait time).
(b) The mean time spent waiting and being served (combined).
(c) The mean number of taxicabs waiting to be serviced.
(d) The mean number of taxicabs either waiting or being serviced.
(e) The probability that there is a taxicab being serviced.

11.5. (Problem 11.3 continued) Assume that the arrival rate and service rate are Poisson-distributed. Use the computer program to find the optimal number of mechanics to hire.

11.6. (Problem 11.3 continued) Assume that management is considering renting special equipment to improve maintenance. This equipment rents for $160/week and will be used 40 hours/week. With this equipment, the mean time spent for different numbers of mechanics is:

Number of Mechanics	1	2	3
Mean Time Spent (min)	35	15	12

Assume that each mechanic requires his own piece of equipment.

(a) Find the optimal number of mechanics (and pieces of equipment) to hire.
(b) Should the new equipment be rented?

11.7. (Problem 11.6 continued) Assume that arrival and service rates (with the equipment) are Poisson-distributed and that, with the equipment, a mechanic can service a car in an average of 12 minutes. Assuming one mechanic, find:

(a) The mean time spent by taxicabs waiting for maintenance.
(b) The mean time spent at the maintenance facility (waiting plus service).
(c) The mean number of taxicabs waiting for maintenance.
(d) The mean number of taxicabs either waiting or being serviced.
(e) The probability that the mechanic is servicing a car.

11.8. (Problem 11.6 continued) Assume that arrival and service rates are Poisson-distributed. Use the computer program to find the optimal number of mechanics (and pieces of equipment) to hire.

11.9. An airport has one runway, used for both takeoffs and landings. Planes arrive for either takeoff or landing at the rate of one each 5 minutes. Takeoffs and landings take the same amount of time, an average of 4 minutes, and are scheduled on a first-come, first-served basis. Both arrival and service rates are Poisson-distributed.

Find:

(a) The mean waiting time for takeoff or landing.
(b) The mean number of planes either waiting to take off or land.
(c) The probability that the runway is in use.

11.10. (Problem 11.9 continued) Use the computer program to find the minimum number of runways such that the mean waiting time is no more than 2 minutes. For this number of runways, what is the probability that the runway is in use?

11.11. An emergency room of a hospital serves patients who arrive, on the average, every 10 minutes. Treating a patient takes, on the average, 9 minutes. Both arrivals and treatments are Poisson-distributed. Patients are treated on a first-come, first-served basis.

Assuming only one doctor, find:

(a) The mean waiting time before being treated.
(b) The mean time spent at the hospital for patients.
(c) The mean number of patients waiting for treatment.
(d) The mean number of patients either waiting or being served.
(e) The fraction of the time the doctor is busy.

11.12. (Problem 11.11 continued) Use the computer program to find the minimum number of doctors required so that the mean waiting time for patients is no more than 5 minutes and the fraction of patients who must wait at all is no more than 0.2.

11.13. A minicomputer company assembles its made-to-order computers on a company operated assembly line. Orders for individual computers arrive at an average rate of 9 per month and the assembly line rate is, on the average, 10 per month. The company makes a $1000 profit on each minicomputer delivered immediately. As a sales incentive, the company reduces the purchase price by $50 for each day the customer must wait for delivery. To set up each additional assembly line costs the company $40 per day. Orders are filled on a first-come, first-served basis and the computers are delivered as soon as they come off the assembly line. The mean time spent on an order (from arrival to delivery of final product) for different numbers of assembly lines is:

Number of Assembly Lines	1	2	3	4
Mean Time Spent (days)	10	6	3	2

Assume 30 working days per month. Find the optimal number of assembly lines to operate.

11.14. (Problem 11.13 continued) Assume that the company is considering installing new automated equipment for the assembly lines. This equipment will cost $10 per day for each assembly line. The improved values for the mean time spent by an order for different numbers of assembly lines is:

Number of Assembly Lines	1	2	3
Mean Time Spent (days)	6	3	1

(a) How many assembly lines should be operated?
(b) Should the new automated equipment be used?

11.15. In Problems 11.13–11.14 assume that the arrival rate and service rate are Poisson distributed. Use the computer program to find the optimum number of service facilities that should be utilized. Assume that with the new equipment, 12 minicomputers per month can be assembled.

11.16. A shipping company is planning to build a loading–unloading dock to service its own ships. Ships will arrive at an average rate of 8 per month and the proposed dock will load–unload (in one operation), on the average, 10 per month. The ships each earn $1000 per day in profit when they are in operation at sea. Assume all arrivals and services are Poisson distributed. No limit is imposed on the queue, and service is first-come, first-served (1 month = 30 days, 1 year = 12 months).

(a) For the proposed dock, find the
  (1) Average time spent by a ship (waiting plus loading–unloading) at the dock.
  (2) Average number of ships at the dock (waiting or loading–unloading).
  (3) Probability that a ship is being loaded or unloaded.
(b) The company is considering two additional alternatives to the above dock:
  (1) Special equipment costing an additional $480,000 per year which will permit 11 ships per month to be loaded–unloaded.
  (2) A second dock costing an additional $600,000 per year. Ships will wait in a single queue and use the first available dock. Average time spent at the dock by a ship (waiting plus loading–unloading) is 3.6 days.
Which of the three alternatives should be chosen?

BOOKS OF INTEREST

See bibliography of Chapter 12 on page 435 for a list of applicable readings.

CHAPTER TWELVE

Analytical Solutions to Queueing Problems

OBJECTIVES: The purpose of this chapter is to acquaint you with the following introductory considerations in solving queueing models analytically.

1. *The Poisson process.*
2. *Analysis of the basic single-server queueing system.*
3. *Special cases of single-server queueing systems.*
4. *Multiple-server queueing systems.*

A detailed introduction to queueing problems was presented in Chapter 11. Included was a comprehensive description of the characteristics of queueing systems and a discussion of the various measures of system performance. It was pointed out that these system measures can be derived by using either simulation or analytic methods. In general, quantitative solutions usually represented by an algebraic expression or formula are more exact; however, except for a limited number of queueing problems, they are extremely difficult to derive.

In this chapter a selected group of basic queueing models will be presented. Included in the presentation will be a discussion of the Poisson process and descriptive and mathematical versions of the models and their analytical solutions. Where practical, within the scope of this text, a sketch of the derivations of the analytic solutions will be presented. Two general classes of models are treated, the single-server and the multiple-server models. They are compared with respect to the impact on a business system decision maker having control of the system and requiring a decision as to the size of the service facilities.

SECTION 12.2. *The Poisson Process*

Two of the elements of a queueing system are the arrival process and the service process. As was pointed out in Sections 11.3 and 11.5, these processes can be represented by probability distributions so as to describe the occurrence of an arrival and the occurrence of a service. Furthermore, this description may be defined in terms of either the arrival rate or the interarrival time for the arrival process and for the service process by either the service rate or the time required to complete a service. It can be easily shown that the two definitions for each process are identical and interchangeable.

Of the many probability distributions that can be used to describe arrival and service processes are the special distributions characteristic of a system meeting the conditions of a Poisson process. A *Poisson process* is a random process with the following requirements:

419   1. The process has no memory. The probability of an event occurring during a unit of time does not depend on what happened during previous units of time.

2. The process rate (say the arrival rate λ or the service rate μ) is assumed to be constant for the entire time period being examined.

3. The probability of exactly one event occurring during a small unit of time is equal to the process rate times the unit of time duration. The probability of two or more events occurring during a small unit of time is very small and we will assume that it approaches zero as the unit of time gets very small.

4. The distribution that provides probabilities for the number of events (arrival or service completions) that occur during a specific time period of the process is the Poisson distribution (see Section 2.10).

5. The distribution that provides probabilities for the times between the occurrence of events (arrivals or service completions) of the process is the exponential distribution (see Section 2.11).

Many actual queueing situations can be described as Poisson processes, and thus the arrival and service elements are represented by either the Poisson or the exponential distributions. It can be shown that the arrival rates for a process defined by a Poisson distribution with a mean arrival rate λ will also have the interarrival times distributed according to the exponential distribution with a mean interarrival time $1/\lambda$. The usual convention in queueing systems described by a Poisson process is to define the arrival process by a Poisson distribution with a mean arrival rate λ or an exponential distribution with a mean interarrival time $1/\lambda$. In addition, the service process is defined by an exponential distribution with a mean service time $1/\mu$, where μ equals the mean service rate.

SECTION 12.3. *Basic Single-Server Model*

Consider a queueing system with a single service facility (i.e., only one service occurs at a time), and those waiting in the queue enter service on a first-come, first-served basis, or FIFO queue discipline. In addition, no balking or reneging takes place. We assume that the system is described by a Poisson process with the Poisson probability distribution defining the arrival process and the exponential distribution defining the service process. Finally, we assume that the mean service rate is larger than the mean arrival rate, $\mu > \lambda$, so that the possibility of serving all the arrivals is realistic. If $\lambda > \mu$, the queue will get larger and larger indefinitely.)

In order to derive analytic results for the system- and user-oriented statistics, such as the mean number of users in the system or the mean time spent in the system, it is necessary to find the probability distribution for the number of users in the system. We will denote by n the *state* of the system at a given instant of time (i.e., the number of users either waiting for or receiving service). P_n will denote the probability that there are n users in the system at a given instant of time, or

$$P_n = \text{probability of being in state } n$$

Consider now a system in state n at some time $T, n > 0$. For this system one of three events occurred during a small interval of time just prior to T.

1. The first possible event is that the system was in state $n-1$ (i.e., there were $n-1$ users in the system) and a new arrival occurred, bringing the total to n.
2. The second possible event is that the system was in state $n+1$ (i.e., there were $n+1$ users in the system) and a service completion occurred, reducing the total to n.
3. The third possible event is that the system was in state n and no arrivals or service completions occurred, thus leaving the system in the same state n. (We assume that the time interval is so small that two arrivals or two service completions or an arrival and a service completion during the time interval cannot take place.)

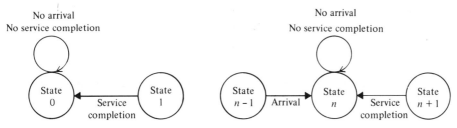

FIGURE 12.3.1. *Schematic of possible events for single-server model.*

If $n = 0$, only the second and third events could have occurred. These various events are shown schematically in Figure 12.3.1. It can be shown that in steady state or equilibrium,[†] the following equations are valid:

$$\lambda P_0 = \mu P_1$$
$$\lambda P_1 + \mu P_1 = \lambda P_0 + \mu P_2$$
$$\lambda P_{n-1} + \mu P_{n-1} = \lambda P_{n-2} + \mu P_n$$

Solving these equations recursively yields the following result

$$P_n = \left(\frac{\lambda}{\mu}\right)^n P_0$$

[†]*Steady state* or *equilibrium* means that the probability of being in state n remains the same over time. Mathematically, it states that if the number of customers in the system at time T is given by the probability distribution P_n, then for any $h > 0, P_n$ is the probability that n customers are in the system at time $T + h$.

Since P_n is a discrete probability distribution, it must satisfy the requirement that

$$\sum_{n=0}^{\infty} P_n = 1$$

or

$$\sum_{n=0}^{\infty} \left(\frac{\lambda}{\mu}\right)^n P_0 = 1$$

which yields

$$P_0 = 1 - \frac{\lambda}{\mu}$$

Thus,

$$P_n = \left(\frac{\lambda}{\mu}\right)^n \left(1 - \frac{\lambda}{\mu}\right)$$

The value λ/μ, also denoted by ρ, is called the *traffic intensity* or the system's *utilization factor*. Since the probability of the system being empty is P_0, the probability of the service being busy is

$$P_b = 1 - P_0 = \frac{\lambda}{\mu}$$

To find the mean number of users in the system, L_s, we must find the expected value of n [i.e., $E(n)$]. This is found from

$$E(n) = \sum_{n=0}^{\infty} n \cdot P_n$$

which can be shown to equal

$$L_s = E(n) = \frac{\lambda}{\mu - \lambda}$$

To find the mean number of users in the queue who are waiting for service, L_q, let us note the following:

$$\text{queue length} = \begin{cases} \text{number in system} & (\text{if } n = 0) \\ \text{number in system} - 1 & (\text{if } n > 0) \end{cases}$$

Therefore,

$$E(\text{queue length}) = 0 \cdot P_0 + \sum_{n=1}^{\infty} (n-1)P_n$$

$$= \sum_{n=0}^{\infty} n \cdot P_n - \sum_{n=1}^{\infty} P_n$$

$$= E(n) - (1 - P_0)$$

Thus,

$$L_q = E\,(\text{queue length}) = \frac{\lambda}{\mu - \lambda} - \frac{\lambda}{\mu}$$

$$= \frac{\lambda^2}{\mu(\mu - \lambda)}$$

It can also be shown that the mean time spent in this system is

$$T_s = \frac{1}{\mu - \lambda}$$

The mean time spent in the queue is

$$T_q = \frac{\lambda}{\mu(\mu - \lambda)}$$

The mean length of a busy period

$$L_b = \frac{1}{\mu - \lambda}$$

The mean number of customers served per busy period

$$N_b = \frac{\mu}{\mu - \lambda}$$

EXAMPLE. Assume that customers for the only local bakery of a large community arrive randomly following a Poisson process. The single salesperson can serve customers at an average rate of 20 per hour; the service time is exponential. The mean arrival rate of customers is 12 per hour. The bakery operates 12 hours/day. We thus have

$$\lambda = 12 \text{ customers/hour}$$
$$\mu = 20 \text{ customers/hour}$$

Hence, the mean number of customers in the bakery is

$$L_s = \frac{\lambda}{\mu - \lambda} = \frac{12}{20 - 12} = 1.5 \text{ customers}$$

and the mean time spent by the customers in the bakery is

$$T_s = \frac{1}{\mu - \lambda} = \frac{1}{20 - 12} = \frac{1}{8} \text{ hour} = 7.5 \text{ minutes}$$

In addition, the mean number of customers waiting to be served is

$$L_q = \frac{\lambda^2}{\mu(\mu - \lambda)} = \frac{(12)^2}{20(20 - 12)} = 0.9 \text{ customer}$$

and the mean waiting time of a customer is

$$T_q = \frac{\lambda}{\mu(\mu - \lambda)} = \frac{12}{20(20 - 12)} = 0.075 \text{ hour} = 4.5 \text{ minutes}$$

The system's utilization factor, or the probability that the salesperson will be busy, is

$$P_b = \frac{\lambda}{\mu} = \frac{12}{20} = 0.6$$

Finally, the mean length of a busy period is

$$L_b = \frac{1}{\mu - \lambda} = \frac{1}{20 - 12} = \frac{1}{8} \text{ hour} = 7.5 \text{ minutes}$$

and the average number of customers served per busy period is

$$N_b = \frac{\mu}{\mu - \lambda} = \frac{20}{20 - 12} = 2.5 \text{ customers}$$

Let us now determine some average costs for this queueing system. Assume that the salesperson receives \$3.00/hour, whereas customers value their time at \$8.00/hour. Thus, the daily cost for the bakery salesperson is

$$\$3 \times 12 = \$36$$

while the mean cost for a customer's time in the system based on $T_s = \frac{1}{8}$ hour is

$$\$8 \times \tfrac{1}{8} = \$1$$

Since there are 12 arrivals/hour for 12 hours, 144 customers request service, at a total cost of

$$\$1 \times 144 = \$144$$

Hence, the average total daily cost for serving the bakery customers (with one salesperson) is

$$\text{TC} = (\text{queueing cost}) + (\text{salesperson cost})$$

$$= \quad \$144 \quad + \quad \$36$$

$$= \quad \$180$$

Assume management is considering installing some self-service equipment that increases the salesperson's service rate up to $\mu = 42$ customers/hour. Thus, the mean time spent by customers in the bakery would be

$$T_s = \frac{1}{42 - 12} = \frac{1}{30} \text{ hour} = 2 \text{ minutes}$$

and the mean daily customer queueing cost is reduced to

$$144 \times \$8 \times \tfrac{1}{30} = \$38.40$$

If the self-service equipment costs an extra \$30/day, the average total daily cost would be

$$TC = (\text{salesperson cost}) + (\text{equipment cost}) + (\text{queueing cost})$$

$$= \quad \$36 \quad + \quad \$30 \quad + \quad \$38.40$$

$$= \quad \$104.40$$

a savings of $75.60 over the system with no self-service capability.

SECTION 12.4. Limited Queue

Assume that the bakery queueing system can accommodate only a limited number of customers at any one time. Thus, if the system can handle a maximum of M customers then a maximum of $M - 1$ customers can be waiting in the queue at some given time and any additional customers that arrive do not enter the system and are lost. This type of system is called a *loss-delay system* or a *limited-queue model*. An important characteristic of this model is that steady state or equilibrium is reached for any value of the utilization factor λ/μ. This is true because we are sure that the queue cannot grow to a length greater than $M - 1$. The balance equations for this model are:

$$\lambda P_0 = \mu P_1 \qquad\qquad (n = 0)$$

$$\lambda P_n + \mu P_n = \lambda P_{n-1} + \mu P_{n+1} \qquad (n = 1, 2, \ldots, M-1)$$

$$\lambda P_{M-1} = \mu P_M \qquad\qquad (n = M)$$

Solving these equations for P_n, the probability of n customers in the system, we obtain for $n = 0, 1, \ldots, M$,

$$P_n = \begin{cases} \left(\dfrac{1 - (\lambda/\mu)}{1 - (\lambda/\mu)^{M+1}} \right)(\lambda/\mu)^n & (\text{for } \lambda \neq \mu) \\[3mm] \dfrac{1}{M+1} & (\text{for } \lambda = \mu) \end{cases}$$

If $\lambda < \mu$ and $M \to \infty$, then P_n appproaches the value given in Section 12.3; that is, $P_n = (1 - \lambda/\mu)(\lambda/\mu)^n$.

To find the mean number of customers in the system, we find $E(n)$. Thus,

$$L_s = E(n) = \begin{cases} \dfrac{\lambda/\mu}{1 - (\lambda/\mu)} - \dfrac{(M+1)(\lambda/\mu)^{M+1}}{1 - (\lambda/\mu)^{M+1}} & (\text{for } \lambda \neq \mu) \\[3mm] \dfrac{M}{2} & (\text{for } \lambda = \mu) \end{cases}$$

It should be noted that for $\lambda < \mu$, the number of customers in this system is smaller than for the case of an unlimited line length. $[L_s = (\lambda/\mu)/(1 - \lambda/\mu).]$

As was shown in Section 12.3,

$$E(\text{queue length}) = E(n) - (1 - P_0)$$

Therefore,

$$L_q = L_s - (1 - P_0)$$

The mean time in the system is

$$T_s = \frac{L_s}{\lambda(1 - P_M)}$$

or

$$T_s = \begin{cases} \dfrac{1}{\mu[1 - (\lambda/\mu)]} - \dfrac{M(\lambda/\mu)^M}{\mu[1 - (\lambda/\mu)^M]} & (\text{for } \lambda \neq \mu) \\[2ex] \dfrac{1}{\mu}\dfrac{M+1}{2} & (\text{for } \lambda = \mu) \end{cases}$$

Similarly, the mean time spent in the queue is

$$T_q = \frac{L_q}{\lambda(1 - P_M)}$$

EXAMPLE. Consider now the single-server system of Section 12.3 with $M = 6$. Thus,

$$L_s = \frac{\frac{12}{20}}{1 - \frac{12}{20}} - \frac{(6+1)\left(\frac{12}{20}\right)^7}{1 - \left(\frac{12}{20}\right)^7}$$

$$= 1.5 - \frac{0.196}{0.972}$$

$$= 1.5 - 0.20$$

$$= 1.3 \text{ customers}$$

and

$$T_s = \frac{1}{20\left(1 - \frac{12}{20}\right)} - \frac{6\left(\frac{12}{20}\right)^6}{20\left[1 - \left(\frac{12}{20}\right)^6\right]}$$

$$= 0.125 - 0.015$$

$$= 0.11 \text{ hour}$$

$$= 6.6 \text{ minutes}$$

Hence, both the average number of customers in the system and the average time spent in the system is less than for the basic single-server model. If M gets very large, the finite queue model becomes the infinite queue model.

SECTION 12.5. *Limited-Source Model*

In some queueing situations the queue is limited because the population of potential customers is limited. For example, a machine repairman in a factory may be responsible for maintaining M machines. They enter the queueing system when they need repair, and the queue length is at most $M-1$ machines. If M is the maximum number of customers in the system, the steady-state or equilibrium equations are as follows.

$$P_0 = 1 / \sum_{n=0}^{M} \left[\frac{M!}{(M-n)!} \left(\frac{\lambda}{\mu} \right)^n \right]$$

$$P_n = \frac{M!}{(M-n)!} \left(\frac{\lambda}{\mu} \right)^n P_0 \qquad (\text{for } n = 1, 2, \ldots, M)$$

$$L_s = M - \frac{\mu}{\lambda}(1 - P_0)$$

$$L_q = M - \frac{\lambda + \mu}{\lambda}(1 - P_0)$$

$$T_s = \frac{L_s}{\lambda(M - L_s)}$$

$$T_q = \frac{L_q}{\lambda(M - L_s)}$$

EXAMPLE . For the single-server system with $M=6$, we get the following:

$$P_0 = \cfrac{1}{\left[\begin{array}{c} \frac{6!}{6!}\left(\frac{12}{20}\right)^0 + \frac{6!}{5!}\left(\frac{12}{20}\right)^1 + \frac{6!}{4!}\left(\frac{12}{20}\right)^2 + \frac{6!}{3!}\left(\frac{12}{20}\right)^3 \\ + \frac{6!}{2!}\left(\frac{12}{20}\right)^4 + \frac{6!}{1!}\left(\frac{12}{20}\right)^5 + \frac{6!}{0!}\left(\frac{12}{20}\right)^6 \end{array} \right]}$$

$$= \frac{1}{1 + 6(0.6) + 30(0.36) + 120(0.216) + 360(0.130) + 720(0.078) + 720(0.047)}$$

$$= \frac{1}{178.12}$$

$$= 0.0056$$

Hence,

$$L_s = 6 - \frac{20}{12}(1 - 0.0056)$$

$$= 4.34 \text{ customers}$$

and

$$T_s = \frac{4.3}{12(6 - 4.3)}$$

$$= 0.21 \text{ hour}$$

$$= 12.6 \text{ minutes}$$

Thus, both the average number of customers and the average time spent in the system are significantly larger than for either the basic single-server model or the limited queue model.

SECTION 12.6. *Arbitrary Service Distribution*

In many queueing situations the service process is not defined by an exponential distribution. However, it is still possible to derive basic queueing results if the interarrival distribution is exponential and the service distribution is arbitrary, as long as we know the mean service time $1/\mu$ and the variance, σ^2, of the service time distribution. The results are:

$$P_0 = 1 - \frac{\lambda}{\mu} \qquad (\text{where } \lambda < \mu)$$

$$P_n = \left(\frac{\lambda}{\mu}\right)^n \left(1 - \frac{\lambda}{\mu}\right)$$

$$L_s = \frac{\lambda}{\mu} + \frac{\lambda\sigma^2 + (\lambda/\mu)^2}{2[1 - (\lambda/\mu)]}$$

$$L_q = L_s - \frac{\lambda}{\mu}$$

$$T_s = \frac{L_s}{\lambda}$$

$$T_q = \frac{L_q}{\lambda}$$

Note that the steady-state equations are the same as in the basic single-server model, but that the expected times and number of customers depend on σ^2, the variance of the service time distribution. It can be easily verified that when service time is exponential, so that $\sigma^2 = 1/\mu^2$, the basic single-server model equations result. Furthermore, if the service time is constant $1/\mu$, so that $\sigma^2 = 0$, then

$$L_q = \frac{\lambda^2}{2\mu(\mu - \lambda)}$$

which is exactly half the value for the basic single-server model. Hence, when the service time is a constant $\frac{1}{20}$ hour,

$$L_q = \frac{(12)^2}{2(20)(20 - 12)}$$

$$= 0.45 \text{ customer}$$

$$L_s = 0.45 + \frac{12}{20}$$

$$= 1.05 \text{ customers}$$

and

$$T_s = \frac{1.05}{12}$$

$$= 0.0875 \text{ hour} = 5.25 \text{ minutes}$$

SECTION 12.7. *Multiple-Server Model*

Let us consider a queueing situation where the system is composed of many identical servers. For example, the department store checkout or the checking and savings bank service windows will consist of several servers each capable of handling service at a rate of μ customers per unit time. We assume that the arrivals follow a Poisson process and that each server's service time is an exponential distribution. Let

$$S = \text{number of servers.}$$

We assume that the individual service times for each of the servers are all mutually independent (i.e., for each server and among servers). Finally, we assume that arrivals wait in a single queue and proceed to the first available server. Thus, if there are fewer people in the system than the number of servers $(n < S)$, no queue develops and there is no waiting time. However, if $n > s$, then S customers will be served and $n - S$ will wait in a queue. The combined service rate of all the servers is then $S\mu$ and this quantity must be larger than λ, the arrival rate, in order to derive meaningful results.

It can be shown that in steady state or equilibrium the following equations are valid:

$$(\lambda + n\mu)P_n = \lambda P_{n-1} + (n+1)\mu P_{n+1} \quad (\text{for } 0 \leqslant n < S)$$

$$(\lambda + S\mu)P_n = \lambda P_{n-1} + S\mu P_{n+1} \quad (\text{for } n \geqslant S)$$

Solving these equations yields the following results:

$$P_n = \begin{cases} \dfrac{(\lambda/\mu)^n}{n!} P_0 & \text{(for } 0 \leqslant n < S) \\[3mm] \dfrac{(\lambda/\mu)^n}{S! \cdot S^{n-s}} P_0 & \text{(for } n \geqslant S) \end{cases}$$

Where the probability of no customers in the system, P_0, is given by

$$P_0 = \frac{1}{\displaystyle\sum_{n=0}^{S-1} \frac{(\lambda/\mu)^n}{n!} + \frac{(\lambda/\mu)^S}{S!} \frac{1}{1-\lambda/S\mu}}$$

To find the remaining relevant expressions, we first find L_q, the expected number in the queue. This is found from

$$L_q = E(n - S) = \sum_{n=S}^{\infty} (n - S) \cdot P_n$$

which yields

$$L_q = \frac{(\lambda/\mu)^S \lambda/S\mu}{S!(1-\lambda/S\mu)^2} P_0$$

Hence,

$$L_s = L_q + \frac{\lambda}{\mu}$$

$$T_s = \frac{L_q}{\lambda} + \frac{1}{\mu}$$

$$T_q = T_s - \frac{1}{\mu}$$

We can also find the probability of a busy period, that is, the probability that $n \geqslant S$ as

$$P(n \geqslant S) = \frac{(\lambda/\mu)^S}{S![1-(\lambda/\mu S)]} P_0$$

As an example, consider the mechanics supply problem of Section 11.7, with mechanics arriving at a rate of 2 per minute and the service rate of an attendant equal to 3 machines/minute. Assume there are two attendants serving on a FIFO basis and that arrivals are Poisson and service is exponential. Thus,

$$S = 2 \text{ servers}$$

$$\lambda = 2 \text{ mechanics/minute}$$

$$\mu = 3 \text{ machines/minute}$$

Hence, the probability of no mechanics in the system is

$$P_0 = \cfrac{1}{\cfrac{(\lambda/\mu)^0}{0!} + \cfrac{(\lambda/\mu)^1}{1!} + \cfrac{(\lambda/\mu)^2}{2!}\cfrac{1}{1-(\lambda/2\mu)}}$$

$$= \cfrac{1}{\cfrac{\left(\frac{2}{3}\right)^0}{0!} + \cfrac{\left(\frac{2}{3}\right)^1}{1!} + \cfrac{\left(\frac{2}{3}\right)^2}{2!}\cfrac{1}{1-[2/2(3)]}}$$

$$= \frac{1}{1+0.667+0.333}$$

$$= 0.5$$

The mean number of mechanics waiting to be served is

$$L_q = \frac{\left(\frac{2}{3}\right)^2 [2/2(3)]}{2! [1-2/2(3)]^2}(0.5)$$

$$= 0.083 \text{ mechanic}$$

and the mean number of mechanics in the system is

$$L_s = 0.083 + \tfrac{2}{3} = 0.75 \text{ mechanic}$$

The mean time spent in the system is

$$T_s = \frac{0.083}{2} + \frac{1}{3} = 0.37 \text{ minute}$$

(see the table in Section 11.7) and the mean waiting time per mechanic is

$$T_q = 0.37 - \tfrac{1}{3} = 0.04 \text{ minute}$$

SECTION 12.8. *Comparison of Single- versus Multiple-Server Queues*

Assume that the supply bin has a single attendant that can serve at the rate of 4.5 mechanics/minute. He thus operates as the equivalent of 1.5 attendants, each at a rate of 3 per minute. However, letting $\mu = 4.5$ in the single-server model yields for the mean number of mechanics waiting in line

$$L_q = \frac{\lambda^2}{\mu(\mu-\lambda)} = \frac{(2)^2}{4.5(4.5-2)} = 0.356 \text{ mechanic}$$

which is more than four times as large a number compared to the figure found for the two slower attendants. Furthermore, the mean time each mechanic would spend waiting with one attendant is

$$W_q = \frac{L_q}{\lambda} = \frac{0.356}{2} = 0.178 \text{ minute}$$

much longer than for two attendants.

On the other hand, the average time spent in the system with one fast attendant is

$$T_s = \frac{1}{\mu - \lambda} = \frac{1}{4.5 - 2} = 0.4 \text{ minute}$$

which is slightly more than for the case with two attendants.

From the management's point of view, it may be well worth the small additional cost of the idle time for the mechanics in order to save the cost of a second attendant.

Thus, it is not possible to generalize a solution to the multiple-server case and treat it as if it were a single server with the same total service rate. Each individual situation must be analyzed and evaluated based on its operating characteristics and the relevant cost involved.

SECTION 12.9. *Summary*

In this chapter we have presented analytic solutions to a selected number of queueing situations. These models were of two basic types, the single-server model and the multiple-server model. For the single-server case several modifications were considered and the results presented. To develop these models, several simplifying assumptions were made. First, we assumed that all arrivals follow a Poisson process. Second, we assumed that the queue discipline was first-come, first-served. Third, we assumed (except in Section 12.6) that the service distribution was exponential.

The appropriateness of these assumptions for solving real situation queueing problems is left for a more advanced analysis of queueing theory. It should be pointed out that many complicated queueing models have been formulated, the solutions of which can only be found by numerical methods such as Monte Carlo simulation. Several such models and their solutions will be presented in Chapter 13.

PROBLEMS   For all problems, assume that arrivals and service follow a Poisson process. The basic single-server and multiple-server problems can be solved using the computer program described in Section 11.11.

12.1. For each of the following single-server queueing systems, find values for the following performance measures: L_s, L_q, T_s, T_q, P_b, and N_b.

(a) $\lambda = 10$, $\mu = 15$
(b) $\lambda = 6$, $\mu = 12$
(c) $\lambda = 0.2$, $\mu = 0.3$

12.2. For each of the following single-server queueing systems with a limited queue length, find values for L_s, L_q, T_s, and T_q.
(a) $\lambda = 10$, $\mu = 15$, $M = 5$
(b) $\lambda = 6$, $\mu = 4$, $M = 8$
(c) $\lambda = 10$, $\mu = 10$, $M = 20$

12.3. For each of the following single-server queueing systems with a limited source, find values for L_s and T_s.
(a) $\lambda = 10$, $\mu = 15$, $M = 4$
(b) $\lambda = 6$, $\mu = 12$, $M = 6$

12.4. For each of the following multiple-server queueing systems, find values for L_s, L_q, T_s, and T_q.
(a) $\lambda = 1$, $\mu = 2$, $S = 2$
(b) $\lambda = 2$, $\mu = 1$, $S = 4$

12.5. A service station has only one lift for servicing cars. If cars arrive while a car is being served, they will wait. Cars arrive at a rate of 5 per hour and can be serviced in 8 minutes.
(a) What is the average number of cars waiting?
(b) What is the average time a car spends in the station?
(c) If a second lift is added, how would that affect the answers to parts (a) and (b)?

12.6. Working a 7-hour day, a one-man staple-gun repair shop services staple guns at a rate of 10 per hour. The cost of a staple gun not being available for production is $10/hour. Staple guns arrive for repair at the rate of 8 per hour.
(a) What is the average number of staple guns in the service system?
(b) What is the average time spent waiting for service?
(c) What is the probability that three or more staple guns will be waiting?
(d) If it is possible to increase the mean service rate to 12 per hour by making changes in personnel and equipment costing $100/day, would this change be worthwhile?

12.7. (Problem 12.6 continued). If the cost of a second similar service facility were $200/day, would it be worthwhile to add this second facility?

12.8. A quick-service retail store bargain table is served by a salesperson whose service rate is 30 transactions/hour. Shoppers arrive at a rate of 15/hour and are served on a first-come, first-served basis.
(a) What is the probability that there will be 3 or more shoppers in the system?

(b) If arriving shoppers leave (i.e., don't wait) when there are two shoppers in the system, what proportion of arriving customers will actually make purchases?

12.9. (Problem 12.8 continued). If more efficient equipment and forms are used to improve the productivity of the sales clerk to serve 36 transactions/hour, what is the probability there will be three or more shoppers in the system? If the marginal profit per transaction is $0.50, how much additional profit can be expected from the improved service in a 10-hour day? Assume all customers stay with service.

12.10. An office is staffed by two secretaries that perform the same basic duties. One of the activities involves typing letters dictated by a supervisor. Suppose that each secretary can type five letters per hour and the letters arrive at a rate of four per hour for each secretary.

(a) Assuming that each secretary does her own work, what is the expected waiting time for a letter?
(b) Suppose that the two secretaries pool their work. Letters arriving at the office are typed by whoever is free in the order they arrive. What is the expected waiting time for a letter in this system?

12.11. A ticket agency has one telephone reservations clerk on duty at a time answering requests for ticket information and making reservations. If the clerk is busy, a telephone answering service asks the caller to wait. When the clerk becomes free, the call of the person waiting the longest is transferred to the clerk. Calls arrive at a rate of 15 per hour and the clerk can service a call in 3 minutes, on the average.

(a) What is the average number of calls waiting to be connected to the clerk?
(b) What is the average time a caller must wait before reaching the ticket reservations clerk?

12.12. The local savings and loan association currently has two sidewalk tellers, each serving customers at the rate of 15 per hour. Customers arrive at a rate of 25 per hour and wait in a single queue until a teller is free.

(a) What is the probability that the service facility will be idle?
(b) What is the probability that only one teller will be busy?
(c) What is the average time spent waiting in the queue?

12.13. The East Coast Dry Dock has the responsibility of servicing the Atlantic fleet of five aircraft carriers. The mean service time is 6 months, and arrivals occur on the average of three times every 2 years. What is the probability that an aircraft carrier desiring service will be required to wait?

12.14. A new minicomputer system which runs only one program at a time can process on the average 60 programs/hour. Users submit programs at a mean rate of 45 per hour.

(a) What is the utilization factor for this computer?

(b) What is the probability that no programs are being processed?

(c) What is the average turnaround time for a program?

12.15. The local public library currently checks out books at one desk. The mean arrival rate is one user every two minutes. The checkout time has a mean of 1.5 minutes and a standard deviation of 0.5 minute, with an unknown distribution. Find the mean time spent waiting for checkout and the number of users waiting.

12.16. A fast-food store is planning to provide curbside service for cars and must decide how many spaces to assign for waiting cars. It is expected that cars will arrive every 6 minutes unless the waiting area is full, in which case the customer goes elsewhere. The mean service rate is 15 cars/hour. Determine the expected number of potential customers that would be lost because of inadequate space if the following number of spaces were to be provided (not including the car being served):

(a) Zero

(b) One

(c) Three

BOOKS OF
INTEREST

Cooper, R. B., *Introduction to Queueing Theory*. New York: Macmillan Co., 1972.

Cox, D. R. and W. L. Smith, *Queues*. London: Methuen & Co., Ltd., 1961.

Gross, D. and C. M. Harris, *Fundamentals of Queueing Theory*. New York: Wiley-Interscience, 1974.

Lee, A. M., *Applied Queueing Theory*. New York: St. Martin's Press, 1966.

Morse, P. M., *Queues, Inventories, and Maintenance*. New York: John Wiley & Sons, Inc., 1958.

Newell, G. F., *Applications of Queueing Theory*. London: Chapman & Hall, Ltd., 1971.

Prabhu, N. U., *Queues and Inventories*. New York: John Wiley & Sons, Inc., 1965.

Saaty, T. L., *Elements of Queueing Theory*. New York: McGraw-Hill Book Co., 1961.

CHAPTER THIRTEEN

Simulation

OBJECTIVES: The purpose of this chapter is to present
to you the following concepts essential
to the construction of simulation models.

1. *Basic elements of simulation for
   solving problems.*
2. *The Monte Carlo sampling technique.*
3. *The distinction between static and
   dynamic problems.*
4. *Dynamic simulation procedures.*
5. *Queueing simulations.*
6. *The relevance of computer simulation
   languages.*
7. *Statistical considerations.*

Simulation is a technique used for developing the measures of performance for those decision problems where various components of the problem are random. It is generally applied when the problem is too complex for analytical methods to yield a solution. In practice, many people consider simulation merely as a "last resort" solution, since an analytical solution, if obtainable, is always preferable. However, many real-life decision problems that involve random activities are much too complex to be adequately treated by analytical methods, but are easily handled by simulation procedures. It is for these situations that simulation proves most useful.

There is a basic difference between an analytical model and a simulation model. In general, an analytical model will define an objective function which relates the measure of performance variable to the controllable variables. This function may consist of expected values of some of the random variables. A simulation model, on the other hand, only provides a means for *generating representative samples* of the measure of performance variable. Thus, it is necessary to repeat the process of using the simulation model to generate samples, from which we obtain a set of sample values. We then compute the average value of the samples, and consider this the best estimate of the mean of the measure-of-performance random variable. This process of generating one sample after another may be called *executing* or *running* the model. Usually a computer is used to execute the model since the operations are too time-consuming to be performed by hand. Clearly, the more samples we generate (i.e., the longer we run the model), the better our estimate will be.

In this chapter we shall discuss the general techniques of constructing simulation models. However, every simulation we perform is essentially a new problem to which the same general set of techniques apply. Thus, this chapter will contain a variety of problems, each of which will demonstrate the simulation methodology.

There are two basic types of situations which involve random elements and which lend themselves to simulation. However, each must be treated slightly differently from the simulation point of view.

The first type of problem involves finding probability distributions (means, standard deviations) of variables where there is no time element present. For example, finding the length of a part which is made by joining together two parts whose lengths vary is essentially a problem of this type. In this case we are not concerned with how the lengths change over time. This type of problem will be referred to as a *static problem*.

The second type of problem, which will be referred to as a *dynamic* or *time-dependent problem*, involves not only random variations but also changes that occur over time. Mathematicians use the term *stochastic* for such problems. An example of such a variable is a company's daily sales which are growing gradually on the average (upward trend) and, in addition, vary randomly from day to day. The model must include both the random and time-dependent elements of sales. Another example is the number of cars waiting at a toll booth to pay their tolls. The number is random and also changes over time, and thus both elements must be considered.

These two types of problems will be modeled somewhat differently, although many of the simulation techniques are common to both.

SECTION 13.2. *Static Simulation Model I—*
A Parts-Production Problem

13.2.1. Statement of the Problem. A manufacturing process assembles a part (called part C) from two other parts (called A and B), which are to be purchased from suppliers. Part C is made by joining together parts A and B. Therefore, the length of each part C is equal to the length of the part A used plus the length of the part B used. Like all production processes, the production processes that produce the A and B parts are variable (i.e., not every part A is of the same length nor is every part B of the same length). We can describe the lengths of the A and B parts by probability distributions as shown in Table 13.2.1. Let us assume that the lengths are given in inches (centimeters could just as easily have been used). Although we have described the lengths by discrete probability

TABLE 13.2.1. *Probability Distributions of the Lengths of Parts A and B*

LENGTH OF PART A		LENGTH OF PART B	
Length	*Probability*	*Length*	*Probability*
10	0.25	17	0.07
11	0.25	18	0.14
12	0.25	19	0.23
13	0.25	20	0.38
		21	0.12
		22	0.06
Mean = 11.5		Mean = 19.52	
Standard deviation = 1.12		Standard deviation = 1.24	

distributions, in reality the lengths are continuous. However, the discrete distribution is used throughout the chapter, primarily for simplicity in the presentation. Assume that our objective is to estimate the mean and standard deviation of the length of part C. These values directly affect the quality of the final product in which part C is used. This problem has a simple analytical solution but will be used to develop the basic simulation approach.

13.2.2. Physical-Sampling Approach to the Parts-Production Problem.
Before considering the simulation solution to this problem, let us consider how we might find the mean and standard deviation of the length of part C by physical sampling. We would begin by taking a batch of part A's and a batch of part B's. In order to generate sample lengths of part C's we would:

1. Select a part A at random and measure its length.
2. Select a part B at random and measure its length.
3. Add the length of part A to the length of part B. This yields one random sample of a part C length.

If we repeat this procedure 100 times, we will generate 100 random samples of part C lengths. One such random sample set is shown in Table 13.2.2. The sample average $(\overline{C})$ of 30.86 is an estimate of the true mean, and the sample standard deviation (S) of 1.42 is an estimate of the true standard deviation. If we repeated the sampling process again,

TABLE 13.2.2. *Sample of 100 Part C Lengths Found by Sampling 100 Part A Lengths and 100 Part B Lengths*

Sample Number	Sample Part A Length	Sample Part B Length	Computed Part C Length $C=(A+B)$	C^2
1	12	21	33	1,089
2	10	17	27	729
3	11	20	31	961
4	10	19	29	841
5	13	22	35	1,225
6	11	18	29	841
7	12	17	29	1,225
⋮	⋮	⋮	⋮	⋮
100	10	22	32	1,024
			3,086	95,433

$$\overline{C} = \text{average} = \Sigma \frac{C}{n} = \frac{3,086}{100} = 30.86$$

$$S = \text{standard deviation} = \sqrt{\frac{\Sigma C^2 - n\overline{C}^2}{n-1}} = 1.42$$

with different batches of *A* and *B* parts, we would obtain different values for $\bar{C}$ and *S* due to random variation.

The simulation technique resembles in many ways this physical sampling procedure. The major difference is that it will not be necessary to physically obtain the batches of *A* and *B* parts and measure them. Instead, an analytical technique is used for generating samples of the parts and their lengths without actually physically performing any measurement. In effect, the technique, known as the *Monte Carlo sampling technique*, is a procedure for generating random samples in such a way that over the long run these samples conform to any designated probability distribution. The technique itself is an analytical technique and can be easily programmed for use on a computer.

SECTION 13.3. *Monte Carlo Sampling Technique*

13.3.1. General Theory. Let us consider how we can generate random samples of lengths of part *A*. In essence we need a procedure for randomly selecting a value of either 10, 11, 12, or 13, but in such a fashion that over the long run, 25% of the values will be 10, 25% will be 11, 25% will be 12, and 25% will be 13 (see Table 13.2.1). To generate random samples, we will generate random digits and use these to generate our sample values. Let us assume that we have a source of random digits such as a random-number table as given in Appendix C. Each time we wish to generate a sample value for a part *A* length we shall select a few (let us use four) random digits from the table. It will be more convenient if the random numbers selected from the table are between 0 and 1, so let us simply place a decimal point in front of the random digits each time a set is chosen which will give us a range of values from 0.0000 up to 0.9999 or 10,000 different possible values. Since we place a decimal point in front of the digits, the number of digits used does not alter the range of the random numbers (i.e., 0 to 1).

Our procedure for generating part *A* lengths will be first to select a random number as described and, depending on its value, determine whether the part *A* length associated with this random number is to be 10, 11, 12, or 13. We desire that this procedure select the value 10, 25% of the time. Let us, therefore, make the following rule:

> *RULE 1.* If the random number is between 0.0000 and 0.2499, consider the part *A* length to be 10.

The reasoning for this is as follows: 0.0000 through 0.2499 is 2,500 out of the possible 10,000 possible values of the random number and therefore will occur 25% of the time (i.e., a part *A* length of 10 will be generated 25% of the time).

For the part *A* length of 11 the rule will be:

RULE 2. If the random number is between 0.2500 and 0.4999, consider the part *A* length to be 11.

Again, 0.2500 through 0.4999 is 2,500 out of 10,000 possibilities, or 25%. For length 12 the range of random numbers is 0.5000 to 0.7499, and for length 13 it is 0.7500 to 0.9999.

Thus, each time we wish a part *A* length we select a random number and find the range into which it falls. For example, if the random number selected is 0.6382, we have generated a part *A* length of 12. We have discussed generating random numbers by using a random-number table only for its simplicity and ease for hand computations. However, procedures for generating a sequence of values which are random, statistically speaking, do exist for use with computerized techniques. An initial integer value called the "seed" is supplied by the user and is used to generate the sequence of random numbers.

A straightforward method exists for determining the range of values of the random number (i.e., 0.0000–0.2499, 0.2500–0.4999, etc.). We first form the *cumulative probability distribution*, which is defined as the probability that the part *A* length is less than or equal to some designated length, say 10 (≤ 10), or less than or equal to 11, or 12, or 13. This distribution and the random-number range are shown in Table 13.3.1. The probability of 10 or less is equal to the probability of 10 since 9, 8, 7... are not possible (i.e., have probability zero). The probability of 11 or less is the probability of 10 or 11, which equals $0.25 + 0.25 = 0.50$. Another way of stating it is that the probability of 11 or less equals the probability of 10 or less plus the probability of 11, again $0.25 + 0.25 = 0.50$. The probability of 12 or less is the probability of 10, 11, or 12 ($0.25 + 0.25 + 0.25$), or alternatively the probability of 11 or less plus the probability of 12 ($0.50 + 0.25$), which equals 0.75; and so on. Notice that the upper limit of the random-number range is always just less than the cumulative probability. This approach of forming and using the cumulative probability distribution simplifies the selection of the random-number range for a

TABLE 13.3.1. *Cumulative Probability Distribution and Random-Number Range for Part A Lengths*

Length	Probability	Cumulative Probability	Random-Number Range
10	0.25	0.25	0.0000–0.2499
11	0.25	0.50	0.2500–0.4999
12	0.25	0.75	0.5000–0.7499
13	0.25	1.00	0.7500–0.9999

TABLE 13.3.2. *Cumulative Probability Distribution and Random-Number Range for Part B Lengths*

Length	Probability	Cumulative Probability	Random-Number Range
17	0.07	0.07	0.0000–0.0699
18	0.14	0.21	0.0700–0.2099
19	0.23	0.44	0.2100–0.4399
20	0.38	0.82	0.4400–0.8199
21	0.12	0.94	0.8200–0.9399
22	0.06	1.00	0.9400–0.9999

given probability distribution. Table 13.3.2 presents the distribution and random-number values for the part *B* length.

13.3.2. Simulation Approach of the Parts-Production Problem Using Monte Carlo Sampling. Our simulation procedure for generating sample part *C* lengths is as follows:

1. Select a random number, considered to be of the form .xxxx, where xxxx indicates random digits.
2. Determine into which range of the values, as shown in Table 13.3.1, the random number falls and determine the part *A* length accordingly.
3. Select a (different) random number.
4. Determine into which range it falls and thus the corresponding part *B* length by using Table 13.3.2.
5. Add the part *A* length to the part *B* length, giving one random sample of a part *C* length.

Steps 1–5 are repeated for as many times as the sample size requires. Table 13.3.3 lists one such simulation of 100 samples.

If we repeated this process using another set of random numbers, we would obtain a completely different set of sample values and a different mean and standard deviation estimate, as a result of random variation. This is also true if we chose a different physical sample. This variation in the sample results is usually called *sampling error* and exists with simulation as well as physical sampling. The statistical considerations will be discussed later in the chapter, but in general we should note that the larger the sample size (*n*), the smaller the variation in our sample results.

Another important point is that we have generated this sample using the probability distributions given in Table 13.2.1. If another supplier of part *A* was being considered, with a different probability distribution of part *A* lengths, the simulation would have to be repeated (i.e., rerun). In this respect, both physical sampling and simulation are less general than analytical methods.

TABLE 13.3.3. *A Simulation of Part C Lengths n = 100 Samples Generated*

Sample Number	Random Number	Part A Length	Random Number	Part B Length	Part C Length $C = A + B$	C^2
1	0.2837	11	0.1709	18	29	841
2	0.8942	13	0.6385	20	33	1,089
3	0.0783	10	0.0392	17	27	729
4	0.4261	11	0.9647	22	33	1,089
5	0.5320	12	0.8037	21	33	1,089
6	0.7731	13	0.4156	19	32	1,024
7	0.1986	10	0.0684	17	27	729
⋮	⋮	⋮	⋮	⋮	⋮	⋮
100	0.6382	12	0.7863	20	32	1,024
					3,178	101,135

$$\bar{C} = \text{mean} = \Sigma \frac{C}{n} = \frac{3,178}{100} = 31.78$$

$$S = \text{standard deviation} = \sqrt{\frac{\Sigma C^2 - n(\bar{C})^2}{n-1}} = 1.88$$

The problem we have considered has served the purpose of presenting the simulation techniques. In fact, it could have been solved far more simply using analytical methods. We can compute the mean part *A* length and part *B* length from the probability distributions of Table 13.2.1 and the mean part *C* length will equal the sum of the two means:

$$\text{mean part } C \text{ length} = \text{mean part } A \text{ length} + \text{mean part } B \text{ length}$$

$$= 11.5 + 19.52$$

$$= 31.02$$

SECTION 13.4. *Static Simulation Model II—*
New-Product-Introduction Problem

13.4.1. Statement of the Problem. A clothing company is considering making a new coat which will be offered for sale only for the current winter season. The cost of producing each unit is not known with certainty, but company management estimates the following probability distribution for the cost per unit:

Cost Per Unit ($)	7	8	9	10	11	12
Probability	0.05	0.15	0.20	0.30	0.25	0.05

443

The company must decide on both a selling price and a production quantity, since the coats will be produced in advance of when they are sold. Unsold coats can be sold to discount outlets for salvage at $5/coat at the end of the season. The demand for the coats cannot be known with certainty and will depend on the selling price. For example, company management estimates that for a selling price of $20/coat, the probability distribution of demand is:

Demand	500	600	700	800	900
Probability	0.10	0.20	0.40	0.20	0.10

The company wishes to know what price to charge and how much to produce so as to maximize expected profit.

13.4.2. Simulation Model of the Problem. The controllable variables of the problem are selling price (s) and production quantity (q). The uncontrollable variables are the salvage value (v), which is considered certain and equal to $5/coat, and the production cost per unit (c), which is considered a state-of-nature variable with a known probability distribution. Demand (d) is a partially controllable variable, affected by selling price. For a selling price of $20 per coat, it is described by the probability distribution shown. However, different selling prices would generate different demand probability distributions. The objective is to maximize profit (P). Let us write an equation relating profit to all our variables.

$$P = \begin{cases} ds + v(q-d) - qc & \text{(if } q > d) \\ qs - qc & \text{(if } q \leqslant d) \end{cases}$$

Profit equals revenue minus costs. Thus, if the quantity produced exceeds the demand, revenue equals demand (d) times selling price (s) plus the salvage value ($v = \$5$ per unit) times the number of unsold units [i.e., production quantity (q) minus demand (d)]. The cost is always the quantity produced (q) times the cost per unit (c). If the quantity produced (q) is less than the demand (d), the revenue is quantity produced (q) times selling price (s) minus quantity produced (q) times cost (c).

As an example, consider the following data for selling price $s = \$20$, production quantity $q = 800$ units, cost $c = \$8$, and demand $d = 700$ units. The profit would be

$$P = (700)(20) + (5)(800 - 700) - (800)(8)$$
$$= 14,000 + 500 - 6,400$$
$$= \$8,100$$

If the production quantity $q = 600$ units, the profit would be

$$P = (600)(20) - (600)(8)$$
$$= 12,000 - 4,800$$
$$= \$7,200$$

Let us now construct a simulation model of this problem. The general procedure is to generate random samples of cost (c) and demand (d) for a given selling price (s) and production quantity (q), and compute the profit as above. This will yield one random sample value of profit. We then repeat this process, generating as many random samples of profit as we choose, compute the average profit, and use this as an estimate of the expected profit for the given strategy (s, q). Notice that simulating different strategies requires performing the simulation procedure over again using different values for selling price (s) and production quantity (q). Of course, a different selling price would also have a different demand distribution.

In order to generate random samples of cost (c) and demand (d), we shall use the Monte Carlo technique. This requires forming the cumulative distributions and determining the random number ranges. These are shown in Tables 13.4.1 and 13.4.2. The simulation itself is shown in

TABLE 13.4.1. *Cumulative Probability Distribution and
Random Number Range for Cost per Unit (c)*

c	*Probability*	*Cumulative Probability*	*Random-Number Range*
7	0.05	0.05	0.0000–0.0499
8	0.15	0.20	0.0500–0.1999
9	0.20	0.40	0.2000–0.3999
10	0.30	0.70	0.4000–0.6999
11	0.25	0.95	0.7000–0.9499
12	0.05	1.00	0.9500–0.9999

TABLE 13.4.2. *Cumulative Probability Distribution and
Random-Number Range for Demand (d)
Assuming Selling Price (s) = $20*

d	*Probability*	*Cumulative Probability*	*Random-Number Range*
500	0.10	0.10	0.0000–0.0999
600	0.20	0.30	0.1000–0.2999
700	0.40	0.70	0.3000–0.6999
800	0.20	0.90	0.7000–0.8999
900	0.10	1.00	0.9000–0.9999

SIMULATION FOR S =   20.00   Q =   600.00

SAMPLE NO	RANDOM NO 1	COST	RANDOM NO 2	DEMAND	PROFIT
1	0.7852	11.00	0.5751	700.00	5400.00
2	0.3838	9.00	0.1270	600.00	6600.00
3	0.3078	9.00	0.7039	800.00	6600.00
4	0.4535	10.00	0.3853	700.00	6000.00
5	0.2307	9.00	0.9166	900.00	6600.00
6	0.4231	10.00	0.2888	600.00	6000.00
7	0.9252	11.00	0.9518	900.00	5400.00
8	0.3834	9.00	0.7348	800.00	6600.00
9	0.9580	12.00	0.1347	600.00	4800.00
10	0.1856	8.00	0.9014	900.00	7200.00
11	0.7385	11.00	0.3183	700.00	5400.00
12	0.2635	9.00	0.7158	800.00	6600.00
13	0.9233	11.00	0.0979	500.00	3900.00
14	0.2774	9.00	0.7835	800.00	6600.00
15	0.2041	9.00	0.1732	600.00	6600.00
16	0.2021	9.00	0.6536	700.00	6600.00
17	0.1029	8.00	0.7352	800.00	7200.00
18	0.4852	10.00	0.2945	600.00	6000.00
19	0.4002	10.00	0.7505	800.00	6000.00
80	0.8996	11.00	0.9494	900.00	5400.00
81	0.5998	10.00	0.0541	500.00	4500.00
82	0.9262	11.00	0.0706	500.00	3900.00
83	0.0878	8.00	0.8915	800.00	7200.00
84	0.5592	10.00	0.3315	700.00	6000.00
85	0.9561	12.00	0.7528	800.00	4800.00
86	0.9122	11.00	0.6976	700.00	5400.00
87	0.9756	12.00	0.5755	700.00	4800.00
88	0.6728	10.00	0.8567	800.00	6000.00
89	0.0854	8.00	0.8019	800.00	7200.00
90	0.0428	7.00	0.0396	500.00	6300.00
91	0.8523	11.00	0.7574	800.00	5400.00
92	0.8736	11.00	0.4251	700.00	5400.00
93	0.6881	10.00	0.3025	700.00	6000.00
94	0.6216	10.00	0.0073	500.00	4500.00
95	0.4498	10.00	0.6328	700.00	6000.00
96	0.7488	11.00	0.7978	800.00	5400.00
97	0.0472	7.00	0.1032	600.00	7800.00
98	0.1947	8.00	0.2393	600.00	7200.00
99	0.6840	10.00	0.9496	900.00	6000.00
100	0.5420	10.00	0.7057	800.00	6000.00

STRATEGY   2   SELLING PRICE   20.00   PRODUCE   600.00 UNITS
AVG PROFIT =   5985.00   STD DEV =   904.90

FIGURE 13.4.1. *Simulation for selling price (s)=$20 and production quantity (q)=600 units.*

Figure 13.4.1 for selling price $(s) = \$20$ and production quantity $(q) = 600$ units. We have arbitrarily chosen to simulate 100 random profit samples. The estimate of expected profit for $s = \$20$ and $q = 600$ units from the simulation is $5,985.00. Naturally, a different sequence of random numbers would generate a different estimate, owing to sampling variability. However, increasing the sample size, n, reduces this variability.

Evaluating a different strategy for production quantity q, but the same selling price $s = \$20$ requires rerunning the simulation with the value of q changed. To evaluate strategies with other selling prices requires knowing the probability distributions of demand for these selling prices. Let us assume that for a selling price of $19, the probability distribution of demand is

Demand	500	600	700	800	900
Probability	0.05	0.15	0.40	0.25	0.15

and for selling price $s = \$21$ it is

Demand	500	600	700	800	900
Probability	0.20	0.30	0.35	0.10	0.05

To evaluate all the strategies, we would have to repeat the simulation shown in Figure 13.4.1 first for $s = \$19$ and various values of q using the demand distribution shown above, and similarly for $s = \$21$. The simulated average profits for each of these simulations (generated by computer) is shown in Figure 13.4.2. From these estimated profits we would select as the optimal policy strategy 3:

selling price $s = \$20$

production quantity $q = 700$

estimated expected profit $P = \$6,700.00$

SECTION 13.5. *Dynamic Simulation Problems*

As previously discussed, dynamic or stochastic simulation problems involve a study of the situation (system) over time. In general, each sample value of interest will depend on the values of the prior samples. For instance, in an inventory problem, today's inventory level will almost certainly be dependent on yesterday's inventory level. If the inventory level was high yesterday, it is more likely to be high today rather than low, and vice versa. Thus, simulating the inventory level will require tracking the inventory level over time and using the prior day's inventory level in addition to today's demand and any receipt of goods, in determining the current inventory level. Another example is a queueing system where each user's waiting time is highly dependent on the values for the user in front of him in the queue. Obviously, he cannot enter service until the user in front of him has entered service. If the prior user's wait time is long, the current user's wait is more likely to be long rather than short.

SIMULATION RESULTS

STRATEGY	1	SELLING PRICE	20.00	PRODUCE	500.00 UNITS
		AVG PROFIT =	5165.00	STD DEV =	651.52

STRATEGY	2	SELLING PRICE	20.00	PRODUCE	600.00 UNITS
		AVG PROFIT =	5985.00	STD DEV =	904.90

STRATEGY	3	SELLING PRICE	20.00	PRODUCE	700.00 UNITS
		AVG PROFIT =	6700.00	STD DEV =	1296.28

STRATEGY	4	SELLING PRICE	20.00	PRODUCE	800.00 UNITS
		AVG PROFIT =	6493.00	STD DEV =	2043.16

STRATEGY	5	SELLING PRICE	20.00	PRODUCE	900.00 UNITS
		AVG PROFIT =	6360.00	STD DEV =	1864.47

SIMULATION RESULTS

STRATEGY	6	SELLING PRICE	19.00	PRODUCE	500.00 UNITS
		AVG PROFIT =	4665.00	STD DEV =	651.51

STRATEGY	7	SELLING PRICE	19.00	PRODUCE	600.00 UNITS
		AVG PROFIT =	5510.00	STD DEV =	816.17

STRATEGY	8	SELLING PRICE	19.00	PRODUCE	700.00 UNITS
		AVG PROFIT =	6174.00	STD DEV =	1096.13

STRATEGY	9	SELLING PRICE	19.00	PRODUCE	800.00 UNITS
		AVG PROFIT =	6168.00	STD DEV =	1849.86

STRATEGY	10	SELLING PRICE	19.00	PRODUCE	900.00 UNITS
		AVG PROFIT =	6007.00	STD DEV =	1744.14

SIMULATION RESULTS

STRATEGY	11	SELLING PRICE	21.00	PRODUCE	500.00 UNITS
		AVG PROFIT =	5665.00	STD DEV =	651.53

STRATEGY	12	SELLING PRICE	21.00	PRODUCE	600.00 UNITS
		AVG PROFIT =	6092.00	STD DEV =	1075.48

STRATEGY	13	SELLING PRICE	21.00	PRODUCE	700.00 UNITS
		AVG PROFIT =	6310.00	STD DEV =	1633.25

STRATEGY	14	SELLING PRICE	21.00	PRODUCE	800.00 UNITS
		AVG PROFIT =	6032.00	STD DEV =	2203.16

STRATEGY	15	SELLING PRICE	21.00	PRODUCE	900.00 UNITS
		AVG PROFIT =	5463.00	STD DEV =	2186.84

FIGURE 13.4.2. *Simulated average profit for selling price (s)=$19, $20, $21 and for production quantity (q)=500, 600, 700, 800, and 900 units. Sample size (n)=100.*

To simulate such dynamic or stochastic systems, we must design a simulation model that tracks the system over time and collects statistics. This differs from static simulations, where we simply generate independent random samples of the measure of performance of interest. The general dynamic simulation techniques will be developed by considering several problems.

448

13.6.1. Statement of the Problem. Assume that we are considering the selection of a reorder point (R) for an inventory policy that will be of the form: Order $Q = 120$ units when inventory equals R units. The probability distribution of daily demand is

Daily Demand (units)	17	18	19	20	21	22	23
Probability	0.05	0.10	0.20	0.30	0.20	0.10	0.05

mean [daily demand (units)] = 20 units

The lead time period is also variable and has the following probability distribution:

Lead Time (days)	1	2	3	4	5
Probability	0.10	0.20	0.40	0.20	0.10

mean = 3 days

Let us assume that the quantity to be ordered each time, $Q = 120$ units, is predetermined and that we wish to select a reorder point R which minimizes the sum of expected inventory carrying costs per year and expected stockout costs per year. All stockouts are assumed to be backordered (i.e., customers wait until goods are available for delivery). The inventory carrying cost is $k_c = \$10/\text{unit} \cdot \text{year}$ and the stockout or backordering cost is $k_s = \$100/\text{unit} \cdot \text{year}$.

The equation for the total variable cost per year is

(1) $\text{TC} = k_c \, (\text{average inventory}) + k_s \, (\text{average backorder level})$

In this case the variable TC includes only those costs which are variable with respect to the decision variable R [Q has been previously determined, and therefore the ordering costs are determined (i.e., KD/Q)].

We wish to find the value for the reorder point R which minimizes TC.

13.6.2. Simulation of the Inventory Problem. The simulation methodology is to first simulate each day's activity (i.e., demand and arrival of orders) and thus determine a closing inventory or level of backorders for that day. We can then compute the average inventory and level of backorders, considering the values for each day as one sample. Our

†This section uses material from Chapter 10.

measure of performance is

$$\begin{pmatrix} \text{total cost} \\ \text{per day} \end{pmatrix} = \frac{\$10}{\text{unit} \cdot \text{year}} \begin{pmatrix} \text{average} \\ \text{inventory} \end{pmatrix} + \frac{\$100}{\text{unit} \cdot \text{year}} \begin{pmatrix} \text{average level} \\ \text{of backorders} \end{pmatrix}$$

For each day we randomly generate a demand and subtract it from the opening inventory (or backorder level), giving a closing inventory (or backorder level). If, during the day, the inventory has passed below the reorder point R, an order will be placed. The day on which it will be scheduled to arrive will be determined by randomly generating a lead-time period. We will assume that the order is available to fill demand on the morning following the day of its arrival. For example, if the inventory reaches the reorder point on March 1 and lead time is 3 days, the order will be added to inventory at the beginning of March 5.

To generate random samples of daily demands and lead-time periods using the Monte Carlo technique, we form the cumulative distributions and random-number ranges for daily demand and lead-time period. These are shown in Tables 13.6.1 and 13.6.2.

Let us begin our simulation by assuming an initial inventory of 120 units (i.e., the order quantity Q) and simulate 100 days of inventory movement. The simulation results (generated by computer) are shown in Figure 13.6.1 for a reorder point of 70 units.

TABLE 13.6.1. *Cumulative Probability Distribution and Random-Number Range for Daily Demand*

Daily Demand	Probability	Cumulative Probability	Random-Number Range
17	0.05	0.05	0.0000–0.0499
18	0.10	0.15	0.0500–0.1499
19	0.20	0.35	0.1500–0.3499
20	0.30	0.65	0.3500–0.6499
21	0.20	0.85	0.6500–0.8499
22	0.10	0.95	0.8500–0.9499
23	0.05	1.00	0.9500–0.9999

TABLE 13.6.2. *Cumulative Probability Distribution and Random-Number Range for Lead-Time Period*

Lead-Time Period	Probability	Cumulative Probability	Random-Number Range
1	0.10	0.10	0.0000–0.0999
2	0.20	0.30	0.1000–0.2999
3	0.40	0.70	0.3000–0.6999
4	0.20	0.90	0.7000–0.8999
5	0.10	1.00	0.9000–0.9999

DAY	ORDER ARRVS	OPEN INV	OPEN B/O	RANDOM NO 1	DEMD	CLOSE INV	CLOSE B/O	PLACE ORDER	RANDOM NO 2	LEAD TIME	ARRIVES BEG DAY
1		120.	0.	0.6872	21.	99.	0.				
2		99.	0.	0.4420	20.	79.	0.				
3		79.	0.	0.3654	20.	59.	0.	YES	0.9377	5	9
4		59.	0.	0.2538	19.	40.	0.				
5		40.	0.	0.1629	19.	21.	0.				
6		21.	0.	0.6015	20.	1.	0.				
7		1.	0.	0.5861	20.	0.	19.				
8		0.	19.	0.6164	20.	0.	39.				
9	YES	81.	0.	0.7411	21.	60.	0.	YES	0.7930	4	14
10		60.	0.	0.1482	18.	42.	0.				
11		42.	0.	0.7405	21.	21.	0.				
12		21.	0.	0.7366	21.	0.	0.				
13		0.	0.	0.5110	20.	0.	20.				
14	YES	100.	0.	0.7660	21.	79.	0.				
15		79.	0.	0.4276	20.	59.	0.	YES	0.2484	2	18
16		59.	0.	0.4123	20.	39.	0.				
17		39.	0.	0.8704	22.	17.	0.				
18	YES	137.	0.	0.8146	21.	116.	0.				
19		116.	0.	0.4146	20.	96.	0.				
20		96.	0.	0.7398	21.	75.	0.				
⋮											
99		76.	0.	0.0768	18.	58.	0.	YES	0.1142	2	102
100		58.	0.	0.9323	22.	36.	0.				

```
STRATEGY  2   R =       70.00 UNITS        AVG INV =       48.79 UNITS    STD DEV =    36.79 UNITS
                                           AVG B/O =        2.66 UNITS    STD DEV =     8.06 UNITS
                                           COST =        753.90 $/TIME
```

FIGURE 13.6.1. *Simulation for R=70 units.*

The sample average for inventory and backorders are estimates of the true mean inventory and backorder level. We can thus evaluate our total cost per day using equation (1) as:

$$TC = k_c \text{ (average inventory)} + k_s \text{ (average backorder level)}$$
$$= (10)(48.79) + (100)(2.66)$$
$$= \$753.90/\text{year}$$

Thus, we can consider one possible strategy:

Order 120 *units when inventory equals* 70 *units.*

Estimated total cost per year = \$753.90

13.6.3. Simulation Solution to the Problem. To simulate other inventory decision rules we would rerun the simulation again for each different value of the reorder point. These runs have been performed for reorder points of 60, 70, 80, and 90 units, and the results are tabulated in Figure 13.6.2. From these results it would appear that strategy 3, order 120 unites when inventory equals 80 units, has the lowest simulated average cost per year and can be chosen as the best strategy. We must realize that the simulated average costs are estimates of the true mean costs and are

451

INVENTORY SIMULATION

CARRYING COST = 10.00 $/(UNIT*TIME)   STOCKOUT COST = 100.00 $/(UNIT*TIME)
ORDER QTY = 120.00 UNITS   NO. SAMPLES = 100

PROBABILITY DISTRIBUTION OF DAILY DEMAND

D	17.00	18.00	19.00	20.00	21.00	22.00	23.00
PROB	0.05	0.10	0.20	0.30	0.20	0.10	0.05

PROBABILITY DISTRIBUTION OF LEAD TIME DAYS

L	1	2	3	4	5
PROB	0.10	0.20	0.40	0.20	0.10

SIMULATION RESULTS

STRATEGY 1 R = 60.00 UNITS   AVG INV = 41.43 UNITS   STD DEV = 35.38 UNITS
                             AVG B/O = 3.78 UNITS   STD DEV = 9.30 UNITS
                             COST = 792.30 $/TIME

STRATEGY 2 R = 70.00 UNITS   AVG INV = 48.79 UNITS   STD DEV = 36.79 UNITS
                             AVG B/O = 2.66 UNITS   STD DEV = 8.06 UNITS
                             COST = 753.90 $/TIME

STRATEGY 3 R = 80.00 UNITS   AVG INV = 59.67 UNITS   STD DEV = 37.61 UNITS
                             AVG B/O = 0.85 UNITS   STD DEV = 3.49 UNITS
                             COST = 681.70 $/TIME

STRATEGY 4 R = 90.00 UNITS   AVG INV = 76.03 UNITS   STD DEV = 39.92 UNITS
                             AVG B/O = 0.16 UNITS   STD DEV = 1.60 UNITS
                             COST = 776.30 $/TIME

FIGURE 13.6.2. *Inventory simulation.*

subject to sampling variability. If we reran the simulations using a different sequence of random numbers, the results would be different and could conceivably indicate a different strategy as being optimal. These statistical considerations will be discussed later. Furthermore, there is no guarantee that $R=75$ or $R=85$ would not yield a higher simulated average profit. The search for an optimal value of R would require rerunning the simulation for other values of R.

SECTION 13.7. *Simulation of Queueing Systems*[†]

13.7.1. Introduction. It has already been discussed in Chapter 11 that analytical solutions to queueing problems are frequently difficult to obtain and simulation is often used. The general objective of a simulation model of a queueing system is to generate for each user representative

[†]The sections on simulation of queueing system use material from Chapter 11.

samples of:

1. Time at which the user arrives (TA).
2. Time at which the user begins to be served (time at which service entered) if the user waits for service (TE).
3. Time at which user leaves (TL) either due to service being completed, balking, or reneging.

If these three values are known for each user (either by physical sampling or simulation), statistics can be computed for the user-oriented measures of performance of the system, such as:

1. Mean time spent in the system: average of $(TL - TA)$.
2. Mean time spent waiting: average of $(TE - TA)$.
3. Probability that the user balks (number of users that balk, divided by the total number of users).
4. Probability that a user renegs (number of users who reneg divided by total number of users).

Let us assume that at present we are only interested in obtaining user-oriented statistics from the simulation, for example the mean wait time and mean time spent in the system. The objective of the simulation is therefore to generate representative sample values of the three times (TA, TE, TL) for a series of users using the system. From these values the sample values of the wait time (WT) and the time spent in the system (TS) can be computed:

$$(1) \qquad\qquad WT = TE - TA$$

$$(2) \qquad\qquad TS = TL - TA$$

We can then collect sufficient statistics of these sample values to estimate mean wait time and mean time spent in the system.

It will be seen that queueing simulations are of the dynamic type in that each user's time of arrival, wait time, time at which service entered, and so on, is highly dependent on prior users. Thus, it is necessary to construct a model that tracks the system over time, as was done for the inventory simulation model.

13.7.2. Simulation Methodology. Our objective is to construct a model that randomly generates representative values for the time at which a user arrives, TA; the time at which the user enters service (if he enters service), TE; and the time he leaves, TL, whether due to finishing service, balking, or reneging. This will require randomly generating samples from the probability distributions which describe the arrival and service processes. Using the interarrival and service-time values, we will compute TA, TE, and TL, and from these values the measures of performance can be computed.

In order to generate the time at which a user arrives we shall randomly select a value from the interarrival time probability distribution to determine how long after the prior arrival this new user arrives. For example, if the prior user arrived at TA=9:01:15 and the interarrival time for the current user is 20 seconds, his time of arrival is TA=19:01:35.

In order to determine the time at which the user enters service (TE), the system must be examined at the time at which the user arrives to determine whether he actually enters service (there may be balking and/or reneging) and, if so, at what time. For example, if balking occurs when there is already one user waiting, the system must be examined at the time each user arrives (TA) to determine whether there is already one user waiting. If so, no value for TE is computed (the user leaves immediately, i.e., balks) and the time that the user leaves (TL) is set equal to TA. If the user waits for service, the time he enters service (TE) will be determined by when a server is free to serve him, which is dependent on the status of the system when he arrives.

If the user enters service at TE, the time at which he leaves (TL) is determined by

$$TL = TE + \text{service time}$$

The service time will be randomly generated using the probability distribution of service times and the Monte Carlo technique. From the three values TA, TE, and TL we can compute, for example, the wait time (WT) and time spent in the system (TS) using equations (1) and (2).

This basic methodology will apply for all queueing simulations. Let us consider the simulation of a variety of queueing systems with the objective of obtaining at present only user-oriented statistics. Recall that user-oriented statistics are those for which each user provides one additional sample data value.

SECTION 13.8. *Simulation of a Single-Server Queueing System*

13.8.1. Statement of the Problem. Let us consider simulating a simple queueing system defined as follows:

1. One server.
2. One unlimited queue; first-in, first-out; no priority users; no balking; no reneging.
3. The interarrival-time (IAT) distribution is

IAT (seconds)	10	15	20	25	30
Probability	0.10	0.25	0.30	0.25	0.10

mean = 20.0 seconds

4. The service-time (ST) distribution is:

ST (seconds)	5	10	15	20	25	30
Probability	0.08	0.14	0.18	0.24	0.22	0.14

mean = 19.0 seconds

The problem is then to simulate 100 users of the system and estimate the mean wait time and mean time spent in the system.

13.8.2. Simulation Methodology. We shall develop a model which tracks each user of the system and determines for each his time of arrival (TA), the time at which he enters service (TE), and the time at which he finishes being served and leaves (TL). To do this we consider the movement of time to be represented by a "clock" which takes on higher values as time advances. Let us start the clock running at time equal to zero at the beginning of the simulation and select a unit by which to measure time. Since our interarrival- and service-time distributions are given in terms of seconds, let us select a time unit of 1 second. Thus, if we state that for a given user, the time of arrival (TA) equals 25, this is to be interpreted that the user arrives at a point in time 25 seconds after the start of the simulation.

For each user we shall randomly select an interarrival time (IAT) and determine the time of arrival by adding the time of arrival of the prior user to the interarrival time of the current user. To determine the time at which he enters service, we will determine whether or not there is someone in service when he arrives. This can be determined by observing the time at which the prior user leaves service (TL). The current user cannot enter service earlier than the TL for the prior user. To determine the time at which the user finishes being served and leaves (TL), we randomly sample a service time (ST) and compute TL = TE + ST. The random generation of interarrival times (IAT) and service times (ST) will be accomplished using the Monte Carlo technique. The cumulative distributions and random-number ranges are shown in Tables 13.8.1 and 13.8.2. The simulation, for 100 users, is shown in Table 13.8.3. Notice that the column headings for TA, TE, and TL are shown as "clock times," indicating that these values are points in time on the clock. The sample values of the user statistics, wait time (WT) and time spent in the system (TS), are computed from the TA, TE, and TL values using equations (13.7.1) and (13.7.2) and are shown in the right-hand columns.

Notice that when the first user arrives at clock time 15, no one is being serviced and he enters service immediately (TE = 15). User 2 arrives at clock time TA = 40 and also does not wait. User 3 arrives at TA = 55 and must wait until user 2 finishes. Therefore, the clock time at which user 2 enters service is TE = 60 instead of being equal to his time of arrival, TA = 25. He therefore waits WT = TE − TA = 60 − 55 = 5 seconds.

TABLE 13.8.1. *Cumulative Probability Distribution and Random-Number Range for Interarrival Time (IAT)*

IAT (seconds)	Probability	Cumulative Probability	Random-Number Range
10	0.10	0.10	0.0000–0.0999
15	0.25	0.35	0.1000–0.3499
20	0.30	0.65	0.3500–0.6499
25	0.25	0.90	0.6500–0.8999
30	0.10	1.00	0.9000–0.9999

TABLE 13.8.2. *Cumulative Probability Distribution and Random-Number Range for Service Time (ST)*

ST (seconds)	Probability	Cumulative Probability	Random-Number Range
5	0.08	0.08	0.0000–0.0799
10	0.14	0.22	0.0800–0.2199
15	0.18	0.40	0.2200–0.3999
20	0.24	0.64	0.4000–0.6399
25	0.22	0.86	0.6400–0.8599
30	0.14	1.00	0.8600–0.9999

TABLE 13.8.3. *Single-Server Queueing Simulation for 100 Users*

User Number	Random Number 1	Interarrival Time	Clock Time of Arrival, TA	Clock Time Service Entered, TE	Random Number 2	Service Time, ST	Clock Time of Exit, TL	Wait Time, WT	Time Spent in System, TS
1	0.2068	15	15	15	0.2648	15	30	0	15
2	0.7384	25	40	40	0.4350	20	60	0	20
3	0.3026	30	55	60	0.9841	30	90	5	35
4	0.9983	30	85	90	0.8712	30	120	5	35
5	0.6648	25	110	120	0.5827	20	140	10	30
6	0.8304	25	135	140	0.9013	30	170	5	35
7	0.3276	15	150	170	0.8436	25	195	20	45
8	0.7519	25	175	195	0.6093	20	215	20	40
9	0.0468	10	185	215	0.0846	10	225	30	40
10	0.1580	15	200	225	0.5063	20	245	25	45
11	0.2984	15	215	245	0.3762	15	260	30	45
12	0.6281	20	235	260	0.4246	20	280	25	45
13	0.3746	20	255	280	0.2893	15	295	25	40
14	0.6835	25	280	295	0.8461	25	320	15	40
15	0.9467	30	310	320	0.6587	25	345	10	35
⋮	⋮	⋮	⋮	⋮	⋮	⋮	⋮	⋮	⋮
100	0.5032	20	2,010	2,040	0.7407	25	2,065	30	25
					Sum =			3,584	5,585
					Number of users =			100	100
					Average =			35.84	55.85

His time spent in the system may be computed from either $TS = TL - TA$ or $TS = WT + ST$ and is equal to 35 seconds.

From the 100 samples of wait time (WT) and the time spent in the system (TS), we compute the average,

$$\overline{WT} = \frac{\Sigma WT}{100} = 35.84 \text{ seconds} \quad \text{and} \quad \overline{TS} = \frac{\Sigma TS}{100} = 55.85 \text{ seconds}$$

These are estimates of the true mean wait time and the true mean time spent in the system. As is the case with all simulation estimates, they are subject to sample variability. A longer run length (i.e., a greater number of samples) will give a more precise estimate.

The average time spent in the system can then be used to solve decision problems for queueing systems such as was shown in Section 11.10.

SECTION 13.9. *Simulation of a Multiple-Server Queueing System*

13.9.1. Statement of the Problem. In order to determine the required adjustments to our simulation model when there are multiple servers, let us assume that a second server is added to the queueing system described in Section 13.8. We shall see that this assumption requires only a minor modification to the procedures already developed and allows us to perform the required simulation.

13.9.2. Simulation Methodology. The methodology developed for simulating a single-server system can be adapted to simulate a multiple-server system. The only modification that is required is that if a user arrives and finds only one user in service, he does not have to wait but is served immediately by the second server. Therefore, the only change in the simulation procedures is to redefine how we determine the time at which the user enters service, TE. Since two users can be served simultaneously, we must now observe the time at which the prior two users leave (TL) in order to determine TE for the current user. The current user can, thus, enter service when one of the prior two users leaves. In order to make the problem more interesting we use the service-time distribution shown in Table 13.9.1. This distribution causes more queueing (longer lines) than that of Table 13.8.2. The interarrival-time distribution is still that of Table 13.8.1. The simulation for 100 users is shown in Table 13.9.2.

Notice that the second user can enter service immediately upon arrival since there are two servers. The same is true for the third user, since he arrives at clock time 55 and the first user has left at clock time 45. Thus, one of the servers is free when he arrives at clock time 55. The fourth user arrives at clock time 85 and does not wait since user 2 exits at

TABLE 13.9.1. *Service-Time Distribution for Server Simulation*

ST (seconds)	Probability	· Cumulative Probability	Random Number Range
10	0.08	0.08	0.0000–0.0799
20	0.14	0.22	0.0800–0.2199
30	0.18	0.40	0.2200–0.3999
40	0.24	0.64	0.4000–0.6399
50	0.22	0.86	0.6400–0.8599
60	0.14	1.00	0.8600–0.9999

TABLE 13.9.2. *Server Queueing Simulation for 100 Users*

User Number	Random Number 1	Interarrival Time	Clock Time of Arrival, TA	Clock Time Service Entered, TE	Random Number 2	Service Time, ST	Clock Time of Exit, TL	Wait Time, WT	Time Spent in System, TS
1	0.3261	15	15	15	0.2846	30	45	0	30
2	0.8741	25	40	40	0.6275	40	80	0	40
3	0.1413	15	55	55	0.9827	60	115	0	60
4	0.9685	30	85	85	0.8732	60	145	0	60
5	0.6783	25	110	115	0.5013	40	155	5	45
6	0.7934	25	135	145	0.9146	60	205	10	70
7	0.2604	15	150	155	0.6830	50	205	5	55
8	0.8307	25	175	205	0.3874	30	235	30	60
9	0.0647	10	185	205	0.1864	20	225	20	40
10	0.1965	15	200	225	0.4165	40	265	25	65
11	0.6217	20	220	235	0.8416	50	285	15	65
12	0.4347	20	240	265	0.6087	40	305	25	65
13	0.3382	15	255	285	0.2741	30	315	30	60
14	0.6856	25	280	305	0.7013	50	355	25	75
15	0.9016	30	310	315	0.6429	50	365	5	55
⋮	⋮	⋮	⋮	⋮	⋮	⋮	⋮	⋮	⋮
100	0.4086	20	1,960	2,055	0.8387	50	2,105	5	55

Sum = 1,152 4,785
Number of users = 100 100
Average = 11.52 47.85

clock time 80. The fifth user arrives at clock time 110 and must wait until clock time 115 to enter service, when user 3 exits.

Notice also that although user 9 arrives after user 8, he exits before user 8.

The average wait time is now 11.52 seconds and the average time spent in the system is now 47.85 seconds.

13.10.1. Statement of the Problem. Let us reconsider the problem of Section 13.8, the single-server queueing system simulation, but now assume that users may balk. If the user arrives and finds the server (or in general, all servers) busy, he may leave immediately and not wait for service (i.e., balk). Let us also assume that users are different with respect to when they balk. Some are impatient and will balk even though there is no one else waiting. Others may stay even though there are five users already waiting. A probability distribution can be used to describe the fraction of users who balk when there is zero or more (any) users waiting, one or more, two or more, and so on. A user who balks when there are two or more users already waiting in line when he arrives, stays if there are fewer than two users waiting in line when he arrives. Let us assume that the probability distribution of the number of users that must already be waiting in order that the current user balks (balking tendency distribution) is as follows:

Number of Users Already Waiting	> 1	> 2	> 3	> 4
Fraction who Balk (probability)	0.20	0.30	0.30	0.20

Therefore, 20% of the users will balk if one or more users are already waiting, 30% will balk if two or more users are already waiting, and so on.

Let us again simulate the system to find the average wait time (WT) and average time spent in the system for those users who stay for service. Let us also find the fraction of users who arrive and balk (P_B), since this is an important measure of performance of the service provided to users.

13.10.2. Simulation Methodology. The simulation methodology is quite similar to that for the single-server queueing system without balking except that we must determine whether or not a user balks when he arrives. If there is a server free when a user arrives, he enters service. If there is no server available and one or more users already waiting, we must determine the user's tendency to balk (i.e., determine if he will balk when there is one or more users already waiting, two or more, etc.). We shall randomly sample a value from the balking-tendency distribution using the Monte Carlo technique to simulate balking tendency. The cumulative probability distribution and random-number range for this distribution is shown in Table 13.10.1. If there are fewer users than this value already waiting, he stays for service; otherwise, he balks. For each customer we will indicate whether or not he balks so as to be able to compute the fraction of customers who balk. For each customer who balks, TE will have no value.

Number of Users Already Waiting for a Balk	Probability	Cumulative Probability	Random-Number Range
1 or more	0.20	0.20	0.0000–0.1999
2 or more	0.30	0.50	0.2000–0.4999
3 or more	0.30	0.80	0.5000–0.7999
4 or more	0.20	1.00	0.8000–0.9999

The simulation for 100 users using the same interarrival and service times as used in Section 13.9 is shown in Table 13.10.2. The first user finds the server free and therefore does not balk. The second and third users arrive and find no one waiting and therefore will not balk. When the fourth user arrives at clock time 80, there is one user in service (user 2, who will leave service at clock time 115) and one user waiting (user 3, who will enter service at clock time 115). Therefore, there is a chance that user 4 will balk. A random sample from the balking-tendency distribution is generated (i.e., the value 3). Since there is only one user waiting (less than 3) user 4 does not balk but stays for service. When user 5 arrives at clock time 100 there are two users waiting (user 2 is still in service and users 3 and 4 are waiting). The random sample from the balking-tendency distribution is the value 2. Since there are two users waiting, user 5 balks. No wait time or time spent in the system is recorded for the user. These statistics will only be computed for users who actually enter service.

At the end of the simulation we count the number of users who balk. The estimate of the probability that a user balks P_B (fraction of users who balk) is computed as the number of users who balk divided by the total number of users. This is equal to $\frac{41}{100} = 0.41$. The average wait time and average time spent in the system are computed using the values for the 59 users who were served and are equal to 66.39 seconds and 101.25 seconds, respectively.

SECTION 13.11. *Simulation of a Queueing System with Reneging*

13.11.1. Statement of the Problem. Let us again reconsider the problem of Section 13.8, the single-server queueing system simulation without balking. Let us now also assume that some users will wait for service for only a given amount of time, and if they must wait longer, they leave and do not enter service (renege). Moreover, assume that users differ in their tendency to renege; some will wait longer, others less before reneging. A user who reneges at 30 seconds waits and enters service if he can do so within 30 seconds after arriving. However, if he must wait for service

460

TABLE 13.10.2. Single-Server Queueing Simulation with Balking for 100 Users

User Number	Random Number 1	Interarrival Time, IAT	Clock Time of Arrival, TA	Random Number 2	Number Waiting for a Balk	Balk?	Clock Time Service Entered, TE	Random Number 3	Service Time, ST	Clock Time of Exit, TL	Wait Time, WT	Time Spent in System, TS
1	0.8732	25	25				25	0.2864	30	55	0	30
2	0.5382	20	45				55	0.8705	60	115	10	70
3	0.2873	15	60				115	0.9832	60	175	55	115
4	0.3716	20	80	0.7809	3		175	0.0238	10	185	95	105
5	0.6207	20	100	0.2830	2	Yes	—		—	100	—	—
6	0.6798	25	125	0.9654	4		185	0.3542	30	215	60	90
7	0.1079	15	140	0.0476	1	Yes	—		—	140	—	—
8	0.8463	25	165	0.5187	3		215	0.7890	50	265	50	100
9	0.6682	25	190	0.1643	1	Yes	—		—	190	1	—
10	0.7834	25	205	0.8235	4		265	0.5138	40	305	60	100
11	0.4819	20	225	0.6842	3		305	0.6217	40	345	80	120
12	0.9624	30	255	0.4861	2	Yes	—		—	255	—	—
13	0.8176	25	280	0.7462	3		345	0.1743	20	365	65	85
14	0.0652	10	290	0.9467	4		365	0.0641	10	375	75	85
15	0.5902	20	310	0.1568	1	Yes	—		—	310	—	—
⋯	⋯	⋯	⋯	⋯	⋯	⋯	⋯	⋯	⋯	⋯	⋯	⋯
100	0.7651	25	2,025	0.3136	2		2,085	0.3817	30	2,105	60	80

Number balking = 41
Fraction balking = 0.41

Number of users = 59

Sum = 3,927
Average = 66.39

Sum = 5,974
Average = 101.25

longer than 30 seconds, exactly 30 seconds after arriving he leaves (reneges). The probability distribution of how long a user will wait before reneging (reneging tendency distribution) is as follows:

Renege Time (seconds)	15	30	45	60	75	90	105	120
Probability	0.05	0.10	0.15	0.20	0.20	0.15	0.10	0.05

Therefore, 5% of the users will renege after waiting 15 seconds, 10% will renege after waiting 30 seconds, and so on.

Let us simulate the system to find the average wait time and average time spent in the system for those users who stay for service. We will also find the fraction of users who renege before being served.

13.11.2. Simulation Methodology. The simulation methodology is similar to that for the single-server queueing system with balking (Section 13.10). Before a user enters service we must determine if the time he would have to wait before entering service is greater than the time he will wait before reneging. This latter time is determined by randomly sampling from the known probability distribution. The reneging tendency cumulative probability distribution and random-number range is shown in Table 13.11.1.

TABLE 13.11.1. *Cumulative Probability Distribution and*
Random-Number Range for the Reneging-Tendency Distribution

Wait Time Before Reneging (seconds)	Probability	Cumulative Probability	Random-Number Range
15	0.05	0.05	0.0000–0.0499
30	0.10	0.15	0.0500–0.1499
45	0.15	0.30	0.1500–0.2999
60	0.20	0.50	0.3000–0.4999
75	0.20	0.70	0.5000–0.6999
90	0.15	0.85	0.7000–0.8499
105	0.10	0.95	0.8500–0.9499
120	0.05	1.00	0.9500–0.9999

The simulation for 100 users is shown in Table 13.11.2. The first and second users do not wait and therefore cannot renege. The third user has to wait only 5 seconds, which is less than the minimum renege time, and therefore cannot renege. The fourth user must wait 35 seconds before entering service and therefore would renege if his policy is to wait only 15 or 30 seconds before reneging. The randomly generated value for user 4 is 90 seconds, so he does not renege. Similarly, the fifth user will wait 35 seconds, since the randomly generated wait time for a renege is 105

TABLE 13.11.2. Single-Server Queueing Simulation with Reneging for 100 Users

User Number	Random Number 1	Interarrival Time, IAT	Clock Time of Arrival, TA	Random Number 2	Wait Time for a Renege	Renege?	Clock Time Service Entered, TE	Random Number 3	Service Time, ST	Clock Time of Exit, TL	Wait Time, WT	Time Spent in System, TS
1	0.3219	15	15				15	0.3876	30	45	0	30
2	0.9076	30	45				45	0.1940	20	65	0	20
3	0.1416	15	60				65	0.6136	40	105	5	45
4	0.0592	10	70	0.7583	90		105	0.0873	20	125	35	55
5	0.6382	20	90	0.8642	105		125	0.8817	60	185	35	95
6	0.3715	20	110	0.3276	60	Yes	—	—	—	170		
7	0.7396	25	135	0.2874	45	Yes	—	—	—	180		
8	0.2413	15	150	0.9783	120		185	0.5379	40	225	35	75
9	0.8713	25	175	0.6316	75		225	0.2573	30	255	50	80
10	0.3388	15	190	0.3847	60	Yes	—	—	—	250		
11	0.0138	10	200	0.1609	45	Yes	—	—	—	245		
12	0.6614	25	225	0.4793	60		255	0.4278	40	295	30	70
13	0.0872	10	235	0.0218	15	Yes	—	—	—	250		
14	0.4351	20	255	0.5813	75		295	0.9395	60	355	40	100
15	0.2874	15	270	0.9364	105		355	0.6207	40	395	85	125
⋯	⋯	⋯	⋯	⋯	⋯	⋯	⋯	⋯	⋯	⋯	⋯	⋯
100	0.5918	20	2,045	0.8215	90		2,075	0.3469	30	2,105	30	60

Number of users who renege = 44

Fraction who renege = 0.44

Sum = 2,886

Number of users = 56

Average = 51.54

Sum = 5,034

56

89.89

seconds. The sixth user cannot enter service until clock time 185, and he therefore would have to wait 75 seconds before entering service. The randomly selected value for his wait time before reneging is 60, which is less than the 75 seconds he must wait before entering service, and he therefore reneges. The time he leaves the system is 60 seconds after arriving. No wait time or time spent in the system is recorded for a user who reneges. At the end of the simulation, we count the number of users who renege. The estimate of the probability that a user reneges (fraction of users who renege) is computed as the number of users who renege divided by the total number of users and is equal to 0.44. The average wait time and time spent in the system is computed using the 56 samples of users who were served and are equal to 51.54 seconds and 89.89 seconds, respectively.

SECTION 13.12. *Computing System-Oriented Statistics from Queueing Simulations*

The queueing simulations that we have developed so far have computed only user-oriented statistics (i.e., those for which each user provides one additional sample value). There are other types of statistics, such as number of users in the system, which have values at each point in time, and these values change with changes in time. The procedures for computing statistics for these types of time-dependent or stochastic variables are considerably different than those for the calculations of the user statistics. To compute averages, we must first determine the value of the number of users in the system at each point in time. This is most clearly displayed by a graph. For the simulation of Section 13.8 (Table

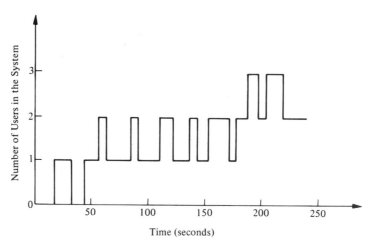

FIGURE 13.12.1. *Number of users in the system single-server queueing simulation of Section 13.8 (see Table 13.8.3).*

13.8.3), the single-server queueing system simulation, the graph appears in Figure 13.12.1. Each time a user arrives, the number in the system increases by one. Each time a user finishes service and leaves, the number in the system decreases by one.

In order to construct this graph it is necessary to determine at which points in time the number of users in the system changes value. In general, the term given to any occurence that causes the system to change its status is an *event*. For the single-server queueing system there are only two events:

1. Arrival (occurs at clock time TA).
2. End of service (occurs at clock time TL).

If we examine Table 13.8.3, looking at the values of TA and TL for the users, we can determine the points in time at which the number of

TABLE 13.12.1. *Computation of Average Number of Users in the System Single-Server Queueing Simulation of Section 13.8 (see Table 13.8.3)*

Clock Time	Event[a]	Old Number in System	New Number in System	Length of Time Since Last Change	$\left(\begin{array}{c}Length\ of\\ Time\\ \times(Old\ Value)\end{array}\right)$
15	A	0	1	15	0
30	E	1	0	15	15
40	A	0	1	10	0
55	A	1	2	15	15
60	E	2	1	5	10
85	A	1	2	25	25
90	E	2	1	5	10
110	A	1	2	20	20
120	E	2	1	10	20
135	A	1	2	15	15
140	E	2	1	5	10
150	A	1	2	10	10
170	E	2	1	20	40
175	A	1	2	5	5
185	A	2	3	10	20
195	E	3	2	10	30
200	A	2	3	5	10
215	E	3	2	15	45
:	:	:	:	:	:
2,065	E	3	2	10	30
				2,065	4,275

Average number in the system $= 4,275/2,065 = 2.07$

[a]A, arrival; E, end of service.

users in the system changes its value. Table 13.12.1 shows, for each event, at which clock time the change occurs, the type of event, and the "old" and "new" values for the number of users in the system. The number of users in the system remains at its old value until the next event occurs, at which time it changes to its new value. The length of time during which the number of users remained at the old value (length of time since last change) is also shown in Table 13.12.1, since it is necessary for computing the average number of users in the system. From Table 13.12.1 the graph of Figure 13.12.1 can be constructed.

Let us next consider the computation of the average number of users in the system. Table 13.12.1 indicates the values for the number of users in the system and how long the number of users in the system has remained at that level. For example, at the beginning of the simulation, there were zero users in the system for 15 seconds, then there was one user in the system for 15 seconds, zero users in the system for 10 seconds, one user in the system for 15 seconds, and so on. In effect, each second can be considered a sample. Thus, we have 15 samples of value zero, 15 samples of value 1, 10 samples of value 0, 15 samples of value 1, and so on. Since the total time period of observation is 2,065 seconds, it is as though there were 2,065 equally spaced samples of number of users in the system. The last column of Table 13.12.1 shows the old value times the length of time that the number of users in the system has maintained this value. Summing this column gives the weighted sum necessary to compute the average. The weighted sum divided by the number of seconds observed (2,065) gives the average number in the system.

The same approach can be used to develop statistics for mean number in the queue or average number of servers busy. The average number of servers busy is equivalent to the probability that the server is busy when there is only one server.

SECTION 13.13. *Computer Simulation Languages*

The simulation approach that views the system as changing over time only when events occur is generally used when writing computer programs to simulate queueing systems. This approach is termed *event-based*. Rather than handling each user one at a time, from the time he enters the system until the time he leaves, the program updates the clock to the next event scheduled to occur and makes whatever changes to the system and the statistics that are necessary. Since these programs tend to be extremely complicated, special-purpose computer simulation languages have been developed to simplify the programming involved.

One of the most widely used simulation languages used in the United States is GPSS (General-Purpose System Simulator), developed by IBM. The programmer states the sequence of steps (or events) that a user must take from the time he enters the system until he leaves. The statements are of the form GENERATE (arrivals), QUEUE (join the queue), ENTER (the service system), DEPART (the queue), ADVANCE (the clock, i.e., spend time in service), LEAVE (the service system), and TERMINATE (leave the system.) From these simple statements, the rather complex simulation program is compiled. However, a computer program (the GPSS Compiler) must be available to generate the simulation program from the statements. Since GPSS is so powerful (i.e., a few simple statements describe the system), it is easy to learn and therefore is widely used. A sample GPSS program and output are shown in Figures 13.13.1 and 13.13.2. The program describes a queueing system with one unlimited FIFO queue, two servers, no priorities, no balking or reneging, and interarrival and service time uniformly (equiprobably) distributed. The statistics generated are:

1. Average number of users in the system.
2. Average number of servers busy and server utilization.
3. Average number of users in the queue.
4. Average time spent in the system.
5. Average wait time.
6. Probability that a user does not wait.

The annotated program output indicates where each of these statistics is found.

Another widely used simulation language is SIMSCRIPT, developed by the RAND Corporation. Writing a program in SIMSCRIPT is far more complicated than GPSS, since the description of the system pertains to the events of the system (arrival, end of service, renege, etc.). Although the programming is more complicated, there is more flexibility, that is, programs written in SIMSCRIPT can accomplish tasks not possible in GPSS. Like GPSS, SIMSCRIPT requires a computer program

```
BLOCK
NUMBER   *LOC    OPERATION   A,B,C,D,E,F,G,H,I          COMMENTS
                 SIMULATE
         SERVR   STORAGE     2               2 SERVERS IN SERVICE FACILITY
         SYSTM   STORAGE     10000000        SYSTEM UNLIMITED IN CAPACITY
1                GENERATE    20,10           IAT IS UNIFORM 20 + OR - 10
2                ENTER       SYSTM           ARRIVAL ENTERS THE SYSTEM
3                QUEUE       QUE             ARRIVAL JOINS THE QUEUE
4                ENTER       SERVR           ENTER SERVICE WHEN FREE
5                DEPART      QUE                AND LEAVE QUEUE
6                ADVANCE     30,15           SERVICE TIME UNIFORM 30 + OR - 15
7                LEAVE       SERVR           LEAVE SERVICE FACILITY
8                LEAVE       SYSTM           EXIT FROM SYSTEM
9                TERMINATE   1
                 START       10,NP           WARMUP RUN FOR 10 USERS, NO PRINTOUT
                 RESET                          CLEAR STATISTICS AFTER WARMUP RUN
                 START       100             RUN FOR 100 USERS
                 END
```

FIGURE 13.13.1. *GPSS queueing simulation program.*

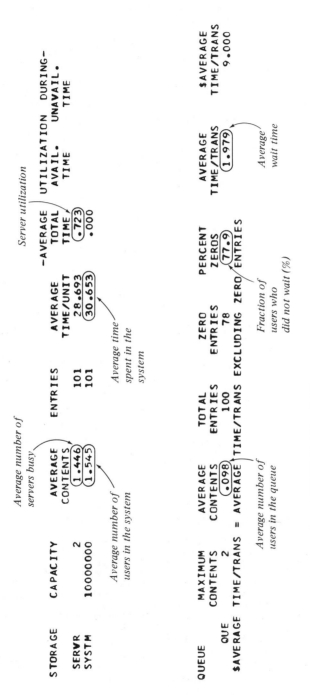

FIGURE 13.13.2. GPSS queueing simulation program output.

(SIMSCRIPT Compiler) to generate the simulation program from the statements in the SIMSCRIPT program.

Another "language," known as GASP, is available, but it is not a true language like GPSS. GASP is a series of procedures (subroutines) written in the FORTRAN language which the programmer appends to his FORTRAN program. These subroutines do many of the complicated operations necessary for queueing system simulation programs. Although GASP is the least powerful of languages mentioned, it has the advantages that no compiler (computer program to generate the simulation program from programmer statements) is necessary and the program generally requires less computer storage. Thus, GASP can be run on small computers.

There are many other simulation languages, such as SIMULA, that are used almost exclusively outside the United States. However, all simulation languages have one element in common. They enable the programmer to write a simulation program with less effort than writing it in a general-purpose language such as FORTRAN. Almost all queueing system simulations written today are written in one of these languages. Were it not for languages such as GPSS and SIMSCRIPT, the job of writing simulation programs would be far more complicated than it is. The popularity of using simulation has increased with the development of simulation languages which simplify the work necessary to develop the computer simulation programs.

SECTION 13.14. *Statistical Considerations*

13.14.1. General Considerations. As mentioned previously, the random nature of the simulation sample values yields statistics that are estimates of the true theoretical values and are subject to sampling variability. If a simulation is rerun using a different sequence of random numbers, the statistics derived will have different values. These statistics (e.g., average profit or average cost) are used as measures of performance in a decision problem, and it is important that the strategy with the highest average profit (or lowest average cost) really does have the highest true mean profit. It is possible, however, that the simulated average profit is higher than the others only because of random variation. It is, therefore, necessary to determine the amount of variability for each simulation estimate. The measure of variability is stated in the form of a *confidence limit* (e.g., 100 ± 10) at a given *level of confidence* (e.g., 95%). A 95% confidence level for a confidence limit of 100 ± 10 would be interpreted as:

> We are 95% confident that the true value is between 90 and 110; that is, the procedures used to determine the confidence limit will be correct (true mean is between confidence limit points 95% of the time.

The determination of a confidence limit will depend on the variability (standard deviation) of the sample average. If the standard deviation of the sample average (frequently referred to as the *standard error of the mean*) is small, the confidence limit will be "tighter," and our estimate is more precise than if the standard deviation is larger. Therefore, it is important to determine the standard deviation of the sample average and use it to determine a confidence limit on the true values. It will be seen that the standard deviation of the sample average decreases as the number of samples on which the average is computed increases. Thus, the decision maker can achieve more precise estimates by running the simulation longer and generating more samples. The sample size should be chosen such that the confidence limits on the true values are small enough that it is highly likely that the strategy selected with the best average measure of performance does have the highest true mean value.

13.14.2. Static Simulation Statistics. The statistical techniques regarding averages of independent samples was presented in Sections 2.14 to 2.16.

Let us examine the results of the new product simulation of Section 13.4 in light of these considerations. The two strategies with highest average profit are strategies 3 and 4:

Strategy	Sample Average Profit, $\bar{P}$	Sample Standard Deviation of Profit, S_P	Standard Deviation of $\bar{P}$, $S_{\bar{P}} = S_P/\sqrt{100}$	95% Confidence Limits on True Mean
3	6,700.00	1,296.28	129.63	6,570.37–6,829.63
4	6,493.00	2,043.16	204.32	6,288.68–6,697.32

Notice that the confidence limits on the two true average profits overlap. This, in general, implies that it is not "relatively unlikely" that the true mean profit for strategy 3 is lower than strategy 4. We would have to increase the run size to reduce the confidence intervals. Below is shown the results for runs of $n = 10,000$ samples.

Strategy	Sample Average Profit, $\bar{P}$	Standard Deviation of Profit, S_P	Standard Deviation of $\bar{P}$, $S_{\bar{P}} = S_P/\sqrt{10,000}$	95% Confidence Limits of True Average Profit
3	6,608.04	1,350.01	13.50	6,594.54–6,621.54
4	6,572.23	1,739.86	17.40	6,554.83–6,589.63

Now, since the confidence limits do not overlap, we may conclude that strategy 3 has a higher expected profit than strategy 4. We are also

95% confident that the expected profit is between $6,594.54 and $6,621.54.

The decision as to the sample size for a simulation should be based on the confidence limits obtained. The criteria for deciding how long to run (when to stop) are often called *stopping rules*.

13.14.3. Dynamic Simulation Statistics. Dynamic simulation statistics differ from static simulation statistics in that generally the sample values are not independent of each other. For example, the wait time of one user in a queueing simulation is dependent on the prior user, and the end-of-day inventory is dependent on the prior day's inventory. This invalidates certain results stated for static simulation statistics which assumed independent samples. Before considering the statistical properties of the simulation estimates, let us consider the generating of the sample.

Frequently, dynamic simulation models are begun (initialized) at a system status level that is not representative of the system at a later point in time. For example, consider a simulation of a queueing system which is considered heavily loaded (e.g., an average number of users in the queue of 20 and an average wait time of 10 minutes). We may begin the simulation with no one in the system, and consequently the first few users will have zero or very low wait times. These sample values are not representative of the system in equilibrium or steady state and should not be included in the sample of wait times with the wait times of users who arrive later in the simulation. This initial period of time, before the system reaches steady state, is known as the *warm-up* or *transient* period. The sample values during the warm-up period actually come from a different sample population than those obtained after the system has stabilized (steady state). Combining sample values from the warm-up period and the steady state period is statistically invalid.

There are two approaches to overcoming this difficulty. If it is not too difficult, we can initialize the simulated system to a set of conditions which are representative of the steady state. We have actually done this for the inventory simulation of Section 13.6. The initial inventory was set at the order quantity, Q, which is a reasonable value for inventory in the steady state. Hence, for this case it is valid to include all the inventory samples in the averages, since there really is no warm-up period.

In other simulation problems, however, it may be extremely complicated to initialize the system so as to be representative of steady state conditions. This is usually the case in queueing simulations. The alternative approach used is to start the simulation in the empty condition and allow the simulation to run for a while and warm up, but not to include the sample values generated during this warm-up period in the final averages. After the simulation reaches a representative steady state, the collection of the relevant statistics begins. For example, consider the single-server, no-balking, no-reneging simulation of Table 13.8.3. In the text we have used all 100 sample values of wait times and time spent in the system in computing the average. The average wait time and the average time spent in the system of the first few users is low relative to the later users who are more representative of the steady state. In this example the system warms up very quickly since the values for the sixth user are lower than for the fifth, indicating that the system is stabilizing. If we recomputed the averages using only the sample values for users 7 through 100 (i.e., 94 samples), the recomputed average wait time and the average time spent in the system differ very little from the previous values that used all 100 samples. This is because the system reaches steady state so quickly (i.e., very few samples with low values were included in averages). In fact, there is a small, but not negligible probability in the steady state (approximately 0.05) that the server is idle and a user will not have to wait, as was the case for the first user. Thus, our averages computed using all 100 samples are not very biased. In other, more complicated simulations, using the values generated during the warm-up period may bias the results significantly and should be avoided.

Let us now consider the question of the statistical properties of the simulation estimators. The major difference between static and dynamic simulation samples is that for dynamic simulations, the sample values are not independent of each other. This violates only one assumption stated for the static simulation averages. The standard deviation of the sample average ($\sigma_{\bar{x}}$) is *not* equal to $\sigma_x / \sqrt{n}$; it is actually much greater. The theoretical methods for computing $\sigma_{\bar{x}}$ are quite complicated and are not used very frequently. However, we can estimate the standard deviation of our sample averages by running many independent simulation runs of 100 samples, each using different sequences of random numbers each time. If we perform 10 independent runs, we have 10 independent random samples, and our averages ($\bar{x}$) can be used to estimate the standard deviation of these sample averages. This has been done for the single-server, no-balking, no-reneging simulation of Section 13.8. The average wait-time values for 10 independent runs of 100 users each is shown in Table 13.14.1. We have also computed the overall average ($\bar{\bar{x}}$) and the standard deviation of the sample average ($S_{\bar{x}}$). Notice that the value of $S_{\bar{x}}$ computed, 25.03, is considerably larger than $S_x / \sqrt{100}$, which would be in the range $30/10 = 3$.

The overall mean ($\bar{\bar{x}}$) is essentially the average computed over 1000 samples and can be used as the best available estimate of the mean wait time. The 10 independent runs taken together constitute a sample of 1,000 users, and the estimated standard deviation of this average ($\bar{\bar{x}}$) is $S_{\bar{\bar{x}}} = S_{\bar{x}} / \sqrt{10} = 7.92$, since the sample of 1,000 is 10 times as large as the sample of 100.

We can now state the confidence limit on the true average wait time for runs of 1,000 samples as:

$$\bar{\bar{x}} \pm 1.96 S_{\bar{\bar{x}}} = 31.24 \pm (1.96)(7.92)$$
$$= 31.24 \pm 15.52$$

TABLE 13.14.1. *Computation of Standard Deviation of Sample Average for Wait Time from 10 Independent Runs of 100 Users*

Run	Average Wait Time, $\bar{x}$	$(\bar{x})^2$	Standard Deviation of Wait Time, S_x
1	8.32	69.22	9.65
2	20.99	440.58	16.32
3	13.15	172.92	10.98
4	19.31	372.88	17.04
5	23.81	566.92	24.22
6	37.62	1,415.26	30.30
7	81.63	6,663.46	47.98
8	15.20	231.04	14.12
9	70.69	4,997.08	34.04
10	21.67	469.59	16.68
	$\Sigma\bar{x}=312.39$	$\Sigma\bar{x}^2=15,398.95$	

Overall average $\bar{\bar{x}}=31.24$

Standard deviation of sample average $(\bar{x})$

$$S_{\bar{x}} = \sqrt{\frac{\Sigma\bar{x}^2 - n(\bar{\bar{x}})^2}{n-1}}$$

$$= \sqrt{\frac{15,398.95 - (10)(31.24)^2}{9}}$$

$$= \sqrt{\frac{5,640.199}{9}}$$

$$= 25.03$$

The run length (n) can be selected so as to reduce the confidence limit to an acceptable value.

SECTION 13.15. *Using the Computer*

13.15.1. Introduction. As has been discussed, computers play an important role in sumulation studies. To illustrate their usefulness, three simulations presented in this chapter have been programmed:

1. New-product simulation.
2. Inventory simulation.
3. Queueing simulation.

473   Each of the programs is discussed separately.

13.15.2. New-Product Simulation Program. The program simulates the new-product-introduction problem of Section 13.4. The simulation is performed for all possible production quantities (i.e., all possible demand values).

The input to the program is:

1. The salvage value.
2. The number of samples to use.
3. The random-number seed, which may be any odd integer not ending in 5. If none is supplied, one is selected by the program.
4. An indication of whether or not a detailed printout of each sample demand, cost, and profit is desired.
5. The probability distribution of cost.
6. The selling price and probability distribution of demand for the given selling price.

Additional runs may be performed by submitting other selling prices and demand distributions. The program output was presented as Figures 13.4.1 and 13.4.2.

13.15.3. Inventory Simulation Program. The program performs the inventory simulation of the problem presented in Section 13.6. All reorder-point strategies are simulated; that is, the reorder point is set equal to all values of demand greater than or equal to the mean.

The input to the program is:

1. The carrying cost k_c.
2. The stockout cost k_u.
3. The order quantity Q.
4. The number of samples (days) to use.
5. The random-number seed. It may be any odd integer not ending in 5. If none is given, the program selects one.
6. An indication of whether or not the detailed printout of daily activity is desired.
7. The probability distribution of daily demand.
8. The probability distribution of lead time.

The program output was in Figures 13.6.1 and 13.6.2.

13.15.4. Queueing Simulation Program. The program performs a simulation of an infinite queue system with or without multiple servers, balking, and reneging as described in Sections 13.7–13.11. The input to the program is:

1. The number of servers.

FIGURE 13.15.1. *Queueing simulation program output.* ⟶

```
                    QUEUEING SIMULATION

NO. OF SERVERS =  2    BALKING YES    RENEGGING YES
WARMUP =   5 USERS        RUN =   20 USERS

                 PROBABILITY DISTRIBUTIONS
IAT    10.00    15.00    20.00    25.00    30.00
PROB   0.1000   0.2500   0.3000   0.2500   0.1000

ST     10.00    20.00    30.00    40.00    50.00    60.00
PROB   0.0800   0.1400   0.1800   0.2400   0.2200   0.1400

         BALKING TENDANCY DISTRIBUTION - NO. OF USERS WAITING
NO.     1.00     2.00     3.00     4.00
PROB   0.2000   0.3000   0.3000   0.2000

          RENEGGING TENDANCY DISTRIBUTION - WAIT TIME
WT     15.00    30.00    45.00    60.00    75.00    90.00   105.00   120.00
PROB   0.0500   0.1000   0.1500   0.2000   0.2000   0.1500   0.1000   0.0500

         USER PRINTOUT - WARMUP RUN
TIME OF   TIME SVC   TIME OF    WAIT     TIME
ARRIVAL   ENTERED    EXIT       TIME     SPENT
  15.       15.        45.       0.       30.
  40.       40.        80.       0.       40.
  55.       55.       115.       0.       60.
  85.       85.       145.       0.       60.
 110.      115.       155.       5.       45.

                 USER PRINTOUT
TIME OF   TIME SVC   TIME OF    WAIT     TIME
ARRIVAL   ENTERED    EXIT       TIME     SPENT
 200.        0.       200.       0.        0.     BALK
 135.      145.       205.      10.       70.
 150.      155.       205.       5.       55.
 185.      205.       235.      20.       50.
 175.      205.       245.      30.       70.
 285.        0.       285.       0.        0.     BALK
 215.      235.       295.      20.       80.
 240.      245.       295.       5.       55.
 260.      295.       315.      35.       55.
 310.      310.       360.       0.       50.
 330.      330.       370.       0.       40.
 340.      360.       420.      20.       80.
 360.      370.       420.      10.       60.
 440.        0.       440.       0.        0.     BALK
 375.      420.       460.      45.       85.
 415.        0.       430.      15.       15.     RENEG
 390.      420.       470.      30.       80.
 505.        0.       505.       0.        0.     BALK
 470.      470.       510.       0.       40.
 455.      460.       520.       5.       65.
 485.      510.       550.      25.       65.
 530.      530.       570.       0.       40.
 550.      550.       590.       0.       40.
 570.      570.       590.       0.       20.
 595.      595.       625.       0.       30.

                SIMULATION RESULTS
USER STATISTICS
        AVG WAIT TIME  =    12.89      STD DEV =    14.65
        AVG TIME SPENT =    56.50      STD DEV =    18.07
        PROB OF BALK  =     0.17
        PROB OF RENEG =     0.05
SYSTEM STATISTICS
        AVG NO IN SYSTEM =     2.49    STD DEV =    0.90
        AVG NO IN QUEUE  =     0.62    STD DEV =    0.72
        AVG NO SERVERS BUSY =  1.87    STD DEV =    0.36
        SERVER UTILIZATION =  93.62%
```

2. An indication of whether or not balking and/or reneging is permitted.
3. The random-number seed to be used. It may be any odd integer not ending in 5. If none is supplied, a seed is selected by the program.
4. The warm-up run length.
5. The run length over which statistics are taken.
6. An indication of whether or not a detailed user printout is required.
7. The interarrival-time distribution.
8. The service-time distribution.
9. The balking-tendency distribution (if balking is permitted).
10. The reneging-tendency distribution (if reneging is permitted).

The program output is shown in Figure 13.15.1. Notice that in cases of balking, the printout for the user is not in sequence by time of arrival. This is because the printout for users who remain occurs when they exit from the system. Also, the run length is stated in terms of the users who are served, not including those who balk or renege.

SECTION 13.16. *Summary*

The technique of simulation and its relevance to a variety of business problems has been presented. These techniques were applied to two types of problems, static and dynamic. In each case the detailed methodology was developed so that the reader can perform simulations of his own on real-life problems. We have also shown that the computer is very important in any simulation project. Several of the simulations developed in this chapter have been programmed, and the outputs are given in the various sections.

A detailed analysis of the statistical considerations regarding simulation has also been presented in this chapter. This aspect is omitted in most texts but is very important in practical real-life simulation projects.

PROBLEMS

13.1. Reconsider the parts-production problem of Sections 13.2 and 13.3, but assume the probability distribution of parts' lengths is as follows:

Length of Part A	5	6	7	8	9
Probability	0.07	0.19	0.38	0.25	0.11

Length of Part B	14	15	16	17
Probability	0.23	0.41	0.27	0.09

Generate 5 random samples of part C lengths and compute the average part C length.

13.2. A craftswoman makes carved wooden statues and each day sells her output to a gift shop in town. The number of statues she makes each day is variable and is described by the following probability distribution:

Number Made	1	2	3	4
Probability	0.15	0.25	0.35	0.25

The price she is paid *per statue* by the gift shop also varies and is described by the following probability distribution:

Price per Statue ($)	5	6	7	8
Probability	0.13	0.24	0.46	0.17

Assume that she is paid the same price each day for all her statues. Generate five random samples of the craftswoman's daily sales in dollars, and estimate the mean.

13.3. Repeat Problem 13.2 assuming that she is paid an independent price for each statue, each of which is described by the price probability distribution of Problem 13.2.

13.4. Reconsider the new-product-introduction problem of Section 13.4, assuming a selling price of $20 and the following probability distributions of demand and cost:

Cost ($)	8	9	10	11
Probability	0.13	0.26	0.39	0.22

Demand	500	600	700	800	900
Probability	0.37	0.26	0.18	0.12	0.07

(a) Generate five random samples of profit and estimate the mean profit assuming that the quantity produced is 600.
(b) Use the computer program to find the optimal production quantity.

13.5. A manufacturing process is highly dependent on the temperature and humidity each day, which are random. When temperature and humidity are high, the process produces more defectives. The number of units produced is independent of the weather but is also random. The probability distributions of daily production and fraction defective are as follows:

Daily Production Units	1,000	1,250	1,500	1,750	2,000
Probability	0.1	0.2	0.4	0.2	0.1

Fraction Defective	0.05	0.10	0.15	0.20	0.25
Probability	0.31	0.27	0.21	0.16	0.05

Simulate 5 days of production and estimate the mean number of good (nondefective) units produced each day.

13.6. (Problem 13.5 continued) Assume that the cost of each unit produced is $2 and that each good (nondefective unit) is eventually sold for $10.

(a) Use the samples generated in Problem 13.5 to estimate the mean net profit per day.
(b) Using your estimate from part (a), what is the economic value of equipment that would cause the process to produce 2,000 units with 5% defectives each day?

13.7. Reconsider the inventory simulation of Section 13.6 with the following probability distributions of lead time and daily demand:

Daily Demand (units)	10	20	30	40	50
Probability	0.15	0.20	0.30	0.20	0.15

Lead Time	1	2	3
Probability	0.25	0.50	0.25

Simulate 20 days of inventory movement using the rule:

Order 200 units when inventory equals 60 units.

Assume the opening inventory equals 200 units.
(a) Estimate the average inventory and average backorder quantity from these samples.
(b) Using the carrying cost and backorder cost of Section 13.6, find the average cost per year, not including ordering cost.

13.8. (Problem 13.7 continued) Use the computer to simulate 100 days of inventory activity for reorder points of 60, 80, 100, and 120 units. Which appears to have the lowest cost?

13.9. An investor is considering a series of 1-year investments which can be made at the beginning of the next 3 years. Each year he will invest $\frac{1}{2}$ of his existing funds and buy bonds paying 10%/year with the other half. The investment is risky and has the following probabilities of various yearly returns:

Yearly Return (%)	−50	−25	0	25	50
Probability	0.1	0.15	0.25	0.3	0.2

Each year's return is independent of all other years. The investor wants to find the expected value of his cash holdings at the end of the 3-year period. Simulate five samples of 3-year periods and estimate the expected cash holdings at the end of the 3-year period if he starts with $10,000.

13.10. A company maintains a checking account at a bank with a special provision for automatic borrowing. If the account balance falls below $2,000, the bank automatically transfers $5,000 into the account as a loan. The probability distributions of the company's net daily deposits and withdrawals are:

Daily Deposits	1,000	1,500	2,000	2,500
Probability	0.21	0.37	0.25	0.17

Daily Withdrawals	2,000	2,500	3,000	3,500	4,000	4,500
Probability	0.04	0.09	0.18	0.26	0.28	0.15

Simulate 10 days to determine
(a) The average bank balance.
(b) The average time between $5,000 loan transfers into the account.
Assume that the initial balance is $2,000.

13.11. A gasoline station sells one grade of gasoline and has a single pump and attendant. Cars arrive for gas, wait in a single queue, and are served on a first-come, first-served basis. The interarrival-time probability distribution is as follows:

IAT (minutes)	2	3	4	5	6	7	8
Probability	0.07	0.14	0.26	0.22	0.16	0.10	0.05

The probability distribution of time to be served is:

Service Time (minutes)	2	3	4	5	6	7	8
Probability	0.08	0.17	0.28	0.20	0.14	0.09	0.04

Simulate 10 customers buying gas and find the average wait time and the average time spent at the gas station.

13.12. (Problem 13.11 continued) Use the computer program to simulate 100 users being served. Compare your results with those of Problem 13.11.

13.13. (Problem 13.11 continued) Assume that balking occurs. The probability distribution which describes when users balk is:

Number of Users Already Waiting for a Balk to occur	1 or more	2 or more	3 or more
Probability	0.5	0.3	0.2

(a) Simulate 10 customers buying gas and find the average wait time, average time spent in the system, and the fraction of customers who balk.
(b) Assume that the average profit on a sale is $2. What profits are lost as a result of customers who leave without buying gas?

13.14. (Problem 13.13 continued) Use the computer program to simulate

100 customers buying gas. Compare your results to those of Problem 13.13.

13.15. (Problem 13.11 continued) Assume that reneging takes place. The probability distribution which describes when users renege is:

Renege Time (minutes)	2	4	6	8
Probability	0.2	0.4	0.3	0.1

(a) Simulate 10 customers buying gas and find the average wait time, average time spent, and the fraction of users who renege.
(b) Assume that the average profit on a sale is $2. Estimate the lost profits due to reneging.

13.16. (Problem 13.15 continued) Use the computer program to simulate 100 customers buying gas. Compare your results to those of Problem 13.15.

13.17. (Problem 13.11 continued) Assume that the gas station is considering installing a second pump and attendant. Because attendants talk to each other, the service-time distribution will become:

Service Time (minutes)	7	8	9	10	11	12	13
Probability	0.08	0.17	0.28	0.20	0.14	0.09	0.04

Simulate 10 customers buying gas and find the average wait time and time spent at the gas station.

13.18. (Problem 13.17 continued) Use the computer program to simulate 100 customers buying gas. Compare your results to those of Problem 13.17.

13.19. (Problem 13.17 continued) Assume that although two attendants are serving customers, balking occurs as described by the distribution of Problem 13.13.

(a) Simulate 10 customers buying gas and find the average wait time, average time spent at the gas station, and the fraction of customers who balk.
(b) Assume that the profit on a sale is $2. Estimate the lost profits due to balking.

13.20. (Problem 13.19 continued) Use the computer program to simulate 100 users buying gas. Compare your results to those of Problem 13.19.

13.21. (a) Using the simulation data of Problem 13.2, find the 95% confidence limits of mean daily sales.
(b) Find the mean number made, mean price, and mean daily profit from the probability distributions.
(c) Does the confidence limit developed in part (a) contain the mean found in part (b)?

(d) What sample size is necessary to achieve a 95% confidence limit of ±$2?

13.22. Reconsider Problem 13.12. Perform 10 independent runs of 100 customers buying gas and use these results to establish the standard error of the mean wait time $(S_{\bar{x}})$ for runs of 100 users. What is the estimate of the 95% confidence limits for runs of 1,000 users?

13.23. Reconsider Problem 13.11. From the simulated data, construct a table and graph of number of customers at the gas station versus time. Find the average number of customers at the gas station.

**ARTICLES
AND BOOKS**

Bonini, C. P., *Simulation of Information and Decision Systems in the Firm.* Englewood Cliffs, N.J.: Prentice-Hall, Inc., 1963.

Emshoff, J. R. and R. L. Sisson, *Design and Use of Computer Simulation Models.* New York: Macmillan Co., 1970.

Evans, G. W., G. F. Wallace, and G. L. Sutherland, *Simulation Using Digital Computers.* Englewood Cliffs, N.J.: Prentice-Hall, Inc., 1967.

General Purpose Simulation System/360: Introductory User's Manual. White Plains, N.Y.: IBM Corporation, 1967.

Gordon, Geoffrey, *System Simulation.* Englewood Cliffs, N.J.: Prentice-Hall, Inc., 1969.

——, *The Application of GPSS V to Discrete System Simulation.* Englewood Cliffs, N.J.: Prentice-Hall, Inc., 1975.

Kleijnen, J. P. C., *Statistical Techniques in Simulation.* New York: Marcel Dekker, 1973.

Markowitz, H. M., "Simulating with SIMSCRIPT," *Management Science,* June 1966, pp. B-396–404.

Martin, F. F., *Computer Modeling and Simulation.* New York: John Wiley & Sons, Inc., 1968.

Meier, R. C., W. T. Newell, and H. J. Pazer, *Simulation in Business and Economics.* Englewood Cliffs, N.J.: Prentice-Hall, Inc., 1969.

Naylor, T. H., J. L. Balintfy, D. S. Burdick, and K. Hu, *Computer Simulation Techniques.* New York: John Wiley & Sons, Inc., 1968.

Pugh, A. L., *DYNAMO User's Manual,* 2d ed. Cambridge, Mass.: MIT Press, 1963.

Schmidt, J. W. and R. E. Taylor, *Simulation and Analysis of Industrial Systems.* Homewood, Ill.: Richard D. Irwin, 1970.

Schriber, Thomas J., *Simulation Using GPSS.* New York: John Wiley & Sons, Inc., 1974.

Shannon, Robert E., *Systems Simulation: The Art and Science.* Englewood Cliffs, N.J.: Prentice-Hall, Inc., 1975.

Tocher, K. D., *The Art of Simulation.* London: The English University Press, 1963.

CHAPTER FOURTEEN

PERT-CPM

OBJECTIVES: The purpose of this chapter is to present
to you the following concepts that are
important in the study of PERT.

1. *Viewing projects as a sequence of
   activities and events.*
2. *Representing a project by the PERT
   chart.*
3. *The computation of completion times
   and slack times.*
4. *The concept of the critical path.*
5. *Allowance for variable time estimates.*
6. *The relevance of linear programming
   to project scheduling.*

All organizations frequently engage in large, complex projects that require many different steps or operations to be performed in order to complete the project. The introduction of a new product is a good example of a complex project, since it requires many operations, such as research and development, product testing, market research, and package design. In such cases the job of planning and control of the project becomes difficult.

The concern of managers involved with implementing the project focuses around the question of when the project will be completed. Since many variables affect the time of completion of the project, it is important to have a decision making aid to assist in answering such questions as:

1. When do we *expect* to complete the project?
2. If any operation takes longer then expected, what effect will this have on the overall completion time of the project?
3. What is the probability of completing the project by the scheduled date?
4. If there are additional funds that can be spent to reduce the time to perform certain operations, how should they be spent (i.e., how much on which operations)?

PERT (program evaluation and review technique) and CPM (critical path method) provide a methodology for planning and control of project implementation and for answering questions such as those listed. Because of their success in performing these functions, they are widely used in government and industry.

All projects may be viewed as being composed of operations or tasks called activities, which require the expenditure of time and resources for their accomplishment.

DEFINITION. An **activity** is an operation or task that requires the expenditure of time and resources for its accomplishment.

483

For example, in building a house the activities might be:

1. Architects draw plans.
2. Excavation.
3. Foundation masonry work.
4. Building the frame.
5. Roofing.
6. Electrical work.
7. Plumbing.
8. Interior work.

Each of these activities requires time and resources (man-power, materials, money) to complete. We will denote each activity of the project by a letter name (*A, B, C,* etc.). The choice of the activities that describe the project is an important part of the modeling process. For example, we could have combined activities *B* and *C* for the house-building project into one activity, calling it simply "lay the foundation." By doing this we would reduce the number of activities but risk combining two distinctly different activities into one and thereby lose some degree of control. The proper choice of the activities that describe the project is a skill which comes only with experience.

In general, not all activities can begin at once, although some can proceed at the same time. For example, we cannot begin building the frame of the house until after the foundation is complete. The plumbing and electrical work can both begin after the frame is completed. For each activity we must determine if the activity can begin at the beginning of the project or whether other activities must be completed before this one begins.

> *DEFINITION.* **Predecessor activities** *are those activities which must be completed before a given activity can begin.*

The predecessor activity to *D* (building the frame) is *C* (foundation masonry work). The predecessor activity to activities *E, F,* and *G* is activity *D*. We consider as predecessor activities only those that must be completed immediately before this activity can begin. We do not list *A*, *B*, and *C* as predecessors, even though they must be completed first, since listing *D* as a predecessor activity accomplishes this. Activity *H* has as its predecessor activities *E, F,* and *G*, which must be completed first.

If we wish to know when the project will be completed, we must know (i.e., estimate) how long each activity will take.

> *DEFINITION.* t_e *is the* **expected time** *(duration) to complete an activity.*

We may measure it in hours, days, weeks, months, or whatever, but we must measure all activity durations in the same time unit. Given the activities, their predecessor activities, and their expected durations, PERT allows us to develop useful information about the overall project.

Since some activities cannot begin until certain other activities are completed let us make the following definition:

> *DEFINITION. An **event** is a point in time at which a given set of activities are all completed.*

For example, in our house-building project, activity H cannot begin until activities E, F, and G are completed. We can therefore define an event that occurs at the moment when all three activities E, F, and G are completed. When this event occurs, activity H can begin. We shall name the events of the project by numbers (1, 2, 3, etc.). Event 1 will be the start of the project, and the highest numbered event will be the completion of the project (i.e., all activities completed).

SECTION 14.4. *The PERT Chart*

The *PERT chart* or *network* is a diagrammatic representation (or model) of the sequence of activities and events necessary to complete the project and is helpful to the manager in visualizing how the project must proceed. Since the project is composed of activities and events, we choose the following means of representing them on the PERT chart:

> *RULE.* Represent all activities by arrows and all events by circles or nodes.

For example, if activity A can begin at the beginning of the project, we shall indicate this in the PERT chart as in Figure 14.4.1. The beginning of the project is event 1, and the arrow coming out of event 1 indicates activity A being performed. When activity A is completed, we consider event 2 to have occurred.

In our house-building project we indicated that activities E, F, and G cannot begin until activity D is completed. This would be represented as in Figure 14.4.2.

Also, we noted that activity H could not begin until activities E, F, and G were completed. This is represented as in Figure 14.4.3.

In general, we will define events for the starting and ending points of all activities. Let us draw a PERT chart for the house-building project. The activities and their predecessor activities are shown in Table 14.4.1. The PERT chart that represents this relationship is shown in Figure

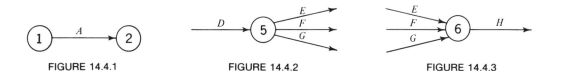

FIGURE 14.4.1   FIGURE 14.4.2   FIGURE 14.4.3

TABLE 14.4.1. *Activities of the House-Building Project*

Activity	Description	Predecessor Activities
A	Architects draw plans	None
B	Excavation	A
C	Foundation masonry work	B
D	Building the frame	C
E	Roofing	D
F	Electrical work	D
G	Plumbing	D
H	Interior work	E, F, G

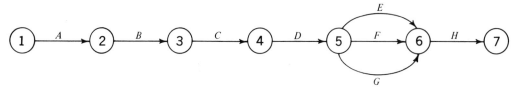

FIGURE 14.4.4. *PERT chart for the house-building project.*

14.4.4. We have defined seven events. Event 1 is the beginning of the project and event 7 is the completion of the project.

Let us consider a more complicated project, which is shown in Table 14.4.2. This project will be the case study for this chapter around which the PERT methodology will be developed. We have also indicated for each activity the expected duration (t_e) in days (i.e., how long to complete the activity). The PERT chart that represents this project is shown in Figure 14.4.5.

Since activities A, B, and C have no predecessor activities, they can begin immediately and are shown coming out of event 1, the start event. The project is completed when all activities have been completed. Since activities G, I, and J are the last to be completed, they are shown terminating in an event, event 7, which is the project completion. Since

TABLE 14.4.2. *Activities for the Case-Study Project*

Activity	Predecessor Activities	Expected Duration, t_e (days)
A	None	12
B	None	20
C	None	14
D	C	16
E	A	28
F	B, D	15
G	B, D	36
H	C	22
I	E, F	18
J	H	24

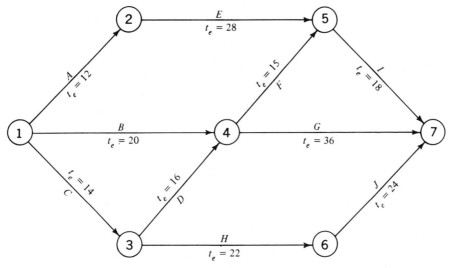

FIGURE 14.4.5. *PERT chart for the case study project.*

activities F and G both have activities B and D as predecessors, activities B and D terminate in the same event (4), and activities F and G start at event 4. Notice that the expected duration times (t_e) are shown for each activity which will be useful in the analysis that follows.

SECTION 14.5. *Paths in a PERT Network*

One of the primary questions we wish to answer is: When can we expect the project to be completed? One method of analysis is to find all the *paths* in the network.

> *DEFINITION. A **path** is a sequence of activities that connect the start event (1) to the end event (7) for the case project.*

For a large, realistic project, this can be a tedious if not almost impossible job and is, therefore, not useful in practice. We present the procedure, however, since it reveals many of the concepts involved.

Table 14.5.1 lists all the paths for the case project and the time required to reach the end event via that path. For example, if we are only concerned with completing activities A, E, and I (path 1), we expect that it will take 58 days, the sum of the duration times of activities A, E, and I. However, completing A, E, and I does not mean that the project is complete, since all activities must be completed. However, the time taken to complete the path with the longest duration (i.e., path 5 with 66 days) will give sufficient time to complete all activities. Therefore, the expected time of completion of the project is 66 days after the beginning.

TABLE 14.5.1. *Paths of the Case Project*

Path Number	Path	Duration
1	A–E–I	12 + 28 + 18 = 58
2	B–F–I	20 + 15 + 18 = 53
3	B–G	20 + 36 = 56
4	C–D–F–I	14 + 16 + 15 + 18 = 63
5	C–D–G	14 + 16 + 36 = 66
6	C–H–J	14 + 22 + 24 = 60

DEFINITION. *The* **critical path** *is the path with the longest duration, and it determines project duration.*

It must be remembered that this total path-enumeration analysis should be limited to small problems and, in general, will not be useful in large problems. We shall next discuss the general PERT methodology, which yields much more information and is a more efficient technique for handling large projects.

SECTION 14.6. *Expected Time of Completion*

An important question regarding the project is when do we expect each activity to be completed and when will each event occur.

DEFINITION. T_E *is the* **earliest expected point in time** *at which an activity is completed. Similarly, the T_E for events is the earliest expected point in time at which an event occurs (i.e., all activities that terminate in the event are completed).*

The term "earliest expected time" is used, since we expect it to occur no earlier than indicated. We must, however, always identify the T_E value with either an activity or event specifically. These values, for activities and events, will be a primary element of the planning and control capabilities of PERT.

Let us compute the earliest expected time of completion (T_E) for each activity and the earliest expected time of occurrence (T_E) for each event. The results are shown for activities in Table 14.6.1 and, for events on the PERT chart of Figure 14.6.1, next to each event. We shall measure time by a "clock" that starts at time 0 days (or whatever time unit is appropriate) and advances as the project proceeds. All point-in-time measures will be in number of days after the beginning of the project. Thus, if an event occurs at time 17, this is to be interpreted as 17 days after the beginning of the project.

We assume that the project begins at time 0, which is T_E for event 1. Let us find T_E for activity A. It is expected to begin at time 0 (T_E for

TABLE 14.6.1. *Earliest Expected Completion Times* (T_E)
for Activities

Activity	Earliest Expected Completion Time, T_E	Activity	Earliest Expected Completion Time, T_E
A	12	F	45
B	20	G	66
C	14	H	36
D	30	I	63
E	40	J	60

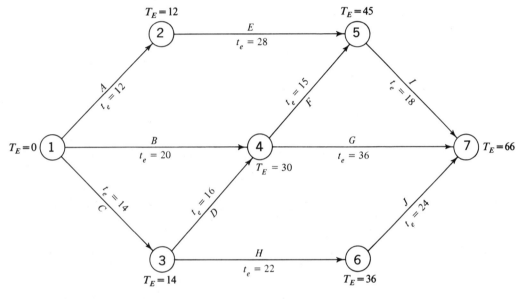

FIGURE 14.6.1. *PERT case study project.*

event 0) and take 12 days to complete. Thus, we expect it to be completed at time $0 + 12 = 12$. Similarly, T_E for activity B is $0 + 20 = 20$ and for activity C is $0 + 14 = 14$. Let us next consider event 2. Since event 2 occurs when activity A is completed, T_E for event 2 equals T_E for activity A, which is 12. Similarly, T_E for event 3 equals T_E for activity C, which is 14. Event 4, however, does not occur until *both* activities B and D are completed. We expect activity B to be completed at time $T_E = 20$, but we have to find T_E for activity D. Activity D can begin as soon as event 3 occurs, which we expect to be at time $T_E = 14$. Since we expect activity D to take $t_e = 16$ days to be completed, T_E for activity D is $16 + 14 = 30$. Therefore, we expect activity B to be completed at $T_E = 20$ and activity D at $T_E = 30$. Event 4 does not occur until *both* activities B and D are completed, and thus we will expect event 3 to occur at time $T_E = 30$, the *later* of the completion times for the activities terminating in event 4.

489

Proceeding in the same manner, we compute T_E for all activities and events. Notice that T_E for event 7 is found by considering T_E for three activities G, I, and J (i.e., 66, 63, and 60) and selecting the latest of them, 66, for activity G.

We now have an estimate of the time at which each activity will be completed and the time at which each event will occur. The expected completion time of the project is T_E for the ending event, event 7, and is, as before, 66 days. Notice also that it was activity G with $T_E = 66$ which determined T_E for event 7. It was path 5 C–D–G, ending in activity G, which was our longest or critical path.

SECTION 14.7. *Latest Allowable Times*

Our expected durations (t_e) are estimates, and therefore our earliest expected times of completion for activities and earliest expected time of occurrence for events are also estimates. Some activities may take longer to complete than were estimated, and this delayed project completion. A useful piece of information about each activity and each event would be the latest point in time at which the activity could be completed or the event occur and still not delay the project completion beyond the expected completion time (66 days in this case).

An example may serve to illustrate this concept. Assume that I must take two trains to get to work. The first leaves the station at 8:00 A.M. and always leaves on time. It arrives at 8:20 (a 20-minute trip), when I get off and wait for the next train, which arrives at the station at 8:25. The second train arrives at my job at 8:55, just in time for me to be at work at 9:00. Sometimes, the first train takes longer than 20 minutes. Considering the first train ride as an activity, it must be completed no later than 8:25 or I miss my connection and am late to work (project completion). Similarly, the event "arrival at the connecting station" must occur no later than 8:25 or I miss the connection and am late to work. If the first train is delayed or late, I am not concerned as long as my arrival at the connecting station is *no later* than 8:25 (the latest allowable time). We therefore define latest allowable time, denoted by T_L, as follows:

> DEFINITION. T_L, for an activity, is the **latest allowable point in time** at which the activity can be completed and not delay the project completion beyond the expected time of completion. Similarly, T_L for an event is the latest allowable point in time at which the event can occur and not delay the project completion beyond the expected time of completion.

Let us compute T_L, the latest allowable time, for all activities and events of our case project. The results are shown, for activities, in Table 14.7.1 and for events, on the PERT chart of Figure 14.7.1. The concept of slack (S) which also appears will be discussed in the next section.

TABLE 14.7.1. *Latest Allowable Completion Times (T_L)*
and Slacks for Activities

Activity	Earliest Expected T_E	Latest Allowable T_L	Slack $S = T_L - T_E$
A	12	20	8
B	20	30	10
C	14	14	0
D	30	30	0
E	40	48	8
F	45	48	3
G	66	66	0
H	36	42	6
I	63	66	3
J	60	66	6

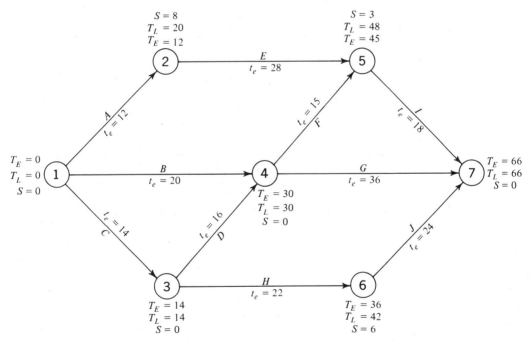

FIGURE 14.7.1. *PERT case study project.*

To find T_L values we begin at the end of the PERT network. The expected completion time for the project is T_E for event 7, or 66 days. Since event 7 is project completion, it must occur no later than time 66 days or else the project will be completed later than expected. Thus, for event 7, $T_L = T_E = 66$ days. We now work backward through the network. Consider activity I. Activity I terminates in event 7. The time of occurrence of event 7 is never earlier than the completion time of activity I.

491

If event 7 must be completed no later than $T_L = 66$ days, activity I must be completed no later than $T_L = 66$ days.

RULE. T_L for all activities equals T_L for the event in which they terminate.

Therefore, once we find T_L for an event, we have found T_L for all activities terminating in that event.

Let us consider event 6. T_L for activity J (and event 7) is 66 days and the expected duration of activity J is 24 days. Thus, activity J must begin no later than $T_L = 66 - 24 = 42$ days. For example, if activity J did not begin until day 43, it would not be completed until day 67 ($43 + 24 = 67$), that is, 1 day later than T_L for activity J (and event 7). Activity J cannot begin until event 6 occurs. Since the latest time for activity J to *begin* is 42, event 6 can occur no later than time 42 days if the project completion is not to be delayed (i.e., $T_L = 42$ days for event 6). In a similar fashion, T_L for event 5 can be computed as $66 - 18 = 48$ days.

Event 4 is a more complicated situation. Both activities F and G begin at event 4. The latest allowable time T_L for event 4 must be sufficiently early to allow *both* activities F and G to be completed no later than their latest allowable times. For activity F, $T_L = 48$ and its expected duration $t_e = 15$. Thus, activity F must *begin* no later than $T_L - t_e = 48 - 15 = 33$. Activity G must *begin* no later than $T_L - t_e = 66 - 36 = 30$. Thus, event 4 must occur no later than the earliest of these times (i.e., $T_L = $ minimum $\{33, 30\} = 30$). If event 4 occurs at time 31, activity G will be late getting started and the project completion will be later than 66 days.

Continuing in this fashion, the remainder of the latest allowable times (T_L) for all events are obtained. The T_L value for the start event, event 1, is always equal to T_E for the event (i.e., zero).

Latest allowable times are important information, as they indicate how late an activity may be completed before there is any cause for concern. For example, if after the project is begun it is learned that activity B will not be completed until time 25 days instead of time 20 days as originally estimated, will this change affect the overall project completion time? The answer is no, assuming that all other activities remain as estimated, since T_L for activity B is 30 days. The ability to answer this type of question during during project implementation is thus a very important feature of the PERT methodology.

SECTION 14.8. *Slack*

The question of how much longer than expected the duration of an activity may take before it becomes critical (i.e., before it will delay the project completion) is a function of the earliest expected completion time (T_E) and the latest allowable completion time (T_L) and is called primary slack.

*DEFINITION. **Primary slack (S)** is the difference between the latest allowable time (T_L) and the earliest expected time (T_E), that is, $T_L - T_E$, and is calculated for both activities and events.*

For an activity, slack is interpreted as how much longer than the expected duration t_e an activity may take to complete without delaying the overall completion of the project. For an event, slack is interpreted as how much later than expected (T_E) an event may occur without delaying the projected completion beyond the expected point in time. In either case slack time $S = T_L - T_E$.

The slack times for all activities are shown in Table 14.7.1 and for events on the PERT chart in Figure 14.7.1. The slack time of 5 days for activity E means that activity E can take 5 days longer (duration) than expected ($t_e = 28$) or that activity E may be completed 5 days later than the earliest expected completion time ($T_E = 40$) without delaying the project beyond 66 days. The slack time of 7 days for event 2 means that event 2 may occur 7 days later than the earliest expected occurrence time ($T_E = 12$) and still not delay the project beyond its expected completion time of 66 days.

SECTION 14.9. *The Critical Path*

From our investigation of the paths of the PERT network, we determined that activities C–D–G formed the *critical path*.

> We have previously defined the *critical path* as that sequence of activities which require the longest time to complete and therefore determine the project completion time.

The PERT analysis we are now performing will yield the critical path without having to identify all possible paths in the network. All activities with zero slack time cannot be delayed, or else the project will be delayed beyond the expected completion time. Therefore, they determine the project completion time and constitute the critical path. We can therefore state the following rule for finding the critical path as follows:

> *RULE. The critical path is formed by those activities with zero slack time.* Furthermore, all events with zero slack time will be events along the critical path.

Let us apply this concept to our case project. Those activities with zero slack time are C, D, and G. Hence, our critical path is C–D–G as was previously determined. The events with zero slack time are 1, 3, 4, and 7. Notice that these events connect activities C, D, and G, and also indicate the critical path. In general, individuals working on a project are familiar with specific activities only, since the events are defined by the project director and the PERT analysts. It is therefore always preferable to state the results in terms of activities rather than in terms of events.

The activities that form the critical path are those which must be most carefully monitored, since any delay in their completion delays the entire project. The other activities may be delayed by as much as their respective slack times without delaying the overall project.

SECTION 14.10. *Dummy Activities*

In some cases activities in a project share predecessor activities, but not all the same ones. For example:

Activity	Predecessor Activities
X	T, U, V
Y	T, V

In this case we cannot define an event in which activities T, U, and V terminate, which is also the start event for activities X and Y, since activity Y does not have activity U as its predecessor. The approach is to define a *dummy activity* which takes no time to complete (i.e., $t_e = 0$) and is shown as a dashed line on the PERT chart. The PERT chart representation of this situation is shown in Figure 14.10.1. In effect, as soon as event 12 occurs (activities T and V completed), event 13 occurs immediately if activity U has been completed. Otherwise, event 13 occurs as soon as activity U is completed.

Dummy activities are treated the same as all other activities in the PERT analysis, and since they have $t_e = 0$, never cause the delay of the event in which they terminate.

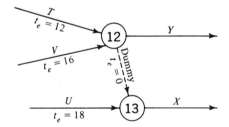

FIGURE 14.10.1

SECTION 14.11. *Schedule Times*

In many cases a project has a scheduled date of completion. For example, the owners may have planned to move into the new house on a certain date and completing the building of the house by that date is of primary concern. We have computed all latest allowable times (T_L) and slack times (S) with respect to not delaying the project beyond the earliest expected completion time of the end event. We can also compute these values with respect to the scheduled completion time.

Let us therefore define the following:

DEFINITION. *Let T_S be the latest allowable point in time for completing an activity or for an event occurring without delaying the project beyond the scheduled completion time.*

DEFINITION. *Let S_s be the secondary slack time (i.e., $T_S - T_L$).*

Thus, T_S for the final event of the network will be set equal to the scheduled completion time of the project. All other T_S values for activities and events are computed precisely, as are the T_L values, but using the scheduled completion time of the final event as reference. For example, if our case-study project is scheduled to be finished by day 75, since the earliest expected completion time for the project is 66 days, then all T_S values are 9 days later than the corresponding T_L values and all secondary slack times $(S_s = T_S - T_E)$ are 9 days greater than the corresponding primary slack times $(S = T_L - T_E)$. The T_S and S_s values are shown for activities in Table 14.11.1 and for events on the PERT chart of Figure 14.11.1.

TABLE 14.11.1. *Schedule Times (T_S) and Secondary Slack (S_S) for Activities*

Activity	Earliest Expected T_E	Schedule Time T_S	Secondary Slack $S_S = T_S - T_E$
A	12	29	17
B	20	39	19
C	14	23	9
D	30	39	9
E	40	57	17
F	45	57	12
G	66	75	9
H	36	51	15
I	63	75	12
J	60	75	15

The S_s value of 9 for the start event, event 1, is to be interpreted so that we can start the project 9 days late and still complete it by day 75 if all activities take just as long to complete as expected.

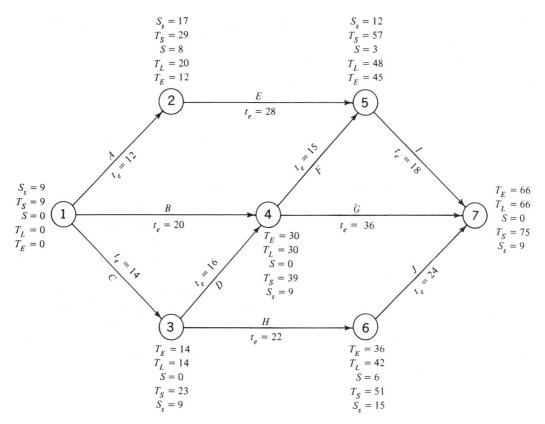

FIGURE 14.11.1. *PERT case study project.*

SECTION 14.12. *Variable Time Estimates*

14.12.1. Activity Durations. Our expected durations for activities (t_e) are actually only estimates. In general, however, activities do not take exactly as long as estimated to complete. Sometimes they take more time and sometimes less time. A more accurate model of the duration of an activity is to describe the duration by a probability distribution. One probability distribution that has been used extensively to model activity durations is the *beta distribution*, because it contains one very important property. We shall not express the beta distribution mathematically, but only describe this important property, which makes it so convenient to use to model activity durations.

Assume that instead of supplying a single time estimate for the duration of each activity (t_e), we supply three:

a. The optimistic estimate. The time duration that is the shortest possible for completing the activity. The actual duration should be less than this value only 1% of the time.

496

m. The most likely estimate. The time duration that has the highest probability of occurrence. This is the mode of the distribution, not necessarily its mean.

b. *The pessimistic estimate.* The time duration that is the longest possible for completing the activity. The actual duration should be greater than this value only 1% of the time.

The useful property of the beta distribution is that if we know the three values *a*, *m*, and *b* for an activity, we can compute the mean or expected duration (t_e) and the variance of duration (σ_e^2) as follows:

$$t_e = \frac{a + 4m + b}{6}$$

$$\sigma_e^2 = \left(\frac{b - a}{6}\right)^2$$

The beta distribution, unlike the normal distribution, is not necessarily symmetrical. We can have an optimistic estimate (*a*) very close to the most likely estimate (*m*) and the pessimistic estimate (*b*) much greater than *m*, or vice versa. This is known statistically as a *skewed distribution*. Figure 14.12.1 indicates representative skewed and symmetrical beta distributions for an activity duration.

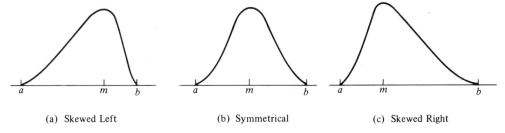

| (a) Skewed Left | (b) Symmetrical | (c) Skewed Right |

FIGURE 14.12.1. *Representative beta disturbance for activity durations.*

Let us reconsider our case project, but use three time estimates, *a*, *m*, and *b*; the expected duration (t_e) and variance of duration (σ_e^2) are shown for each activity in Table 14.12.1.

For example, for activity *A*,

$$t_e = \frac{8 + 4(12) + 6}{6} = \frac{72}{6} = 12$$

$$\sigma_e^2 = \left(\frac{13 - 8}{6}\right)^2 = (1.33)^2 = 1.78$$

TABLE 14.12.1. Expected Duration (t_e) and Variance of Duration (σ_e^2)
for Activities

Activity	Optimistic, a	Most Likely, m	Pessimistic, b	Expected $t_e = \dfrac{a+4m+b}{6}$	Variance $\sigma_e^2 = \left(\dfrac{b-a}{6}\right)^2$
A	8	12	16	12.00	1.78
B	13	19	31	20.00	9.00
C	8	14	20	14.00	4.00
D	4	16	28	16.00	16.00
E	19	23	57	28.00	40.11
F	9	15	21	15.00	4.00
G	24	36	48	36.00	16.00
H	14	22	30	22.00	7.11
I	13	18	23	18.00	2.78
J	14	24	34	24.00	11.11

For activity B,

$$t_e = \frac{13+4(19)+31}{6} = \frac{120}{6} = 20$$

$$\sigma_e^2 = \left(\frac{31-13}{6}\right)^2 = (3)^2 = 9$$

Notice that the three estimates a, m, and b have been chosen such that the expected duration t_e for each activity is precisely the same as the previous single estimate values (see Section 14.4). Since the expected duration (t_e) derived from the three estimates is used precisely as if it were the single estimate, all the analyses $(T_E,\ T_L,\ S,$ etc.) done so far is still valid. Let us, however, incorporate a measure of variability into our analysis.

14.12.2. *Project Duration.* The single most important question concerning the variability of the project completion time is what is the probability of completing the project by a given point in time, such as the scheduled completion time of 75 days? We have computed the earliest expected completion time as 66 days, using the expected duration, t_e, of each activity. We need a measure of the variability of this 66-day estimate (i.e., the standard deviation or variance). In general, we can associate a variability measure, say the variance, for any activity earliest completion time (T_E) or earliest event occurrence time (T_E). However, we are now concerned only with the variance of the completion time of event 7, the final event. We shall denote σ_E^2 as this measure of variability.

DEFINITION. σ_E^2 is the **variance** of either completion time for an activity or time of occurrence for an event.

We now model the completion time of the project (event 7) as having expected value $T_E = 66$ days, and variance σ_E^2, which is as-yet undetermined. The estimate of 66 days was derived assuming that the project duration (and earliest expected completion time) would be the sum of the durations of the critical path activities, C, D, and G. Let us maintain this assumption, as it is usually a reasonable and convenient assumption in PERT analysis.

If the project duration is the sum of three random quantities, the duration of activities C, D, and G, its distribution is the sum of three independent random variables. Let us use the *central limit theorem*,[†] which states that the distribution of sums of random variables is approximately normally distributed with mean equal to the sum of the means and variance equal to the sum of the variances. Thus, the mean project duration (T_E for event 7) is $14 + 16 + 36 = 66$ days as before, and the variance is $\sigma_E^2 = 4.00 + 16.00 + 16.00 = 36.00$ days, and therefore the standard deviation $\sigma_E = \sqrt{36.00} = 6.00$ days. Thus, we can view the project duration and the probability of completing it by $T_S = 75$ days as shown in Figure 14.12.2.

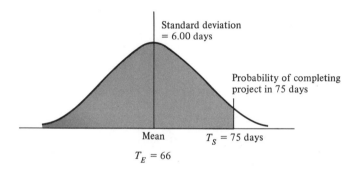

FIGURE 14.12.2. *Probability distribution of project duration.*

In order to compute the probability of completing the project by 75 days, we must use the Cumulative Normal Probabilities Table (see Appendix B) which give areas for a normal distribution with mean zero and standard deviation 1. To use this table, we must convert our question from

What is the probability that a random sample from a normal distribution with mean 66 and standard deviation 6 is less than 75?

to

What is the probability that a random sample from a standard normal distribution is some value (usually called z) above the mean (or zero)?

[†]See Section 2.13 for a full discussion of the central limit theorem.

We can compute this value by subtracting the mean 66 from 75 and dividing by the standard deviation:

$$z = \frac{75 - 66}{6} = 1.5$$

Thus, 75 days is 1.5 standard deviations above the mean. From the table (Appendix B) the probability that a random sample is less than or equal to 1.5 standard deviations above the mean is 0.93319. Thus, there is a 93% chance of completing the project by 75 days, assuming that the project duration is determined by activities *C*, *D*, and *G*.

The assumption that the critical path, *C–D–G* in this case, is the one which actually determines the project duration is one that is usually made in PERT analysis for convenience. Let us examine why path *C–D–G* may not actually determine project duration. Consider path *A–E–I* with mean duration $12 + 28 + 23 = 63$ days, variance $1.78 + 40.11 + 2.78 = 44.37$ days and standard deviation $= \sqrt{44.37} = 6.66$ days. There is a reasonable probability the path *C–D–G* can take longer than path *A–E–I*. For example, path *C–D–G* can take longer than 64 days, while path *A–E–I* can take less time than 64 days. Figure 14.12.3 illustrates this possibility. It should

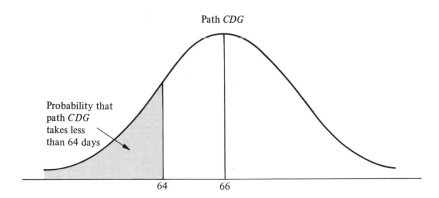

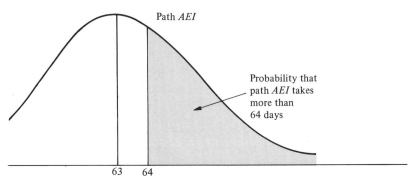

FIGURE 14.12.3. *Probability distributions of durations for paths C–D–G and A–E–I.*

be clear that there is always some probability that a path other than the one determined as critical may actually be critical (determine project duration). Simulation (discussed in Chapter 13) has also been used to determine the probabilities of various paths being critical.

14.12.3. Event Occurrence Times.

The duration of the project is equivalent to the earliest expected occurrence time (T_E) of the end event, since all points in time are measured relative to zero days (i.e., T_E for the start event). We can also compute a variance associated with T_E for each event (σ_E^2). We shall assume that the variance of the duration (σ_e^2) for the activity which determines the T_E for the event is used to determine σ_E^2. For each event the variance of time of occurrence (σ_E^2) equals σ_E^2 for the prior event plus σ_e^2 for the activity connecting them. The variances for each event are shown on the PERT chart of Figure 14.12.4. For event 1, $\sigma_E^2 = 0$, by definition. Consider event 2. T_E for event 2 was found by adding T_E for event 1 plus T_E for activity $A = 0 + 12 = 12$. Thus, σ_E^2 for event 2 equals σ_E^2 for event 1 plus σ_e^2 for activity $A = 0 + 1.78 = 1.78$. Similarly, for event 3, $\sigma_E^2 = 0 + 4.00 = 4.00$. To find σ_E^2 for event 4, we must recall which activity (B or D) determined $T_E = 30$ for event 4. It was activity D (and event 3) which gave $T_E = 14 + 16 = 3$. Using σ_E^2 for event 3 and σ_e^2 for activity D, we obtain $\sigma_E^2 = 4.00 + 16.00 = 20.00$. Therefore, our estimate of the occurrence time for event 4 is normally distributed with mean equal to 30 days and variance equal to 20 days. We can, if we wish,

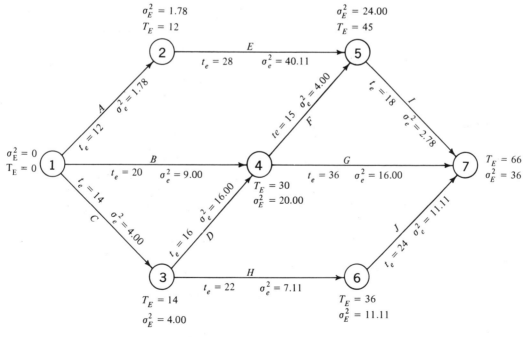

FIGURE 14.12.4. *PERT case study project.*

compute the probability that event 4 occurs by the 35th day. We first compute

$$z = \frac{35 - 30}{\sqrt{20}} = 1.12$$

Then from the Cumulative Normal Probabilities Table (Appendix B), we find that the probability of $z \leqslant 1.12$ equals 0.56864. Continuing in this fashion we can compute σ_E^2 for all the events. Notice that σ_E^2 for event 7, the end event, is 36, the same value obtained using the path-duration approach.

14.12.4. Activity-Completion Times. In a similar fashion, σ_E^2 for each activity can be computed as σ_E^2 for the start event plus σ_e^2 for the activity duration. This computation has been done for each activity and is shown in Table 14.12.2.

TABLE 14.12.2. *Expected Completion Time* (T_E) *and*
Variance of Completion Time (σ_E^2)
for Activities

Activity	Expected T_E	Variance σ_E^2	Activity	Expected T_E	Variance σ_E^2
A	12	1.78	F	45	24.00
B	20	9.00	G	66	36.00
C	14	4.00	H	36	11.11
D	30	20.00	I	63	26.78
E	40	41.89	J	60	22.22

The use of variable time estimates is more realistic, since it incorporates the inherent variability of projects.

SECTION 14.13. *Linear Programming Model of Project Completion*

It is possible to formulate for any given project a linear programming model that will determine the expected occurrence times (T_E) for the end event and therefore the completion time of the entire project. This approach will be useful when considering the resource-allocation problem of Section 14.14.

To simplify the formulation, let us change our notation slightly as follows. For each activity we have defined t_e as the expected duration. Let us now define

$$t_A = t_e \text{ for activity } A$$
$$t_B = t_e \text{ for activity } B$$
$$t_C = t_e \text{ for activity } C \qquad \text{etc.}$$

502

For each event we have defined T_E as the earliest expected occurrence time. Let us now define

$$T_1 = T_E \text{ for event 1}$$
$$T_2 = T_E \text{ for event 2}$$
$$T_3 = T_E \text{ for event 3} \qquad \text{etc.}$$

Our linear programming model will have as its controllable variables the earliest expected occurrence times for each event (T_1, T_2, etc.). For each activity there will be a constraint that relates the earliest expected occurrence times for the activity's start and end events to the activity duration. Let us consider a small portion of the case PERT network as shown in Figure 14.13.1. We shall write two constraints, one for activity I and one for activity G. Consider how T_7 for event 7 is determined: $T_7 = T_4 + t_G$ or $T_5 + t_I$, whichever is larger. Thus,

(1) $\qquad\qquad\qquad\qquad T_7 \geqslant T_4 + t_G$

(2) $\qquad\qquad\qquad\qquad T_7 \geqslant T_5 + t_I$

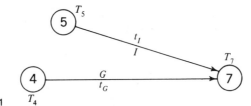

FIGURE 14.13.1

For our PERT network, one of the expressions will be "equal to" and the other will be "greater than" the right-hand side. For example, since we have already solved the PERT problem, we know that

$$t_G = 36 \qquad T_4 = 30$$
$$t_I = 18 \qquad T_5 = 45$$
$$T_7 = 66$$

Substituting these values into equations (1) and (2), we obtain

$$66 = 30 + 36$$
$$66 > 45 + 18 = 63$$

Thus, as long as we try to make T_7 as small as possible (minimize), equations (1) and (2) accurately compute the earliest expected occurrence time for event 7. However, the expected occurrence time for event T_5 can be any value between 45 and 48 and equation (2) will still hold. This is because event 2 has a slack of 3 days. Thus, the linear programming solution will guarantee the correct T_E values only for the end event and those on the critical path. In addition, it will be shown that by determining the shadow prices we can find the critical path activities.

Let us now formulate the linear programming model of the case-study PERT network. We shall write all the activity constraints in the same format as equations (1) and (2). Our objective function will be to minimize the earliest expected occurrence time of end event 7. The model is shown in Figure 14.13.2. The right-hand sides are the activity durations, $t_A, t_B, \ldots$.

$$\text{minimize } Z = T_7$$
s.t.

Activity A:	$T_2 - T_1 \geqslant 12$	
Activity B:	$T_4 - T_1 \geqslant 20$	
Activity C:	$T_3 - T_1 \geqslant 14$	
Activity D:	$T_4 - T_3 \geqslant 16$	
Activity E:	$T_5 - T_2 \geqslant 28$	
Activity F:	$T_5 - T_4 \geqslant 15$	
Activity G:	$T_7 - T_4 \geqslant 36$	
Activity H:	$T_6 - T_3 \geqslant 22$	
Activity I:	$T_7 - T_5 \geqslant 18$	
Activity J:	$T_7 - T_6 \geqslant 24$	

$$T_1, T_2, T_3, T_4, T_5, T_6, T_7 \geqslant 0$$

FIGURE 14.13.2. *Linear programming model of the PERT case study.*

The solution to this linear programming model (using the computer) yields the T_E values for each event as previously computed (see Section 14.6). The dual-variable values from the computer solution are:

Activity	Constraint	Dual-Variable Value
A	1	0
B	2	0
C	3	+1
D	4	+1
E	5	0
F	6	0
G	7	+1
H	8	0
I	9	0
J	10	0

The dual-variable values indicate that for activities C, D, and G, increasing the activity duration (right-hand side) by 1 day will increase the overall project duration (objective function is T_7) by 1 day. These activities, therefore, constitute the critical path.

14.14.1. General Considerations. Assume for the moment that we have additional money (or other resources such as manpower) to expend so as to complete the project more quickly. Let us further assume that we can reduce the duration of any activities we choose and that the cost for a 1-day reduction in the duration of any activity is $1,000, a 2-day reduction is $2,000, and so on. We have a fixed amount to spend and we wish to determine the activities on which to spend the money so as to minimize the project duration. This resource-allocation type of problem is generally referred to as the critical path method (CPM), PERT cost, or "crashing." Clearly, the activities to crash for our case project are the critical path activities, *C*, *D*, and *G*, since they determine project duration. Consider crashing activity *G*. We must determine how many days we can reduce the duration of activity *G* before it no longer has any effect on the project duration (T_E for event 7). To find this we must look at the slack on the other activities, *I* and *J*. The slack for these activities are 3 and 6 days, respectively. If we reduce the duration of activity *G* by more than 3 days, T_E for event 7 will be reduced, but it cannot go below 63 days, the T_E for activity *I*. After a 3-day reduction in the duration of activity *G*, the critical path changes to *C–D–F–I*, and any additional reduction has no further effect on project duration.

However, after a 3-day reduction in activity *G*, we can reduce the duration of activity *F* or possibly reduce the other activities which are along the critical path. In general, this type of approach is too complicated for practical applications and has been introduced only to show the basic concepts. Furthermore, the problem is unrealistic in assuming that the cost per 1-day reduction ($1,000) applies to all activities.

A more realistic problem arises where the per-day cost of the reduction differs for each activity and there is a limit on the maximum reduction possible for each activity. The decision problem then becomes one of determining each activity budget so as to minimize project duration. This problem is more complex than the one for which the cost of the one-day reduction is constant for all activities. Various algorithms for solving this problem have been developed which tend to be complex and often require delineating the paths of the network. Under certain assumptions, however, the problem may be simply formulated as a linear programming problem.

14.14.2. Linear Programming Model of the Resource-Allocation Problem. We assume that all activities can have different durations (t_A, t_B, etc., using the notation of Section 14.13), depending upon the amount of money spent (X_A, X_B, etc., the cost). We shall also assume that the duration is linearly related to the amount of money allocated (X), as

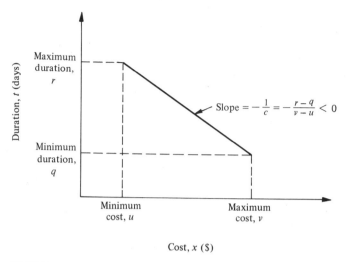

Slope $= -\dfrac{1}{c} = -\dfrac{r-q}{v-u} < 0$

Maximum duration, r

Minimum duration, q

Minimum cost, u

Maximum cost, v

Duration, t (days)

Cost, x ($)

FIGURE 14.14.1. *Activity duration versus cost,* $t = r - (1/c)(X - u)$.

indicated in Figure 14.14.1. Finally, we assume that there is some minimum cost (u) we must spend which yields the maximum duration (r) and that the project duration can be no less than a given value (minimum duration, q) which will cost the maximum allocation (v). We can write the equation of activity duration as

$$t = r - \frac{1}{c}(X - u) \qquad \text{(for } u \leqslant X \leqslant v\text{)}$$

(1)
$$= r - \frac{r - q}{v - u}(X - u)$$

The variable c is the cost of a 1-day reduction, which was \$1,000/day for the problem of Section 14.14.1. The slope of the curve is $-1/c$, which measures the change in duration (which is negative) for each additional dollar spent. We shall use a convention similar to that of Section 14.13 and denote which activity is being considered by a subscript. For example:

$$t_A = \text{expected duration of activity } A$$

$$r_C = \text{maximum duration for activity } C$$

$$X_B = \text{allocation to (cost of) activity } B, \qquad \text{etc.}$$

Let us assume that we are given the pertinent data for the activities of our case-study project as in Table 14.14.1. We formulate a linear programming model of this resource allocation problem, which determines for any given amount of money (called M) how to spend it so as to minimize project duration.

The controllable variables for our problem are the amounts of money to spend on each activity (i.e., X_A, X_B, etc.). Each of these

TABLE 14.14.1. *Resource-Allocation Data*

Activity	Minimum Duration, q	Maximum Duration, r	Minimum Cost, u (\$)	Maximum Cost, v (\$)	Cost of Daily Reduction, c
A	6	12	5,000	11,000	1,000
B	12	20	10,000	16,400	800
C	9	14	8,000	14,000	1,200
D	10	16	12,000	17,400	900
E	16	28	14,000	29,600	1,300
F	5	15	3,000	7,000	400
G	20	36	17,000	29,800	800
H	7	22	11,000	21,500	700
I	11	18	13,000	20,000	1,000
J	14	24	16,000	27,000	1,100
			109,000	202,700	

variables must be constrained so as to be within the range u and v, the minimum and maximum amounts permitted. Each activity will thus have two constraints of the form

$$(2) \qquad X_A \geqslant u_A \qquad \text{(for } X_A \leqslant v_A)$$

$$(3) \qquad X_B \geqslant u_B \qquad \text{(for } X_B \leqslant v_B)$$

The other constraints will be essentially the same as shown in the linear programming model of Section 14.13. For example, for activity A we had the constraint

$$(4) \qquad T_2 - T_1 \geqslant t_A = 12$$

In the resource-allocation problem, t_A is dependent upon X_A, the amount of money to be spent on activity A. From equation (1), we have

$$t_A = r_A - \frac{1}{c_A}(X_A - u_A)$$

$$(5) \qquad = 12 - \frac{1}{1,000}(X_A - 5,000)$$

Combining equations (4) and (5), we obtain

$$T_2 - T_1 \geqslant 12 - \tfrac{1}{1,000}(X_A - 5,000)$$

$$(T_2 - T_1 - 12)1,000 \geqslant -X_A + 5,000$$

$$1,000T_2 - 1,000T_1 - 12,000 + X_A \geqslant 5,000$$

$$1,000T_2 - 1,000T_1 + X_A \geqslant 17,000$$

This is now in a form acceptable for a linear programming model. The general form for the constraint is

507 $\qquad$ (6) $\qquad cT_t - cT_s + X \geqslant rc + u$

where the subscript t stands for the event in which the activity terminates. The subscript s stands for the event at which the activity starts.

The linear programming model is shown in Figure 14.14.2. Equations (1), (2), and (6) have been applied to each activity to form the constraints. In addition, a constraint that indicates how much money is available to spend $(X_A + X_B + \cdots + X_J \leqslant M)$ has been added. We can run the model with M anywhere between \$109,000 and \$202,700 (i.e., the

Constraint Number		Minimize $Z = T_7$ s.t.

Activity Duration Constraints

1.	A:	$1000\,T_2 - 1000\,T_1 + X_A \geqslant 17{,}000$
2.	B:	$800\,T_4 - 800\,T_1 + X_B \geqslant 26{,}000$
3.	C:	$1200\,T_3 - 1200\,T_1 + X_C \geqslant 24{,}800$
4.	D:	$900\,T_4 - 900\,T_3 + X_D \geqslant 26{,}400$
5.	E:	$1300\,T_5 - 1300\,T_2 + X_E \geqslant 50{,}400$
6.	F:	$400\,T_5 - 400\,T_4 + X_F \geqslant 9{,}000$
7.	G:	$800\,T_7 - 800\,T_4 + X_G \geqslant 45{,}800$
8.	H:	$500\,T_6 - 500\,T_3 + X_H \geqslant 26{,}400$
9.	I:	$600\,T_7 - 600\,T_5 + X_I \geqslant 31{,}000$
10.	J:	$1100\,T_7 - 1100\,T_6 + X_J \geqslant 42{,}400$

Minimum Dollars for Activities

11.	A	$X_A \geqslant 5{,}000$
12.	B	$X_B \geqslant 10{,}000$
13.	C	$X_C \geqslant 8{,}000$
14.	D	$X_D \geqslant 12{,}000$
15.	E	$X_E \geqslant 14{,}000$
16.	F	$X_F \geqslant 3{,}000$
17.	G	$X_G \geqslant 17{,}000$
18.	H	$X_H \geqslant 11{,}000$
19.	I	$X_I \geqslant 13{,}000$
20.	J	$X_J \geqslant 16{,}000$

Maximum Dollars for Activities

21.	A	$X_A \leqslant 11{,}000$
22.	B	$X_B \leqslant 16{,}400$
23.	C	$X_C \leqslant 14{,}000$
24.	D	$X_D \leqslant 17{,}400$
25.	E	$X_E \leqslant 29{,}600$
26.	F	$X_F \leqslant 7{,}000$
27.	G	$X_G \leqslant 29{,}800$
28.	H	$X_H \leqslant 21{,}500$
29.	I	$X_I \leqslant 20{,}000$
30.	J	$X_J \leqslant 27{,}000$
31.	Project Cost	$X_A + X_B + X_C + X_D + X_E + X_F + X_G + X_H + X_I + X_J \leqslant M$

FIGURE 14.14.2. Linear programming model for the resource-allocation problem case study project.

highest and lowest possible values) and determine the optimal allocation $(X_A^*, X_B^*,$ etc.) and the minimum project duration, T_7. Notice that the maximum durations shown in Table 14.14.1 are equal to the t_e values used throughout the chapter. Thus, the minimum project duration obtainable for an expenditure of $109,000 is 66 days.

Let us assume that management is willing to spend $M = \$150,000$ for the project and wishes to know how much to spend on each activity and how long the project will take. This question can be answered by running the model for $M = \$150,000$. The solution is shown in Table 14.14.2. The values for the variables X_A through X_J indicate how much to spend on each activity. The values for the variables T_1 through T_7 indicate the earliest expected occurrence times for events 1–7. The activity durations can be found by substituting the allocations (X_A for activity A, etc.) into equation (1), i.e., $t = r - (1/c)(X - u)$. These values are also shown in Table 14.14.2. Using these activity durations and solving for earliest expected completion times (T_E), latest allowable completion times (T_L), and slacks (S) for all activities yields the fact that all slack values are zero [i.e., all activities are critical (see Table 14.14.2)]. This is not surprising, since it would be pointless to spend money on activities to shorten their duration so as to create slack.

Of interest is the shadow price associated with the project cost. In our problem the maximum expenditure M is $150,000. The shadow-price value is -0.00031, which may be interpreted as: *an additional dollar*

TABLE 14.14.2. *Optimal PERT Allocation for M=$150,000*

Objective Function: $Z = T_7 = 44.59$

Description	Variable	Solution Value	Duration, t_e	Earliest Expected Completion Time, T_E	Latest Allowable Completion Time, T_L	Slack, S
Activity A	X_A	$11,000	6.00	6.00	6.00	0
B	X_B	$10,000	20.00	20.00	20.00	0
C	X_C	$14,000	9.00	9.00	9.00	0
D	X_D	$16,500	11.00	20.00	20.00	0
E	X_E	$14,528	27.59	33.59	33.59	0
F	X_F	$ 3,562	13.59	33.59	33.59	0
G	X_G	$26,125	24.59	44.59	44.59	0
H	X_H	$18,284	11.59	20.59	20.59	0
I	X_I	$20,000	11.00	44.59	44.59	0
J	X_J	$16,000	24.00	44.59	44.59	0
Event 1	T_1	0.00 days				
2	T_2	6.00 days				
3	T_3	9.00 days				
4	T_4	20.00 days				
5	T_5	33.59 days				
6	T_6	20.59 days				
7	T_7	44.59 days				

available would reduce project duration by 0.00031 day, or each additional $1,000 spent decreases project duration by 0.31 day.

SECTION 14.15. *Using the Computer*

A computer program has been prepared which computes PERT statistics. The input to the program is:

1. The number of activities and events.

PERT ANALYSIS

ACTIVITY	START EVENT	END EVENT	************* ACTIVITY DURATIONS *************				
			A	M	B	TE	VAR
A	1	2	8.00	12.00	16.00	12.00	1.78
B	1	4	13.00	19.00	31.00	20.00	9.00
C	1	3	8.00	14.00	20.00	14.00	4.00
D	3	4	4.00	16.00	28.00	16.00	16.00
E	2	5	19.00	23.00	57.00	28.00	40.11
F	4	5	9.00	15.00	21.00	15.00	4.00
G	4	7	24.00	36.00	48.00	36.00	16.00
H	3	6	14.00	22.00	30.00	22.00	7.11
I	5	7	13.00	18.00	23.00	18.00	2.78
J	6	7	14.00	24.00	34.00	24.00	11.11

PERT RESULTS

ACTIVITY	TE	VAR	TL	PRIMARY SLACK	CRITICAL	TS	SECONDARY SLACK
A	12.00	1.78	20.00	8.00		29.00	17.00
B	20.00	9.00	30.00	10.00		39.00	19.00
C	14.00	4.00	14.00	0.00	YES	23.00	9.00
D	30.00	20.00	30.00	0.00	YES	39.00	9.00
E	40.00	41.89	48.00	8.00		57.00	17.00
F	45.00	24.00	48.00	3.00		57.00	12.00
G	66.00	36.00	66.00	0.00	YES	75.00	9.00
H	36.00	11.11	42.00	6.00		51.00	15.00
I	63.00	26.78	66.00	3.00		75.00	12.00
J	60.00	22.22	66.00	6.00		75.00	15.00

EVENT	TE	VAR	TL	PRIMARY SLACK	CRITICAL	TS	SECONDARY SLACK
1	0.00	0.00	0.00	0.00	YES	9.00	9.00
2	12.00	1.78	20.00	8.00		29.00	17.00
3	14.00	4.00	14.00	0.00	YES	23.00	9.00
4	30.00	20.00	30.00	0.00	YES	39.00	9.00
5	45.00	24.00	48.00	3.00		57.00	12.00
6	36.00	11.11	42.00	6.00		51.00	15.00
7	66.00	36.00	66.00	0.00	YES	75.00	9.00

PROB OF COMPLETING PROJECT BY TIME   75.00 EQUALS 0.93319

FIGURE 14.15.1. *PERT computer program output.*

2. A code indicating whether one or three time estimates are given.
3. The scheduled completion time T_S.
4. For each activity:
   (a) A description.
   (b) The start and end event numbers.
   (c) Three (or one) time estimates (a, m, b).

The program prints:

1. For activities:
   (a) All input information.
   (b) t_e, σ_e^2.
   (c) $T_E, \sigma_E^2, T_L, S, T_S, S_s$.
2. For events: $T_E, \sigma^2, T_L, S, T_S, S_s$.
3. The probability of completing the project by T_s.

   The output of the program is shown in Figure 14.15.1.

SECTION 14.16. *Summary*

The basics techniques of PERT–CPM have .been developed and its use described by means of a detailed case-study project. Methods for finding the project completion time and the critical path were discussed. A detailed analysis of the variability of the estimates was presented to show its importance in PERT problems. Two applications of linear programming were also presented. The first dealt with a model of project completion and the second was a model of resource allocation.

A computer program was presented that supplies the important values T_E, T_L, and so on, for both activities and events and also provides the probability of completing the project by T_S.

PROBLEMS

14.1. Consider the following project:

Activity	Predecessor Activity	Expected Duration (*days*)
A	—	15
B	—	12
C	A	7
D	A	34
E	B, C	28
F	B, C	18
G	F	14

(a) Construct the PERT chart.

(b) Find all the paths in the network and which path is the critical one.
(c) Find the earliest expected times, latest allowable times, and slack times for all activities and events. Find the critical path.
(d) Assume that the project is scheduled to be completed 60 days after it is begun. Find the latest allowable times and secondary slack times with respect to this schedule date.

14.2. (Problem 14.1 continued) Assume that the project has already begun and that activity A took 17 days and activity B took 14 days. Find the revised earliest expected times, latest allowable times, slack times for all activities and events, and find the critical path.

14.3. Consider the PERT chart given in Figure P14.3 (all the estimates are in weeks).

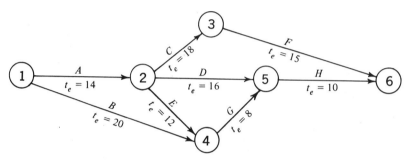

FIGURE P14.3

(a) Find the earliest expected times, latest allowable times, and slack times for all activities and events. Find the critical path.
(b) Assume that the project is scheduled to be completed by 52 weeks after it is begun. Find the latest allowable times and secondary slack times with respect to this schedule date.

14.4. (Problem 14.1 continued) Assume that instead of a single time estimate for the duration of each activity, three are given: a, optimist estimate; m, most likely estimate; b, pessimistic estimate:

	Activity						
Estimate	A	B	C	D	E	F	G
a	9	3	4	20	20	9	8
m	15	12	7	36	26	18	14
b	21	21	10	40	44	27	20

(a) Repeat parts (a)–(d) of Problem 14.1.
(b) Find the variance of the earliest expected times for all activities and events.

(c) Find the probability of completing the project by the schedule time of 60 days.

(d) Run this problem on the computer to check your results.

14.5. Consider the following project with the optimistic (*a*), most likely (*m*), and pessimistic (*b*) estimates of duration in days.

Activity	Predecessor Activities	a	m	b
A	—	5	8	11
B	—	5	10	15
C	—	15	18	33
D	A	25	43	61
E	A	6	15	18
F	A	2	5	8
G	B, F	6	12	18
H	C	18	25	44
I	C, E, G	17	32	47

(a) Construct the PERT chart.

(b) Find the expected duration and variance of duration for all activities.

(c) Find the earliest expected times and variance, latest allowable times, and slack times for all activities and events. Find the critical path.

(d) Assume that the project is scheduled to be completed by 50 days after it is begun. Find the latest allowable times and secondary slack times for all activities and events with respect to this schedule date.

(e) Find the probability of completing the project by 50 days.

(f) Run this problem on the computer to check your results.

14.6. (Problem 14.3 continued) Assume that three time estimates of duration are given:

Estimate	A	B	C	D	E	F	G	H
a	11	11	13	10	8	9	3	5
m	14	20	18	14	12	15	7	10
b	17	29	23	30	16	21	11	15

(a) Repeat parts (a) and (b) of Problem 14.3.

(b) Find the variance of the earliest expected times for all activities and events.

(c) Find the probability of completing the project by the schedule date of 52 days.

14.7. Consider the project described by the PERT chart of Figure P14.7 (all time durations are in weeks).

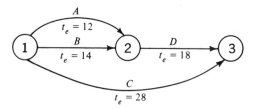

FIGURE P14.7

(a) Formulate the linear programming model to find the project duration.
(b) Run this problem on the computer.
(c) Find the critical path from the shadow price values.

14.8. (Problem 14.7 continued) Assume that the duration of each activity is determined by how much money is spent. The activity duration–cost relationships are as follows:

Activity	Minimum Duration	Maximum Duration	Minimum Cost ($)	Maximum Cost ($)	Cost of a 1-Week Reduction ($)
A	8	12	6,000	8,000	500
B	6	14	3,600	10,000	800
C	14	28	3,200	6,000	200
D	12	18	8,400	12,000	600

(a) Formulate the linear programming model to determine the optimal way in which to spend a fixed amount (M) on the activities so as to minimize project duration.
(b) Run this model on the computer, assuming $30,000 is to be spent for the project.
(c) By how much will project duration be reduced for each additional $1,000 that can be spent? Rerun the model, assuming that $31,000 can be spent to verify your answer.

14.9. In planning a project to introduce a new product, the company lists the various activities as shown in the table below:

Activity	Description	Expected Time To Complete (weeks)	Immediate Predecessor
A	Product design	5	–
B	Market research	2	–
C	Production analysis	4	A
D	Product model	4	A
E	Sales brochure	3	A
F	Cost accounting	1	C
G	Product testing	4	D
H	Sales survey	5	B,E
I	Price and demand report	2	H
J	Project report	3	F,G,I

(a) Construct the PERT chart for this project.

(b) Find the earliest expected times, latest allowable times, and slack times for all activities and events.

(c) List the activities which are on the critical path.

(d) Assume that the project must be completed within 20 weeks after it is begun. Find the latest time that the production analysis activity can begin.

ARTICLES AND BOOKS

Baker, B. N. and R. L. Ellis, *An Introduction to PERT/CPM*. Homewood, Ill.: Richard D. Irwin, Inc., 1964.

Evarts, H. E., *Introduction to PERT*. Boston: Allyn and Bacon, 1964.

Ford, L. R., Jr. and Fulkerson, D. R., *Flows in Networks*. Princeton: Princeton University Press, 1962.

Levin, R. I. and C. A. Kirkpatrick, *Planning and Control with PERT/CPM*. New York: McGraw-Hill Book Co., 1966.

Levy, F. K., Thompson, G. L., and Wiest, J. D., "The ABC's of the Critical Path Method." *Harvard Business Review*, September–October 1963.

Lockyer, K. G., *An Introduction to Critical Path Analysis*. New York: Pitman, 1964.

MacCrimmon, K. R. and C. A. Ryavec, "Analytical Study of the PERT Assumptions," *Operations Research*, January 1964, pp. 16–37.

Miller, R. W., "How to Plan and Control with PERT." *Harvard Business Review*, March–April 1962.

——, *Schedule, Cost, and Profit Control with PERT: A Comprehensive Guide for Program Management*. New York: McGraw-Hill Book Co., 1963.

Moder, J. J. and C. R. Philips, *Project Management with CPM and PERT*, 2d ed. New York: D. Van Nostrand, 1970.

Murdick, Robert G. and Joel E. Ross, *Information Systems for Modern Management*. Englewood Cliffs, N.J.: Prentice-Hall, Inc., 1971.

Wiest, J. and F. K. Levy, *Management Guide to PERT/CPM*. Englewood Cliffs, N.J.: Prentice-Hall, Inc., 1969.

CHAPTER FIFTEEN

Competitive Situations:
Game Theory

OBJECTIVES: The purpose of this chapter is to acquaint you with the following introductory concepts of game theory.

1. *The framework of competitive situations.*
2. *The two-person zero-sum game.*
3. *Games with saddle points.*
4. *The concept of a mixed strategy.*
5. *Finding the optimal mixed strategy.*
6. *The use of linear programming to solve games.*

SECTION 15.1. *Introduction*

In Chapter 3 we discussed decision problems where the choices are made by a single individual. The decisions were affected by the existence of uncontrollable variables that were either known or, if unknown, were considered state-of-nature variables. In many situations these uncontrollable variables will be considered competitive-strategy-type variables. There exists a second (or several) individual(s) whose interests are in conflict with first decision maker and may be said to be in competition with him. Thus, a decision by each individual must take into account the decisions of the other competitors, and the outcomes that result are based on the combination of actions independently chosen by these individual decision makers.

In this chapter some introductory concepts of game theory will be presented. In addition, several procedures will be developed for analyzing and solving simple competitive-strategy decision situations.

SECTION 15.2. *Game Theory versus Subjective Probabilities*

Game theory is concerned with competitive situations wherein both competitors' decisions could be predicted with certainty *if each competitor had perfect information as to the other's decision.* For example, in the game of poker, or blackjack, if one player knew the cards of the other, we could predict with certainty what his decision would be. The technique of game theory assumes this prediction capability.

For many competitive situations, however, this is not the case. For example, if one company raises its price, they cannot predict whether their competitor will also raise his price. In such cases the company can best represent the competitor's actions as random and use subjective estimates of the probabilities of each competitive strategy and then apply the EMV decision rule.

However, when the competitive strategy can be predicted with certainty if perfect information is available, game theory may be used. Let us now consider the simplest of games, the two-person zero-sum game.

The simplest kind of game to analyze is one involving two players, each of whom has a set of alternative strategies from which to make a choice. When each player has made his choice, there will be a payoff to each player. For this simple game the sum of the payoffs to both players is zero (i.e., the winnings of one player equals the loss to the other). Each player chooses his strategy so as to maximize his payoff, which at the same time minimizes the payoff to his opponent. Many competitive situations follow this structure. Military tactics have often been portrayed as two-person zero-sum games, since, for example, the territory gained by one combatant equals the loss to the other. Also, if two competitors bid on a fixed-amount contract that may be divided between them, awards to one bidder are funds not awarded to the other.

Let us consider a simple two-person zero-sum game. Assume that an individual (called A) plays a game with a second individual (called B). They each simultaneously display one, two, or three fingers and exchange different amounts of money, depending upon the number of fingers showing for each player. We shall use the payoff to player A as our measure of performance, but we should recognize that the payoff to player B is always the negative of that for player A. We consider a negative payoff as a loss. Figure 15.3.1 shows the payoff (winnings) to player A for each combination of fingers displayed (competitive strategies). We denote the strategies for player A as A_1, A_2, and A_3, and those for player B as B_1, B_2, and B_3.

Player A Strategies	B_1 1 Finger	B_2 2 Fingers	B_3 3 Fingers
A_1: 1 Finger	−2	12	−4
A_2: 2 Fingers	1	4	8
A_3: 3 Fingers	−5	2	3

Payoff: Winnings to player A

Note: Loss to player B = Winnings to player A

FIGURE 15.3.1. *Payoff table for the "finger game."*

Thus, if both players display two fingers (A_2, B_2), player A wins \$4 (i.e., player B loses and pays player A \$4). If they both display one finger (A_1, B_1), player A wins −\$2 (i.e., he pays player B \$2). The sum of winnings to both players is always zero:

$$\text{winnings to } A + \text{winnings to } B = 0$$

$$\text{for } (A_2, B_2): \quad (+4) + (-4) = 0$$

$$\text{for } (A_1, B_1): \quad (-2) + (\;\;2) = 0$$

518

Let us view the situation from the point of view of player A. Suppose that he decides to use strategy A_1: one finger each time. Soon, player B will realize this and always use strategy B_3: three fingers, which makes player A's winnings the lowest (i.e., worst for player A). Thus, if player A always uses the same strategy, he should assume that after a short while player B will always select a strategy so as to yield the worst (lowest) payoff to player A. In choosing a strategy, player A is therefore wise to use the *pessimistic* or *maximin criterion*.

Figure 15.4.1 indicates the application of the pessimistic criterion to this game. The worst, or lowest, payoff for each strategy for player A is shown and the actual value is circled within the payoff table. For player A, the worst outcome for each strategy is the minimum value of each row. Thus, the pessimistic criterion leads player A to select strategy A_2 and expect to receive a payoff *no worse* than \$1 (i.e., a win of \$1). He wins more if player B chooses either B_2 or B_3.

Let us consider the situation from the point of view of player B. Whichever strategy he selects (B_1, B_2, B_3), player A will soon realize it and select a strategy so as to yield to player B the worst possible outcome. Since the values shown are actually losses to player B, the worst outcome is the highest value. Figure 15.4.2 shows the pessimistic or minimax criterion applied for player B. We have placed squares around the worst payoff for each of the strategies for player B. Player B therefore will select strategy B_1 and lose to player A no more than \$1. (He loses less if A chooses A_1 or A_3.)

SECTION 15.5. *Saddle Points*

Figure 15.5.1 shows the pessimistic criterion for both players. Notice the interesting result that has happened in this game. *Both players*, using the

	B_2: 1 Finger	B_3: 2 Fingers	B_3: 3 Fingers	*Worst* *Outcome for A*
A_1: 1 Finger	-2	12	$\boxed{-4}$	-4
A_2: 2 Fingers	$\boxed{1}$	4	8	1 *Select* A_2
A_3: 3 Fingers	$\boxed{-5}$	2	3	-5

Payoff: Winnings to player A

Note: Loss to player B = Winnings to player A
Negative value = Loss

FIGURE 15.4.1. *Payoff table for "finger game" with pessimistic criterion for player A. Circle indicates row minimum.*

	B_1: 1 Finger	B_2: 2 Fingers	B_3: 3 Fingers	
A_1: 1 Finger	-2	$\boxed{12}$	-4	
A_2: 2 Fingers	$\boxed{1}$	4	$\boxed{8}$	
A_3: 3 Fingers	-5	2	3	
Worst Outcome for Player B	1	12	8	Select B_1

Payoff: Winnings to player A

Note: Loss to player B = Winnings to player A
Negative value = Loss

FIGURE 15.4.2 *Payoff table for "finger game" with pessimistic criterion for player B. Rectangle indicates column maximum.*

pessimistic criterion, have selected strategies that guarantee a payoff *no worse than $1* (winnings for A, loss for B). Thus, the payoff for each game must be exactly $1 from B to A (i.e., $1 win to player A, $1 loss for player B). We call this value of $1 the *value of the game* and denote it by a variable V. Notice also that the value in the payoff table which yielded the "best of the worst" values (1) is the same value for both players, as indicated by having both a circle and a square around it. This value is called a *saddle-point value* and will always indicate the optimal solution to the game if it exists. We can thus state the optimal solution to the game as

FOR PLAYER A: Select A_2 and win
no less than $1

FOR PLAYER B: Select B_1 and lose
no more than $1

The value of the game is $1 to player A and $-$1 to player B.

	B_1: 1 Finger	B_2: 2 Fingers	B_3: 3 Fingers	Worst Outcome for Player A	
A_1: 1 Finger	-2	$\boxed{12}$	$\boxed{-4}$	-4	
A_2: 2 Fingers	$\boxed{1}$	4	$\boxed{8}$	1	Select A_2
A_3: 3 Fingers	-5	2	3	-5	
Worst Outcome for Player B	1	12	8	Select B_1	

Payoff: Winnings to player A

Note: Loss to player B = Winnings to player A
Negative value = Loss

FIGURE 15.5.1. *Payoff table for "finger game" with pessimistic criterion for both players. Circle indicates row minimum, worst for player A; rectangle indicates column maximum, worst for player B.*

The reason that this solution is considered optimal is that if one player uses his optimal strategy and the other does not, the player deviating from his optimal strategy will do worse than if he used his optimal strategy. For example, assume that player A always uses A_2 (i.e., displays two fingers), but player B considers strategies other than B_1. Strategy B_2 yields a win to player A of \$4 instead of \$1, and strategy B_3 yields a win to player A of \$8 instead of \$1. Both cases are worse from the point of view of player B, and he will therefore stay with strategy B_1. A similar analysis holds for player A.

Thus, when trying to find the optimal solution to a game, we may begin by looking for a saddle point. If one exists, it indicates the optimal solution.

SECTION 15.6. *Games Without Saddle Points—Mixed Strategies*

In the preceding game, the optimal solution indicated that each player select the same strategy each time, since a saddle point existed. In such cases the solution calls for each player to use a *pure strategy* (i.e., only one out of the many possible). It can be shown that when no saddle point exists, the best approach is for each player to randomly select a strategy each time the game is played. This type of decision rule is called a *mixed strategy*. The optimal solution to a game without a saddle point will indicate which strategies each player is to use and with what frequency (i.e., probability).

Let us assume that the two players change the payoff for the two-finger, one-finger (A_2, B_1) case from 1 to 6. The new game, along with the pessimistic criterion for both players, is shown in Figure 15.6.1. Notice that there is no longer a saddle point, since in no case does a row

	B_1: 1 Finger	B_2: 2 Fingers	B_3: 3 Fingers	*Worst Outcome* *for Player A*
A_1 : 1 Finger	-2	12	-4	-4
A_2 : 2 Fingers	6	4	8	4 Select A_2
A_3 : 3 Fingers	-5	2	3	-6
Worst Outcome *for Player B*	6 Select B_1	12	8	

Payoff: Winnings to player A

Note: Loss to player B = Winnings to player A
Negative value = Loss

FIGURE 15.6.1. *Payoff table for revised "finger game" with pessimistic criterion for both players. Circle indicates row minimum, worst for player A; rectangle indicates column maximum, worst for player B.*

minimum (worst for A) and column maximum (worst for B) coincide. To prove this, let us assume that player A begins by using only the strategy selected by the pessimistic criterion, A_2; similarly, player B initially uses only strategy B_1. The result will yield a payoff of \$6 to player A. However, player B will quickly see that player A is using only strategy A_2 and will decide to switch to strategy B_2, since then the payoff to A will only be \$4.

If player B uses only strategy B_2, player A will soon switch to strategy A_1, with a payoff of \$12. This switching will continue as long as each player uses only one pure strategy; that is, no matter which pure strategy player A selects, player B will select a strategy that makes player A's strategy nonoptimal.

The optimal solution can occur only when both players use a combination of strategies known as a *mixed strategy*. For example, player B may elect to use strategy B_1 with probability $\frac{1}{4}$ (25% of the time), strategy B_2 with probability $\frac{1}{2}$, and strategy B_3 with probability $\frac{1}{4}$ on a random basis. If he does so, let us find the expected value to player A for each of his pure strategies A_1, A_2, and A_3. These computations are shown in Figure 15.6.2. Since strategy A_2 yields the highest expected value, 5.5, player A might consider using A_2 as a pure strategy against player B's mixed strategy. However, then player B will abandon his mixed strategy and use only B_2, since the payoff to player A will be lowest (i.e., \$4). This will cause player A to switch from strategy A_2 to strategy A_1, since his payoff will be 12 instead of 4, and so on. From this discussion it is clear that the mixed strategy stated for player B is not optimal, since he will switch from it in order to improve the payoff (i.e., reduce his losses).

Let us define each player's mixed strategy as follows:

FOR PLAYER A: Select strategy A_1 with probability p_1
Select strategy A_2 with probability p_2
$\vdots$

FOR PLAYER B: Select strategy B_1 with probability q_1
Select strategy B_2 with probability q_2
$\vdots$

Let us try to understand what the optimal mixed strategy means for each player. The procedures for finding the optimal mixed strategies will be covered later. Assume that the optimal mixed strategies are as follows:

Player A	*Player B*
$p_1 = \frac{1}{8}$	$q_1 = \frac{1}{2}$
$p_2 = \frac{7}{8}$	$q_2 = \frac{1}{2}$
$p_3 = 0$	$q_3 = 0$

	B_1: 1 Finger	B_2: 2 Fingers	B_3: 3 Fingers	Expected Value
A_1: 1 Finger	-2	12	-4	$E(A_1) = 4.5$
A_2: 2 Fingers	6	4	8	$E(A_2) = 5.5$
A_3: 3 Fingers	-5	2	3	$E(A_3) = 0.5$
	$P(B_2) = \frac{1}{4}$	$P(B_1) = \frac{1}{2}$	$P(B_1) = \frac{1}{4}$	

Payoff: Winnings to player A

Note: Loss to player B = Winnings to player A
Negative value = Loss

FIGURE 15.6.2. *Payoff table for revised "finger game" showing expected value for player B. Mixed strategy.* $P(B_1) = \frac{1}{4}$; $P(B_2) = \frac{1}{2}$: $P(B_3) = \frac{1}{4}$.

That is, strategies A_3 and B_3 will not be used since the probability of their selection is zero (p_3 and $q_3 = 0$).

The expected values for each player's pure strategies against his opponent's mixed strategy are found as follows:

FOR PLAYER *A*

$$E(A_1) = 2q_1 + 12q_2 - 4q_3$$
$$= -2\left(\tfrac{1}{2}\right) + 12\left(\tfrac{1}{2}\right) - 4(0) = 5$$
$$E(A_2) = 6q_1 + 4q_2 + 8q_3$$
$$= 6\left(\tfrac{1}{2}\right) + 4\left(\tfrac{1}{2}\right) + 8(0) = 5$$
$$E(A_3) = -5q_1 + 2q_2 + 3q_3$$
$$= -5\left(\tfrac{1}{2}\right) + 2\left(\tfrac{1}{2}\right) + 3(0) = -1.5$$

FOR PLAYER *B*

$$E(B_1) = -2p_1 + 6p_2 - 5p_3$$
$$= -2\left(\tfrac{1}{8}\right) + 6\left(\tfrac{7}{8}\right) - 5(0) = 5$$
$$E(B_2) = 12p_1 + 4p_2 + 2p_3$$
$$= 12\left(\tfrac{1}{8}\right) + 4\left(\tfrac{7}{8}\right) + 2(0) = 5$$
$$E(B_3) = -4p_1 + 8p_2 + 3p_3$$
$$= -4\left(\tfrac{1}{8}\right) + 8\left(\tfrac{7}{8}\right) + 3(0) = 6.5$$

523   These computations are shown in Figure 15.6.3.

	B_1 $q_1 = \frac{1}{2}$	B_2 $q_2 = \frac{1}{2}$	B_3 $q_3 = 0$	
$A_1 : p_1 = \frac{1}{8}$	-2	12	-4	$E(A_1) = 5$
$A_2 : p_2 = \frac{7}{8}$	6	4	8	$E(A_2) = 5$
$A_3 : p_3 = 0$	-5	2	3	$E(A_3) = -1.5$
	$E(B_1) = 5$	$E(B_2) = 5$	$E(B_3) = 6.5$	

FIGURE 15.6.3. *Summary of expected-value computations.*

Notice that for the pure strategies used by player A (A_1 and A_2), the expected value, $E(A_1)$ or $E(A_2)$, against player B's mixed strategy (B_1, B_2) is the same (5), while the unused strategy, A_3, has a worse (lower) expected value, -1.5. Thus, player A has no reason to switch from using only A_1 and A_2. The same is true for player B. Strategies B_1 and B_2 also have expected value 5 against player A's mixed strategy, and the unused strategy, B_3, has worse (higher) expected value.

We call the expected value of all strategies used by the players, the *value of the game V*. In this case the value of the game is $V = 5$. This is interpreted as the *expected* (or average) winnings to player A is \$5, or that the expected losses to player B for each play of the game is \$5.

SECTION 15.7. Dominance

The principle of *dominance* is often useful in reducing the size of the game which need be considered when looking for optimal strategies. A strategy that has, as each of its payoffs, values that are all worse than those of another strategy will never be selected by the decision maker. This occurs because we have assumed that each player is intelligent and chooses his best option. Considering the game as shown in Figure 15.6.1, we see that all the payoffs to player A for strategy A_3 are worse than for strategy A_2. Thus, player A can always do better by selecting strategy A_2 than by selecting strategy A_3. Strategy A_3 is therefore dominated by strategy A_2 and need not be considered further. Thus, our revised finger game reduces to the 2 by 3 game shown in Figure 15.7.1.

Dominance may be used to eliminate strategies from all decision problems. It is for this reason that in Chapter 1 we spoke of only including in the model those strategies that could conceivably be optimal.

	B_1 1 Finger	B_2 2 Fingers	B_3 3 Fingers
A_1 : 1 Finger	-2	12	-4
A_2 : 2 Fingers	6	4	8

FIGURE 15.7.1. *Reduced "finger game."*

A graphical procedure exists for finding a solution to games wherein one player has only two strategies. These are referred to as *2 by n games*. We shall use the reduced finger game of Figure 15.7.1 to illustrate the technique.

Denote the mixed strategy for player A as follows:

Select strategy A_1 with probability p_1.
Select strategy A_2 with probability $p_2 = 1 - p_1$.

Indicating the value of p_1 fully specifies the mixed strategy. If player A uses the mixed strategy above, the expected value of player A's winnings for each of player B's pure strategies is as follows:

FOR STRATEGY B_1: $E(B_1) = p_1(-2) + (1 - p_1)(6)$

FOR STRATEGY B_2: $E(B_2) = p_1(12) + (1 - p_1)(4)$

FOR STRATEGY B_3: $E(B_3) = p_1(-4) + (1 - p_1)(8)$

We can represent the expected value graphically by plotting each $E(B)$ versus p_1. This graph is shown in Figure 15.8.1 for B_1, B_2, and B_3. The B_1 curve is obtained from the fact that when $p_1 = 0$, $E(B_1) = 6$, and when $p_1 = 1$, $E(B_1) = -2$. A similar approach yields the curves for B_2 and

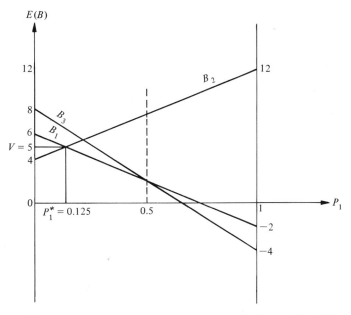

FIGURE 15.8.1. *Expected value of strategies B_1, B_2, and B_3 versus p_1.*

B_3. The optimal value of p_1, labeled p_1^*, is equal to 0.125 and is shown on the graph. Let us explain why this is the optimal value of p_1.

Suppose that player A arbitrarily selects $p = 0.5$. The expected values for player B's pure strategies are $E(B_1) = 2$, $E(B_2) = 4$, and $E(B_3) = 8$, as read from the graph. Thus, if player B knew that player A was using $p_1 = 0.5$ and $p_2 = 0.5$, he would select strategy B_1, since it has the lowest expected value, and pay player A an *average* of \$2 per play of the game.

However, player A can see from the graph that as he decreases the value of p_1, $E(B_1)$ increases, yielding him a greater average winnings. For example, from the graph: for $p_1 = 0.4$, $E(B_1) = 2.8$; for $p_1 = 0.3$, $E(B_1) = 3.6$; for $p_1 = 0.2$, $E(B_1) = 4.4$. If p_1 goes below the value indicated as $p_1^* = 0.125$, player B will switch to strategy B_2, since the expected payoff, $E(B_2)$, to player A will be lower. For example, for $p = 0.1$,

$$E(B_1) = 5.2$$
$$E(B_2) = 4.8$$

However, when $p_1 = p_1^* = 0.125$, both strategies B_1 and B_2 yield the same expected value, 5, against player A's mixed strategy of $p_1^* = 0.125$, $p_2^* = (1 - p_1^*) = 0.875$. No further improvement is possible for player A, assuming that player B makes logical decisions. The expected value of $V = 5$ is the value of the game.

We can solve algebraically for the value p_1^*, instead of reading it from the graph, since at $p_1 = p_1^*$, $E(B_1) = E(B_2)$. Thus,

$$p_1^*(-2) + (1 - p_1^*)(6) = p_1^*(12) + (1 - p_1^*)(4)$$
$$-8p_1^* + 6 = 8p_1^* + 12$$
$$16p_1^* = 2$$

Hence,

$$p_1^* = \tfrac{2}{16} = \tfrac{1}{8} = 0.125$$
$$p_2^* = 1 - p_1^* = 0.875$$

We can also find player B's optimal mixed strategy. The probabilities used by player B are q_1, q_2, and q_3. The graph indicates that player B will not use strategy B_3, if $p_1 = 0.125$, since $E(B_3)$ is larger than $E(B_1)$ and $E(B_2)$, and therefore $q_3^* = 0$. The values of q_1^* and q_2^* may be found from the fact that for the optimal strategy for player B, the expected value of each of player A's pure strategies must be equal, and we already know they will equal 5, the value of the game. Thus,

$$E(A_1) = q_1(-2) + q_2(12)$$
$$E(A_2) = q_1(6) + q_2(4)$$

Since $q_1 = 1 - q_2$, and for $q = q^*$, $E(A_1) = E(A_2)$, we get

$$q_1^*(-2) + (1 - q_1^*)(12) = q_1^*(6) + (1 - q_1)(4)$$

$$-14q_1 + 12 = 2q_1 + 4$$

$$16q_1 = 8$$

or

$$q_1^* = \tfrac{1}{2}$$

$$q_2^* = 1 - q_1^* = \tfrac{1}{2}$$

Let us check that for these values, the expected value of each of player A's pure strategies equals 5.

$$E(A_1) = q_1(-2) + q_2(12)$$

$$= \tfrac{1}{2}(-2) + \tfrac{1}{2}(12)$$

$$= -1 + 6$$

$$= 5$$

$$E(A_2) = q_1(6) + q_2(4)$$

$$= \tfrac{1}{2}(6) + \tfrac{1}{2}(4)$$

$$= 3 + 2$$

$$= 5$$

Thus, the expected value of all pure strategies used by either player against the opponent's mixed strategies equals 5, and there is no advantage to either player to deviate from their optimal mixed strategies. The value of the game is 5; that is, the *average* winnings for player A is \$5/play of the game and B loses on the average \$5/game.

We can summarize the optimal solution as follows:

FOR PLAYER A: Select strategy A_1 with probability $p_1 = \tfrac{1}{8}$
                 Select strategy A_2 with probability $p_2 = 1 - p_1 = \tfrac{7}{8}$

FOR PLAYER B: Select strategy B_1 with probability $q_1 = \tfrac{1}{2}$
                 Select strategy B_2 with probability $q_2 = 1 - q_1 = \tfrac{1}{2}$

The value of the game is 5.

If player B has two strategies and player A has more than two, the game may be solved in the same graphical fashion by simply reversing the rows and columns and multiplying all payoffs by -1, since payoffs are assumed to be the winnings of the player selecting the row strategies.

The optimal solution to a game may be found by formulating it as a linear programming problem. Let us formulate the LP problem for player A, that is, the LP model that will yield the choice of the probabilities for player A's mixed strategy, p_1 and p_2. We have shown that player A's selection of p_1 and p_2 will result in player B's strategies yielding an expected value of V (the value of the game) or greater to player B. However, the strategies for player B which have expected value greater than V will not be used in player B's optimal mixed strategy, since he wishes V to be as small as possible. At the same time, player A wishes V to be as large as possible so as to maximize his average winning. Table 15.9.1 shows the linear programming formulation of the game for both players. Notice that V is also a variable and has been subtrated from both sides of all constraints so as to appear on the left-hand side only. Since V is a variable, it is also restricted to be nonnegative (i.e., $V \geqslant 0$), which means that no solution is obtainable for a game whose value is negative. We shall discuss procedures for overcoming this difficulty later in the section.

TABLE 15.9.1. *Linear Programming Formulation of the Revised Finger Game*

	For Player A
maximize $Z = V$	
s.t.	
$E(B_1) \geqslant V$:	$-2p_1 + 6p_2 - V \geqslant 0$
$E(B_2) \geqslant V$:	$12p_1 + 4p_2 - V \geqslant 0$
$E(B_3) \geqslant V$:	$-4p_1 + 8p_2 - V \geqslant 0$
	$p_1 + p_2 = 1$
	$p_1, \quad p_2, \quad V \geqslant 0$

	For Player B
minimize $Z = V$	
s.t.	
$E(A_1) \leqslant V$:	$-2q_1 + 12q_2 - 4q_3 - V \leqslant 0$
$E(A_2) \leqslant V$:	$6q_1 + 4q_2 + 8q_3 - V \leqslant 0$
	$q_1 + q_2 + q_3 = 1$
	$q_1, \quad q_2, \quad q_3, \quad V \geqslant 0$

From the point of view of player B, he must choose q_1, q_2, and q_3 such that the expected values of each of player A's pure strategies is no more than V, and at the same time he wishes V to be as small as possible. This leads to the formulation for player B in Table 15.9.1.

Notice that the linear programming formulation for player B is very similar to the dual problem for player A, and vice versa. It can be shown that the dual-variable or shadow-price values for either player's problem are the solution to the other player's problem if we ignore the negative sign that appears in the shadow prices for player A's LP problem. Figure 15.9.1 presents the computer solution to the linear programming problem for player A. The solution is $p_1^* = 0.125$, $p_2^* = 0.875$, and $V^* = 5$, as before. Notice also that the shadow-price values on constraints 1 and 2 are the negative of the optimal mixed strategy values for player A (i.e., $p_1^* = 0.5$ and $p_2^* = 0.5$).

Consider now the situation where the value of the game V is negative, and therefore no feasible solution to the problem would be obtained. We can convert this game to one with a positive value by

LINEAR PROGRAMMING

MAXIMIZE Z =   0.0   0.0   1.000

SUBJECT TO THE FOLLOWING CONSTRAINTS

NO.	TYPE	RHS		CONSTRAINT COEFFICIENTS	
1	GE	0.0	-2.000	6.000	-1.000
2	GE	0.0	12.000	4.000	-1.000
3	GE	0.0	-4.000	8.000	-1.000
4	EQ	1.000	1.000	1.000	0.0

VARIABLES
    ORIGINAL VARIABLES 1 THROUGH   3
    SURPLUS VARIABLES   4 THROUGH   6 ADDED TO CONSTRAINTS 1 THROUGH   3
    ARTIFICIAL VARIABLES 7 THROUGH 10 ADDED TO CONSTRAINTS 1 THROUGH   4

OPTIMAL SOLUTION

OBJECTIVE FUNCTION   5.000

BASIS VARIABLES   6   1   2   3

VARIABLE	SOLUTION VALUE	OBJECTIVE FUNCTION RANGES		
		LOWER	GIVEN	UPPER
1	0.125	-8.000	0.0	8.000
2	0.875	-6.000	0.0	8.000
3	5.000	0.0	1.000	999999.000
4	0.0	-999999.000	0.0	0.500
5	0.0	-999999.000	0.0	0.500
6	1.500	-2.000	0.0	0.400

CONSTRAINT	SHADOW PRICE	RIGHT HAND SIDE RANGES		
		LOWER	GIVEN	UPPER
1	-0.500	-1.200	0.0	2.000
2	-0.500	-2.000	0.0	6.000
3	0.0	-999999.000	0.0	1.500
4	5.000	0.0	1.000	999999.000

FIGURE 15.9.1. *Computer solution of game using linear programming.*

reversing the rows and columns (players A and B) and multiplying all payoffs by -1, since the payoff table always shows winnings to the player choosing the row strategies. The game of Figure 15.7.1 with reversed players is shown in Figure 15.9.2. The solution to this game will give identical probabilties p_1, p_2, q_1, q_2, and q_3, and V will be equal to the negative of the V of the original game.

PLAYER A

		A_1 1 Finger	A_2 2 Fingers
P L A Y E R B	B_1: 1 Finger	2	−6
	B_2: 2 Fingers	−12	−4
	B_3: 3 Fingers	4	−8

Payoff: Winnings to player B

FIGURE 15.9.2. *Revised "finger game" with players reversed.*

SECTION 15.10. *Summary*

In this chapter we have examined a class of decision problems involving competitive situations. Although there may be two, three, or more conflicting interests, we considered only the simplest situation, which is the two-person zero-sum game. The value of the game is found by either the existence of a saddle point or by finding optimal mixed strategies for each player. We showed that the game could be structured as a linear programming problem, the solution of which provides the optimal mixed strategies. For the special case where one player has exactly two possible strategies to choose from, a graphical procedure for solving the game was described.

For more complex games (e.g., non-zero-sum or three or more players), solutions are beyond the scope of this text.

PROBLEMS

15.1. Find the optimum strategy for each player and the value of the game for each of the following two-person zero-sum games.

(a)

	B_1	B_2
A_1	8	4
A_2	9	−2

(b)

	B_1	B_2	B_3
A_1	−3	6	12
A_2	0	7	2
A_3	−2	5	1

(c)

	B_1	B_2	B_3	B_4	B_5	B_6
A_1	2	2	3	5	6	-4
A_2	4	-2	5	4	3	5
A_3	7	3	4	6	8	6
A_4	3	2	4	5	7	1

15.2. (Problem 15.1 continued) Show that by using the rule of dominance, the payoff matrix can be reduced to either a single row or a single column. Further show that the value of the reduced game is the same as was obtained in Problem 15.1.

15.3. Using the graphical technique, find the optimal mixed strategies for both players and the value of the game for the following competitive situations:

(a)

	B_1	B_2
A_1	6	5
A_2	1	8

(b)

	B_1	B_2
A_1	65	45
A_2	50	55

(c)

	B_1	B_2	B_3	B_4	B_5
A_1	5	-1	11	-3	13
A_2	-3	9	-5	3	1

15.4. (Problem 15.3 continued) Formulate each of the games in Problem 15.3 as a linear programming problem and solve using the computer program for LP problems.

15.5. Reduce each of the following games by using the rule of dominance and then solve the reduced game by the graphical technique:

(a)

	B_1	B_2	B_3
A_1	3	8	5
A_2	6	2	7
A_3	4	5	6

(b)

	B_1	B_2	B_3	B_4	B_5
A_1	8	7	6	-1	-2
A_2	12	10	12	0	4
A_3	14	6	8	14	16

15.6. (Problem 15.5 continued) Formulate each of the reduced games in Problem 15.5 as a linear programming problem and solve using the computer for LP problems.

15.7. Two airlines presently share a fixed market for passenger travel. Under new government guidelines, the airlines can engage in competitive advertising to increase their share of the market. Three strategies are available to each airline. The percentage increase in market share for airline A is given in the table.

	B_1: no advertising	B_2: light advertising	B_3: heavy advertising
A_1: no advertising	2	-4	-10
A_2: light advertising	7	0	-2
A_3: heavy advertising	12	-8	10

(a) What is the optimal strategy of each airline?

(b) Do the solution strategies necessarily maximize profits for either of the airlines?

(c) How might the two airlines maximize their joint profits?

15.8. A small supermarket A has been serving four small population centers about 4 miles apart along a major highway. The total population is distributed such that center 1 contains 25%, center 2 contains 30%, center 3 contains 10%, and center 4 contains 35% of the population. Although the supermarket has had the whole market to itself, rumors are spreading that a major competitor B will locate in one of the four population centers. Supermarket A has been contemplating moving to larger quarters and can relocate in any of the four centers.

Both supermarkets are aware that the market split will be determined by travel distance and somewhat by loyalty according to the following rules:

(1) If supermarket A is closer than supermarket B to a population center, it will capture 75% of that center's business.

(2) If both supermarkets are equally distant from a center, supermarket A captures 55% of that business.

(3) If supermarket B is closer to a population center, it wins 65% and supermarket A gets only 35% of that center's business.

The supermarkets are considering their alternatives in anticipation of the choice to be made by their competitor.

(a) Set up the payoff matrix for supermarket A as a two-person zero-sum game.

(b) What are the optimal strategies for both supermarkets?

15.9. In the game of matching coins, each of two players A and B tosses a coin. If they both show the same side, A wins both coins. Otherwise, B wins both coins. Develop the payoff table for this game, and solve it graphically. Show that the expected value of the game is zero and that both players should select heads or tails with equal probabilities.

15.10. Two service stations share the sale of gasoline equally in a small Midwestern community. Both would prefer not to offer a free premium to customers at this time; however, both suspect that the other is readying a premium offer, and if it is offered, some sales will be lost to the competitor. If neither introduces the premium offer or if both introduce the premium offer, the status quo will be maintained and both will continue to get their same relative share of the customers. If, however, one introduces free premiums and the other does not, there will be a gain of 10% in the share of the market to the station offering the free premiums. What is the best strategy for the two stations to use with respect to introducing free premiums?

15.11. For each of the following payoff tables, transform the game into an equivalent linear programming problem and find the mixed strategies for each player and the value of the game by using the computer program for LP problems.

(a)

	B_1	B_2	B_3
A_1	10	2	5
A_2	1	7	4
A_3	6	3	9

(b)

	B_1	B_2	B_3	B_4	B_5
A_1	0	10	5	2	11
A_2	7	1	-3	3	5
A_3	2	6	-1	10	5
A_4	8	3	11	-3	1

**BOOKS OF
INTEREST**

Davis, M. D., *Game Theory: A Nontechnical Introduction*. New York: Basic Books, Inc., 1970.

May, F. B., *Introduction to Games of Strategy*. Boston: Allyn and Bacon, 1970.

McKinsey, J. C. C., *Introduction to the Theory of Games*. New York: McGraw-Hill Book Co., 1952.

Owen, G., *Game Theory*. Philadelphia: W. B. Saunders Co., 1968.

Von Neumann, J. and O. Morgenstern, *Theory of Games and Economic Behavior*. Princeton, N.J.: Princeton University Press, 1947.

Williams, J. D., *The Compleat Strategyst*. Rev. ed. New York: McGraw-Hill Book Co., 1965.

APPENDIX A   *Exponential Functions*

x	e^x	e^{-x}	x	e^x	e^{-x}
0.0	1.000	1.000	**5.0**	148.4	0.0067
0.1	1.105	0.905	**5.1**	164.0	0.0061
0.2	1.221	0.819	**5.2**	181.3	0.0055
0.3	1.350	0.741	**5.3**	200.3	0.0050
0.4	1.492	0.670	**5.4**	221.4	0.0045
0.5	1.649	0.607	**5.5**	244.7	0.0041
0.6	1.822	0.549	**5.6**	270.4	0.0037
0.7	2.014	0.497	**5.7**	298.9	0.0033
0.8	2.226	0.449	**5.8**	330.3	0.0030
0.9	2.460	0.407	**5.9**	365.0	0.0027
1.0	2.718	0.368	**6.0**	403.4	0.0025
1.1	3.004	0.333	**6.1**	445.9	0.0022
1.2	3.320	0.301	**6.2**	492.8	0.0020
1.3	3.669	0.273	**6.3**	544.6	0.0018
1.4	4.055	0.247	**6.4**	601.8	0.0017
1.5	4.482	0.223	**6.5**	665.1	0.0015
1.6	4.953	0.202	**6.6**	735.1	0.0014
1.7	5.474	0.183	**6.7**	812.4	0.0012
1.8	6.050	0.165	**6.8**	897.8	0.0011
1.9	6.686	0.150	**6.9**	992.3	0.0010
2.0	7.389	0.135	**7.0**	1,096.6	0.0009
2.1	8.166	0.122	**7.1**	1,212.0	0.0008
2.2	9.025	0.111	**7.2**	1,339.4	0.0007
2.3	9.974	0.100	**7.3**	1,480.3	0.0007
2.4	11.023	0.091	**7.4**	1,636.0	0.0006
2.5	12.18	0.082	**7.5**	1,808.0	0.00055
2.6	13.46	0.074	**7.6**	1,998.2	0.00050
2.7	14.88	0.067	**7.7**	2,208.3	0.00045
2.8	16.44	0.061	**7.8**	2,440.6	0.00041
2.9	18.17	0.055	**7.9**	2,697.3	0.00037
3.0	20.09	0.050	**8.0**	2,981.0	0.00034
3.1	22.20	0.045	**8.1**	3,294.5	0.00030
3.2	24.53	0.041	**8.2**	3,641.0	0.00027
3.3	27.11	0.037	**8.3**	4,023.9	0.00025
3.4	29.96	0.033	**8.4**	4,447.1	0.00022
3.5	33.12	0.030	**8.5**	4,914.8	0.00020
3.6	36.60	0.027	**8.6**	5,431.7	0.00018
3.7	40.45	0.025	**8.7**	6,002.9	0.00017
3.8	44.70	0.022	**8.8**	6,634.2	0.00015
3.9	49.40	0.020	**8.9**	7,332.0	0.00014
4.0	54.60	0.018	**9.0**	8,103.1	0.00012
4.1	60.34	0.017	**9.1**	8,955.3	0.00011
4.2	66.69	0.015	**9.2**	9,897.1	0.00010
4.3	73.70	0.014	**9.3**	10,938	0.00009
4.4	81.45	0.012	**9.4**	12,088	0.00008
4.5	90.02	0.011	**9.5**	13,360	0.00007
4.6	99.48	0.010	**9.6**	14,765	0.00007
4.7	109.95	0.009	**9.7**	16,318	0.00006
4.8	121.51	0.008	**9.8**	18,034	0.00006
4.9	134.29	0.007	**9.9**	19,930	0.00005

From Robert L. Childress, *Calculus for Business and Economics* (Englewood Cliffs, N.J.: Prentice-Hall, Inc., 1972).

$P(Z \le z)$

z	0.09	0.08	0.07	0.06	0.05	0.04	0.03	0.02	0.01	0.00
−3.5	0.00017	0.00017	0.00018	0.00019	0.00019	0.00020	0.00021	0.00022	0.00022	0.00023
−3.4	0.00024	0.00025	0.00026	0.00027	0.00028	0.00029	0.00030	0.00031	0.00033	0.00034
−3.3	0.00035	0.00036	0.00038	0.00039	0.00040	0.00042	0.00043	0.00045	0.00047	0.00048
−3.2	0.00050	0.00052	0.00054	0.00056	0.00058	0.00060	0.00062	0.00064	0.00066	0.00069
−3.1	0.00071	0.00074	0.00076	0.00079	0.00082	0.00085	0.00087	0.00090	0.00094	0.00097
−3.0	0.00100	0.00104	0.00107	0.00111	0.00114	0.00118	0.00122	0.00126	0.00131	0.00135
−2.9	0.0014	0.0014	0.0015	0.0015	0.0016	0.0016	0.0017	0.0017	0.0018	0.0019
−2.8	0.0019	0.0020	0.0021	0.0021	0.0022	0.0023	0.0023	0.0024	0.0025	0.0026
−2.7	0.0026	0.0027	0.0028	0.0029	0.0030	0.0031	0.0032	0.0033	0.0034	0.0035
−2.6	0.0036	0.0037	0.0038	0.0039	0.0040	0.0041	0.0043	0.0044	0.0045	0.0047
−2.5	0.0048	0.0049	0.0051	0.0052	0.0054	0.0055	0.0057	0.0059	0.0060	0.0062
−2.4	0.0064	0.0066	0.0068	0.0069	0.0071	0.0073	0.0075	0.0078	0.0080	0.0082
−2.3	0.0084	0.0087	0.0089	0.0091	0.0094	0.0096	0.0099	0.0102	0.0104	0.0107
−2.2	0.0110	0.0113	0.0116	0.0119	0.0122	0.0125	0.0129	0.0132	0.0136	0.0139
−2.1	0.0143	0.0146	0.0150	0.0154	0.0158	0.0162	0.0166	0.0170	0.0174	0.0179
−2.0	0.0183	0.0188	0.0192	0.0197	0.0202	0.0207	0.0212	0.0217	0.0222	0.0228
−1.9	0.0233	0.0239	0.0244	0.0250	0.0256	0.0262	0.0268	0.0274	0.0281	0.0287
−1.8	0.0294	0.0301	0.0307	0.0314	0.0322	0.0329	0.0336	0.0344	0.0351	0.0359
−1.7	0.0367	0.0375	0.0384	0.0392	0.0401	0.0409	0.0418	0.0427	0.0436	0.0446
−1.6	0.0455	0.0465	0.0475	0.0485	0.0495	0.0505	0.0516	0.0526	0.0537	0.0548
−1.5	0.0559	0.0571	0.0582	0.0594	0.0606	0.0618	0.0630	0.0643	0.0655	0.0668
−1.4	0.0681	0.0694	0.0708	0.0721	0.0735	0.0749	0.0764	0.0778	0.0793	0.0808
−1.3	0.0823	0.0838	0.0853	0.0869	0.0885	0.0901	0.0918	0.0934	0.0951	0.0968
−1.2	0.0985	0.1003	0.1020	0.1038	0.1057	0.1075	0.1093	0.1112	0.1131	0.1151
−1.1	0.1170	0.1190	0.1210	0.1230	0.1251	0.1271	0.1292	0.1314	0.1335	0.1357
−1.0	0.1379	0.1401	0.1423	0.1446	0.1469	0.1492	0.1515	0.1539	0.1562	0.1587
−0.9	0.1611	0.1635	0.1660	0.1685	0.1711	0.1736	0.1762	0.1788	0.1814	0.1841
−0.8	0.1867	0.1894	0.1922	0.1949	0.1977	0.2005	0.2033	0.2061	0.2090	0.2119
−0.7	0.2148	0.2177	0.2207	0.2236	0.2266	0.2297	0.2327	0.2358	0.2389	0.2420
−0.6	0.2451	0.2483	0.2514	0.2546	0.2578	0.2611	0.2643	0.2676	0.2709	0.2743
−0.5	0.2776	0.2810	0.2843	0.2877	0.2912	0.2946	0.2981	0.3015	0.3050	0.3085
−0.4	0.3121	0.3156	0.3192	0.3228	0.3264	0.3300	0.3336	0.3372	0.3409	0.3446
−0.3	0.3483	0.3520	0.3557	0.3594	0.3632	0.3669	0.3707	0.3745	0.3783	0.3821
−0.2	0.3859	0.3897	0.3936	0.3974	0.4013	0.4052	0.4090	0.4129	0.4168	0.4207
−0.1	0.4247	0.4286	0.4325	0.4364	0.4404	0.4443	0.4483	0.4522	0.4562	0.4602
−0.0	0.4641	0.4681	0.4721	0.4761	0.4801	0.4840	0.4880	0.4920	0.4960	0.5000

From Marvin H. Agee, Robert E. Taylor, and Paul E. Torgersen, *Quantitative Analysis for Management Decisions* (Englewood Cliffs, N.J.: Prentice-Hall, Inc., 1976), pp. 361-362.

z	0.00	0.01	0.02	0.03	0.04	0.05	0.06	0.07	0.08	0.09
+0.0	0.5000	0.5040	0.5080	0.5120	0.5160	0.5199	0.5239	0.5279	0.5319	0.5359
+0.1	0.5398	0.5438	0.5478	0.5517	0.5557	0.5596	0.5636	0.5675	0.5714	0.5753
+0.2	0.5793	0.5832	0.5871	0.5910	0.5948	0.5987	0.6026	0.6064	0.6103	0.6141
+0.3	0.6179	0.6217	0.6255	0.6293	0.6331	0.6368	0.6406	0.6443	0.6480	0.6517
+0.4	0.6554	0.6591	0.6628	0.6664	0.6700	0.6736	0.6772	0.6808	0.6844	0.6879
+0.5	0.6915	0.6950	0.6985	0.7019	0.7054	0.7088	0.7123	0.7157	0.7190	0.7224
+0.6	0.7257	0.7291	0.7324	0.7357	0.7389	0.7422	0.7454	0.7486	0.7517	0.7549
+0.7	0.7580	0.7611	0.7642	0.7673	0.7704	0.7734	0.7764	0.7794	0.7823	0.7852
+0.8	0.7881	0.7910	0.7939	0.7967	0.7995	0.8023	0.8051	0.8079	0.8106	0.8133
+0.9	0.8159	0.8186	0.8212	0.8238	0.8264	0.8289	0.8315	0.8340	0.8365	0.8389
+1.0	0.8413	0.8438	0.8461	0.8485	0.8508	0.8531	0.8554	0.8577	0.8599	0.8621
+1.1	0.8643	0.8665	0.8686	0.8708	0.8729	0.8749	0.8770	0.8790	0.8810	0.8830
+1.2	0.8849	0.8869	0.8888	0.8907	0.8925	0.8944	0.8962	0.8980	0.8997	0.9015
+1.3	0.9032	0.9049	0.9066	0.9082	0.9099	0.9115	0.9131	0.9147	0.9162	0.9177
+1.4	0.9192	0.9207	0.9222	0.9236	0.9251	0.9265	0.9279	0.9292	0.9306	0.9319
+1.5	0.9332	0.9345	0.9357	0.9370	0.9382	0.9394	0.9406	0.9418	0.9429	0.9441
+1.6	0.9452	0.9463	0.9474	0.9484	0.9495	0.9505	0.9515	0.9525	0.9535	0.9545
+1.7	0.9554	0.9564	0.9573	0.9582	0.9591	0.9599	0.9608	0.9616	0.9625	0.9633
+1.8	0.9641	0.9649	0.9656	0.9664	0.9671	0.9678	0.9686	0.9693	0.9699	0.9706
+1.9	0.9713	0.9719	0.9726	0.9732	0.9738	0.9744	0.9750	0.9756	0.9761	0.9767
+2.0	0.9773	0.9778	0.9783	0.9788	0.9793	0.9798	0.9803	0.9808	0.9812	0.9817
+2.1	0.9821	0.9826	0.9830	0.9834	0.9838	0.9842	0.9846	0.9850	0.9854	0.9857
+2.2	0.9861	0.9864	0.9868	0.9871	0.9875	0.9878	0.9881	0.9884	0.9887	0.9890
+2.3	0.9893	0.9896	0.9898	0.9901	0.9904	0.9906	0.9909	0.9911	0.9913	0.9916
+2.4	0.9918	0.9920	0.9922	0.9925	0.9927	0.9929	0.9931	0.9932	0.9934	0.9936
+2.5	0.9938	0.9940	0.9941	0.9943	0.9945	0.9946	0.9948	0.9949	0.9951	0.9952
+2.6	0.9953	0.9955	0.9956	0.9957	0.9959	0.9960	0.9961	0.9962	0.9963	0.9964
+2.7	0.9965	0.9966	0.9967	0.9968	0.9969	0.9970	0.9971	0.9972	0.9973	0.9974
+2.8	0.9974	0.9975	0.9976	0.9977	0.9977	0.9978	0.9979	0.9979	0.9980	0.9981
+2.9	0.9981	0.9982	0.9983	0.9983	0.9984	0.9984	0.9985	0.9985	0.9986	0.9986
+3.0	0.99865	0.99869	0.99874	0.99878	0.99882	0.99886	0.99889	0.99893	0.99896	0.99900
+3.1	0.99903	0.99906	0.99910	0.99913	0.99915	0.99918	0.99921	0.99924	0.99926	0.99929
+3.2	0.99931	0.99934	0.99936	0.99938	0.99940	0.99942	0.99944	0.99946	0.99948	0.99950
+3.3	0.99952	0.99953	0.99955	0.99957	0.99958	0.99960	0.99961	0.99962	0.99964	0.99965
+3.4	0.99966	0.99967	0.99969	0.99970	0.99971	0.99972	0.99973	0.99974	0.99975	0.99976
+3.5	0.99977	0.99978	0.99978	0.99979	0.99980	0.99981	0.99981	0.99982	0.99983	0.99983

04433	80674	24520	18222	10610	05794	37515
60298	47829	72648	37414	75755	04717	29899
67884	59651	67533	68123	17730	95862	08034
89512	32155	51906	61662	64130	16688	37275
32653	01895	12506	88535	36553	23757	34209
95913	15405	13772	76638	48423	25018	99041
55864	21694	13122	44115	01601	50541	00147
35334	49810	91601	40617	72876	33967	73830
57729	32196	76487	11622	96297	24160	09903
86648	13697	63677	70119	94739	25875	38829
30574	47609	07967	32422	76791	39725	53711
81307	43694	83580	79974	45929	85113	72268
02410	54905	79007	54939	21410	86980	91772
18969	75274	52233	62319	08598	09066	95288
87863	82384	66860	62297	80198	19347	73234
68397	71708	15438	62311	72844	60203	46412
28529	54447	58729	10854	99058	18260	38765
44285	06372	15867	70418	57012	72122	36634
86299	83430	33571	23309	57040	29285	67870
84842	68668	90894	61658	15001	94055	36308
56970	83609	52098	04184	54967	72938	56834
83125	71257	60490	44369	66130	72936	69848
55503	52423	02464	26141	68779	66388	75242
47019	76273	33203	29608	54553	25971	69573
84828	32592	79526	29554	84580	37859	28504
68921	08141	79227	05748	51276	57143	31926
36458	96045	30424	98420	72925	40729	22337
95752	59445	36847	87729	81679	59126	59437
26768	47323	58454	56958	20575	76746	49878
42613	37056	43636	58085	06766	60227	96414
95457	30566	65482	25596	02678	54592	63607
95276	17894	63564	95958	39750	64379	46059
66954	52324	64776	92345	95110	59448	77249
17457	18481	14113	62462	02798	54977	48349
03704	36872	83214	59337	01695	60666	97410
21538	86497	33210	60337	27976	70661	08250
57178	67619	98310	70348	11317	71623	55510
31048	97558	94953	55866	96283	46620	52087
69799	55380	16498	80733	96422	58078	99643
90595	61867	59231	17772	67831	33317	00520
33570	04981	98939	78784	09977	29398	93896
15340	93460	57477	13898	48431	72936	78160
64079	42483	36512	56186	99098	48850	72527
63491	05546	67118	62063	74958	20946	28147
92003	63868	41034	28260	79708	00770	88643
52360	46658	66511	04172	73085	11795	52594
74622	12142	68355	65635	21828	39539	18988
04157	50079	61343	64315	70836	82857	35335
86003	60070	66241	32836	27573	11479	94114
41268	80187	20351	09636	84668	42486	71303

Based on parts of *Table of 105,000 Random Decimal Digits*, Interstate Commerce Commission, Bureau of Transport Economics and Statistics, Washington, D.C. Reproduced from John E. Freund, *Modern Elementary Statistics*, 4th ed. (Englewood Cliffs, N.J.: Prentice-Hall, Inc., 1973).

Index

541